THE NINTH STATE

THE NINTH STATE

NEW HAMPSHIRE'S FORMATIVE YEARS

LYNN WARREN TURNER

THE UNIVERSITY OF NORTH CAROLINA PRESS

Chapel Hill & London

© 1983 The University of North Carolina Press
All rights reserved
Manufactured in the United States of America

Library of Congress Cataloging in Publication Data

Turner, Lynn W.
   The ninth state.

   Includes bibliographical references and index.
      1. New Hampshire—Politics and government—
1775–1865. I. Title.
F38.T87 1983   974.2'03   82-13386
ISBN 0-8078-1541-1

The University of North Carolina Press gratefully
acknowledges the generous support of Phi Alpha Theta
in the publication of this book.

TO VERALYN AND BRUCE,
*who grew up knowing more about
the history of New Hampshire than
of the state in which they lived*

CONTENTS

FOREWORD

Lynn W. Turner—professor, college president, editor, author, educator, scholar—did not live to see this work published. He did all the research and he prepared the manuscript and he submitted it for evaluation and he received Phi Alpha Theta's annual manuscript award for his work in 1978. He was preparing the book for publication by the University of North Carolina Press when he died—early in 1982.

Professor Turner's finished work, *The Ninth State: New Hampshire's Formative Years*, is a pioneer study, unusual at this late date in the development of American historiography, covering the history of New Hampshire from the revolutionary period into the miscalled Era of Good Feelings. His emphasis is upon the political developments within the state.

He bases these developments upon the four geographical sections that existed in the state when the Revolution began—the Old Colony in and around Portsmouth; the Merrimack Valley, originally peopled by migrants from Massachusetts; the Connecticut Valley, a kind of extension of the land of steady habits; and the Frontier. Though they all belonged—not always willingly—to the same political entity, the people of these areas were sadly lacking in any sense of union or concert in the management of public affairs. Their discord was readily reflected in their inability to write a satisfactory fundamental law. Six times they tried after 1776, but it was not until 1792 that they produced even a semirational compromise. Meantime, they engaged in passionate conflicts, typical of other states, over other substantive issues—the fate of Tory property, conflicting land claims, financial delinquency, the use of paper currency—until the conservative elements throughout the state began to assert themselves.

The touchstone for their activity was the new federal Constitution, which was supported by mercantile interests in the Old Colony and by farmers, mostly those in the Connecticut Valley, who had access to an outside market. These elements, interestingly, did not form a Federalist party. In national politics they were Yankees first and Federalists by happenstance. In New Hampshire they formed an elite, content to be firmly in control; their rivalries were personal. Among them the most important were those between John Sullivan, frequently governor, and John Langdon, United States senator for twelve years and a strong centralist.

It was the French revolutionary wars and their effect upon American commerce in the Atlantic, Professor Turner maintains, that created the traditional party lineups in New Hampshire. Initial events—epitomized by the Jay Treaty—angered the mercantile and shipping interests of the Old Colony. They found the French more compatible; led by John Langdon, they joined the developing Republican coalition. But second thoughts—as expressed in the reaction to the French attacks on shipping in the Caribbean and to the arrogant behavior of the XYZ envoys—affected a larger contingent, the freehold farmers, who on issues involving President Adams (himself a freehold farmer) became unexceptionable Federalists. Although their posture toward other issues involving state matters ranging from imposition of taxes on unsurveyed lands to reform of the judiciary remained controversial, Federalists, under the governorship of John Taylor Gilman, maintained their ascendancy until 1805.

Four interrelated factors undercut and destroyed the Federalist position: Jefferson's victory in 1800; Langdon's return from the Senate to private life; the formation of a carefully organized party structure; and the Federalist effort to uphold the monopoly character of their Bank of New Hampshire against a Republican effort to charter a rival Union Bank in Portsmouth. Jefferson's victory weakened the hearts and minds of Federalists all over the Union; Langdon's return opportunely provided the Republicans with their first effective leader, along with the skill needed to produce a political organization and the will to use the bank issue to convince farmers—a new, rising, hungry generation which had not formed any affiliations—that more banks meant more credit and better prices. Helpful, as well, was the booming commercial prosperity of the time.

Led by Langdon, Republicans took over control of the state in 1805 and kept it through the first year of the Embargo. Although Portsmouth's commercial interests and their collaterals remained loyal, sufficient numbers of the state's younger farmers became discontented enough with the decline of agricultural prices to turn against the party, and the Federalists revived their spirits enough to take control once more. It lasted one year. When commerce revived, as it did for a while under Madison's commercial policies, Langdon and the Republicans returned and some Federalists joined them—among them William Plumer, who succeeded Langdon as Republican governor in 1812.

Plumer was an unhappy war governor. Although he begged Federalists to unite behind the war effort, they ignored him. New Hampshire experienced much less of the hostility to the Madison administration that characterized Massachusetts and Connecticut during the Anglo-American War, but its antiwar sentiment was obvious: the militia, for example, refused to respond to federal or gubernatorial requisitions—even to protect the harbor at Portsmouth—until the probability of an invasion became overwhelming. There was much backsliding from former Republican affiliations, and following the intransigent trend elsewhere, Federalists ultimately organized a "Peace party" to secure the electoral vote for De Witt Clinton.

In 1813 the Federalists, led once more by John Taylor Gilman, won control again and adopted a policy of noncooperation with the Madison administration; they remained in a majority until after the war, when their constituency, particularly the younger element, lost enthusiasm and began to drift away, partly because of embarrassment over the party's war record and partly because of the declining economy. By 1820 the Federalist candidate for governor was able to win only 3 percent of the vote. Meantime, Republicanism revived; Plumer won reelection by ever-increasing majorities in three successive elections. When Samuel Bell succeeded him in 1819, with another overwhelming Republican majority in the legislature, the party seemed destined for a bright, united, and long-lived future.

Within this broad and full political account, Professor Turner also conjoins careful expositions of the forces and issues that influenced the state. In addition to the traditional economic pressures that affected all classes of society and were quickly reflected in political activities, he points to social rank—the elite had greater influence in all places—and religion as the most important forces influencing institutions and events. He gives particular attention to religious doctrines and structures, which were dominated by Congregational clergy and laymen and their conservative persuasions, but which were ultimately effectively challenged by various dissenting religious groups, most notably the Baptists and Methodists, who not only joined the Republican opposition but won a full measure of religious freedom.

Issues, as he also points out, were plentiful in every year of his study, but few of concern to the state were provocative enough to cause much controversy and division until after the Federalists began to lose power. After that, the issues became notable; lengthy controversies over banking monopolies, over reform of the judiciary, and over the effort to transform privately controlled Dartmouth College into a Republican-controlled state university dominated the whole two decades at the beginning of the nineteenth century.

While his focus is political, Professor Turner has not neglected those other aspects of history needed to complete an explanation of New Hampshire's development: analyses of foreign trade (out of Portsmouth), turnpikes, canals, banks and insurance companies, workshops and mills (factories were still in the adolescent stage), the common school system and prison reform, and (as the period ended) the movement to abolish imprisonment for debt—a forerunner of the social reform movements of the next generation—provide a well-rounded understanding of New Hampshire's history in the early years of the Republic.

He completes his work with a compendium of maps which record statistics gleaned from town records, state papers, newspapers, and legislative votes.

Joseph G. Rayback, Chairman
Manuscript Committee
Phi Alpha Theta

PREFACE

*The discovery of tomorrow's truth depends largely
upon today's zeal and yesterday's ambition.*

This sentence, which I found after my husband's death in one of the speeches made during his college presidency, expresses a credo by which he lived. Although his professional career left him with very little time for research, he used vacations, sometimes the early morning and late evening hours during summers, and eventually his retirement years to complete this book, the culmination of a lifetime's interest. He finished revising it only two weeks before his death. To the best of my ability as a research assistant trained by him, I have worked with the staff of the University of North Carolina Press in the publication of this book—a labor of love in his memory. Our two children have aided me in this task.

Vera Arbogast Turner

THE NINTH STATE

CHAPTER I

REVOLUTIONARY
NEW HAMPSHIRE

Before the Revolution, the people of the different parts of New-Hampshire, had but little connexion with each other. —Jeremy Belknap

"On the 30th of November [1782]," wrote a young New Hampshire farmer, "the provisional treaty was signed, in which Great Britain explicitly acknowledged the independence of the United States. . . . The evils & privations occasioned by a war of eight years, made the tidings of an honorable peace a joyful event to the nation."[1] News of the treaty did not actually reach the people of New Hampshire generally until March 29, 1783, when the *New Hampshire Gazette* published the announcement in a letter which had been received from John Taylor Gilman, delegate to the Continental Congress. With becoming gravity, President Meshech Weare and the committee of safety postponed formal celebration of this event until the twenty-eighth day of the following April, after Congress had proclaimed the end of hostilities.[2] Then, from daybreak until midnight, the assembled magistrates, lawmakers, aristocrats, clergymen, and townspeople in Portsmouth, the old social capital of the state, made merry over the return of peace with bells, guns, sublime anthems, prayers of grateful eloquence, an elegant dinner, a splendid ball, illuminations, and fireworks.[3] The humble people of the state, who probably disapproved of Portsmouth's extravagance, were equally and dutifully thankful for England's capitulation. Matthew Patten of Bedford paused at the end of his customary round of duties to record in his diary, "10th was a day of Rejoicing in this town on acct of the peace and I Recd a dollar from William Duncan toward his note. . . . and in the afternoon and Evening several thunder showers which produced a great deal of Rain."[4] Thus, in their various ways, did the people of New Hampshire celebrate the major turning point in our national history.

New Hampshire's participation in the struggle for independence had perhaps been as wholehearted as that of any of the thirteen original states. Although some of the oldest English "plantations" in the New World lay within its borders, the royal colony of New Hampshire ranked only tenth among the original thirteen in population and contained less than 4 percent of the total number of inhabitants living between Maine and Georgia in 1775. Nevertheless, it had been one of the earliest to expel a royal governor and to attack the royal arsenals on its soil. It had sent delegates to the First and Second Continental Congresses and had been the first colony to request from the latter body its advice in the construction of a new state government. New Hampshire minutemen had marched swiftly to the aid of Massachusetts after hearing the news of Lexington and Concord. Thereafter, until 1781, the Granite State had kept three regiments in the Continental Line and its soldiers had fought courageously at Bunker Hill, Trenton, Saratoga, Monmouth, and Yorktown.[5]

By 1780, however, it could well have been said that New Hampshire had almost lost interest in the war. Alone among the thirteen revolting colonies, it had escaped British invasion (G. B. Shaw, in "The Devil's Disciple," to the contrary notwithstanding). Less than a tenth of its men of fighting age had seen active service, either with the regulars or the militia. The black clouds of war had, for New Hampshire, a silver lining. Privateers and naval contracts brought wealth to Portsmouth's merchants and employment to its artisans. The gross inflation of the currency aided the shrewd farmer who kept his prices in proportion. Taxes were high, but as long as they could be paid in paper money, the state was more likely than the taxpayer to suffer. Readers of the dull weekly gazettes found a great deal more space devoted to advertisements of lands for sale on the northern frontier than to accounts of campaigns in Virginia, or even to debates in the New Hampshire legislature. Nine-tenths of the people went about their daily business of plowing, shopkeeping, lumbering, and pioneering in much the same way that they always had, oblivious to the world war into which they had been drawn.

That is not to say that the war, and the events of the preceding twenty years, was not to have profound effects upon the northern province. Population had increased from 52,700 in 1767 to 103,179 in 1780,[6] and the number of incorporated towns had nearly doubled. The French and Indian menace had been removed, allowing a burst of expansion toward the north and west. The Revolution produced political and social stress that, even among a conservative people, inevitably loosened the bonds of authority. The Tory aristocracy was banished and dispersed. Democratic ideas were propagated, and found a degree of acceptance in the provisional government. The Congregational clergy lost its firm grip on the religious establishment. Into every crevice and cranny of society, as Jeremy Belknap, the contemporary historian, ruefully admitted, the hidden roots of revolution penetrated, to nourish new growth by slowly demolishing the old.

New Hampshire, though so small a state, was perhaps the least homogeneous one in New England. Belknap noted that "before the Revolution, the people of the different parts of New-Hampshire, had but little connexion with each other."[7] Twenty-five years later, Timothy Dwight found little change in this respect. "One of the chief evils, under which New-Hampshire labours," he wrote, "is the want of union and concert in the management of public affairs. The sense of a common interest appears to be loosely felt by the inhabitants. Those in the eastern counties are apparently little connected with those in the western; and those in the middle of the state still less perhaps with either."[8] This tripartite division, noted by a keen outside observer, was partly due to geography, which, until the railroad era, presented difficult barriers to communication between the seaboard and the valleys of the two great rivers, the Merrimack and the Connecticut. Almost equally effective in promoting division, however, was the fact that much of the population had emigrated from other colonies and retained older loyalties after settling upon lands that happened to belong to New Hampshire. The geographical, economic, and sentimental barriers between the distinct regions in the state produced conflicts that troubled its history throughout the four decades following 1780. It would be impossible to draw precise lines between each of these areas, but for descriptive purposes such boundaries may be assigned. The state might be divided into four regions, arbitrarily named (1) the Old Colony, (2) the Merrimack Valley, (3) the Connecticut Valley, and (4) the Frontier. Within each of these areas appeared lines of cleavage, denoting economic, racial, religious, and social differences.

The Old Colony was the original New Hampshire, containing some of the earliest English settlements in America. It comprised the eighteen-mile strip of coastline between the Massachusetts border and Old Kittery in Maine, together with the tidewater reaches of the Piscataqua River and its tributaries. Here the four ancient towns of Portsmouth, Dover, Exeter, and Hampton had existed through three-quarters of the seventeenth century almost as tiny independent republics. By subdivisions, by accretions, and by adjustment of the boundary with Massachusetts, these four towns had become thirty-seven in 1780, long established, settled largely by "first families," and tributary to Portsmouth. Here, in colonial days and to some degree until 1820, was the political, economic, and social focus of the state.[9] In this southeastern corner 28 percent of the population and 58 percent of the wealth of the state was concentrated.[10] In colonial times this area had governed the province. It had two capitals: Portsmouth, where the Wentworths, well beloved by their Hanoverian monarchs, had held their little courts until 1775, and Exeter, where the sober God-fearing Weares and Bartletts and Gilmans had established the power of the succession.

During the colonial times New Hampshire had been virtually synonymous with Portsmouth. In the little port and capital, closer by ship to London than by land to Georgia, a Tory aristocracy of merchant princes and civil servants had aped Beacon Hill splendor with creditable success. John Adams, in his own more plebeian days, wrote of "the pomps and vanities and ceremonies of that little world, Portsmouth."[11] When the Revolution scattered this earliest ruling class, its place was promptly taken by self-made rebels from a lower social stratum: sea captains, smuggling merchants, and ambitious physicians. This new aristocracy, combined with remnants of the old, soon restored to Portsmouth its air of distinction. Trade with the West Indies, Halifax, and Europe was ruined by the war, but privateering kept sailors at work and merchants in profits until the peace brought a partial resumption of normal commerce. Portsmouth in 1780 was not relatively so important as it had been in 1700, yet it looked forward confidently to continued prominence in the new republic. Its five thousand merchants, seamen, tradesmen, artisans, shopkeepers, farmers, and dependents kept it in the list of the twelve largest cities in the United States, while French dancing-masters, Scotch admirals, and Negro slaves gave it a cosmopolitan air.

In 1780, however, Portsmouth was no longer the political capital of New Hampshire. That position had been usurped by Exeter. Men in rebellion against their king had first transferred the government to this less exposed spot, but the move had been symbolic as well as strategic. Somber homespun replaced crimson silk; the landed gentry ousted the merchant princes. The Portsmouth ruling class had been mercantile, Anglican, closely allied with England; the Exeter people were landowners, Congregationalists, and descendants of Massachusetts emigrants. It was the "country party" led by Meshech Weare of Hampton, Matthew Thornton of Londonderry, the Bartletts of Kingston, and the Gilmans of Exeter which seized power from the nerveless grasp of the king's servants in 1775 and maintained its powerful grip until the end of the war. Thus, even within the narrow limits of the Old Colony, there was an economic, social, and religious conflict, symbolized by a shift in the political center of gravity.

The region, however, was an economic unit, with Portsmouth as its trading center. The inland towns brought lumber, cattle, and, in some years, grain to Portsmouth and there exchanged them for English merchandise. Shipbuilding was carried on all along the shores of Piscataqua Bay and up its tributary rivers. The coastal towns maintained fishing fleets. Rudimentary manufactories grew up at the falls of the rivers when the English supply of better and cheaper goods was shut off. But the great majority of people, even in this region so near the sea, were farmers who depended reluctantly upon the Portsmouth merchants to buy their surplus produce and sell them imported necessities. Shifting price levels or disturbed external conditions frequently aroused bitter antagonism between these classes. To that was added religious animosity when the merchants turned from the prevailing Congregationalism to the Anglican church. Finally, it may be noted that the government had introduced further confusion by dividing this economic unit between two counties, the larger part of it being in Rockingham with shire towns at Portsmouth and Exeter, but the northern part being in Strafford County with its capital at Dover.

Beyond the farthest limits to which the four original towns had pushed themselves lay the second New Hampshire, which was the growth entirely of the eighteenth century. Under a strained interpretation of its royal charter the Massachusetts Bay Colony had claimed the entire Merrimack Valley and proceeded, after 1690, to grant it to its citizens. There had sprung up, in consequence, a host of vigorous new settlements along the river, with Rumford (now Concord) at their center. They were divorced from Portsmouth not only by incompatibility but by geography, since roads from the coast to the interior were only nominal, whereas the Merrimack provided easy access to the older settlements in Massachusetts. More than once during the confusion of the Revolutionary War the towns of the upper Merrimack were made acutely conscious of their dependence on Newburyport and Boston, and they were inclined to seek economic union with Massachusetts in spite of their political connection with Portsmouth.

Other factors, however, tended to divide this region within itself. Although Massachusetts had made nearly all the original town grants, both the New Hampshire government and the Masonian proprietors had maintained their original claims to the area and had frequently made grants of previously settled townships to second or even third parties. There resulted an uncertainty of title which led to bitter quarrels and almost to pitched battles. The most notorious example was that in which the Rumford patentees, under the title of Massachusetts, and the Bow settlers, under a New Hampshire grant, fought through all the courts to the throne itself before a settlement, symbolized by the new name Concord, was determined.[12] Massachusetts also contributed an ethnic diversity to New Hampshire by granting Londonderry to a body of Scotch-Irish emigrants. These tough Gaelic Presbyterians prospered by combining linen manufacture with husbandry. They soon made Londonderry the second most populous town in the colony and spread abroad until some fifteen towns in the Merrimack Valley had a large admixture of Scotch-Irish people.[13] There was economic divergence as well in this area, for the towns that included rich intervale land in the valleys of the Merrimack and its tributaries were far more prosperous than the hilly, rock-strewn upland towns.

The Merrimack Valley was still of secondary importance in 1780. The falls at Amoskeag and Dunstable provided good fishing places but were nuisances to navigation. The harnessing of water power and the transfer of wealth and population to the industrial cities that arose at these sites lay far in the future. Nevertheless, the valley was on the threshold of greater things. Along the banks of the river lay twenty flourishing farming towns, and within the limits of Mason's patent were thirty-five more corporations, although many were still but sparsely settled. These towns contained 37 percent of the population of New Hampshire in 1780, but not nearly so large a proportion of the wealth. The region had outstripped the Old Colony in numbers and was growing fast. When the general court met at Concord for the first time in 1782, it was tacit recognition of the increasing importance of the central area. United against the Old Colony, the Merrimack Valley could have controlled New Hampshire, but it was too much divided against itself to do this consistently. Scotch-Irish Presbyterian regarded Massachusetts Puritan with distrust, the barren upland farms of Hillsborough County bred discontent against the rich intervale lands of the valley, and the isolated, self-sufficient areas had little in common with the towns that floated their logs to Newburyport and bought their luxuries from Boston. To add to the confusion, government had divided the area among three counties, with Strafford being given a few towns in the north and the line between Rockingham and Hillsborough snaking back and forth across the Merrimack with no regard for geography but with, perhaps, a tender solicitude for political expediency. This situation was particularly galling to Concord and Londonderry; both these large towns had aspirations for leadership, but both remained in Rockingham County under the shadows of Exeter and Portsmouth.

Across the range of hills which separates the Connecticut and the Merrimack valleys lay the third New Hampshire. Massachusetts had pushed her claim to this region also and had established fortified border settlements as far north as Charlestown (Old No. 4) before 1741, when the king fixed the present boundary line between the two provinces. From that point northward, on both sides of the Connecticut River, Governor Benning Wentworth of New Hampshire had erected tier upon tier of regular townships and granted them wholesale after the Peace of Paris. Because nearly all the actual settlers were from Connecticut, a New Connecticut grew up in the northern valley of the river, closely associated with the mother colony in trade, religion, and sentiment. If the Merrimack settlements had originally been remote from Portsmouth, those on the Connecticut were practically in another world, separated by a hundred miles of trackless forest from the seacoast and shut off even more effectually from the political capital by a mutual lack of sympathy. On the other hand, the broad Connecticut flowed southward to the parent colony, carrying the produce of the upper settlements and encouraging the return of supplies, Yale schoolmasters and ministers, and new recruits for the labor of reducing the forest.

Two unusual and important characteristics of this frontier region in the decade before 1780 had powerfully affected its development. One was the presence of Dartmouth College, New Hampshire's only seat of higher learning, yet situated on its farthest frontier. Dartmouth provided a leadership and a cultural cohesion of which few frontiers could boast. The other characteristic was the simple fact that the Connecticut River did not definitely become the western boundary of New Hampshire until 1782. Before that time, there was not even an artificial political line to separate the neighbors on either side of the stream. The population in the upper valley of the Connecticut was one of the most homogeneous groups in New England, except for the fact that the settlers below Plainfield had come from Massachusetts, while those above had originated in Connecticut. The assembly at Portsmouth probably had this distinction in mind when it set the boundary between Cheshire and Grafton counties along the northern line of Plainfield town in 1769.

Isolated and suffering from a feeling of neglect, the Connecticut Valley region contained some fifty incorporated towns in 1780. Their inhabitants formed about 27 percent of the state's population, thus nearly balancing the Old Colony. The towns in Cheshire county were well settled, and those along the eastern bank of the river as far north as Bath were beginning to take on the aspect of civilized communities. Many of the others had hardly any existence as yet, outside the surveyor's plots in the possession of their proprietors. Their inhabitants regarded them as little independent republics, free to cast their lot with whatever political body pleased them most. Their trade, their religious ideas, their sympathies extended across and down the river. In 1780 they did not consider themselves a part of New Hampshire.

To the northward, beyond these three areas, extended a frontier region whose settlement had only begun in 1780 and whose political importance was negligible. The day was long distant when the scenic beauties of Lake Winnepesaukee and the White Mountains were to become the chief economic resource of the state. They were rather regarded in 1780 as disappointing barriers to agricultural exploitation. The pioneers filtering into this wild country in 1780 were a heterogeneous lot, drawn from all of the New England states and bringing a variety of social and cultural ideas with them. Sober yeoman farmers from Connecticut settled next to speculating land barons from Portsmouth and Boston. Baptist and Methodist classes almost threatened to crowd out the few orthodox churches that got a foothold in the wilderness. The region contained barely 8 percent of the state's population, but it was growing more rapidly than any of the other three sections. In the absence of good roads southward, the frontiersmen did their trading downriver to Connecticut and Portland or across the border into Canada. In 1780 this entire northern region, including the Connecticut River towns, lay within the bounds of Grafton County, an artificial creation whose only claim to identity was that all of its settlements were approximately in the same rudimentary stage of civilization.

This Gallic division inevitably reflected itself in the politics of New Hampshire. In colonial times the Old Colony was as zealous in defending its right to rule against the new towns as it was against royal governors. In the last provincial assembly, which met in 1775, the area of the four original towns had twenty-one representatives, while all the rest of the colony had only sixteen. Eight delegates, among whom incidentally there was none from Concord, were all that spoke for the Merrimack Valley in that assembly, while only six towns in the Connecticut region were represented. Of those six, three sent representatives for the first time, only to have them barred from the assembly by vote of the older members. More than one hundred incorporated towns were completely unrepresented.[14]

The sudden loosening of restraint brought about by the Revolution encouraged an immediate change in this situation. The province was being governed in 1775 not by the legally elected assembly just analyzed but by an extralegal congress or convention of revolutionaries, in which the Merrimack and Connecticut towns had more than fully represented themselves. Such was their excess of zeal that Hanover with only 434 people had sent two delegates, and Dunstable, population 705, had sent three. Seventy-seven towns that had never been represented in the assembly were participating in the revolutionary decisions of the fourth provincial convention. Yet the older settlements had managed to increase their own delegations enough to retain the balance of power.[15] Accordingly, when New Hampshire made its first constitution, a system was devised by which representation of the newer towns was drastically reduced. Under this plan, Hanover, which had sent two delegates to the convention, was combined with five other towns for the purpose of electing a single representative to the new general court. Such sudden deflation of their ambitions was too much for the frontier settlements. It gave impetus to their defection and the long struggle over the "New Hampshire Grants."

There were times in the dark days which followed when the authority of the Exeter oligarchy did not actually extend much beyond the limits of Rockingham County, and even within the Old Colony was sorely challenged. No sooner was the new constitution adopted on January 5, 1776, than the government had to face a mild rebellion on the sea coast. Portsmouth, jealous of Exeter and fearful of the drift toward independence, induced a dozen eastern towns to join it in a spirited protest against the new form of government.[16] This revolt subsided quickly, but the western towns were more jealous of their "liberty." In matters of trade and finance, the Merrimack towns felt more dependent upon their parent, Massachusetts, than upon the assembly at Exeter. Frequent conventions were held with the towns along the lower course of the river for the regulation of currency and river-borne commerce.[17] But the most serious defiance of Exeter came from the Connecticut Valley. From 1776 until 1782 a part or the whole of this region was completely independent. In 1781 the rebellion reached its climax when thirty-five towns in Grafton and Cheshire counties seceded from New Hampshire and joined the self-styled State of Vermont. The Exeter government threatened to maintain its authority by force, and civil war was averted only by congressional intervention.[18]

Sectional conflict as an element in the history of colonies to the southward, especially Pennsylvania, Virginia, and the Carolinas, has long been recognized, but New England has often been cited as an area of homogeneous population and internal political peace. New Hampshire historians have been guilty of such generalizations. A careful reading of the record, however, makes it abundantly clear that the basic sectional pattern outlined in this chapter was a strong determinant in the history of the state for the next four decades. Yet it was by no means the only determinant, nor, in itself, a simple one. Religious dissension, class feeling, clashing economic interests, social change—all played their part in making the transition from the eighteenth to the nineteenth century an exciting process in New Hampshire.[19]

CHAPTER 2

CONSTITUTION MAKING

You and I, my dear friend, have been sent into life at a time when the greatest lawgivers of antiquity would have wished to live. How few of the human race have ever enjoyed an opportunity of making an election of government for themselves or their children!—John Adams

Independence had been won in 1783 not by a new nation but by a loosely federated group of thirteen individual and separate states.[1] Even that congeries had not been formalized until Maryland's ratification of the Articles of Confederation on March 1, 1781, less than eight months before the surrender of Cornwallis and the virtual end of the war. Generally speaking, the smaller states—Delaware, Georgia, Maryland, and New Jersey—were reluctant to ratify the Articles, despite their having equal voices with the larger states in Congress, because the proposed union failed to nationalize the trans-Appalachian west. New Hampshire had not raised this objection, but its delegates had opposed the provisions that requisitions for meeting the expenses of the "common" government should be assessed according to the value of surveyed land in each state and that levies for the armed forces should be in proportion to the number of white inhabitants. The ground of objection in both instances was the great number of Negro slaves in the southern states, who would neither be taxed nor counted as manpower—an ominous foreshadowing of future bitter disputes.[2]

These scruples, however, did not prevent New Hampshire's early ratification of the Articles, on March 4, 1778. In April 1781, furthermore, the New Hampshire legislature readily agreed to give Congress the requested authority to raise a 5 percent duty on imports. Until 1782 the Granite State met congressional requisitions for both men and money with commendable promptitude. It could fairly be said, when peace came, that New Hampshire had carried its share of the war burden.

The northernmost state, however, entered the postwar period under the embarrassment of a state constitution that declared that it was to prevail only "during the present unhappy and unnatural contest with Great Britain." This anomaly was only one of many that New Hampshire experienced as it sought, in common with the other states, to find a new and suitably republican basis for the exercise of government. Unlike the other New England colonies, it had no charter that could serve this purpose, even temporarily. Consequently, as did ten others of the "original thirteen," New Hampshire went through the painful process of excavating, reexamining, and rebuilding the very foundations of legally constituted society.

Yet New Hampshire's experience was in many ways unique. It was the first of the thirteen states to create a "constitution"—a woefully makeshift piece of machinery—but the last to form a fundamental law under which a sovereign state could operate. The obliging efforts of its statesmen to produce a document that would satisfy its people involved six distinct "constitutions" and no less than fourteen sessions of the conventions that assembled to create them. No other state endured such travail. Yet these apparently futile efforts might well be viewed as sacrifices on the altar of Democracy. For reasons that were partly accidental and partly ideological, the citizens of New Hampshire became the first people in the world's history to attempt the creation of a constitution by electing a body of delegates for that purpose alone and then subjecting the work of the convention to a popular referendum. A more democratic—and more difficult—procedure can hardly be imagined.

New Hampshire had entered the rebellion under the guidance of a series of popularly elected "provincial congresses," the fourth of which, assembling in May 1775, had progressively assumed all the powers, functions, records, and assets of the legitimate royal government before the end of the year. Disturbed at the cessation of the courts and at the exercise of so much responsibility on so slender an authority, the provincial congress had, in October, presented a request for advice to the Continental Congress—an act which proved to be a landmark in the march toward independence. The "radicals" in Congress—Sam Adams, John Adams, Richard Henry Lee, et al—seized the opportunity to press for a step toward self-government, and November 3, Congress recommended to New Hampshire that "a full and free representation of the people . . . if they think it necessary, establish such a form of government, as . . . would best produce the happiness of the people."[3] With this carte blanche in hand, New Hampshire became the first colony to adopt a new constitution, three months ahead of any of the others and half a year before it declared its independence.[4]

The fourth provincial congress complied with Philadelphia's prescription for a "full representation of the people" by providing for the election of a fifth congress consisting of eighty-nine delegates to be chosen from the one hundred and fifty incorporated towns in the colony. "Free representation" was approached even more closely by a reduction of the property qualification for voting from an estate worth £50 simply to one on which taxes were paid, while eligibility for the office of representative, which had formerly rested on a property of £300 value, was now opened to owners of £200 freeholds. Having thus provided government both for the existing crisis and, it was hoped, for the future, the fourth provincial congress dissolved itself and went home in time for Thanksgiving.

Poverty, disaffection, and electoral irregularities made the fifth provincial congress something of a rump parliament from the beginning, reducing its potential membership of eighty-nine to sixty-six. On January 5, 1776, this body officially promulgated New Hampshire's first constitution. It was a flimsy platform of sovereignty, yet it remained in service until 1784, buffeted by the storms of war, depression, rebellion, and inflation. It had no legal basis for existence, resting only upon adoption by an extralegal convention that had been elected according to precepts issued by a preceding extralegal body. For eight years after New Hampshire declared its independence on June 15, 1776, this constitution continued to declare "that we never sought to throw off our dependence upon Great Britain, but felt ourselves happy under her protection while we could enjoy our constitutional rights and privileges." Revolutionists, to be sure, are seldom anxious about trifling inconsistencies such as these.

A much more serious defect of this constitution was that the convention that had been elected for the express purpose of creating it turned itself into the legislature for which it had provided and to which it gave virtually unlimited powers. The constitution was presented to the people as a fait accompli, to which the only alternative was treason. Their first opportunity for an expression of opinion did not come until the following September when, without reference to the possible effect of independence upon the dependent constitution, precepts were issued for the election of another legislature.[5] The towns in Grafton County registered their disapproval by ignoring their precepts; nor were all of them represented again in the New Hampshire legislature until the constitution of 1776 had been superseded by a better one. It was discontent with this revolutionary frame of government that brought about the eventual secession of thirty-seven towns in the Connecticut Valley and the various schemes for their union with Vermont or the creation of a New Connecticut on the upper banks of the river. The seceders clothed their principles in abstractions about the sovereignty of the incorporated town, but their actual quarrel was with the oligarchical dictatorship that the constitution of 1776 had set up to replace the king's government in New Hampshire. "It is a thousand pities," declared the widely circulated Grafton Address, "that when we are engaged in a bloody contest, merely to oppose arbitrary power without us, we should have occasion to contend against the same within ourselves;—especially by those who profess to be friends of liberty."[6]

An exaggerated local pride, a consciousness of geographic, economic, and historic remoteness from Exeter, and an opportunistic desire to achieve independence from a state whose hands were tied by war moved the western towns as much as did a genuine love of liberty, yet their criticism of the Exeter government was not unfounded. The provisions of the constitution concentrated power in the hands of a dangerously small clique. It created an upper legislative chamber called a council, the members of which were originally selected by the assembly out of its own membership. This bicameral legislature then proceeded to appoint all the judicial and executive officers for the state and counties by concurrent resolutions. These included the committee of safety, necessarily chosen from the legislature, which was the only executive authority known to the state until 1784. The constitution did allow the people, in case the "present unhappy dispute with Great Britain should continue longer than this present year," to elect their councillors "in such manner as the Council and House of Representatives shall order."[7] The people's share in their government was thus confined to an annual vote for a representative and a councillor, whose power, after election, was subject to few restraints. The inevitable result was a despotism, on the whole benevolent, in the hands of the landed gentry, who controlled the legislature. It has been frequently pointed out, for example, that Meshech Weare was president of the council, chairman of the committee of safety, and chief justice of the superior court for the entire period of the Revolution. That he exercised these combined legislative, executive, and judicial powers with tact and restraint in no way lessens the fact that they were virtually totalitarian. It has not been so generally recognized that the virus of pluralism affected not only the highest officials in state government but spread throughout the lower ranks as well. During the first year of their tenure under the constitution, the legislators took advantage of their unparalleled opportunities by appointing themselves and their friends to virtually every post of power and profit, military as well as civil, in the state, thus making of the government a tightly held, closed corporation with its center in Exeter and the Old Colony.[8] A Connecticut River town, looking at this oligarchy in December 1776, thought that the state had been "influenced by the Iniquitous Intreagues and secret Designations of persons unfriendly to settle down upon the Dregs of Monarchical and aristocratical Tyranny."[9]

The constitution of 1776 was accepted because it suited the exigencies of wartime government. The absence of a bill of rights permitted the legislature to suppress newspapers and persecute loyalists without having to worry over constitutional scruples. The constitution had simply assumed that the ordinary functions of government, such as the administration of justice, would proceed without prescription, which left the legislature free to decide which would continue and which would not. But there was one serious omission which was destined to become a permanent affliction in New Hampshire. This was the touchy question of the basis of representation in the assembly. The harried committee that perpetrated the constitution of 1776 left this matter for future legislative decision. It had already, in fact, been decided, since the legislature simply retained the plan by which it itself had been elected in 1775. This plan was a rough compromise between representation according to population and representation of incorporated towns. It provided that each town containing one hundred freeholders was entitled to one representative, that more populous towns could have another representative for each additional one hundred freeholders, and that smaller towns should be combined in such a way as to have the requisite number of freeholders and thus send a composite delegate to the legislature. Freeholders or voters were defined as "Legal In-habitant[s] paying Taxes," and representatives were required to own £200 real estate within the colony.[10]

This scheme of representation appears to have been as equitable as could be expected in the eighteenth century, and it was, in fact, the most democratic plan that existed at that time. It had the practical effect, however, of securing to the older towns in New Hampshire that decisive influence which they had always exercised but which they had been in danger of losing to the newer settlements during the first upheaval of the Revolution. For example, the area of the four original towns, which contained 32 percent of the population in 1775, elected 57 percent of the representatives to the provincial assembly.[11] But in the fourth provincial convention, which also met in 1775, and in which towns were represented by the number of delegates they saw fit to elect, the Old Colony was overwhelmed by homespun representatives from the hinterland, and its proportion of representation dropped to that of its share of the population, that is, 32 percent.[12] Although the apportionment of 1776 gave it a still smaller portion, 30 percent, it also reduced drastically the representation from the upstart frontier regions, which had been grossly swollen in the fourth convention. Thus Grafton County's delegation was sliced from sixteen to six, Hillsborough County's from thirty-one to seventeen. This reduction gave the experienced contingent from the older towns a chance to operate without being overwhelmed by sheer numbers. Its advantage was even more pronounced in the council, where Rockingham County, with its five councillors, needed to be joined by only one of the remaining four counties in order to have a voting majority. Thus did the Rockingham squires, who had controlled the assembly in the days when its chief business was to quarrel with the royal governor, defend their prerogative against the western upstarts who wished to take over direction of the more serious quarrel with the royal armies.

While necessarily acknowledging the existence of this oligarchy, New Hampshire historians have tended to take a romantic view of it. Thus

Jeremy Belknap accounted for Meschech Weare's extraordinary powers in the following words: "So great was the confidence of the people in this gentleman, that they scrupled not to invest him, at the same time, with the highest offices, legislative, executive, and judicial; in which he was continued by annual elections during the whole war."[13] Actually, Weare's only elective office, that of councillor, was one to which the people of Rockingham County alone elected him. His other offices were the gifts of the legislature. Frank B. Sanborn, more than a century later, put it this way: "Weare and Gilman . . . had a hereditary claim on the popularity they enjoyed, and their justice and good faith were known throughout the country which they had served in offices, humble or important, but always neighborly, for a whole generation."[14] While these statements may have been perfectly true of the immediate area in which Squires Weare and Gilman lived—that is to say, the area that they had restored to preponderance in the state government—they were somewhat euphoric when applied to the whole state, one-third of which was in continuous altercation with these same gentlemen throughout the war.

The Connecticut River towns detested the new state government for the very reason that Exeter approved it—because it deprived them of importance. Instead of looking at the statistics of population or of wealth, they held up the statistics of charters, and these showed that sixty-eight incorporated towns in Grafton and Cheshire counties were entitled to only twenty-one representatives in the new legislature, while sixty-four towns in Rockingham and Strafford counties were given fifty-one representatives. Hanover itself, the seat of Dartmouth College and the center of civilization west of the Merrimack River, which alone had sent two delegates to the fourth provincial convention, was now expected to combine with five other towns to elect a single representative. Here was ample basis for the resentment that the Connecticut Valley held against the Exeter oligarchy. Accordingly, the political scientists at Hanover evolved the doctrine, appealing enough to any New Englander, that sovereignty resided in the town corporation rather than in the aggregation of towns called the state and that any possible union between these miniscule sovereignties must be on a basis of complete equality, just as was the union of the colonies in the Continental Congress.[15] Adhering to this principle, the upper Connecticut towns refused to federate until the combined weight of New Hampshire, Vermont, and the Continental Congress bore down upon them in 1782, and only then after a compromise with their views had been written into the new constitution. The incorporated town was fixed so firmly in the fundamental law as the basis of representation that no subsequent effort could remove it. It is there today, making the New Hampshire lower house almost as large as the national House of Representatives.[16]

It may be presumed that the people, at least in the eastern parts of the state, acquiesced temporarily in the wartime dictatorship that flourished under the reticences of their primitive constitution, but what they did to the proposed constitution of 1778 shows that they had no intention of permitting the oligarchy to become a permanent one. The arrival of the Articles of Confederation in December 1777 apparently reminded the New Hampshire legislators that it would be somewhat anachronistic to enter an American confederation under a constitution that still looked forward to reconciliation with the mother country. Accordingly, they determined, on February 26, 1778, to call a constitutional convention "for the sole purpose of forming and laying a permanent plan or system of Government for the future Happiness and well-being of the good people of this State."[17] Seven days later they ratified the Articles of Confederation.[18]

The constitutional convention that met at Concord on June 10, 1778, was the first body in the world's history to be elected by a people for the sole purpose of making a constitution, although proposals for such a convention had been made in Massachusetts as early as October 1776.[19] The journal of this convention, unfortunately, has never been found, and only a few facts about it are known. A fairly complete roster of the delegates, compiled from town records, indicates that most of them came from the Old Colony and the Merrimack Valley, while the western and northern regions of the state were scantily represented. There were several obvious reasons for this imbalance. Since the assembly had placed no restrictions upon the number of delegates which each town could send, the older, wealthier towns nearest Concord elected more delegates to the convention than they were entitled to send to the legislature.[20] Thus Portsmouth sent five, Exeter three, Pembroke, Epping, and Dunstable two each, and so on. Furthermore, since the towns had to pay the expenses of their own delegates, the newer and poorer settlements in the hills and on the frontier could not afford to send any representatives at all. Finally, the disaffection in the Connecticut Valley was rising to full tide, making many of the western towns indifferent to the internal affairs of New Hampshire. Just one day after the convention assembled at Concord, sixteen New Hampshire towns joined the new state of Vermont, and the constitution-makers were deprived of whatever expert assistance the intellects of Dartmouth might have afforded. For these various causes at least fifty-five towns, chiefly in the western and northern parts of the state, were unrepresented in the convention. While the Old Colony and the Merrimack Valley combined, regions which were entitled to sixty-six representatives in the assembly, sent only five less than that number to the convention, the Connecticut Valley and the Frontier, entitled to twenty-five representatives, sent less than half that number of delegates to Concord.

Thus it appears that the constitution of 1779 was made by much the same group of men which had made the constitution of 1776 and had been ruling the state since its inception. By actual count, twenty-two of the seventy-five delegates were also members of the coexistent legislature, which had issued the call for the convention, and seventeen of them had been members of the assembly that created and adopted the first constitution. The majority of these repeaters were from Rockingham County. Furthermore, the heads of the revolutionary junto were present to direct the work of the convention. Meshech Weare was its chairman; John Langdon and Ebenezer Thompson signed the finished product as chairman pro tempore and secretary, respectively; and the committee that framed the plan of government consisted of the flower of the squirearchy, Meshech Weare, Matthew Thornton, Timothy Walker, John Langdon, Nathaniel Peabody, Ebenezer Thompson, and Samuel Livermore from Rockingham and Strafford counties, together with five other men to represent the western part of the state.[21]

Although the convention represented mainly those parts of the state that already controlled the government, the debates soon indicated the existence of a party which desired some radical changes. Two letters from one of the delegates reveal the important fact that "a large number [insisted] upon having the supreme executive authority lodged in one man with the advice of a Privy Council . . . but the greater number that it is most safe in the hands of the Council and Assembly."[22] A further effort to break the existing monopoly was embodied in a motion to increase the representation of the western towns, but this also was defeated by the stand-patters. There is no hint as to how the convention divided on these important questions, but it is not improbable that the Portsmouth delegates led the minority fight against Exeter and Concord, and that this debate represented an early reaction of the mercantile interests against the squirearchy.

When a constitution finally emerged in June 1779, it bore ample evidence of its parenthood.[23] The new document left the legislature exactly as it had been, and with only slightly diminished powers. It remained the source of all legislative and executive authority. It was to continue exercising all appointive power. The degree of democracy in the existing government was to be diminished by a measure mandating higher property qualifications for elected officers and the addition of a religious qualification for both officers and electors. As for the basis of representation in the legislature, not the slightest concession was made; it was to remain exactly as it had been since the fifth provincial congress was elected. This seems particularly inept, since there appeared to be a strong possibility at the moment that not only the Grafton County seceders but many of the towns in Vermont as well might rejoin New Hampshire if a few inducements were offered.[24] But the oligarchy yielded only three points to popular demand. It included a strong clause against pluralism in succeeding legislatures, a weak amending clause, and the Declaration of Rights, which included a guarantee of jury trial and of freedom of conscience coupled with protection for the Protestant religion, but nothing about free speech or a free press.

When this unedifying instrument was submitted to the people during the summer of 1779, it met with a scornful reception. "*At Pennycook in New-Hampshire*, A LARGE *Speckled* Hen which had been sitting on her nest, at times, for a twelvemonth, did on the fifth of June last produce an egg of an uncommon kind, which is now carrying about for a sight," wrote Belknap in a satirical apologue, which he sent to a Boston newspaper. Unable to assign any other reason why the hen should have labored to such poor purpose, the whimsical minister blamed it on the Tories, who were the scapegoats for all the sins of the age, saying that "a cock of that species, has of late been seen hovering about the yard where the hen was kept."[25]

Someone writing under the pseudonym of PHILOTEKNON in the *New Hampshire Gazette* attacked the inconsistencies in the proposed constitution with savage sarcasm, but leveled his keenest shafts at the bald attempt to maintain unhampered legislative tyranny. "Some men who would fain have been deemed wise, have imagined that the safety of a State consisted in its being governed by Laws and not by Men. But your Constitution-Mongers have with superior Wisdom, vested the supreme Power of the State in a set of Men, who are to give Law to Law itself, who are to controul, alter and repeal the Common and Statute Laws of England, and the ancient Laws of this State, and even to propose Alterations in the Constitution itself."[26]

According to Belknap, this constitution was rejected by a decisive margin of 1700 out of 2800 popular votes cast.[27] It would be interesting to have a tabulation of the vote, but, unfortunately, none has been discovered. Belknap asserted that Portsmouth gave only two favorable votes, and it may have been his influence which caused Dover to reject the "Egg" unanimously.[28] Keene also voted unanimously against the new constitution, while Concord and Canterbury approved it by margins of a single vote. The convention delegates, who reassembled in September, recognized the decisiveness of their defeat and "dissolved themselves from any further proceedings in the formation of a Constitution."[29]

This result has been interpreted as a vote of confidence in the government of Squire Weare and his colleagues, but since these men had themselves made the constitution, it would seem rather to have been a vote against their making their system perpetual.[30] The people knew that their makeshift government with all its defects could last only until the end of the war, but the constitution of 1779 would have continued it indefinitely. Yet even though the constitution itself was a recognized failure, the process by which it had been stillborn was a triumph for democracy. Here, for the first time in history, the people had elected representatives entrusted with the important task of creating a permanent government and then had exercised their own sovereign will as to whether or not that government was acceptable. Although Massachusetts produced the first goods with this machinery, New Hampshire must be given credit for having made the earliest trial run.

The success of Massachusetts, during the spring of 1780, in writing and establishing an excellent constitution encouraged New Hampshire to try again in 1781. The time was ripe for a turn toward vigor and firmness in government. Many elements in society were thoroughly disgusted with the conduct of the war and the inflation, feebleness, and poverty of spirit that it engendered. One evidence of counterrevolution was the repeal of all state legal tender laws, on the fifth anniversary of the Declaration of Independence.[31] The same legislature that passed this bill agreed to call another constitutional convention to meet in Concord in June.[32] Profiting by the experience of Massachusetts, the assembly directed that the people should not only vote upon the constitution to be framed but should give their reasons for any adverse votes, so that if the constitution were rejected, the same convention might proceed to draft another one more agreeable to the popular mind. Little did the constitution-makers realize that success lay three drafts, seven sessions, and nearly twenty-nine months in the future.[33]

It is again an irritating circumstance that we do not have the journals of this convention, any intimation of the debates that must have rent it at times, or the record of votes by which the towns expressed their opinions of its work. The only surviving evidence consists of the three drafts of a constitution which the delegates prepared, two drafts of an address which they sent to the people to accompany the constitution, a few fragments of votes in town records, letters, newspaper references, and a list of probable delegates compiled in 1852. This is slender evidence on which to base conclusions, and it is not without its own contradictions. Such as it is, however, it has been largely neglected, and it does not altogether support some of the easy assumptions that have been made in regard to New Hampshire's constitutional progress.

The reconstructed roster of delegates, while probably not exactly accurate, is reliable enough to show that the convention of 1781 was quite different from the convention of 1778 in several respects. Its membership was smaller by at least one-third: poverty, hostility, and indifference had reduced the delegation from seventy-five to fifty-eight. At least eighty incorporated towns, possibly more, were unrepresented in the 1781 convention. The twenty-five or more towns that had lost interest in constitution making between 1778 and 1781 were the poor interior towns in Rockingham and Hillsborough counties. This loss probably fell mostly upon the party which had been the majority and had written the constitution in 1779. Subsequent events showed that the balance of power had shifted to the group that favored a drastic remodeling of the government.

The meager response to the call for the drafting of a constitution in 1781 was undoubtedly an indication of impoverishment and war weariness. Some of the unrepresented towns, such as Epping and Wolfeborough, were more interested in religious revivals in 1780 than in the surfeit of war, politics, and constitutions. The Connecticut Valley boycotted the convention, however, for political reasons. Virtually all of the towns west of Mason's patent line, including eight which were represented in the convention, had joined themselves once more with Vermont in April.[34] It seemed clear that unless the convention made some effort to meet the demands of these secessionists, any constitution that it turned out would apply only to a remnant of the state.

The membership of this convention is also interesting. Twelve of the fifty-eight delegates had participated in the convention of 1778–79, but these repeaters were not the southeastern squires. They were homespun, small-town leaders, such as John Dudley of Raymond and Ebenezer Smith of Meredith—men who had cooperated loyally with the revolutionary government but were in no sense a part of the inner clique that dominated it. Meshech Weare, Josiah Bartlett, Matthew Thornton, John Wentworth, and many others of the earlier revolutionary leaders were absent; this was to be the first enterprise since 1775 in which they had not borne a substantial part. John Langdon was present, it is true, and John Sullivan joined the convention for its later sessions, but neither of these men was deeply in sympathy with the Exeter oligarchy. The actual leaders of the convention were probably its legally trained members: John Pickering and Jonathan M. Sewall of Portsmouth, Daniel Newcomb of Keene, and John Sullivan of Durham. The two Portsmouth lawyers were chairmen of the committees that drew up the two parts of the constitution; Sewall acted as secretary and Sullivan was secretary pro tempore for at least one session.[35] Thus it appears that the convention consisted of a relatively inexperienced group of men, led by attorneys and merchants who were not altogether in sympathy with the government then in power and were certainly eager to change the system by which it prevailed.

In the address that accompanied their newly made constitution to the town meetings, the delegates pointed out that opposition might be expected from those who had gathered complete power—legislative, executive, and judicial—into their own hands under the old constitution and had been able to resist any change in spite of the government's manifest defects.[36] The weapons with which they proposed to unseat the oligarchy were two: the separation of powers, involving the creation of a strong executive and judiciary which could check the legislature, and an exclusion clause, which would prevent the same individuals from dominating all three branches. They defended both of these principles with further indirect arraignments of the existing government.

> These three important powers [legislative, judicial, and executive] we have thought proper to keep as separate and distinct as possible for the following reasons:
>
> If they should be all united the maker of the law would be the interpreter thereof, and might make it speak what language best pleased him, to the total abolition of justice.
>
> If the executive and legislative powers should be vested in one body still greater evils would follow. This body would enact only such laws as it wished to carry into execution, and would, besides, entirely absorb and destroy the judicial power, one of the greatest securities of the life, liberty, and property of the subject; and, in fine, would produce the same system of despotism first mentioned.
>
> And, lastly, should the executive and judicial powers be combined the great barrier against oppression would be at once destroyed; the laws would be made to bend to the will of that power which sought to execute them with the most unbridled rapacity.[37]

As for the "Exclusion Bill," the absence of it was considered a serious defect in the 1776 constitution. "In consequence of which many of the individuals who compose [the legislature] assist in enacting laws, in explaining and applying them, and in carrying them into execution."[38] The results of this pluralism, according to the address, were so bad as to be obvious to everyone. "Besides the interference of several offices held by the same person in point of time, which we have too often *seen*, and the difficulty of one man's giving his attention to many matters sufficiently to understand them all, which we have too often *felt*, there is a still stronger reason, which is the difficulty of a man's preserving his integrity in discharging the duties of each unstained, at least by suspicion."[39] Here was a direct and almost personal indictment of the men who *had been* the government since 1776.

The remedy that the constitution-makers proposed for these evils was a heroic one, amounting to a legal revolution.[40] An entirely new executive department was proposed, to consist of a governor, elected annually by the people, with sole command of the militia, and a council of five, chosen by the joint ballot of the legislature, which was to advise and consent to the governor's appointments of militia and civil officers and judges. The executive was also given a limited veto over the legislature and the power of pardon. The tenure of judges was made dependent upon good behavior, "as they ought, in a peculiar manner, to feel themselves independent and free, and as none would be at the pains to qualify themselves for such important places if they were liable to be removed at pleasure."[41] All justices were to be appointed by the governor and council, but removable by the address of both houses of the legislature. Finally, the architects of this civil structure proposed to keep its features distinct by a series of measures which prevented the holding of more than one important office by the same man and thoroughly insulated the members of the legislature from the temptations of officeholding.

This convention, however, sought to make the government not only more stable but also less democratic. The constitution proposed in 1781 would not only have wiped out the democratic gains that the revolutionary congress of 1775 had made but would have created a narrower electorate than that of colonial times.[42] It required a £100 freehold for voters, £200 to be a representative, £400 to be a senator, and £1,000 to be governor. Officeholding was furthermore confined to Protestants. Finally, the legislature was to be composed in such a way as to give it a definitely aristocratic caste. The twelve senatorial districts into which the state was to be divided were to be equal not in population but in taxable property. The house was to consist of fifty members, distributed at the beginning by counties as follows: Rockingham twenty, Hillsborough ten, Strafford eight, Cheshire eight, Grafton four. These fifty men were to be elected not directly by the people but by and from county conventions, and it was only the delegates to these conventions who were to be elected from the towns, one delegate for every fifty ratable polls, with the usual plan for combining the smallest towns.

This complicated scheme was borrowed in its entirety from the "Essex Result," that contribution to the Massachusetts constitution-making process contributed by Theophilus Parsons in the spring of 1778. The New Hampshire constitution-makers, however, had the wit to see that it was perfectly adapted to their purposes, for it combined three desirable principles: (1) a legislature once removed from direct responsibility to the people, (2) limitation of the legislature to a reasonable size, (3) retention of the deeply cherished system of town representation. While a representative under this plan would have no very definite constituency, yet nearly every town in New Hampshire would be able to elect one of its inhabitants to a county convention.

The address argued that the limited house would contain a larger proportion of able men, "they being twice sifted," that it would proceed with more dispatch, and that it would be less expensive. Then followed an amazing piece of logic: "The objection that in this way each town will not know, nor have the power of designating its own Representative, will, perhaps, on examination, be found one of the strongest arguments in its favor. Those interested views, that party spirit and zeal for rivalry, which too often takes place in towns on such occasions, will be hereby in a great measure destroyed; and the people will be under a necessity of acting upon higher and better principles."[43] Unfortunately, the people did not appreciate this summons to a higher ethics and voted down the convention's interesting forecast of soviet government. It is not altogether impossible that its advocates realized its possibilities of manipulation as well as its moral advantages.

It seems quite clear from the constitution itself that its creation was a part of that conservative reaction that led ultimately to the establishment of the United States Constitution and the reign of the Federalist party. The evidence that would fully establish this conclusion—that is, the debates of the convention and the town votes on ratification—is missing, but all other facts point that way. There is the internal evidence of the constitution itself, with its curtailment of legislative power and its return to aristocratic principles. There is the fact of a heavy delegation from the seaboard regions, a delegation which contained merchants and lawyers who transacted merchants' business, men who were distrustful of an unrestrained lawmaking body made up of farmers, physicians, speculators, and Yankee storekeepers, men who had been injured by that body's amateurish experiments with the currency, with confiscation of loyalist property, and with arbitrary interference in executive and judicial matters. Since members of this delegation filled all the offices in the convention and since two of them, Pickering and Sewall, virtually wrote the constitution, it seems fair to assume that they led the fight for a more responsible government.[44]

But they faced a strong opposition in the convention itself. Referring to the part that Pickering played, William Plumer wrote that "his task was arduous, for the prejudices which the Revolution had engendered against the arbitrary government of Great Britain, made the people jealous of giving to their own officers so much power as was necessary to establish an efficient government."[45] The bitter debate over an independent executive, which had consumed two days in the convention of 1778, probably occupied even more time in 1781.[46] The constitution itself, however, shows that the strong government advocates were victorious. Taken together with the adoption of a conservative constitution by Massachusetts in 1780 and the rise of the Essex Junto, these facts indicate that the orgy of legislative license had reached its peak in New England and that the conservative classes—merchants, lawyers, and clergymen—were ready to swing the balance in the other direction.

It was still too early, however, for their triumph. When the constitution was placed before the people, no one seemed to have a very clear idea of its true significance. Belknap, who certainly favored a conservative revision, complained of the shortness of time allowed for the public discussion of so vital a question.[47] The moment was ill chosen for calm and unhurried consideration of a fundamental issue. As the town of Hampton pointed out, less than half the towns in the state had been able to send delegates to the convention; Grafton and Cheshire counties had seceded from New Hampshire, and the currency was in a state of uncertainty.[48]

All of these were reasons, of course, why a new constitution was sorely needed, but they also filled men's minds with anxiety to the exclusion of thoughts about a permanent plan of government. There seems to have been very little public discussion of the scheme, and what little there was tended to center about the details of the plan, rather than face the great central issue. There was concern about the insidious danger inherent in a revival of the hated word *governor*. One timorous writer in the *New Hampshire Gazette* was fearful lest the power given to the governor of destroying fortifications in time of war would lead to tyranny; another wanted to amend the Bill of Rights so as to deprive Tories of any protection against retroactive laws.[49] The most intelligent objection from the democratic point of view was made by TRUE REPUBLICAN on the ground that the convention method of electing representatives to the legislature would shield the representative from responsibility to his constituents. He wrote: "But though this representative is to act agreeably to his own judgment, where he is uninstructed, yet relative to points where he receives positive instructions, he is bound to follow them, whatever may be his private sentiments. If the contrary was to be allowed, representation would be but an empty sound."[50]

To these feeble or irrelevant objections, the conservatives made weak and insincere answers, completely ineffectual in overcoming the popular antipathy to "high-toned government." The consequence was that the constitution failed to receive the two-thirds vote in its favor required for ratification. No record of the town vote was preserved, so it cannot be determined whether the defeat was narrow or overwhelming or whether the vote had any sectional character. Concord voted unanimously against the plan, insisting upon the existing practice of town representation, the elimination of the "Privy Council," and the reduction of the governor to a mere presiding official in the legislature.[51] Hopkinton, Canterbury, Sanbornton, and Plymouth in the same area found similar fault. Hampton in Rockingham County and Hollis in Hillsborough also voted against the strong executive and the indirectly elected assembly. Keene, the shire town for Cheshire County, gave a favorable vote, but even here it was desired that the power of appointing judges be placed in the legislature's rather than the governor's hands.[52] It is apparent that the lawyers who wrote the repudiated document completely overestimated the people's willingness to trust in their wisdom. As someone wrote on the back of a contemporary copy of the constitution, "This Plan was rejected—perhaps because it was too good."[53]

The convention reassembled in January 1782 and learned that their handiwork had been rudely shattered by the sovereign people. With a semblance, at least, of good grace, they once more bent to the thankless task of creating a constitution which no one seemed to want. In March they were compelled to publish an appeal in the newspapers for towns to send delegates so that they could make some pretense of representing a majority of the state.[54] Conflicts of jurisdiction and of authority arose with the assembly, and the convention had to order that a recent voter's oath imposed by the assembly be ignored in order to find enough qualified voters to ratify a constitution. Another draft was submitted to the people, and rejected, in 1782. "We have a Constitution as often as we have an almanac," wrote Belknap, "and the more we have the worse."[55]

As the people grew more fractious, the necessity for a conclusion of the business became imperative. Cornwallis had surrendered in the previous October, and from that time everyone assumed that the war would soon end. In November 1782 the provisional treaty of peace was signed. Yet New Hampshire was still operating under a constitution limited to the duration of the war. Since it seemed likely that the constitution-makers would require more time than the peacemakers, the people were called to town meetings once more in March 1783 and asked to extend their "temporary" constitution for another year.[56] Thus reprieved, the convention hastened its work to a conclusion, produced a third draft in June, met again in October to learn (probably to their astonishment) that this effort had been successful, ordered that the new government should go into operation on June 2, 1784, and hurried home to continue celebrating the news of the Treaty of Paris.

The prolongation of the convention's life had been partly due to its effort to save something from the wreckage of its first constitution. The second draft, sent out in August 1782, was a compromise in which aristocracy had been sacrificed in order to preserve "vigor and dispatch."[57] Property qualifications for voting were removed and the suffrage given to all adult males who paid a poll tax. Property qualifications for officeholding were reduced by one-half. The unlucky system of county conventions was replaced by the old plan of town representation, modified in such a way as to favor small communities at the expense of

Portsmouth. All this the convention surrendered in order to keep the governor and his powers intact. But the sacrifice was in vain; the people were adamant. In the third and final draft, the governor, with his royalist flavor, was replaced by a plain, republican president, who was not an independent executive with a veto power, but was merely the chairman of the senate with a simple legislative vote.[58] The council was to consist of two senators and three representatives rather than five men chosen from the people at large, and was given equal authority with the president in making appointments.[59] By this evisceration of its original plan, the convention finally produced a constitution acceptable to the people. Belknap was indignant that the plan of 1781 had been "spoiled," and conservatives everywhere believed that the new constitution had fundamental weaknesses.[60] Seven years of experience proved the truth of this opinion. In 1792 many of the provisions that had been forced out of the first draft by the people were voted in again. But for the time being the spirit of local individualism was too well entrenched to be overthrown by the advocates of strong government.

The original draft of 1781 was closely modeled upon Massachusetts's constitution of 1780 and therefore owed its origin chiefly to John Adams rather than to John Pickering. Since, however, New Hampshire had always been a political, economic, and ideological satellite of its larger neighbor to the south, Pickering is certainly not to be criticized for copying ideas that were themselves the embodied tendencies of all New England history. He changed them to suit local circumstances, and Ebenezer Hazard thought that some of the changes were improvements.[61]

Wherever they could, however, Sewall and Pickering copied the Massachusetts document verbatim and *sans apologie*, so that many clauses of the two constitutions are identical to this day.[62] The "Declaration of Rights" in both instruments was so long as to suggest excessive penitence for years of neglect, but New Hampshire's after the burden of an extra year of reflection, was the longer, by thirty-eight articles to thirty. Both constitutions firmly separated the three departments of government and set up checks and balances. Both devised a bicameral legislature, the lower house to represent population and the upper to represent property. Pickering even embodied the county convention scheme of the Essex Result in the New Hampshire constitution, whereas Parsons was plainly unable to get a hearing for it in Massachusetts.

The simpler circumstances of New Hampshire made it possible for Pickering to devise a much saner system for electing senators and councillors than Massachusetts's awkward scheme of drawing them out of the same hat. Pickering followed Massachusetts in creating a governor and clothing him with the veto power, but he did not think it necessary to provide a lieutenant-governor for New Hampshire. The Massachusetts constitution preserved the paralyzing selection of militia officers by those whom they commanded, while the New Hampshire convention was able to reverse that age-old practice and cause officers to be appointed by their superiors. The guarantee of a strong and independent judiciary was a feature of both constitutions. Property qualifications, both for suffrage and for office, were higher in the New Hampshire draft of 1781 than in the Massachusetts constitution. John Adams's cherished mandate for "The Encouragement of Literature, &c" was reproduced with pious exactness for the benefit of future New Hampshire legislatures. Dartmouth College, however, was prevented by its royal charter and perhaps by its then-current attitude of defiance from sharing specifically in constitutional blessings as did Harvard. Finally, whereas the Massachusetts constitution-makers could not see the likelihood of their work standing in need of revision before 1795 and subsequently never again, Pickering was more modest and provided for a mandatory revision within seven years.

Most of this similarity, though, existed only between what Massachusetts adopted in 1780 and what would have been New Hampshire's constitution in 1781 if Pickering had had his way. When the people of the state had finished their dissections by 1783, the family resemblance had been excised, and it was difficult to recognize the patient as a spiritual offspring of the Essex Result. For reasons which the paucity of evidence makes only conjectural, the story of New Hampshire's constitutional convention had quite a different ending from that of Massachusetts. Perhaps the men of substance in New Hampshire lacked the courage to engineer a coup d'état such as that effected by the Massachusetts conservatives in 1780.[63] Perhaps they were not clever enough to devise that same advantageous system for counting votes by which, after a little manipulation, the Massachusetts convention was able to show a two-thirds majority for their constitution. It may even have been that the returns from the towns were so overwhelmingly adverse as to leave them no possible margin of manipulation. Whatever the explanation, the fact is that the Massachusetts convention assumed for itself the responsibility of ratifying a constitution which had not clearly been approved by two-thirds of the people, while the New Hampshire convention deferred ratification to the people and humbly accepted their amendments. Massachusetts achieved a more splendid result, but New Hampshire was more democratic. It may even be that its leaders, by being more patient, tempered the winds of discontent.

CHAPTER 3

PEACE AND DEPRESSION

The war with all its Calamitys did not seem near so distressing as the present times.—New Hampshire State Papers

In the years that immediately followed the proclamation of peace the people of New Hampshire were to learn that the liquidation of an eight-year war was a slow and painful process.[1] The conflict left a heritage of festering wounds that monopolized the attention of legislators to the detriment of constructive measures. The journals of the general court, for a decade after the nominal establishment of peace, are fraught with the aftermath of war—with pleas of soldiers for back pay, compensation, and pensions; with payrolls and accounts for requisitioned supplies, bounties, provisions, and services to be adjusted between a bankrupted state treasury and importunate creditors, including Congress; and with a miscellany of demands that drove legislators to distraction. When the political uncertainty growing out of defective state and national constitutions and the financial chaos produced by an enormous debt, unpaid taxes, and inflated currency were added to this, they made the task of reconstruction during the 1780s one that would have tried even experienced statesmen working under the most favorable conditions. But the New Hampshire leaders of that period were experimenting with a new form of government and facing an economic depression in addition to all their inherited difficulties.

A sharp difference of opinion over postwar treatment of the loyalists was one of the earlier evidences of the shape of the future. Such leaders as John Adams, John Jay, and George Washington approved the fourth, fifth, and sixth articles of the treaty of peace and believed that they should be carried out as fully as though Congress had sovereign power to execute them. The men who governed New Hampshire after 1783 were in at least partial agreement with this opinion. Even before Congress acted, John Sullivan, the attorney general of the state, properly interpreted the sixth article of the treaty as nullifying a New Hampshire law of 1782 which provided for the confiscation of all absentee loyalists' property and brought no further actions under that statute.[2] When Congress sent out its proclamation of January 14, 1784, enjoining the states to observe their obligations under the treaty, the New Hampshire legislature responded more loyally than did most of the states. In November it repealed a law that had prevented British subjects "and all other persons inimical to the United States" from instituting actions in the courts.[3] But it was not until two years later, and then only after a sharp struggle, that a bill was carried which repealed the proscription and confiscation laws of the war period and allowed the Tories one year in which to return and settle their affairs in the state courts.[4] By this legislation New Hampshire came as near to implementing the Treaty of Paris as it was possible for a single state legislature to do. When Lord Carmarthen made out his bill of particulars on treaty violations in 1786, it contained no indictment against New Hampshire.[5]

This honorable result was not altogether the result of a highly developed ethical sense in New Hampshire. It was the work chiefly of Portsmouth merchants, lawyers, and the "property interest" of the southeastern towns in general, and it coincided exactly with their interests. Sullivan's tenderness toward the Tories was partially due to the fact that he was employed as counsel for one of the wealthiest of them.[6] The Portsmouth gentry had from the first been opposed to the policy of confiscation and had voiced their objections in resolutions from town meetings to the legislature.[7] Their reasons were candidly stated: the balance between British and New Hampshire merchants was very much in favor of the latter, and if confiscations were to be indiscriminately indulged, they would be the losers. This contention was validated by the accounts of the British merchants themselves, who listed New Hampshire as the least of their debtors, excepting New Jersey.[8] A clever writer in the *New Hampshire Gazette* (possibly Jeremy Belknap) pled for reconciliation with the loyalists on the pragmatic grounds that continued persecution simply exiled them to Nova Scotia, where, aided by state legislation that drove British trade from Portsmouth to Halifax, their products and shipping would soon replace New England's in the West Indian markets. "What fatal consequences this system will have upon the commerce of the United States and particularly upon that of New Hampshire and Massachusetts our children, and children's children will relate in tears."[9]

Against the merchants and conservatives in general, who believed in the necessity of honoring treaties, there were arrayed powerful forces in favor of unrelenting war on the Tories. At the head of these were the relatively few men who had speculated in or been corrupted by the confiscated loyalist property and who faced exposure and ruin if their deeds were bared in the courtroom. A much larger group of ordinary farmers who had purchased small portions of the confiscated estates were equally fearful that their titles might not hold against judicial review. Towns such as Londonderry, where valuable loyalist properties had fallen into other hands, were especially hostile to legislation in compliance with the treaty, and the interior towns in general, indifferent to the interests of the merchants, were more susceptible to ancient grudges than to arguments based on expediency.

Accordingly, there were bitter protests at the leniency of the government and little disposition to cooperate in carrying out the treaty. Sullivan was attacked in the newspapers for "suffering the estates of absentees to remain unappropriated, thereby withholding from the soldier his stipend, from the distressed widows and helpless orphans the means of support."[10] The sovereign people, in town meetings, on county juries, and in angry mobs, took matters into their own hands. Resolutions were passed to refuse admittance to Tory refugees in spite of the treaty,[11] and when some of the bolder ones returned anyway, immediate demonstrations were made of the fact that while Congress might ratify treaties, it could not enforce them. John Stinson, who had served in the king's army during the war, came to his old home in Dunbarton and overstayed his year of grace, whereupon his unforgiving neighbors sent a protest to the general court, which ordered Stinson's removal from the state.[12]

When Elijah Williams, who had also fought on the wrong side in the war, took advantage of the treaty to return to Keene for a settlement with his debtors, he was seized by a mob and carried before a justice of the peace. The magistrate was too lenient, so the local patriots, "aggravated probably by the arts of those who were indebted to him," attempted to substitute the rope for the statute book. Only the strenuous exertions of the more responsible citizens prevented a lynching.[13] To patriotic violence had been added the malignant influence of religious intolerance in Claremont, where a forlorn group of Episcopalians had been persecuted throughout the war for loyalism. The treaty brought no surcease to them, and finally in March 1784 they petitioned the British governor of Canada to be granted lands on Lake Memphremagog in order to escape oppression in New Hampshire.[14] Those Tories who had remained in the state and who managed to recover their influence after the war, such as Joshua Atherton, James Sheafe, and George Jaffrey, were objects of deep suspicion to their less artful countrymen. The town of Chester instructed its representatives in 1783 "to endeavor likewise, that no Person or Persons of whatever denomination, whom you have just Cause to suspect, have been, or are enemical to American Measures; have aided her enemies, or been Idle Spectators during the Contest with Great Britain shall sustain, or hold any office of Trust, Profit or Honor, in the State."[15]

In spite of such sentiments, Governor Bartlett appointed Atherton attorney general in 1793, and other "Idle Spectators" soon crept into many of the highest offices. As the plain people of the state, the people who had done most of the fighting and the suffering during the war, saw the squires, the merchants, the lawyers, and the clergymen begin to band together once more, oblivious to their temporarily divided loyalties and mutually interested in recapturing the profitable trade with England and reestablishing a virile executive government, they wondered if their struggle for liberty had been in vain. Seeds of suspicion were sown that, by assiduous Republican watering, sprouted into the later conviction that the Federalists were simply the old Tories in disguise.

The confiscation acts had been passed, less perhaps for the purpose of punishing loyalists than of filling the empty war chest. Their failure, however, to do more than enrich a few speculators and war profiteers amply justified Belknap's mild statement that the revolutionary government was "unskilled in the art of finance."[16] The desperate necessity of paying for an eight-year war drove the financial amateurs at Exeter into every fiscal expedient known to man, except such as might have been too unpopular. Taxation, being within the latter category, was avoided as much as possible. Although the assessment of £2,160,000 in 1780 looks formidable enough for a poor community of 90,000 people,[17] there were two mitigating circumstances: the sum was fixed in a currency inflated some 400 percent, and only a small part of it was collected. By reason of poverty, depreciated paper money, suspension of the courts, secession, and the legislature's absorption in other matters, tax payments during the war depended almost entirely upon local whim. Year after year the total of delinquent taxes grew, until it reached the sum of £399,877 in 1781.[18] This mountain of debt, owed by towns to the state, became a sectional issue because it was the poorer towns that were delinquent and these were concentrated in the interior regions of the state. The sectional implications of the problem are clearly indicated by the petitions for tax abatement received by the assembly; these came from a wide arc of towns on the frontier, stretching from Conway and Wakefield in the northeastern edge of settlement through New London, Cardigan (Orange), and Unity in the thinly settled interior, and turning northward again up the Connecticut River.[19]

Tax delinquency, a frontier problem, was attended by the familiar frontier complaints against neglect, absentee ownership, and uncertain land titles. The townsmen of Concord, alias Gunthwaite, now Lisbon, in the northern part of Grafton County, petitioned for an abatement of back taxes in 1786, claiming that, in spite of their poverty and small numbers, they had defended themselves, without assistance, against "the Ravage of the savage Enemy," and had sent more than their share of soldiers to the Continental Army. Yet no sooner did the legislature grant their request than the tax collecting stopped again because of a dispute between the inhabitants and a well-known speculator, who claimed the township by a rival grant.[20] Pleas for permission to assess nonresident proprietors, many of them living in other states, who refused to pay their share of the taxes came from a number of towns. An amazing injustice, which could have occurred only within the town system of New England, was revealed by some petitioners who had only recently migrated to the northern frontier from other states, yet were held responsible for a share of all the delinquent taxes of their newly chosen hometowns.[21]

The petition of Dorchester, a newly settled town in Grafton County, gives almost a complete picture of the frontiersman's state of mind. It began with the complaint that the petitioners were overtaxed and always had been, which explained why "there is considerable sums in back-rearages which we are now called upon for; which at present appears impracticable For us to pay and support our Families in this uncultivated Wilderness." The town's growth had been seriously hindered by its isolated position, lack of town organization, and "the Dispute In these parts about Jurisdiction." Before the settlers were given a civil organization, the selectmen of a neighboring town had assessed them much too high, and during the Vermont controversy they "lost [their] Meeting" and assessed no taxes at all.

> We sensibly Feeling the Before innumerated Dificulties together with our Arduous Strugles in Begining and setling this Rugged Wilderness Our Lands Being something Broken and not so fertile as most Towns round about us—Therefore we pray Your Honors to take our Dificult Scituation into Your Wise Consideraton and Grant us such releaf in the Premises as in Your Wisdom You may think fit, that thereby our heavy burthen May be lightened and we incouraged to exert ourselves in every Possible way to discharg what may be found to be our Just proportion.[22]

Another serious difficulty is revealed by this petition—namely, that for eight years some of the towns in Grafton County had refused to recognize the sovereignty of New Hampshire and to pay taxes into its treasury. When they returned to their allegiance in 1784, they encountered heavy bills for delinquent taxes. Owing perhaps to the adroitness of Jonathan Freeman, agent for the town of Hanover, and Russell Freeman, his brother and Hanover's representative in the general court, the Connecticut Valley towns received lenient treatment at the hands of the government which they had defied. The legislature made full allowance for the soldiers and supplies the towns had furnished during the war and accepted the balance due in state notes at face value.[23] This compromise marked an end to the jealousy between Hanover and Exeter and the beginning of a political entente which endured for decades. Exeter was not always so generous, however, with other delinquent towns. A petition from Unity for abatement of taxes was summarily dismissed, a similar one from Cardigan (Orange) received favorable treatment by the house but was rejected by the senate, and upon numerous others the journals record no decision.[24] Already a line of cleavage was beginning to appear in the Connecticut Valley between the flourishing, conservative intervale towns and the poor, struggling settlements back in the hills.

Tax delinquency greatly augmented the appalling problem of the state debt—a problem which would have strained the resources of New Hampshire even if every penny of tax had been paid promptly into the treasury. In spite of a partial repudiation of its paper currency, New Hampshire emerged from the war with a state debt that Timothy Pitkin estimated at $500,000.[25] To the interest on this sum was added the state's annual obligation to the national treasury, which for the year 1785 was fixed at $105,416.[26] State and national debt together created a per capita burden of more than eighteen dollars for every farmer in New Hampshire—a large sum for those days.

Until 1782 New Hampshire had met the requisitions of Congress faithfully, standing behind only Massachusetts, Connecticut, Virginia, and Pennsylvania in the amount of money furnished the common treasury.[27] Congress, however, had refused to act upon its protest that it was assessed more than its just portion, and after 1782 the state began to fall behind in its payments. From then until the end of the Confederation, New Hampshire dropped from fifth among the states in the size of contributions to fourth place in the amount of its delinquency.[28]

The conservative classes and sections regarded this financial infidelity with shame and apprehension, but the legislators from interior towns could not be persuaded to vote the necessary appropriations. A bill to raise part of the Continental requisition of 1785, for example, was defeated by a vote of 17-44, with only the commercial towns in its favor.[29] Nevertheless, the legislature struggled manfully with the state debt and managed to reduce the principal to approximately $300,000 by 1790.[30] This was accomplished by grinding taxation, which fell with peculiar severity upon the poor. Taxes of £25,000, of which £23,000 went to payment of interest and reduction of principal on the state debt, were being levied in 1784.[31] It is not surprising that such a tax, falling almost entirely upon polls and real estate, aroused class and sectional animosity.

Taxes, debts, claims, and confiscations alone would have made the problems of public finance difficult during the 1780s, but they were magnified by the indescribable confusion into which all fiscal relations had been thrown by the currency problem. Unable, both for political and economic reasons, to finance more than a small part of the war by taxation, New Hampshire, like all the other states and the Continental Congress, had resorted to paper money. The legislature had indeed been moderate, for it had only printed some £150,000 in notes and had stopped the presses in 1778.[32] But this sum was augmented by the paper of other states that had found its way into New Hampshire and by more than $5,000,000 in Continental bills which had been poured into the state.[33] The Continental currency was exchanged for a new issue at 40 to 1 in 1780, and by January 1 of the next year paper money was worth only one seventy-fifth of its face value.[34]

It is difficult for the imagination to translate this figure into the experience of people who witnessed the price inflation that necessarily accompanied currency depreciation. A few pages from the matter-of-fact diary kept by Matthew Patten of Bedford, judge of probate for Hillsborough County, give the figures some semblance of reality. In June 1780, Patten paid $100 for an eighteen-pound salmon and $24 for twelve rows of pins. In July two and one-half bushels of corn cost him $100, four pounds of tobacco $30, three pounds of sugar $30. Clothing himself, even with garments of household manufacture, was a formidable task when broadcloth cost $187 for half a yard, cotton was $30 a pound, a pound of sole leather cost $24, and a quarter-pound of indigo was $70. Even when the worthy judge stopped at the tavern for refreshment, he had to carry a large purse, for rum was $16 a quart, and a mug of toddy cost $8. The situation in regard to his own income was cogently stated in this reference to a fee for judgment in a certain probate case. "I charged 3 Dollars the old way and submitted it to themselves what Discount to give me in continental bills they gave me 230 dollars which was 76 and ⅓ for one."[35]

Already familiar in American experience and destined to recur later, this situation created a hard-money party, determined to end the reign of paper. It was composed chiefly of merchants whose far-flung enterprises suffered from the chaotic state of the currency, professional men whose fixed incomes were reduced to invisibility by the depreciation, and all those individuals who formerly had had specie to lend at interest who were now being repaid one-fiftieth of its value. The wartime woes of this group were epitomized by Belknap, who had contracted to preach to the people of Dover for £100 a year and who could have legally been paid for all his services during the year 1781 in currency worth nine bushels of corn.[36] His parishioners were not so un-Christian as to take full advantage of this opportunity, but that his salary had failed to keep pace with inflation was evident in his letter to Ebenezer Hazard in October 1783. "I have long felt that the concerns of a family are a great hindrance to scientific labours, and especially during the late reign of war, paper money, regulation-acts, beggars on horseback, &c., &c., &c., when the most of my attention was engaged in keeping the belly and back from grumbling, the kitchen-fire from going out."[37]

The current of reaction against paper money, loose finance, and legislative dictatorship was flowing strongly by the end of 1780. In Philadelphia, John Sullivan, New Hampshire's delegate to Congress, joined the party of nationalist leaders who gained control of that body and undertook a complete reorganization of the war effort.[38] New Hampshire delegates participated in two conventions, at Boston in August and at Hartford in November, which advocated strong measures for increasing the authority of Congress, giving it taxing power and compulsory sanctions over delinquent states.[39]

At home, the movement toward a more vigorous state constitution was accompanied by a policy of fiscal retrenchment. Taxes were levied to meet the interest on state securities and to redeem the paper currency. A drastic law for the collection of delinquent taxes was written.[40] But the hard-money party won its really notable victory on September 1, 1781, when, by a majority of one vote, it enacted a law making gold and silver once more the legal tender for all debts. This bill was carried by the seaboard and Merrimack Valley towns against the interior towns of Rockingham and Hillsborough counties.[41] A great number of towns failed to participate in this decision, however. The vote was taken on the last day of a special session in the harvest season when thirty-three of the representatives from the interior parts of the state were absent and when at least a third of the towns in the state were not even represented. It is almost certain that the vote would have been reversed, had all these towns been able to speak their minds.

In January 1782, however, the legislature followed up this bill with another one which partially repudiated the paper currency. A scale of depreciation was drawn at what was approximately the rate of exchange between paper and silver for every month between February 1777 and June 1781.[42] Holders of old bills were then allowed to exchange them for specie notes according to the scale of depreciation: that is to say, a £100 note issued prior to February 1777 could be exchanged for a new £100 bill, but it would require £7500 in bills issued after December 1, 1780, to exchange for the same value. The bills thus drawn into the treasury were sent to Congress for specie credit or were destroyed. Certificates receivable for taxes were issued for the interest on the old notes. This measure was certainly drastic, but it was far from being a complete repudiation. The opportunities it afforded for speculation and the comfort it gave to those who had already speculated can easily be grasped.

For a few months the deflationary policy was supported by a continuing artificial war prosperity. Prices remained high, even in the new currency, and specie, brought in by privateers and the French fleet, was plentiful.[43] The renewal of foreign trade after the peace, however, produced a very unfavorable balance of trade and quickly drained the country of specie. By November 1783 the agricultural towns were complaining of the complete absence of gold and silver.[44] People were not destitute of goods or property, but their surpluses were of no value unless they could be exchanged. Domestic exchange was impossible, except by barter, because of the lack of a medium. Foreign exchange might have brought in specie if the proper trade regulations, tariffs, and treaties could have been enacted. But experience soon showed that to be successful such regulation of commerce had to be uniform throughout the United States, and neither the state legislature nor Congress had the authority to make such regulations. Consequently, specie did not flow into New Hampshire. In the absence of legal currency, no amount of hard work or good intentions would pay debts or taxes. This was the vicious circle of futility into which not only New Hampshire but every one of the thirteen states had been drawn. A group of malcontents put the whole matter succinctly in November 1783, when they said, "The war with all its Calamitys did not seem near so distressing as the present times."[45]

It appeared that New England's primary necessity was a revival of commerce, but such a revival presented a curious triangular problem of internal conflict, interstate hostility, and international complication. When Portsmouth harbor was reopened to British ships on June 18, 1783, the people of New Hampshire anticipated the dawning of a golden commercial era. In their relief at the end of wartime restrictions and in the enthusiasm that the European concert against Great Britain had engendered, they assumed that their trade would now be worldwide. Reaction against the British mercantilist system caused them to swing to the opposite extreme of free trade, and for a few months New Hampshire merchants enjoyed the delusion that Portsmouth harbor would be crowded with Piscataqua vessels, loading lumber, fish, and beef for all parts of the world or bringing back the produce of the globe in free exchange.

The dream was soon shattered. France, Holland, and Spain did not rush to buy New Hampshire lumber. England turned the Navigation Acts against its former colonies, permitting only limited exports of American goods to its own shores and completely cutting off the lucrative trade with the British West Indies in American ships. Meanwhile, England immediately recaptured the American states as markets for its own manufactures. Taking advantage of the brief enthusiasm for free trade, and the subsequent inability to agree on retaliatory measures, British merchants dumped cheap goods in American ports in such quantities as to destroy the infant war industries that had recently sprung up and to drain the country of specie.[46] "Powder and ball, muskets and bayonets, could not conquer us, but we are to be subdued by British gewgaws," wailed a Boston newspaper.[47]

Demands for retaliation against Great Britain arose, but who was to do the retaliating? It was obvious that New Hampshire, acting alone and able to affect by legislation only the Piscataqua trade, could not hope to intimidate the British giant. Massachusetts urged that the New England states, acting in concert, could regulate their commerce effectively, but New Hampshire preferred to have Congress exercise that power.[48] The explanation for the state's dependence upon Congress lay in its geographical position; New Hampshire lay like a sponge within the grasp of Massachusetts, and only the small area around Piscataqua Bay could claim a measure of freedom from that grip. The northern frontier was tributary to Portland, the Merrimack Valley to Newburyport, and even the traffic of the upper Connecticut towns had to pass through Massachusetts on its way to and from Hartford. The peculiar geographical situation of the interior towns dictated a nationalist attitude in preference to economic existence at the mercy of the Massachusetts legislature. Even Portsmouth could hope to compete more favorably with Bay State ports under uniform commercial regulations, enforced by national authority. This explains the promptness with which, on April 6, 1781, New Hampshire ratified the proposal to give Congress the power to levy a 5 percent tariff.[49]

Rhode Island's obduracy killed the 5 percent plan, however. The states hastened to levy their own tariffs, and New Hampshire reluctantly fell into line by passing an impost act on April 17, 1784.[50] In November a second congressional plan for a uniform tariff appeared to offer a reprieve, but New York gave it the death blow, and New Hampshire was left to the mercy of its powerful neighbors.[51] The Massachusetts tariff, growing constantly more oppressive, soon drove the Portsmouth merchants to petitioning the legislature for relief, and a committee was appointed to confer with the Bay State officials, but nothing was accomplished.[52] By June 1785 the legislators had learned that mutual restrictions on commerce benefited no one, and New Hampshire agreed to suspend the operation of its impost insofar as it affected imports from Massachusetts if that state would make a similar concession.[53] Commissioners from each state were named for another conference, again with no results. In the spring of 1786 New Hampshire felt compelled to levy a new tariff, with rates as high as 15 percent on some commodities.[54]

In the meantime, both New Hampshire and Massachusetts were struggling with the more difficult problem of the carrying trade. On June 23, 1785, New Hampshire enacted a Navigation Act, designed to aid its shipping at the expense of foreign vessels. This brought protests from French merchants to Congress that such laws were not only discriminatory and unfriendly but actually violated the treaty of amity and commerce with France. Secretary Jay agreed and denounced the New England states vigorously.[55] New Hampshire was also induced to join Massachusetts and Rhode Island in a sorry attempt to retaliate for loss of the West

Indies trade by completely excluding British vessels from its ports. Such measures had little effect on England as long as Connecticut and New York refused to join in them.[56] They aroused immediate protest among some merchants whose imports from Britain were cut off, as well as among farmers who could find no market for their lumber and cattle. The legislature could withstand the pressure only until November, when the Navigation Act was suspended "until all the other New England States and the State of New York shall adopt similar acts."[57] The bewilderment resulting from thirteen state legislatures attempting to regulate commerce with a single, powerful cosmopolitan trading nation is clearly revealed in a wistful resolution passed in October 1785:

> *Voted*, that His Excellency the President be desired to write the several Executives in the union & request to know whether their Assemblies have, or are likely to join with this State & Massachusetts in their commercial opposition to great Britain—whether they have empowered Congress to regulate Commerce or have passed or probably will pass Acts similar to those enacted by this & the Massachusetts States in June last respecting Navigation & Commerce and lay such information before the General Court at their next session.[58]

Further embarrassment was caused when the legislature attempted to revive state industries by offering bounties and exemption from taxes and by making regulations to improve the quality and uniformity of the products.[59] An act to encourage the export of native iron, steel, and glass manufactures by allowing ships of any nation to lade them free of duties or charges ran directly counter to the simultaneous attempt to embargo British shipping. When the trading interests offered an amendment to exclude British ships from this concession, it was defeated, 34–42, with the towns tributary to Portsmouth contributing most of the votes against it.[60] An act to regulate the size and quality of sawmill products brought an immediate cry of rage from that part of the country where lumber served as both currency and export.[61] Petitions came from Rochester, Wakefield, and Dover, praying that the law be repealed, that British ships be allowed to carry lumber to the West Indies, and that "the Duty Layed on tunnage on Ships or Vessells belonging to foreigners which Duty we Look Upon to be Equal to Shuting up our ports against them" be removed.[62] The next legislature was compelled to suspend the law.[63]

Thus, the attempt of this small and economically vulnerable state to regulate its own commercial relations had eventuated in trouble not only with France, Great Britain, Congress, and Massachusetts but between the sectional interests within the state. The interior towns wanted a tariff for revenue, but opposed trade restrictions that deprived them of a market for their produce.[64] The Portsmouth merchants felt that the impost fell chiefly upon them and benefited the ports of Massachusetts, while the Navigation Act gave them some hope of building up their own merchant marine.[65] Between the big shippers' demand for protection and the small producers' demand for a market, futile resentment against Great Britain and the necessity of trading with it, anger at Massachusetts's imposts and the desire to raise a revenue from Massachusetts's exports, efforts to stimulate industry and efforts to stimulate trade, the legislature gyrated in painful indecision. Small wonder that it sought to transfer the burden to broader shoulders. In December 1786 a committee was appointed "to draught an address to Congress, stating the situation of the publick affairs of this state and the improbability of ever supplying the Treasury of the United States, unless some method can be devised for regulating the commerce of the said United States."[66]

New Hampshire bore one cross during the troubled 1780s that its neighbors were spared—a trial which was uniquely its own. By the sudden revival of an ancient dispute the title to every acre in the richest and oldest two-thirds of its territory was put in jeopardy. In 1622 the original area of New Hampshire had been granted to Captain John Mason by the Council for New England in one of those curious patents that betrayed the deplorable ignorance of American geography prevalent among seventeenth-century bureaucrats. In 1746 the heir of Captain Mason sold his title claim to a group of twelve wealthy and prominent New Hampshire men, who were thenceforth known as the Masonian Proprietors. They issued quit-claim deeds to all persons actually in possession of improved property within their domain, thus laying to rest the quit-rent quarrel between settlers and proprietors that had constantly agitated New Hampshire history. They then proceeded in *ex parte* fashion, to survey the inland limit of their patent, which they interpreted as a line sixty miles distant from the sea at all points running in a great curve from Richmond to Ossipee. This line can be followed on the map today in the boundaries of towns and counties. Between 1746 and 1783 the Masonian Proprietors had proceeded to grant some thirty-seven new townships within the unsettled portion of their territory on terms similar to those of all typical New England town charters.[67]

The Masonian Proprietors granted their land on easy terms and so conducted their gigantic speculation that no serious complaint had risen against them until 1783. Unfortunately for their continued peace and comfort, they were members of the old Portsmouth aristocracy, and during the war serious doubts had been cast upon their individual loyalties to the American cause. The general discontent that arose as an aftermath of the war singled out these Tories and land-grabbers as objects of popular wrath. The trouble was apparently touched off by the town of Marlow, lying in Cheshire County, whose southeastern corner had been cut off by the curved patent line.[68] The Masonian Proprietors, with their customary tact, had settled the problems that originally grew out of this conflict to everyone's satisfaction, but during the war the blundering state government had assessed Marlow its full tax bill while at the same time assigning those taxpayers who had been cut off by the Masonian line to another jurisdiction.[69] As a solution to both their land problem and their tax problem, the outraged inhabitants of Marlow, and of other towns similarly affected, conceived the idea of denying the curved line's validity.[70] There suddenly appeared the convenient suggestion that Mason's patent contained no warrant for a curved line; that a proper interpretation of its wording entitled the proprietors only to a straight line between the two points sixty miles from the sea; and that all of the considerable area lying between the two lines had always belonged to the state.

Since the land in question had long since been formed into townships by the proprietors, and much of it had been settled and improved, the insinuation that the proprietary title was invalid immediately created great unrest. But the men who had probably originated the idea of attacking the curved line had given even greater grounds for uneasiness. These men were the so-called Allen Proprietors. At one time in the turbulent history of the Mason family, their claim to New Hampshire had been sold to a London merchant named Samuel Allen. The sale had been of dubious legality; the Allen claim had never been recognized by the people of New Hampshire, and since 1715 it had been entirely quiescent. Suddenly in 1783 this antiquated claim to the richest two-thirds of the state was revived, ostensibly by the Allen heirs, but actually by a group of speculators that included Dr. Nathaniel Peabody of Atkinson, an unscrupulous land-grabber, and Peter Green, a Tory lawyer of Concord. General Sullivan was retained by the Allenites to act as their attorney and to provide a respectable front for their blackmail. The scheme can hardly be called anything less harsh, for at a time when the people of Rockingham, Strafford, and Hillsborough counties were already suffering an infinite variety of evils, these men brought the very ownership of their homes into question in order to squeeze concessions from the Masonian Proprietors. Contemporary testimony indicates that each group of proprietors aroused public distress and confusion by spreading evil rumors about the other, and some people even came to believe that "it was the intention of those proprietors [the Allenites] to establish lordships, & reduce the people to vassallage."[71]

Public resentment against both the Allenites and the Masonians, particularly in the Merrimack Valley region, flared to such intensity that for a time it eclipsed even the currency situation.[72] The farmers whose lands

were in jeopardy believed that both sets of proprietors were only attempting to revive the aristocracy that they had beaten down by arms. Was not
attorney Sullivan of the Allenites also employed by the "refugees," and
was not Peter Green a notorious loyalist? As for the Masonians, the
revolutionary hero John Stark, who had a quarrel with them over a piece
of land, expressed the popular prejudice when he petitioned for a settlement by the legislature on the ground that "the expence and hazard of a
law-trial with men of their oppulence is such a serious matter, that he
cannot think of entering into, and without the aid of the General Court,
must sit down under the loss, wholly occasioned by a set of men, who
have made a great stride to monopolize a great part of this State for a
very trifling consideration."[73]

The fullest expression of popular feeling in this controversy appeared
in the petitions that poured in upon the legislature during the summer of
1786. Two of these, coming from a convention of delegates representing
ten towns in Hillsborough County and from sixty inhabitants of western
Rockingham County, are particularly explicit, and especially interesting
since these areas were most vitally concerned in the Mason-Allen dispute.
The petitioners expressed the true frontier philosophy that a proprietary
title granted to an English captain by "the Usorped authority of the
britash Court" under right of "bare Discovery" was invalid against oc-
cupancy by citizens whose "Ancestors purchesed of the native Lords of
the Soile & Defended it with their blood & treasure."[74] Now the quarrel
between Allenites and Masonians was not only throwing doubt upon the
title to land occupied for generations but was greatly retarding the settlement of waste lands, since would-be settlers were afraid to purchase from
either party. The petitioners urged the legislature to intervene and determine whether the title belonged to Allenites, or Masonians, or neither.
If it legally rested in either of the claimants, the petitioners "earnestly
pray[ed] that the Lines may be fairly run according to their Grant that
they may have their Right; & if they are honest Men they can wish no
more." But the petitioners strongly hinted their belief that neither party
had good title, and that the land actually belonged to the state, at least
beyond the straight line. If a committee of the legislature found this to be
the case and ran the proper line, then "the Unimproved Land without s^d
patton line now in the possesion of Said Claments may be Sold to Redeem our publick Securitys or in Such other way as your wisdom may See
meet." They neglected to add the happy conclusion that such a method of
retiring the public debt would deliver the farmers of the Merrimack
Valley from a heavy tax burden and make everyone but Allenites and
Masonians happy.

The assault on the Masonian patent was a clear-cut issue between
mass and class involving the destruction of sacred property rights. It

would have been a hopeless attack before 1775, for in colonial days the Masonian Proprietors were almost synonymous with the governor's council. But in 1786 the syndicate was tainted with Toryism and was regarded with jealousy even by the more conservative patriots. Furthermore, it could be shorn of part of its property without the hazard of a lawsuit but under color of legality simply by the appointment of a "disinterested" committee to resurvey the western limit of the patent according to the new interpretation.

This the house of representatives proposed to do in 1786, but the senate maintained its true function as protector of property rights by refusing to concur in the resolution, "which excited much alarm among the people."[75] Public opinion was too strong for the senate to resist, however. In 1787 the disinterested committee was appointed, and it performed its duty by running a straight line to connect the sixty-mile terminal points. The end of the matter was sordid for all parties concerned. The Masonian Proprietors were in no mood to fight for their rights, and the state was interested only in obtaining revenue, regardless of its source. Accordingly, a bargain was effected by which the state sold its newly discovered lands to the proprietors, who had for years been in possession of them, for $40,800 in public securities and specie. The Allenites were bought off even more easily with £5 in cash and 8500 acres of land. The great monopolizers retained their title, but the state treasury was enriched, speculators could continue to improve their opportunities, and the uncertainty that had hovered over New Hampshire land titles for one hundred and sixty years was finally dispelled. It was one of the most efficient, if not the most honorable, pieces of work that the government performed during the distracted decade of the 1780s.[76]

The overwhelming difficulty, one which permeated every other problem in this troublesome period, was the mass of private debts, which, added to public indebtedness, delinquent taxes, the stagnation of commerce, and the general economic insecurity, drove men to the verge of rebellion. These debts had accumulated imperceptibly during an upward swing of the business cycle. The war had brought prosperity, in general, to two classes of men—farmers and speculators—of whom Belknap said, "They have been growing rich on the spoils of their country, and you know the adage, 'Crescit amor nummi quantum ipsa pecunia rescit.'"[77] The reversal of economic conditions after 1780, and particularly the state's policy of deflation, threw many individuals from both these classes into serious difficulties.

"Public and private credit was much impaired," wrote William Plumer, who lived through these years as a young farmer and public official, "& creditors pressed their debtors for payment. . . . The scarsity of money reduced the value of property very low. . . . In this state of things the people murmured & complained. Many petitioned the legislature for releif, but obtained none. Paper money was what they requested; nothing else would satisfy them, tho every well informed man knew, if it was made, it would depreciate, & prove a fertile source of fraud & iniquity."[78]

Murmur and *complain* were mild words to describe the wave of discontent that mounted steadily during the 1780s. It began as early as 1782, when the legislature received several petitions for paper money from the Merrimack Valley and from Cheshire County. They indicated genuine suffering on the part of tradesmen and farmers, who "with all their industry are unable to carry on any Commerce or Trade even with their Neighbors to pay any debt, tho' never so just or trivial. . . . As a consequence of the above recited grievances we are threatened with speedy and inevitable ruin by the multiplicity of lawsuits which with the extravagancy of Lawyers fees in many instances tend to the Destruction of the unfortunate Debtors and will if not speedily mitigated end in the utter annihilation of all good order and harmony in this state."[79]

Since the law allowed a creditor to keep his debtor in prison until his demands were met in specie, no matter how much property the debtor may have owned, an actual shortage of gold and silver obviously produced appalling injustice. For this reason many people advocated a law to make real estate a legal tender for certain debts. A petition in favor of such a measure, from "People in the upper part of this State," attributed the distress of debtors to the fact that the state itself had failed to meet its obligations, thus depriving of funds the people who "have lent the Publick large Sums of Money in order to carry on the late war to Effect." It assumed that the defalcation of both public and private debts was due to the scarcity of money, not to any wish to evade obligations.

> Nothing but gold or Silver (which is not to be had) or the Imprisonment of the Debtor, will Satisfy a great part of the Creditors. Numbers of Gentlemen of handsome Fortunes Obliged to leave their Familys, Farms and Stocks, without any overseer or Labourer and imbrace a Loathsome gaol, and many more in Daily Expectation of Shareing the fate of their Neighbours, and at the Same time have in their hands a Plenty of Real and Personal Estate and ready to deliver the Same, besides the great Cost they are put to by unnecessary law Suits and Great fees when there is not money in Circulation to pay one fourth part of the Cost.[80]

The hand of the ruined speculator is evident in this curious document. At the same time, however, the legislature received dozens of petitions on this subject from agricultural towns, expressed in dubious orthography but unquestionable sincerity. The freeholders of Grafton, a frontier settlement, complained of "the Deplorable & Shocking Situation of the People of this Town Paper Currency So ameadiately Sinking & the Great Scarcity of Cash almost None Surculating in this Part of the State that the Like was Never Experienced by a Free People." Their taxes were enormous, they said, but they did not have enough money "to Pay Even for the Copy of the Rits & if there is Not Somthing Done we Shall Soon be reduced to a State of abel Begary therefore we Pray your honours to Pass an act to inable the People to Pay there Debts without money for we have Property."[81] Such a situation might have been merely chronic on the frontier, but in 1783 it was equally the subject of complaint in old and normally prosperous towns, such as Amherst and Londonderry.

For all these ills, the panacea that was hawked most persistently in petitions and the public prints was the issuance of paper money. A writer from Hillsborough County informed subscribers to the *New Hampshire Gazette* that taxes that could not be paid, commerce that profited only Great Britain, public officers who thought only of sinecures, and foreclosures that drove the honest husbandmen to migrate from the state were difficulties for which there was an easy solution—"a bank of paper money." But what had the legislature done about it? "Why, in effect, NOTHING. . . . The people should assert their own MAJESTY, as the origin of power. Instruct your representatives to vote for the making a paper currency, and to pledge themselves in behalf of their constituents for the support of its credit; and let laws be made Enacting Banishment to those who shall dare to refuse or depreciate it, as unworthy the name of fellow citizens.[82]

Later articles attacked those who opposed a paper money issue, "gentlemen of fortune who would wish to become the nobility of our country" and merchants who imported meat and grain rather than buy from the farmers in their own state. "If it be objected by Gentlemen in trade, who owe money in England and elsewhere, that this money will be instrumental in carrying away the silver and gold out of the State; Suppose it does for the present: They have already sent the most of it off, and the Legislature will want this money for the use of the inhabitants."[83] Until the autumn of 1786, the *New Hampshire Gazette* was crowded with expressions similar to these, and the editors themselves, although admitting opposing views to those expressed in their columns, were mildly enamored of the paper money sorceress. The easy-money advocates claimed well-nigh universal support and threatened the legislators with retribution at the polls unless their wishes were gratified.[84]

Conservative writers answered those arguments by claiming that the resources of the state were not equal to the task of maintaining a paper currency without depreciation. If state notes were lent to farmers on real estate as security, the "government would be under all the embarrassments of poverty, while the public chest was crouded with paper bills, and in this case, all the end that this paper money could answer, would be enabling the dishonest members of society to defraud the honest and industrious creditors, by discharging debts, without paying one fifth or tenth part of the value."[85] A FRIEND TO THE RIGHTS OF MANKIND clinched his argument by stating flatly that any law making paper money a legal tender was prohibited by the constitution. Even if three-quarters of the towns in the state petitioned for a note issue, the legislature could not legally comply with their wishes.

This may have been sound law and economics, but it offered no solution to the problems for which the paper-money people thought they had the answer. To meet the crying needs of the time, the conservatives advanced nothing but platitudes. A writer in the *New Hampshire Mercury* insisted that the delinquent taxpayers be brought to book; this would fill the treasury and pay off the state debt.[86] But no one explained how frontier towns could satisfy the treasury when specie was unobtainable, and the amount of state tax certificates in circulation amounted to less than half of the outstanding taxes.[87] "In circulation" would be euphemistic if the charges that speculators had engrossed these certificates and were holding them for appreciation were true. But the conservatives argued that if farmers were unable to pay their debts, it was simply due to their own imprudence or indolence. Hard work, renunciation of foreign luxuries, and encouragement of domestic manufactures would improve their lot.[88] Asked a paternal champion of law and order:

> What, then, my friends, are we after? it is true we are distressed. But when complaining will not pay our taxes, nor insurrections discharge our debts; and when we cannot any way get free from them, but by industry and frugality, and these will easily get us well rid of them. . . . Let us keep our eyes fixed on the constitution, and neither infringe it ourselves, nor suffer others to infringe it; for no personal advantage can be so great, as the chance of injury to ourselves and posterity, if we attempt the subversion of the present constitution.[89]

The propertied men who made up the state legislature voted almost unanimously against a bill entered in 1785 to create a "land bank" of paper currency. However, they "thot something must be done," and on November 3, the house of representatives passed a tender act which exempted debtors from imprisonment if they offered real or personal property equivalent to the specie value of the debt. Creditors were not obliged to accept such tenders, but could, if they preferred, continue the debt at 6 percent interest, a rate probably lower than that at which most debts had been incurred.

On the whole, this was not a radical measure, and it passed the house by an overwhelming majority, 64-17, the latter votes coming from Portsmouth and the southeastern towns, where liquid capital was concentrated. Strenuous efforts were made in the senate, however, to modify or limit the bill and then to repeal it after a few weeks of operation.[90] According to William Plumer of Epping, one of the seventeen opponents of the measure in the house, it proved to be a defective palliative. "Instead of the law being a remedy it increased the evil—it impaired credit, & locked up much of the small remains of money. People were afraid to loan their money, lest when they called for it they should receive a tender of old houses, uncultivated lands, or property of little value, or be obliged to wait long for more favorable times for payment."[91]

Debtors defrauded their creditors by concealing valuable property or making it over to third persons.[92] An outraged creditor protested that "the horrors of a gaol, the sovereign prompter to payment, and the creditor's best security, are taken away. . . . Inroads upon the Constitution, are like the swellings of mighty rivers over their antient banks— slow and unalarming, at the beginning—rapid and tremendous in their progress—a deluge and destruction in the end."[93]

The legislature of 1785 made another inroad upon the constitution by passing an act for the expeditious recovery of small debts, which allowed justices of the peace to try civil suits involving £10 or less. This was an ill-digested effort to stop the clamor against the lower courts and the excessive fees that were sometimes piled up on these small suits. It bore a taint of self-interest, since a great majority of the legislators who passed it were justices who would profit by the resulting increase in their business. This act was pronounced unconstitutional by the courts within a few months, after it had led to some ridiculous miscarriages of justice.[94] The other enactments of this addled parliament of 1785 were in the same character. When its final session had stumbled to adjournment, Belknap wrote to his friend Hazard, "Our G.C. Quarrelled among themselves, and broke up. Some wanted the Navigation Act repealed, and others the Tender Act; but neither are done. Fine times!"[95]

The radicals were as much displeased with the legislature's failure to issue paper money as the conservatives had been with its temporizing proclivities. After the March elections in 1786 a writer in the *New Hampshire Gazette* issued a statement in the nature of an ultimatum.

> The inhabitants of this State, seeing in the public prints, that some of
> the richest States in the union, are now rejoicing in the happy fruits

of a paper medium, without the least depreciation, and that others are preparing to adopt the same measures, and they are labouring under every discouragement themselves with no prospect of relief, and only the certainty of death and taxes before them, murmur and repine at the situation of their public affairs, and have made a great change in the Representative body for the approaching session, in hopes that at length, they may be happy enough to find men of such firmness as to withstand the browbeating, stale and worn-out arguments of those who are against the adopting of any public measures which may militate with their own private interest.[96]

The leaders of the paper-money group did make strenuous and concerted efforts to bring their campaign to a victorious conclusion in the legislature of 1786. They were encouraged by the triumphs of paper-money metaphysicians in seven states of the Union, including nearby Rhode Island. The journals were replete with essays on the beneficial effects of these experiments, and since they were all still in their infancy, it was difficult to refute arguments in their favor. To the hard-pressed farmers, it seemed outrageous that their own government should conspire with the aristocrats of Massachusetts and Connecticut to keep the life-giving waters out of parched New England.

The popular movement that germinated in the spring of 1786 was in many ways reminiscent of prerevolutionary history. Apparently spontaneous, it was actually directed, or at least stimulated, by a few visionary enthusiasts, clever demagogues, and selfish agitators. In April someone wrote anonymous letters to selectmen in many towns, urging the election of delegates to a state convention that was to meet in June at Concord, simultaneously with the legislature, and to guide the decisions of the people's representatives into the proper channels. Spontaneous conventions and mobs gathered at various places in the Merrimack Valley in May to intimidate Allen claimants and compose far from humble petitions to the legislature. Just prior to the meeting of the general court a convention at Hampstead decided upon the form of a statement of grievances, which later found its way to the assembly in the identical language of petitions from Hawke, Hampstead, Sandown, and Londonderry. Men who recalled the methods by which John Wentworth had been dispossessed of his government in 1775 began to fear for the continuance of the squirearchy in the seats of power.[97]

The first session of the general court of 1786–87, which met in Concord in June, was relieved from serious paper-money pressures by an extraordinary tour de force. A number of towns in the Merrimack Valley had responded to the anonymous call for the election of delegates to the self-styled convention scheduled to meet in Concord simultaneously with the legislature. Control of this convention was seized by a group of conservative young men, who persuaded it to bring to the legislature a list of demands so extreme that they were laughed out of court, and the convention dissolved in confusion.[98] It soon became evident, however, that rural despair was not to be dispelled by ridicule. In July a self-styled Rockingham County convention met in Londonderry, chaired by a simple, gullible farmer from Hampstead named Joseph French, who aspired to be the Daniel Shays of New Hampshire. The leading spirit, however, was Colonel Benjamin Stone, who was closely connected with General Nathaniel Peabody of Atkinson. Peabody was a remarkable man—vain, boastful, blasphemous, well-informed, hospitable to excess, aristocratic in pretensions, and democratic in politics. In 1785 his unscrupulous speculations in frontier lands and intrigues in politics had so damaged his reputation that the house of representatives asked for his dismissal from the militia on the ground that "gentlemen of character and fortune will not serve under him."[99] Because he was deeply involved in a hopeless tangle of debt and because he wished to divert public attention from the Allen claim, of which he was a proprietor, Peabody favored an inflation of the currency.[100]

Much more open in his leadership of the paper-money party was a similar character, General Jonathan Moulton, who presided over two conventions in Strafford County during the summer. Moulton, now sixty years of age, had been a prominent and wealthy land speculator long before the Revolution. He had owned a vast extent of land around the shores of Lake Winnepesaukee, where his name is perpetuated in the town of Moultonborough, and he was still offering to sell eighty thousand acres in that region in 1785.[101] Depression, over-extension, and popular hostility had caught him short after the war. He engaged in endless litigation and "often attempted to corrupt judges, bribe jurors, suborn witnesses, and seduce the Counsel employed by his opponents."[102] By such dealings, Moulton lost his standing with the upper classes, and his financial straits urged him toward any debtor's expedient in 1786. Inflamed by the exhortations of such leaders, the Rockingham Convention, meeting in an adjourned session at Chester in August, voted to use armed force against the legislature if its demands were ignored.

When the general court convened at Exeter in September, it received an enormous number of petitions from county conventions, towns, and groups of clamorous citizens. Most of the petitions for paper money came from towns in the back regions of the Old Colony and the lower part of the Merrimack Valley—the areas most harassed by debt and depressed prices. The petitions from the frontier towns were concerned primarily with abatement of taxes. Only one petition for paper money came from the Connecticut Valley, and there is evidence that this one, from Hanover, was a product of Dartmouth College student satire rather than a genuine town paper.[103]

A petition from the town of Atkinson (home of Nathaniel Peabody) contained the most imposing and well-reasoned, as well as the most verbose, arguments for paper money. After a recital of the unparalleled sacrifices that they had made in a war to "establish their feet upon the stable mountain of peace, plenty, liberty, and happiness—and lay a pleasing foundation for the future freedom and glory of unborn millions, their progeny" the petitioners said that they had expected peace to bring "the dear earned promised happy day—But alas to their chagrin and disappointment they find it not, though they have sought it diligently with tears, but instead of enjoying the blessings of peace heretofore predicted, and with confidence accepted, the Citizens of this State now find themselves in a labyrinth of difficulty and distress, like Issachar of old crouching under the weight of complicated burdens." The burdens were then enumerated: an enormous public debt which they would find difficult to discharge even in normal times, private debts greatly augmented by the war, "the train of needless and expensive law-suits, which alone would be an insupportable burden," and heavy taxes. None of these obligations could be met "for want of a suitable medium of trade. . . . Silver and gold hath taken wings and flown to the other side of the Atlantic, without leaving a substitute or even its shadow." Neither the United States nor New Hampshire minted its own money, but depended on foreign coinage. Yet in spite of this both the state and private creditors made their demands in specie. "To require the making of brick without straw was formerly deemed arbitrary in rulers." The people of Atkinson said they had no wish to countenance disorder or to violate the constitution or the laws, and they were "full determined . . . to promote manufactures, agriculture, economy and industry, and in a word to restore and establish public credit." They were also fully aware that no scheme of issuing paper money could avoid some injury to someone, but in their circumstances they felt that such injury would be less than nearly everyone received from the scarcity of money.[104]

This logic was not easy to refute. The author of the Atkinson petition showed an equally intelligent understanding of the problem of foreign commerce. In addition to the domestic debt, he said, New Hampshire was "vastly in arrears" on its quota of the foreign debt, which could be paid only in specie; specie could be drawn in only by exporting native products; such export depended upon the prosperity of shipbuilding, navigation, and commerce; these could revive only if a medium of trade "sufficient to purchase the produce and manufactures of the Country" was in circulation. Thus, by this avenue also, he arrived at the necessity for paper money. His premises may have been false, and his conclusions were certainly shaky; but granted the first, his logic led inescapably to the second, and it was the kind of logic which plain people could understand.

Under the weight of this deluge of petitions for paper money, the legislature felt compelled to take some action. A committee of nine, including representatives from both conservative and radical towns, was appointed to ponder the situation. This committee reported in favor of issuing £50,000 in state notes, bearing 4 percent interest, one-fifth of which would be appropriated for government expenditure and the remainder to be loaned to individuals on mortgages of real estate. The bills were not to be a tender for debts or taxes, but might be received for any other governmental demand. The £10,000 portion was to be retired by four equal tax assessments between 1789 and 1792, while the £40,000 was expected to be repaid by the borrowers.[105]

This report was obviously a compromise between those who thought that paper money was a panacea and those who considered it a curse. It would have afforded no relief to debtors, since the paper was not to be a legal tender; taxpayers would derive little benefit from its limited application to governmental obligations; landowners would have mortgaged their land to no purpose if the bills failed to circulate. Its chief result, if it had been adopted, would have been to throw the state fiscal system into still more confusion. It is difficult to escape the conclusion that the committee expected its report to be rejected.

The report was neither rejected nor accepted. The legislature ordered it to be printed and sent to the towns for a referendum vote, then washed its hands of the annoying subject. In the meantime, the bill for compliance with the British treaty by removing legal impediments to the collection of debts by British subjects came under discussion. On September 14, it failed to pass the house of representatives, 32-34, obviously owing to bad management on the part of its advocates. The next day, however—the same day on which the paper-money issue had been short-circuited—the senate passed a similar bill and sent it to the house. John Pickering of Portsmouth made an eloquent plea for sustaining the honor of the state; a dozen laggard conservatives were rounded up for roll call, and the bill passed 44-34.[106] Runnels and McMurphy, the members from Londonderry, and Peabody, who was apparently present in Exeter, immediately spread the report that the lawmakers had authorized Tories to return and reclaim their confiscated property.

Joseph French, chairman of the self-constituted Rockingham Convention, no sooner received this news from Peabody through Colonel Stone than he gathered an armed mob of two hundred men and boys and marched them from Londonderry to Exeter. They encamped outside the town on the afternoon of September 20 while one more appeal was sent to the rulers. In surprisingly good English it read: "Inasmuch as we consider the prayer of our former petition has not been granted, & as we are *determined to do ourselves that justice which the laws of God & man dictate to us*, therefore we pray your honors to grant us the request of our former petition, & not drive us to a state of desperation. We pray your honors to give us an immediate answer."[107]

The house of representatives weakened to the point of voting that a joint committee be appointed to consider the petition, but the more conservative senate unanimously nonconcurred. Receiving no answer to his petition, French then arranged his mob into files and marched them into town, up old Court Street to the Town House with colors flying, drums beating, and arms clubbed. Here they treed the wrong game, for it was the superior court rather than the general court which was in session at the Town House. Chief Justice Livermore ignored the rioters and sternly forbade anyone inside the courtroom to look out the windows.[108] Then the mob marched back to the meetinghouse where the two houses of the legislature were in convention.

Succeeding events might have turned out very differently if Major General John Sullivan had not been president of the state and chairman of the senate. The energetic Irishman's military career had not been notably successful, but he had never lacked courage. He invited some of the insurgent leaders into the meetinghouse and then made a bold and powerful speech to the legislature, arguing that to answer the petition of the insurgents would be a betrayal of its trust; that even if the mob's demands had been constitutional, they had not come from a majority of the people; and, finally, that even if the cry for paper money were both right and popular, the legislature ought never to accede to it under armed threat.[109] French's answer to this was to surround the meetinghouse with armed sentinels and threaten to keep the court indoors until it complied with the petition.

As the hours of darkness drew near, the townspeople of Exeter grew alarmed at the possible consequences of an armed rabble in their midst during the night. A volunteer company was formed and marched toward the meetinghouse with the intention of disarming the sentries. A possible "effusion of blood" was prevented by Sullivan, who obtained permission to speak with the Exeter volunteers. While this parley went on, Sullivan sent an aide to inform French that the legislature would do no further business that night but would take up the petition in the morning. French agreed to withdraw his men to his encampment on the plain, and the day of peril passed without any fighting.

In spite of President Sullivan's promise the legislature reconvened as soon as the insurgents were out of town. The previous six hours' experience had temporarily dispelled the dread of a powerful executive; Sullivan was authorized "to call forth a sufficient number of the militia to protect the General Court in their present session."[110] Orders were immediately dispatched to officers of nearby regiments, and during the night militia companies marched toward Exeter and a possible civil war. Early in the morning the Exeter volunteers arrested a man from Londonderry who was "lurking" in town "as a spy" and committed him to gaol, soon adding to his cell six insurgents whom French sent to demand his release. By eight o'clock several militia companies had arrived in Exeter, and were organized under the command of Major General Joseph Cilley, the Revolutionary War hero. In the meantime, French and Major Cochran, military commander of the insurgents, led them to within a mile of the meetinghouse. General Cilley marched out and ordered a cavalry charge, and the mob dispersed. Those who were better armed rallied at a bridge two miles from town, where Cochran ordered them to fire, but again the cavalry drove them off, capturing thirty-nine prisoners in the process. These were brought back to town, forced to march between the ranks of the victorious militia to the tune of "The Rogues March," and lodged in jail. The "Riot of '86"—the New Hampshire counterpart of Shays' Rebellion in Massachusetts—collapsed utterly.

Conservatives and advocates of strong government everywhere were elated by the outcome of this affair. Jeremy Belknap, who happened to be in Exeter on the eventful twentieth of September, exulted that the "riotous spirit has met a severe check, which will give a deep wound to the knavish system; the hands of lawful government will be strengthened."[111] A week later the *New Hampshire Mercury* exclaimed rapturously that "*a free government, the people's government* shone with a splendor that never was excelled, seldom equalled!"[112] William Plumer, a future governor of the state who was then studying law in Londonderry and who served as a volunteer in General Cilley's law and order forces, felt that "by this event the government gained much." It was fortunate, he thought, that, unlike the insurgents in Massachusetts who attacked the inferior courts, those of New Hampshire "made a bold assault upon the legislature, the fountain head of authority. This brot the question to a single point, whether the people would maintain their government & right, or submit to the will & caprice of an ignorant and lawless mob."[113]

The small state was distinguished likewise from its great neighbor in the clemency that it displayed toward the defeated rebels. This was probably due in great part to the fact that important men, even members of the legislature, might have been implicated and compromised if the affair had been investigated too thoroughly. Everyone was convinced that the prisoners were well-meaning, if misguided, creatures—"privately urged on by men of influence . . . who had studiously avoided taking an active part with them in the business."[114] On September 22 they were examined by the legislature. French produced a suspicious letter from General

Moulton, who, as a militia officer, was present at the examination "and blushed whilst it was read."[115] Other prisoners testified that they had been "deceived by false representations."[116] Sullivan publicly arraigned "certain crafty and designing persons wishing to make these conventions (however innocent in their first formation) a cover for the most injurious and unjustifiable conduct, and, under colour of conventional authority, to subvert the constitutional power of the state."[117] Belknap wrote that "the principal directors . . . endeavoured to conceal themselves, whilst they persuaded a considerable number of persons of various characters, to appear openly in support of the petitions. They took pains to spread false reports through the country."[118] There seemed to be no doubt in the minds of contemporary observers that the insurgents were cat's-paws.

Daniel Shays was hounded out of Massachusetts after his rebellion; Joseph French confessed that he had forfeited his life in New Hampshire and was granted a full pardon. The senate was inclined to be severe, the house lenient; they compromised by dismissing most of the prisoners and remanding eight of the ringleaders to the superior court for trial as rioters only. These were released on bail and ultimately tried, found guilty, and punished with light fines. The militia officers among the insurgents were court-martialed, and eight of them were deprived of their commissions.[119] Ecclesiastical discipline was likewise imposed by the two Presbyterian churches in Londonderry, which required those of their members who had participated in the riot to make public confession and repentance.[120]

The humiliating collapse of the Exeter rebellion rendered further consideration of paper money in New Hampshire academic, but the final disposition of the legislative committee's paper-money plan remained an item of unfinished business. Town meetings were accordingly held in the late autumn to vote upon a financial theory already suffering tremendous psychological deflation. According to the report of another legislative committee in January 1787, only 400 persons had voted for the plan proposed by the court, while 1238 persons had voted against paper money on any plan. The legislature immediately took the following action: "On motion, can the legislature consistently with the constitution and their oaths, pass an act making paper bills of credit a tender to discharge private contracts made prior to the passing such act, the motion being put, *Voted*, unanimously in the negative. On the motion whether paper money be emitted on any plan that has been proposed, *Voted* in the negative."[121]

While the legislature chose to interpret the people's votes on its plan as a mandate against paper money, this was at best a dubious conclusion. The fact that the vote was taken at special town meetings in the winter season, after the fall of both French and Shays had discredited the paper-money movement, coupled with the customary political inertia of the times, prevented more than a sixth of the qualified electorate from expressing their opinions. Even the opposition vote is suspect; it includes many who voted against the legislative plan because they wanted more paper issued or wanted it made legal tender. It is difficult to make the reported figures support any final conclusion except that the legislature wanted them to be inconclusive.

The paper-money issue was to some extent sectional, but to a much larger extent it was a class question, creating horizontal rather than vertical lines of cleavage.[122] Petitions and votes in favor of paper money came more thickly from the Merrimack Valley than from other sections of the state, but there was much support for inflation even in the Old Colony. The evidence that a majority of the people of New Hampshire—the plain people who vastly outnumbered merchants, lawyers, squires, and clergymen combined—wanted paper money is abundant. Yet the legislatures from 1783 to 1787, subjected to continuous pressure and dependent upon annual elections by all taxpayers, held out against paper issues. The reason for their irresponsiveness to public demands can only be attributed to the fact that they would not have been legislators if their individual property holdings had amounted to less than £100. Men with even so small a stake as this in the status quo were not easily persuaded to tinker with the currency. Nevertheless, the submission of the question to popular decision in 1786 showed signs of weakening. What would have been the outcome if the paper-money advocates had not committed the irreparable blunder of attempting a rebellion is of course a purely conjectural matter. But the actual effect of the rebellion was clear enough; hundreds of moderate farmers who had signed petitions for paper money repudiated their cause and joined hands with the triumphant upper class to support their chosen government.

Thus ended New Hampshire's 13th Vendémiaire. It was at the same time the dying gasp of the Revolution and the triumph of counterrevolution. President Sullivan made this clear when on September 30 he issued a proclamation to discourage any further meetings of conventions. They "have a tendency to overturn and destroy all constitutional authority and government," he said.[123] No one was better qualified as an expert on this subject than Sullivan, who had been a leading member of that provincial convention which first undertook the destruction of the king's government in 1774. But twelve fateful years had elapsed, and new "events [had] proved the danger of setting up even the resemblance of a government or authority, within a constitutional government to which the former is unknown."[124] This was exactly the view that Governor Wentworth had taken of the Exeter conventions in 1775, and subsequent events may well have been part of that proof which Sullivan cited. The Revolution had been initiated and sustained by extralegal conventions—county conventions, provincial conventions, continental congresses. The Hillsborough towns had elected delegates to conventions of one kind or another nearly every year since 1774. It is not surprising that when they had a grievance in 1786, their first impulse was to organize a convention. In their innocence they had not learned that conventions were no longer considered respectable. The belated lesson was sufficiently well inculcated by the militia on Exeter plain, and New Hampshire relapsed into its ancient habits of respect for authority. The old order had been swept away; the period of confusion and readjustment had run its course; now it was time to build again.

CHAPTER 4

PERSONAL POLITICS

If you are at a loss for quacks and jockies, in the science of government, we can abundantly supply you, and be no losers.—Jeremy Belknap

The decade following the adoption of the constitution of 1784 presents a fascinating picture of political transition in New Hampshire.[1] A small and remote colony, whose participation in imperial government had been minimal and whose internal affairs had been largely in the hands of royal officials, changed into a self-governing commonwealth and an equal participant with the other twelve new states in a federated nation. The adult male possessors of real estate of the value of more than fifty pounds, who were qualified to vote in colonial days, had full control of their town governments, but above that level they elected only a representative to the lower house of the provincial legislature. After 1792 the village voter, who by this time needed only to be a taxpayer, elected representatives to both houses of the state legislature, a member of the governor's council, the governor himself, three congressmen, and five electors of the president and vice-president of the United States. This heady accession to power had a transforming effect upon political folkways.

It was a decade, furthermore, of groping toward political party organization. Colonial government had been dominated by the Wentworth family connection. Opposing factions within the Portsmouth aristocracy had surfaced only rarely. Most of the resistance to the governor and the royal prerogative came from the popularly elected assembly, which generally stood united when it chose to contest such matters as control of the purse. The struggle against parliamentary taxation and the measures of ministerial "oppression" leading to the War for Independence forced men, of course, to choose sides or to eschew politics altogether. Few colonials were completely on the side of the British government; these were quickly deprived of any part in local affairs. Among the "patriots" who took charge of the province and the state under the provincial congresses and the constitutional government of 1776 were some more zealous for independence than others, some who wanted to move faster than others, and some who were more sympathetic toward intercolonial union than others, but none of these differences of degree led to any kind of organized contention.

With independence won, however, major antagonisms that might have been made the basis of political parties came quickly into existence. The spectral outline of a debtor party rising up in arms against a creditor party was apparent to everyone at Exeter in September 1786. From the beginning of the decade until 1792, a protracted struggle went on between the advocates of a government wherein all power was centered in an annually elected legislature and the proponents of a more balanced form. Finally, there was the deep-rooted conflict between aristocratic and democratic views of social control, expressed in daily work and conversation as well as in every vote in the legislature. Here certainly were the raw materials out of which political parties are fabricated.

For many reasons, however, aside from the mere confusion of issues, politics remained an unorganized business during this decade. Until the new constitution went into effect in 1784, the spoils of office fruited from domination of the legislature rather than from victory at the polls. Even during the latter part of the decade an ambitious man found it easier and more profitable to cultivate goodwill among a few dozen legislators than among several thousand voters. In the days of the Wentworths patronage had been dispensed by the royal governor and a closely knit, aristocratic council, which also acted as the upper house of the legislature. Politics had inevitably resolved into nepotism. The immediate effect of the Revolution had been to change this arrangement much less than might have been expected. The Wentworths were displaced, it is true, but members of the legislature moved quickly into the vacuum and carried on in the same old tradition. Rewards that had formerly been bestowed by a royal council dependent upon the king were henceforth given by a state council dependent upon the general court, and popular approval was hardly more necessary in the latter case than in the former. Consequently, political organizers continued to bend their skills toward building up personal followings in the legislature rather than seeking votes among the people. Only the handful of men who aspired to the state presidency or a seat in the senate found it necessary to go outside the boundaries of a single town for a popular following.

Popular elections were no revolutionary innovation in New Hampshire—they were coeval with the first settlements. According to immemorial custom, ballots for everything from hog-reeve to president were cast at the annual town meeting in March. This was the one occasion when nearly all the town's inhabitants gathered together, something of a substitute for the ancestral English fairs. While the male taxpayers assembled in the meetinghouse to make their civic decisions, the women gathered in nearby houses for gossip, the young people improved the opportunity for courtship, and the boys worked off their excess energy on the village common. Something of the festive nature of this great occasion may be gleaned from a characteristically laconic entry in Matthew Patten's diary. "I gave james 77 Dollars to Divide between him and

Robert and David for Election tomorrow."[2] In 1781, seventy-seven dollars would just have purchased each of the three boys a quart of rum with a little to spare, and it is not unlikely that the money found its way eventually into the taverner's cash drawer. As the day waned, the crowd in the meetinghouse grew smaller and that in the tavern larger. Since local business usually preceded state affairs on the agenda, it is not surprising to find more votes cast for a fence-viewer than for a senator in many a town record. After the settlement of those affairs that most immediately affected them, the voters grew indifferent to the blessings of free suffrage and allowed governors to be elected and constitutions to be ratified by the persistent minority. Voting was especially light upon questions that required a special town meeting in an unaccustomed season. Not more than a ninth of the qualified electorate was interested in fundamental constitutional changes, while even the annual average of 8500 votes cast for president of the state came from less than one-third of the voters.

Election of state (and later national) officers was by ballot, but was not very secret. Voters wrote the names of their candidates on pieces of paper and handed them to the town clerk, who counted and recorded the votes and sent attested copies of the record to the proper county or state official. This system encouraged a delightful promiscuity in orthography and permitted clever politicians to cast out many an honest vote because the *i*'s and *e*'s had been interchanged. Moreover, it is difficult to imagine that in a small town the clerk, the moderator, and all the spectators did not know who had given in each slip of paper as it was opened and read. Under these circumstances it was easy for a powerful landowner or formidable moneylender to exercise a considerable influence over humble voters, and it is certain that local, personal leadership carried more weight in New England than it does today. Politicians learned very early to furnish indolent voters with printed ballots, properly spelled and easy to recognize.[3]

New Hampshire politics had always been a function of the social system. By definition, all voters were freeholders, but the property owners in most New Hampshire towns fell naturally into two social groups. The upper class consisted of the squires, the merchants, and the professional men, particularly the minister, who were the natural leaders of the New England town democracies. Their prestige, education, ability, and wealth gave them an influence far greater than their numbers and enabled them under ordinary conditions to manage the political activity of the much larger but more inert class below them. The financial heresies and political irresponsibilities of the 1780s caused these naturally conservative leaders to welcome the federal Constitution, as Sullivan's and Belknap's writings clearly show. Only a few of the less responsible among them, such as Joshua Atherton and Nathaniel Peabody, led their communities against it.

The mass of small farmers, though enfranchised by the Revolution, played little part in politics other than to vote in town meetings. In ordinary times they were content to follow the advice of the minister or the squire. Not all of them even attended town meetings regularly, and those who did were accustomed to elect one of the local aristocracy as moderator, to listen to the citizens with "larnin'" discuss the issues, and to vote as the squire or the minister or the town lawyer suggested. There was nothing particularly menial about this relationship. It was a natural tribute to wisdom, heredity, influence, or proven ability, which, in normal times, the New England yeomanry was accustomed and willing to pay. As a property owner, a church member, and a responsible participant in town affairs, the poor farmer was ordinarily as conservative as the rich one. It was only in abnormal times, and usually under the stimulus of adverse economic conditions, that the small fellow took the bit in his teeth and ran away from the guiding hand of the local aristocracy. Thus, in the debt-ridden 1780s the yeomanry of Londonderry threw off all restraint and took up arms against their own government, only to be punished for it afterward by their church as well as by the magistrates. When prosperity was restored, the Presbyterian conservatism of the town led it firmly into Federalism. The complexion of politics was largely a question of the degree to which normal relations existed between the two classes in rural New Hampshire society.

The economic depression of the 1780s came closer to driving a wedge between these classes than had any previous event; yet the social antagonism did not become an organized partisan battle. The reason was that the leaders during this decade were nearly all on the same side. The very conditions that produced a class struggle denied leadership to the aggrieved class. This phenomenon was strikingly illustrated at the federal convention, where Sullivan, the Langdons, Pickering, Gilman, West, Bartlett, Livermore, Toppan, and Payne defended the Constitution, while Atherton was the only forceful speaker against it. It was plain that the proto-Federalist party needed no organization while it commanded such overwhelming talent and that the proto-Republican party lacked the talent to effect organization. Even Atherton was only temporarily enrolled with the malcontents in 1788; his later career showed that he had no real quarrel with the ruling classes.

Nathaniel Peabody might have organized an opposition party, had his fortunes been more secure. He had ability, and in 1784, when he was a member of the council, he made unblushing use of the patronage to ingratiate himself with his fellows.[4] But Peabody's sands were already running out. He failed of reelection to the council, he was implicated in the

Exeter riot, and within a few years, he became the permanent inmate of a debtor's prison. Leadership for the Jeffersonian element in New Hampshire had to come from disaffected Federalists.

The absence of any fundamental quarrel between the great men of New Hampshire made their personal rivalry all the more intense. For twenty years they were all crowded together on the same platform, first tearing down the British Empire and then building up an American state on the ruins. It was inevitable that while this work was being completed, they should jostle one another and each think himself entitled to a larger share of his countrymen's gratitude. So long as there were more exciting things to be done on the field of battle, in Congress, or in the navy yards at home, they were content to allow old Meshech Weare to monopolize the state government. By tacit agreement the political truce was even extended for a year after the adoption of the new state constitution, although Weare was "quite superannuated."[5] But in 1785 the veteran patriot was obliged to retire, and the battle for his place became a major contest.

The two chief antagonists were John Sullivan and John Langdon. Both of them had unimpeachable reputations for patriotism, beginning with the two December days in 1774 when they had directed the dismantling of the king's fort on Castle Island. In 1775 they had represented New Hampshire at the Second Continental Congress, but thereafter their paths separated. Congress, for no ascertainable military reason, gave Sullivan a brigadier's commission, and he spent the ensuing five years in the army acquiring a reputation for bravery, bombast, and bad luck. In 1780 he resigned his commission and was sent again to Congress, where he gave two years of useful service marred somewhat by constant complaints about the nonpayment of his salary and by the suspicion that he sold out to the French interest.

Sullivan's return to New Hampshire in 1781 and his appointment as attorney general came at an unfortunate time. He had hardly become accustomed to his new title before the superior court was confronted with an outraged mob at Keene, and he felt it necessary to don his old uniform in order to overawe the rioters.[6] Then the press began to bristle with accusations that he was too lenient with Tories. Sullivan had exposed himself to these attacks by his efforts in 1782 to gain permission for Mrs. Holland, the wife of a proscribed loyalist, to visit her children in Londonderry and by his continuing to act as attorney for the family of a prominent Portsmouth merchant, Colonel George Boyd, who had lived in England during the war.[7] These actions were both justifiable and honorable, but they gave Sullivan's opponents a chance to smear him with the Tory label. The suspicions of the plain people were further raised against him when he took the lead in organizing the New Hampshire branch of the Society of the Cincinnati and became its first president. Farmers who were already complaining about the Continental Congress's commutation of half pay for pensioned-off revolutionary officers to full pay for five years were quick to scent aristocracy in this new military, secret, and hereditary society. In 1785 the Durham lawyer made another political faux pas by consenting to champion the Allen claim. This not only arrayed the "unthinking multitude" against him but antagonized the influential and wealthy Masonian proprietors.

Sullivan deserved well of his countrymen for his important services during the Revolution. His tumultuous eloquence, Celtic humor, and commanding appearance were calculated to make him popular. But he had unfortunate defects of character which detracted from his stature. The worst of these was an intense egotism which made him too sensitive to criticism and too susceptible to flattery. "I never knew mortal so greedy of flattery," wrote young William Plumer. "He swallows the grossest."[8] Belknap confirmed Plumer's opinion of the "Hibernian General."[9] Yet, on the whole, Sullivan was the logical candidate of the conservatives, and most of them supported him, however reluctantly.

Langdon's career after 1775 had been less spectacular but far more profitable than Sullivan's. He had the wit to realize that he lacked military skill and the wisdom to leave Congress before the folks back home forgot about him. Returning to Portsmouth in 1776, he spent the remaining years of the war at home, building ships for the new Continental Navy, fitting out privateers for his own emolument, and being elected annually to the speakership of the house. These occupations permitted him to become wealthy while serving his country and guarded him from the appearance of sordid avarice which attached to Sullivan's constant complaints about money.[10]

Langdon was adept at making a sensational show of patriotic generosity and then quietly recouping himself. The legend about his offering his entire fortune to equip Stark's expedition against Burgoyne is retailed in every New Hampshire history. The newspapers heralded his advancing the expenses of himself and Nicholas Gilman to the Constitutional Convention, but failed to mention the fact that the legislature later repaid the money. Unlike Sullivan, Langdon was also able to acquire military glory without running much danger of being captured by the British. He became a resplendent colonel in the militia, and joined the expeditions to Bennington and Rhode Island without getting close enough to the battlefront to smell powder. Altogether he managed to come through the revolutionary years with enhanced reputation and estate and to escape the misfortunes that dogged Sullivan. It is a great tribute to his talents that he was so constantly engaged in public life, made a fortune out of a war which ruined many men, took his stand boldly on the important questions of the day, yet had few enemies.

Political etiquette in the eighteenth century required that office-seekers emulate Caesar's reluctance to assume the proffered crown. All candidates adhered to this rule in public, protesting on every occasion that only an inviolable attachment to the welfare of their country and profound respect for the wishes of their fellow citizens induced them to leave the circle of domestic felicity for the stormy scenes of public life. Consequently, when it became certain that Meshech Weare would retire at the end of his term in 1785, there was no public campaign by his would-be successors, but their friends were not so reticent. Each group accused the other of that most heinous of crimes—actually seeking office. The newspapers flamed with charge and countercharge. Just before "election day" in March "runners"—gentlemen of persuasive speech—were employed to visit as many taverns as possible and drop a few good words for their respective candidates.

It must have been a shock to Sullivan and Langdon when the votes were counted and George Atkinson was found to have more than either of them. Atkinson was a sober Portsmouth merchant "of decent talents, strict integrity, and . . . irreproachable character," who had quietly earned an excellent reputation as speaker of the house of representatives during 1784–85.[11] Many conservatives apparently preferred his Weare-like solidarity to the more brilliant talents of the younger candidates. No aspirant had a majority of the votes, however. The house of representatives sent the names of Atkinson and Langdon, who was next highest, to the senate, where Langdon was chosen president of the state by a vote of seven to one.[12] Sullivan had to content himself with being attorney general, speaker of the house, major general of the militia, and a member of the council. It was embarrassing for these men to be, by the vagaries of the constitution, so closely associated and not surprising that an open breach soon occurred. During Sullivan's absence from a council meeting, President Langdon got his brother Woodbury appointed to the superior court bench, and Sullivan protested vigorously. "You will see, by our papers," wrote Belknap to Postmaster General Hazard, "that our Major General has resigned his offices. The big fellows cannot agree. . . . I suppose he [Sullivan] expects to be biggest of all next year, and there will be a pull for it between him and J.L."[13]

Belknap's prognostication was quite accurate; Sullivan was girding himself for a supreme effort in 1786. Conservative sentiment swung toward him in reaction against the Tender Act and some of Langdon's political appointments.[14] Sullivan received a decisive verdict from the people, outdistancing his rival by some seven hundred votes. The ex-president was sent to the house of representatives by Portsmouth and was promptly elected speaker. "They have changed places," observed a visitor to the legislative session where the votes were counted. "Their [*sic*] is much animosity between them."[15]

Whatever Sullivan's defects may have been, he proved to be a forceful executive in the troubled year 1786. As he himself said, he came "to the chief seat of government at a time when our trade is embarrassed, our finances deranged, and for want of a sufficiency of circulating cash, even the requisitions of Congress but in part complied with."[16] His proposals for relief had none of the earmarks of a New Deal, but followed the tried and true virtues dear to the conservative mind: "encourag[ing] Industry, and frugality, . . . promoting agriculture, . . . discouraging the consumption of foreign Luxuries."[17] By his fearless and decisive conduct in the September riot at Exeter, Sullivan rendered a great service to his state and raised himself much higher in the estimation of many good men. "Sullivan has really done himself honour, and the State service," said Belknap. "We could not have had a better *military* governour, and certainly one of this character is necessary at this day."[18] Sullivan, indeed, devoted a great deal of attention to the militia, bringing it to such an unusual peak of perfection that it became the subject of a long dispatch to Louis XVI's foreign minister from his vice-consul at Portsmouth.[19] Perhaps the excellence of its military establishment had something to do with preventing a Shays' Rebellion in New Hampshire.

Sullivan's firmness, however, generated popular resentment as well as respect. Feeling ran so high in the insurgent centers that, for many weeks after the riot, General Reid of Londonderry, who had served with the victorious militia, was threatened by anonymous letters and night mobs.[20] It was quite natural that the disappointed paper-money advocates should blame Sullivan for their discomfiture and seek revenge at the polls in 1787. On the other hand, the advocates of a firm policy were likewise stirred to unwonted action. The result was the highest popular vote of the decade, but it was scattered among four candidates, so that none of them had the requisite majority. Sullivan had four hundred votes fewer than Langdon, but when their names were sent to the senate, he received the reward of good deeds and was chosen for another term.[21]

The fact that the people were willing to see their two heroes assume the first and second positions of honor almost interchangeably shows how little partisan spirit there was in these elections. The state was not then deprived of the services of a defeated candidate; before parties solidified he could readily continue to serve in a secondary post. Opposition at the polls did not prevent Sullivan and Langdon from cooperating in the legislature at the heads of their respective houses. In the meantime, lesser men formed combinations, sought alliances, and grasped for office in a manner which had no visible foundation in principle or consistency. The Langdons alienated the powerful Livermore family in an intrigue by which Samuel Livermore was to be elected to Congress and then forced to resign as chief justice so that Woodbury Langdon could be appointed to his vacant place. The judge outwitted the Langdons by holding both appointments in spite of outraged protests from the legislature, but he did not, as might have been expected, rush into an alliance with Sullivan. Instead, he ran for the presidency himself in 1787 and helped to throw the election into the legislature. Although Livermore was as strongly conservative as any man in New Hampshire at the time, he received nearly all of the insurgent vote in Londonderry.[22] Looking upon these incomprehensible intrigues, carried on in the midst of public distress and national futility, Belknap sorrowfully wrote to his good friend Hazard, "If you are at a loss for quacks and jockies, in the science of government, we can abundantly supply you, and be no losers."[23]

When the legislature assembled in June 1788, Sullivan and Langdon were members both of the house and of the federal ratifying convention. Langdon was unanimously elected speaker; two days later the votes from the March meetings were counted, and it was confirmed that he had been elected president by a majority of *two*! Thereupon the house unanimously elected Sullivan speaker, but he refused the office. Sullivan's adherents were apparently as disappointed as their chief, since, for the first time on record, they voted against the legislature's reply to the president's inaugural.[24] The most significant statement in Langdon's speech was one, however, with which the Sullivanites were in perfect agreement, except, perhaps, for the matter of punctuation. "The deranged State of our finances the almost annihilation of our commerce are objects truly important, but I look forward with pleasure to the time which I trust is not far distant when by the blessing of divine providence we shall be relieved in a great measure from those and many other embarrassments by the adoption of the proposed federal constitution."[25] Langdon's prophecy was fulfilled fifteen days later when New Hampshire's ratification put the Constitution into effect.

President Langdon had only said officially what nearly every articulate man in New Hampshire had been saying for four years, in private correspondence, in newspaper articles, in sermons, and in public speeches. Fully two years before Shays' Rebellion had aroused such apprehensions in the minds of Washington, Hamilton, and Jay, Belknap had attacked the weaknesses of the Confederation in a long letter to Hazard. In 1786 this letter became a powerful piece of national propaganda for the new government when Hazard published it in the *New Haven Gazette*.

In vivid language, Belknap contrasted the responsibilities of the Confederate Congress with its futility and poured scorn upon the idea of a "*combined sovereignty*, subject to be checked, controuled, and negatived by thirteen *individual sovereignties*." How are our debts to be paid? he had asked. Land sales will not produce cash, the southern states will not have a poll tax on Negroes, the northern states object to a property tax on their stony acres, Rhode Island gives a mortal stab to any proposal for import duties. "Our federal government is a huge, complicated, unwieldy machine, like . . . thirteen *independent* clocks, going all together, by the force of their own weights, and carrying thirteen *independent* hammers fitted to strike on *one bell*. . . . The plain English of all this is that our present form of federal government appears to be inadequate to the purpose for which it was instituted."[26]

Belknap here expressed, probably better than any other person in New Hampshire could have done it, the hardheaded disillusionment that drove like-minded men to seek escape from "the tyranny of state legislatures." New Hampshire had not been as refractory as some other states, but there were still enough uncertainties in its situation in 1787 to make conservatives long for greater stability. The paper-money party was not altogether suppressed. The effort to create a strong state government was still far short of success. Commerce was still inert, and New Hampshire paid daily tribute to Massachusetts for its importations. In addition to all this, there were not lacking anomalies in the relations between the state and the Confederate Congress.

The awkwardness of state and congressional relations in negotiations with foreign powers was impressed upon New Hampshire merchants by no less a person than Captain Horatio Nelson, then in command of H.M.S. *Boreas*, on duty in the West Indies. In March 1786 the future admiral, "by mere dint of power, without colour of law," seized a valuable brig belonging to William and James Sheafe of Portsmouth and carried it to an unknown court for condemnation. The unfortunate owners, having "no where else to look for redress but to this honorable Court," sent a petition to the state legislature.[27] It was a poor place to look. All that the honorable court could do was to instruct its delegates to move Congress to order their minister at London to demand compensation, and thus add another item of humiliation to the burden of poor John Adams.[28] The delegates were probably ashamed even to ask for this fruitless favor, given their state delinquencies to the national treasury. Men who were conscious of the latent power within their newborn nation, and jealous of its honor, looked upon these accumulated impotencies with burning shame and took their resolutions for a bold remedy when the opportunity offered.

Opportunity knocked three times, however, before New Hampshire fully recognized it. Five commissioners were appointed by the legislature to attend the Annapolis Convention in 1786, but the Potomac was far away and trouble was brewing at home in September.[29] None of the five attended the convention, although they were certainly in sympathy with its purpose. Joshua Wentworth regretfully declined his appointment, but wrote to President Sullivan: "I hope two of the Gentlemen will attend, who are appointed, as I view the state of our Commerce almost at an end, and if some measures are not adopted to secure what little remains and open a door to further advantages these Eastern states will consequently be ruined, & the whole Confederacy broken up."[30]

The invitation that proceeded from Annapolis for a general convention to be held in Philadelphia was favorably received by New Hampshire's house of representatives in January 1787. The senate, conservative and suspicious of a movement which seemed to be growing out of another revolutionary convention, withheld its assent until the project had been approved by Congress. This approval was given in February, and when the new state legislature convened in June, it was decided to send delegates to the Philadelphia convention, then already in session. After a dispute over the method of choice, which came dangerously close to resulting in no choice at all, the two houses agreed upon four suitable delegates, any two of whom might represent the state if they could get to Philadelphia.[31] The four were John Langdon, who had just resigned from the legislature; John Pickering, author of the state constitution; Nicholas Gilman of Exeter, a delegate to the Confederation Congress; and Benjamin West of Charlestown, the most eloquent lawyer in the state but overly cautious and conservative. All four were from old, wealthy centers of population, men of substance and property, members of the provincial aristocracy, enemies of legislative licentiousness, advocates of a stronger national government, and consequently well fitted to represent the cause of the dominant party in New Hampshire.

New Hampshire might have played a larger part in the framing of the Constitution if Pickering and West could have been persuaded to go to Philadelphia, but neither of them was venturesome enough to make the journey. The task devolved upon Langdon and Gilman, but the state treasury was not sufficiently prosperous to advance their expense money. Fortunately, Langdon was willing to subsidize the delegation and take repayment afterward.[32] Even if he had borne the expense without remuneration, as the *New Hampshire Gazette* reported it, he would hardly have been the "disinterested patriot" that the paper proclaimed him to be. As a considerable merchant and shipowner, Langdon had made his interest perfectly clear as early as April 1784, when he wrote:

> I wish I could see better prospects in commerce, but I despair of
> that until the several states can be prevailed on to give up this great
> object (which concerns the whole) to congress, their head; for, while

thirteen different states, in thirteen different parts of the continent, undertake to regulate trade, it will not only destroy that social intercourse that ought to be cultivated between the states, but bring on the utmost confusion. However, I hope ere long we shall all see the necessity of leaving this business to congress, who only can, and ought to, regulate commerce.[33]

After Langdon, as speaker of the house or president of the state, had signed his name to three distinct bills granting this power of regulation to Congress on behalf of New Hampshire, only to see each bill become worthless through the unwillingness of some other state legislature to make a similar grant, he was eager enough to lay an axe to the root of the evil.[34] Langdon had consistently, if not ostentatiously, opposed the debtor party in the New Hampshire legislature, and he welcomed those constitutional provisions which ended the struggle by forbidding states to emit bills of credit or "impair the obligation of contract." As a large holder of Continental securities, he was not averse, either, to creating a government with enough financial power to meet its obligations.[35]

Although a much younger man than Langdon, Nicholas Gilman had similar interests to serve. He belonged to a family that was peculiarly identified with the fiscal affairs of the state and had easier access to large sums of money than did most men in that bankless era. His father and his elder brother, between them, had held the office of state treasurer from 1775 to 1788, and his brother was one of the three commissioners appointed by Congress to settle accounts with the various states. The Continental Loan Office had been in his father's house at Exeter throughout the war, and the Gilmans had not failed to lend large sums of their own to the patriotic cause.[36] Although Gilman had not been present in the state legislature to record his vote on the issues that developed in the 1780s, he had led a volunteer company against the insurgents at Exeter, and his views were thoroughly acceptable to the dominant party in the state government.

The New Hampshire delegates arrived at Philadelphia after most of the basic work had been done, and they contributed little to the final result except their votes and some commonsense observations. But their presence, Gilman reported, "notwithstanding we are so late in the day ... is a circumstance, in this critical state of affairs, that seems highly pleasing to the Convention in general."[37] Except for the distinction of being one of the youngest and handsomest men in the convention, Gilman was of small importance.[38]

Langdon, however, made a number of minor observations which are particularly significant in the light of New Hampshire's experience. As the representative of a small, poor frontier state he advocated extensive powers for the federal government: to call out the militia (shades of Joseph French and Daniel Shays), to regulate the slave traffic, to veto state laws that were incompatible with the interests of the Union, to acquire a national capital, distinct from any state capital. As a merchant, he insisted that states should have nothing to do with tonnage duties, which "was an essential part of the regulation of trade." New Hampshire's suffering at the hands of Massachusetts led him to insist that no state should be allowed to tax exports from another state. Because of the difficulties that the New Hampshire Grants had caused his state, he favored the admission of new states, but not necessarily on a basis of equality. New Hampshire's poverty was reflected in his insistence that congressmen be paid by the general government. Its broad franchise suggested to him the idea that the Constitution might be rejected by the people if it included property qualifications for congressmen. Finally, so indelible were his impressions of the evils of a paper currency that he agreed to forbid an indulgence in it not only to the states but also to the national legislature.[39] It is especially interesting to note that Langdon held no conscientious scruples on the shibboleth of state sovereignty. "As one of the people," he remarked, "the National government is mine, the State Government is mine. In transferring power from one to the other, I only take out of my left hand what it cannot so well use, and put it into my right hand where it can better be used."[40]

When the proposed constitution was finally revealed to the public and the extent of its renovating power became apparent, the New Hampshire conservatives were overjoyed. "Men of talents, information, & attachment to their country seem to have turned their whole attention to the Constitution reported by the late *Federal Convention*," wrote Plumer in December 1787. "'Tis an object of much importance to this nation."[41]

The young lawyer did not at all exaggerate the quality of the federalist party in New Hampshire; it included most of the leaders in the state. New Hampshire's last delegates in the old Congress, Nicholas Gilman and Paine Wingate, exchanged congratulations with delegates from other states that their days of impotence would soon be over. Sullivan, president of the state, gave the Constitution his official endorsement and called an extraordinary special session of the legislature in frigid December to plan for a ratifying convention.[42]

Samuel Livermore, the chief justice, Thomas Bartlett, speaker of the house, John Taylor Gilman, state treasurer, John Pickering, the senior senator—indeed, all the chief officers of the state—were unanimously for it. Josiah Bartlett, at the head of the medical profession, Benjamin West, who stood at the forefront of the bar, the Langdons, Sheafes, and Longs, who spoke for the merchants of Portsmouth, all favored ratification. The benediction of the clergy was added from virtually every pulpit, and the tiny New Hampshire press seemed altogether favorable. All the people who counted wanted the new Constitution, and assumed they would have no trouble getting it. The confident majority in the legislature permitted itself a premonitory gratulation. "This State hath been ever desireous to act upon the liberal System of the general Good of the United States without circumscribing its views to the narrow & selfish Objects of partial convenience; And has been at all times ready to make every concession to the safety & happiness of the whole, which Justice and sound policy could vindicate."[43]

The response to Sullivan's call for a special session of the legislature on December 5, however, was not enthusiastic. There had already been a regular session in September, and another one was scheduled for February. A week passed before a quorum had assembled, and even then fewer than half the towns in the state were represented.[44] Nevertheless, the delegates were relatively well distributed, except that the areas closest to Exeter, the Old Colony and the Merrimack Valley, had a slight preponderance.[45] This did not seem to have any discernible effect upon the planning procedures. Resolutions to submit the proceedings of the federal convention to a "convention to be chosen by the people" and to print four hundred copies of the proposed new Constitution for distribution to the town meetings were adopted without a division.

The only apparent controversy was caused by a curious motion that the towns should be permitted to elect twice as many delegates to the ratifying convention as they were entitled to send to the legislature. This led to the only roll-call vote of the session and was soundly defeated, 14 to 34, with towns that later ratified the Constitution generally in the opposition.[46] It was determined instead that delegates to the convention should be the same number as representatives in the legislature, elected in the same way except that unrepresented towns would have the privilege of electing delegates and the religious test would not apply. To these generous and democratic concessions was added the remarkable provision that delegates' expenses were to be paid out of the state treasury rather than by the towns they represented.[47] This virtually guaranteed a maximum number of delegates for the ratifying convention; it became, in fact, the largest representative body that had met in New Hampshire since the fourth provincial convention.[48] The federalist leaders, in their supreme confidence, put no obstacle in the way of "a full and free" representation of the voters on this momentous question.

During the winter of 1787–88, the present Constitution of the United States was on trial before that most independent of all tribunals, the New England town meeting. It is not likely that many of the citizens had been enlightened by a reading of *The Federalist* essays or even by such mediocre discussions as appeared in the New Hampshire journals, for newspaper circulation was not extensive. Nor did the federalists seem to have felt any necessity for propaganda or exertion; most of the activity came from opponents of the Constitution. Langdon explained their methods in a letter to General Washington.

> Just at the moment that the choice for members of our Convention, in one of our principal counties [probably Hillsborough], took place, a report was circulated by a few designing men, who wished for confusion, that the Massachusetts Convention, who had just met, were against the plan, and would certainly refuse it; that the liberties of the people were in danger, and the great men, as they call them, were forming a plan for themselves; together with a thousand other absurdities, which frightened the people almost out of what little senses they had.[49]

This kind of agitation among poor, isolated, suspicious farmers, who had seen men of their kind hunted down in the winter snow by Massachusetts troops, some of whom had themselves been routed and humiliated at Exeter by "the great men," who had petitioned their legislature in vain for redress and who were simple enough to believe that paper money would solve all their problems, was highly effective.[50] A majority of the delegates who appeared at Exeter in February were opposed to the Constitution, and many of them had been bound by inflexible instructions from their towns to vote against its ratification.

The discovery of this fact was a stunning blow to the overly optimistic federalists, although they should have been prepared for it if they had read better the signs of the times. Massachusetts had ratified only by the narrow margin of 187 to 168; the federalists and anti-federalists comprised much the same groups in both states, but in Massachusetts, with its long coastline and many ports, the trading and investing towns were far more numerous than the few in New Hampshire, clustered around the Great Bay. If the vote of the rural districts was so formidable in Massachusetts, its preponderance in New Hampshire might have been predicted. Actually, however, the anti-federalist majority, according to Langdon, was only about four.[51] After nine days of debate, the federalist orators had been able to convert a few of their opponents, but as these men felt bound by their instructions they could not vote for ratification without first consulting their constituents. They combined with the federalist minority to vote, 56-51, for an adjournment of the convention until the following June.[52]

New Hampshire's unexpected failure to ratify in February was a sore disappointment to federalists throughout the country and a source of mortification to the leaders who had so confidently promised the state's acquiescence. Letters passed between Washington, Madison, and Knox, deprecating New Hampshire's behavior and expressing the apprehension that its conduct would have a chilling effect upon the conventions in other states, especially in Virginia. Nicholas Gilman, attending the moribund congress in New York, wrote to Sullivan that the people at home

> can hardly imagine what pernicious effects our Convention business has produced in a number of the States—New Hampshire had been counted on by friends & foes as being perfectly federal—so that from the ratification of the new System in Massachusetts—the opposers began to make excuses and change sides in all Quarters but immediately on your adjournment they augmented their forces, took possession of their old ground and seem determined to maintain it at all hazards. . . . This being the case I hope no pains will be wanting to secure a Majority in the next meeting of our Convention— I do assure, Sir, Our present situation appears truly alarming and I am more and more confirmed in an opinion I have long entertained that the tranquility of our Country is suspended solely on the great question of the day.[53]

Yet New Hampshire was not so influential as these apprehensive gentlemen believed it to be. Two more states ratified during the spring, making eight altogether. The federalists really exerted themselves in the doubtful towns, and when the convention met again in June, New Hampshire had a prospect of being the ninth state to ratify, thus gaining the honor of putting the Constitution into effect. The June session therefore was less a reconsideration of the Constitution on its merits than a race to ratify before Virginia could rob New Hampshire of this distinction. On the fourth day, Saturday, June 21, at 1:00 P.M., the vote was taken, and New Hampshire approved the Constitution by a majority of ten, 57–47.[54] The state's position as the "keystone of the arch" was incidentally secured by Patrick Henry, who kept the Virginia convention at odds until five days later when it ratified by the same majority of ten.

The official records of these momentous events give no answers to many questions that immediately leap to the mind. One wonders about the membership of the convention: whether the opponents and proponents of the Constitution fell into distinct classes, and who were the half-dozen men whose change of opinion turned federalist defeat into victory. It can be stated without hesitation that the federalist delegates were representative of the talent and wealth of the state, if not of its virtue. They were led by Samuel Livermore, the chief justice, owner of a baronial estate in Holderness on the northern frontier, an eloquent speaker and a shrewd parliamentary tactician. But Livermore was only primus inter pares, with John Langdon, John Sullivan, Josiah Bartlett, and John Pickering. It would have been difficult to find five other men in New Hampshire to equal these. They had occupied the highest executive, legislative, and judicial offices in the state government and had represented New Hampshire in Congress and in the Continental Army.

Still other prominent federalists in the convention were Peirce Long, a Portsmouth merchant and shipper who had commanded a regiment in the war and afterward became collector of customs at the port; John Taylor Gilman, the state treasurer; Christopher Toppan of Hampton, a landowner with extensive holdings, shipbuilder, and merchant, who had been mildly loyalist throughout the war, but immediately afterward had been elected to the house, council, and senate; Thomas Bartlett of Nottingham, speaker of the house; John Calfe of Hampstead, who had been clerk of the house for many years; Benjamin West of Charlestown, the eloquent lawyer whose great influence was wielded in private for the adoption of the Constitution; General Benjamin Bellows of Walpole, one of the influential citizens of Cheshire County who had remained loyal to New Hampshire during the Vermont controversy, a man "of strict integrity, and great prudence"; Jonathan Freeman of Hanover, a prominent citizen of that influential town; and Colonel Elisha Payne of Lebanon, a Connecticut emigrant who had led the New Hampshire towns in their secession from the Exeter government and had, for a time, been the lieutenant-governor and chief justice of Vermont as well as a major general in its militia.[55]

A peculiar feature of the convention of 1788 was the number of ministers and physicians who came to represent their towns. These professional men were preponderately federalist. Of the seven clergymen, five Congregationalists voted for and one against ratification; the other clergyman was a religious as well as a political dissenter—William Hooper, of Madbury, a Baptist minister. Pastor Benjamin Thurston of Northampton and the Reverend Samuel Langdon of Hampton Falls, a former president of Harvard, were prominent advocates of the Constitution in the debates. Of the seven physicians who were elected to the convention, five voted for ratification and two against it. If the delegates were in any way representative of their classes as well as of their constituencies, the federal party was made up of substantial landowners, merchants, shipbuilders, security holders, lawyers, physicians, and orthodox clergymen—leaders who were accustomed to guide public opinion and direct public affairs.

In addition to the official delegates, however, a number of interested persons used their influence outside the convention for the adoption of the Constitution. "The three principal 'Lobby-members' of the Convention, were Wingate, N. Gilman, & Tim Walker," wrote a commentator.[56] Wingate and Gilman, representing the state in New York, were certainly doing all they could by way of correspondence to urge ratification.[57]

Gilman was so sanguine of the result that he began speculating in Continental securities and urged the state government to purchase its quota "of the public Securities now in circulation, while they are to be had at the present low rate."[58] George Barstow, the Democratic historian of New Hampshire, lived close enough to this period to remember something of public feeling on such matters.

> Speculators, who had bought, at a ruinous discount, from the officers and soldiers of the revolution, a large amount of continental certificates, naturally looked to the establishment of an energetic general government as the only chance for their redemption. This class of men, therefore, regarded the constitution with favor, rather as the sun which was to bring their own golden harvests to maturity, than the means of dispensing the blessings of equal rights and free institutions upon a great nation.[59]

The anti-federal party was poor in all but numbers. It had but one orator who could compete with Livermore, Langdon, and Sullivan— Joshua Atherton. Although this able attorney had been a Tory during the war, he had so regained public confidence that the town of Amherst sent him to the convention. He became the leader of the anti-federal party and virtually its sole support in debate, although he was more inclined to dramatic posturing than to expressing the real opinions of his constituents. Through John Lamb of New York, Atherton kept in touch with the anti-federalist leaders in other states, and fought a vigorous rearguard action against what he called the "consolidarians."[60]

Another wealthy opponent of the Constitution, Captain Charles Barrett of New Ipswich, had also been suspected of loyalism during the Revolution. When Barrett and Atherton objected to allowing cases to go from state to federal courts on appeal, General Sullivan replied in exasperation: "It seems singular that gentlemen who considered the British king was as eligible as that of any people could be, complain of this regulation as a hardship, and destructive of the rights of the people. They quietly suffered an appeal to Great Britain in all causes of consequence. They then boasted of their liberties; boasted of the liberty of appealing to judges ignorant of our situation, and prejudiced against the name of an American."[61] Barrett's presence and attitude in the convention are even more remarkable for the fact that the federalist candidate whom he defeated in New Ipswich was Timothy Farrar, who had been a prominent patriot and leader in the revolutionary government.[62] Atherton and Barrett were symbols of the resentment that Hillsborough County felt against a state government that had spurned their pleas for economic relief. The other anti-federal delegates of more than average distinction were Joseph Badger of Gilmanton, one of the early settlers in the Lake

Winnepesaukee region, an officer in the New Hampshire militia who had
helped to capture Burgoyne, and a councillor in 1784; Colonel Ebenezer
Webster of Salisbury, father of the great defender of the Constitution, a
revolutionary soldier, county judge, and senator; and Abel Parker of
Jaffrey, a highly respected revolutionary veteran and farmer. Also among
the party were Runnels and McMurphy, the two Londonderry representatives in the legislature; Colonel Benjamin Stone of Atkinson, the intimate of Nathaniel Peabody, who had been court-martialed for complicity in the Exeter riot; and Colonel Joseph Hutchins of Haverhill (one
of the Grafton County towns that had voted for paper money), who
probably attended the June session expressly to swell the vote against
ratification.

The six anti-federal members who had also been members of the assembly in 1786 had all voted for the emission of paper money and
against the act to give effect to the British treaty. Others had signed their
names to petitions for paper money. John Sullivan, who, of course, was
hardly an unprejudiced witness, characterized his opponents in the convention as "a motley mixture of Ancient Torys, friends to paper money,
Tender Laws, Insurrection, etc.; persons in Debt, distress & poverty,
either real or Imaginary; men of blind piety, Hypocrites, & Bankrupts;
together with Many honest men bound by Instructions to Vote against
the Constitution at all Events."[63]

Unfortunately, no contemporary bothered to record the names of the
men whose change of opinion between February and June secured a
majority for ratification. Only one town, Hopkinton, is positively known
to have released its delegate from its original adverse instructions, and
the record shows that he voted for ratification.[64] Daniel Webster always
insisted that his father was one of the converts, but the record shows that
although Ebenezer Webster was in Concord on June 21 and was marked
on the roll as attending the session, he did not vote either way.[65] All
accounts agree that the town of Salisbury, which he represented, originally instructed him to vote against the Constitution, but the traditions
differ as to whether the town changed its mind while the delegate did
not—or vice versa—or whether Webster was tricked into absence while
the final vote was being taken.[66] There is a half-authenticated story that
Judge Timothy Walker of Concord invited several anti-federalists to his
home for a dinner which was so well appreciated that they tarried too
long and thus failed to record their votes against the Constitution.[67] This
may account for the fact that four delegates who attended the convention
on the last day did not vote, since at least two of them had been definitely
instructed to oppose the Constitution.[68]

The journal of the convention bears evidence that both sides may have
stirred themselves after the adjournment of the first session to rally their

forces. Haverhill, which had not sent a delegate to Exeter, now elected an anti-federalist to represent the classed towns of Haverhill, Coventry, Piermont, and Warren. The federalists of Grafton County did not allow this maneuver to pass unchallenged; they elected Isaac Patterson of Piermont, a federalist, to represent Piermont and Warren, which had just won the right to be represented in the legislature separately from the other two towns.[69] Four interior towns in Cheshire County, unrepresented in the first session, sent two delegates with negative votes in June, but these were offset by the appearance of Elisha Payne from Lebanon and John Hall of Derryfield (Manchester). Thus, each side merely gained three votes by its interim exertions. However, the delegates from Hancock, Peterborough, Lee, and Hinsdale, who had attended the first session, failed to return. The first two of these towns had instructed their delegates against ratification, and the history and local circumstances of the latter two indicate that they also were opposed to the Constitution. The absence of these four men at the final session, through poverty or indifference, probably resulted in a loss of four anti-federalist votes.[70] The anti-federalist elected from Epping did not attend the convention, and two other anti-federalist towns, Andover and Protectworth, which were entitled to elect delegates, did not do so. If the four anti-federalists who succumbed to Judge Walker's hospitality, the four who did not return for the second session, the one from Epping who did not attend at all, and the two more who might have been elected had all voted on June 21, ratification might have been defeated by one vote, as it certainly would have been defeated by more than one vote in February.[71]

Very little of what was said in the convention was recorded, and that little is not very illuminating. Young John Quincy Adams, who drove up to Exeter from Newburyport in February to hear the debate, reported that Atherton assailed the proposed union because it went beyond the limits to which a proper construction of derivatives from the Latin word *foedus* should confine it and that Parson Thurston threatened the anti-federalists with immediate reconquest by Great Britain if they voted to remain outside the union.[72] The only speech made in the convention that found its way into a contemporary newspaper was one by Sullivan in defense of the jurisdiction of the federal courts. This was a sensible performance, but the subject was too narrow to give any general idea of the entire debate.[73] An alleged speech by Atherton against the provision that allowed continuance of the slave trade was printed in 1827, when the northern conscience was stirring on the subject of slavery. As reproduced, it was an impassioned tirade unlikely to have been uttered by the Amherst Tory, and the idea it was used to foster—that the opposition to the Constitution had been based upon the highest moral and religious principles—was a nineteenth-century afterthought.[74] Daniel Webster also furnished his official biographer with a short, sturdy speech which his father was supposed to have made, announcing his conversion to federalism, owing chiefly to his profound faith in General Washington. As the commentator remarked, the speech "certainly has the Websterian ring," and it probably served the great constitutionalist well by furnishing him with an impeccable background. Unfortunately, no explanation was made of the fact that Ebenezer was said to have ended his speech with the flat assertion "I shall vote for its adoption," and then failed to do so.[75]

The sketchy journal of the convention shows that the debate on Article 1, Section 8, which defines the powers of Congress, occupied three half-day sessions in February. Next to that the most time was taken up by a discussion of biennial elections to Congress. The anti-federalists obviously feared a strong central government, made up of "consolidarians." Colonel Benjamin Stone was reported as doubting whether "our situation could be much happier by changing one set of tyrants for another— British for American tyrants."[76] This remark was made in opposition to the right of appeal from state to federal courts, a subject to which an entire session was devoted. From these lofty heights, the delegates descended to petty prejudices, objecting for half a day to the prohibition of religious tests contained in Article 6. Under such laxity, declared one delegate, "a Turk, a Jew, a Roman Catholic, and what is worse than all a universalist may be president of the United States." Sullivan gave much credit to the Reverend Samuel Langdon for puncturing this argument with his firm insistence that religion could stand on its own feet without the support of the civil arm.[77]

The journal shows that the leaders on both sides were more skilled in parliamentary tactics than in constitutional theory. The convention settled three disputed seats in favor of delegates who later voted for ratification.[78] Langdon's motion to adjourn the Exeter session was a masterstroke, which Atherton tried in vain to avert. So also was the appointment in June of a committee consisting of eight federalists and seven anti-federalists to report amendments. This committee was appointed at the morning session, June 20; by three o'clock that afternoon it was able to report a list of twelve amendments, which were accepted. Such extraordinary speed was accomplished by adopting verbatim the nine amendments that Massachusetts had formulated and adding three which required that the upkeep of a standing army depend upon the three-fourths vote of Congress, that Congress make no laws to infringe the rights of conscience, and that citizens have the right to bear arms.[79] These twelve amendments were well calculated to remove many of the fears that honest people entertained in regard to a concentrated, centralized power.

At this point, Atherton shrewdly took the offensive by moving that the convention "ratify the proposed Constitution, together with the amendments; but that said Constitution do not operate in the State of New Hampshire without said amendments."[80] Livermore countered quickly by moving to postpone Atherton's motion and substitute for it a motion "that in case the Constitution be adopted . . . the amendments reported by the Committee be recommended to Congress."[81] To do this, Atherton argued, was "to surrender our all, and then ask our new Masters if they will be so gracious as to return to us, some, or any part of, our most important Rights and privileges."[82] Nevertheless, both of Livermore's motions carried. On the next day, Atherton played his last card by moving that the convention adjourn again, but this time the federalists voted against adjournment. Livermore then called for the final vote, and the struggle was over.

Langdon hurried off in jubilation to send the good news to Hancock, King, Hamilton, and Washington, while Sullivan posted a message by fast relays to the New York and Virginia conventions.[83] Although New Hampshire's action in February had grievously disappointed General Washington and his friends, its ultimate ratification as the ninth state secured the new government and was therefore cause for universal rejoicing.[84] This was all the more true because in New Hampshire alone among the small states had there been any serious opposition to the Constitution, and the opposition had been overcome by what appeared to be reason and enlightenment.

The geographical distribution of the final vote in the state convention reveals more of the motivation behind both parties than do the debates.[85] From the appended map it can be seen at once that the bulk of the opposition to the Constitution came from the central part of the state and that the favorable votes came largely from the Old Colony, the Connecticut Valley, and the Frontier (see Map 10). Mercantile, shipping, and trading interests were clearly lined up behind the Constitution. The agricultural interest was divided. Towns in which farmers had access to an outside market, such as those in the Connecticut Valley, and towns in which great proprietary interests existed, such as Holderness and Moultonborough, were federal. The upland, relatively isolated towns, in which agriculture was almost entirely self-sufficient and the small freeholder predominated, were anti-federal. A general correspondence between the vote on ratification and such economic facts as taxable property, density of population, delinquent taxes, and votes on paper money and tender laws is also demonstrable.[86] But this economic coincidence can be, and has been, overemphasized. It would be naive to believe that the ordinary voter of New Hampshire even understood the economic implications of the Constitution, much less governed his attitude toward it by such a comprehension. The factors of social control, class antagonism, tradition, orthodoxy, sectional feeling, and suspicion of any new project determined the result in at least as many towns as did specific economic considerations.

A limited degree of correlation between the paper-money fever and the opposition to the federal Constitution is demonstrable, although it is far from perfect. Table 4–1, based on very incomplete data, is nevertheless illuminating.[87]

Of the representatives who voted for the paper-money plan of 1786, 60 percent came from towns that later elected delegates who voted against the federal Constitution. An even higher degree of correlation—65 percent—shows for the towns which voted in favor of the paper-money referendum and then elected delegates who voted against ratification, although the remaining 35 percent indicates that a longing for paper-money was not incompatible with federalism. A comparison of maps that show the distribution of the vote on adoption of the Constitution and of paper-money sentiment throughout the decade serves to illustrate two facts: that the paper-money issue divided the classes horizontally much more sharply than did the constitutional question, and that paper-money sentiment and anti-federalism show the greatest degree of coincidence in the isolated, interior areas, away from the means of communication (see Map 9 and Map 10).[88]

It is quite reasonable to suppose that the Constitution's prohibition of state currency influenced the merchants of Portsmouth, the oligarchs of Exeter, and the squires of Grafton County in its favor. But the representatives of the country towns had less reason to fear such a prohibition than to hope that a federal government would grant them the relief that their state legislature had not given. It is less likely that the paper-money party

TABLE 4-1

	Federal	Anti-federal
Towns that petitioned for paper money between 1780 and 1787	9	20
Towns whose representatives in the legislature voted in favor of the paper-money plan of 1786	27	41
Towns whose representatives voted against the paper-money plan of 1786	22	2
Towns that voted in favor of the paper-money plan of 1786	20	28
Towns that voted against the paper-money plan of 1786	15	13

voted against the Constitution than that paper-money agitation and anti-federalism were products of the same adverse economic conditions.

A further breakdown of the vote within the four areas of the state shows interesting results. The Old Colony was overwhelmingly federal. Here there were twenty-four votes for ratification and only eight against. This area, which contained now much less than a third of the total population of the state, produced 40 percent of the affirmative vote in the convention. Every one of the towns on the seacoast or on one of the inlets of Piscataqua Bay—in other words, every town affected by commerce, fishing, or shipbuilding—gave its vote for ratification. They formed a part of the federal belt which stretched almost the entire length of the Atlantic seacoast, and their unity is a striking feature of the map. Among the anti-federal minority, however, were Atkinson, the most vigorous petitioner in 1786 for paper money; Madbury, in which most of the people were Baptists; and Rochester, which may have feared the effect of federal regulations upon the lumber trade. Portsmouth, Exeter, Hampton, Durham, and Dover were the chief federal towns. In this oldest and most institutionalized part of New Hampshire, the instinct toward conservatism and authority had regained predominance by 1788 and was a powerful factor in bringing the Constitution into functional life.

The Merrimack Valley was as decisively anti-federal as the Old Colony was federal. The middle part of the state gave only eleven votes for ratification to twenty-five against. It was a part of that anti-federal hinterland which stretched almost unbroken from Lake Winnepesaukee to Narragansett Bay.[89] The Merrimack Valley was still an agricultural and lumbering region in 1788, still relatively isolated and self-sufficient. Like Middlesex and Worcester counties in Massachusetts, it was a region of small, debt-burdened farms, with little opportunity to develop a market for surplus produce. Consequently, its inhabitants were forced to exchange their scanty supplies of currency for a few necessities imported from the seaboard at high prices. The economic burdens of the postwar depression had fallen upon these Merrimack farmers with peculiar severity, and their clamors for relief had gone unheeded. Londonderry had been the very fountainhead of the paper-money agitation, and Goffstown, Amherst, and Canterbury were not far behind.

It is difficult to account for the scattered federalist votes in this region upon any other ground than the personal preferences of the delegates. The pattern of religious organization may have had some influence. Hopkinton and Henniker, for example, may have been inspired by their Congregationalist orthodoxy rather than their politics to vote for the Constitution, for they later became inalterably Democratic towns. The fact that twelve of the fifteen Scotch-Irish communities in New Hampshire were anti-federal probably reflects religious prejudice as much as ethnic or economic differences.[90] Sectarian resentments may also have influenced the anti-federal sentiment in Salem, Chichester, Canterbury, Gilmanton, and Sanbornton, where Baptist churches had been organized. Concord's vote against the Constitution is peculiar, since the town had decidedly opposed paper money and was to become consistently Federalist in later years. In 1788, however, Concord had not yet become a trading center. It was engaged in a double quarrel with the state government over the location of the capital and the formation of a new county on the upper Merrimack. Its adverse vote may have been chiefly an expression of pique against Exeter.

The Connecticut Valley, as it was described in the first chapter, sent twenty-eight delegates to the Concord convention. These divided sixteen for and twelve against the Constitution, and the line of cleavage was almost strictly an economic one. Nine of the adverse votes came from the poor interior towns in the heights above the river valley and adjacent to Hillsborough County—towns such as Unity, Marlow, and Jaffrey, which had appealed in vain to the eastern squires for tax abatements or currency increases. In the whole length of the actual Connecticut Valley, though, where rich intervale land and ready access to markets made the farmers more content, there were only three anti-federal towns. The older and wealthier communities in the south, Charlestown, Walpole, and Keene, were federalist, while in the northern part of the valley every town except Haverhill followed the lead of Hanover and Lebanon in favor of the Constitution. The three river towns that voted against the Constitution had voted for paper money. Religious prejudice may have played some part in determining the line of division; the Congregationalist towns in general supported the Constitution, while Claremont, an Episcopalian center, and Croyden, Newport, Marlow, and Richmond, with Baptist churches, were all anti-federal. The parallel fracture between the valley towns and the hill towns determined later division into Federalist and Republican sections.

The great river itself was the decisive factor in giving this area its federalist majority. It was an artery not only of commerce but also of ideas, and the decisive acceptance of the Constitution by the state of Connecticut was a potent influence with her sons in the upper valley. The western towns were probably much better informed upon the Constitution and its obvious advantages than were the central parts of New Hampshire, and Connecticut was the source of their information. A writer in the *Connecticut Courant* thus addressed the river towns: "New York, the trading towns on the Connecticut river, and Boston, are the sources from which a great part of your foreign supplies will be obtained, and where your produce will be exposed for market. In all these places an import is collected, of which, as consumers, you pay a share without deriving any public benefit. You can not expect any alteration in the private systems of these states unless effected by the proposed government."[91]

The nearly unanimous federal vote of the Grafton County towns reflected the recollection of events that had embittered the previous decade. The long struggle for an Upper Connecticut state was over but not forgotten. These people of the upper Connecticut were no lovers of either Exeter or Bennington. A strong federal government would save them from utter subjection to the dominant sections of their states; it would preserve the upper Connecticut as an economic unit even if its political solidarity was shattered; it would guarantee the statehood of Vermont and bring to an end the long period of turmoil and uncertainty. Thus, even in defeat, the New Hampshire Grants might survive with victory for their cherished principle of local autonomy. That is why Elisha Payne, who had once led the militia of the Grants against the authority of New Hampshire, came to Concord in June to vote for the new Constitution.

The Northern Frontier consisted of the settled territory between the Connecticut Valley towns and the Maine border, stretching northward from the shores of Lake Winnepesaukee. Some thirty-three towns in this wilderness were represented at the convention by nine delegates, of whom six voted for and two against the Constitution. Ebenezer Smith of Meredith failed to record his vote; he may have been a guest at Judge Walker's dinner. As the vote stands, it shows a precise geographical division, the two anti-federal votes coming from towns lying against the Maine border and the six federal votes from those to the westward.

The eastern half of this frontier area was geographically a part of Maine rather than of New Hampshire. It was drained by the Saco River, and its outlets to the world were through Portland and old Biddeford. It was separated from Portsmouth by lakes and mountains; when David Page of Conway traveled to the convention at Exeter, he went by way of Alfred, Maine. It is not surprising that the border towns from Rochester northward to Conway voted, as did the neighboring Maine towns, against the Constitution. It is more difficult to assign a reason for the federalism of the towns north of Lake Winnepesaukee and in the Pemigewasset Valley. New Hampshire historians ascribe it to the personal influence of Judge Livermore, who lived in Holderness. This may well be true, for his impact was not only intellectual but economic. Livermore was typical of an important factor on the New England frontier—the great proprietor who often owned half of the land in the town and who, when he chose to live upon his estates, exercised an irresistible weight in his community. Such men as Livermore and Francis Worcester of Plymouth could easily dominate the politics of an entire county.

The importance of the federalist votes in this frontier area can hardly be exaggerated. If the region be extended westward to take in the Grafton County towns on the Connecticut River, which were actually a part of the frontier so far as recent settlement was concerned, it can be said that it gave the decisive majority for the adoption of the Constitution. The Old Colony, the Merrimack Valley, and Cheshire County—the southern, long-settled part of the state—divided almost evenly in the ratifying convention—federalist votes 45, anti-federalist 44. It was the raw northern frontier, bringing in twelve federalist votes, which gave the real margin of victory for the Constitution.[92] If ratification had depended upon the commercial sections of the state alone, New Hampshire would never have become the ninth pillar, or the keystone in the arch, of union.

One of the easy assumptions of American history is that the federalists and anti-federalists of 1788 became the prototypes or ancestors of all the subsequent rival organizations in our two-party system. While there is a limited degree of truth in this opinion, which was widely held by contemporaries, time and place eroded much of its accuracy in New Hampshire. In 1788, the Old Colony, the Connecticut Valley, and the Northern Frontier were decidedly federalist, while the Merrimack Valley, plus the eastern part of Cheshire County, was strongly anti-federalist. In the nineteenth century, after the two parties had achieved relatively stable positions, only the Connecticut Valley remained staunchly Federalist. The Merrimack Valley became less thoroughly Republican than it had been anti-federalist; the Frontier came to be pretty equally divided; but, strangest of all, the Old Colony changed to Republicanism. This could mean either that a great social or economic revolution came over New Hampshire or that the political issues of the nineteenth century affected the voters in a very different way than did the constitutional question. The choice of explanations is easy to make, for New Hampshire's social and economic pattern underwent no such radical change as would account for so great a shifting on the map.

The evidence does not deny a certain fundamental economic pattern which underlay the consistent federalism or anti-federalist republicanism of well-defined areas from 1788 to 1820. The thin soil of the central part of Hillsborough County, for example, continued to produce rugged individualists in the form of anti-federalists, Jeffersonian Republicans, and Jacksonian Democrats through three generations. Likewise, the prosperous Connecticut Valley did not fail to befriend the party with a high regard for property rights until long after 1820. But the towns and sections that formed exceptions to this generalization were so numerous as to render it suspect. One of the most important of these changes was the defection of Portsmouth to Republican ranks. Equally interesting on the other side was the conversion of Londonderry, Sanbornton, and Peterborough to consistent Federalism.

The fact that so many of these radical changes occurred makes any thesis linking the federalism of 1788 with the Federal party of 1800 subject to so many exceptions as to become pointless. What does appear evident is that the federalism of each period had certain common characteristics that attracted the people of Exeter and Hanover, but that the bonds that held Portsmouth and Henniker in 1788 were not present in John Adams's Federalism. Economic factors were important, but not necessarily decisive elements in the composition of the parties that fought not only the battle for ratification of the Constitution but the long campaigns for its interpretation and enforcement.

CHAPTER 5

A FRAGMENT OF

SOCIAL HISTORY

*Taxes laid by the British Parliament upon America are not more con-
trary to civil freedom, than [ecclesiastical] taxes are to the very nature of
liberty of conscience*—Isaac Backus

The social changes that occurred in New Hampshire during the American Revolution could hardly be called revolutionary.[1] New England's life-
style probably changed less during these fateful years than that of any
colonial region, and New Hampshire's less than any other part of New
England. Such institutions as the state-supported church, the paternalistic
government, the village school, the militia company, the country merchant, and itinerant courts seemed to emerge from the war years un-
scathed and unimproved. Yet colonial society itself had not been static,
and the rate of normal change was undoubtedly accelerated by the disturbances of the war. The spirit of inquiry, furthermore, which the quarrel with Great Britain had fomented in the realm of political theory,
inevitably, even if imperceptibly, penetrated all other aspects of life, and
eventually, though often many years later, led to profound alterations in
the social fabric.

THE CHURCH

Next to the economic processes of "getting and spending," religion was
the most important influence in the lives of New Hampshire people;
indeed, Calvinists made little distinction between God and mammon.
Prior to the American Revolution the Congregational church was established by law in New Hampshire, as it was in all parts of New England
except Rhode Island. Its political position rested upon a statute of 1714
that authorized towns to erect meetinghouses and engage ministers at
public expense, levying taxes for that purpose and collecting them in the
same manner as any other regular town rate. The statute contained a saving clause, declaring that it was not intended to "interfere with her Majesty's grace and favour in allowing her subjects liberty of conscience,"
but it further stipulated that only those who "constantly" attended "the
publick worship of God on the Lord's-day according to their own per-

swasion" should be excused from paying toward the support of the "settled" minister.[2]

Although the Congregational church was nowhere mentioned in this act, it was firmly established and linked with the civil power, since the law gave the majority of the legal voters in every New Hampshire town the privilege of setting up *their* church and forcing the minority to help them support it. There was not a parish in New Hampshire in 1714 in which Congregationalists were not an overwhelming majority; consequently, there were none but Congregational ministers engaged under the terms of this act. For that matter, there was really no minority to be oppressed. It was for the benefit of future dissenters that the proviso quoted above had been added.

New Hampshire's religious establishment was never at any time as harsh and unyielding as those of Massachusetts and Connecticut. The reason may have been that the colony's first settlers came to Piscataqua for the fishing or to escape religious persecution in Massachusetts rather than with any idea of establishing a new Zion in the wilderness. At any rate, church membership was never made a qualification for the suffrage, as was the case to the southward; in fact, when the Bay Colony wanted to annex the New Hampshire towns in 1641, it had to make an exception for them in its voting restrictions.[3] Not only were the laws less severe but the spirit of intolerance had less hold upon the people. When the Reverend Arthur Browne came to Portsmouth in 1738 as the first Anglican priest, he thus described his situation: "And I must add in commendation of the People in general, that the same inveterate Prejudices don't prevail, nor is the same Spirit of Obstinacy and Disaffection gone forth among them, that reigns triumphant in the neighbouring Provinces."[4] Isaac Backus, the Baptist historian, also testified to this relative mildness of temper, but attributed it to the royal government in New Hampshire, which, in fact, tended to make the Anglican rather than the Congregational influence supreme in official circles.[5]

Except for the Scotch-Irish settlers of Londonderry and other Merrimack Valley towns, who brought their Presbyterianism with them to America in the 1720s, the Anglican Portsmouth aristocrats who began worshiping at Queen's Chapel in 1734, and a few Quakers and Baptists scattered throughout the colony, New Hampshire was still uniformly Congregationalist on the eve of the Revolution. The rebellion, however, which the Congregationalist clergy fostered against George III and his threat to establish an Anglican bishop among them, turned against their own establishment. It was inevitable that revolutionary sentiment, once unloosed, could not be restricted to political channels alone, but would sap at the foundations of all structures formerly upheld by awe and authority. Dissenting churches found a great release of energy during the

Revolution, and people were more inclined to join them because of the troubled times.

The immediate beneficiaries of this new freedom were the Baptists, who had been active in southern New England for a century, but did not establish their first church in New Hampshire until 1755. In 1770, Dr. Samuel Shepard, a Stratham physician of dubious standing in the medical profession, was converted to the Baptist faith by reading a tract which he had idly picked up from a table during a sick call. He soon organized a church at Brentwood, which, with its five branches, provided him with a parish of seven hundred members, by far the largest in New Hampshire.[6] Shepard was a forceful, uncouth character, zealous enough to be a successful evangelist, but practical enough to remain a physician and to build up a competent property from his two professions. He was typical of the shrewd and resourceful men who led the religious revolt against Congregationalism in New England.

The political revolution in New England was accompanied by a religious struggle in which the Baptists were the Whigs and Isaac Backus their Samuel Adams. The religious revolutionary pointed out to the political rebel in 1774 "that taxes laid by the British Parliament upon America are not more contrary to civil freedom, than [ecclesiastical] taxes are to the very nature of liberty of conscience."[7] Unfortunately, the Baptists were in the peculiar position of rebelling against rebels, and this is the unpardonable political sin. There was a strong tendency during the war to tar Baptists with a Tory brush. Although in general the Baptists were nothing worse than neutral in sentiment, their position was rendered even less secure by the Declaration of Independence. Previously, they could petition the king to enforce their rights against colonial legislatures; after 1776 there was no external power to whom they might appeal.

In spite of persecution, however, the Baptists persisted in their penetration of New Hampshire. Even in the older settlements where Congregationalism was well entrenched, they made converts, but on the frontier the Baptist itinerant, with his contempt for settlement contacts, his willingness to preach without first being educated, and his ability to cover parishes hundreds of square miles in extent, had a peculiar advantage over the Congregationalist missionary. Hence it was in the newly settled areas and in the poorer towns that the Baptists reaped their greatest harvests. During the war Baptist enthusiasm spread until there were some twenty-four distinct congregations in the state, extending as far northward as Rumney and Holderness.[8] Young converts such as William Plumer enthusiastically toured the farther reaches of Strafford and Grafton counties, ignoring the war against England in their assaults upon a much older enemy of mankind.

As far as any visible results are concerned, the Revolutionary War tended to increase intolerance in New Hampshire rather than to validate any suggestion of religious freedom. Of the nine colonies which had established churches, six achieved a separation of church and state during the Revolution, but Connecticut, Massachusetts, and New Hampshire continued into the nineteenth century with their tax-supported churches.[9] In the proposed constitution of 1779 for New Hampshire a Protestant test for officeholding was suggested for the first time. At the end of the war this requirement was written into the permanent constitution. This same document fully guaranteed rights of conscience and promised that no individual should be "hurt, molested, or restrained in his person, liberty, or estate for worshiping God in the manner and season most agreeable to the dictates of his own conscience."[10] Yet Article 6 of the Bill of Rights maintained that the greatest security of good government lay in the inculcation of morality and piety through public worship of the Deity and empowered the legislature to authorize "the several towns, parishes, bodies corporate, or religious societies within this state to make adequate provision at their own expense for the support and maintenance of public Protestant teachers of piety, religion and morality." Finally, it declared that "no person of any one particular religious sect or denomination shall ever be compelled to pay towards the support of the teacher or teachers of another persuasion, sect, or denomination."[11]

In 1791 the legislature implemented Article 6 of the constitution by passing an act "for Regulating Towns and the Choice of Town Officers," which replaced the statute of 1714 as the legal basis for the ecclesiastical establishment. Among other things, it provided that the qualified inhabitants of any town might "vote such sum or sums of money as they shall judge necessary for the settlement, maintenance, and support of the ministry . . . to be assessed on the polls and estates in the same town as the Law directs."[12] Under this law, if a town corporation, by majority vote, contracted for a minister's services and then levied a tax upon all members of the corporation to raise the money for his salary, an individual taxpayer would be legally obligated to pay, even though he had voted against hiring the minister and objected to his sermons. He could escape the obligation only by proving, in court if necessary, that he was a bona fide member of a legally recognized sect distinct from that of which the minister was a part.

It should be obvious that the enforcement of this obligation to maintain public worship would have encountered difficulties, even if there had been no differences of religious opinion among the people. A large proportion of the towns in New Hampshire had their origins in church quarrels, when the people in one end of the town refused any longer to attend services in the same house with the people in the other end and petitioned the legislature for parish privileges and the right to hire their own minister.[13] Congregationalist ministers were as much injured by the eternal bickering under this system as were dissenting preachers. After years of starving on an insufficient salary, only half paid, the long-suffering clergyman might finally sue the town for fulfillment of contract. In the meantime, the town collector might have been proceeding against refractory townspeople for payment of the ministerial tax. The people might begin a countersuit, perhaps alleging fraud in the contract, such as the improper counting of votes by the clerk in town meeting. Some sympathy should be reserved for earnest and humble Congregationalist ministers during these trying years. Beset on one side by what they felt to be heretical zealots whose proselyting tactics were anything but gentlemanly and on the other by skinflint selectmen and congregations who felt encouraged by the law to drive as sharp a bargain for salvation as they dared, many an obscure scholar wore out his life in loyal support of what he truly believed to be a system organized according to God's will, only to be labeled a bigot and a fogy by his successors.

Article 6 in the New Hampshire Bill of Rights seems to be a cynical contradiction of the guarantee of freedom of conscience which precedes it, but the sincerity of the statesmen who framed it need not be brought into question. Obvious as it now seems, the people of that day required a good deal of bitter experience to learn that freedom of conscience was incompatible with support of religion by taxation. Even so wise and fair-minded a man as Jeremy Belknap could state with calm conviction in 1791 that there was "as entire religious liberty in New-Hampshire, as any people can rationally desire."[14]

Yet the appearance of Presbyterians, Episcopalians, Quakers, and Baptists in New Hampshire had abundantly demonstrated the irrational character of the system. In some cases the sects had used the law to the disadvantage of the Congregational order. In frontier towns where the Baptist itinerant arrived before the orthodox minister and built up his following, the first town meeting might result in a vote to settle a Baptist minister and tax the Congregational minority for his support. This happened so frequently that a minister of the standing order was moved to publish a complaint against the situation in a Boston newspaper. "Alas, the consequence of the prevalence of this sect! [Baptists] They cause divisions everywhere. In the State of New Hampshire, where there are many new towns, infant settlements, if this sect gets footing among them, they hinder, and are like to hinder, their settling and supporting learned, pious and orthodox ministers; and so the poor inhabitants of those towns must live, who knows how long? without the ministry of the gospel, and gospel ordinances."[15]

The sects, however, caused most trouble in places where the Congregational church had long been established and supported by town funds. When religious minorities grew up in such places, there were several ways to settle the problem. On rare occasions the minority became a majority and captured control of the town meeting. Such reverses turned the Congregationalists into a minority subject to persecution by their former victims.[16] A more frequent solution, which was possible when the minority was large enough to support a church of its own, was for the former congregation to divide into two parishes and each continue in the good work of taxing for the support of its own preaching. But when the religious minorities were too small or too scattered to support a separate church, the law and the constitution made them liable to be taxed for the preacher of the majority. In such cases the efficacy of Article 6 in guarding their liberty of conscience depended entirely upon local opinion and the energy of the magistrates.

Unlike Massachusetts and Connecticut, New Hampshire made no effort to force dissenters to attend public worship or to see that they contributed to the support of their own ministers. The problem of the unincorporated sectarian was left largely to the discretion of local officers. In most of the towns, year after year, it is evident that the officers were lenient or that the dissenters paid their tax quietly.[17] Some dissenters or deists were exempted from the ecclesiastical tax merely upon their affidavit that they differed in religious opinion from the settled minister. Public opinion, however, usually insisted that *every* property owner should be made to pay toward the support of *some* church.

There is no question that the system did make it possible for town officers to persecute a religious minority, in spite of the "no subordination" language of the constitution. In the typical New Hampshire town, where there was a single meetinghouse controlled by the Congregationalists and where all the prudential affairs of the church were settled in town meeting, a handful of Baptists might have a hard time. They would be legally free to attend the meetings of their society whenever a Baptist itinerant visited the town for a service, but in the meantime, having no regular church of their own, they might be expected to pay their share toward the support of the town's established minister.

The Methodists and Baptists had many practical grievances against this grudging toleration. Their technique of itinerancy, in contrast to the Congregationalist ideal of a settled pastorate, made for an unequal incidence of the law. A circuit rider served many societies, but he could be settled, and therefore eligible to receive public support, in only one town. A handful of loyal Baptists, who had opportunity to hear their own minister only infrequently as he traveled his huge circuit, might have to spend all their other Sundays in the Congregational meetinghouse or else be charged with such lax support of their own church as to preclude them from the saving provisions of the law. Under these conditions Baptists and later sectarians were inclined to blanket all their grievances under the single demand for complete religious freedom, rather than fight each irritation separately. Their greatest leaders, Backus and Manning, were consistent in their advice that the Baptists take advantage of *none* of the exemptions in their favor but rather stand fast in opposition to the entire system. Not all had either the courage or the stubbornness to do so. Many a layman paid his tax under protest, and some ministers accepted, or even sued for, their share of the public treasury. But most resisted the union of church and state in its entirety and refused to pay taxes that they considered to be in violation of their consciences as well as their rights. It was in these cases that persecution continued to stain the history of New England after 1800.

The judicial annals of Connecticut and Massachusetts are full of arrests, imprisonments, fines, attachments of property, and sale at vendue for nonpayment of religious taxes. When the sectarians employed attorneys and attempted to vindicate their rights in the courts, they often had difficulty in obtaining even the most elementary justice. Selectmen, collectors, constables, judges, and jurors were usually Congregationalist, and they frequently conspired to defeat the benevolent purposes of the law. The courts were inclined to recognize only the Congregational church as a distinct sect and to place a heavy burden of proof upon any one who wished to demonstrate that there were others. New Hampshire judges sometimes failed to be convinced even of differences between Calvinists and Universalists—and ordered the latter to pay for support of the former.[18]

It is difficult to determine the exact extent of this kind of persecution in New Hampshire. The absence of controversial literature, of spectacular court battles, and of repeated legislation would seem to indicate that there was much less outright persecution and dissension in New Hampshire than in the states to the south. On the other hand, it must be noted that most of the great sectarian leaders lived and fought in southern New England, and that New Hampshire was the scene of skirmishes rather than of the main battle. Here and there a concrete story of persecution can be found. Baptists in Richmond complained that their brethren in a neighboring town "have suffered much by the inhabitants of their town, who have taken away their cattle and sold them at the post for their minister's rates, and they are threatened still to be used in like manner."[19] The Baptist church in Londonderry owed its independence to the boldness of one of its members, who threatened to sue the constable who arrested him for nonpayment of taxes, and was subsequently unmolested.[20] In

1799 a quarterly meeting of the Free Will Baptists found it necessary to protest to the selectmen of Wolfeborough against their seizure of one Thomas Cotton's cow for nonpayment of religious taxes.[21] These are enough examples at least to prove that the law was capable of becoming an engine of persecution in the hands of intolerant magistrates.[22]

While the system of supporting religion by law thus caused dissenters to hate the standing order as persecutors, it had the equally unfortunate effect of convincing Congregationalist leaders that the sectarians were merely tax evaders of the most despicable sort. Exemption laws and "no subordination" clauses, devised for the sincere purpose of accommodating tender consciences, provided loopholes for persons of a very different sort who had no wish to be taxed for the benefit of any parson—a class of unwelcome recruits to the dissenting churches who were called "neuters" for lack of a more suitable designation.[23] In some cases, entire congregations deserted their pastor in order to form a Methodist or Baptist church as a tax shelter. In the very nature of things, therefore, the rush to join dissenting sects could not be interpreted solely as a thirst for salvation—unless it were from the tax-gatherer.

Some Congregationalist divines could see no motive in the movement but a selfish one. When Belknap, after being underpaid by his Dover congregation for years, finally negotiated a settlement which would involve a larger ecclesiastical tax for the ensuing year, he wrote with weary cynicism to a friend, "It will have one effect, which, however irksome in the operation, will finally produce solid good. . . . Some will fall off and turn Baptists, but those who remain will be the more closely united and zealously engaged."[24] Other members of the establishment were less philosophical about the growth of the Baptist sect in New Hampshire. President Dwight gave his opinion of it in prose of withering scorn:

Of all religious sects, those which owe their existence to the reluctance, felt by every avaricious man, to support the public worship of God, are the worst in their character, and the most hopeless of reformation. Arguments to enforce the duty of opening the purse are addressed to a heart of stone, and an intellect of lead. The very fact, that a man has quitted on this ground a religion, which he approved, for one which he disapproved, will make him an enemy to the former, and a zealot for the latter. Conviction and principle are here out of the question. The only inquiry, the only thought, is concerning a sum of money, so pitiful, that the proprietor is ashamed of being even suspected of his real design. Hence he becomes enthusiastic, bigoted, censorious, impervious to conviction, a wanderer after every struggling exhorter, and every bewildered tenet;

and thus veers from one folly and falsehood to another, and another, throughout his life. This conduct is often challenged as a mere exercise of the rights of conscience; but conscience is equally a stranger to the conduct and the man.[25]

Whether the sects grew by feeding upon hypocrisy or heroics, their shattering effects upon the orthodox establishment were the same. Everywhere it gave ground after the Revolution, losing both influence and adherents. No Jefferson arose in New Hampshire, however, to lead the way to immediate separation of church and state or to write an immortal statute of religious freedom. This work was accomplished in New England by gradual erosion of the old society and through the efforts of many men.

EDUCATION

For an ambitious youth growing up in New Hampshire during the revolutionary era, the process of obtaining a formal education could well have been a frustrating experience. Depending upon exact time, place, and circumstance, there could have been a vast difference between the schooling to which he was entitled by law and that which was offered him in fact. The system of education that appeared in the statute books of New Hampshire, first established when the Piscataqua settlement had been within the jurisdiction of Massachusetts in 1647, required all towns of fifty families to support an elementary school and those of one hundred "howsholders" to "sett up a grammar schoole."[26] When New Hampshire became a separate province this law was retained and strengthened from time to time until it provided a fine of twenty pounds not only for towns but also for parishes that evaded their educational obligations.

A lamentable disregard for the statute, however, is betrayed by numerous petitions to the legislature setting forth excuses for not observing it and dispensations allowed by the general court. In the years of expansion after 1760 dozens of border towns were incorporated and settled without attracting the fifty families that made a school legally necessary. Subsequently, the dislocations of the revolutionary struggle, and particularly the disintegration of centralized authority, made a mockery of the high-sounding intention of the law and left the matter of schooling entirely in the hands of local magistrates. These selectmen, in turn, found that the quarrel with the royal government added confusion and unaccustomed responsibilities to their already burdened office and that war taxes and school taxes could not be squeezed out of the same thin pocket-books.

Evasion of the school law was generally overlooked in a period when the very existence of a free people seemed to be at stake. Enforcement rested not on an administrative officer but upon the grand juries of the counties, which were expected to bring indictments against towns and selectmen who neglected their duties.[27] Judges might charge grand jurors in the most solemn tones to bring the full weight of the law upon refractory magistrates, but the jurors were their neighbors, shared their anxiety as well as their cupidity, and felt that a fine of twenty pounds levied upon an official for saving the town's money was worse tyranny than parliamentary taxation. Juries could easily be satisfied that the law was obeyed. A favorite method of furnishing such satisfaction was to hold school for a few weeks just before and during the term of court. Since courts themselves were held very irregularly during the period from 1775 to 1780, even this subterfuge was not always necessary. If worst came to worst and juries and judges were obdurate, the town might vote to pay the fine, as cheaper than paying a schoolmaster.[28]

Belknap expressed the outraged sensibilities of friends of learning in a letter which described conditions in Dover, one of the largest and most affluent towns in the state.

> I have long thought, and do still think it one of the greatest misfortunes of my life to be obliged to rear a family of children in a place and among a people where insensibility to the interests of the rising generation, and an inveterate antipathy to literature, are to be reckoned among the prevailing vices; where there is not so much public spirit as to build a schoolhouse; where men of the first rank let their children grow up uncultivated as weeds in the highway; where grand jurors pay no regard to their oaths; and where a judge on the bench has publicly instructed them to invent subterfuges and evasions to cheat their consciences and prevent the execution of the laws for the advancement of learning, which in another part of the same charge he pretended to extol, as a means of preserving the country from slavery.[29]

Belknap recognized a fact which later American history has demonstrated to be infallible: that war is always accompanied by "a most unhappy prostration of morals."[30] Interest in education fell to an even lower level during the postwar period of economic depression and political uncertainty. The constitution-makers paid lip service at the shrine of learning in 1783 when they enjoined future legislatures to cherish the interests of seminaries and public schools and to encourage all other means and expressions of knowledge, but Belknap soon discovered that this injunction was little more than a pious hope.[31] After repeated solicitation of the legislature for financial aid in publishing his *History of New Hampshire*, a work which certainly merited official encouragement if any ever did, he was finally, in 1791, granted fifty pounds.[32] Even this modest sum was voted only after acrimonious debate.

Efforts to encourage better schools were only auxiliary to the basic educational process, which then, as now, depended upon two fundamentals—the skill of the teacher and the aptness of the pupil. Since the beginning of the eighteenth century Massachusetts had required some kind of certification for teachers, but New Hampshire did not do so until 1789.[33] Consequently, in the hiring of teachers selectmen had no requirements to meet except the parsimony of their constituents.[34] The miserable salaries of five to eight dollars per month paid to teachers by local officials encouraged an unfortunate tendency to regard school keeping as a short ladder to more worthy and lucrative occupations. The great majority of the teachers were male transients. It was customary for college students, especially at Dartmouth, to alternate a term of study with a few months of teaching, and thus to earn their way through college. Among the famous men of the period who at one time or another devoted a small part of their lives to school teaching were Benjamin Thompson, who kept the school at Concord before he left for Europe and became Count Rumford; Daniel Webster, who taught the youth of Fryeburg, Maine, for a season; Jeremiah Smith, later chief justice and governor of New Hampshire; and John Phillips, who abandoned teaching for commerce and made a fortune, which he then turned back to the uses of education.

Only a very few professional teachers in this period commanded public respect through their skills and services. One such was Owen O'Sullivan, a highly educated immigrant from Ireland, conversant with five languages, who kept the schools in Berwick, Maine, and Somersworth, New Hampshire, for fifty years and became the father of two governors.[35] An even more notable career was that of Major Samuel Hale, who presided over the Latin grammar school on King Street in Portsmouth for forty years and who could number his famous pupils by the score. Hale graduated from Harvard College in 1740, participated in the memorable capture of Louisbourg by the New England militia in 1745, represented Portsmouth for many years in the legislature, and performed innumerable civic duties in addition to his teaching. He might have had a notable career in the army, the courts, or as a statesman, but he preferred to serve in the humble capacity of a schoolmaster and to train others to occupy the positions he forswore.[36]

As the new nation emerged from the difficulties of war and depression, an increasing solicitude for better schools began to manifest itself in New Hampshire. The process began in 1789 with the passage of an act that repealed all former legislation on the subject and provided that school taxes in each town should henceforth be levied according to a proportion fixed by state law.[37] The opportunity to evade obligations was thus taken away from the local official, and from that time control of the schools centered more and more in the state government. By 1818 school legislation had assumed something of the proportions of a complete code. The school tax in that year was increased to ninety thousand dollars for the entire state; this sum was to be expended for the maintenance in each town of a school in which English grammar, reading, writing, arithmetic, and geography should be taught. The larger towns were also required to maintain a Latin grammar school. Teachers were expected to hold certificates of qualification and of moral character, and annual inspections of schools by town committees were required.[38]

Although these laws were only imitations of legislation that Massachusetts had long before enacted, they spelled progress in every direction but that of secondary education. In this field the state was anticipated and outdone by private enterprise in the academies that arose to take the place of the neglected grammar schools. John Phillips of Exeter, "excited," as Belknap said, "by the melancholy prospect," founded and endowed Phillips Exeter in 1781, a few years after having aided his nephew in the establishment of the Andover academy.[39] Academies multiplied phenomenally in New Hampshire thereafter, so that the state became distinguished in the early nineteenth century for its leadership in this field of education.[40] By 1833 thirty-eight academies had been incorporated by the state, and thirty were still flourishing. Some of these rank today among the leading preparatory schools in the country.

The only institution of higher learning in New Hampshire during the early nineteenth century was Dartmouth College, which had been chartered by Governor Wentworth in 1769. Its uncertain financial and physical condition until 1820 suggested not only that another college in the state would have been superfluous but that there was hardly enough support in northern New England for the one that already existed. In 1790 Dartmouth was housed in a single building; it maintained a faculty of only three professors and served a student body of 150.[41] In spite of the attempted secession of that part of the Connecticut Valley to Vermont, which had been instigated in some part by the Dartmouth authorities, New Hampshire was proud of its one college. In the state legislature there was as much disposition to aid Dartmouth as there was to contribute to any educational purpose. On several occasions the legislature authorized lotteries by which venturesome people were seduced into furnishing funds for Dartmouth buildings. In 1789 a tract of forty thousand acres in the northern wilderness was granted to the college.[42]

The legislature insisted upon adding the governor and council to the body of trustees whenever they acted upon returns from the sale of this township. This, perhaps, was evidence of a growing suspicion on the part of many state leaders that the institution's willingness to accept public support was equaled by its reluctance to accept public accountability. In spite of frequent requests only one further grant of land was made to "those importunate beggars, the trustees of Dartmouth College."[43] As the democratic principle in education made headway during the nineteenth century, a feeling arose that institutions of higher learning as well as public schools should be made more responsive to the public will. This sentiment supported the attack on the Dartmouth College charter in 1816 and played a large part in the political maneuvering of the years after 1800.

The educational renaissance of the 1790s was not confined to the schools, but spread its benefits as well for those institutions and agencies that were the means of adult education. On the eve of the Revolution, New Hampshire boasted only one newspaper, the *New Hampshire Gazette*, which was circulated among a mere handful of wealthy patrons. By 1790 the state supported six newspapers, and the press had pushed inland as far as Keene and Walpole. News reporting was still in its infancy, however, and the arid, microscopically printed folio sheets contained little more than advertisements, political diatribes, and "the latest" dispatches from abroad—usually as much as three months late. New Hampshire intellectuals who really thirsted for news subscribed to Massachusetts and Connecticut papers or to those party organs which came to be printed at Philadelphia and Washington. The quality of the New Hampshire press improved steadily, however, and the number of papers grew until in 1820 twelve were being published in towns as far apart as Portsmouth, Keene, and Haverhill.[44]

Newspapers lost much of their effectiveness for lack of means to circulate. Until the establishment of the federal government the national postal service did not extend beyond a route from Boston to Portsmouth, and the latter town contained the only post office in New Hampshire. Gentlemen either called at the printer's office for their newspapers or sent a servant; if there was need, the printer might hire a horseman to deliver his papers privately. In 1791 the state took matters into its own hands and established four postal routes which carried mail once weekly to all parts of the state as far north as Sandwich and Haverhill.[45] When the federal postal system was fully set up, it absorbed this state establishment.

The whole process of communication and transportation received a considerable stimulus during the next few years by a great zeal for public improvements. Roads and bridges were built, ferries established, canals cut around the falls in the rivers, and stagecoach lines projected. If the people of New Hampshire in 1820 did not inform themselves of public events, it was not due to lack of opportunity. The desire to improve knowledge and skill by the pooling of resources and the association of effort touched every level of society and found a curious reflection in the journals of the legislature.

As soon as the country had recovered from depression and the unrest of the 1780s, the legislature began to receive petitions for the incorporation of "social libraries." These were voluntary groups of persons who sought to borrow each other's books and discuss their mutual literary interests.[46] Villagers also banded together and sought cultural uplift in musical societies, for which they asked legislative incorporation. In 1799 the first agricultural society in the state was established, not by dirt farmers, but by landed lawyers, physicians, and merchants who wished to learn and discuss whatever improvements in agriculture might make their farms more profitable. The advantages of interchange of ideas had already spurred the lawyers to organize a state bar association in 1788 and the physicians to follow with a medical association in 1791.

THE PROFESSIONS

It is a strange fact that in the years just before the Revolution physicians outnumbered either lawyers or clergymen in New Hampshire.[47] The doctors were not only numerous but were held in high esteem. Matthew Thornton and Josiah Bartlett, two of New Hampshire's three signers of the Declaration of Independence, were physicians. The latter served as chief executive of the state for four years and during that term of office became the first president of the New Hampshire Medical Society.[48] Dr. Nathaniel Peabody of Atkinson became a major general in the state militia. Another famous medical warrior, who did more actual fighting, was Dr. Henry Dearborn, who was practicing medicine in Nottingham, N.H., when the news of Lexington sent him off to war. Dr. Ebenezer Thompson of Durham graduated from the practice of medicine to the state judiciary in which he successively held nearly every position on the bench to which a man could be appointed. Dr. Samuel Tenney of Exeter stepped from medicine into politics and became a congressman and a leader of the Federalist party.

One encounters, in fact, the names of so many physicians in the political annals of the state that their preoccupation with politics suggests itself as a strong reason for the backward state of medical knowledge.

Virtually nothing was yet known about the causes of disease. Preventive medicine had advanced to the point of inoculation for smallpox, but it was an advance still being resisted by a great many physicians; the art of curing disease still rested almost entirely upon a blind prescription of "simples" and liberal phlebotomy. Preparation for a medical career consisted of attaching oneself to a practicing physician for a few months, reading his books, attending him on sick calls, mixing his drugs, sweeping out his office, learning the names of a few ailments, and assuming the prefix "Dr." One lone medical school had existed in Philadelphia since 1765, and a second one was founded at Harvard twenty years later, but few indeed were the students who attended either of them.[49] In the absence of any regulative laws or ethics, quackery flourished on every hand, and the profound ignorance of even the honest practitioner seems appalling when contrasted with modern knowledge.[50]

New Hampshire was no center of scientific progress, but the physicians of the state were not slow to avail themselves of advances that had first been made elsewhere. In 1791, following examples already set in four other states, the New Hampshire Medical Society was launched with considerable prestige; the instigator, organizer, and first president, Josiah Bartlett, was also the president of the state.[51] This respected patriot summarized both the ideological and practical purposes of the organization in a letter which he wrote in 1793:

> I have long wished that the practice of Medicine in this State (upon which the lives and Healths of our fellow Citizens depends) might be put under better regulations than it has been in times past and have reason to hope that the incorporation of the New-hampshire Medical Society (if properly attended to by the Fellows) will produce effects greatly beneficial to the Community by encouraging Genius & learning in the Medical Science and discouraging Ignorant & bold pretenders from practizing an art of which they have no knowledge.[52]

The society immediately raised the standards of training for medical students, established a medical library, held frequent meetings for the discussion of professional subjects, and organized a lobby to press the legislature for restrictive laws governing medical practice. In 1811 the society heard its first formal paper read by a member who had done research on the arteries, and in 1817 it held its first clinic in conjunction with an annual meeting.[53] Dartmouth College, in 1797, became the fourth institution in the country to develop a medical school, founded by Dr. Nathan Smith, a genuine pioneer in the field of medical education.[54] During the next thirteen years forty-five bachelors of medicine were produced by this infant establishment.[55] The quality and quantity of medical aid increased, public health and sanitation became matters of conscious inquiry, and hospitals were erected. By 1820 the citizens of New Hampshire had access to far better medical care than had been available to even the most favored of their prerevolutionary forebears.

Even in their backwoods simplicity, the people of rural New Hampshire were subject to ills of the flesh and the devil, and they acknowledged their debts in ample support of physicians and parsons. They recognized no similar need for professional help, however, in their frequent resort to the law courts. In 1767 there had been only eight lawyers in New Hampshire, but no one had complained of a deficiency in the supply. During the early part of the war the courts had been entirely suspended. A few of the younger lawyers, such as John Sullivan, became professional patriots, but the majority of them retired into timid neutrality and waited for a de facto settlement of the dispute before they were willing to gamble upon its de jure aspect. *Inter arma silent leges.* The burden of the war grew so great, the currency so worthless, and prices so uncertain that even New Englanders felt it necessary to forgo the luxury of litigation.

The same conditions helped to create a tremendous popular prejudice against lawyers. Men who believed that the unlimited printing of paper money would solve their economic problems were easily persuaded that the legal profession was instituted by rapacious creditors for the sole purpose of perverting justice. In the presumed alliance of wealthy merchant, orthodox clergyman, and shyster lawyer against the common people, the supposed role of the last was suggested by its phonetic resemblance to the word *liar*.[56] Popular suspicions were cleverly phrased in a newspaper jingle that appeared shortly after the legislature, in response to complaints about short measure in the lumber trade, had passed an act regulating the length and thickness of sawn boards.

> There's a report the General Court,
> To regulate the sawyer,
> Of late in fact have pass'd an act,
> But quite forgot the Lawyer.[57]

Even the judges, who until 1800 were usually men of no legal training, shared this general distrust and sometimes warned juries to be on their guard against particularly clever young barristers.[58] Merchants, physicians, clergymen, and newspaper editors were often as much affected by suspicion, and perhaps jealousy, of lawyers as were the lesser folk. Little as they were loved, however, the members of the bar were indispensable political allies and leaders. They played an important part in giving the Federalist party that intellectual superiority which it enjoyed almost to the end of its existence. The fact that the great majority of them were to be found in the Federalist ranks only made them the more unpopular with the mass of the people, who eventually drifted into the Jeffersonian camp. "Pettifogarchy" was a favorite epithet with which Republican journalists taunted their opponents.

The unsavory reputation of the legal profession was at least partially justified and explained by the weakness of legal education in 1780, although the process of imbibing enough law to become a lawyer was identical with that of learning enough medicine to become a doctor. The student simply attached himself to a practicing attorney for a few months, read through his library, acted as his clerk, ate at his table, slept in his bed, and paid him a consideration. The most famous lawyers in the United States, from Patrick Henry to Abraham Lincoln, were trained in this way. A few wealthy southerners had been sent to the Inns of Court in London, but these somehow failed to outshine their more humbly educated brethren. The first law school in the United States was not founded until 1784, and none was attached to any college in New England until 1817.[59] Before that time the quality of legal education depended upon the knowledge, sympathy, conscientiousness, and industry of a single instructor, who was also a practicing lawyer and, if a good one, presumably a very busy man. It might more accurately be said, therefore, that the quality of legal education depended almost entirely upon the industry, intelligence, and initiative of the apprentice.

If the instructor had an adequate library, his aspiring student might begin with *Coke upon Littleton* or, after 1769, Blackstone's *Commentaries on the Laws of England*, although the latter authority, with his exaltation of parliamentary supremacy, was not popular in revolutionary America. In spite of the hostility against things English, however, it would have been impossible for a fledgling lawyer to read an American legal textbook, for the simple reason that none existed. His education in the English common law gave him a strangely impractical basis for pleading in the American courts. Much more to the point was the actual observation of his preceptor in action and the help afforded in drawing up legal papers in the office.

In contrast to the patriot parties in Massachusetts and Virginia, in which lawyers played leading roles, New Hampshire's revolutionaries were, with few exceptions, merchants, physicians, clergymen, and country squires. The faction that ruled the state during the war was devoid of legal talent—a fact which may explain why New Hampshire suffered so from amateur constitution making until after the fighting was over. Out of a list of eighty names compiled by a state historian to include all those who held important civil offices during the war, only ten were lawyers.[60] Of those ten, only half were included within the select circle of patriots who determined policy and dispensed offices. One of these, Wyseman

Claggett, was a remarkable and able man, a native of England, attorney general of New Hampshire under the crown, who turned completely against his native land and, in his old age, became a zealous revolutionary.

Among the remaining, less ardent leaders, Samuel Livermore, John Pickering, and Benjamin West were very capable lawyers, but they avoided committing themselves to the cause of independence until Burgoyne's defeat gave them a rational expectation of its being achieved. They then entered the service of the government and aided considerably in bringing about the conservative reaction that marked the later years of the war. In contrast to this rather cautious record of Whiggism on the part of a few lawyers, the loyalty of many to the Revolution was under serious doubt. At least three lawyers were included in the list of Tories who were proscribed in 1778.[61] To these might be added several whose Tory principles were well known but who remained in the state and generally on their good behavior. Among these were Joshua Atherton of Amherst, John Prentice of Londonderry, Peter Green of Concord, and Simeon Olcott of Charlestown.

Once the issue with Great Britain was settled by the amateur warriors, diplomats, and statesmen who were willing to risk their necks and their reputations, the lawyers of New Hampshire came out of hiding and assumed their natural posts of leadership in the work of reconstruction. They were soon joined by an able group of younger men whose names recur frequently in these pages: William Plumer, self-educated son of an Epping farmer; Jeremiah Smith of Peterborough and Exeter, Harvard graduate, gifted with acid wit and profound legal sense; Edward St. Loe and Arthur Livermore, sons of the chief justice and inheritors of his vigorous independence; Clifton Claggett, another son of a famous lawyer, inheriting all of his father's belligerence but none of his wit; two students of Joshua Atherton, his son, Charles Humphrey, who achieved greater eminence at the bar than his father, and William Gordon, who like many another apprentice married the master's daughter; a similar duo from the office of John Sullivan, son George and son-in-law Jonathan Steele; Thomas W. Thompson of Salisbury, a shrewd and affable Harvard graduate in whose office young Daniel Webster served his apprenticeship; William H. Woodward of Hanover, grandson of Eleazer Wheelock, the founder of Dartmouth College; and John Samuel Sherburne, an able but somewhat devious protégé of John Langdon in Portsmouth. Into this society, with something of the effect of a meteor, flashed Jeremiah Mason, who opened an office in Portsmouth in 1797. A physical and intellectual giant with a persistent Yankee nasal twang, Mason soon earned the reputation of being the greatest lawyer who had ever practiced in New Hampshire. He retained that reputation only for ten years until Daniel Webster descended from the north and quickly displayed the evidences of unmatched genius. When it is realized that the brilliant Massachusetts lawyers Theophilus Parsons, Samuel Dexter, and Theophilus Bradbury, also practiced in the New Hampshire courts, it may well be understood that battles of epic proportions resounded within their modest walls during this heroic period.[62]

By 1787 there were twenty-nine licensed attorneys in New Hampshire, one for every 4600 inhabitants.[63] In June 1788 a majority of these men met at Concord and organized the New Hampshire Bar Association. Rules for raising the standards of the profession were immediately drawn. County bar associations were organized in the following year and further regulations adopted.[64] These events had more than an incidental significance. Until 1780 the clergy was the only common-interest group, professional or otherwise, with any degree of organization, and even its was slight. It was enough, however, to have given it a solidarity and weight which greatly enhanced its influence. The organization of the legal profession was evidence that lawyers as well as ministers had come to recognize the benefits of self-discipline and combined effort. When the physicians followed with their association in 1791, a powerful trinity of the learned professions was completed.

THE COURTS

The revolutionary age in New Hampshire was one of judicial experimentation. Prior to 1771 the only courts in the province had been held at Portsmouth, and men in the Connecticut Valley had had to travel to the seacoast for justice at the hands of the king's judges. Long agitation against this inconvenience had finally resulted in the organization of five counties and an itinerant judiciary.[65] The county courts had barely begun to function, however, when the suspension of the royal government and the outbreak of war put a complete stop to the machinery of justice. Extralegal committees of safety tended to assume criminal jurisdiction, and civil causes were suspended; only gradually did the regular courts resume their functions, but under very different auspices. Judges, justices of the peace, sheriffs, coroners, and other officials who had formerly been appointed by and responsible to the royal governor now became the appointees and, to a large extent, the dependents of the legislature.

The provincial court of appeals, consisting of the governor and council, to which cases could formerly be taken from the lower courts, was abolished, as was also, of course, the right to appeal important cases to the king in council.[66] Being a completely sovereign body, the state legislature established an admiralty court, which was soon busily engaged in condemning prizes brought in by New Hampshire privateers. Otherwise, the regular state courts became the ultimate arbiters of justice for New Hampshire citizens, except that appeals from the decisions of the courts could be taken to the legislature. Disturbingly, this practice, which had been invoked only occasionally in colonial times, became embarrassingly common after 1776. Such appeals came to the assembly in the form of petitions praying that judgments of the courts be set aside, rectified, or vacated or that the petitioner be "restored to his law," that is, granted a review, a rehearing, or a new trial. The general court was more than willing to listen to these petitions and, if necessary, to pass special acts directing the judicial courts to reconsider or setting aside their verdicts. Such improper interference of the legislative body in judicial matters became increasingly irritating to the legal profession.

On the whole, it is doubtful if the Revolution benefited the administration of justice in New Hampshire. While it removed certain arbitrary and injurious elements inherent in a royally appointed and controlled judiciary, it substituted a no less arbitrary and much more capricious control by an ever-changing body of popularly elected legislators. It became the mission of a group of young reformers, including Jeremiah Smith and William Plumer, to bring the judicial establishment into a golden mean of usefulness midway between the absence of accountability in colonial times and the servility that marked its character in the early republic.

The Revolution did not greatly change the actual structure of the judiciary, which remained based on the law of 1769 that had established the five counties.[67] At the broad bottom of the judicial pyramid were the justices of the peace, who still retained, in the eighteenth century, much of the importance that had marked them in the days of Queen Elizabeth. In addition to a large number of purely administrative and prudential duties, they were given jurisdiction over petty criminal cases and civil disputes that involved sums varying from forty shillings to ten pounds, according to the whims of the legislature. The justice's office was of sufficient importance that men sought the appointment, towns petitioned for them, and politicians built up party machines through their calculated distribution. Courts of general sessions, consisting of three or more justices within each county, were required to be held quarterly. These courts were responsible for the general conservation of the peace, had jurisdiction over a few specified misdemeanors, and carried on the prudential business of the county. They were a relic of English medieval jurisprudence, and the lawyers of 1790 were inclined to regard them as archaic, if not worse. Reformers made repeated attempts to abolish this anachronism, finally succeeding in 1794.[68]

Only a little less cumbersome were the inferior courts of common pleas. The inferior court for each county consisted of four judges who, until 1797, held quarterly sessions and had original jurisdiction over all cases involving title to real estate (except probate) and all civil causes that were beyond the jurisdiction of justices.[69] The possibilities for the perversion of justice in these courts were almost infinite. Any of their judgments, except in cases carried to them by appeal from the justices, could be appealed to the superior court, and the judges were inclined to grant postponements and continuances upon the slightest grounds. A correspondent to the *New Hampshire Gazette* in 1786 wished to be informed

> whether the institution of our Inferior Courts are intended as Sinecures for Judges Clerks and Lawyers, or whether judgments and verdicts, from which there are constant appeals, can be of any advantage to the people? Whether extravagant bills of costs for fees, entries and attendancy are justifiable upon any principle? And whether defaulting, appealing, pleading of demurrers and abatements, continuing, referring and receiving what little money the contending parties have, are not the principle transactions of these courts? If so, in the name of justice, and for the benefit of an already too heavily oppressed State, "Let them be abolished", and all the people will Heartily say Amen.[70]

The feature of these little courts that strikes the modern eye as most eccentric is the plurality of judges. Four men were required to do what is now performed by one, indicating an excess of suspicion on the part of the people. "What an absurdity in jurisprudence!" exclaimed a young lawyer in complete frustration while attending one of these courts.[71] The influence of twenty local politicians who enjoyed the moderately lucrative and fairly secure positions on the inferior benches, however, made it difficult to modify or abolish their courts.

The highest court of justice in New Hampshire, save for the general court, was the superior court of judicature. Its bench consisted of a chief justice and three puisne justices, who, as did the dignitaries of the Supreme Court of the United States, rode circuit for a good part of the year. They were required to hold semiannual sessions of the court in each of the five counties, and this necessitated traveling to points as far distant from each other as Portsmouth and Haverhill.[72] Three of the four judges were required to make a quorum. If one of them failed to appear at the opening of court, as did Judge Woodbury Langdon in 1790 when the unexpected arrival of a brig inspired him to put his mercantile business ahead of his judicial duties,[73] or as did Chief Justice John Pickering in 1794 after an attack of nervous aquaphobia,[74] or as did Chief Justice Simeon Olcott in 1796 because he consulted his almanac rather than the statute for the opening date,[75] the responsibility for justice fell completely on the remaining three. If one of these became ill, was related to a party in the suit, or had an ulterior interest in the case, there would be an expensive postponement and an addition to the growing heap of resentment. The superior court had original jurisdiction in all criminal cases of any consequence and appellate jurisdiction over all important civil cases. The Revolution increased its responsibility by making it (saving the legislature) the ultimate repository of justice for the citizens of New Hampshire and by forcing within its jurisdiction the chancery powers that had formerly been exercised by the royal court of appeals.

For these arduous services the justices of the superior court had, until 1771, been paid nothing except their fees, and these, in 1748, had not exceeded ten pounds a year.[76] In 1789 the salary of the chief justice was still only six hundred dollars. It is not surprising, then, for this reason if for no other, that the executive authority had difficulty in finding capable men who would accept appointment to the highest judicial offices. Until after the Revolution there was scarcely a single judge who had been trained in the law. Most of them were hard-headed, practical merchants or farmers who consented to attend court as an avocation. Meshech Weare, who was chief justice during the war as well as president of the council and chairman of the committee of safety, had been educated for the ministry but had turned country squire. Among the associate judges who had appeared on the bench after 1780 were Matthew Thornton and Josiah Bartlett, physicians; Woodbury Langdon and William Whipple, merchants; and John Dudley and Timothy Farrar, farmers.

Such men did not interpret the law with professional purity but they were often better judges than the second-rate lawyers who could be persuaded to accept office. Of Simeon Olcott, for instance, a contemporary wrote: "As he had not that clear discriminating mind which is requisite for the bench, he was not distinguished as a judge. His reputation for honesty and integrity was great and, I believe, never questioned on any occasion. This inestimable quality inspired the people with great confidence in him, and covered with the mantle of charity, his blunders in fact, as well as his errors in law."[77]

For the period between 1791 and 1795 the superior court achieved an unprecedented degree of stability, retaining the same personnel for more than four years. The chief justice was John Pickering, who "brought to the position more law learning than any judge who had sat there before him."[78] His associates were Olcott, Farrar, and Dudley. While Pickering's timidity was offset by his learning and Olcott's mediocrity was overlooked because of his integrity, both Dudley and Farrar compensated for their lack of a legal education by persistent study and native acumen. After Pickering had been replaced by Daniel Newcomb, a less-noted lawyer, Jeremiah Smith gave it as his opinion that "though there are now two lawyers on the bench I think they are by no means the two best of the four—Farrar and Dudley in my judgment greatly overmatch them."[79]

Theophilus Parsons, who was himself an oracle of the law, declared that Dudley was the best judge he had ever known in New Hampshire.[80] Yet this man, whose judgment and faithfulness to duty were never questioned, was almost illiterate.

It was not until 1802, when Jeremiah Smith, at great personal sacrifice, accepted the office of chief justice, that the New Hampshire judiciary began to attain the respectability and character that it ought to have had. The difficulty, even at that time, lay in the niggardly salaries that the legislature grudgingly offered the judges. A good lawyer could earn much more in leisurely practice, or even as clerk of the court, than he could in the highest judicial position in the state. Almost certain that capable, well-trained men would not accept an office with such meager compensation, executive officers were inclined to forestall refusals by appointing mediocrities. Men who were appointed in this way, realizing their own weakness and feeling that the miserable salaries were no inducement to self-improvement, were not careful about administering the law with exactness or regularity. This convinced the legislature that the people were hardly getting even their little money's worth and encouraged them not only to refuse higher salaries but constantly to hector the judges with investigations, overrulings, and threats of removal. Reformers found this vicious circle of incompetence extremely difficult to break through.

From the lawyer's point of view, the overwhelming necessity for reform lay in the instability and uncertainty of judicial decisions. Prior to Smith's accession to the bench, the judges spurned the common law, ignored precedent, and even swept aside the statutes when equity seemed to illumine the path of justice more clearly. Chief Justice Samuel Livermore, though himself a lawyer, reversed his own decisions without compunction, claiming that "every tub must stand on its own bottom."[81] He was also responsible for the ruling that English law reports made prior to the Declaration of Independence might be cited in his court, not as binding precedents but as helpful suggestions, but that those after 1776 were completely irrelevant.[82] In one of his inimitable charges to the jury, Judge Dudley began by abusing the lawyers who had just argued the case, and continued somewhat in this fashion: "They talk of law. Why, gentlemen, it is not law that we want, but justice. They would govern us by the common law of England. Trust me, gentlemen, Common sense is a much safer guide for us,—the common sense of Raymond, Epping, Exeter and the other towns which have sent us here to try this case between two of our neighbors. A clear head and an honest heart are worth more than all the law of all the lawyers."[83]

THE LAW

The judges, however, were not altogether to blame for New Hampshire's eccentric courts. Much of the difficulty lay in the amorphous condition of the law itself. Even before the Revolution no man could say whether the law in New Hampshire was based on the English common law, the Pentateuch, or the laws of nature. The colonial courts administered a confused mixture of all three. This had acquired the character of a New Hampshire common law, growing out of the peculiar customs of the people and adapted to their particular circumstances.[84]

Many provincial laws were derived from the Old Testament and Puritan theology, reflecting New Hampshire's early connection with Massachusetts, and were directly contrary to English law. The laws of inheritance, for example, disregarded English primogeniture and followed the ancient Hebrew principle of giving only a double portion to the oldest son. Marriage, which the Puritans looked upon as a civil contract rather than a religious sacrament,[85] was performed by a justice of the peace, and divorces could be obtained only by special acts of the legislature.[86]

The influence of the frontier was also potent in modifying the principles of English law when it was introduced into the northern wilderness. Even the English authorities recognized this stubborn fact and conceded that colonial officers, in making and applying the law, should be "as consonant and agreeable to ye Laws and Statutes of this Our Realm of Engd, as ye prent state and condition of our subjects inhabiting within ye limits aforesaid, and ye circumstances of ye place will admit."[87] Great sections of the complicated English common law relating to the tenure and conveyance of land were completely useless in the primitive culture of New Hampshire, and were discarded for simpler forms.

Laws based upon such vague and conflicting principles should have been flexible enough to satisfy the most latitudinarian judges. The Revolution, however, introduced a further uncertainty—whether the English common law had any further standing in independent American courts. Judges such as Livermore, Bartlett, and Dudley were inclined to confirm their patriotism by substituting New Hampshire common sense for English common law and by denying the validity of English authorities. When a lawyer once cited Lord Mansfield as his authority, Judge Dudley exclaimed in irritation that, according to his memory, Mansfield was that damned clever Scotchman who had plotted with Lord North and George III to enslave America. William Plumer carried a point with this same judge against no less an opponent than Theophilus Parsons, backed by Coke and Blackstone, simply by quoting a Mosaic law which contradicted the Englishmen.[88] It is not to be wondered at that lawyers spent little time in scholarly study of the great commentators when they were so little regarded by the courts.

The leaven that was introduced into so many institutional lumps by the Revolution did not fail to perform its transforming work within the body of the law. In 1784 the extraordinary practice of granting divorces only by special act of the legislature was abolished, and jurisdiction was transferred to the judicial courts where it belonged. In 1789 New Hampshire abandoned the Jewish law of inheritance and instituted equal division of property among heirs to intestate estates.[89]

A growing sense of social responsibility was reflected in a new law for the support of paupers passed in 1798 and a comprehensive statute of 1792 to regulate sanitary conditions in the larger towns. It cannot be said, however, that the law carried New Hampshire from medievalism to enlightenment in one leap. The first New Hampshire law code, in 1680, had mandated capital punishment for seventeen crimes.[90] In the revision of 1792 as many as eight offenses, namely, treason, murder, rape, arson, sodomy, burglary, robbery, and counterfeiting, still incurred the death penalty. But perhaps the least civilized portion of the code, and one that persisted for many years after the Revolution, was the prescription of imprisonment for debt. It is true that in 1782 the legislature greatly ameliorated the plight of imprisoned debtors by providing that those who gave bond not to escape could occupy chambers within the jail yard and that poor debtors could be discharged upon oath after sixty days' imprisonment unless their creditors wished to pay their board.[91] These laws made New Hampshire much more liberal in the treatment of imprisoned debtors than were most of the other states.[92]

Nevertheless, it remained possible in the nineteenth century for once prominent Dr. Nathaniel Peabody to be forced to spend the last twenty years of his life within the limits of a jail yard simply because he could not pay his debts. The law was even interpreted to apply to the dead body of the debtor, which continued to belong to the creditor after the last possibility of satisfying the debt had been destroyed.[93] It was not until 1844 that the struggle for abolition of this barbaric anachronism met with complete success.

In the meantime, a group of younger lawyers, including especially Jeremiah Smith, William Plumer, and Jeremiah Mason, worked diligently over a period of several decades to bring order and reason into New Hampshire's chaotic system of judicature. In 1789, Jeremiah Smith, then a member of the legislature, was made chairman of a committee "to select, revise, and arrange all the laws and public resolves then in force, whether passed before or since the Revolution." Doing most of the work himself, Smith produced within three years a compilation which was published in 1792 and constituted the first reliable codification of the statutes.[94] Smith also kept a careful record of the arguments presented in cases that came before the highest state court during the period of his chief justiceship, 1803–16, and thus initiated in New Hampshire the publication of court records. As practicing attorney, legislator, writer, and, most eminently, judge, Smith spent a long lifetime, with only a few political lapses, in the service of the blind goddess.

Plumer strove manfully in the courts themselves, in the state legislature, in the constitutional convention of 1791–92, and as governor of the state to improve the quality of the courts and of the justice they dispensed. He constantly advocated more adequate compensation for the judges and made heroic efforts as governor to create a bipartisan judiciary through his appointive power. It was a source of great regret to him that he could not persuade Jeremiah Mason to accept the chief justice's office. Both men had been instrumental during the early years of their legal practice in bringing about the cessation of legislative meddling with the decisions of the law courts.

In *McClary* versus *Gilman*, a case in 1792, Plumer, representing the defendant, argued against an act of the legislature that "restored the plaintiff to her law," that is, ordered the court to reconsider her case after rendering an initial decision against her. Plumer insisted that this order either reversed the court's judgment or required a new trial without reversing the court's judgment. Either position, he said, was a violation of the Bill of Rights. The superior court agreed with his logic, declared the legislature's act unconstitutional, and dismissed the case out of hand.[95] At about the same time, Mason, just beginning to establish his practice in Westmoreland, argued a similar case on similar grounds and won it. Both Plumer's and Mason's cases involved the rightful ownership of pigs, which seemed to be a favorite subject of litigation in New Hampshire. In Mason's case the legislature twice ordered the case reopened and the second time transferred to the court of common pleas. Here, too, the court declared the legislative interference to be unconstitutional and both of the pig cases became causes célèbres that tended, Mason reported, "to bring such special acts of the Legislature . . . into ridicule and deserved contempt."[96]

Since law and politics are so closely intertwined, the relationships of these and other would-be reformers, often in harmony, sometimes in discord, will be detailed in future pages of this book. Suffice it to say here that their efforts succeeded to the extent that New Hampshire jurisprudence in 1820 had kept pace with the general progress of life and society that had transformed the Granite State since the colonial era.

CHAPTER 6

IN THE FEDERAL UNION

Do you wish to know in what light I am considered here?—an illiberal, ignorant fellow, who has never seen the world, who is startled at the mention of millions.—Jeremiah Smith

By its belated ratification of the federal Constitution, New Hampshire had indicated its willingness to participate with some enthusiasm in the experiment of a stronger national government.[1] To the state legislature elected in March 1788 fell the exciting privilege of giving legal effect to the new partnership by putting the federal machinery into motion. The Constitution's directives were general: the same New Hampshire electors eligible to vote for representatives to the more numerous branch of the state legislature (all male taxpayers) were entitled to elect three of their fellow citizens to the House of Representatives; the state legislature was to choose two others to the Senate; and the state was entitled, before January 7, to select five electors who should then vote for two American citizens, from different states, as president and vice-president. In the process of implementing these new responsibilities, the general court developed some interesting antagonisms.

Perhaps because of the familiar habit of electing delegates to the Continental Congress, the legislature, in its November session, turned first to the choice of its two United States senators. The two houses of the general court decided to do this by concurrent resolution, as had been their custom. Although John Sullivan, probably because of ill health, was not a candidate for this office, John Langdon, Samuel Livermore, Josiah Bartlett, and Nathaniel Peabody were all supported by various factions. Langdon's election was a foregone conclusion, but no other candidate commanded a sure majority. Strangely enough, there was some sentiment for Peabody, even among the Exeter politicians, but he was decisively defeated in the senate.[2] Paine Wingate, already serving in the old Congress, was eventually elected to the second senatorial post as a compromise candidate.

A sharp difference of opinion developed over procedures in the election of the remaining federal officers. It was finally agreed that the people should vote both for their three representatives to Congress and their five electors by general ballot. In case the elections were not completed on the first ballot (and no one expected them to be), the people would meet a second time and select their representatives from double the number wanted of the names standing highest on the list. In the case of electors, however, the legislature reserved final selection to itself, should the people fail to give the necessary majorities.[3] The absence of party machinery made these elections extremely difficult. The candidates for Congress were so numerous that not a single one of them received a popular majority in December. At the second trial, Benjamin West, Samuel Livermore, and Nicholas Gilman were elected, but West declined the office. This necessitated the passage of another law to authorize a third popular election, at which Abiel Foster of Canterbury was chosen to fill out New Hampshire's complement of representatives.[4] All five members of the New Hampshire delegation to the First Congress were strong supporters of the Constitution.

The popular vote for electors in December was scattered among all the local heroes in the state. According to law, the legislature was accordingly required to choose the five electors from the ten highest candidates, but the law had not specified the method by which the legislature was to proceed. Consequently, two days were spent in wrangling over this question. The house wanted to complete the election by joint ballot in convention, but the senate held out for concurrent resolution. The convention method was equivalent to destroying the senate's voice in the matter; forty-eight members of the house might choose all the electors against the combined vote of a house minority and the entire senate. The electors, however, had to be chosen before midnight of January 7. As the winter shadows lengthened in the old Exeter meetinghouse on that day, frantic efforts were made on both sides to wear down the opposition. The house resolved that a joint committee choose the electors; the senate suggested that the committee merely nominate electors for the concurrence of the general court; the house then proposed to choose the electors by lot, but the senate refused.[5] General Sullivan had led the fight in the house against senate equality, but shortly before midnight he gave up the struggle. The house then concurred in a resolution which had just come down from the senate, naming as electors the five candidates who had received the highest popular vote, including Sullivan himself. The disagreement had nothing to do with personalities or parties—it was simply a struggle for the future control of electoral machinery, in which the conservative instinct prevailed.

Langdon's elevation to the national sphere of government left the way to the state presidency open again to Sullivan.[6] He made his plans for the 1789 campaign carefully, striving to build up his following in the legislature and making good use of the *New Hampshire Spy*, his own newspaper published in Portsmouth. By these efforts, he recovered much of the ground he had lost in 1787. John Pickering ran him so close a race, how-ever, that the election was again thrown into the senate, where Sullivan was chosen president for the third time.

President Sullivan began his last administration with an inaugural ad-dress of inimitable coyness. "Neither my own inclinations or the state of my health led me to expect the Honour of being called to the chair of Government," he assured the legislature.[7] The only serious problems he had to face were the embarrassments arising from the transfer of many functions from state to national authority. In September his love of pomp was gratified by the ceremonies accompanying President Washington's visit to New Hampshire, the last time a president entered the state until 1817, when Monroe repeated the performance. After the federal judi-ciary was organized by Congress, President Washington appointed Presi-dent Sullivan, his old companion-in-arms, to the Portsmouth District Court. Sullivan marred the latter months of his last term in elective office by insisting upon retaining both of his public posts. In June 1790 he retired to the relative obscurity of the federal bench, and died five years later. John Sullivan had been undoubtedly one of New Hampshire's greatest and most useful citizens, yet his career was flawed by petulance, frequent failure, and ethical myopia.

In the distribution of federal offices in New Hampshire, Senator Lang-don's influence over the patronage was obvious. His brother-in-law John Samuel Sherburne became the first federal district attorney, and his brother Woodbury Langdon, the superior court justice, was rescued from an impeachment by appointment to a federal commissioner's post in Philadelphia. With Langdon and Sullivan both in federal office the presi-dency of the state became in 1790 a prize for lesser men. So many candi-dates entered the field that the choice devolved for the fourth time in six years upon the legislature, which passed over both John Pickering and Joshua Wentworth at the head of the list and chose Dr. Josiah Bartlett.[8] The conduct of this eminent physician and revolutionary patriot proved to be so noncontroversial that he was reelected for three succeeding terms by nearly unanimous votes. Bartlett appointed his foremost rival, Pickering, to the office that he had just vacated, chief justice, and Joshua Atherton, a man whom he, as a member of the committee of safety, had imprisoned during the Revolution, to the post of attorney general. At the same time other and younger politicians were coming to the fore. In 1791 the thirty-one-year-old lawyer from Epping, William Plumer, was elected speaker of the house of representatives in his fourth year as a member of that body.[9] In the previous year his friend Jeremiah Smith, a rising young lawyer from Peterborough, had succeeded Abiel Foster in New Hampshire's congressional delegation.

In this era of personal politics New Hampshire's leaders often found themselves in curious alliance with or opposition to each other upon different issues at the same time or upon the same issue at different times. The state's entire delegation to the First Congress and most of the leaders in state government had been strong advocates of the federal Constitution, but they did not find this a satisfactory basis of common action in the years immediately after 1788. If support of Washington's administration may be considered the acid test of Federalism, New Hampshire's statesmen hardly qualify. According to the criteria selected by one student of the period, New Hampshire's representatives in the lower house between 1789 and 1793 voted with the administration a combined total of ninety-three times and against it forty-three times.[10] Support for only two-thirds of his measures is not the kind of loyalty upon which a party leader can build a solid administration.[11]

The national measures introduced during these four years brought out three indistinct antagonisms, none of which was an accurate forecast of things to come. Two of these were geographical. In 1792 a bill to increase the regular army to six thousand men was introduced at the behest of Washington and Knox. It was an administration bill, and it embodied the Federalist principle of an expensive standing army, which Jefferson was to use as a rallying cry against Adams in 1799. Yet the chief purpose of these troops was to push the Indians out of the Northwest Territory and open up more land for settlers. Senator John Langdon, destined to become the leader of the Jeffersonian Republicans in New Hampshire but always a great nationalist, voted for the bill. Senator Wingate, a frugal Yankee farmer who spent the last forty-five years of his life in unwavering Federalism, voted against it on the ground that "it would be a gulf to absorb the treasury of the United States."[12] Representative Jeremiah Smith, who later became an ardent supporter of the administration, also voted against this "ministerial bill," not because he had any fear of a standing army, but because it would only "gratify . . . Land-jobbers and a set of rascals on the frontiers."[13] If Wingate and Smith had prevailed, Wayne's famous victory at Fallen Timbers could hardly have been possible. Here was one of the earlier indications of New England's antagonism to the West, and on this occasion, Wingate and Smith were Yankees first and Federalists not at all.

The bill to reapportion the House of Representatives according to the first census evoked the latent antagonism between North and South. A ratio of one representative to every thirty thousand inhabitants favored the southern states and injured the northern because it left there large unrepresented fractions. New Hampshire, for example, with 142,000 people, would gain one representative but have almost enough left over for a fifth one. If the ratio were one to thirty-three thousand, the larger unrepresented surpluses would exist in the southern states. This measure, consequently, was determined in favor of the larger ratio by a sectional vote, with the New Hampshire delegation voting in harmony with the northern interest.[14] Jeremiah Smith believed that he had rendered his country a service by voting to leave as many southerners as possible unrepresented. "I am clearly of Opinion that the people Southward of Pennsylvania are in a state of barbarity when compared with the New England States," he wrote to Plumer.[15]

New Hampshire delegates treated the remaining measures of the first two Congresses according to their economic interests. Providing a revenue for the new government by establishing impost duties was certainly a federal measure, and the New Hampshire members supported it, but not without guardianship of their state's particular necessities. "Mr. Langdon spoke warmly against" a duty on cables and cordages, which would injure shipbuilding on the Piscataqua.[16] Langdon and Wingate were not quite able to carry out Dr. Belknap's injunction "for the honour of New England, not to consent to the duty on molasses," but they did beat the tax down from five cents to two and one-half cents per gallon.[17] Molasses and rum were still as important to the New England economy as they had been in the days when they were potent ingredients of rebellion.

It is commonly asserted that our first national political parties grew out of the debate over Hamilton's great financial measures. If this is true, it is a fact to which contemporary New Hampshire statesmen were exceptions. Far from pleasing New Hampshire's federalist delegation in Congress, Secretary Hamilton's brilliant proposals for funding the national debt and assuming state debts split it asunder. John Langdon, the future Republican leader, was a rich man and an investor in United States securities; his brother Woodbury had speculated in soldiers' certificates. Langdon was one of Hamilton's staunchest supporters. When asked if assumption would not be unfair to his own state, he admitted the fact, but answered, "It is a *great national* measure! New Hampshire does not contribute her proportion of the public revenue."[18] He helped Hamilton with the log-rolling that finally carried the assumption bill, and he had no constitutional scruples over the United States Bank. After the bank bill had passed, Langdon bought stock and urged his state to do the same. Langdon's vote on assumption, however, was offset by the opposition of Senator Wingate, who owned no securities and was shocked at the enormous debt that Hamilton was blithely assuming.

Abiel Foster, one of New Hampshire's three representatives, also championed assumption. He argued against Madison's plan for discriminating between original holders and speculators as unjust to many towns in New Hampshire which had hired their quotas of drafted soldiers at a very high price, paid in the soldiers' depreciated certificates, which they still held.[19] Foster's votes in this case were consistent with his life-long career as a Federalist, but they probably lost him his seat at the next election. His successor, Jeremiah Smith, a future Federalist governor, was as bitter against the advocates of assumption as any Jeffersonian. "After the most painful search and inquiry," he wrote, "I have never yet been able to find that they were actuated in managing this business by any principles at all, unless those principles which govern sharpers, right or wrong to get the best bargain they can, may be denominated such."[20]

Representative Nicholas Gilman, a future Republican who speculated in the funds and had lobbied for the Constitution, voted against the assumption bill, although he probably had no objection to the general principle. The plan brought down from the Senate, he explained in a letter to General Sullivan, looked too much like one formed by a combination of Tories and "advocates of Public fraud."[21] New Hampshire's remaining congressman, Samuel Livermore, who was certainly no democrat, favored the secretary's report in April, but changed his mind during the summer and voted against it in August. Thus the New Hampshire delegation stood three to two against Hamilton's favorite project, and one of the two supporters later became a prominent Jeffersonian.[22]

With the possible exception of Langdon, the New Hampshire congressmen simply did not recognize the deep political significance of Hamilton's measures, as the letter from Jeremiah Smith plainly indicates. To the founder of the Federalist party, the fact that speculators were unduly enriched by funding, or some states unfairly treated in the assumption, was of small importance compared to the major objective of winning to the support of the national government those moneyed men whom he considered the backbone of society. This was the great principle that Smith failed to discover in the plan. To the young congressman, assumption was simply a measure for transferring part of Massachusetts's and New York's debts to the taxpayers of New Hampshire. The final roll call found New Hampshire and Virginia voting against Massachusetts and South Carolina.[23]

The state of public opinion in their constituency undoubtedly influenced Gilman and Livermore to vote against assumption. New Hampshire, with its very small investing class, had little interest in the speculative possibilities of Hamilton's scheme, but was certain that its obvious features did the state injury. In 1795 only five states held fewer federal securities than New Hampshire.[24] Yet Hamilton had arbitrarily assigned to each state the amount of its debt to be assumed before the accounts between the states and the general government had been adjusted. When that adjustment was completed, New Hampshire was certain that it would show the state to have contributed $375,055 more than its equitable share toward the war and New York to have expended $874,846 less than its part. Yet the assumption bill provided for assuming only $300,000 of New Hampshire's debt, while including four times that amount of New York's indebtedness.[25]

In the state legislature of 1790 a committee was appointed to draw up a remonstrance to Congress against assumption, but it "was winked out of sight" when "the attention of the House was arrested upon the subject of *Tender laws*."[26] A second committee reported a censorious resolution declaring that the Assumption Act was "an infringement on the rights of the legislature of this state."[27] Because of its strong language this was defeated. In June 1791 the state legislature finally adopted a protest, one which was based on economics rather than constitutionality. This memorial complained that the state had paid one-twenty-eighth of the cost of the war, but was to be relieved of only one-seventieth of the assumed debt; by "the most rigid Oeconomy" and "burthensome Taxes" the state had "extinguished a large part of their debt," but would now be forced to pay $600,000 of the debts of other states. The end of this eloquent remonstrance, however, was something of an anticlimax. "If said Assumption must be carried into effect," it concluded, let there be another reckoning so that New Hampshire's share of the whole will be equal.[28] Upon receiving this document for presentation to Congress, Jeremiah Smith dryly remarked that New Hampshire, having been cheated on the first assumption, was in a peculiar position as champion of a second one.[29]

The debate on the bill to establish the United States Bank furnishes historians with another test for party affiliation: namely, a fondness for loose construction of the Constitution and centralized power as opposed to strict construction and state sovereignty. New Hampshire and its representatives, however, would appear to have been confused on this important point. The New Hampshire delegation did not share Madison's constitutional scruples and voted solidly for the establishment of the bank.[30]

The Judiciary Bill, however, aroused their small-state jealousy and antagonism. Both Langdon and Wingate voted against it because they felt that the lower federal courts would not only be too expensive but would encroach upon the state judiciaries and too greatly centralize the administration of justice.[31] Samuel Livermore conducted a major campaign against the Judiciary Bill in the House. The Union had managed to get along for fourteen years without federal courts, he said, and why should they be thought necessary now? They would prove obnoxious, expensive, and conflicting. "This new-fangled system would eventually swallow up the State Courts"; it "would entirely change the form of Government," insisted the former chief justice of New Hampshire and leader of the federalist forces in 1788.[32]

New Hampshire's fear of a powerful federal judiciary grew out of a long-standing conflict between the state and the Confederation over the

McClary case. In the early years of the Revolution a group of New Hampshire entrepreneurs had outfitted the *McClary* as a privateer, commissioned by Congress. Soon afterward, the *McClary* captured a Boston brig, the *Susanna*, whose papers gave her the character of an enemy ship. The state courts, at that time exercising admiralty jurisdiction, condemned the vessel and cargo, and the prize money was widely distributed among the owners and crew of the *McClary*. The Boston owners of the *Susanna* obtained from the court of appeals under the Confederation a reversal of this judgment, but Congress had done nothing to dispute New Hampshire's assertion that no foreign court could interfere with its sovereignty in the matter. After the establishment of the new federal courts, however, the *Susanna* owners obtained a confirmation of their favorable judgment and an order for $31,721.36 in restitution from the *McClary* owners.[33]

Among those whose purses were imperiled by this decision were some of the most influential citizens in New Hampshire, federalist and otherwise. The legislature showed its anxiety for their welfare by sending a spirited protest against the decision to Congress.[34] The *McClary* owners had, in the meantime, appealed to the Supreme Court, and the newly elected governor, John Taylor Gilman, called a special session of the legislature to strengthen their position. The federalist governor laid the issue before the federalist legislature, and there emerged a remonstrance against federal usurpation which was not matched again for vigor and indignation until Jefferson tried his hand at a similar document in 1798. The federal court's decision was called a "violation of State independence and an unwarrantable encroachment in the courts of the United States." The memorial went on to say "that the attempts repeatedly made to render the laws of this State in this respect null and void is a flagrant insult to the principle of the revolution. . . . Can the rage for annihilating all the power of the States, and reducing this extensive and flourishing country to one domination, make the administrators blind to the danger of violating all the principles of our former Government, to the hazard of convulsions in endeavoring to eradicate every trace of State power except in the resentment of the people?"[35]

This strong language had no effect, for the Supreme Court had already confirmed the decision against the *McClary* owners,[36] and Congress ignored the memorial. But it gave to a federalist state the dubious distinction of being the first to attack the jurisdiction of that court which Jefferson later called "the last refuge of Federalism."

The record of the first two Congresses makes it clear that New Hampshire representatives were not guided by any discernible party principles in giving their votes. Neither Hamiltonian economics nor constitutional theory had persuaded them to line up in perfect support of the administration. The best proof of this is found in the correspondence of Jeremiah Smith, who in 1792 was unaware of the fact that he was destined to become an unflinching Federalist. "Do you wish to know in what light I am considered here?" he wrote from Philadelphia, "—an illiberal, ignorant fellow, who has never seen the world, who is startled at the mention of millions . . . I am of too little consequence to be courted by the ministry. We have no opposition, else I believe I should enlist."[37]

The principal issues of purely local significance which faced New Hampshire politicians in the early years of the republic were the state's fiscal policy, the weakness of its judiciary, and the final remaking of the state constitution. The last story will be reserved for a separate chapter. As for financial questions, the growing prosperity of the 1790s solved many problems, but did not necessarily create harmony among farmers, merchants, speculators, and artisans. The squirearchy of the Old Colony, allied temporarily with the merchants of Portsmouth, had the Hamiltonian view of fiscal policy. They were eager to continue the state's practice of heavy taxation, even after Congress had assumed the state debt, in order to habituate the people to paying taxes.[38] At the same time, the speculators in state securities, including the Gilmans and other Exeterites, fought vigorously, but unsuccessfully, against taxing these and other forms of intangible property.[39] There was an obvious difference of opinion during these years between the financiers who attempted to preserve the total sum of outstanding state securities as a fertile field for speculation and less sophisticated statesmen who believed that the paper should be called in by taxation and the debt reduced.[40]

Early in 1792 the first bank in New Hampshire, located at Portsmouth, was incorporated. The proprietors and shareholders in the bank included the Langdons and Sherburne, James Sheafe, John Peirce, the Gilmans, and other members of the Exeter Junto, a group of remarkably able politicians who made their homes in that town. The bank was therefore certainly not a partisan institution but one which divided farmers and small businessmen from rich merchants and speculators. The incorporation act received vigorous support from John Taylor Gilman, the state treasurer, and was signed into law by Governor Bartlett. Several of the original proprietors sought to promote the bill in the legislature by offering shares of their own stock at par to its opponents.[41] The latter, including William Plumer, failed to prevent the incorporation, but they did succeed in defeating a bill that would have made the state a heavy stockholder. The twenty-seven votes in favor of thus combining public and private financial interests came from a solid block of towns in the Old Colony, including Portsmouth, Exeter, and Dover, supported by such interior towns as Amherst, Londonderry, Charlestown, and Hanover. It was defeated by thirty-two assemblymen representing forty-five towns, nearly all except Concord, Walpole, Plainfield, and Haverhill distant from the existing transportation routes.[42] In a later session, however, this bill was passed. Like the first Bank of the United States, the state banking system of New Hampshire began as a semipublic enterprise.

New Hampshire's rising young lawyers were as dissatisfied as were the common people with the delay and uncertainty of justice, if not with its expense. They attributed these faults not to themselves but to untrained and indifferent judges. Better judges, they reasoned, could never be obtained so long as the legislature was free to bully and humiliate, as well as to starve, the bench. Consequently, the young reformers found the root of all judicial evil in the fact that the general court and the other courts were still insufficiently differentiated. The ancient name, which was then the one most frequently applied to the legislature, indicates that a large part of its business was, as it had been in early colonial days, actually judicial. The assembly often spent more than half of its time in private business, leaving public affairs to be settled hastily at the end of each session. Such paternalism may have been necessary for a tiny colony consisting of four small settlements, but it was an anomaly for an independent state of 150,000 people.

Several rather notorious cases tried in the courts between 1786 and 1792 helped to dramatize the unwarranted interference in judicial business that had become habitual with the state legislature. The two famous "Pig Cases," in which William Plumer and Jeremiah Mason were involved, have already been described.[43] Another cause célèbre was the McGregore case, which had grown out of an act of 1786 allowing civil suits involving £10 or less to be tried before a justice of the peace, an official who was likely to know even less law than a judge. Under that law, Colonel McGregore of Londonderry, an excise master and a powerful politician, had sued for £10 damage before a justice of the peace and obtained a favorable judgment, but the defendant had appealed to the inferior court of common pleas and secured an annulment of the verdict on the ground that the legislature's act was unconstitutional.[44] The assembly then ordered the decision of the inferior court annulled and gave McGregore leave to carry his case to the superior court on the same basis as an appeal. It even considered impeaching the justices of the inferior court, but a majority of fourteen defeated this display of legislative pique.[45]

In 1790 the ambiguous relations between the legislature and the judiciary led to the actual impeachment of Judge Woodbury Langdon and ended in farce and humiliation for the lawmakers. Langdon's appointment as an associate justice of the superior court in 1785 had been generally popular at the time. Woodbury's career as a merchant and shipowner had not included much time spent in the study of the law, but he "readily discovered the prominent features in a cause, and dispatched business with great facility."[46] For attending some fourteen terms of court each year in all parts of New Hampshire, riding through mountains and forests and fording unbridged rivers, Judge Langdon was paid the annual salary of $520. It is, therefore, not surprising that at times he regarded his business in Portsmouth as more important than traveling through the woods to Plymouth to hold court. Since other judges frequently felt the same kind of disinclination, the terms in Grafton and Cheshire counties failed several times for want of a quorum on the bench. A legislative committee to investigate the causes was appointed at the behest of the western representatives, and three of the judges made properly obsequious explanations of their dereliction. Langdon, however, seized the opportunity to lecture the assembly on its own irresponsibility. "I conceive *ergo*," wrote the forthright judge, "that the Legislature have no more rights to make enquiry why the judges of the Superior Court adjourn than to know the reasons for their decisions in any matter that legally come before them or than sd Judges have to enquire the reasons why the Legislature adjourn or decide on any matter within their province."[47]

Langdon's defiance enraged the western delegates to the point of moving a resolution to address the executive for his removal; when that failed, they carried a vote for his impeachment, 35–29.[48] In July, the senate met at Exeter as a court of impeachment; the managers and the defendant attended and stated their readiness to proceed; but it was suddenly realized that the senate could not constitutionally act in the absence of the house. Langdon's sardonic talents took full advantage of this opportunity to humiliate his opponents. He insisted that the court proceed; when the senior senator, attempting to gloss over the true reason for their impotence, remarked that several of the senators were absent, Judge Langdon replied that they had a quorum; *he* took no exception to the absence of *his* judges; "he was even willing to dispense with the attendance of some who were present." The senate was forced to adjourn in deep embarrassment, finding itself unable to make a court for reasons very similar to those for which the defendant had been impeached.[49]

When the senate met again in January, with the house duly in concurrent session, Woodbury Langdon was in Philadelphia, having been appointed to federal office at a salary more than four times the sum he received as a judge.[50] He had likewise resigned from the New Hampshire judiciary, and accompanied his resignation with a philippic that stated in forceful and biting language the complaints that the judiciary could logically bring against the legislature.

> I will only observe that it appears to me exceedingly surprizing that the honorable house of Representatives (unless individuals thereof

have some private ends to answer) should be so very anxious about the neglect of duty in me or any other of the Judges when they are so often culpable in this respect themselves. Why do they blame those who follow their example? And how unreasonable it is for them to expect punctuality in the Judges when their small salaries (tho' I am no advocate for large ones in a young & republican government) are so badly paid while the members of the general Court were so scrupulously attentive to their own pay (if I am rightly informed) as to even make use of money for that end that was lodged in the Treasury for other purposes—When too the Judges are so liable to be harrassed & persecuted for a reasonable absence; & much more especially when the members of the late legislature discovered such a disposition to nullify the most solemn decisions of the Courts of law!—What gentleman will accept do they suppose of a seat on the bench or if he does be so attentive to his duty as he could wish when subject to such inconvenience and indignities! In fine where is the Independence of the judicial department! And if this be destroyed where is the security of the subject?[51]

The rage of the western members upon hearing the clerk read this insulting letter, added to the frustration they already felt at being robbed of their prey, drove them to ridiculous extremes. Dr. William Page of Charlestown, who was the vocal agent of his section's animosity against the Portsmouth judge, bullied the house into passing a resolution that Langdon ought not be permitted to resign while under impeachment. He followed this immediately with another resolution censuring the language of Langdon's communication.[52] The senate had meanwhile adjourned the trial again, but Page was determined to have his revenge. For the second time he introduced a resolution to address the president and council for Langdon's removal and then obtained instructions from the house for the managers to nol-pros the impeachment. These two resolutions were then entered in reverse order in the journal of the house. Three weeks later the senate sensibly terminated the affair by unanimously nonconcurring in the address for removal.[53]

Although the impeachment had ended in a fiasco, it had the merit of revealing constitutional weaknesses, judicial ills, and political uncertainties. It was demonstrated that under the constitution of 1784 the president and council, in their executive capacity, might appoint a judge to office; then, as members of the two branches of the legislature, vote to address themselves for his removal; and finally, in their executive capacity again, remove him from office.[54] Langdon's case also revealed the organic ills in the judiciary: the lack of dignity, responsibility, and authority which so seriously hampered its usefulness.

Jeremiah Smith, who had accepted appointment as a manager of the prosecution with a rather uneasy conscience, seized what he thought would be this opportunity to demand a reform in the judiciary. He had composed a speech which of course was never given, but which would have used Woodbury Langdon as an instrument for probing into the diseased tissues of the courts. Judges, he declared, could not also be merchants; they could not serve God and mammon. It was due to such amateur and untrained judges that

> our courts of law, when they have pretended to sit to dispence justice, have rather dispersed than dispensed it. To the same cause it has been owing, that difficult cases of law have been determined without any deliberation, and the very same question has received different determinations. In short, instead of justice running in a clear, a steady and broad channel, it has all the impetuosity of a torrent, and, like a torrent, bears down all before it. The consequence has been, that nobody rests satisfied with our legal determinations.[55]

The strangest feature of Woodbury Langdon's impeachment was the alignment of animosities which it displayed. Undertaken principally by the western delegates, led by Colonel William Page, "a wild enthusiastic projector, fond of shew & parade," it had also enlisted the support of such eastern lawyers as Edward Livermore and Jeremiah Smith, but had encountered the strong opposition of William Plumer.[56] Yet before the year was out, Plumer, Page, Livermore, and Smith were working smoothly together on the revision of the constitution and supporting each other in their respective candidacies for public office. Plumer's enthusiasm for Langdon, whom he was soon to find in bitter political opposition, was a clear sign that politics were still purely personal in 1791.

New Hampshire gained a member in the House of Representatives by the reapportionment of 1791, and the new plum was the object of considerable grasping. Since there were no party issues or party machines to bring about the nominations, that necessary work was accomplished by personal intrigue. Members of the general court that met at Dover in June 1792 spent most of their spare time attempting without much success to form quadrumvirates for the August election.[57] Page, Plumer, Sherburne, Foster, and many others were supported more or less seriously against the incumbents, Jeremiah Smith, Nicholas Gilman, and Samuel Livermore. The result betrayed no discernible political trend. Although Smith was triumphantly reelected, receiving the vote of nearly every elector in the three western counties, Gilman and Sherburne prevailed in the east. A second election had to be held to determine the fourth place, and Paine Wingate, whose term as senator had expired, won over Abiel Foster at this trial. Samuel Livermore had been elected to the Senate in June, so that he and Wingate exchanged places. This election gave Rockingham County four of the six New Hampshire delegates to Congress.

One will search in vain for any kind of consistent principle displayed in these political events from 1789 to 1793. In Philadelphia there was vague talk of a "ministerial party" and an "opposition party," but the votes in Congress were determined by economic, geographic, and personal considerations, with small relation to past or future parties. In New Hampshire the word *party* referred to a group of men determined to push a certain bill through the legislature or to elect a certain candidate, without regard to other bills or other offices. One finds the words *federalist* and *republican* used only in a very general sense, and not used so frequently as *Whig* and *Tory*. Neither the votes in the legislature nor those in popular elections show anything more than a rough and confused approximation of the later political situation. "The people appear divided," Plumer had written, "& trifles light as air unite and divide them."[58]

CHAPTER 7

CONSTITUTIONAL REVISION

I have seen men so inattentive to their acknowledged right that, when they have been called upon for their votes for a form of government for themselves and their posterity, not one of them in ten cared so much about it as to give their vote pro or con; a few busy men did all that was or could be done, and the rest acquiesced. —Jeremy Belknap

One of the most remarkable features of nearly all the state and national constitutions written during the revolutionary period was the inclusion of means for their own revisions.[1] Our modest forefathers thus acknowledged their fallibility and gave their descendants legal processes by which the fundamental structure of government could be modified to meet changing conditions without resort to rebellion or the coup d'état.[2]

The New Hampshire constitution of 1784 *required* that seven years after its adoption the general assembly should provide for the election of a constitutional convention which might propose whatever changes in the fundamental law it saw fit and submit these to the voters, two-thirds of whom would have to approve them. This mandatory exercise in reflection came most opportunely for New Hampshire in 1791. Seven years of actual experience under the constitution of 1784 had disclosed innumerable weaknesses. For the most part, these had gone to prove that the convention of 1781 had been right the first time and that many of its original proposals which the people had rejected needed to be restored. The federal Constitution, in its marked contrast to the old Articles of Confederation, had served as a good example of a successful reform and as an object lesson in vigorous government.

Moreover, the operation of the new federal government, with its assumption of powers formerly exercised by the states, rendered anomalous many provisions of a constitution designed for a supposedly sovereign state in a loosely confederated league. Minor difficulties arose because the chief executives both of the Union and of New Hampshire were styled "President" and because the state constitution still required the legislature to elect delegates to Congress. A more serious problem grew out of the lack of a proper sense of discrimination in certain persons who held both state and federal offices. Pluralism was endemic in New Hampshire. Samuel Livermore had ignored pointed hints that he resign as chief justice of the superior court after he had been elected a congressman, and John

Sullivan had seen no conflict in holding at the same time the presidency of the state and a federal judgeship.

Seven years of experience had furthermore demonstrated that the executive power in New Hampshire's government was inadequate, the legislative power ill-defined, and the judicial arm too weak. Citizens were learning that simple devices that had seemed to work well enough when lubricated by revolutionary ardor threatened to break down through internal friction when self-defense was no longer the paramount issue. The stage was set for the climax of the counterrevolutionary movement that had begun in 1781 with the policy of deflation and the first draft of the "Essex constitution."

The 108 delegates who assembled in Concord for constitution making during the month of September 1791 were a highly composite group. Several familiar figures—Sullivan, Bartlett, the Langdons, and the Gilmans—were absent because of other duties. But there was a strong contingent of the older men who had been leaders since colonial times: Pickering, Livermore, Peabody, Atherton, Payne, and Toppan, to name the most notable. All of these except Nathaniel Peabody had been members of the convention of 1788 and leaders in the struggle over the ratification of the federal Constitution. Several of them had served in earlier state constitutional conventions, and one, John Pickering, had been elected to every such body meeting in the state since 1776. These men, however, were too old, or too busy elsewhere, to play an active role in this convention. Livermore was elected president, but after the first session he took his seat in Congress and did not return until the work was nearly finished. John Pickering served as president pro tempore and Nathaniel Peabody as chairman of the committee of the whole, but both men were past their prime and found it difficult to conduct the exacting business of the convention.[3]

The mantle of actual leadership fell from these aging shoulders upon younger men. From the Connecticut Valley came Daniel Newcomb, who had helped to shape the constitution of 1784, and Dr. William Page of Charlestown, another of those politico-physicians so often to be met with in those days. Page had tried diligently to lead Cheshire County into union with Vermont and was now endeavoring with equal energy to increase western influence in the government of New Hampshire.[4] One of the boldest and most restless of the younger leaders was Edward St. Loe Livermore, son of the convention's president, who had left the parental domain in Holderness to practice law in Portsmouth. Another promising newcomer was Jeremiah Smith of Peterborough, who had already made his mark in the courts and legislature and would have been much more influential in the convention if he had not also been a congressman and therefore unable to attend all the sessions.

Perhaps the most influential man in the convention, certainly the most indefatigable, was William Plumer of Epping. A sixth-generation descendant of Newburyport Puritan ancestors, Plumer had virtually educated himself in the law and was rapidly building up a vigorous practice in the courts of Rockingham County. In 1791 he was serving his fourth term as Epping's representative in the general court and had been elected speaker of the house. Plumer was an ardent advocate of constitutional reform. Throughout the first seven-day session of the convention he was in constant attendance, vigilant in debate and active upon a number of important committees. At the end of the week's discussion the convention elected a grand Committee of Ten (two from each county), which, during the interval of adjournment, was to consider all the amendments that had been suggested, together with any others that it might deem suitable, and report at the next session. Plumer and Peabody representing Rockingham County, Joshua Atherton for Hillsborough, William Page for Cheshire, and Elisha Payne for Grafton were the most influential members of this committee.[5] The others—Nathan Hart of Moultonborough and Ebenezer Smith of Meredith representing Strafford County, Robert Wallace of Henniker in Hillsborough County, Sanford Kingsbury of Claremont for Cheshire County, and Jonathan Freeman from Hanover in Grafton County—though somewhat less articulate and original, were solid and capable men. Throughout the winter of 1791–92 the committee met whenever a session of the general court or of the law courts gave opportunity for the members to come together. Peabody and Freeman tended to oppose all the reforms introduced by Plumer and Page, while Atherton, "fickle as Proteus," held the balance between them.[6]

In spite of these obstacles, Plumer drove the committee to the completion of its report and the preparation of an explanatory letter to accompany it in time for the second session of the convention, which began on February 8. The real work of the convention was done at this February session of sixteen days, but the records of its votes would be incomprehensible without a key supplied by Plumer's autobiography. He makes it clear that most of the far-reaching changes proposed in the fundamental structure of the government were the work of a small group of authoritarians, seconded by the moderate majority of the convention. At the other extreme stood the leaders of the malcontents who were dissatisfied with the existing government not because it lacked vigor but because it was already too unresponsive to their particular interests. These two minority groups and the moderate element in the center formed combinations and engaged in struggles that depended largely upon the immediate problem under debate, and not upon any well-conceived, general lines of cleavage. On many issues, especially those which envisaged some sweeping change, the two extremes found themselves in alliance against the timid center; but on other proposals which would benefit only one of the smaller groups, the minority would be crushed by the combined weight of radicals and moderates. Thus the record of votes in the convention shows apparent confusion and strange alliances between Portsmouth aristocrats and backwoods delegates, deistical lawyers and pious Calvinist elders.

Plumer fought doggedly throughout the convention to remove religious restrictions from the constitution, but in this effort he failed. On the first day of the convention he introduced a resolution to expunge Article 6 from the Bill of Rights and substitute for it a new guarantee of religious freedom which would have swept away tax support for any established church.[7] But Plumer was twenty-eight years ahead of his time; his motion was crushed by an 89–15 vote. Three days later, however, a proposal to remove the Protestant test for officeholders received much greater support and was defeated by only eighteen votes, 33–51.[8] Plumer boldly persuaded the Committee of Ten to expunge the Protestant qualification in spite of the convention's decision and justified the step in daring language. "The Religious test is omitted because it is incompatible with the principles of a free government, and inconsistent with the bill of rights which secured to all the free enjoyment of their Religious sentiments and the right of electing and being elected into office; and because it is not sufficient to exclude the wicked and designing but may prevent the honest and virtuous."[9]

In the February session Article 6 was again subjected to a verbal attack —this time by the religious conservatives. The convention accepted, 57–35, a substitute article which would have made it impossible for any person to escape religious taxation by changing his denominational allegiance.[10] Curiously enough, the people of New Hampshire proved to be more liberal than the convention majority, but less radical than Plumer. The new Article 6 was spurned by four-fifths of the popular vote, but the omission of the Protestant test, although approved by a majority, failed to receive the two-thirds vote necessary for ratification.[11]

The convention showed a much greater degree of unanimity on the necessity of a clearer separation of powers in the state government. There was substantial agreement that this feature of the emasculated constitution of 1781 needed to be restored, and the restoration was the chief triumph of the convention. The representatives of the mercantile and urban property interests, which favored a potent executive, combined with delegates from rural constituencies, disgusted with an impotent legislature, to effect these changes. The test came early, on a vote to remove the chief executive from the senate, and the victory was decisive, 65–14.[12] Thereafter, the convention proceeded, without a record vote, to order that the members of the executive council should be elected by the people, one from each county, rather than be selected from and remain within the legislature, and that councillors could not hold seats in either house of the general court. The Committee of Ten built upon this broad foundation by giving the governor a qualified veto over the legislature and a clear negative against nominations by the executive council. They also introduced a lieutenant-governor and made him the presiding officer in the senate. This latter resurrection was too much for the delegates, who remembered the long years of colonial history when New Hampshire had been governed, not too well, by royal lieutenant-governors, and the ghost was laid again, but the other changes were accepted.[13] Thus an independent, responsible executive, no longer entangled with and subservient to the legislature, was erected.

At this point the convention began to wrestle with the difficult and intricate problem of legislative apportionment. The constitution of 1784 had created an elective senate of twelve members, divided among the counties presumably according to wealth. It had at the same time authorized the legislature to divide the state into equal districts for the election of senators, but this the legislature had never done. No matter how closely the original apportionment may have corresponded to the distribution of wealth, the census of 1790 revealed a considerable disparity as regards population.[14]

Rockingham County, the old seaboard area, was overrepresented, while the two western counties, Hillsborough and Cheshire, were rather seriously underrepresented. The representation of Grafton and Strafford was approximately proportional to their population, but these were the frontier counties, growing rapidly and expecting soon to be underrepresented, as were Hillsborough and Cheshire. This condition was recognized in the convention, and the remedy adopted without a record vote. It was agreed that the legislature should be *required* to "divide the State into twelve [senatorial] districts having respect to the proportion of public taxes and nearly equal as may be without dividing Towns or places." Thus the preponderance of Rockingham County was destroyed, and the basis for future gerrymandering laid. In an effort to save something from the wreckage, the conservatives proposed raising the property qualification for senatorial candidates to £500 and giving them two-year terms, but these proposals were brushed aside by the convention.[15]

Reform of the senate was child's play compared to the task of making the house of representatives truly proportional. Ghosts of colonial assemblies in controversy with royal governors, of the great Connecticut Valley secession, of the county convention scheme which had been slain in 1782—these and other dread specters rose to haunt the man who laid impious hands on the sacred principle of town representation in the assembly. It will be recalled that the convention of 1781–83 had struggled heroically with this problem and finally surrendered, allowing each town with 150 male taxpayers to elect a representative, but withholding the privilege of electing another until the number reached 450. Smaller towns were combined into constituencies of 150, unless peculiar circumstances justified the legislature in granting them individual representation. These circumstances were discovered frequently after 1784. Preposterous over-representation of rural hamlets and gross injustice to towns of more than 300 voters resulted from this situation.[16] The doctrine of town autonomy simply could not be reconciled with the principle of representation according to population. The situation was most galling to such small but ambitious villages as Exeter, Dover, and Concord, which aspired to leadership in state politics and had sent as many as five delegates to the provincial congresses in their day, but could not now find the 300 additional polls that would distinguish them from such remote, poverty-stricken and unenlightened communities as Hinsdale.

Plumer, with his customary boldness, made a frontal attack on the problem. He introduced an amendment which would have given New Hampshire a modern house of representatives by limiting the membership to sixty and having these elected from equal districts to be determined by the legislature.[17] His proposal was defeated, 22–73. Sixteen of the favorable votes came from towns in Rockingham and Strafford counties that felt overwhelmed by the annual deluge of representatives from the hinterland.[18] Efforts to limit the size of the assembly by increasing the number of voters which entitled a town to representation or to equalize the representation of the larger towns by lowering the "mean increasing number" were defeated by a solid block of seventy votes. Invariably these came from small towns already entitled to one representative with no prospect of ever having more than one.[19]

Against their solid entrenchment in the status quo it was impossible to effect a breach in the system. The Committee of Ten made one more effort by reporting an amendment that the house should never consist of more than 110 members or less than 80. The convention threw out this proposal without a record vote.[20] In the end the reformers were completely defeated and forced to leave the composition of the house exactly as it stood, without amendment. The only change effected was a provision for the payment of representatives' salaries by the state, rather than by the towns, which made the rural victory even more complete. This amendment was endorsed by more than two-thirds of the voters and added to the constitution.[21] Membership in the house immediately spurted and grew annually thereafter more rapidly than the population, until in 1821 it had reached 192 and was nearly equal to that of the national House of Representatives.

This failure in 1791 to reconstruct the state legislature along rational lines proved in the long run to have historic consequences. No subsequent convention had quite the same opportunity, and the follies of the system grew more ridiculous with time. The senate has resisted every democratic impulse from Jackson to Kennedy and remains to this day representative of taxable property rather than people.[22] As the lower chamber grew to gargantuan proportions, the senate became disproportionately small, even though its size was doubled by an amendment in 1878.[23] Thus, the inability to create a working compromise between town autonomy and proportionate representation has saddled New Hampshire with the most grossly inflated lower house in the United States, while the upper chamber has remained one of the smallest in existence. Such a legislature became not only an undemocratic anachronism but, as the reformers clearly foresaw in 1791, an inefficient and easily corrupted machine.[24]

When the convention reached that part of the constitution dealing with the judicial branch of the government, it embarked upon a stormy sea indeed. A large proportion of the convention's members had been intimately connected, as judges or lawyers, with the state judiciary, and whether or not they approved of reform, they knew that it was needed. Complaints about the administration of justice in New Hampshire had been mounting in a crescendo of dissatisfaction since the courts had resumed full operation at the end of the Revolutionary War. Suitors complained about the law's delays, the expense of trials, the tricks of the lawyers, and the denials of justice to the poor. To their lament was now added the critical voice of professional discontent, made vocal by such rising young lawyers as Plumer, Smith, and Livermore.

The widespread discontent was fully reflected in the convention. In a series of bold resolutions, which were carried by majorities of nearly two to one, the delegates decided to sweep away the entire judicial structure and empowered their Committee of Ten to build anew. This task occupied most of the committee's time and attention.[25] During the session of the legislature in December the committeemen who were also members of the general court met in Plumer's lodgings every night to continue their work. Plumer obtained leave from the legislature to examine the dockets of the courts, and thus secured a fund of valuable data to support his theories.[26] When the committee finally revealed its plan, it proved to be a complete remodeling of the judiciary.

The backbone of the new system was to be a supreme court consisting of a chief justice and from six to nine associate justices. This court was to hold three terms annually in each county, but the individual judges were to be relieved of excessive burdens by the division of the state into two circuits and by the provision that only three of the nine judges were necessary to make a court. In addition to all the authority exercised by the old superior court, the new court was to have original civil jurisdiction in cases involving more than £4. The third term in each county was to be the law term, in which difficult points of law, appeals for new trials and restorations to law, and causes in equity were to be decided. Thus the new supreme court would have replaced entirely the old common pleas courts as well as the superior court. The increase of jurisdiction of justices of the peace to £4 cases took up the remainder of the civil cases. Minor criminal trials, formerly handled by the cumbersome courts of general sessions, were to become the province of new county courts consisting of five to seven judges. Appeals from both the county courts and justice's courts were to go to the supreme court. The probate courts were to be left unchanged.[27]

The chief authors of this plan were probably Plumer and Smith, although the latter was in Philadelphia during the winter of 1791–92. Many of its features were discussed in correspondence between the two friends. Smith had attempted to use his position as a prosecutor of the Woodbury Langdon impeachment to indict the existing judicial system, and Plumer had proposed comparable changes in a legislative study committee on which he had served in June. The best argument for the change was given by Plumer himself in the explanatory report of the Committee of Ten which he drafted. "The Courts of common pleas doth not appear to us a court of trial but of defaults," he wrote. In three of the county dockets that he had studied, only 110 actions had gone to jury trial out of 2,388 entered, and 81 of the 110 verdicts had been appealed to the superior court.[28]

No part of the committee's report caused such stormy debate in the second session of the convention as did this section. The dissenting minority of the committee carried its fight to the floor and was strongly supported by Chief Justice Pickering, whose character and experience gave him great influence. Some of the advocates of reform were either, like Colonel Payne, too old to bear the brunt of battle or, like Edward Livermore, so tactless and violent as to stir up needless opposition. An angry pamphleteer, writing shortly after the convention had adjourned, made capital of Livermore's intemperate behavior toward "the venerable Chairman" (Pickering) and his injudicious assault, not on the judicial system, but on the incumbent judges, several of whom were present. Livermore in fact had bluntly stated that he expected the opposition to come from the twenty judges of the inferior courts and the five times that number who "were gaping for the office." The anonymous writer pretended to be horrified to hear Payne, Page, and Plumer propose to abolish the existing courts. "What, said I, can these gentlemen be after! at one stroke level a judiciary system, that has cost the wisdom of ages to erect! When such a proposition comes forward to lay the axe at the root of the tree, it behooves every good citizen not only to examine carefully and see what we are to receive in return: but to take a retrospective view of the conduct of those who bring it forward."[29]

Thereupon he reminded his readers that Payne and Page had led the secession to Vermont and were not altogether free of suspicion in regard to certain letters that had passed between Vermont authorities and the governor of Canada during the Revolution. As for Plumer, the pamphleteer charged him with preaching "the doctrines of passive obedience and non-resistance" during a tour of the New Hampshire frontier which he had made in 1780 as a Baptist missionary. "How came it about," asked the writer, "that these gentlemen should be so anxious to alter our laws and judiciary system. Is it out of pure regard to the love of liberty, and the citizens of this State? Or is it because they once had an antipathy to our government, and still retain it?"

The author of this pamphlet was Thomas Cogswell of Gilmanton, a judge in one of the inferior courts that the new system proposed to eliminate and therefore a highly interested party to the combat.[30] Whether sincerely or for self-preservation, Cogswell gave apt expression to the extremely conservative viewpoint on the judiciary. He thought, with Blackstone, that it was better to suffer inconveniences than constantly to change a system. "In free states the trouble, expense, and delay of judicial proceedings, are the price that every subject pays for his liberty." The judicial system disposed of cases as a new mill grinds flour, he said, slowly but surely. The present government cost only sixpence per head per year to operate, "and the man who is not content thus far, with our government, would not be content with any."

As for the new proposals, he continued, a court of chancery was superfluous, for equity jurisdiction was inherent in all the courts. The new courts would be arbitrary and expensive; they would favor the rich and mulct the poor; the only people to benefit by them would be the pettifogging lawyers and a new train of twenty judges at £200 each. The proposal to increase the jurisdiction of the justices would create five hundred petty tyrants. As for legal training, the courts that presently had no lawyers on the bench were the best in the system. The writer concluded with a little jeu d'esprit. The judicial system would be perfect as it stood, he declared, if the legislature would only remove the trial of bastardy from the general sessions to the common pleas. "It really appears a farce, for forty justices to assemble, to hear a matter which originated in so much love and good nature, and now disputing who shall pay the shot."

These were powerful arguments, whether they appealed to reason or to prejudice, and it soon appeared that the temper of the delegates had softened considerably since the previous September. The heart of the committee's proposal—to erect a supreme court—was submitted again to a vote. In September it had been assented to by a majority of twenty-seven; it was now defeated 48–54.[31] Reforming zeal now gave way to discretion, and the convention decided to dump the entire problem into the lap of the legislature. Four amendments were devised which made it the duty of the legislature "to make a reform in the Judiciary System," including a transfer of equity jurisdiction and the power of granting new trials to the courts, but they authorized merely a reorganization of the existing courts "if they shall judge it necessary for the public good."[32]

Only a small part of the committee's work survived. It had recommended retirement for judges at the age of sixty-five; the principle was retained, but the venerable judges in the convention procured an elevation of the age limit to seventy. There was also a sufficient number of justices of the peace in the convention to retain that part of the report which increased their jurisdiction. Their influence can be gauged pretty accurately by the vote, which was 63–35.[33] It should be noted that as a part of the original plan of reorganization the increased jurisdiction of the justices would have substituted for much of the business of the court of common pleas, but when this court was not eliminated, the justification for enlarging the scope of justices' power lost much of its force. The convention also proposed five amendments that were designed to remove minor abuses in the judiciary connected with probate courts, clerks' fees, and the all too prevalent tendency of officials to confuse their public and their private business.

The strong prejudice against lawyers welled up several times in the convention from the debt-ridden hinterland, only to be blocked by the more sophisticated communities. A proposal to exclude lawyers from seats in the legislature was crushed by a vote of 79 to 15. William Plumer, however, himself a lawyer, was responsible for one entirely reasonable limitation upon the fraternity. Lawyer members of the legislature had long been accustomed to act as counsel and even to plead for parties whose petitions or memorials were under consideration by the general court, thus playing at the same time the incompatible roles of advocate and judge. The people were inclined to believe that lawyer members even encouraged appeals to the legislature in cases in which they had an interest, intending to use their influence for a more favorable settlement than could be had before a judicial tribunal.[34] A motion by Plumer in the legislature itself to prohibit this abuse had failed, but he introduced it into the convention, and it passed without a record vote.[35]

The convention was now virtually finished with its labors, but the puzzling problem of how to present so complicated a structure to the public for approval remained to be solved. Page, Plumer, and Livermore were made a committee to find the solution. Experience had shown that town meetings could mangle a beautifully constructed constitution beyond recognition without really intending to destroy it. The problem was to present the amended constitution in such a way that a fair expression of public opinion might be registered upon the whole as well as upon each separate part. The committee recommended first that the entire constitution, as it would appear if the amendments were adopted, should be printed and distributed to every town. Then the amendments were arranged in seventy-two paragraphs and printed beside ruled columns so that the votes for and against each amendment might be recorded separately. These tally sheets were also to be sent to each town. The committee's recommendations were adopted, and the convention adjourned to await the decision of the sovereign people.[36]

The leaders most responsible for the amendments felt considerable anxiety as to the result.[37] They had spent the better part of a year in studying, debating, writing, and polishing these seventy-two amendments, yet the people of New Hampshire might destroy their entire work by a few votes. How much time did the people give to consideration of this momentous question? Perhaps the case of Concord provides a typical answer. On April 23, the selectmen ordered the constable to call a town meeting for May 7 to consider the proposed amendments, together with several items of town business. There had been no town meeting since the regular annual one on March 6; therefore it is certain that the amendments were not publicly debated prior to the day on which they were to be considered. How much they may have been discussed privately in Widow Osgood's tavern is not recorded. At any rate, the "freeholders" of Concord met on May 7 at one o'clock in the afternoon, decided not to straighten a road, leased part of the school lot to James Walker, and then voted upon the seventy-two amendments to the constitution.[38]

Not unsurprisingly, such scenes produced a deep distrust of democracy. "I have seen men so inattentive to their acknowledged right," wrote Jeremy Belknap, "that, when they have been called upon for their votes for a form of government for themselves and their posterity, not one of them in ten cared so much about it as to give their vote pro or con; a few busy men did all that was or could be done, and the rest acquiesced."[39] Plumer testified that "the great mass of the people took no interest in the revision. Many of them felt their inability to decide the questions submitted to them, & refused acting."[40] The highest number of votes cast on May 7 for or against any amendment was 4,987, only a little more than half the voter response two months earlier in an almost uncontested gubernatorial election.[41]

Small as it was, however, the popular vote in May was sufficient to riddle the structure that the convention had so laboriously erected. Forty-six of the seventy-two amendments were accepted by the necessary two-thirds vote, but the twenty-six rejected articles contained the very heart of the revised system.[42] The people had vetoed the changes proposed in the senate, had voted against removing the governor and councillors from the legislature and adding to their powers, and had refused to order the legislature to remodel the judiciary. Only the trimmings on the new structure had been accepted; the great internal framework that gave it substance was thoroughly demolished.

The journal of the convention bears mute evidence that a period of bewildered indecision followed the revelation of this popular disapproval. A committee appointed to study the returns discovered that they were full of inconsistencies.[43] Although the people had rejected the amendment that would have removed the governor from his seat in the senate, they had adopted another which authorized the senate to elect its own president, who was to succeed to the governor's chair in case of a vacancy, but while acting as governor was not to remain in the senate. The voters had also rejected the proposal to expunge the existing parts of the constitution dealing with the council, yet they had approved a new phrase, tucked away in the middle of a long exclusion bill, that expressly prohibited councillors from holding seats in the legislature.

The convention faced a thorny difficulty. Since the people had accepted forty-six amendments, it could hardly wash its hands of the entire matter, as had the convention of 1779. Should it submit meekly to public opinion, as had the convention of 1782, and iron out the remaining inconsistencies in the spirit of what was undoubtedly the majority will? It was clear that the people did not want a strong executive, preferred that the legislative and administrative functions continue to be intermingled, and opposed changes in the judiciary. Should the convention bow to that decision and abandon its efforts to separate those three powers?

The answer of the convention was a bold one—to resubmit their entire scheme for a strong, independent executive, and to do so in such a way as to make another rejection most unlikely. The journals do not reveal the mystery of this policy development except in broad outlines. It began with a committee recommendation that the convention proceed to draw up a new series of amendments. Two days later, however, the convention decided "that the seeming inconsistency mentioned in the Report of the Committee of Saturday last, may be fairly reconciled."[44] In other words, the inconsistencies were to be ignored and the original revision sent forth again for the popular benediction. New committees were appointed to remove the minor inconsistencies and to rewrite the amendments, which was done in such a way as to make them differ only in detail from the amendments under the heads of senate, governor, and council originally sent to the people in February. They completely reconstituted the system that the voters had flatly rejected in May.

Furthermore, the convention decided that no opportunity would be afforded this time for contradictions—the reconstituted amendments were to be accepted or rejected as a whole. This proved to be a shrewd stratagem. It took much more brashness on the part of the people to vote against a complete reform recommended by their leaders than it did to peck away at small portions of the structure. The convention met again in September and learned that 2,122 votes had been cast in favor of the amendments and only 978 against them.[45] Thus, although the efforts made to remodel the legislature and the judiciary had been defeated, the reformers by a bold stroke of political strategy had made good their attempts to organize a strong and independent executive department. It was a maneuver comparable in decision and daring to the calculation by which the Massachusetts conservatives had made sure of their victory in 1780.[46] Printed copies of the constitution, as amended, were ordered for distribution, and with this the work of the convention was finished.[47] It had held four sessions, covering thirty-one days, between September 7, 1791, and September 7, 1792. Its leaders had come to the first session with high hopes for a completely remodeled government; much of their planning had been defeated in the convention itself and still more by the people at large, but in the end their efforts had been saved from futility by a resourceful demonstration of wit and courage.

The work accomplished by the convention of 1791–92 was indeed so extensive that even the New Hampshire courts have made the mistake of referring to it as a new constitution.[48] Technically, it was only a revision of the constitution of 1784, which still remains the fundamental law of New Hampshire; but in spirit, certainly, it was a new organic law, or, rather, it was a reestablishment of what the constitution of 1784 would have been if it had been adopted in 1782. The revision of 1792 so strengthened the constitution that it continued throughout the nineteenth century virtually without change. The people did not even authorize another convention until 1850. When that convention met, with William Plumer's oldest son as one of its members, Plumer was the only person still living who had been a member of the 1792 convention. He died while the convention was still in session, too soon to know that the people had rejected all of the numerous amendments suggested by his son's associates. They were still content with what had been known for nearly sixty years as "Plumer's Constitution."[49]

A brief review of the amended constitution in 1792 will show how extensively it had been revised.[50] There were first of all a number of changes in nomenclature: the assembly became the legislature; president was changed to governor, and so forth. These were convenient but hardly fundamental. A second and much more important series of changes was designed to eliminate abuses that had been tolerated by the earlier constitutions. Members of the legislature were prohibited from acting as counsel in cases tried before them; judges, registers, and clerks were forbidden to act as counsel in many cases in which they apparently had been doing so; and, finally, excise collectors and other bonded debtors to the state were excluded from the legislature unless their accounts with the state were settled. A third set of changes was made in order to improve administrative procedures. The secretary of state was required to hire a deputy and to give bond for the faithful performance of his duties. The oath of office was greatly simplified. County officers were held to stricter accountability. The impeachment process was patched up and the amending process was altered to make septennial conventions optional rather than mandatory. A fourth series of amendments made the legislature more responsible to its constituents. These included a provision for the galleries to be opened to visitors and another for the printed reports of each session to contain more information. The most important change perhaps was that which shifted the burden of supporting town representatives from the towns themselves to the state treasury. This meant that the future would see an immediate enlargement of the house of representatives—an enlargement which the older and wealthier towns would subsidize, although they were strongly opposed to it.

The important changes wrought in the framework of government may be summarized under four additional headings. First, senators were no longer to be chosen by county constituencies but from districts equal in ratable property. No such fundamental change was made in the composition of the lower house. Second, the executive head, now called governor, was taken out of the senate and given a veto over legislative acts which could be overridden only by a two-thirds vote of each house. He was also given a negative over nominations and decisions of the council. The method of his election in cases in which a popular majority might not obtain was changed to a simple joint ballot by the legislature. Third, the councillors were no longer to be elected from the two houses of the legislature by their fellow members and to retain their seats in that body while also acting as an executive council. They were now to be elected by the people, one from each county, and were expressly prohibited from being members of the legislature. Fourth, only two slight amendments were retained out of all those suggested for the reform of the judiciary. One of these provided a retirement age of seventy for judges and sheriffs; the other authorized the legislature to increase the jurisdiction of justices of the peace to £4 cases except those involving title to real estate. Fifth and finally, changes made necessary by the new federal Constitution were approved; the chief one was the expunging of the entire section that provided for the election of delegates to the Continental Congress.

One very important matter remains to be considered. Why did the people accept in one lump in September 1792 the same amendments in regard to the senate and executive department that they had rejected piecemeal in May? The absence of complete statistics makes a definite answer to this question impossible. We do not have, for instance, a record of the votes cast in each town for and against the amendments at the May meeting; we have only the totals on each amendment. It cannot be ascertained therefore which part or parts of the state voted in favor of and which against a stronger executive in May. The town votes on the final amendments in September, however, are preserved.

When this vote is plotted on a map, it shows a distribution which is at first glance very surprising (see Map 11). Areas that voted against the ratification of the federal Constitution now favored the amendments to the state constitution—amendments which specifically erected that strong executive power that they were supposed to fear. Londonderry, Rochester, and almost the whole of Hillsborough County, the centers of the paper-money agitation and opposition to the federal Constitution, voted almost unanimously for these amendments.[51] On the other hand, old mercantile towns, such as Exeter, Dover, and Hampton, together with other towns that had supported the federal Constitution, such as Chester, Hopkinton, and Plymouth, were against these amendments. Could it be that towns that had wished to strengthen the hand of government in 1788 had changed their viewpoints in four scant years?

Fortunately, Plumer gives a clue to this puzzling situation. In February 1793 he wrote Jeremiah Smith a letter which described the state of public opinion in Exeter. "The people of that *little village* are uneasy & alarmed at the alterations in the constitution. The representatives being paid by the State will greatly encrease their numbers in the western parts of the State. And a division of the State into equal districts for electing Senators will as the *wise sages* of Exeter say, soon remove the treasury & Secretary's office to Concord."[52] This letter not only explains why Exeter should have opposed the amendments but reveals that the people of New Hampshire saw the issue chiefly as a sectional or geographical one, rather than as a question of economic or abstract principles. Another examination of the map shows that the vote on this issue cut straight across the usual lines of division within the state. Portsmouth and its connecting towns did not agree with Exeter and Dover on this question; Portsmouth had already been robbed of the seat of government and was more jealous of Exeter than of the western towns. The amendments were carried in fact by an alliance of Portsmouth and the interior towns. Every town voting in Strafford County except Dover returned a majority for the amendments; Hillsborough, Cheshire, and Grafton towns voted 49–19 in their favor. This result indicates the successful use of political bribery. The interior towns were so well pleased with the concessions made to them, particularly the payment of their representatives by the state, that they willingly endorsed the strong executive desired by the conservative leaders.

The map, however, shows the opinion of only a small minority. The 3,100 freeholders who turned out to vote on the amendments in September were 1,887 fewer than those who had voted in May and represented only a minor fraction of the total body of voters. What the indifferent majority thought of the proposed changes must remain unknown, except for the self-evident fact that they were not sufficiently opposed to vote against them. Many towns did not even return votes on the proposition, and those that did returned but few. Only thirty-two voters came to the meeting in Portsmouth, while one hundred turned out in Epping and thirty-nine in far-off Rumney, on the frontier of settlements. It is quite evident that the town meetings in which this question was decided were attended by that small group of interested persons who felt that their own vital concerns were at stake. If it shows anything conclusively, the map indicates that the men who determined to resubmit their important amendments to people who had already rejected them were skilled psychologists and knew how to make the most of the indifference as well as the prejudices of their countrymen.

CHAPTER 8

THE RISE OF PARTIES

We are alarmed at the proceedings of your house. . . . You act as if the Devil had taken full possession & presided over your deliberations.
—William Plumer

The constitutional convention of 1791–92 had been convulsed by many factional fights, but of one divisive influence it had been free.[1] There had been no political parties to which the warring factions could adhere. A few of the members—Joshua Atherton, Nathaniel Peabody, Thomas Cogswell—had been anti-federalists in 1788, but no longer used that designation. A much larger number of New Hampshire leaders, including Sullivan, Smith, Pickering, Bartlett, Plumer, the Gilmans, the Livermores, the Langdons, and the Sheafes, still called themselves federalists, simply because they supported the new Union. But these temporary party names had already lost their significance. Nothing except vague and conflicting personal antagonisms divided the leaders of New Hampshire in 1792. Within a few months, however, these men were to find themselves arrayed in hostile ranks under banners inscribed Federalist and Republican, fighting at the side of other men with whom, in many cases, they had exchanged heavy blows during the paper-money struggle or at the ratifying convention.

Not political theory, not economic interest, not class hatreds, but a war raging three thousand miles away divided the people of New Hampshire into hostile political parties. The French Revolution and the continental battles growing out of it had been noticed occasionally in the foreign dispatches printed four or five months after the event in New Hampshire newspapers, but for three years these had aroused little interest. It was only when France and England expanded their war to this side of the Atlantic that New Hampshire began to take notice of it. Not much time was required after that to light a domestic conflagration that did not burn out until Napoleon had been exiled to St. Helena. The differences of opinion in regard to foreign policy were sharp and bitter. In the case of New Hampshire, it is possible to determine with remarkable precision the year, almost the day, on which transient allegiances to former factions were cast aside and the cockades of alien nations adopted with fanatic devotion. It was the crisis of 1793 which gave birth to both the Republican and the Federalist parties.[2]

France met the British threat to its foreign commerce by throwing open its West Indian and home ports to neutral vessels. Many a revolutionary patriot whose ardor for France had cooled since 1783 found it rekindled by this opportunity to bring prosperity back to American shipping. When Britain, under its Rule of 1756, began to seize American vessels engaging in this trade, patriots recalled that they had spilled their blood against British tyranny before, that British soldiers still occupied forts on American soil, that American citizens from Kentucky to Algeria were being captured and enslaved by savages, reputedly encouraged by perfidious Albion. "Under all the foregoing circumstances," wrote level-headed Paine Wingate, "it is not strange that there is prevailing in this country a bitterness of spirit against Great Britain which is not very compatible with a state of neutrality and will render it almost impossible to preserve peace with that country."[3] Anglophobia flourished, however, not so much among New England merchants, whose ships were being seized, as among Virginian planters, whose debts to British factors might be evaded if war with England resulted. Jeremiah Smith was certain that a desire to escape just obligations rather than a tenderness for commerce lay behind Madison's embargo proposal and the plan to sequestrate British property in America.[4]

Nevertheless, England's high-handed seizures caused some vigorous reactions in New Hampshire. The most remarkable one was evidenced in the views of John Langdon. This man, who had given Hamilton's financial measures his complete support, began to change his opinions in 1793, and presently announced himself in opposition to the Federalist administration. He was heard to say, early in 1794, that "he *wished to see the revolutionary spirit of seventy five again revived*," and before long he was writing letters to Monroe in extravagant praise of "the Intrepidity, Justice, and Magnanimity" of France.[5]

The vote on Madison's Non-Intercourse Resolution can be regarded as the first party test in Congress, so far as New Hampshire was concerned. Wingate and Smith voted against it in the House; Gilman and John Samuel Sherburne favored it.[6] In the Senate, Langdon shifted to Madison's support, but Livermore was entirely opposed to any kind of embargo.[7] Thus, at this critical point, the New Hampshire delegation was evenly divided. Langdon, Gilman, and Sherburne, however, did not represent the opinion of half the state, only a faction in the Old Colony.

The European war, which had converted Langdon into a Jeffersonian, led the Livermores, the Sheafes, John Taylor Gilman, Jeremiah Smith, William Plumer, and many other wavering politicians into the ranks of the Hamiltonians. Plumer wrote to Smith in the spring of 1794 that only a few desperate and abandoned men in New Hampshire favored war with Great Britain but that the great majority, even including the merchants who suffered most from British spoliations, were willing to "make many sacrifices for peace."[8] Smith had already announced, in an earlier letter to Plumer, his adherence to Federalism.[9]

Josiah Bartlett, physician turned statesman, had presided over New Hampshire as president and governor from 1790 to 1794, during the emergence of political parties. His influence in this development had been small; he was not essentially a politician. He had served his state and nation well in legislative and administrative posts since 1775, had signed the Declaration of Independence, and had founded the New Hampshire Medical Society. He had not participated in the creation of the state constitution, however, and his role in the federal ratifying convention of 1788 had evidently been a passive one. Having reached the age of sixty-five in 1794, he retired from public life, full of honors. His successor was John Taylor Gilman of Exeter, state treasurer since 1784, who received 75 percent of the popular vote.

Gilman's views of public finance were thoroughly Hamiltonian, in addition to which he and his brothers, Nicholas and Nathaniel, had taken advantage of their offices to speculate in both state and Continental securities. If John Langdon was destined to become the nucleus of the Republican party in New Hampshire, John Taylor Gilman already headed a group of expert politicians in Exeter who served as the core of state Federalism. As state treasurer, Gilman had advocated continuation of taxation at the high war level, even though public expenditures had assumed their prewar simplicity. He argued that citizens should be habituated to paying annual taxes, whether needed or not, and that surpluses should be maintained in the state treasury for unexpected contingencies.[10]

As already noted, however, economic issues were not yet politically divisive in the early 1790s. It was public excitement over the question of foreign relations which in 1794 brought out the largest vote yet to be registered in the state, but the congressional elections were indecisive. Smith, Sherburne, and Gilman were reelected, but Foster moved ahead of Wingate for the fourth place. Avowed Federalists made a strong effort to prevent Langdon's continuation in the Senate, but the former governor still had a loyal following. At its June session in 1794 the house renominated Langdon, the senate named a Portsmouth Federalist, Jacob Sheafe, and a deadlock ensued.[11] During the summer a senator from Strafford County resigned in order to accept an appointment to the judiciary, and the people of his district elevated Thomas W. Waldron from the lower house to fill the vacancy. In December the senate concurred in the house resolution to elect Langdon, with Waldron casting the deciding vote.[12] Federalists cried that the procedure was indelicate, since Waldron had voted in both houses on the same motion, and unconstitutional, because the house resolution should have died with the adjournment in June. The deed was done, however, and the Federalists had to make the best of it.

Jeremiah Smith shrewdly observed that Langdon was less dangerous in Philadelphia than at home, where his resentment would have spurred him into actively hostile measures.[13] Events proved the truth of this prophecy. After 1796, Langdon was the only Republican in the Senate from New England, and was relatively impotent. Whether he could have stirred up a serious opposition in New Hampshire is problematical, but the fact is that Republicanism failed to triumph there until after he did return in 1801.

Not many months after Langdon's reelection, however, his vote came perilously close to defeating the administration in the Senate. President Washington called the senators back to Philadelphia in May 1795 to consider the treaty that John Jay had negotiated with England. Langdon was thoroughly convinced that the treaty betrayed American commercial interests to the British yoke. He voted against it, and if Senator Livermore had agreed with him, their votes would have defeated ratification.[14] When Senator Mason of Virginia revealed the terms of the treaty to the newspapers, Portsmouth, in common with nearly all the commercial centers, found them unsatisfactory. At a town meeting held on July 16 the inhabitants approved an address to President Washington asking him not to sign the treaty on the ground that "the regulations of trade, commerce, and navigation between the two parties . . . hold out the most decided advantage to British subjects, and must in their operation prove destructive to American commerce and navigation."[15] The town also voted its hearty thanks to Senator Langdon for his opposition and to Senator Mason "for his patriotism in publishing the treaty unduly withheld by the Senate from the people."[16]

Some time later, the conservative group in Portsmouth, which had failed to control the town meeting, drew up an address to President Washington commending him for signing the treaty. It was supported by some forty eminent and respectable citizens of the metropolis. When its existence became known to the more volatile elements in the population, a mob gathered, armed with clubs and the revived spirit of '75. Carrying effigies of envoy Jay and Senator Livermore through the streets, the crowd surrounded the homes of men who had signed the address, broke down their fences, trampled their shrubs, and threw stones at their windows. Thomas Sheafe was threatened with ruin if he did not surrender the document, but he manfully refused, and the crowd had to vent its ill humor by burning the effigies.[17]

This outburst of mob violence evoked painful memories of the riot at Exeter in 1786. Ten of the ringleaders were arrested and tried at the next session of the superior court, where spectators imitated the revolutionary tribunals of Paris by applauding and lionizing the defendants. Overawed, perhaps, by this display of sympathy, the judges granted a continuance of the trial to the next term, and the defendants returned in triumph to Portsmouth.[18]

By these events, party lines were drawn so tightly in New Hampshire as to admit of no neutrals. John Langdon and Portsmouth had gone irrevocably Republican, but for the time being they were almost alone. In November the New Hampshire legislature unanimously approved a vigorous Federalist answer to Governor Gilman's strong Federalist address, expressing complete approval of the Jay Treaty.[19] Smith wrote from Philadelphia that New Hampshire's firmness had dismayed the enemies of good government and completely discredited Langdon, Sherburne, and Nicholas Gilman. "As a state we are federal—strictly so," Plumer assured him in reply. "We are ready to go any length that reason can justify in support of the federal government & its administration. The sons of anarchy & misrule in this unhappy country, like Sisiphus, will find their incessant labour unavailing."[20]

While New Hampshire Federalists were rallying to the support of Hamilton's foreign and fiscal policies, they were carrying out at home a determined deflation, which aroused suspicion and opposition. This was largely the work of the Exeter Junto. Exeter had controlled the state treasury almost continuously since 1775. Oliver Peabody, another Exeterite, succeeded John Taylor Gilman at the exchequer in 1794. The Gilman family, together with Peabody, Benjamin Connor, a clever floor leader in the assembly, and Jonathan Clark, also from Exeter, not only controlled the treasury but dictated the fiscal policy of the state.

In 1794 the legislature suddenly decided to liquidate the state debt. The largest part of it, in state notes and certificates, was to be redeemed at 75 percent of face value, while the various issues of state bills were to be called in at a much less favorable rate. Creditors were to receive half of their money in specie and the other half in new state notes bearing 6 percent interest and payable in eighteen months.[21] On the face of it, this looked like a partial repudiation of the state's debt, a measure which the country towns might have carried against the conservative east. Actually, the vote on the bill showed the opposite sectional alignment. It was interpreted as an administration measure, supported by Exeter and the conservative centers.

Even more heroic measures would have been justified by the flourishing condition of the state treasury. As a result of the assumption of state debts, it contained $300,000 in United States securities and a large sum of specie; its assets also included a block of shares in the New Hampshire Bank, £11,000 loaned at 6 percent interest to individuals, and large sums due from collectors, excise masters, and the Masonian proprietors. In spite of this wealth, however, the legislature was persuaded to authorize Peabody and Gilman to borrow £25,000 at 6 percent in order to have funds on hand for the conversion of notes into specie. The treasurer was also authorized to issue extents against all state debtors, *except* those to whom the £11,000 had been loaned, unless their accounts were promptly settled.[22]

Neither the terms of this extraordinary bill nor its sponsorship is easy to explain. Connor, the Exeter representative, had introduced the legislation authorizing the state treasurer to lend public money to private individuals. He and Clark, together with three brothers of the governor, were among the nine men to whom the £11,000 had subsequently been lent. It seemed strange to some observers that the state should have to borrow money when its own reserves were in the hands of speculators. The partiality that spared the governor's brothers but demanded of other state debtors immediate payment did not go unchallenged. Nathaniel Peabody, one of the excise masters who felt peculiarly injured by the law's harsh demands, moved in the next session of the legislature for a committee to investigate the treasurer's transactions.[23] Oliver Peabody was thus forced to name the nine men to whom the state's money had been lent and the Boston broker from whom he had borrowed $40,000 (£25,000). He affirmed that a small part of this money was deposited in the New Hampshire Bank and the remainder was in his care. When the committee transmitted this reply to the legislature, it was voted to be unsatisfactory, but at that point everyone seemed to agree that the investigation had gone far enough. The general assembly ordered the treasurer to discharge his obligation to Bond, the Boston broker, immediately and to collect the debts due the state as soon as possible. In order to carry through its redemption plan, it was then forced to levy a tax of £8,000.[24]

Although a scandal was thereby averted, suspicion, ill will, and discontent were increased. The people grumbled at their unexpected tax; the handful of Republicans complained that justice had failed; and many of the lesser Federalists became seriously dissatisfied with the Exeter leadership. Plumer, for example, was convinced that the whole scheme had been a gross speculation in state securities, carried on with money borrowed from the state, and obligating the state itself to a further paper debt at high interest rates.[25] It is impossible to say, so long afterward, whether any such scheme was actually tried or whether the Exeterites had that much imagination, but the fact that others suspected them of it is in itself significant.

The intrusion of national issues into state political life determined that local questions would no longer be decided on their merits, but would become partisan tests. This was evident not only in the delicate investigation of the treasury but in every other issue that arose after 1794. In the early stages of the *McClary* case, all New Hampshire statesmen, regardless of party affiliations, had sympathized with the defendants. Governor

Gilman had called a special session of the legislature to defy the federal courts, and Smith and Plumer had applauded his action. After the rise of Jacobin clubs, the Jay Treaty riots, and a few other assaults on order and good government, Federalist sentiment changed. Representative Smith complained that the home state was pushing things in an unseemly manner; then, when the Supreme Court pronounced its decision, he abandoned the *McClary* owners altogether in admiration of the federal judiciary. "Patterson delivered one of the most elegant correct perspicuous & convincing arguments I ever heard delivered in a Court of law," Smith said of a decision which transferred $32,000 from the pockets of New Hampshire citizens to a Boston estate.[26]

Plumer agreed with Smith and reported that "the candour & integrity of the judge commands the respect & esteem of even the Portsmouth democrats. . . . It would have been more fortunate," however, he wrote, "had the judgment . . . been against these men. The respondents, with the exception of Joshua and George Wentworth, are, I believe, all federalists."[27] Smith supposed that the *McClary* faction would combine with the Langdons against Gilman.[28] This was a natural expectation, and the *McClary* case should have furnished the Republicans with excellent propaganda in New Hampshire against despotic centralization. The fact, however, that the Republicans were too nationalistic to take advantage of a cause célèbre and that the Federalists abandoned their former championship of state sovereignty is interesting.

In addition to new-found admiration for the federal judiciary, New Hampshire Federalists began to cherish their state judges more consistently. The problem was more complicated here, for the Federalist lawyers wavered between contempt for the ignorant men who occupied the bench and respect for the bench regardless of its occupants. Unfortunately, in 1795, only three years after the Langdon impeachment, the superior court was again under fire for the same remissness in holding all of its terms. Governor Gilman recommended an inquiry into the conduct of the judges, and the house of representatives responded by introducing a resolution to address the governor for the removal of Chief Justice Pickering and Associate Justice Dudley. Pickering was saved from disgrace only by the casting vote of the speaker, John Prentice.[29]

The irony in this narrow escape was that although Pickering was the first really well informed lawyer to occupy the supreme judicial seat in New Hampshire, he probably deserved to be removed. He was only fifty-eight years of age, but ill health and nervous disability were already pointing toward the insanity that was to blight his useful career. He had been far more guilty of absence from court than had Woodbury Langdon in 1792; he had irritated lawyers and spectators for years with constant complaints of poverty and sickness; he had threatened many times to resign and then had humbly apologized to the legislature and promised to reform. Even his Federalist friends were beginning to recommend his resignation.[30]

A month after Pickering's reprieve, Judge Sullivan died and thereby furnished an easy solution to the problem. Here was an opportunity to provide Pickering a sinecure and remove him from the superior court at the same stroke. It would be good politics too, since Pickering had abandoned his alliance with the Langdons and become a firm Federalist. Accordingly, the Federalists of New Hampshire petitioned Washington for his appointment. John Langdon and Sherburne supported Woodbury Langdon, but their credit at the national capital had disappeared since 1794, and although Smith was not enthusiastic in Pickering's cause, the Portsmouth lawyer received the appointment. This elevation to the federal bench of a man so nearly expelled from the state judiciary upon the recommendation of Federalist leaders who admitted that he ought no longer to be a judge provides some interesting lessons in politics. Nine years later, in the inevitable epilogue, Pickering was impeached and removed from office by the Jeffersonians.

The elections in 1796 offered something a little more accurate than riots and memorials to test the people's attitude on the momentous issues of the day. In the seaboard area the Republicans made much of the discontent over the terms of the Jay Treaty, but the governor had also given them an issue which might attract votes in the western part of the state. In the winter session of the legislature, Gilman had vetoed a bill for raising the tax on unimproved lands. The house had repassed the measure by the necessary two-thirds margin, but the senate had then defeated it.[31] A tax on unimproved lands provided the clearest possible issue between settlers in the frontier towns and speculators in the older section of the state. Gilman consequently aroused great resentment outside the Old Colony by his veto, while land speculators praised his "firmness & independence" and thought that it atoned for some of his past misconduct.[32] Unfortunately for the Republicans, it was not easy to combine the resentment of merchant speculators against the treaty with that of frontiersmen against the merchant speculators. That great combination did not come to pass in 1796. Instead, the western towns scattered their dissenting votes among several favorite sons, and Gilman was reelected by a 72 percent majority.[33]

The situation in the legislature was not so comforting to the Federalists. Pierce Butler, a United States senator from South Carolina, upon reading accounts of the March elections in New Hampshire, discovered that a number of prominent Federalists would not be resuming their seats in the June session. He immediately spread the word in Philadelphia that the people of the northernmost state had disciplined their late legislators for their disgraceful truckling to Great Britain.³⁴ While this would have been hard to demonstrate, it was clear that Londonderry had reverted to the paper-money faction and that Portsmouth and Rye were completely lost.³⁵ The Portsmouth Federalist representatives of the previous year had been replaced by a Republican trio. Two of these, John Goddard and Woodbury Langdon, were capable and influential men, whom the Federalists could oppose only with difficulty. The third, Timothy Drowne, was actually still under recognizance to the superior court for his participation in the late riots. There were men of "talents and property" on the Federalist side in Portsmouth, but they were not in a majority.³⁶

The Federalists had not ceased to worry about the Republican leaven in their new house before the House of Representatives gave them a greater fright. In Philadelphia the opponents of Jay's Treaty were making a determined fight to strike it down from behind by refusing the appropriations necessary to carry it into effect. Langdon warmly approved of this project. "A vast Majority of the people are opposed to the Treaty," he assured Madison, "and are lookg. up to the House of Representatives, to save us from distruction."³⁷ Plumer took a very different view of the situation. "We are alarmed at the proceedings of your house," he wrote to Smith. "You act as if the Devil had taken full possession & presided over your deliberations."³⁸ Apparently, the people in general agreed with Plumer rather than Langdon. When the bill eventually passed, the New Hampshire delegation was unanimous in its favor. Even Nicholas Gilman swung back to the Federalist side, and Sherburne obtained leave of absence on the excuse that he had important cases to argue in the state courts in order to extricate himself from the dilemma of voting against either his "Virginia friends" or his constituency.³⁹

The congressional elections in August 1796 became the first definite and decisive party contest in New Hampshire history. Jeremiah Smith received an ovation from "the honorable judges, . . . the gentlemen of the bar, the grand jury, and a number of respectable citizens of this and the neighboring towns" when he returned to Amherst in June.⁴⁰ It contrasted vividly with the lack of enthusiasm that greeted Gilman and Sherburne at home. In July these two declined reelection. Sherburne might have saved himself the trouble, said Plumer, "but some men who have no other make a merit of necessity."⁴¹ He also doubted that even John Taylor Gilman's influence could have secured a reelection for his brother. A few days before the town meetings were held, Plumer reported to Smith that the voters in New Hampshire were "divided into two parties, federalists & anti-federalists. The latter have announced Woodbury Langdon, Nathaniel Peabody & Thomas Cogswell as their candidates. They are very industrious & intent in bringing in their men."⁴² Unfortunately, he continued, the Federalists were divided, with Jonathan Freeman, John Prentice, Edward Livermore, and William Gordon vying for a place on the ticket with Smith, while the Jeffersonians encouraged this free-for-all.

The Republican strategy of dividing votes, however, proved to be a complete failure. Woodbury Langdon received only 978 out of 6,418 votes cast;[43] Smith and Foster were reelected, and two western Federalists took the vacant places of Gilman and Sherburne. Not one of these Federalist congressmen was from the Old Colony, where wealth and commerce were concentrated. Foster lived in Rockingham County, but in its extreme northwestern corner (Canterbury); Smith and Gordon were both from Hillsborough County, and Freeman's home was in Hanover, in Grafton County. In the November presidential election the Federalists completed their triumph. Five of the party candidates for electors commanded popular majorities, and the legislature chose the remaining elector from the two men who stood sixth and seventh on the list, both Federalists. New Hampshire cast its six ballots for John Adams and Oliver Ellsworth. Without them, Adams would have lost, and Thomas Jefferson would have become president of the United States in 1797.

CHAPTER 9

FEDERALISTS AND REPUBLICANS

All, all came down, a motley nation,—
As tho' "in hell there were vacation,"—
Burning with Jacobinic zeal
To overturn the public weal.
                    —Amherst Village Messenger

Both France and England employed in this period the age-old technique of intervention in the political affairs of neutrals.[1] American politics would have been less bitter if the European belligerents had not stood each behind one of the parties and fought their battles with American ballots as well as with European bullets. Until 1796 France enjoyed an advantage in this game of penetration because of its treaty of alliance with America, and because American merchants had serious economic grievances against England. After 1796, however, France played its hand badly. Measuring all republics by the decadence and corruption that had permeated its own, France reasoned that the Federalists might be frightened and the Republicans bribed into submission to French will. The Adams administration, therefore, became a protracted war of nerves which had its effect in producing a high degree of American hysteria.

The French began by warning of the dire results that would follow ratification of the Jay Treaty. When that measure finally squeezed through Congress, France broke off diplomatic relations, ordered Charles Pinckney to leave the country, turned its privateers loose upon American shipping, and tried to boost Jefferson into the presidency. This violent behavior had an immediately unfavorable effect upon opinion in New Hampshire. "The piratical conduct of the French very much alarms our merchants," wrote a formerly moderate Federalist. "Our Frenchified patriots are now cursing the *terrible Republic*! . . . If the french robberies should extirpate french politics in our Country, we shall profit by the losses of our Merchants."[2] New Hampshire conservatives, however, were apparently less apprehensive of French belligerence than of the tactics of the Republicans, whom they regarded as a fifth column. "I fear more from our Democrats, our frenchified Americans, than from the French themselves," declared William Plumer. "The time is come when our country's *foes are those of our own household*."[3]

The March elections of 1797 proved to be a smashing Federalist triumph. Only a handful of avowed Republicans, including Woodbury

Langdon, John Goddard, Timothy Drowne, and Thomas Chadwick, all from Portsmouth, returned to the state legislature. John Taylor Gilman was reelected governor by 89 percent of the largest vote yet cast in a state election.[4] Senator John Langdon had allowed his name to be used on the opposition ticket, but received only six hundred votes, all but nineteen of these from Rockingham County. The victors celebrated with a "moderate firm & federal" election sermon by the Reverend Asa Peabody and a public dinner, at which preachers and legislators alike "drank a number of federal toasts" while Goddard and Langdon made wry faces.[5]

An interesting carry-over from colonial legislative protocol, which became a convenient means of testing party loyalty in early American assemblies, was the governor's opening address and the answers made by each of the houses. Governor Gilman opened the June session of 1797 with a strongly worded demand for support of President Adams's foreign policy. The reply of the house of representatives, firmer even and more federal than the governor's address, was written by a young lawyer from Keene, Peleg Sprague, who later succeeded Jeremiah Smith in Congress. At the following debate on the committee's report the galleries of the old Concord meetinghouse were crowded with important spectators, including visitors from Massachusetts. Goddard and Langdon attacked the document vigorously; Sprague conducted a strong and ingenious defense. It was adopted by the house without amendment by a vote of 104 to 27, and the senate concurred unanimously, although the senator from district one was supposed to be a Republican. This vote may be accepted as a fairly accurate estimate of relative party strength in 1797.[6] The two centers of opposition to the address were Portsmouth, whose influence obtained eight negative votes in the Old Colony, and the Merrimack Valley, where thirteen contrary votes appeared. The Connecticut Valley was almost solidly Federalist, and only three representatives from the Frontier voted with Portsmouth.

In March 1798 the national Republican leaders made the serious mistake of trying to embarrass President Adams by calling for the correspondence from America's three unrecognized ministers in France. The notorious XYZ Papers, with which Adams satisfied the demand, were read in Congress on April 3. Within a few days a flame of indignation swept the country as the full significance of the clumsy French solicitation of a bribe became clear to the American people. Even in Portsmouth, Republicans felt forced to retreat, and the effect elsewhere in the state was even stronger. Arthur Livermore wrote from his home in Holderness on the northern frontier, "What few there are of us . . . are perfectly federal— ready to sign addresses—pay taxes—fight—or anything else that is chosen."[7] Prominent men who had hitherto paid little attention to politics wore the black cockade to signify their antagonism to France. Counties, towns, revolutionary veterans, and voluntary associations of gentlemen astonished President Adams with messages of approval and pledges of support. The inhabitants of Salisbury held a town meeting, with the revolutionary veteran Ebenezer Webster in the chair, and adopted the following resolution: "Resolved, That altho' we are small and remote, compared with many other towns, yet at a period like the present, when the honour and independence of the United States have been outraged, we consider it our duty to declare to the world, our unshaken attachment to our national Honour, Independence, Constitution, and Government; and to support these, we pledge our hard earned property, and even our lives."[8]

The unexpected swing in public opinion toward administration policies was as discouraging to "the democrats" as it was inspirational to Federalists. Some people had feared that the winter session of the legislature, held in Portsmouth, would be cowed by the democratic rabble, in imitation of Parisian models, but it had been the democrats themselves who were silenced. Goddard gave up the struggle and declined reelection, advising other Republicans to follow his example, since they could effect nothing against the overwhelming majority.[9] Londonderry returned to the Federalist fold, and the Republican delegation in the legislature was reduced to trifling proportions. Governor Gilman, Senator Livermore, and all four of New Hampshire's Federalist congressmen were triumphantly reelected.

The legislature met at Hopkinton in June, with the full heat of indignation at the XYZ exposure still burning in every breast. According to the pious custom of the times, the minister of the place, who happened to be a young candidate, was invited to act as chaplain. In his first morning prayer the youthful preacher made some enthusiastic comments about France and neglected to commend the president and Congress to divine favor. He was thereupon notified that his further services were not required, and when he preferred a memorial in his own defense, it was promptly dismissed by a committee. "For the Court to live without prayers," Plumer, speaker of the house, wrote his wife, "will, I beleive, be less offensive to Heaven than jacobinical sacrifices."[10]

The reply to Gilman's forceful address was written by Plumer, who probably expressed the reaction of the great majority of New Hampshire's citizens:

'Tis with regret and indignation we find [the French] republic
wantonly destroying our commerce, insulting our government,
treating our ambassadors with scorn and contempt, and insidiously
endeavouring to weaken and destroy the confidence of our citizens
in the constituted authorities of our country. Although we believe

that the blessings of honorable peace are worthy of great sacrifices, yet even peace purchased with the loss of our liberty and independence is a greater evil than war. The unanimity and harmony, the firm, yet steady attachment of the citizens of the United States in general, and of this State in particular to the government of their choice, will be a strong and never failing resource in every event.[11]

This address was accepted without a division; a similar memorial to President Adams was approved by a vote of 134 to 4 in the lower house and unanimously in the senate.[12] To prove that their patriotism was not confined to words, the assembly authorized the purchase of artillery for the militia and appropriated four thousand dollars for the erection of fortifications at Portsmouth if the governor should deem them necessary.

Swept onward by the growing war fever as French and American vessels fought at sea, New Hampshire Federalism reached the pinnacle of success in March 1799. Governor Gilman was elected to his sixth successive term by 86 percent of the popular vote, and the Republican delegation in the state legislature was nearly wiped out. In Portsmouth the conservative merchants rallied to beat Langdon's machine and send Federalists to replace Drowne and Woodbury Langdon. Only nine of the twenty-seven representatives who had voted against the Federalist answer to Gilman's speech in 1797 were returned to this legislature, and even they gave their support to the national administration. As the end of the eighteenth century approached, New Hampshire was as nearly unanimous in political sentiment as it is possible for a freely democratic people to be.

No state legislature in the Union gave President Adams more loyal support than did New Hampshire's during 1799. Governor Gilman's opening speech, which breathed fire and brimstone against France and its American adherents, was echoed by an antiphonal blast from the house of representatives, adopted unanimously by 137 votes, with only three members absent.[13] The *Oracle of the Day*, Federalist organ in Portsmouth, looked at the harmonious scene with sublime satisfaction.

> We congratulate our readers on the progress of federalism in Virginia, and on the success of the federal ticket in the city of New-York.—Truth it is seen triumphs, while falsehood stands confounded. The present may be considered as a new era in American politics.—Our government may be said to rest on a more sure foundation than ever, and bid defiance to the clamors of noisy demagogues, and the restless spirit of that faction which has so long labored to destroy all law & liberty that does not coincide with its licentious principles. It is now decided by the great body of the

people of America, that it is better "to stand on our own, than on foreign ground;" that uniting under the *federal standard* is the best way to preserve our liberty & independence, to promote our individual & publick interest, to make us strong and powerful as a nation, and to give us respectability in the eyes of the world.[14]

Administration policies, which were looked upon with distrust in some quarters, received nearly unanimous support in New Hampshire. The Granite State delegation in Congress had voted for a navy, a standing army, war taxes, and suspension of commerce with France, all of which seemed to be highly acceptable to the home state.[15] Merchants approved measures of defense against French "pirates," and farmers rejoiced in steadily rising prices for their produce.[16] None of the "wise and good" majority thought that the national government had done wrong in protecting itself against fifth columnists by a new Naturalization Act, an Alien Bill, and a Sedition Law; they were even disposed to believe that the restrictive measures were too lenient.

William Gordon made an able and eloquent argument in favor of the constitutionality of the Alien Act, ending with a peroration which would not look out of place in the *Congressional Record*. Could the government be so deficient in power as not to prevent a peacetime invasion by potential enemies, he asked. Gentlemen were afraid to give the president extraordinary powers, but the ordinary laws would not detect the alien revolutionists' peculiar brand of poison. It was said that this law had no precedent; it might also have been said that the United States had never before faced so dangerous a situation. He trusted therefore that the bill would pass.[17]

The Concord *Courier* called the Sedition Act "the mildest law ever made to suppress seditious practises" and added that "we hope it will be promptly executed on every occasion."[18] The Portsmouth *Oracle*'s comment betrayed its location in the hotbed of Jacobinism. "When a man is heard to inveigh against this law, set him down as a man who would submit to no restraint which is calculated for the peace of society. He deserves to be suspected."[19] The opposition here inferred must have been confined to conversation, for little of it appeared in the newspapers, even though some of them still claimed to be open to the writers of both sides.

With such universal agreement, at least among the literate elements of society, it is not surprising that the Kentucky and Virginia resolutions received scant courtesy in New Hampshire. The newspapers treated them as military threats and replied with sinister foreshadowings of civil war.[20] "We think it highly probable that Virginia and Kentucky will be sadly disappointed in their infernal plan of exciting insurrections and tumults," proclaimed the *Oracle*.[21] The legislature's reply to these expressions of wisdom from other states was blunt and straightforward.

> Resolved that the Legislature of New Hampshire unequivocally express a firm resolution to maintain and defend the Constitution of the United States, and the Constitution of this State against every agression either foreign or domestic, and that they will support the Government of the United States in all measures warranted by the former. That the State Legislatures are not the proper tribunals to determine the Constitutionality of the laws of the General Government—that the duty of such decision is properly and exclusively confided to the Judicial department.[22]

This being the case, the New Hampshire legislature saw no particular reason for expressing its mere opinion of the Alien and Sedition Acts, but if other state legislatures wanted it, it was that the laws "are constitutional and in the present critical situation of our country highly expedient." If the Virginia lawmakers wanted arguments in favor of this sentiment, added the New Hampshire assembly, they could refer to the able exposition by the minority of their own legislature, upon which it was superfluous to elaborate. Such was the unanimous sentiment of the New Hampshire legislature, and again the name of *every* member present was recorded as having voted in the affirmative.[23]

Party warfare had not existed long enough in this period to have produced the civilized amenities. Like the Whigs and Tories of Stuart times, the Federalists and Republicans of Adams's day were inclined to regard each other as engaging in treasonable rather than legitimate opposition. "The spirit of party ran high," recalled a contemporary, "divided families, neighborhoods, towns & states; &. blind to public interest, embittered the sweets of social life, & hazarded the rights of the nation."[24] A notable example of this rancor was the village of Amherst, where the northwest parish, which later became the town of Mount Vernon, was Republican, while the older settlement was Federalist. Reporting with bitter resentment a town meeting in which the northwesterners had crowded down to vote a remonstrance against the Sedition Law and direct taxes, the *Village Messenger* found adequate expression only in verse:

> All, all came down, a motley nation,—
> As tho' "in hell there were vacation,"—
> Burning with Jacobinic zeal
> To overturn the public weal.[25]

In order even to approach an understanding of the violent abuse that filled the press on both sides, a modern reader must recall that fundamentals deeper than economic advantage or political patronage were thought to be at stake. Jeremiah Smith, for example, wrote that "a real jacobin, in my opinion, is never made by want of knowledge only. It is the qualities of the heart that constitute the essence of this detestable character. He hates the light, because it reproves his deeds."[26]

It was due to such thought processes that the Federalists of Adams's period, in both the national and local spheres, indulged in overkill against their political opponents. The hysteria was strong enough in New Hampshire to lead to demands that the president remove from office three Portsmouth Republicans—Joshua Wentworth, supervisor of the customs, Joseph Whipple, collector of customs, and William Gardner, commissioner of the loan office. Early in 1798 Wentworth was dismissed as a defaulter, and Nathaniel Rogers, a capable man but a notorious ex-Tory, was appointed in his place. The other two Republican officeholders, Whipple and Gardner, were efficient and popular. They had held many offices under the state government and had been fervid patriots during the Revolution. Their connections were mercantile, and they belonged to families long established in the Portsmouth aristocracy. But as the French crisis deepened, Gardner and Whipple became open partisans of France, indulged in abuse of Adams, and lent their weight to the democratic organization growing up in Portsmouth. When these facts became so notorious as to arouse political comment even in the Boston *Centinel*, the secretary of the treasury, Oliver Wolcott, obtained the dismissal of the Portsmouth officers.[27] Unfortunately, President Adams replaced them with two more former Tories, one of whom would have been imprisoned for errors in his accounts if his friends had not protected him.[28]

This business had a pernicious influence. It placed upon the Federalist party the odium of introducing the doctrine that officeholders should be active supporters of the administration in order to hold their jobs. This was all the justification that Jefferson needed in 1801 to dismiss Adams's appointees and reinstate Whipple and Gardner. The Virginian can hardly be accused of inventing the spoils system when the major half of the principle had been laid down by his Federalist predecessors. Furthermore, the intrigue against the Portsmouth men had immediately unfortunate political effects. It gave the Republican party two influential martyrs in New Hampshire. Adams's replacement of sterling rebels by men whose loyalism during the Revolution was candidly admitted substantiated the charge that the Federalist party was more pro-British than anti-French.

New Hampshire Federalists not only followed the bad example of their national leaders in the matter of intolerance but adopted the same fatal tendency toward disunity which characterized the councils of President Adams. While the younger Federalists felt compelled to stand with Governor Gilman in common support of the nation's foreign policy, they did not by any means endorse the Exeter program for the state. Gilman himself created one difficult issue by threatening to resign in 1797 unless his salary was raised from $1,000 to $1,200. The senate approved this measure, but the house adamantly refused to adopt it until Gilman took the extraordinary step of refusing to sign the resolution for the lower salary. Under this pressure the house acquiesced, but Gilman's behavior had been so objectionable that he lost 1,500 votes to other Federalist candidates in the 1798 election.[29]

Governor Gilman and his Exeter friends accepted the Hamiltonian thesis that the power to tax ought to be exercised as a political principle whether or not it was required for the production of revenue. The national government had already aroused strong hostility by applying this doctrine in Washington and, for the first time since the adoption of the Constitution, by levying a direct federal tax. To add annual state taxes, equally unfamiliar to people who expected one levy to carry the government through several normal years, seemed to some of the younger Federalists to be asking for trouble. The Republican leaders were happy to provide it. Goddard shrewdly argued against the tax bill in 1797, but helped to secure its passage in a convention of the two houses.[30] He could then point to both state and national taxes as Federalist measures, designed to drain all the surplus wealth of New Hampshire into the gaping treasuries at Exeter and Washington. Such accusations received even more popular credence when the annual examinations of the treasurer's accounts by the legislature revealed an inability to produce immediate evidence of cash supposedly on deposit in the New Hampshire Bank.[31] There was always strong suspicion that the state's money was actually on loan to privileged private individuals.[32]

The Federalist leaders not only quarreled over fiscal policies but worked at cross purposes in the regulation of the state judiciary. A rift at this point developed between some of the Federalist lawyers and such nonprofessional leaders as Gilman and Freeman. In their persistent efforts to dignify the courts, Plumer, Smith, and their colleagues had to overcome the hostility not so much of their political opponents as of unsympathetic colleagues within their own party.[33] The two factors that seemed most influential in guiding legislative and executive policy toward the judiciary were niggardliness and a prejudice against lawyers. Neither of these was confined to one party. Nevertheless, as long as virtually all lawyers were Federalists, which was the case until 1800, Republican leaders could exploit the universal dislike for the profession in the interests of their party.

The situation was clearly revealed in legislation enacted during the last decade of the eighteenth century. In 1793 the superior court was invested with certain chancery powers previously exercised by the legislature, and during the next year the courts of general sessions were abolished.[34] In spite of the additional burden that the act of 1794 placed upon the inferior courts of common pleas, their terms were reduced by half in 1796, while the jurisdiction of justices of the peace was extended to include suits involving £4 or less. These reforms were readily made because the bulk of the country members thought that they "would lessen the business & influence of lawyers."[35] The truth was that although the laws were hastily drawn, partial, and lacking in the proper safeguards, intelligent lawyers approved of their fundamental purpose. In revising the fee table, however, the legislature was frankly discriminatory against the legal profession. Fees to jurors and witnesses were raised, but those that went through a lawyer's hands were allowed to remain at their low figure. Langdon and Goddard had used the debate on these measures to proclaim Republican sympathy for the little man who fell into the clutches of the lawyers. However, a Federalist speaker, Russell Freeman, had been as vociferous as Goddard in denouncing lawyers' fees, and the bills passed by strong Federalist majorities.

The rise of strictly defined parties in New Hampshire coincided with turbulent changes in the personnel of the superior court. After John Pickering had escaped possible removal from the chief justiceship in 1795 by transfer to the federal bench, Simeon Olcott, an associate justice, was raised to the chief place and Ebenezer Thompson of Durham was appointed to fill the vacancy. Thompson held the office for little more than a year and was succeeded by Daniel Newcomb of Keene. In 1797 uncouth John Dudley reached the legal retirement age established by the constitutional amendments of 1792, and was persuaded to resign. Edward St. Loe Livermore, talented but erratic, was appointed to fill the vacancy, and astonished nearly everyone by his excellent conduct on the bench. The superior court now consisted of Olcott, Newcomb, Livermore—all members of the bar with adequate legal training—and Timothy Farrar, who had succeeded Woodbury Langdon and who, even without benefit of legal education, was considered to be the equal of his colleagues.[36] All four of these judges were firm Federalists, and three of them lived west of the Merrimack River. In the spring of 1798, however, Livermore and Newcomb resigned. Within the brief space of eight years, the highest court in the state had suffered seven resignations, one impeachment, and innumerable threats of removal.

The responsibility for this woefully unstable condition in the judiciary lay upon several shoulders. In some cases the judges themselves were at fault, either in accepting positions for which they soon felt themselves to

be unqualified or in being too readily disillusioned with offices that originally appeared attractive. In other cases the responsibility lay with the
governor and council in the exercise of their power of appointment.
Governors Bartlett and Gilman were both prejudiced against lawyers on
the bench and tended to select judges on the basis of their military or
genealogical records rather than their legal attainments. These officials
were limited in their choices, however, to men who would accept the
inadequate salaries provided for the judiciary. The governor was by public opinion held responsible for the character of the judicial establishment, yet frequently he was forced to appoint a wealthy farmer with an
independent income when he would have preferred a promising young
lawyer who could not afford to abandon his practice. Thus the ultimate
responsibility fell upon the legislature, which refused to provide judges
with the "honorable salaries" prescribed by the constitution. By maintaining judicial salaries at a point only a little above the subsistence level,
the legislature kept the judges as subservient and the judicial establishment as unstable as either would have been if the judges had been subject
to annual elections.

At the beginning of the decade the salary of the chief justice was $600,
and he had to account for his fees. It would be tedious to recount the
herculean efforts made annually by a few persistent legislators to raise
this figure. Federalist as well as Republican towns resisted the increases.[37]
In the face of opposition from the conservative senate as well as the rural
constituencies the reformers in 1797 pushed the remuneration of the
chief justice to $850 and of his associates to $800 each.[38] Prior to his
resignation, Livermore had assured his friends he would remain on the
bench if his salary was raised to $1,000, but repeated efforts to obtain
this increase had been unavailing.[39]

To fill the two vacancies in the superior court, Governor Gilman and
his council appointed Paine Wingate and Ebenezer Smith of Durham.
"Previous to this," said Plumer wryly, "the governor had been considered
by lawyers as being hostile to the bar; these appointments confirmed that
opinion."[40] Wingate, after his six years in Congress, had virtually retired
to his farm in Stratham and was now nearly sixty years of age. He was a
man of unquestioned talent and integrity, but he had never studied law
and had little experience with judicial proceedings. Furthermore, his
firmness of character approached obstinacy, a fact that lawyers soon
discovered to their sorrow. Theophilus Parsons said of him "that it was
of great importance that Judge Wingate should form a correct opinion
before he pronounced it, for after that, law, reason, and authority would
be unavailing."[41] Wingate remained on the bench for ten years and,
everything considered, made an adequate judge. Even in 1798 he was
better qualified for the office than was Ebenezer Smith, although the

latter was by profession a lawyer. Smith was a pleasant, accommodating nonentity who had read law with General Sullivan and then subsided into a scrivener's practice. He seldom appeared in the courts to argue a case and had enjoyed very little experience in public affairs.

Fortunately, Smith recognized his limitations and, at the urging of his own friends, decided to decline his appointment. William Plumer and Jeremiah Smith thereupon urged the governor and council to appoint Arthur Livermore, younger brother of the resigned judge and son of the former chief justice. Livermore was only thirty years old at the time, but he possessed a full portion of the talents and temper that distinguished his entire family. Unfortunately, the Livermores and the Gilmans were not friendly, and this suggestion was received without enthusiasm by the council. When Arthur and Edward both appeared in Hopkinton during the June session in order to dragoon the legislature into continuing their aged father in the Senate, and especially when Edward lost his temper and engaged in personal abuse, the council decided to get along without any more Livermores on the bench.[42] In September, John Prentice, speaker of the house, was appointed to the vacancy, but he neither accepted nor declined his commission. He was hopeful of succeeding Samuel Livermore in the Senate, but wished to have the judgeship to fall back on if his election failed. As a result of all this Byzantine maneuvering, the vacancy on the superior court bench continued unfilled from March until December.[43]

The business of electing a Senator in 1798 strained the Federalist party in New Hampshire almost to the breaking point. Samuel Livermore's Federalism was unimpeachable, and he had been a useful member of Congress, but in 1798 he had reached the age of sixty-six and had become too fond of adding alcohol to a constitutional intemperance which needed no stimulant. He had likewise the misfortune of having antagonized the Exeter Junto by too many sarcastic comments about their political pretensions.[44] The unforgiving Exeter influence fell in behind Prentice, even though he had been appointed to the superior court. Other Federalists supported James Sheafe, a Portsmouth merchant and former Tory, for the senatorship. The Federalist majority was so divided that the election had to be deferred from June until December

John Prentice, the speaker, appeared at the winter session with a judge's commission in his pocket, but still intriguing for the senatorship. A session of the superior court in Grafton County had failed for lack of a quorum because he had not attended. The Concord *Courier* printed a violent attack on him, and many Federalist members became disgusted with his conduct.[45] Taking advantage of this situation, the Republicans gave their votes to Livermore, the least popular of the Federalists, and the incumbent senator was renominated in the house by a majority of one vote. Realizing now that his temporizing was likely to influence the senate adversely as it had already injured him in the house, Prentice hastened to return his judge's commission to the governor. His decision came too late. Wearied with the struggle, the senate concurred in the election of the elder Livermore, and on the same day the governor and council appointed his son Arthur to the position that Prentice had surrendered.[46]

Stung by this double defeat, Prentice descended from the chair on the last day of the session and made a violent speech denouncing the article in the *Courier* and vilifying William Plumer, to whom he attributed its authorship. Since Plumer had been Prentice's law student a dozen years earlier and had just preceded him in the speaker's chair, and since the newspaper piece in question had actually been written by Edward Livermore, this was an extraordinary performance. The handful of Republicans present must have looked on in unreserved delight as they witnessed Federalists tearing each other apart in public.

On the surface, however, New Hampshire was unanimously Federalist in 1799, and this requires some explanation. Those who delight in attempting to reduce the contradictory mass of human affairs to least common denominators have labeled Federalism the party of merchants, shippers, bankers, speculators, and capitalists and Republicanism the party of the landed interests, particularly the yeoman farmers. If this had been strictly true, no state in the Union should have been more Republican than New Hampshire in 1799. At least nine-tenths of its population consisted of self-sufficient yeoman farmers and their families. The state had the smallest stretch of seacoast among the original thirteen states, except Pennsylvania, and only one port of any consequence. Yet Portsmouth, the center of shipping and mercantile interests, was also the fountainhead of Republicanism within the state, and the Langdons, Wentworths, Goddards, and Whipples, who furnished leadership for Democracy, were among the foremost merchants in Portsmouth. Federalism, on the other hand, found its strength in the agricultural towns of the interior and its leaders among the country squires.

That New Hampshire's interests were primarily agricultural was a fact clearly recognized whenever the welfare of the state as a whole rather than of a particular part was considered. Thus it had been rural frugality which had caused New Hampshire's earlier representatives in Congress, though good Federalists, to oppose national extravagance and Hamilton's assumption scheme. It was the towns of the Connecticut and Merrimack valleys, not those of the Old Colony, that wanted to protest against the assumption of state debts. Proposals to raise taxes on real estate or prevent taxation of intangibles, to increase salaries, to encourage banking, manufacturing, and internal improvements, to spend the state's money for the benefit of individuals, and to protect the rights of creditors continued to find Portsmouth and the Exeter Junto combined against the hill towns as invariably after they had fallen out over politics as before.[47]

Economic cleavages were certainly present during the decade of the 1790s, as they had been during the 1780s, even though the prosperity of the period made them less sharp. But they were not the basis of political divisions. The persistent antagonism between poor towns and rich towns might have been exploited to advantage by political parties. But the opportunity was only partially recognized. The issues that created the parties were at once more remote and more superficial than economic questions. Thus it was possible for mercantile Portsmouth and back-woods Deering to form a political alliance against mercantile Exeter and backwoods Holderness.

It was not economic but social conservatism that accounted for New Hampshire's devotion to the Federalist party in 1799. Even though nearly all the voters were freehold farmers, they divided readily into distinct social groups. The gentleman farmers, whose primary interests were in law, trade, speculation, medicine, the pulpit or politics, continued as before to exercise the privileges and obligations of leadership. The genuine farmers, who made their precarious livings from the rocky soil of New Hampshire, continued to be too much absorbed in that effort to meddle with politics. They were inclined by heredity and environment to practice the habit of deference. It need hardly be repeated that the political destiny of New Hampshire after the Revolution was determined by the state of relations between these classes—the leaders and the followers.

The complete unanimity that characterized New Hampshire's attitude on foreign policy in 1799 could only have been achieved by absolute harmony between these two groups in society. Such harmony had been lacking in the 1780s, when the agitation for paper money had created a sharp horizontal cleavage between the poor farmer and the wealthy land-owner. The struggle had continued over the ratification of the federal Constitution, which had been a victory for the upper class, and the adoption of the 1791 amendments to the state constitution, in which the poor farmer was appeased. The domestic policies of Washington's administration had done little to affect the status of social antagonisms in New Hampshire, but the growing prosperity of the country had softened them. Sectional and economic interests could not be entirely erased, but they became increasingly academic. The most illuminating testimonial to the efficacy of this golden influence was the constant reelection of John Taylor Gilman to the chief magistracy, in spite of his vigorous independence and a line of conduct which did not favor the yeoman farmer.

After the issue between federalists and anti-federalists was settled by the adoption of the Constitution, nothing resembling concerted political action by a definite sectional, economic or social group was discernible again until the latter part of Washington's administration. Neither the federalist nor the anti-federalist parties, if they may be called parties, survived the issue that gave them birth. During the following six years, no issue, either in state or national affairs, succeeded in dividing the people into permanent partisan groups. The yeas and nays registered on important votes in the legislature show, for example, that the sections of the state that had no objection to Hamilton's assumption plan were the very ones to remonstrate against the Supreme Court's decision in the *McClary* case, and vice versa. They show also that the voting on both of these issues corresponded not to later political divisions but to what was more nearly a division between wealthy trading areas and poor, remote districts.

The indecisive and contradictory character of New Hampshire's attitude toward national questions between 1789 and 1794 stands in contrast to the growing unanimity of opposition to France and Jacobinism in the succeeding period. In 1794 only 32 determined Federalists had voted against Langdon's reelection to the Senate, but by 1799 the Federalist vote against the Kentucky Resolutions had increased to 140, comprising the entire membership of the house of representatives. Federalism encroached steadily upon the chief Republican strongholds in the Portsmouth area and the Merrimack Valley during these years.

It would be absurd to suppose that the legislature's unanimous stand in support of President Adams meant that every voter in New Hampshire had become a Federalist. It was due primarily to honest indignation against the French Directory's tactless behavior that avowed Republicans as well as Federalists rallied to support the national foreign policy. There was no such agreement on other acts of the federal administration, nor on any question of purely local interest, either between members of the same party or between sections of the state. The same legislature that unanimously rejected Kentucky's nullification proposals divided sharply on the question of increasing taxes for public education. A house which was in complete agreement with Gilman's eulogies of the Jay Treaty in 1795 carried a bill to tax the unimproved lands of nonresident proprietors over the governor's veto by a vote of 96–25.[48] Sectional antagonisms, based upon a variety of economic, social, and geographic interests, were more apparent in state politics than were party programs.

It is a matter of considerable wonder that in the face of so much diversity upon nearly all local issues, the Federalist party maintained so strong a position in New Hampshire until after 1800. But the situation is easily explained by the lack of Republican strength and by the growth of hostility to France. The Republican cause in New Hampshire suffered from a lack of leadership. Goddard and Woodbury Langdon were able men, but they had to struggle almost alone against the combined weight of Gilman, Smith, Freeman, Prentice, Plumer, the Sheafes, the Livermores, and a host of others. A large majority of the lawyers, the Congregationalist clergy, the physicians, the squires, and perhaps also the merchants remained with the Federalist party as they had been with the federalist group in 1788. In other words, the governing class tended to form the Federalist party, and only a small part of the aristocracy became Republican before 1800. Had the yeoman farmer been ever so much disposed toward Republicanism in the 1790s, he would have lacked guidance in his search for it.

A natural consequence of poorly distributed leadership was that neither party developed an organization worthy of the name until after 1800. Since the Federalists enjoyed victory without much effort, they had no need of a machine, while the Republicans lacked the opportunity or the intelligence to create one until after John Langdon came home from the Senate. As in the 1780s, politics continued to be a gentlemanly occupation, or at least an occupation confined to gentlemen, and such matters as nominations and exchanges of support were considered in the light of class privilege. Such had been the tradition of New England for a century and a half. Writing in 1795 to his fiancée, who lived in Maryland, Jeremiah Smith tried to explain the phenomenon. "The phrase 'being a candidate' has not the same meaning here as at the southward. It means with you a person who expresses a desire for an office, solicits votes, perhaps treats the electors. *Here* it only means a person *talked of* for an office; not by himself or particular connections, for in that case he certainly would not be elected."[49]

With no one to solicit his vote, the yeoman farmer remained as indifferent to the blessings of the suffrage in the 1790s as he had been in the 1780s. The annual vote for governor fluctuated between 8,000 and 12,000, rising to the latter height only under the stimulus of XYZ excitement. This represented a little more than one-third of the electorate: the upper third, no doubt, three-fourths of whom were usually willing to vote for Gilman and Adams. This minority represented the articulate portion of the eighteenth-century population—the portion which, by reason of social standing, education, *noblesse oblige*, or a strong sense of duty, attended the town meetings and transacted the state's business. The remaining 65 percent of the electorate looked on with indifference or humble acquiescence. So long as no pressure of any kind was brought to bear, it might have remained indifferent or acquiescent forever. By controlling 75 percent of a 35 percent minority of the electorate, the Federalist party controlled the state like a holding company.

It must be presumed, however, that the silent two-thirds concurred in the policies of their leaders; else they would certainly have used the ballot to effect a political revolution. The Federalist hold on New Hampshire was based upon a remarkable unanimity of public opinion—a cementing of classes such as seldom has occurred in American history. The common bond that united merchants, squires, lawyers, clergymen, farmers, and artisans in support of Federalist foreign policy was hatred of the French Revolution. It was not an economic hostility, except in a very indirect sense, for the only people directly injured by French outrages were the merchants and sailors of Portsmouth, who were most ready to condone them. It was a fear and hatred that went deeper than the pocketbook and aroused the innate social conservatism of all classes.

The deeds of the revolutionists outraged the sense of decency which was so firmly bred into the fiber of Puritan, agrarian New England. One can hardly imagine a scene occurring in New Hampshire such as was reported to have taken place at a banquet in Philadelphia, where each of the diners placed a liberty cap on his head and stabbed the severed head of a pig, emblematic of Louis XVI.[50] The New Hampshire farmer's reaction to the guillotine can be gathered from the simple entry in a Stratham diary for the year 1794. "By News-paper Accounts, Such Destruction was Never before known to be made of mens lives & properties, as has been for a year or two, in France, & the Nations at War; beheading & Murdering their principle Men; and thousands Slain in Battles &c and they by their New invented Masheens, to cut off 6 or 7 Mens Heads at a Blow, Seem to make no more Difficulty in Cutting off their great Mens Heads, than we do of a Sheeps Head."[51]

The impression made upon the mind of a patriarchal farmer in Stratham was no more profound than the horror with which these events were viewed by the greatest genius in New Hampshire at the time. Daniel Webster, still a junior at Dartmouth College, spent a winter evening in 1800 reading Mallet du Pan's *History of the Destruction of the Helvetic Nation*. "I read till I saw Switzerland ravaged and depopulated," he told a friend, "her sons barbarously butchered, and blood flowing in torrents from the side of the Alps! All this I saw done by the intrigue of perfidious France."[52] From the most unlettered to the most cultured minds in New Hampshire, from the lowest ranks in society to the highest, detestation of France grew apace and found political expression in the policies of the Federalist party. The growth of this feeling was summarized as well, perhaps, as anywhere in the speech that Governor Gilman delivered to the legislature in November 1798:

> When we see a foreign nation overturning ancient systems of
> government without any regard to their form, extending robbery
> and devastation as far as their forces can reach; when we see them
> contemning all moral and religious obligation; despising national

compacts; plundering our citizens while in pursuit of lawful commerce; insulting our government, and threatening us with the fate of
nations it has degraded and destroyed; at such a time as this we
should highly prize the blessing of good government, and determine
with one voice and mind to support and defend our rights and
privileges against all hostile attempts whatever. . . . While the
French nation was apparently pursuing measures for the promotion
of liberty, they had the good wishes, at least, of a large proportion
of the citizens of these United States; but unfortunately for our
country they have had much encouragement from the conduct of
many citizens when it seemed almost impossible that anyone should
entertain an idea that the freedom of man was their object; after
they had prostrated governments once free and tyrannized over the
citizens, and after it had become apparent that universal domination
was its object.[53]

Undoubtedly, the most significant phrase in this denunciation was that
which mentioned moral and religious obligation. Any movement which
convinced New Englanders that it was hostile to morals and religion
immediately transcended economic or social questions and became the
paramount peril. The answer of the house of representatives to Gilman's
speech in 1799, although antiphonal as usual, expressed the public attitude in even more vigorous terms:

Well might the citizens of the United States who are so ardently
desirous of liberty and freedom themselves, wish success to the
French nation while endeavouring a reform in their government; but
when she lost sight of her object, driven on by enthusiastic revolutionizing principles, aiming at universal domination, butchering her
own citizens, and the citizens of every other government she by
perfidy and corruption could divide and conquer, trampling on and
despising every civil and religious right, profanely voting the majesty
of heaven out of existence—our feelings revolted, and we turned
indignantly from the scene.[54]

These statements were composed, of course, by Federalist politicians,
with an eye to political advantage. They enjoyed the privilege of being
able to represent their opponents as enemies of morality and religion,
and the satisfaction of being supported so solidly by public opinion that
the Republican leaders could hardly dispute the charge. It was hammered
home by the New Hampshire newspapers, which, until the rise of political parties, had maintained some pretense of impartiality but which had
all become Federalist after 1794. The few Republicans in the state had to
depend on such distant papers as the Boston *Chronicle* for journalism to

their taste. In reply to an article in one of these "foreign" and consequently insidious sheets, the Concord *Courier* wrote: "To hear the partizans of France, and consequently the advocates of confusion and impiety, calling upon the friends of *order* and *religion*, to oppose those measures of Government which are intended to vindicate our rights, lest they provoke the 'terrible Republic' to chastise us, is enough to fire the resentment of the most torpid friend to religion and his country."[55]

The Federalist press played constantly upon the religious prejudices of the people, and in this pursuit no paper was so indefatigable or so successful as the *Newhampshire and Vermont Journal: or The Farmer's Weekly Museum* of Walpole. The contributions of Joseph Dennie, its brilliant editor, who wrote under the pen name of "The Lay Preacher," and of Royall Tyler, witty dramatist and critic, gave this village paper a remarkable circulation far beyond the boundaries of New England and an extensive influence with the yeomanry.[56] "The Lay Preacher" was not the man to ignore the doubtful religious opinions of the head of the Republican party. During the campaign of 1796 he wrote:

> It is whispered, nay it is affirmed with an air of assurance, that such is Mr. Jefferson's admiration of the French, and such his belief of the profligate writings of Voltaire that his mind is tainted with the Deism of France and his confidence weakened in the great truths of Christianity. Now, however indulgently Catholicism might tolerate the closet and speculative skepticism of Jefferson; yet every watchman of the public weal may echo the cry of alarm, should such men be generally talked of, as eligible to sign the laws and guard the morals of his country.[57]

An even more potent force in leading the yeomanry was the pulpit, which joined in the anathemas against France after *The Age of Reason* appeared in 1794. "Tom Paine has kindly cured our clergy of their prejudice," wrote Fisher Ames.[58] Taking advantage of the national Thanksgiving Day proclaimed in February 1795, Congregationalist ministers announced their abhorrence of Jacobinism and their approval of the administration in a barrage of sermons. Their enlistment in the cause was bound to have an immense political effect. They had already led New England, as on crusade, into the Revolution, and their influence was still strong enough to project another holy war against their former ally. To "the clergy . . . in a great measure . . . it is owing . . . that the substantial yeomanry of Massachusetts and New Hampshire have on every late occasion exhibited the most honorable traits of unadulterated Federalism," proclaimed the Boston *Centinel*.[59] Preached before officers of government and assembled guests at each annual meeting of the legislature, the election sermons offered a convenient sounding board for clerical exhortations to vote the Federalist ticket. In 1799, the Reverend Seth Payson of Rindge flew to the defense of the national administration with these words:

> Why is every measure of our Federal Government, though evidently marked with wisdom, and especially every measure calculated for our defence, the object of censure? Why in particular cannot a dangerous alien be required to depart, nor a seditious citizen punished . . . but immediately a cry of unconstitutional oppression is sounded through the Union? And still more to astonish us, we find those very persons who have such a refined sense of the liberties of the subject, and such a jealous concern for the freedom of mankind, approving in the gross all the measures of the French Government— even . . . of that, which compels every citizen to open his doors to customers on the christian Sabbath, however disposed he may be to spend the sacred hours in devotion. And why, we may further ask, are the greatest exertions of the yet firm friends of America, necessary to prevent her from flying, like a fascinated bird, into the ravenous maw of that monster, which has already devoured so many nations, whom she first deceived with her wiles?[60]

On the next such occasion, Noah Worcester of Thornton thought it expedient to warn those deluded citizens who had voted Republican of the possible consequences of their act. "Would it afford you pleasure to see the guillotine erected in your own land?" he inquired. "Would it be to you a delightful employment to be the managers of this deadly machine, or to be the carriers of human blood, in buckets, from morning to evening?"[61] The Calvinist technique for converting Jacobins was not very different from that employed in saving lost sinners. It is worth noting that the Federalism of the pulpit arose not in defense of the capitalist politics of Hamilton but against the threat to the established social order inherent in the French Revolution, a threat that seemed to imperil the small landowner as much as the great one. Thus, in the common front presented by squire and yeoman against France, the minister was the strongest link.

Francophobia encouraged a noticeable resurgence of fanaticism toward the end of the decade. The same legislature that had unanimously upheld President Adams passed without division a more rigid bill to prevent Sunday travel, enabling village tithing men to become little despots on the Sabbath Day.[62] Governor Gilman reduced this legislation to absurdity in the following year. The legislature finished its business on Saturday, June 14, 1800, and informed the governor that it was ready to adjourn. Fearing that some of the lawmakers who lived at a great distance from Concord might be tempted to violate their own statute in their eagerness to get home, Gilman took the unprecedented step of refusing to adjourn them until the following Monday. It is not known whether the Reverend Asa McFarland's congregation at the old meetinghouse was larger than usual on Sunday, June 15, but it is a matter of record that the legislature adjourned promptly after assembling on Monday morning and that the state had been put to $600 extra expense in order to maintain legislative Sabbatarianism.[63]

When the representatives of the people reassembled in November, Governor Gilman thought it necessary to lecture them upon their duty in regard to the "revolutionizing spirit . . . in manners and morals" which threatened to infect New Hampshire. "How important is it," he intoned, "that legislators and magistrates should seriously and deliberately contemplate the precepts they may give, and be equally careful to set a good example to all around them; how important is it to our existence as a free people that morality and religion should be preserved in purity."[64] Perhaps in response to this injunction, a zealous member of the legislature introduced a mandatory bill "for the support of public teachers of religion and morals," which died in committee not because anyone was disposed to weaken religion and morals but because the bill alienated sectarians who were not one whit behind the orthodox in their detestation of France.[65] Thus the legislature added to the general sentiment that the religious braces of society needed tightening if America was not to follow the disastrous course of a nation ruled by deists and atheists.

The Federalism of New Hampshire in 1799 was owing not to economic interests, to an agreement upon national or state domestic policy, or to an absence of class consciousness. It was due, rather, and in spite of the existence of all these divisive forces, to a close union of upper and lower classes upon the single paramount issue of foreign policy, induced by social and religious conservatism. While the state as a whole showed a remarkable diversity on national issues before 1795 and on such domestic questions as judicial reform and the governor's salary, it displayed an incredible unanimity on national issues after 1796. Economic questions, however, continued to find the state divided more or less strictly between an eastern and a western influence. In order to study the interplay of these forces more accurately it might be worthwhile to examine briefly each section of the state.

THE OLD COLONY

The rise of political parties produced a great change in the Old Colony which had been strongly federalist in 1788. While Exeter, Durham, Dover, Barrington, and Nottingham remained generally true to the new Federalism, Portsmouth led the neighboring towns in a great defection over the Jay Treaty and thus split the oldest and wealthiest part of the state into irreconcilable halves. The leadership of Portsmouth, the trading center of New Hampshire, in the Republican cause does not fit into the theory that Federalism was the party of merchants and capitalists. John Langdon and other leaders of the party were merchants who had deprecated the paper-money agitation and supported the federal Constitution. Langdon's biographers have not satisfactorily explained his conversion to Republicanism. Whether it arose from a rekindling of his youthful ardor against England, from an undying admiration for France, from a genuine fear that Washington squinted at monarchy, or from some more personal and consequently more secret reason, one thing at least is certain—he was not a Republican in the egalitarian sense. He frequently expressed contempt for the opinions of the common people and in 1800 welcomed "gentlemen of property and influence" into the ranks of his party.[66] Langdon remained a princely capitalist to the end of his life and, incidentally, became a fervent Congregationalist, finding all this quite compatible with his Republicanism.

Langdon was gifted with some of the arts of a demagogue and the skills of an organizer. The Republican hold on Portsmouth was undoubtedly due to his popularity and the efficiency of his political machine. The apparent source of his strength was the south end, below Buck (now State) Street, where the sailors, artisans, dockworkers, and rope makers were always ready to turn out for a riot or an election.[67] The combination of Republican aristocrats and "the sovereign mob" was strong enough to control every town meeting except in years of unusual public excitement, such as 1795 and 1799, when the Federalists were able to rally enough normally indifferent citizens to outvote the south end. The leadership of the Federalist party in Portsmouth was in the aristocratic tradition, drawn from old merchant families such as the Sheafes, Peirces, and Ladds, together with able young lawyers such as Edward Livermore, attracted by their patronage. They lived in beautiful Georgian houses which gave an air of Old World charm to Portsmouth, and carried on the Tory tradition as best they could in a changing world. But their own class was divided, and it was seldom that they could unite with enough of the "middling" sort to win a victory.

Jealousy of Exeter may have encouraged Republicanism in Portsmouth, for Exeter was the epicenter of Federalism in New Hampshire. The Exeter Junto consisted of an extraordinary collection of men to be gathered within the confines of so small a town. John Taylor Gilman, Jeremiah Smith, Oliver Peabody, Benjamin Connor, and Samuel Tenney were all aristocrats of the sort who have been traditionally assigned to the leadership of the Federalist party. But so also were Nicholas and Nathaniel Gilman, who deserted their older brother to seek after Jeffersonian loaves and fishes. Their influence, however, was small in Exeter, which remained stubbornly Federalist until Federalism had completely disappeared.

Between these two poles of party influence the remaining towns in the Old Colony shifted, as the political currents favored first one and then the other. Each was usually able to control its own senatorial district made up of contiguous towns. Outside its own district Portsmouth was not very effective until after 1800. Politics indeed became something of a sham battle after 1795, when support for the national administration grew so rapidly. On domestic issues, except those which were definitely political, such as increasing Gilman's salary, Portsmouth and Exeter often voted together. Both were willing to increase judicial salaries, to escape taxation of their intangibles, and to incorporate turnpike companies. Both voted against the assumption memorial and in favor of the *McClary* memorial. The Republicans who represented Portsmouth were usually aristocrats, too, and quite as unwilling as the Exeter squires to see their economic interests attacked, even by Merrimack Valley men professing Republican principles.

The remaining towns of importance in the Old Colony—Dover, Rochester, Barrington, Durham, Epping, and Nottingham—were conservative on a majority of the issues of the decade. The smaller and poorer towns, however, such as Atkinson and Sandown of paper-money persuasion, often voted against their wealthier neighbors on economic questions. The ecclesiastical establishment was strongly supported in the Old Colony, only four of its representatives in the constitutional convention showing any marked predilection for reform of that institution. Considered as a whole, the Old Colony can safely be labeled conservative throughout the decade, in spite of Portsmouth's defection.

THE MERRIMACK VALLEY

The chief towns near the river—Londonderry, Concord, Amherst, Chester, Gilmanton, and Sanbornton—voted Federalist in 1800 or in a majority of the years for which records have been found. Londonderry, it appears, definitely abandoned the heresies of paper-money days. Concord frequently voted for its own citizen, Judge Timothy Walker, rather than for Gilman as governor. On a majority of the leading issues of the decade these towns voted conservatively, but not with the consistency that characterized Exeter. The river towns were joined in the elections by a block of towns stretching across the southern boundary of the state, including Hollis, New Ipswich, and Peterborough. Most of these had originally been settled by Massachusetts. But the remaining towns of the interior region, from Fishersfield and Hopkinton to Francestown and New Boston, voted Republican, at least in 1800. This occasional pattern of a Federalist reversed L along the river and the southern border and a Republican inner angle became stabilized in later years. It was only approximately repeated, however, in the legislature. The area was slightly more liberal than the Old Colony on issues of religious freedom. Economic issues tended to throw a majority of the Merrimack Valley towns against the Old Colony, although with some surprising variations, such as the little hill town of Deering voting against relief from taxation of rural property and Amherst voting against all projects of judicial reform. In 1800 the Merrimack Valley was neither disposed to act as a unit nor certain of how it should divide.

THE CONNECTICUT VALLEY

In politics the Connecticut Valley was more firmly united in Federalism than it had been in favor of the federal Constitution. Cheshire and Grafton counties, stretching along the river bank, became notable strongholds of conservatism at a time when the Old Colony was being shaken by Republican incursions. On matters that did not immediately affect their pocketbooks—that is to say, on national issues, religious freedom, judicial reform, turnpikes, and the general encouragement of economic growth—the valley towns maintained a high degree of conformity with Exeter. But on measures that might have added to their own economic burdens, such as the increase of salaries, both judicial and gubernatorial, and taxation, the Connecticut Valley delegates lost cohesion and voted every man for himself. It is particularly noticeable that the interior towns, six miles or more from the river, tended on many occasions to split away from the towns occupying the rich intervale, although Hanover, Walpole, and Chesterfield showed an equal reluctance to spend money.

This surprising paradox of political Federalism and economic Democracy was actually more consistent than its obverse in Portsmouth. The Connecticut Valley's Federalism was born in Connecticut and was attributable, as in its birthplace, to "steady habits." But economically, the valley towns were strictly agricultural and only a little way removed from the frontier stage. Consequently, while Governor Gilman on more than one occasion had this long stretch of transplanted Connecticut to thank for the majorities that placed him in office, he was also doomed frequently to see the projects of his own class and section defeated by its remote influence.

THE FRONTIER

Little information exists to show how the frontier towns voted before 1800, but in that year, at least, they divided almost precisely along the boundary line of Grafton County, the eastern towns voting the Republican ticket and the western towns Federalist. That division, however, had little significance in matters other than politics. So far as economic questions were concerned, the Frontier, like the Connecticut Valley, seemed to favor the expenditure of other people's money but not of its own. This is not difficult to understand in view of the frontier's typical prejudices against absentee landlords and conspicuous luxuries. Nor is it surprising to find the Frontier, where new religious sects flourished, voting more consistently than any other section for religious liberty.

The absence of political uniformity on the frontier was probably due to several factors. After the Revolutionary War settlers on the New Hampshire borderlands tended to move as individuals or families rather than in the traditional New England manner as community groups. The typical town institutions, therefore, particularly the Congregationalist church, failed to appear in many frontier towns until long after they were settled. The scattered farmers were less subject to the influence of the gentry and might consequently be more susceptible to Republican professions of love for the plain people. Yet the frontier was an area in which wealthy speculators held great areas of land, often as much as two-thirds of an entire town. When such a proprietor elected to move to the frontier and live among his tenants, as did Samuel Livermore, he became something of a feudal baron with considerable influence over the politics of his neighbors. More often than not, men of this character represented groups of small towns in the legislature and were certainly less responsible to their constituents than were the representatives of older and better-organized towns. Their votes, on many occasions, may have been completely at variance with the wishes of their fellow townsmen. Finally, voters who migrated to the frontier after 1793 probably carried their political prejudices with them and remained Federalists or Republicans in their new homes in spite of environmental incongruities. Political divisions probably had less real significance on the Frontier than in any of the older regions.

CHAPTER 10

FEDERALIST DECLINE

It is a humiliating circumstance, when a man is conscious he has devoted his time, talents, & money to the public service, & faithfully discharged his duty, to find it difficult to obtain a re-election to an expensive & laborious office. —William Plumer

The newspaper editor who thought that the remarkable unanimity of New Hampshire in 1799 presaged a "new era" in politics was a true prophet.[1] His only error was in assigning to the Federalists, rather than to their opponents, the fruits of this golden age. Though his party then stood at the pinnacle of its five-year climb to success, the succeeding five years were to witness its inexorable descent to a position of apparent hopelessness. Within an even shorter time Federalism was destined to be repudiated by the country at large. It was natural that a four-year lag should occur between the national triumph of the Republicans and their victory in so conservative a state as New Hampshire, but the two reversals were part of the same process. In state as well as nation, Federalist arrogance, over-confidence, abuse of power, and internal dissension were contributing causes to the debacle. Federalist responsibility for heavy taxation, extravagant expenditures, and judicial tyranny, together with Republican promises of democracy, economy, liberty, and peace, affected New Hampshire farmers as surely as it did the backwoodsmen of Kentucky, if more slowly.

Federalists resisted the Republican zeitgeist, but their reign might have been longer if they had fought less strenuously. They were much to blame for their own defeat. During ten years in the saddle the Federalists managed to convince the people of New Hampshire that their continued control of the government would stifle any change toward democracy, deny religious toleration, maintain an expensive administration that favored speculators, and subject them to the total political and financial domination of the Exeter Junto.

Their defiance of France had made the Federalists popular, but the means they adopted to implement that defiance evoked less enthusiasm. "Millions for Defense" proved to be an embarrassing motto after France had backed down and there was nothing left of the glorious dreams of victory but expensive armaments and burdensome taxes. New Hampshire farmers who had signed addresses of commendation to President Adams looked dourly upon his tax collectors. There was some resistance in the town of Weare to federal appraisers; the stamp tax aroused unpleasant memories; and men who accepted appointments to offices created by the new federal laws, such as Joshua Atherton, found their positions uncomfortable.[2] A recruiting party for the frigate U.S.S. *Constitution* was assaulted by a gang of tough sailors in the streets of Portsmouth, and citizens who had been erroneously prosecuted for nonpayment of the carriage tax complained because the United States would not allow itself to be charged for defendants' costs.[3] These were straws in the wind, appearing while New Hampshire legislatures were voting unanimous approval of federal policy, but the Republicans were not so foolish as to overlook them.

The Federalists were much more vulnerable to criticism in their conduct of state affairs than in their support of the national administration against France. They were led by their own theories of government, as well as by their native arrogance, to reject any further democratization of the electoral machinery, believing that the constitutional amendments of 1792 had already carried things too far in that direction. Republican leaders such as the Langdons, who were not a whit less aristocratic than any Federalist, shrewdly exploited this issue by constantly championing reform. Throughout the decade from 1790 Republican legislators had proposed a division of the state into districts for the election of United States representatives and presidential electors. Their control of the first senatorial district made them reasonably certain that by such a division they could elect one congressman and guarantee one electoral vote for Jefferson, but their motive proclaimed for public consumption was a desire to associate public officials more intimately with the voters who elected them. Each such Republican proposal was crushed by a strong Federalist majority, but received consistent support from some Federalist areas.[4] In 1799 such a Republican proposal received twenty-two votes— a poor showing, but significant when compared with the zero that appeared against the legislature's reply to the Kentucky and Virginia resolutions.[5]

The Federalists increased the danger of this situation by clinging to Exeter as the state capital, thus feeding the flame of sectional animosity, which had almost been extinguished by the French crisis. With the governor, the secretary, and the treasurer all resident in Exeter, Republicans could dramatize their claim that the proud little village monopolized the state government to the injury of larger and more centrally located towns. Every session of the legislature witnessed a struggle between half a dozen aspiring hamlets to entertain the ensuing session, and on these votes the Federalist members divided according to their local interests. In 1796 the Federalist newspaper at Concord had struck a double blow at the legislators for voting increases in their own wages and for holding the winter session at Exeter rather than Concord, thus vastly increasing the cost of travel. By this single act the state lost $1,475, according to the *Courier of New Hampshire*.[6] In 1800 the Portsmouth leaders, who would still personally have preferred to bring the capital back to the seacoast, supported a motion to remove the treasurer's office to Concord and secured more than a third of the votes in its favor.[7]

Unquestionably, though, the greatest mistake that the Federalists made in state politics was to allow their opponents to maneuver them into an appearance of ruthless capitalism. In 1799, John Langdon and the other wealthy "Jacobins" in Portsmouth organized the Union Bank, issued notes, and then applied to the legislature for incorporation. This was the second bank to appear in New Hampshire. The Federalist stockholders of the first one, the New Hampshire Bank of Portsmouth, headed by its president, Oliver Peabody, who was also the state treasurer, hastily presented a countermemorial asking not only that the Union Bank's petition be dismissed but that a law be passed to restrain unincorporated institutions from issuing notes. A committee of the house reported precisely in accordance with the wishes of the Peabody memorialists. Up to this point the confident Federalist machine had functioned perfectly, but the next vote brought a rude awakening. The recommendation to dismiss Langdon's petition was carried, although 43 votes were registered against the 89 faithful partisans, but the report in favor of the desired restraining bill was actually defeated, 61–66.[8] The unanimous 137 votes of June 2 had disappeared.

Governor Gilman hastily called a meeting of the Federalist caucus at his house after dinner to discuss the difficult situation. To grant a charter to the Union Bank would be akin to arming the enemy, but to refuse would certainly be an act of partisan politics, which the people, constantly complaining about the chronic shortage of money, would probably not forgive. In addition, there were even darker shadows in the picture. Governor Gilman, Treasurer Peabody, and other prominent Federalist officeholders were heavy stockholders in the old bank. If they used their political power to crush the new one, even from the purest motives of devotion to the state's interest, they would be accused of callow selfishness. The New Hampshire Bank had not been a partisan corporation, for Sherburne and even Langdon himself had been stockholders, but it had largely confined its services to merchants and wealthy landowners. Thus, the Republicans could now easily stigmatize it as a political weapon of the monocrats.

As a matter of fact, Langdon and his friends had been pursuing exactly that course and making no secret of the political nature of their own institution. They had created a formidable organization. Their bank was capitalized for twice the amount of the stock in the New Hampshire

Bank, and the shares were sold in smaller denominations and scattered as widely as possible throughout the state.⁹ The Union Bank made loans on easy terms, particularly to the middle class of farmers, who had been able to "obtain little or no accomodation" from the older bank, and with each loan the new bankers were said to retail gratuitously "the grossest abuse against every officer of government." The mischief had already "spread like a pestilence," as was plainly to be seen in those sixty-six Federalists who voted against Peabody's bill. "It was vain to inform them that it was a Jacobin scheme and they were aiming a blow at the government, the answer was 'there are as many federalists as Jacobins concerned.'" To the dismayed Federalist captains, gathered in secret conclave at Governor Gilman's fireside, it was all too apparent that Langdon's bank was "*a* POLITICAL MACHINE, *and that it would ruin the Politics of the State.*"¹⁰

Some Federalists advocated compromise—for the sake of party supremacy to refuse incorporation to the Union Bank, but for the ease of "accomodation" to allow it to function without incorporation. Gilman and Peabody, however, insisted upon firm adherence to party discipline, and the caucus was finally whipped into line. Consequently, a bill to prohibit unincorporated banks was introduced in the senate, passed by a strong majority, and sent down to the house, which had already rejected the principle on which it was founded. "While the business was pending in this situation," wrote an indignant Republican five years later, "a field was opened for vast intrigue and influence to be exercised on the part of the *interested* proprietors of the *N. H. Bank*, upon members in that body in favor of the bill from the senate. And the field was by no means neglected."¹¹ Gilman was accused of bribing some members with offices and threatening others with pecuniary embarrassment, while his friends asserted that he had nothing to do with the legislature's decisions. Whatever the inducements may have been, there is no question but that at least twenty-one members changed their minds, for the measure which had been rejected earlier by five votes was now accepted, 87–45.¹²

The passage of this bill was probably worth more to John Langdon than an incorporation of his bank. He could send his runners throughout the state with copies of the legislative journals in their saddlebags, asking pointed questions about the conduct of Governor Gilman. "Can it be wise," asked the Republicans, "to place a man in so high and consequential a station, who is willing to make use of the *necessities* of men for *political* purposes, and through *Bank influence* control the politics of the state—who seeks to bind men to government, by their *pecuniary wants*, rather than by the nobler sentiment of FREEDOM?"¹³

Flushed with success and blind to the trap they were digging for themselves, the Exeter politicians now determined to clinch their victory over the Union Bank. At the very end of the session a resolution came down from the senate authorizing the treasurer to purchase twenty-four more shares in the New Hampshire Bank for the use of the state. "The conductors of this arch maneuver certainly deserve credit for their *management*," wrote a Republican editor. "A greater piece of *finesse* was never witnessed in this state—for thus a junto of individuals, at one stroke, benefited both their POLITICS and their PURSES—at least, as they then imagined."[14] This last phrase was appropriate, for by this final act the Federalist politicians destroyed whatever claims to disinterestedness they might have professed in their assault upon the Union Bank. Their opponents quickly pointed out that the purpose of the bill was to give the government so great a financial interest in the old bank that it would never charter a new one, thus assuring the Federalist moneylenders a monopoly in New Hampshire. The fact that the stock, which was selling at a high premium in the market, was offered to the state at par and that the bank was to allow the state the unusual privilege of liquidation at will pointed unmistakably to the political character of the deal. Nor was it justified as an investment when it necessitated additional taxes. The $27,000 tax bill for 1799 indicated that the money invested in bank shares did not represent an idle surplus in the treasury. The entire transaction was in fact such an obvious piece of jobbery that the moderate Federalists turned against it, and it passed the house only by the narrow margin of seven votes.[15]

It is unlikely that the Federalists could have handled the problem of the Union Bank in more disastrous fashion. Even if they had been content with denying Langdon's bank a charter and passing a restraining act, they would have furnished their enemies with strong weapons but they could at least have claimed that such measures were for the protection of the people. Their renewed purchase of New Hampshire bank stock, however, was indefensible. In view of their vulnerability, it would have been expedient for the Federalist stockholders to have allowed the incorporation of the Union Bank and then to have neutralized its political influence by shrewd use of their own institution. But such compliance with the principles of free competition was psychologically impossible for men who had been accustomed to command and to be obeyed, not to say venerated, by their mental inferiors. Since both their personal and their social fortunes were endangered by this new "diabolical" invention of the Jacobins, it was inevitable that they should attack it with their customary arrogance—inevitable too, but fatal, that they carried their counteroffensive too far. The Republicans could not only pose as martyrs to their tyranny but suggest to the common voter that he, too, was being sacrificed to the Moloch of Exeter. They could ask the Hillsborough farmer, "Are you willing to contribute your cash to send down to *Exeter* and *Portsmouth*, for the use of a few private gentlemen there, to speculate with and make their 20, 30, 50 and 100 per cent by its use, allowing you but 6 in return? And in addition to this, are you willing to be taxed to furnish the means of over-awing your own free born minds and binding you in servitude to the policy of a faction?"[16]

Republicans prepared for the elections of 1800 as their Year of Jubilee, while Federalists thought that the contest more nearly resembled Armageddon.[17] Though unincorporated, the Union Bank was still a powerful battering ram for the opposition. It discounted liberally for those who were disposed to enlist in the Republican ranks, and it presented so many New Hampshire Bank bills for collection that the vaults of the pet bank were drained and future bills had to be issued payable at Philadelphia rather than in Portsmouth. The Democratic runners denounced the army, the navy, direct taxes, Alien and Sedition Laws, high salaries (Gilman had asked twice again in 1799 for a raise), and, most of all, the scandalous conduct of the legislature in regard to the Union Bank.[18]

February and March saw the first really vigorous party contest in state history. The Republicans demonstrated their political sagacity and their newfound discipline by supporting Judge Timothy Walker of Concord against Governor Gilman. A "real Jacobin" like Goddard or Woodbury Langdon would hardly have received a vote outside the Portsmouth neighborhood, but Walker cut Gilman's majority from 86 percent to a little less than 62 percent of the votes.[19] Judge Walker attracted a moderate Federalist element as well as the whole Republican electorate. He had been considered a Federalist since the days of the ratifying convention and as a Federalist elector had voted for Adams in 1796. A citizen of Concord, he drew western votes away from the Exeter oligarchs. He favored incorporation of the Union Bank, and during the January session of his court in Portsmouth, according to a Federalist writer, he was frequently invited to dine "where a man would no more expect to get a dinner, than he would 'a beard in the palm of his hand' if he was not a notorious and professed Jacobin."[20] Walker posed in the campaign as a republican Federalist, but the enraged party leaders repudiated him. "If his soul was drawn at full length on the point of a cambrick needle, to discover it, would require the aid of a microscope," grumbled William Plumer.[21] France and Jefferson were still feared in 1800, and the Federalists held firm in New Hampshire. Walker received the greater part of his support from the Old Colony and the Merrimack Valley, but even in Concord his majority over Gilman was only 20 out of 234 votes cast.[22] The final count gave Walker 6,039, Gilman 10,362.

The Union Bank issue, however, had damaged the Federalist cause. Plumer was reelected to the legislature from Epping, where probank sentiment was high, by only two votes. In four of the twelve senatorial districts no candidate obtained a popular majority, and Rockingham County failed to elect a councillor for the same reason. The Federalist majority in the legislature, by a disciplined vote of 126 to 24, filled all these vacancies with their own partisans, going down in some cases to the candidate who stood second or third in popular favor.

Nevertheless, the Republicans had recovered from their setbacks of 1799 at least in Portsmouth, which sent Goddard, Woodbury Langdon, and Drowne to the house of representatives again. Goddard was a host within himself—a man who had been a successful physician and was now an even more successful merchant—"a man of handsome talents, good address, loquacious, & jesuitical."[23] He opened the Republican offensive with a memorial from the proprietors of the Union Bank praying either for an act of incorporation or for the repeal of the law prohibiting unincorporated banks from issuing notes. The Federalist majority on the committee to which this memorial was referred recommended that the memorialists have leave to withdraw their petition—in other words, that it be rejected. This precipitated a vindictive debate in which Goddard lost his temper and Plumer delivered an extemporaneous philippic against banks in general, the Union Bank in particular, and the politicians who were using it for their evil purposes. Ultimately, the committee's report was accepted, 86–59, an ominous increase of nine votes in favor of the Union Bank and all from new members of the house.[24]

Nevertheless, the Federalists had an irreducible majority of some thirty votes, which they used like a bludgeon to impose their will upon the state. John Langdon's term in the Senate was soon to expire, and his implacable foes no longer harbored any sentimental admiration for his revolutionary services. Brushing aside Republican efforts to postpone the election or to distribute the Federalist vote among several favorite sons, the bloc of eighty-seven in the house nominated James Sheafe, a Portsmouth merchant and ex-Tory, to replace John Langdon, the Portsmouth merchant and ex-federalist. Langdon received only twelve votes. The senate concurred in Sheafe's election by ten votes to two, and on March 4, 1801, he took the Senate seat that Langdon had occupied for twelve years.

The New Hampshire delegation in Congress was now unanimously Federalist. In order to preserve its unity the party leaders took unusual measures to elect the right men to the House of Representatives in August. Defying the dangerous publicity that was sure to follow, a caucus of sixty-six Federalist representatives met to nominate a party ticket—perhaps the first time that the dominant party had done so. Four stalwart but undistinguished gentlemen, judiciously drawn from the four sections of the state, were nominated for Congress.

When it came to the choice of presidential electors, the Federalist tacticians left nothing to chance. Since the first election in 1788 New Hampshire had allowed its voters to choose presidential electors on a general ticket, subject to final selection by the legislature if the people failed to make a choice. Together with Massachusetts, which had formed electoral districts, the state had given far more scope to the popular voice than had the Republican South. But in the critical year 1800 there was a general disposition, both North and South, to remove this important matter from the whims of popular fancy and to bring it under strict party control. Virginia changed from district elections to a general ticket, Georgia and Pennsylvania from the general ticket to choice by the legislatures.[25]

By these regressions from democracy, John Adams would certainly lose electoral votes outside New England, and the Yankee politicians were not loath to restore some of them by the same means. Harrison Gray Otis had persuaded the Massachusetts legislature in April to assume the power of naming presidential electors, and the New Hampshire Federalists determined to follow that example.[26] Ignoring the precedents set by their fellow Republicans in half the states of the Union, Goddard and Langdon complained that such a measure would be unconstitutional and would deprive the people of their natural rights. Federalists answered simply with the indubitable fact that the Constitution gave every state legislature the right to choose electors any way it pleased. So the bill passed, but the Federalist majority was whittled down to *seventeen*, with the Old Colony and the Merrimack Valley showing hostile majorities.[27]

This legislation was a piece of gratuitous folly typical of the Federalist inability to trust the people. The effect was bad not because it was unconstitutional (it was not) or even undemocratic (it was) but because it was unnecessary and inexpedient. There is hardly room to doubt that the New Hampshire voters would have chosen Adams electors, but the Federalist legislature feared treachery and the ignorance of the people. The few voters who customarily turned out for the town meetings in November at which the electors were chosen usually voted for one local favorite and five other prominent gentlemen whom they knew by reputation. It was hoped that these six men would vote for Jefferson and Burr, or for Adams and Pinckney, as the case might be, but there was no guarantee that they would. Judge Walker, for example, had cast an electoral vote for Adams in 1796 and still called himself a "federalist," but he had run on the Republican ticket for governor in March. Confused voters might readily have chosen him as a Federalist elector in November, only to see him cast a vote for Jefferson. Under these uncertain conditions, the Federalist legislators preferred to assume that they should express the popular will, rather than organize a disciplined electoral ticket and campaign for its success. By the electoral law of 1800, however, Federalist as well as Republican citizens were deprived of a privilege previously enjoyed. Even though the privilege had not been much exercised, frugal Yankees did not like to lose it. By this act of political highway robbery the Federalists antagonized men upon whom their fate depended.

At the same time that the Federalists changed the political system in order to protect privilege they determined to resist other changes that might threaten it. The original division of the state into senatorial districts had been made in 1792 before parties had been distinctly formed; consequently, they had been based upon pragmatic principles, modified somewhat by local interests. As parties developed and conditions changed during the next eight years, the districts became economically unbalanced and took on the character of a slight Federalist gerrymander. The Republicans, of course, introduced annual resolutions to redistrict the state, and the Federalists annually buried them in committee. In 1800, however, the committee, even with a Federalist majority, decided that the proposal had merit and actually reported out a redistricting bill, which passed the house but was killed in the senate.[28] The stronghold of privilege thus held firm against even a slight concession to democracy.

Federalist discipline in the November session of the legislature prevailed over an attempt to make Walker an elector, and six safe Adams men were chosen.[29] By the end of the year, however, it had become certain that New Hampshire's votes for Adams and Pinckney would be in vain. In January Federalists opened their copies of the *Columbian Centinel* and read with sorrowful agreement a requiem upon the fate of their party. "The period has at last arrived, so often predicted and so justly dreaded from the increase of the force and virulence of faction, in which our happy constitution is surrendered into the hands of its avowed enemies."[30]

New Hampshire's representatives were deeply involved in the desperate attempt to prevent Jefferson's election by elevating Burr to the presidency. On every one of the thirty-six ballots taken in the House of Representatives, even the last one, New Hampshire's four Federalist delegates voted solidly for Burr.[31] Even after the failure of the Burr plot, the Federalists tried to preserve a saving remnant of their system by entrenching themselves in the judiciary—a policy which was to have a considerable bearing upon the careers of several New Hampshire notables. Jeremiah Smith was appointed to one of the circuit judgeships newly created under the Judiciary Act of 1801, and Edward St. Loe Livermore was given a midnight appointment as federal district attorney. Livermore did not long enjoy the emoluments of office, though, for he was promptly removed by President Jefferson and replaced by John Samuel Sherburne. "Are you so unreasonable as to expect an impure fountain will send forth sweet water?" wrote a sarcastic friend to the erstwhile prosecutor.[32]

The New Hampshire Republicans were as elated as the Federalists were depressed by the Republican national victory. Woodbury Langdon's daughter-in-law wrote in a tone of triumphant mockery, "The Jacobins are in high spirits. Mr. Gardner talks of giving or having a ball in consequence of Mr. J———'s election. . . . All the gentlemen of respectability—that is, all the republicans—met at the Sedition Office, or more properly the new Bank, Saturday evening . . . to plan business for the March meeting."[33] Ex-senator Langdon was quite content to leave Washington, even though President Jefferson begged him to remain and preside over the downgrading of the Naval Department. He found a more congenial occupation in returning to the New Hampshire house of representatives and infusing real energy into the local opposition. It is a curious fact that at the moment that the New Hampshire delegation to Congress became completely Federalist it also became part of a hopeless minority, while the lone Republican who had remained at the national capital during the entire twelve years of Federalist supremacy was now removed in the instant of his party's triumph.

It seemed to the local Federalists that Langdon brought a deadly infection of Jeffersonian plague with him from Washington. Republicans began bidding for the old paper-money vote in the farming communities by statements that incorporation of the Union Bank would double the quantity of money in circulation and make it easier for every man to pay his debts. Federalist pessimism was, however, a bit premature. Gilman's majority over Walker for the governorship in 1801 was greater than in 1800, and the Federalists won another comfortable majority in the house of representatives. This enabled them to fill four undetermined seats in the senate with faithful partisans and then to reelect Joseph Blanchard over Levi Bartlett as councillor for Rockingham County by thirty-six votes.[34] John Langdon, however, came within one vote of winning the speakership over John Prentice. The Federalists also encountered some difficulty in electing a senator to fill the vacancy caused by the resignation of septuagenarian Samuel Livermore. There was some sentiment for William Plumer, but the Connecticut Valley faithful insisted upon Simeon Olcott, the ineffectual chief justice of the superior court, and refused to vote for any other candidate. Plumer willingly released his supporters, but Olcott was not an impressive candidate, and it was only by a slender majority of eleven that he was elected.[35]

An advantage in Olcott's election that must have carried some weight was that it left a vacancy at the head of the New Hampshire bench which could be filled by a better man. The entire Federalist leadership turned to Jeremiah Smith for this post in the almost certain event that Congress abolished his circuit court. Pending this outcome, Governor Gilman promoted Judge Farrar to be chief justice, and that exemplary man, with astonishing unselfishness, presided in the court without accepting his new commission until Smith was free to replace him.[36] More amazing still was the legislature's willingness to raise the salary to one thousand dollars in order to induce Smith to accept the appointment.[37] The superior court, now consisting of Smith, Arthur Livermore, Paine Wingate, and William King Atkinson, became a respectable body, capable of maintaining constitutional principles in New Hampshire, as the Supreme Court was to do for the nation.

Judicial restraint might well have been needed, for from the Federalist point of view things did not go well during the single session of 1801. The Union Bank proprietors returned to the attack, and convinced that their opposition would soon be unavailing, some of the rank-and-file Federalists were for extracting what advantage they could out of granting what would ultimately be obtained without their consent. But Plumer, Gilman, and Connor advocated war to the bitter end, and the issue was fought all over again on the floor of the house. A bill of incorporation passed, 84–60, but was defeated by the adverse vote of seven senators, three of whom owed their seats to the Federalist majority in the house.[38] Near the end of the session the Union Bank men presented a bill to exempt their institution from the restraining act of 1799. This was a peculiarly offensive proposal, and it sparked an angry debate in which the Federalist stockholders of the New Hampshire Bank complained that Jefferson had removed federal deposits from their vaults to Boston.[39] In spite of such remonstrances this bill also passed the house and went on to its rendezvous with death in the senate, where the faithful seven again administered the coup de grace. The annual Republican bill for reapportionment of the senate followed exactly the same course.

Against these narrow escapes from defeat, the Federalists won a few solid victories. They transferred the state's printing business from the office of the *New Hampshire Gazette*, which had just been bought out by Republicans, to the printer of the *Courier of New Hampshire*, a staunch Federalist organ. There was laid before the house a letter from the Maryland legislature proposing an amendment to the Constitution which would prevent a repetition of the Burr episode. Such an amendment had been proposed by the New Hampshire legislature itself in 1798 after Jefferson had come uncomfortably close to stealing the presidency from Adams, but the shoe was on the other foot now and the Federalists postponed consideration. In spite of those minor victories, it is significant that three important bills vigorously opposed by the strongest men in the Federalist party had passed the house of representatives by majorities of twenty-eight, twenty-four, and sixteen.[40]

Far more discouraging to the Federalists than these aberrations at home was the destruction of good government which they imagined to be taking place in Washington. After nearly a year of the Jeffersonian revolution, Congressman Tenney wrote to a constituent that "the oeconomy so much vaunted at present by our federal rulers, & so much praised by their friends, is *really a fine* thing tis an *excellent crutch* to support a weak administration; as a cry of extravagance was a *mighty club* to knock down a vigorous one."[41] Some of the Jeffersonian measures struck close to home. Post roads that had been opened by the Adams administration were closed for the sake of economy, and recently commissioned federal officers were quickly deprived of their jobs.[42] Jefferson cleaned out the old Tories whom Adams had installed at Portsmouth harbor and reinstated the former "notorious Jacobins."[43] Furthermore, by the repeal of the Judiciary Act of 1801, the Republican Congress destroyed the federal circuit court to which Jeremiah Smith had been appointed—an office of which he was thus summarily and, in the opinion of all good Federalists, unconstitutionally deprived. "It appears that the President, & a majority of Congress, take peculiar pleasure in demolishing the works of Washington, Adams, & their compeers," wrote Plumer.[44]

Langdon himself became the Republican candidate for governor in 1802, and many Federalists feared that his energy and popularity spelled doom for Gilman. "The Demo's *rise up early, sit up late, & eat the bread of carefulness,*" one alarmed party worker reminded another.[45] Although this Republican zeal did not quite achieve success, it produced tremendous gains, especially in the Old Colony and the Merrimack Valley. Excitement generated by Langdon's entry into the contest, together with the increased efficiency of the Republican machine, brought out 2,500 new voters. Gilman lost only 521 votes to his rival, but Langdon received 3,504 more votes than Walker had attracted in 1801.[46] President Jefferson wrote to Langdon in enthusiasm for this rush toward democracy: "Although we have not yet got a majority into the fold of republicanism in your state, yet one long pull more will effect it. We can hardly doubt that one twelvemonth more will give an executive & legislature in that state whose opinions may harmonize with their sister states, unless it be true as is sometimes said that N.H. is but a satellite of Massachusetts."[47]

The Federalists retained majorities in both houses of the legislature, but Levi Bartlett's victory in Rockingham County finally introduced Republicanism into the council. Gilman met the legislature in a conciliatory mood and suggested that the arrival of peace in Europe was an auspicious moment to patch up quarrels at home. The reply of the house of representatives included the usual warnings against innovations and foreign influence, but was couched in such pleasant generalities that even Langdon voted to accept it. The Federalists were able to pass their bill for raising the salaries of superior court judges by a majority of 73 to 66, but the long struggle over the Union Bank was ended by an act of incorporation which passed the house without a division and the senate, 8–3, with two Federalist senators voting in its favor.[48]

This political ambivalence was also illustrated by the legislature's action in dealing with the sudden resignation of James Sheafe after only one year in the United States Senate—the fifth such desertion of a Washington post by a New Hampshire Federalist within three years. Faced with this unexpected emergency, the Federalist caucus nominated William Plumer as their candidate—a choice not altogether popular with the Exeter Junto. The Republicans shrewdly sought to capitalize on the strain of this situation by selecting as their candidate Nicholas Gilman, younger brother of the governor and a man of indeterminate politics. Plumer was not present during this session of the legislature, but his friends supported him strongly, and the embarrassed Exeter representatives finally decided that they had to vote for "a man of decided principles" and "of talents for business" rather than "a mere gallant for the city Belles."[49]

Thus united, almost by necessity, the Federalists elected Plumer to the Senate on the last day of the session, thereby provoking a bitter attack by Nicholas Gilman upon their honesty and consistency.[50] A Republican newspaper, equally indignant, declared that the state had truly fallen upon strange times. "It cannot escape the notice of the Citizens of New-Hampshire, (who are nearly all republicans) that this is the second or third anti-revolutionary character which has been elected by a small majority in the General Court, to the Senate of the U. States, within the space of one short year!"[51] The *Republican Gazette*, however, had not counted noses very accurately, for in August these citizens came to their town meetings and reelected the four Federalist congressmen, thus guaranteeing New Hampshire a solid Federalist representation in Washington for at least another two years. The Jeffersonians were dominant in the national capital and everywhere south of the Potomac, but they were not yet triumphant in New England.

CHAPTER 11

THE OLD ORDER
YIELDETH

That manufactures, to a certain extent, will be useful to our country
& profitable to the owners cannot be doubted, but I am inclined to think
at this time we are pressing too fast into them, both for the interest of
the country & that of the proprietors. —William Plumer

New Hampshire grew in population during the years between the first census and the fourth but not quite as rapidly as the nation.[1] In 1790 the northernmost state had comprised 3.6 percent of the total population and was tenth in size among the thirteen states; but by 1820 it contained only 2.5 percent of the people and had dropped to fifteenth place among the twenty-seven states and territories.[2] Yet New Hampshire had grown by 72 percent in these thirty years. The distribution and significance of this increase may be seen in Table 11-1.[3]

Every section of the state participated in this advance, although the more recently settled areas of course made the greater proportional gains. During these decades, New Hampshire was still in the "summer" of its development, beckoning the surplus population of southern New England to cheap farms and economic independence.[4] The competition of western soil had as yet diverted only a part of that copious stream of Yankee emigration from the empty land on its own borders. Edward St. Loe Livermore, who visited the Ohio country in 1816 to inspect some of his land purchases, wrote in great disillusionment that "while the people in Mass. and N.H. can so easily obtain lands at home where they are both acquainted with soil climate and productions they are great fools if they emigrate to any of these places."[5] New Hampshire farms still played a part in the dreams of European immigrants. An English cobbler who had settled on a farm in Merrimack wrote in 1821 to a friend still in England, painting the country in glowing colors and stressing the independence that he enjoyed. "I assure you I have made every possible enquiry," he concluded, "and can safely invite you to this happy country."[6]

The constant increase in population and particularly the filling in of the frontier spaces is vividly shown by a comparison of population maps of 1775 and 1820. (See Maps 2 and 21).[7] While Portsmouth was the only

TABLE 11-1

	Population 1790	Total Population 1790 (percentage)	Population 1800	Total Population 1800 (percentage)	Increase since 1790 (percentage)	Population 1820	Total Population 1820 (percentage)	Increase since 1800 (percentage)	Increase since 1790 (percentage)
Old Colony	38,674	27.2	39,893	21.7	3.15	50,143	20.5	25.7	29.
Merrimack Valley	53,509	37.7	69,131	37.6	29.1	86,895	35.6	25.7	62.
Connecticut Valley	38,436	27.1	53,967	29.4	40.4	68,636	28.1	27.1	78.
Frontier	11,399	8.0	20,867	11.3	83.0	38,487	15.8	84.4	237.
Total	142,018		183,858		29.5	244,161		32.7	71.

town with more than three thousand inhabitants in 1775, Gilmanton, Sanbornton, and Londonderry had joined this company by 1820, and twenty-one other towns had more than two thousand, the criterion of urban status. Yet this growing density of population, in the old towns as well as the new ones, was primarily an agricultural phenomenon. The most rural section of all, the Frontier, made by far the greatest relative advance, a fact which was reluctantly recognized by the older towns in the creation of Coös County in 1805. New Hampshire's rural population continued to climb steadily until 1840, when the inevitable decline set in.

A closer examination of maps and charts, however, reveals at least the shadow of changes to come in New Hampshire's population pattern. The rate of increase for the twenty-year period 1800–1820 was only a little greater than it had been for the single decade 1790–1800. The Granite State's forward march had already begun to slow down and was destined to come to a complete halt by 1860.[8] Even more significant is the fact that the rate of growth in the three newer sections of the state—the two river valleys and the Frontier—was less during the last two decades than in the first. Manufacturing in the tiny mills along the fall line in the Old Colony had already begun to develop a greater drawing power than the rocky hillside farms of the north. Even within the Old Colony the rapid growth benefited a few towns at the expense of many others. No less than forty-five towns in the southern part of the state had reached their optimum growth sometime before 1830.[9] Each decade thereafter saw town after town join in this retrogression; more and more young people went west or went to work in the factories, until the tragedy of the abandoned farm had etched itself permanently into the native granite of New Hampshire.

The population changes of these three decades were due not only to the extension of settlement along the frontier but also, in part, to certain economic changes within the older parts of the state. The census of 1820, which for the first time classified Americans by occupation, listed 52,384 people in New Hampshire who gained their livings by agriculture, 1,068 by commerce, and 8,699 by manufacturing. The first of these figures could have been no surprise to contemporaries, but the second must have been a shock to old men who remembered the splendor of Portsmouth's commerce in prerevolutionary days. That only 1.7 percent of the state's breadwinners still followed the sea and the market measured a commercial decline which helped to change the character of New Hampshire society in the nineteenth century.[10]

In colonial times Portsmouth had been one of the chief Atlantic ports, clearing in excess of twenty thousand tons of shipping, of which more than half was destined for the West Indies.[11] The Revolution completely destroyed this trade, leaving not a single square-rigged vessel in seaworthy condition when peace was declared. The wars of Europe, however, revived Portsmouth's prosperity, and by 1806 its shipping had grown to 22,798 tons, exports to $795,263, and imports to more than $800,000.[12]

Embargo, nonimportation, war, and blockade once more swept this commerce from the harbor. With the return of world peace in 1815 and the resumption of mercantile expansion and competition, Portsmouth dropped quickly behind in the race for the world's carrying trade. Tonnage remained stabilized near the 1806 figure, while exports and imports recovered only about half of their prewar value.[13] Boston, Salem, Newburyport, and even Portland grew and flourished during the days when American clippers dominated the sea-lanes, but Portsmouth sank into relative insignificance and would have decayed still further if it had not been sustained by imports of raw materials for manufacturing in the Piscataqua region. The merchant princes disappeared, and their Georgian "palaces" fell into the hands of lawyers, factory owners, and hotel keepers.

This process of decay was due in large part to the fact that Portsmouth had no economic hinterland. The forests in the Piscataqua region which had once supplied the port with great quantities of lumber for export were approaching exhaustion, and the completion of the Middlesex Canal in 1803 diverted the Merrimack Valley's trade to Boston.[14] To overcome this unnatural advantage some visionary Portsmouth people advocated a canal from Lake Winnepesaukee to the Piscataqua. More practical businessmen proposed establishing a freight wagon service on the turnpike from Durham to Concord, believing that they could even reverse the flow of goods from Boston to Concord by way of Portsmouth. A serious step in this direction had been taken in 1793 with the building of the Great Piscataqua Bridge between Newington and Durham, one of the engineering wonders of the time. It was 2,362 feet long, used some five thousand tons of oak and pine timber, and was a genuine monument to the courage of the Portsmouth merchants who provided the $62,000 necessary to pay for it.[15]

Portsmouth remained the metropolis of New Hampshire only until the water power of the Merrimack replaced the winds of the Atlantic as the dynamic of Yankee civilization. When John Langdon, almost the last of the merchant princes, died in 1819, he closed his eyes on a world which retained much of the familiar, old-country charm of the eighteenth century. But when William Plumer died thirty years later, he was a relic of a forgotten past, departing from a strange landscape in which factories and railroads had pulled New Hampshire's center of gravity westward and left Portsmouth little more than "an Old Town by the Sea."

The census takers of 1820 discovered only 8,699 persons in New Hampshire who made their livings by manufacturing. In a state where more than half the population would eventually be employed in industry, this would seem to indicate that Langdon's contemporaries did not appreciate their resources. Ten other states in 1820, including such frontier communities as Ohio and Kentucky, stood above New Hampshire in the number of citizens employed in manufacturing.[16] This should have been no cause either for surprise or mortification to New Hampshirites; indeed, it was probably a matter of rejoicing with them that they ranked so high. Few of them had any vision of the smoking chimneys and whirling spindles that were destined to transform the pleasant river valleys of their acquaintance into hives of industry.

An interesting history could be written of early industrial enterprises in New Hampshire, small though they were. Manufacturing enjoyed at least a propaganda boom in the days of the Confederation when patriots were urged to declare economic independence from England. A few men, of whom President Sullivan, Samuel Hobart of Exeter, and a brother of Jeremiah Smith in Peterborough were notable examples, tried to set up fulling or carding mills on the New Hampshire rivers, but these enterprises were invariably stifled by British competition. Except during periods of embargo and war, when the tiny mills enjoyed a closed market, they only illustrated the dictum that the first enterprisers benefited the public rather than themselves, if indeed the crude products that they turned out could be called public benefits.

The first cotton factory in New Hampshire was erected in the town of New Ipswich in 1804. This enterprise was a grandchild of the Industrial Revolution in England by virtue of its parent—a workman from the Providence mills of Samuel Slater, who, in turn, had acquired his training in the Arkwright factories.[17] The great Amoskeag Mills, which first created and then almost destroyed the city of Manchester, had their humble origin in 1805 when this same pupil of Slater's, Benjamin Pritchard by name, moved to Goffstown and built a tiny cotton mill which was dwarfed by the mighty waterfall it attempted to harness. It was not until 1831 that this enterprise was chartered by the legislature with a capital stock of $1,000,000.[18] Dover, Peterborough, and Pembroke were other towns in which textile mills grew to some importance. In 1814 Keene became the home of a glass factory whose surviving products are now eagerly sought by antique collectors.[19] Gilmanton and Franconia boasted ironworks that were little more than medieval charcoal smelters. All these infant industries, together with hat factories, tanneries, linseed-oil mills, distilleries, nail factories, and paper mills, were worth less than $6,000,000 in 1810. In 1823, when John Farmer and Jacob Moore published their invaluable little gazetteer of New Hampshire, they counted "28 cotton, and 18 woolen factories; 307 carding machines; 256 fulling mills; 22 distilleries; 20 oil mills; 193 bark mills; 304 tanneries; 54 triphammers, and 12 paper mills."[20]

Some of these statistics are misleading. They should evoke pictures not of the gigantic and forbidding brick piles that march for miles along the Merrimack today but of one-story, flimsy wooden structures housing secondhand or handcarved wooden machines that turned fitfully on the energy supplied by an old undershot wheel. New Hampshire's industry of 1820 was so highly decentralized that it hardly affected the distribution of population or the concentration of wealth. Carrigain's map, published in 1816, shows nearly every stream in New Hampshire lined with a similar succession of mills—sawmill, grist mill, fulling mill, carding mill, and, occasionally, a larger cotton mill. These enterprises produced for a local market and were owned by local capital. The Amoskeag Company, for example, was entirely owned by twelve farmers in Goffstown, Bedford, and Manchester until 1822.[21] Under such conditions industrial capital would not be expected to play a very extensive role in the social and political life of the state.

The negative evidence in the journals of the state legislature warrants the deduction that the growth of manufactures excited no political contests prior to 1820. Petitions for the incorporation of manufactories were granted almost automatically, with only a moderate degree of examination. The legislature grew so lax in this regard that Plumer, when governor in 1812, warned against the granting of unlimited charters and secured the inclusion of a forfeiture clause in subsequent grants.[22] Public opinion sanctioned positive aid to new corporations in the form of tax exemptions. Most of the charters included a clause releasing particular companies from taxation indefinitely or for a specific number of years. In addition, an act was passed in 1808 by a Republican legislature granting general exemption for five years to all cotton, woolen, salt, and glass factories.[23] The secretary of state reported in 1819 that $1,995,833 worth of property had enjoyed the benefit of these laws.[24]

This was all the encouragement, however, that the legislature was inclined to extend to manufacturing after 1810. Unlike Confederation times, no bounties were offered for domestic products; nor did New Hampshire look with entire approval upon protective tariffs. The Tariff Act of 1816 received the support of only two of New Hampshire's eight members of Congress; both of these lived in the Merrimack Valley. The other six, men from the Old Colony and the Connecticut Valley, including Senator Jeremiah Mason and Representative Daniel Webster from Portsmouth, opposed a bill which seemed to tax shippers and farmers for the benefit of upstart manufacturers.[25] The vote was probably an accurate gauge of state sentiment on the subject, for it is abundantly clear that few people in New Hampshire foresaw its industrialized future. Writing in 1823, John Farmer expressed the prevalent opinion in typical language: "New-Hampshire is emphatically an agricultural state. Manufactures and commerce engross the attention of a comparatively small portion of its citizens. Young as we are in the arts, it has not yet become our interest to abandon the cultivation of the soil, for the purpose of creating extensive manufactories,—in which must be required large capitals, and a patience and automaton constancy to which we are unused,— while the rewards are uncertain and feeble."[26]

Gradual improvement in transportation accompanied the development of manufactures in New Hampshire. Prior to 1790 the poorly maintained township roads wandered indistinctly through the forests, and one could scarcely have crossed a large stream anywhere except by ferry. Thirty years later the rural scene was very different. Beginning at Portsmouth a traveler in 1820 could have driven his carriage along a good road to the bank of the Piscataqua in Newington and then, after paying toll, across the Great Piscataqua Bridge into Durham. Here he could have taken the stagecoach or continued in his own conveyance by way of the First New Hampshire Turnpike, incorporated in 1796, all the way into Concord township. Paying ten cents for the privilege, he could have crossed the Merrimack on Federal Bridge, built by a corporation of Concord citizens headed by Timothy Walker, and ridden down Main Street from the north, past the "elegant" new state house, which had been finished in 1819. It would have been an easy day's journey and the visitor would probably have agreed that the turnpike had done good service in connecting parts of the state which were greatly in need of closer union.[27]

After spending the night at the Sign of the Eagle, already a famous hostelry, the traveler might have continued westward on the Fourth New Hampshire Turnpike, which connected the Merrimack with the Connecticut at Hanover. The Second and Third turnpikes led southward from Concord and Lebanon into Massachusetts, while the old post road still connected Portsmouth with Boston. A Fifth Turnpike ascended the Connecticut Valley and wound through the White Mountain passes into Maine. Everywhere, the traveler would have found good bridges, comfortable inns and even a few stagecoaches in operation. Between 1790 and 1820 the legislature had incorporated fifty-nine bridge companies and fifty-three turnpike ventures.[28]

This development of internal communications had not come without a political struggle. Turnpikes and bridges too clearly benefited some sections at the expense of others to receive the unanimous benedictions of legislators. The great turnpike boom occurred in the decade 1796–1806. During those years every session of the legislature was flooded with petitions for the incorporation of new companies; the June session of 1804 alone received twenty-two. Many of these failed to go through the law-making mill, and those which succeeded seldom did so with many votes to spare. The motivation behind these votes was exceedingly complex. Much of it was local or sectional, but some of it was based upon genuinely democratic or anti-monopolistic principles. Turnpike proprietors were condemned as monopolists whose grants in perpetuity were dangerous to the state, whose authority to seize private property by right of eminent domain was injurious to landowners, and whose opposition prevented improvement of the public highway system. Inhabitants of the towns through which turnpikes passed were unfairly relieved of highway taxes that had to be paid by residents of less-favored towns. The turnpike mania diverted capital from less speculative and perhaps more beneficial enterprises into a high-cost venture which far exceeded New Hampshire's immediate needs. In spite of all this, it was evident that private enterprise would be drawn inevitably into the area of transportation if government was unwilling to assume the burden.

While the improvement of east to west roads did much to strengthen state unity in the early nineteenth century, canal building had the opposite effect. The natural desire of early canal designers was to make New Hampshire's rapid, southward flowing rivers completely navigable. Success in that effort only increased the economic dependence of western

New Hampshire upon Massachusetts and Connecticut, leaving Portsmouth even more isolated than nature had intended. By 1823 the construction of three canals at a cost of $36,000 had made the Connecticut theoretically navigable for steamboats as far northward as Lyman, just below the Fifteen Mile Rapids.[29] There was little hope, after this, that Connecticut Valley products would ever find their way to the Portsmouth market.

The Merrimack Valley trade was tied even more securely to Boston by the completion of the Middlesex Canal from the Charles River to Chelmsford on the Merrimack in 1803. This enterprise was the most extensive internal improvement in New England before the advent of the railroad, its total cost of construction being $528,000.[30] Its completion was largely due to the vision and persistence of James Sullivan, brother of the New Hampshire president and later a governor of Massachusetts, together with the enthusiasm of his engineer son, John Langdon Sullivan.[31] For sixteen years after its inception, however, the canal lost money, chiefly because the Merrimack channel had to be cleared of numerous obstructions before trade with Concord and the upper valley could be conducted on a large scale. Between Concord and the southern border, the course of the river was interrupted by four cataracts—at Bow, Hooksett, Manchester, and Merrimack. By far the most formidable of these was the forty-five-foot drop of water over Amoskeag Falls, around which Samuel Blodget began to construct a channel as early as 1794. Thirteen years later, after he had exhausted the resources of his stockholders, himself, and three lotteries, the old man was able to ride a raft through the locks and basin of his completed canal. This happy event preceded by only four months the death of the "pioneer of internal improvements in New Hampshire."[32]

It had cost $138,000 to eliminate the four rapids south of Concord, and $68,000 of this had been contributed by the Middlesex Canal Company in order to open the upper Merrimack to its boats.[33] With such an investment in New Hampshire it was inevitable that the Massachusetts corporation should seek legal protection from the legislature of the northern state. There had been opposition to the earlier, smaller enterprises for the improvement of navigation, not of a sectional character but from scattered communities apparently fearful of grants of extensive power to private corporations. This sentiment continued to exist in spite of the obvious advantages to be derived from the improvements, and it grew particularly strong against the powerful, out-of-state corporation that sought a monopoly over the Merrimack River. John L. Sullivan and his partners attempted in 1811 to acquire exclusive rights to canalize the river all the way to Lake Winnepesaukee. Although Sullivan operated behind a screen of New Hampshire lawyers and legislators as the petitioners, his hand was detected and his effort defeated in the senate.[34] In order to secure a monopoly of the canal commerce from Concord, Sullivan organized the "Merrimack Boating Company" and petitioned for a charter. His bill passed both houses but was vetoed by Governor Langdon.[35] In 1812, Sullivan tried again and met a similar rebuff from Governor Plumer. The governor's veto message objected not to the grant itself but to the vague and indefinite terms in which it was made. The bill was written in such language as to convey unlimited use of the entire river for undefined purposes.[36] Plumer's veto was unanimously sustained by the house, and Sullivan's company was subsequently incorporated under a much more carefully guarded charter.[37]

Governor Plumer found himself in opposition to many proposals for internal improvements, not because he disliked progress, but because he foresaw the social cost to the community of surrendering control over its transportation system to groups of monopolists. He was sympathetic with the improvements themselves, and he welcomed rather than feared the prospect of federal aid within state boundaries. He gave his cordial support in 1816 to the survey of a canal route between the Merrimack and Connecticut rivers by way of Lake Sunapee, which was, however, declared impracticable.[38] He also welcomed the congressional resolution of March 30, 1818, which proposed a national survey of internal improvements with a view toward launching a federal program that would benefit all the states.

Governor Plumer appointed Ichabod Bartlett, a promising young lawyer, to make this survey for New Hampshire and his report was submitted to the legislature in June 1819. The people of New Hampshire, it stated, were not indifferent to internal improvements, for they had already invested almost a million dollars in toll bridges, turnpikes, and canals.[39] There remained, however, five projects of great value which were too costly for the state and which might therefore become suitable objects of federal concern. The first of these, a canal from Dover to Alton, would open an area of fourteen hundred square miles to boat navigation and provide easy access for the navy yard at Portsmouth to the inexhaustible supplies of timber on the shores of Lake Winnepesaukee. The second and third were plans to extend navigation on the Merrimack to its source in Lake Winnepesaukee, thus opening another great water route into the heart of New Hampshire. The fourth project was the completion of a road from Plymouth through Franconia Notch to Lancaster, which would provide a highway from Boston to Quebec. The fifth proposal suggested that the Jefferson and Fourth New Hampshire turnpikes, which provided an outlet through the White Mountains to Portland for the settlers of the Upper Coös, be taken over for necessary improvements by the federal government.[40] These dreams were never realized. Political quarrels paralyzed the will of the federal government to make internal improvements, and neither the state nor the private interests of New Hampshire dared to tackle such enterprises unaided. The Granite State had to await the coming of the railroads before it achieved the long-desired highway to Canada.

The relatively large amounts of money that seemed to be available for investment in lands, bonds, and the stocks of private corporations during the three decades after 1790 suggest a rather surprising growth of fluid capital in the little agricultural state of New Hampshire. The evidence is sustained by the rise of banking institutions that not only served to collect this capital in the form of deposits but opened another field of investments. The genesis of New Hampshire's first two banks, both located in Portsmouth, was rooted in politics.[41] Once the Union Bank had broken the barrier erected by Federalist politicians to protect their financial monopoly, a banking fever which put all other manias to shame swept the state. Every session of the legislature from 1802 to 1809 was overwhelmed with petitions for bank charters, and if the aspiring financiers failed in their first attempts to gain legislative favors, they returned each succeeding year until the weary representatives finally surrendered.

In spite of manful resistance, the legislature had yielded up no less than nine charters before 1807—and a population which paid only $30,000 every other year in taxes found itself able to subscribe nearly $1,500,000 in bank capital.[42] Three of New Hampshire's ten banks in 1807 were located in Portsmouth, and there was one each in Dover, Exeter, Keene, Amherst, and Haverhill—the last a village of less than a thousand inhabitants. The remaining two were both in Concord and operated under the same charter, each claiming to be the legal corporation. After the Concord charter had been granted to a mixed group of leading citizens, a quarrel between the Republican grantees, led by Timothy Walker, and the Federalists, led by William Kent, resulted in two banks located at opposite ends of Main Street. Under the statute of 1799 forbidding unincorporated banks to issue notes, a suit was brought against Walker, who engaged William Plumer, the sponsor of the act, as his attorney. Jeremiah Mason, counsel for the plaintiff, had more than a hundred counts in his declaration. The case became a notable one in the New Hampshire courts, but was finally settled by compromise, and both banks continued to operate for twenty years under the same charter.[43]

The cessation of trade under the Embargo Laws created difficulties for the country banks and forced three of them—the Coös Bank at Haverhill, the Cheshire Bank at Keene, and the Hillsborough Bank at Amherst—to suspend specie payments in 1809. The former two eventually recovered, but the last never did, and for many years thereafter anyone connected with the Hillsborough Bank failure was considered a public enemy by the farmers of New Hampshire.[44] The disaster had the good effect, however, of making the legislature more conscious of the need for supervision. Beginning in 1814, banks were required to submit semiannual statements to the governor and council. Men with capital also became more cautious about investing in bank stock until the general economic situation warranted an expansion of credit facilities. Only one new bank was chartered between 1810 and 1820, although a branch of the Bank of the United States opened in Portsmouth in 1817 under the able management of Jeremiah Mason.

In addition to these ten banks, New Hampshire also boasted four insurance companies in 1820, all located at Portsmouth.[45] The most flourishing of these, the New-Hampshire Fire and Marine Insurance Company, had sufficient wealth and taste to house itself in one of the more architecturally perfect buildings of the early nineteenth century.[46] The appearance of so many financial institutions within the brief space of twenty years, after a century and a half in which they had been deemed unnecessary, is strong testimony to the rapid economic development of New Hampshire. It suggests, in fact, overdevelopment and speculation. Yet in spite of the ignorance of sound banking principles, the lack of supervision in the public interest, and the perversion of banks for political purposes, banking in New Hampshire encountered fewer disturbances than were to be found in almost every other part of the Union during those early years.

The leaven of economic change aroused a moderate degree of social consciousness and state pride in New Hampshire during the early nineteenth century. One symbol of its awakening was the new state prison at Concord, first projected in 1804 and finished in 1812.[47] The impulse toward state control of crime and punishment came not only from a humanitarian spirit but from the inadequacy and filth of the county gaols. One of these institutions, at Haverhill, was the scene of a revolting crime in 1805. During the winter of that year three men were crowded into the miserable, one-celled structure. One of the three, Josiah Burnham, was a habitual criminal, imprisoned for forgery. The other two were distinguished but unlucky gentlemen, imprisoned for debt—one, indeed, was Russell Freeman of Hanover, who had not too long before been speaker of the house of representatives. The three men quarreled, and Burnham stabbed his companions to death in a peculiarly brutal manner.[48] The need for penal reform, accented by this notorious crime, could hardly be ignored. Succeeding legislatures, even in frugal New Hampshire, were willing to spend continuously until an excellent prison building, costing $37,000, was erected. Governor Plumer performed the first official inspection in the spring of 1813.

The completion of the state prison made possible a long-needed reform of the criminal code. This work was expertly accomplished in 1811 by a committee consisting of Jeremiah Smith, John Goddard, and Daniel Webster. Capital crimes were reduced from seven to three, and the lash, the pillory, and confinement in the county pestholes were all superseded by terms of imprisonment in the new institution.[49] The New Hampshire authorities availed themselves to the fullest extent of the experience that neighboring states had already gained in prison management, and they tried to set up a model institution.[50] Wholesome work was provided for the inmates, and the Federalist legislature of 1814 was particularly eager to see that they received ample religious instruction.[51] The theory that the prison could be made self-supporting through convict labor proved, however, to be illusory. During the first decade of its operation it cost the state $5,676.67 more than it produced.[52] In 1818, Governor Plumer appointed as warden Moses C. Pillsbury, who became one of the most successful early prison managers in the United States. He not only converted the deficit into a surplus but, through his humanity and vigilance, "made a real contribution to prison management and progress in the country."[53]

In spite of the unusual weight of taxation imposed upon the people by the building of their prison, they were willing to pay for yet another public edifice in Concord—a statehouse. Governor Langdon set the ball rolling for this project in 1806 when, in his address to the legislature, he recommended the fixing of a permanent capital.[54] Prior to this the legislature had convened at one time or another in eight different towns. Sectional jealousy had compelled it to flit from section to section—twice in the Connecticut Valley, once at Amherst, once at Dover. Most of its sessions during the Federalist regime, however, had been shared between Concord and Exeter, with Hopkinton and Portsmouth enjoying frequent visits when Republicans were in power. After 1806 the legislature had adopted Governor Langdon's advice to meet henceforward in Concord, although the jealousy of other towns prevented its immediate recognition as the state capital. It was not until 1808 that all the state records were ordered to be kept in Concord and not until 1814 that the final decision to build a statehouse there was made. In that year a legislative committee reported that New Hampshire was the only state in the Union which lacked a capitol—a regrettable condition which the people would be glad to remedy as soon as the burdens of war were removed.[55] The Federalist legislature of 1815 followed with preliminary plans for this undertaking, and it was completed by the Republicans from 1816 to 1819.

Although there had been so much delay in the decision to build a capitol and a great deal of unpleasant bickering during the actual process of construction, the people of New Hampshire were inordinately proud of their "beautiful edifice" when it was finally finished. Even though the land and stone had been contributed by the people of Concord and $10,000 worth of labor had been performed by convicts in the state prison in dressing the stone, the legislature had expended $67,372.44 in cash—a princely sum for those days. *A Book for New-Hampshire Children*, published in 1823 by one of the nation's early historians, found in the new statehouse a stimulant to civic pride. "I have seen many elegant buildings in the course of my life," declared the boastful author to his juvenile readers, "but I never saw one so elegant as the State House."[56] Whether or not his eulogy was justified, it is certain that the new building symbolized the highest degree of political unity that New Hampshire had been able to achieve since Massachusetts emigrants first established a settlement on the banks of the Merrimack at Penacook.

Not the least of the social changes that occurred during the early nineteenth century was the revolution in religion, which proceeded with accelerated pace after 1800. In the eighteenth century the Congregationalist church had been almost a monopoly not only in the theological sense, but in its symbolism of a way of life which made New England unique. By 1820 the entire picture had changed. Congregationalism still remained the largest and strongest religious organization in the region, but it was only a shell of the mighty organism that had reigned in the day of Cotton Mather. It was now surrounded by a host of dissenting churches, denouncing its theology, proselyting from its ranks, and shearing it of political power. Where once it had bent the magistrates to its will, dictated the laws of the state in its conventions, and molded public opinion from its pulpits, it was now forced to witness the political party of its choice eclipsed and its influence usurped by the press.

Religious historians of all denominations, including Calvinists, unite in their assessment of Congregationalist preaching in 1800 as dull and dismal—devoid of any of the joy and inspiration in religion. It is true that earnest men such as Jonathan Edwards, Samuel Hopkins, and Jonathan Mayhew had stirred the stagnant pool of Calvinism and boiled up new concoctions, some darker and some lighter than the original brew, but these agitations had faded without effecting a permanent change in the "established" church. The way was open, therefore, for attacks on both the substance and the manner of Congregationalist preaching.

The first assault had been delivered by the Baptists, who had forty-one churches and 2,652 communicants in New Hampshire by 1800. The Baptists contended that the Congregationalists were unscriptural, particularly in the matter of infant baptism, that they were not evangelical in their preaching, and that they were oppressive in their settlement of ministers by law. After only a few years of success, however, the Baptists began to resemble those whom they had so roundly denounced. Here and there a Baptist church abandoned its original scorn for legal support, "and from this," complained Elias Smith, "it spread till cattle and horses were taken by force to pay baptist ministers for preaching."[57] Such establishmentarianism stimulated a new protest movement in New Hampshire led by Benjamin Randall, a young Baptist exhorter who was expelled from the fellowship for heresy in 1780. He objected to the Calvinism of Baptist doctrine and to "hireling" preachers in Baptist pulpits. He organized a new, freshly evangelical, Arminian congregation in his own town of New Durham, and his movement spread rapidly along the Winnepesaukee frontier and into Maine. Taking on the designation of Free Will Baptist, the new church claimed 220 congregations and 9,000 members by 1820.[58]

Even the liberalism of the Free Will Baptists did not satisfy Elias Smith, a remarkable evangelist who joined with Elder Abner Jones of Vermont in 1803 to form a new sect which rejected all denominational designations as unscriptural and called itself merely Christian (not to be confused with the Campbellites or Disciples). Besides objecting to everything in all the existing churches which had also offended Randall, Smith toyed with Unitarian and Universalist ideas and savagely attacked the slightest degree of consociation which might inhibit the liberty of a single congregation or, for that matter, of a single Christian. In Smith, the native, popular revolt against lifeless Calvinism reached at least a temporary climax.

At the same time, the outside force of Methodism was penetrating the north. Jesse Lee preached his first sermon in Portsmouth in 1790; the first Methodist circuit in New Hampshire was established in Chesterfield at the opposite corner of the state five years later; and by 1820 some twenty itinerants were riding through every section, preaching salvation to the poor and humble.[59] There were also in New Hampshire six "meetings" of Friends in 1801, and the Shakers had successfully established their peculiar brand of communism in two flourishing villages at Canterbury and Enfield.[60] It is little wonder that a struggling Congregationalist minister, such as the Reverend Jeremy Belknap, felt that he had been called upon to endure "a succession of epidemic disorders."[61]

In addition to what might be called frontal assaults, internal dissension and schism threatened Congregationalism. A liberal reaction against Calvinism took first the extreme form of antithesis in the doctrine that all, rather than a select few, were elected to salvation. One of the earliest Universalist churches in America was gathered in Portsmouth around 1778 by Noah Parker, a remarkably learned and warm-hearted blacksmith.[62] Societies existed in eight other towns in 1821. But the hardest blow that the Puritan church had to suffer came from within the very heart of its fastnesses through the growth of Unitarian ideas. Although the definite parting of the ways did not come until after 1820, the struggle between obdurate Calvinism and the liberalizing tendency had been proceeding for many years, and it had penetrated to New Hampshire. When the break came, five of the most distinguished Congregationalist churches in the state became Unitarian, while two other parishes divided.[63]

This religious ferment did not, of course, end in 1820. It continued vigorously at least until the Civil War, assuming novel and astonishing forms as New England experienced an economic and cultural "flowering." But by the end of the century's second decade, it had already proceeded to the point where the wreckage of ancient institutions lay on every hand. Statistically, its effect upon the unity of the church was measured by John Farmer in 1820 (see Table 11-2).[64]

Even the landscape did not escape alteration. In 1750 a traveler could have made his way through New Hampshire from meetinghouse to meetinghouse, six miles apart, gleaming white and bearing no external sign to indicate that only adherents to the Cambridge Platform preached within. By 1820 there were not many places where the Congregational meetinghouse reigned in solitary splendor. Across the hills, in odd corners of the country parishes, or even daring in some villages to occupy a lot on the opposite side of the green, Baptist and Methodist churches were beginning to appear, sometimes offending the aesthetic as well as the religious feelings of the standing order. Portsmouth, which had only a single church building at the beginning of the eighteenth century, boasted seven by 1805.

The growing strength of the dissenters brought about a great improvement in their legal status after 1800. Eager to gain any allies against the dominant Federalists, the Republican party sought to win sectarian votes

TABLE 11-2

Denomination	Number of Churches or Societies	Number of Members
Congregationalists	164	11,000 to 12,000
Presbyterians	10	1,000
Episcopalians	8	2,000 (200 to 300 communicants)
Baptists	34 (65 societies)	2,658
Free Will Baptists	29 (56 societies)	1,892
Methodists	16 (38 societies)	779
Friends	1 (3 societies)	63
Shakers	2	435
Universalists	2 (9 societies)	
Sandemanians	1	

by proclaiming religious toleration. As soon as they gained control of the legislature, in 1804, they passed a resolution which recognized the Free Will Baptists as a sect, thereby protecting them from persecution by the courts.[65] Similar freedom was granted to the Universalists in 1805 and to Methodists in 1807. None of these laws was opposed by the Federalist party, which seemed somewhat disposed to abandon its ministerial supporters and to compete with the Republicans for the dissenters' suffrages. Even the Federalist judges relaxed in the general atmosphere of good will. In *Muzzy* versus *Wilkin*, the first case involving church taxes to be reported in New Hampshire (1803), Chief Justice Smith rendered an elaborate opinion in favor of the Presbyterian plaintiff by proving that he differed sufficiently from the Congregationalist town minister to be legally exempt from the tax. Judge Wingate dissented. William Plumer, who had defended dissenters in this same court when its attitude was that of Wingate rather than Smith, exclaimed: "What a change since then (say six years) now that court is astute to find reasons & excuses to except sectaries from the support of the Clergy."[66]

These legal exemptions left little but the hollow shell of an establishment in New Hampshire. In the succeeding years many Congregational societies followed the example of their competitors by securing acts of incorporation and separating themselves from the towns in which they were located.[67] Still, the antiquated law of 1791 remained in force, threatening at any moment to place a powerful weapon in the hands of those who sought to revive intolerance. The tribulations that Jeffersonian policy brought upon New England between 1807 and 1815 caused such a resurgence of Federalist-Congregationalist power that the final separation of church and state could not be effected until 1819.

To most of the orthodox clergy the rise of faction within the walls of Zion was a catastrophe, and they sought to stem the current of progress by clinging stubbornly to their outworn ideas and crying "innovation" at every breath of liberalism. Because they were educated, fearless men, and because the other conservative forces in society upheld them, they made a good fight of it and held out with incredible persistence, managing in the end to salvage most of what was useful and worthwhile in their way of life. They fought the doctrinal vagaries of the sects with logic, rhetoric and sarcasm, but not much with the sweetness of the Spirit. This part of the struggle occupied an enormous portion of the output of press and pulpit, and most of it sounds dreary and futile to the modern ear. The titles of the pamphlets were more intriguing than their contents; one is usually disappointed when he looks into "The Clergyman's Looking Glass" or "The High-Flying Churchman stript of his legal Robe appears a Yaho" or "Sunbeams may be extracted from Cucumbers, but the process is tedious." Occasionally, however, the disputant added humor to his arsenal, a prime example of it being John Peck's doggerel on Universalism, published in 1813. The following stanza is a sample:

> O' charming news to live in sin,
> And die to reign with Paul;
> 'Tis so indeed, for Jesus bled
> To save the devil and all.[68]

Congregationalists were firmly convinced that the sectarians came from the lowest orders of society, which was partly true, and that their preachers were ignorant, penniless fanatics, rogues, and demagogues, which was largely false. The sectarian preachers violated the ethics of the profession—they did not prepare themselves in college; they preached crude, extemporaneous sermons; they encouraged excessive emotionalism; they were frequently not even ordained; they proselytized unblushingly; and instead of taking a parish and sticking to it like gentlemen they wandered all over the country poaching on everyone's preserve. The regular ministers sought desperately to warn their people against those "wolves in sheep's clothing." When a prominent and very worthy Baptist minister from Massachusetts came to preach a sermon in Concord, the patriarchal minister of the town, the Reverend Timothy Walker, warned his parishioners in the words that St. Paul addressed to the Christians in Rome: "Now, I beseech you, brethren, mark them which cause divisions, and offences contrary to the doctrine which ye have learned; and avoid them. For they that are such serve not our Lord Jesus Christ, but their own belly; and by good words and fair speeches, deceive the hearts of the simple."[69] One of the good man's auditors remarked that "the old gentleman seemed as much exasperated as a farmer would be, in case a man should break away his fences and let loose a herd of cattle upon the fields."[70] A figure which would more nearly have described the clergyman's state of mind would be that of a ravening wolf let in among his own cattle.

Nowhere did the contrast between archaic institutions and modern needs appear more vividly than in the frontier regions of New Hampshire. While the Congregationalists retained their majorities in most of the older towns, they were beaten almost entirely from the field in vast areas of the newer settlements. It cannot be said, however, that they surrendered the frontiers without a struggle. As early as 1770 the Annual Convention of Congregationalist Ministers, thinking in the familiar terms of church dependence upon state, petitioned the royal governor and the legislature to do something about the deplorable lack of religious teaching in "the back Settlements."[71]

The Revolution prevented any answer to this petition, and subsequently the preachers took the matter into their own hands, arranging to supply a chosen brother's pulpit while he spent four weeks among the benighted frontiersmen. In 1801 the New Hampshire Missionary Society was organized to sponsor the work. The journal of one Jacob Cram, master of arts from Dartmouth and the established minister at Hollis, who was sent by the society on a twenty-six-week itinerancy through the White Mountains and even into Canada in 1808, shows that a Congregationalist could be as full of endurance, woodcraft, sermons, and the Holy Ghost as any Baptist or Methodist.[72]

These laborious efforts bore little fruit, however, and the reason for this failure is not hard to find. The Congregational church suffered from the same handicap on its own frontier that crippled it in the western regions. While its town and church autonomy was well suited to a homogeneous, settled community, or even to a well-knit band of pilgrims who transplanted an old town into the wilderness, it was completely unadaptable to the type of promiscuous, individual homesteading by which New Hampshire's frontiers advanced after the French and Indian War. It could not compete with the Baptist or Methodist itinerant who, after his divine call, did not find it necessary to spend four years in college, wait until a town had enough taxable property to insure his livelihood, sign a contract, undergo an ordination, and then spend the rest of his life in the glebe parsonage. When Cram went into the backcountry in 1808, he found it already full of Methodists; yet the Wesleyans had been in New Hampshire only thirteen years, while the Congregationalists had been there for two centuries. "We have illustrated, afresh, the weakness which has ever beset a democracy in the presence of centralized systems," wrote a prominent Congregationalist, thus explaining at once the physical weakness and the intellectual arrogance that accounted for the failures of his church.[73]

If the religious contestants of the day had confined their assaults to oral denunciation, the bitterness of the struggle might sooner have disappeared. Unfortunately, a minor Book of Martyrs could be compiled from the experiences recorded in the journals of Elias Smith, Benjamin Randall, Amos Kent, and other missionaries who encountered mob violence while attempting to spread the Gospel in New Hampshire. Persecution ranged all the way from locking an itinerant out of a meetinghouse or mocking a sect's rituals to very grim attempts at lynching. Elias Smith seems to have incurred the most persistent opposition, for which his erratic doctrine and warm political partisanship could easily account. On one occasion, Smith's alleged authorship of a scurrilous pamphlet stirred up a serious riot in Portsmouth from which the preacher escaped with a whole skin only because of his congregation's loyal defense.[74] Much of this lawless opposition was only what religious zealots have always met everywhere. In New Hampshire, however, the victims often claimed that their assailants were inspired by the settled minister of the town and that prominent Congregationalists were usually the ringleaders of the mobs.[75] However exaggerated this may have been, the ministers cannot be entirely absolved when they preached from their pulpits that the evangelists were "disturbers of the peace, immoral brawlers, disorderly persons, [and] enemies to learning."[76]

It must be admitted that in most cases at least the last of these epithets was richly deserved. Not only were the itinerants themselves usually unlearned but they expressed the greatest contempt for education and what they believed to be its deadening effects. So many of them were gifted with a warm and spontaneous eloquence that they naturally concluded that "the Lord eddicates his own preachers" and that college training would be a work of supererogation. By reverse logic they also reasoned that the prevailing aridity of Congregational preaching was the result of the preacher's college education, which had dried up the original springs of the Spirit. Elias Smith accused Harvard directly of making ministers "not of the spirit but of the letter, for the spirit giveth life but the letter killeth. . . . That place is . . . a *Volcano* which annually vomits columns of fire and hot lava which makes every green thing die and proves destruction to all around. . . . These men profess to be masters of arts; I have no doubt but they are masters of some arts; they have the art of keeping the people in fear of them; the art of living with little work, of keeping people in ignorance, and of opposing the gospel."[77]

Smith gathered these choice remarks into a pamphlet called "The Clergyman's Looking Glass," in which he set a description of the "scriptural" minister in one column and one of the orthodox clergy in an opposite column on the same page. If he opened his eyes, Smith said, the clergyman could see the contrast between what he should be and what he was. As to the latter, Smith bluntly stated that the settled minister was no less than anti-Christ's and Satan's henchman. Small wonder that a certain amount of indignation greeted the publication of this work.

While the sectarians were the victims of false logic in deducing that dull preaching was the result of education, the orthodox clergy were equally misled in supposing that the evangelists deliberately fostered the scenes of hysterical enthusiasm that often resulted from their sermons. In a mild way they disapproved of the more extreme exhibitions, but they regarded all this as the work of the Holy Ghost operating in power to convict sinners of their guilt, and they were not surprised to see "the aisles covered with the slain," as they quaintly put it.[78] These scenes were the basis of Congregationalist belief that the sectarians were disturbers of the peace and disorderly persons. Regardless of who may have been responsible, the religious orgies that periodically racked New Hampshire did little to increase stability or the sober virtues.

There were a few exceptions to the bad personal relations that characterized meetings between the clergy of different sects. Here and there a generous orthodox minister welcomed into his pulpit a wide variety of dissenting preachers in the belief that all were working for the same cause. Some regretted that "Christians . . . bite and devour one another" and suggested that they might better unite their forces against skepticism and infidelity.[79] One was so magnanimous as to admit that "the Calvinistic Baptists are serious, regular, and to as great an extent as their Calvinistic brethren of other classes, religious."[80] But these expressions of moderate cordiality were the exception rather than the rule. While a typical Methodist circuit rider, lost in a snowstorm in Tuftonborough, fought his way to his next appointment, where he hoped "to call sinners to repentance," he pictured the "settled minister" sitting by a warm fire, selecting portions from the books in his library and writing out a dull sermon to be read to his congregation the following Sunday. "Which of them looks most like a lazy man?" he asked himself, and which "follows the example of Christ . . . in traveling, suffering, preaching, self-denyings, watchings, fastings, and winning souls to Christ?"[81]

It was long before this unfortunate bitterness between workers in the same cause began to disappear. In 1835 a Baptist historian looked back grimly upon these years of contention and wrote: "It should be understood that the opposition that we have been called to meet, has been from the avowed friends of the Savior—the ministers of his religion,—the professed disciples of the Redeemer have come forth and arrayed themselves in opposition. . . . Laws have changed, but the spirit of those who engage in this opposition is the same."[82]

However regrettable it may have been, this spirit was inevitable. The church was so inextricably woven into the pattern of New England life that the rise of a new faith signified not so much the addition of another thread as a decomposition of the original fabric. The Baptists and Methodists were assisting in the process of making New England a part of the United States, but in creating the larger unity they helped to destroy a smaller and older one. New Hampshire provided a clear picture of the ideological clash between the spirit of individualism, which was not native to New England, and the tenacious church-community ideal around which its institutions had developed—a clash that reverberated throughout the westward march of American civilization. With the possible exception of the great physical changes wrought by the Industrial Revolution, no other development in New Hampshire's history transformed the state as profoundly as did the collapse of its Calvinistic society.

CHAPTER 12

DEMOCRACY TRIUMPHANT

Themistocles, when desired at a feast to touch a lute, said he could not fiddle, but he knew how to make a small town a great city. Mr. Jefferson can fiddle . . . but he cannot make a number of small states a great nation. —Jeremiah Smith

During the first five years of the nineteenth century, New Hampshire underwent a political revolution.[1] The Republican forces, which had been in full and ignominious retreat in 1799, suddenly counterattacked and, one after another, captured all of their enemies' strongholds. After John Langdon's return to New Hampshire the battle took on new vigor, with an occasional Federalist rally, but with a Republican boldness that assured ultimate success. Finally, in 1805, Jefferson's followers raised their triumphant banner over the highest battlement.

The president's "destruction" of the internal revenue system, the army, the navy and the new judiciary may actually have raised, in the mind of the average voter, a slight degree of that apprehension which disoriented the Federalist Cassandras. The Republicans lost ground in New Hampshire in 1803. Langdon had assured Jefferson that the Federalists "sicken at the sight of our prosperity" and had promised great things, but his time was not yet come.[2] Gilman gained more new votes than did Langdon and was reelected by a greater majority than in 1802.[3] Both branches of the legislature remained in the hands of the Federalists, who determined upon a short and innocuous session in June. This Republican setback followed a disastrous fire that swept through Portsmouth one night in December 1802, consuming 114 buildings and causing damage estimated at $200,000.[4] With macabre humor, Jeremiah Smith ascribed the tragedy to the vengeance of a righteous God upon the Sodom of Jacobinism, but the effect of his joke was spoiled by the fact that the fire broke out early on a Sabbath morning in the New Hampshire Bank building.[5] At any rate, the Republican Congress in Washington sympathized with the sufferers and appropriated funds for their relief.

In spite of this generosity, Federalists viewed every act of the national government with gloomy suspicion. William Plumer, the new senator, though charmed by President Jefferson's gracious hospitality, declared that "almost every new measure he recommends, recalls to my view Ezekiel's vision, & the declaration made to him by the angel—Turn, & thou shall behold yet greater abominations."[6] High on the list of these abominations were the purchase of Louisiana, the Twelfth Amendment to the Constitution, and the administration's assault upon the national judiciary. Both of New Hampshire's Federalist senators voted against ratification of the Louisiana Purchase treaty, although they dutifully supported the measures to carry it into effect once it became the law of the land. The four New Hampshire congressmen in the lower House, however, voted solidly against every administrative proposal in regard to Louisiana. Although the Federalists raised very persuasive constitutional and legal arguments against the soundness of the Louisiana Purchase, their real objection to it was the fear of adding an illimitable expanse of Republican territory to the Union. "Admit this western world into the union, & you destroy with a single operation the whole weight & importance of the eastern states in the *scale* of politics," wrote Senator Plumer in his journal.[7]

For much the same reasons—fears that it would further weaken the weight of the eastern states in national politics and assure the perpetuation of a Virginia dynasty in the White House—New Hampshire congressmen also unanimously opposed passage of the Twelfth Amendment. In this case, they were in an embarrassingly inconsistent position, for the state legislature of 1798, in which Senator Plumer had been speaker of the house and which had been dominated by Federalists, had demanded a similar amendment in order to prevent Jefferson's reelection to the vice-presidency. New Hampshire's representatives were now inclined to deny any obligation to follow the instructions of constituents and to rely heavily upon the compact theory of the Constitution. Arguing a principle which John Taylor and John C. Calhoun were later to employ in defense of the South, they insisted that the method of electing the president was a fundamental part of the agreement under which the thirteen states originally united and that every partner in the compact had to agree to such a basic change. A generation later, New Hampshire's greatest son, Daniel Webster, was to argue majestically against this doctrine in the same chamber. Able to command the requisite two-thirds majority in each house from within their own ranks, the Republicans of 1803 were indifferent to abstract arguments—they quickly approved the proposed amendment and sent it to the states for ratification. It was taken up in the November session of the New Hampshire legislature, where the Federalist majority secured a simple postponement of consideration rather than an outright rejection. Their margin of victory, even in this weak maneuver, was only 83 to 67.[8] But it was a hollow success, for there were more than enough Republican states to provide the necessary three-fourths majority and the amendment became a part of the Constitution in time to be operative in the election of 1804.

New Hampshire was directly and intimately involved with the Jeffersonian effort to purge and downgrade the federal judiciary. It has already been noted that one of the state's ablest lawyers, Jeremiah Smith, was deprived of a seat on the federal bench by the repeal of the Judiciary Act of 1801. Smith and all of his Federalist friends regarded the repealing statute as unconstitutional, since by destroying their courts it unseated judges who were entitled to life tenure under the Constitution.[9] They surrendered, however, to the authority of a Republican Congress and administration. The short-lived federal circuit court for New England held its last session in Portsmouth in the summer of 1802. This left the district judge, John Pickering, alone to uphold the dignity of federal jurisprudence in New Hampshire. Unfortunately, John Pickering, who had been one of the leading legal luminaries of New England in his younger days, the author of the state constitution and a highly respected judge in the state courts, had been completely disqualified for judicial office by 1803. For five years after his appointment to the federal bench in 1795, he had performed his simple duties competently. But in 1800 his nervous disabilities increased to such a degree that he became completely deranged and sought surcease in alcohol.[10]

The Judiciary Act of 1801 had made provision for such cases as Pickering's by authorizing the circuit judges to appoint one of their own number to exercise the functions of any district judge who became incapacitated.[11] In April 1801 a formal notice of Pickering's insanity had been given to the newly established circuit court, and Judge Smith had quietly taken over his duties.[12] It was therefore a truly backward step when the Repeal Act of 1802 forced Pickering to resume his activity on the bench, and it was a foregone conclusion that he would soon provide the administration in Washington with ample excuse for intervention.

The occasion arose in October 1802, when George Wentworth, whom Jefferson had reappointed to the post of surveyor of customs at Portsmouth, seized the *Eliza* and goods that he claimed had been unladen from her contrary to law. The validity of Wentworth's seizure was challenged, but never actually tested by a competent court of law—it seemed to have been at least open to question.[13] The *Eliza* was owned by Eliphalet Ladd, a prominent Federalist merchant, who applied to Judge Pickering for a release and obtained it without showing the proper bonds and papers. Joseph Whipple, the Republican collector of customs, thereupon sued for a libel of ship and goods, and trial was scheduled for November 11. Edward St. Loe Livermore, who had also been deprived of his midnight appointment as district attorney by President Jefferson, was retained as defense counsel, while John Samuel Sherburne, his successor, was, of course, the prosecuting attorney. The trial was destined to become not merely the case of *United States* versus *Eliza,* but the case of *Republican Surveyor, Collector, Marshal, Clerk and District Attorney* versus *Federalist Claimant, Defense Attorney and Judge.*

On the day scheduled for the trial, Pickering came to the courtroom thoroughly intoxicated. He staggered to the bench and ordered the court to open, then commanded the Republican deputy-marshal to sit beside him. The startled officer demurred, whereupon Pickering cursed him roundly and he hastily took the seat upon the judge's right.[14] At this moment a young lawyer who had been educated in England entered the room, and Pickering, with a drunken notion that the Inns of Court might throw some direct light upon the case, demanded his assistance on the bench. When he refused, the judge started down to cane him, but seeing a former British naval officer among the spectators, he decided that he would be an acceptable substitute and placed him at his left hand. Thus fortified against Jacobins, Pickering roared, "Now damn them, we will fight them," and ordered the parties to proceed. Sherburne, the district attorney, reminded Pickering that the libels had not been read; the Judge replied that he had heard enough about the damned libels and would decide the case in four minutes. Seeing that no trial could be held under such conditions, Livermore obtained Sherburne's consent to a motion for postponement. Judge Pickering instantly brightened. "My dear, I will give you to all eternity," he replied to the Federalist lawyer and ordered the trial postponed until the next day, remarking that he would then be sober.[15]

Unfortunately, he was not. When the court reconvened, Pickering was even more inebriated. After hearing the claimant's brief and a few minutes of argument between the attorneys as to the competence of Sherburne's witnesses, Pickering suddenly ordered restoration of the property to Ladd. "We will not sit here to eternity to decide on such damn'd paltry matters," he declared. Sherburne remonstrated and begged that his witnesses be heard. "Very well," agreed Pickering amiably, "we will hear everything—swear every damn scoundrel that can be produced—but if we sit here four thousand years the ship will still be restored." A few minutes later, however, he shut off the witnesses and again ordered the case dismissed.

Sherburne protested that this decision would injure the revenue. "Damn the revenue," shouted Pickering. "I get but a thousand dollars of it." Sherburne appealed. "Yes, appeal," said Pickering, "and let old Wig try it, but by God, he shan't alter the decree, for I will be alongside him." At this point, Livermore objected that the value of the goods seized was not sufficient to admit of an appeal, and the judge upheld his objection. Sherburne hoped he would be allowed to file a bill of exceptions. "File what you please and be damned," roared Pickering, and ordered the court to stand adjourned.

The trial had, of course, attracted sensation-seeking spectators who laughed at the judge's maudlin sallies, but the Republican officeholders were not at all amused.[16] They had not appeared to very good advantage and their resentments were expressed in immediate complaints to Washington. On February 3, hostile depositions collected by Sherburne were forwarded by President Jefferson to the House of Representatives, "to whom," he delicately suggested, "the constitution has confided a power of instituting proceedings of redress, if they shall be of opinion that the case calls for them."[17] On the last day of its session the House responded by voting, 45–8, to impeach John Pickering, with New Hampshire furnishing half of the negative votes.[18] Not until the following winter, however, did the House draw up actual articles of impeachment. Neither in the depositions furnished by Sherburne nor in this indictment was there any suggestion that Pickering's disgraceful behavior might have been due to insanity. The entire weight of the indictment was concentrated upon the judge's intoxication.[19]

The articles of impeachment omitted any mention of insanity, for the very good reason that this condition was not, nor is it yet, a constitutional ground for removal from federal office. The Republicans, therefore, were forced to picture Judge Pickering as a willful drunkard in order to prove him guilty of impeachable "misdemeanors," while the Federalists emphasized only his insanity in their effort to protect him.[20] From this premise the Pickering case evolved into a sorry display of partisan politics indifferent to the public interest. Pickering was summoned by the Senate to appear for trial on March 2, 1804. This allowed the aged lunatic five weeks in which to engage counsel, gather witnesses, and transport them at his own expense to Washington while the government gathered a small army of willing testifiers in Portsmouth and brought them to the capital to appear against him. Pickering, of course, did not even answer his summons. His son, however, with the undoubted encouragement of wealthy Federalist friends, had employed Robert Goodloe Harper, the able Baltimore attorney who later defended Justice Chase, to ask for postponement of the trial, either in order to issue a writ compelling Pickering's appearance or to allow time for the gathering of defense depositions. This dispensation was requested on the ground that Judge Pickering was insane and mentally incapable either of answering a summons or testifying in his own behalf.[21]

The more extreme Republican senators were opposed even to listening to Harper, but a moderate majority joined with the Federalists to vote that he be heard. Harper's evidence, together with testimony by Olcott and Plumer, the two senators from New Hampshire, established the fact of Pickering's insanity beyond any reasonable doubt.[22] Government witnesses, however, insisted that it resulted from the destructive effects of alcohol and that the judge was responsible for his own condition. The seven men called by the House managers to testify were all Portsmouth Republicans, and five of them had been appointed to federal offices by President Jefferson. Joseph Whipple, the collector, had been removed from that office by President Adams and reappointed by Jefferson. Sherburne, the district attorney, and Jonathan Steele, the clerk of the court, were both aspirants for Pickering's place. Since no representative of the accused was present to cross-examine these witnesses, they reveled in a freedom which would certainly not have been allowed in a regular court. They were permitted to hear and confirm each other's testimony.[23] They were also encouraged to repeat hearsay stories and allowed to contradict each other without reproof. After such irregularities it is not surprising that the Republican majority in the Senate found Pickering guilty "as charged" by the necessary vote of 18–9 and immediately removed him from office.[24]

Ten days after Pickering's removal, Jefferson asked the Senate to confirm his nomination of John Samuel Sherburne to the vacant judgeship and of Jonathan Steele to the district attorney's office vacated by Sherburne. The third star witness, Edward Cutts Shannon, was elevated to the clerkship by Sherburne. Unfortunately for Republican harmony, Steele thought that he should have been made judge and refused the district attorney's office. He returned his commission to Secretary Madison, saying that he had been made a contributing instrument in creating vacancies and a due regard to his reputation prohibited his profiting by that achievement.[25] This scarcely veiled criticism both of Sherburne and of the administration was followed eventually by Steele's withdrawal from the Republican party. Sherburne's hypocrisy excited a considerable degree of hostility among the people of New Hampshire, where Pickering had been generally popular. When, after twenty years on the bench, Sherburne himself became insane, many devout persons in Portsmouth considered it to be a judgment of God visited upon him for his part in Pickering's removal.[26] The circuit court in 1826 took the same action in regard to his disability that had been taken for Pickering in 1801, and he continued to draw his salary until his death in 1830. It is a singular circumstance that each of the first three federal judges in New Hampshire became *non compos mentis* while exercising that office.

The constant defeats in Congress, the acquisition of the illimitable wilds of Louisiana to cast into the balance against New England, and the purging of Federalist officeholders in their very midst brought some of the more intemperate minority leaders to the very verge of treason by

1804. New Hampshire's congressmen, firsthand observers of Republican heresy in Washington, were more vociferous than their constituents in this matter. "I wish the eastern States *knew in this her day the things that belong to their peace*," wrote Senator Plumer, who, as a former Baptist exhorter, was fond of scriptural analogies for his politics. "If New England will not *come out & be separate* from this mass of southern corruption *she must partake of their plagues.*"[27] Several New Hampshire Federalists, including both Senators Plumer and Olcott as well as Congressman Samuel Hunt, nephew of Governor Caleb Strong of Massachusetts and member of a prominent Connecticut Valley family, were involved in the secession plot hatched by Timothy Pickering of Massachusetts in Washington during the winter of 1803–4.[28] It is worth noting, however, that although Pickering succeeded in drawing the Essex Junto into a certain degree of complicity, at least epistolary, their Exeter counterparts in New Hampshire were notably cool to the conspiracy. Chief Justice Smith, probably New England's most acerbic critic of Jefferson's administration, admitted that he did not "see much reason to despair of the republic for this year."[29]

Smith had to admit, however, that the political auguries of 1804, even in Federalist New Hampshire, were far from favorable. The Republicans, he reported, had agreed upon candidates for every state and local office and had organized (apparently for the first time in New Hampshire history) a really formidable political machine, complete from a "grand committee of election & correspondence" composed of a leading citizen from each county to a local chieftain for every town in New Hampshire. All this had been done at a secret meeting of the leading democrats in the office of Philip Carrigain, a hotheaded young Concord lawyer whom the Federalists particularly despised. The purpose of this organization, as expressed by Carrigain, was to promote the cause of republicanism and of pure and undefiled religion. Smith's opinion of this perfectly natural development was that of a horrified conservative. "What think you of pure & undefiled religion under the care of Carigain & French—are you willing to confide your temporal concerns to these worthy citizens? They have leisure and I presume inclination to superintend the management of *your* property—neither of them are much embarrassed or cumbered with any of their own."[30]

To a considerable degree, the state elections in New Hampshire in the spring of 1804 were of national importance. Of the five New England states, Rhode Island and Vermont had already become Republican, while two others, Massachusetts and Connecticut, were conceded to be almost irredeemably Federalist. New Hampshire determined the balance of power; if it remained Federalist, there was some slight chance that a secession might be effected, but if it became Republican, a detachment of

New England from the Union would be hopeless. Jefferson was doubly anxious for the victory of John Langdon, not only for the sake of an old friendship but for the blow which that victory would strike at the "bastard system of federo-republicanism" being hatched by Timothy Pickering and Oliver Griswold.[31] As the Ides of March approached, Jeremiah Smith became increasingly nervous at the signs of violent political feeling and even feared that riots might occur at the town meetings. "Let the event of the election this year be as it may I think . . . federalism is done over in this state," he wrote to Plumer.[32]

Although Smith's prophecy was ultimately fulfilled, he was not immediately justified in his pessimism. Gilman lost only 17 votes from his total in 1803, but Langdon gained so many new voters that the issue was in doubt until the last town had reported. Then it was clear that Langdon had received 3,028 votes more than his total in 1803 and lacked only 208 of becoming the governor of New Hampshire.[33] Rockingham and Hillsborough counties had been won over, and even Cheshire was shaken. The Republicans were disappointed in failing to elect Langdon, but they were very nearly consoled by winning a decided majority in the legislature. This indeed was a momentous victory, for it made the fruition of a secessionist plan virtually impossible and struck a decisive blow at the schemes of Pickering and Griswold.

When this first Republican legislature in New Hampshire's history met in June, it passed resolutions endorsing Jefferson's administration, ratifying the Twelfth Amendment, and dividing the state into congressional districts.[34] Gilman assured his defeat at the next election by vetoing these acts, while Langdon, as speaker of the house, a position in which he always appeared to great advantage, won increased popularity.[35] These developments, together with Burr's defeat in New York and the subsequent death of Hamilton, effectively killed the movement for secession.

A few vigorous Federalists in New Hampshire, however, rejecting the usual pessimism with which their colleagues accepted defeat and reasoning that organized effort should not necessarily be a Republican monopoly, decided to put up a strong fight for the congressional elections in August. Among these men who met secretly in Concord on July 4 were Senator Plumer, Thomas W. Thompson of Salisbury, a Harvard-bred attorney with whom young Daniel Webster was reading law, and William H. Woodward, a lawyer from Hanover and treasurer of Dartmouth College.[36] The apparatus that they put together was even more sophisticated than Carrigain's Republican machine. Under themselves as a state committee, county committees were established which appointed agents in each town and each school district. Provisions were made to secure funds, to support the Federalist newspapers, to enlist new voters and to keep registers of all Federalists.[37] Plumer, under the pseudonym "Impartialis," wrote a far from impartial *Address to the Electors of New Hampshire*, which was printed first in the newspapers and then in pamphlet form.[38] The energy of the Federalist campaign surprised and enraged the Republicans. Gideon Granger wrote to Jefferson that their foes were "making astonishing exertions."[39] The *New Hampshire Gazette* reported that Cheshire County Federalists were employing "immense pecuniary contributions, systematic caucusing, and incredible exertions."[40] The result was eloquent testimony to the effectiveness of such tactics. The Federalist candidates won by an average majority of eight hundred votes, but even more remarkable was the fact that the total vote cast was almost double that of the previous congressional election.

This Pyrrhic victory, which, in effect, made lame-duck congressmen of the five New Hampshire Federalists even before their terms began, proved to be the last triumph of Federalism in the Granite State for nearly five years.[41] Although the new Federalist machine ground out a good deal of propaganda against Jefferson and tried strenuously to defeat his electors at the town meetings in November, the effort failed. The electorate, which had swung from Republican to Federalist between March and August, recoiled even more quickly between August and November. Nearly 4,000 summer voters stayed at home in the fall, but two-thirds of these were Federalists and the Republican electoral ticket prevailed by an average majority of 652 votes.[42] Too many Federalists in New England had deemed it futile to oppose the Jeffersonian juggernaut. Not only New Hampshire but even Massachusetts chose Republican electors. Only Connecticut and Delaware, among all the seventeen states, cast their votes for Charles Cotesworth Pinckney, the inert Federalist candidate for the Presidency. It was the first political landslide in American history, and it buried beyond any hope of recovery the secessionist plot of Timothy Pickering.

If anything more was needed to convince the local disunionists that their time had not yet come, it was added by the New Hampshire legislature in its December session. The General Assembly of Massachusetts had called in June for another amendment to the federal Constitution—abolition of the three-fifths compromise. There is nothing beyond circumstantial evidence to link this resolution with the plottings of Federalist congressmen, and it is unlikely that the majority of Massachusetts Federalists were consciously erecting a standard of separation. Nevertheless, they could hardly have been blind to the disruptive effect that such an amendment, if actually adopted, would have had on the Union. It would have saved New England the trouble of seceding; the slave states would have separated from the North. Governor Strong had been authorized to send copies of the resolution to the other state legislatures and solicit their cooperation in the continued good work of patching up the Constitution.[43]

Governor Gilman laid the Massachusetts resolution before his Republican legislature in November. Roles were strangely reversed. In June, the governor had vetoed his legislature's resolution to ratify the Twelfth Amendment on the ground that "by one change after another the constitution [is] essentially altered and the harmony of the System destroyed."[44] Now the governor championed the principle that one good change deserved another, although his chief argument in favor of the Ely Amendment was that direct federal taxes were levied so infrequently as to cheat New Hampshire of its quid pro quo. Meanwhile, the Republicans, who had so lately insisted that the Constitution needed frequent renovation, now stood staunchly in defense of its sacred compromises. "We believe," they answered Gilman, "that alterations, especially in articles of such importance as the principles of representation and taxation, ought not to be made without mature deliberation and an extensive view of the subject, in its remote as well as immediate consequences." They went on to argue that future wars were inevitable and would have to be financed by direct taxes, "in which event the proposed alteration should it take place, would be severely felt by a State so intirely agricultural as New-Hampshire."[45]

Such ardent admiration for the Constitution by those who were supposed to have opposed its ratification is an excellent illustration of the vicissitudes of politics and of the grievously false position in which the Federalists of New Hampshire had placed themselves. Massachusetts's proposal was rejected by a strict party vote of 87–70 in the New Hampshire assembly. It was similarly spurned by all the other states in the Union except Connecticut and Delaware, neither of which took action upon it.[46] The rebuke was even more stinging than the one administered to Virginia and Kentucky in 1799. Together with the election returns in November, it constituted an overwhelming endorsement of Jefferson and his policies, from Georgia to the District of Maine.

CHAPTER 13

FEDERALIST COLLAPSE

Democracy has obtained its long expected triumph in New Hampshire . . . and [its] success is not owing to snow, rain, hail, or bad roads. It is an incontrovertible fact that the federalists in this State do not compose the majority.—William Plumer.

The political revolution that had brought triumph to the forces of the Democracy on the national scene in 1800 finally achieved an equal victory in New Hampshire in the spring of 1805.[1] The Republicans fought with the boldness of assured victors. The New Hampshire press, which had formerly been devoted exclusively to the service of their enemies, now furnished them with valuable auxiliaries. In 1801 Portsmouth Republicans had acquired control of the state's oldest journal, the *New Hampshire Gazette*, and had immediately filled its columns with blasts at Federalist judges, lawyers, and clergymen.[2]

The next year at Walpole in the overwhelmingly Federalist Connecticut Valley a new democratic journal, The *Political Observatory*, was established by a gifted minister driven out of Connecticut for political heresy.[3] Bristling with shrewd attacks upon religious intolerance and secret caucuses, this paper featured a full exposure of Governor Gilman's past errors in connection with the state treasury and the Union Bank.[4] Ignoring the fact that John Taylor Gilman's two brothers were off-and-on Republicans, the *Observatory* begged that this "aristocratic branch of a most powerful and most numerous family may be lopped, and the genius of liberty no longer shaded and stifled by federalism rise eternally to overpower the rank, poisonous, destructive weeds of tyranny and oppression."[5]

Against such vigorous thrusts the Federalists offered only a halfhearted defense. The well-oiled machine of the previous summer had succumbed to winter rust and failed to respond to the tentative efforts of its creators. Only young Daniel Webster, among all the Federalists, seemed willing to expend energy in the hopeless cause. Seating himself at his father's table in the old farmhouse at Salisbury during a dull winter's day, he composed a stirring *Appeal to the Old Whigs of New Hampshire*, which was published anonymously in February.[6] This first production of a budding genius was superior in literary quality but virtually identical with other pamphlets of its kind in argument, evasion, distortion, and rabble-rousing. "Do we prefer the enemy of WASHINGTON [Langdon] to his friend [Gilman]?" asked Webster, with considerable violence to history. "Do we prefer such a government as the mercy of Jacobinism may hereafter bestow on us, to the National Constitution?" But even young Daniel, with all his untried vigor, was not really optimistic, as his eloquent conclusion demonstrated:

> While our adversaries are making auxiliaries of all the fiery and headstrong passions, shall not Federalists enlist an honest enthusiasm in their cause? Shall there be nothing cold in the Country but real enthusiasm? nothing unanimated but duty?—A united, vigorous, persevering effort, may do much. If it cannot prevent the final catastrophe, it may, at least, delay it—delay it, a few years, till the remnant of the Fathers, who achieved our Revolution, shall be carried to peaceful graves, and their presence no longer reproach the apostacy of their sons?[7]

Webster's jeremiad had no effect on the election, unless it was to sting his opponents into greater activity. Gilman gained only forty-one votes over his 1804 total, while the Republican vote increased more than 25 percent and gave John Langdon a majority of 3,751. The Republicans swept the state, carrying eight of the twelve senatorial districts, electing three of the five councillors and obtaining a majority of forty in the house of representatives.[8] President Jefferson, who had for several years anticipated this victory, sent his felicitations to Langdon as early as February:

> I congratulate you, my dear and antient friend, on the wonderful things which have come to pass in our time. we entered young into the first revolution & saw it terminate happily. we had to engage when old in a second more perilous, because our people were divided . . . but we have weathered this to & seen all come round & to rights. when we parted last, you had to go home & work against wind & tide to bring up the loiterers; I had to lead on those who had just made a breach in the fortress of federalism. all is now settled.[9]

Federalists were convinced that the final seizure of the state government by their enemies would be accompanied by fearful convulsions. They surrendered power grudgingly, and Gilman was so dejected that he even failed to provide refreshment for the honorific escort that saw him home from Concord. Langdon, however, made a mild and undistinguished speech to the legislature, which did nothing much more dangerous than elect Philip Carrigain, Jr. to the post of secretary of state. The Republican legislature of 1804, it is true, had passed the three measures previously mentioned which Gilman had vetoed, but had otherwise only transferred the public printing contract to a good democratic newspaper office and passed a resolution deploring the "abuse and invective" daily appearing in the press "against the constituted authorities of our general government."[10] This resolution had been combined with the endorsement of Jefferson's administration, which Gilman had vetoed. Probably recalling Republican strictures on the Sedition Act, the sober governor had included an unaccustomed touch of irony in his veto message:

> While he declares his readiness to co-operate with the legislature in all constitutional measures for preventing the licentiousness of the press, and is ready to do all in his power for the preservation of our Union, and for supporting such measures as may be best calculated to promote the general welfare, he is compelled to say, that . . . such has been his opinion respecting some measures of the administration, that he is not prepared to express that unlimited confidence which the resolutions seem to purport.[11]

This Republican legislature of 1804 had evinced a surprising degree of respect and patriotic concern for the state judiciary. In spite of Judge Smith's sarcastic remarks about French and Carrigain's managing a little theater of impeachments, he had asked for and received a five-hundred-dollar increase in his salary.[12] This unprecedented grant was made to Smith personally as long as he continued in office, and it made him the highest-paid public official in New Hampshire. The resolution had passed the house by a vote of 101 to 54, which meant that no less than twenty-eight Republicans must have voted for it, in spite of Smith's acknowledged partisanship.[13] The same party that was impeaching federal judges was thus recognizing and rewarding the excellent work that a Federalist judge was doing on the New Hampshire bench.

As a perfectly natural consequence, however, two of the puisne justices, Livermore and Atkinson, conceived themselves to be unjustly discriminated against and petitioned at the December session for favors comparable to Smith's. Repenting perhaps of what they had done in June, the Republican legislators not only rejected the memorial but decided to compensate for the largesse to Smith by limiting the superior court to three judges as soon as one of the four incumbents retired. Smith, sardonically but privately, extolled the legislature for finding a means to extract revenue from the leanest of all sources—the judiciary. Not even Jefferson and Congress had been able to do that![14] Livermore's hot temper flared at this treatment, and he became less punctual in his attendance at court. Complaints inevitably arose, and in June 1805 the Republican legislature launched an investigation that looked like the prelude to a purge. Livermore was a far less pliable man even than Judge

Chase. He answered the questions of the investigating committee with a tart letter, which denied any negligence whatever and contained the following spicy comment:

> It is well known that, formerly in this State, the extreme parsimony of those who composed the General Court had effectually cooled the zeal of most judges for the public service, & tended powerfully to put down the whole government of New Hampshire to the level of contempt. And it is a fact that the little glimmerings of liberality that have at times appeared in the Legislature have uniformly been harbingers of encreased assiduity in judges and in other officers, & productive of much good to the community.[15]

These words did not sweeten the tempers of the legislators. They rejected the report of a committee which had recommended a larger salary for the puisne justices by a crushing vote of 23–119 and refused to create an interim committee to study a reform of the judicial system.[16] At the next session the senate passed a resolution to remove Livermore by address, but the Republican house defeated it 63–71.[17] At a time when the Jeffersonians were straining every nerve to remove a Federalist judge from the Supreme Court, New Hampshire Republicans thus refused to exploit a promising opportunity to begin a local purge. Although removal of a judge required only a majority vote of both houses, the advice of the council, and the signature of the governor—all of which the Republicans could have delivered—they allowed the state judiciary to remain solidly Federalist. At the same time, however, suspicion of the judiciary, encouraged by Livermore's behavior, prevented the completion of a judicial reform like the one that took place in Massachusetts during this period.[18]

John Langdon, indeed, was no longer much of a revolutionary when he returned to the governor's chair in 1805. He was sixty-four years of age, dejected by the recent death of his brother Woodbury, and increasingly devoted to orthodox Congregationalism.[19] Such a man was not likely to enter upon the destruction of New England institutions. The old patriot announced his political principles at the beginning of his administration in sentiments with which the Federalists could hardly quarrel, however much they might criticize the grammar in which they were clothed:

> It is greatly to be lamented that for some years past our citizens have been so much divided in their political sentiments; this makes it in some measure necessary for me to declare mine. I consider myself a republican, and have uniformly (as far as I have been able) from the year 1775 to this day, supported the principles of a free

elective government of the people; from whom all our power and authority originate, being fully convinced that a Republican Government faithfully administered, is the strongest, the freest and the best that has ever yet been experienced.[20]

In later speeches, Langdon showed an even more conciliatory temper. His recommendations were always very practical. He urged particular attention to the militia, the fixing of a state capital, the building of a state prison, encouragement of agriculture and of education. He recommended economy, but found that money was needed to support Republican as much as Federalist measures and had to ask for the usual tax levies. Until 1807, Langdon wisely refrained from stirring up trouble by addressing issues of foreign affairs and national business. In short, had it not been for his constant encomiums on Jeffersonian prosperity, it would have been extremely difficult to tell by his speeches that the governor was not a Federalist. Nor did he differ greatly from Gilman in his conception of his office. When the legislature passed a bill taxing the capital stock of banks, Langdon showed so little respect for the sovereign will of the people's representatives as to give it his veto, thus protecting the stockholders with whom, after all, he was more closely connected.[21]

There was less Republican head-hunting than might have been expected after so long a struggle for power. Oliver Peabody's resignation in 1804 had provided an opportunity to elect a new state treasurer. The Republicans gave the office not to a faithful partisan but to the governor's brother Nathaniel Gilman, a recent and halfhearted convert from Federalism. Nicholas Gilman was also rewarded for his complacency by being sent to succeed Simeon Olcott in the Senate. Thus the remarkable Gilman family remained well entrenched in the citadels of power, even though John Taylor's eleven-year reign had come to an end. A year later, the Republicans not only relegated Joseph Pearson, the secretary of state, to private life after nineteen successive elections, but found him guilty of neglect for not having recorded the public acts passed since the laws had been revised in 1792.[22] The resignation of Jeremiah Mason from the attorney generalship in 1805 gave the Republicans an opportunity to recruit another wavering Exeter Federalist, George Sullivan, by the gift of an office.

For the most part, these appointments and elections evinced a shrewd sense of political strategy rather than a heedless tendency to sweep out the Augean stables. In only one instance did the Republicans use their power to pervert an election. Their candidate for councillor from the strongly Federalist county of Cheshire, Nahum Parker, made an unusually good showing against the Federalist candidate, Moses Hale, in 1805, but Hale gained a small majority. One of the town clerks, however, had spelled the name H-A-L-L on his return, and the legislature decided to deprive Hale of these votes. Even then, the Federalist still had a plurality but lacked the necessary majority. This threw the election into the legislature, which, of course, chose Parker. The steal aroused little protest, however, for it was neither the first nor the last time that the will of the sovereign people had been thwarted by the orthographic vagaries that prevailed among town clerks.[23]

Having definitely established themselves in control, the Republicans settled down to the business of government with little to distinguish them from the Federalists whom they had replaced. It is true that they more readily granted legal recognition to the religious sects that petitioned for it, but the Federalists in the legislature offered no opposition to these bills, letting them pass without division. Governor Langdon's recommendations on behalf of education were met with increased school taxes and a land grant to Dartmouth College. Banks, manufactories, turnpikes, and canals were chartered, a state map was authorized, and the public lands were sold with the same mixture of public spirit and private gain that had animated Federalist administrations.

Even in the realm of national affairs the Republicans acted more like "New England men" than the Federalists had expected. Unwilling to wait even three more years to begin redressing the black balance against the North, the legislature in 1805 instructed New Hampshire congressmen to support an amendment to the Constitution prohibiting immediately the further importation of slaves.[24] When Federalist Senator Plumer received this instruction from Republican Governor Langdon, he was compelled to point out that the amending clause itself rendered such an amendment impossible until 1808, and that even if it were possible, it would probably not be expedient. What a strange reversal of roles![25] Even more surprising, however, was the New Hampshire legislature's refusal to join with Pennsylvania in urging an amendment to restrict the jurisdiction of the federal courts or with Kentucky in a protest against the Ely Amendment advocated by Massachusetts.[26] The house of representatives was so busy during the winter session of 1805 in dealing with these matters that it did not have time to draft the customary memorial of congratulations to President Jefferson.[27]

In one other respect the Republicans showed themselves willing to abandon their former radicalism and to imitate the example of Federalist administrations. This was in regard to the perennial demand for the division of the state into congressional districts. In December 1805 the Federalist senators obligingly called the attention of their opponents to this traditional part of their program, but the Republican majority decided to postpone consideration. In June 1806 a house committee reported that there was too little time to undertake such an important business so soon before the election.[28] Thus did the Republicans pay tribute to the Federalist doctrine of maintaining a united front in Congress. The wisdom of their conversion was demonstrated in August when five Republicans were elected by general ticket and without much opposition to the House of Representatives.[29] After March 1807, when William Plumer was succeeded by Nahum Parker in the United States Senate, the Republicans were as completely in command of the government in New Hampshire as it was possible to be without wrecking the judicial establishment. With real propriety the house of representatives was able to say to Governor Langdon: "We rejoice with you that a collision of parties is no longer felt in the State—that a measure of harmony is restored—and that a fair prospect is before us, which promises concord and happiness."[30]

As for the Federalists, they became astonishingly apathetic after their stunning defeat in 1805. The organization that Plumer and Thompson had so diligently erected a year earlier seems to have collapsed. John Taylor Gilman refused any longer to be a candidate for governor, and the Federalists did not take the trouble to unite on a new one. Their total popular vote shrank almost half between 1805 and 1808, and they lost their hold on every part of the state except the Connecticut Valley. Apologizing to its readers for not printing the spring election returns in 1806, a Federalist newspaper made one of the most remarkable confessions of impotence ever to appear in the political history of the republic.

> The annual meeting for the choice of state, county and other officers, was holden throughout the state on Tuesday last. There is no doubt of the reelection of His Excellency John Langdon.—Indeed no opposition, no systematized exertions have been made to counterbalance the vigilance and adroitness of the democrats. . . .
> The federalists, voting unbiasedly, dependent on no one for instruction for whom to give their suffrages, have supported several of the best men in the state, as their opinions of the abilities and the integrity of the candidates happened to be. . . . Though sensible of the improbability of electing their favourite candidate, it affords a pleasing reflection to know that their principles are still unchanged, and that they still prefer a disciple of the Washington School to the man who now holds the helm of government. The foundation of their political principles is not placed on a crumbling basis of sand, but rests on the stable rock of truth; unmoved by the violent and temporary gusts of party.[31]

The transition to Republicanism in New Hampshire was not as dramatic as the Federalist sweep in 1799. No Republican issue gripped the imagination of all the people, as had the Federalists' anti-French policy at the end of the previous decade. Republican success was due to the lack of an issue and a most satisfying state of prosperity. If the Federalist party had been in a position to claim credit for the peace and national expansion of the period following 1800, it is unlikely that its hold on New Hampshire could have been shaken. The Republican party by reason of its national victory inherited the advantages of a booming commerce and the favorable opportunity to purchase Louisiana. As expressed in his first inaugural address with the practical modifications forced by the Tripolitan War and the Louisiana Treaty, Jefferson's laissez-faire democracy was as perfectly adapted to the political needs and ideals of the New Hampshire farmers as any doctrine they had ever heard.

From a tactical viewpoint the problem of the Republican leaders in New Hampshire had been to break up the close union of squires, merchants, lawyers, clergymen, and yeomen farmers that had formed behind President Adams and Governor Gilman in 1799. This might have been accomplished in either of two ways: vertically, by the detachment of the majority classes in certain geographical areas from their fellows in neighboring sections; or horizontally, by luring the yeomen farmers away from their adherence to the politics of the upper class.

It has usually been assumed that the Republican politicians bent all their efforts toward the latter of these two alternatives. As a matter of fact, the Republican leaders themselves, particularly in Portsmouth, represented a defection from the aristocratic party that had procured the adoption of the federal Constitution, and they always welcomed new recruits from their own class. Thus, Timothy Walker, Nathaniel Gilman, and George Sullivan had each been favored with an important office when they deserted the Federalists. William Plumer was to be welcomed even more generously when the party went over many a veteran's head to nominate him for the governorship in 1812. But this policy indicated a scarcity of adequate leadership in the Republican ranks as much as a genuine desire to convert good men. It was proof in itself that so many of the squires, merchants, lawyers, and ministers remained in the Federalist party as to make it top-heavy and to deprive the Republicans of able leadership.

Thus, the Republican party that dominated New Hampshire from 1804 to 1808 was, much more than in Virginia or Kentucky, a party "of the people." Aside from the Portsmouth aristocrats and a few Federalist apostates, its leadership was drawn almost entirely from a younger generation. Such men as Benjamin Pierce of Hillsborough, Philip Carrigain of Concord, Samuel Bell of Francestown, and the sons of old Josiah Bartlett had all been nurtured from birth in Jeffersonian doctrine. The party attained its supremacy by gradually gaining the confidence of the people, not by any such adventitious popularity as came to the Federalists in 1799. That attainment has perhaps been adequately accounted for by the events narrated in the last few chapters. Nevertheless, certain phases of the story merit some elaboration.

In the first place, it is important to notice the geographical spread of Republicanism. In 1800 it was confined to three restricted areas: the shipping and fishing vicinity of Portsmouth, the more remote agricultural towns of the Merrimack Valley, and the shores of Lake Winnepesaukee.[32] By 1806 it had swept inland over the entire Old Colony, leaving only Exeter and seven other small towns still attached to Federalist principles. In the Merrimack Valley the Republicans captured Concord and Amherst, gaining a strong ascendancy over this region. Their most remarkable achievement, however, was in the Connecticut Valley. In Cheshire County they gained Walpole and eighteen other towns, so upsetting the balance of power that for four successive years they were able to elect a Republican councillor from that Federalist stronghold. Only in the north did they fail to make decisive gains. Some of the thinly settled towns in Grafton County were won over, but almost as many others were regained by the Federalists. In the state as a whole, however, Republican gains on the map are almost as impressive as they were in the vote tally.[33]

The increase in the Republican gubernatorial vote between 1799 and 1805 was greater than the entire Republican and Federalist vote combined at the beginning of the period. In other words, the Langdon machine brought out enough new voters to swamp the entire electorate that had endorsed the Adams foreign policy. The total vote in gubernatorial elections increased by 142 percent between 1799 and 1805. Federalism gained a little more than 21 percent, which was only 4 percent greater than the rate of increase in the voting population—it barely held its own among the new voters. But the Republicans increased their numbers by more than 900 percent during these six years! In 1805, 16,705 more people voted than in 1799, and 99 percent of this additional electorate was Republican.[34]

Clearly, the Republican party achieved its tremendous success not by converting Federalists from the error of their ways but by tapping a new reservoir of latent voting power. It persuaded the common stockholder in the body politic to attend meetings, rather than vote by proxy, and thus destroyed the Federalist directorate. A glance at the record for a few towns confirms the impression that the Republican majorities were made up of new voters (see Table 13-1). Table 13-2 will help to clarify the situation in each section of the state.[35]

It will be seen at once that both parties gained adherents in every section during this remarkable period but that the Republican gain was greater than the Federalist *in every section*. The Federalist increase in the

TABLE 13-1

Towns	Party Vote	1800	1805
Exeter	Federalist	190	143 (lost 47)
	Republican	3	64 (gained 61)
	Totals	193	207 (increased 14)
Hanover	Federalist	128	209 (gained 81)
	Republican	0	58 (gained 58)
	Totals	128	267 (increased 139)
Dover	Federalist	117	108 (lost 9)
	Republican	109	202 (gained 93)
	Totals	226	310 (increased 84)
Amherst	Federalist	123	111 (lost 12)
	Republican	85	266 (gained 181)
	Totals	208	377 (increased 169)
Walpole	Federalist	121	125 (gained 4)
	Republican	1	152 (gained 151)
	Totals	122	277 (increased 155)
Portsmouth	Federalist	183	252 (gained 69)
	Republican	486	722 (gained 236)
	Totals	669	974 (increased 305)
Weare	Federalist	1	13 (gained 12)
	Republican	202	302 (gained 100)
	Totals	203	315 (increased 112)

TABLE 13-2

Sections	Party Vote	1800	1805
Old Colony	Federalist	1,387	1,943 (gained 556)
	Republican	1,579	3,968 (gained 2,389)
	Totals	2,966	5,911 (increased 2,945)
Merrimack Valley	Federalist	3,057	3,707 (gained 650)
	Republican	2,287	6,417 (gained 4,130)
	Totals	5,344	10,124 (increased 4,780)
Connecticut Valley	Federalist	2,896	4,746 (gained 1,850)
	Republican	168	3,860 (gained 3,692)
	Totals	3,064	8,606 (increased 5,542)
Frontier	Federalist	956	1,296 (gained 340)
	Republican	659	1,546 (gained 887)
	Totals	1,615	2,842 (increased 1,227)

Old Colony and the Merrimack Valley was so small as to fall behind the population growth rate, while the Republicans made tremendous strides, completely dominating these two areas. The most interesting development is in the Connecticut Valley, where the Federalists put up a fight and won enough new voters to keep a clear majority. The Republicans, however, took over the Frontier by a small margin, so that in 1805 they controlled three of the four geographical areas in the state. So overwhelming was the Republican victory that it caused an immediate collapse of the Federalist party. Federalist resistance might have vanished completely had it not been for President Jefferson's embargo.

In order to persuade so many indifferent citizens to use their neglected right of suffrage, the Republicans needed and created a well-oiled political machine. That, in itself, was regarded by the Federalists as the deliberate introduction of a plague that had originated in England and had long since corrupted the South.[36] The New Hampshire Republicans had a definite ticket in the congressional election of 1796, and Federalist papers were soon thereafter accusing them of wicked concert. In the heated struggle over incorporation of the Union Bank, both parties had developed their legislative caucuses into effective engines of control. The Republicans, however, were undoubtedly the first to expand their legislative caucus into a vigorous, state-wide machine for "that detestable practice of electioneering."[37] It was their success in that field which galvanized the Federalists into counteraction in 1804 and produced an increase of 117 percent in the popular vote for congressmen. At best, however, the Federalists were slow imitators, as they themselves acknowledged. After 1804 their machine disintegrated from disuse, and its inventors soon relapsed into their former apathy, contemptuously leaving the cultivation of the electorate to their opponents.[38]

Politics and religion had been wedded by the orthodox clergy in the 1790s, when they had joined the Federalist party in the crusade against Jacobinism. Like the Congregational ministers of Massachusetts and Connecticut, those of New Hampshire remained permanently and belligerently Federalist as long as there was a party by that name to support. Their influence had been one of the strong factors in New Hampshire's unanimous Federalism in 1799. So firm in their abhorrence of revolutionary France were the settled clergy that agnostic Federalists such as William Plumer readily contributed to their salaries and helped build their meetinghouses.[39]

The Republican leaders, who, as a group, were no less orthodox than their Federalist opponents, bitterly resented the partisan spirit of their ministers. The first reaction in the Republican press was savage criticism of clerical meddling with matters that were not primarily religious.[40] Since these attacks had no appreciable effect, Republican strategists soon decided to enter the religious arena and to turn the antagonism between the dissenting sects and the standing order to political account. Such tactics fitted in perfectly with the Republican plan of campaign. Baptist and Methodist preachers usually drew their followers from the lower classes, which the Republicans were striving to bring to political awareness.[41] A Republican tactician who did not seek to exploit sectarian discontent for party purposes would have been singularly inept. The turn of the century, therefore, saw such phenomena as a Congregationalist Republican, John Langdon, advocating religious liberty and a deistical Federalist, William Plumer, championing the Calvinist establishment.

The sectarian preachers probably leaned as definitely toward the party of Jefferson as the orthodox did toward Federalism. The most vociferous Republican dissenter was Elias Smith, whose pulpit served without apology as a campaign platform. In 1801, Smith preached a Thanksgiving Day sermon which placed Daniel and the prophets on the side of Jefferson and compared Federalism to the anti-Christ. "Some of the monarchy men attended," he wrote with satisfaction, "but could not relish what was set before them."[42] The *Herald of Gospel Liberty*, which Smith established in 1808, was almost equally a herald of Republican politics and, according to a reputable Congregational minister, "in part supported by the contributions of some leading politicians in this state, for the express purpose of securing his political influence and efforts."[43] One of these supporters was a Republican member of Congress who admitted that "in Mr. Smith . . . he had no confidence, but that his preaching answered a good purpose for his political ends." If Federalist leaders somewhat cynically sought political alliance with the established clergy, it appears that Republican politicians emulated their example in dealing with the sectarian preachers.

There is abundant evidence that the Jeffersonians labored diligently to draw the dissenters within their political net with promises of religious freedom. "Remember my Brethren, that the truth you believe, is not supported by the friends of State Religion," wrote the editor of the *New Hampshire Gazette*.[44] The denunciations thundered against the Republicans by the Federalist press revealed the same campaign technique. The *Portsmouth Oracle* complained, "That party has been continually denouncing the clergy of regular standing as the friends of monarchy and charging them with intermeddling with politics with which they have no concern. But what is their conduct with the Baptists? it is unnecessary to answer."[45]

The evidence points clearly enough to two facts: that the clergy on each side of the state-church question were also political opponents, and that the politicians of both parties exploited the religious issue in order to win votes. This evidence does not, however, answer the more important question of whether the propaganda of press and pulpit was effective with the masses at whom it was directed—whether it brought results.

The acid test of the ballot showed that neither were the Federalist voters so opposed to religious liberty nor the Republicans so devoted to it as has often been represented. It is true that the Republican legislatures from 1804 to 1807 fulfilled their campaign promises in part by legalizing the position of Universalists, Baptists, and Methodists. But in spite of their great majorities they did not attempt a frontal attack upon the legal establishment.[46] On the other hand, the Federalists offered no opposition to these resolutions of religious freedom, allowing them to pass without even a roll call. Religious contention, like political warfare, underwent a period of tacit armistice after 1805.

One of the most effective items of Republican propaganda in the campaigns from 1799 to 1802 grew out of the Federalist legislatures' refusal to incorporate the Union Bank. The final two votes in the house relative to this issue serve to show its relationship to politics.[47] With few exceptions, the towns that voted Republican regularly in gubernatorial elections also favored the Union Bank. Staunch Federalist towns were less consistently opposed to it—note Chester, Kensington, Salisbury, Holderness, and Fitzwilliam on Map 15. The most interesting revelation, however, is the great number of towns, particularly in the Connecticut Valley and the Frontier, that changed from opposition in 1800 to support in 1801. No less than twenty-five of these also deserted Gilman and voted for Langdon during this period. Eighteen other towns whose representatives had persisted in voting against the Union Bank changed from the Federalist to the Republican column *after* 1801—note Epping, Hampstead, Dunstable, Walpole. These facts indicate that the Union Bank issue played an important role in making Langdon governor of New Hampshire.

The voting on the state capitol issue is an interesting example of harmony between Portsmouth and Exeter in spite of politics. In his first address to the legislature in 1805, Governor Langdon recommended a settlement upon a permanent capital. The house voted to hold the next session at Concord, which seemed to be in line with Langdon's policy, but the Republican senate substituted Portsmouth, ostensibly as a compliment to the new governor, and the house concurred.[48] An analysis of these votes shows that, in spite of party policy as announced by the governor, the Old Colony, including Portsmouth, voted almost solidly against Concord on both occasions. The other three sections of the state, Federalist and Republican towns alike, voted almost equally uniformly for Concord on the first trial. Representatives of thirty-eight towns, most of which were Republican, carried the vote for Portsmouth by shifting from their earlier stand.

Exeter and Portsmouth also agreed upon the desirability of giving aid to Dartmouth College. Educational measures, even when they involved heavier taxation or the expenditure of state funds, did not have a marked tendency to become political issues. During the 1790s, the more important and progressive towns—Portsmouth, Exeter, Londonderry, Amherst, Concord, Keene, Charlestown, and Hanover—had generally supported a liberal educational policy, while remote agricultural towns— Atkinson, Weare, Stoddard, Wolfeborough, Plymouth—did not. As far as sentiment toward Dartmouth College was concerned, the situation took a peculiar turn after the Republicans came into power. The larger centers continued to patronize the college, regardless of politics, but the smaller towns shifted about unaccountably and those in the eastern part of the state showed, in general, an attitude of hostility. The northern and southern sections of the Connecticut Valley supported Dartmouth strongly, while a block of towns in its immediate neighborhood turned against it. Fifty-two Republican towns favored Dartmouth's pleas for assistance, but sixty-six opposed them. Among the Federalist towns, only eleven opposed Dartmouth, while fifty-five voted in sympathy. These figures are interesting in the light of a future period when the college was to become a very lively political issue.

The refusal of Federalist legislatures to divide the state into congressional districts appears to have operated in favor of the Republican cause. Prior to 1800 three-quarters of the towns in every section of the state were united in favor of the congressional general ticket.[49] After 1800 Republican propaganda against this undemocratic practice was particularly effective in breaking up this solidarity east of the Merrimack.[50] But a comparison with the political map shows why the Republicans themselves abandoned the districting principle after they came to power. It would have taken a most ingenious gerrymander to have prevented the creation of at least one Federalist district in Grafton County.

The general conclusion to which this analysis leads may be summarized briefly. The Republican party, which in 1799 was a despised and dejected faction, within six years gained control of the government and every part of the state except the Connecticut Valley. It was able to accomplish this miracle by use of a superior organization which drove a wedge between squires and yeomen and won a great mass of lower-class voters, whom the Federalists had never bothered to cultivate. These new voters were persuaded that New Hampshire benefited too much from the Jeffersonian regime to maintain a different system at home. As long as the national territory was increased, the national debt diminished, taxes abolished, and commerce allowed to flourish, it was easy to make Republicans of new voters. New Hampshire slipped naturally into line behind an administration that was ideologically fitted for an agricultural state. So serene did everything become that Federalist opposition disappeared, and, indeed, appeared to have disintegrated. It was only in the domestic problems of church and state, banks, turnpikes, official salaries, and education that lines of cleavage in an old, established society continued to exert some small influence.

CHAPTER 14

BLOCKADE AND EMBARGO

Our ships, all in motion,
Once whitened the ocean,
    They sail'd and return'd with a cargo;
Now doom'd to decay
They have fallen a prey
    To Jefferson, worms, and Embargo.
                                        —Anonymous

In 1804, President Jefferson had won the electoral votes of every state in the Union except Connecticut and Delaware.[1] This Republican landslide was especially savored by Massachusetts Jeffersonians dwelling in the heart of enemy territory. They followed it in 1806 with the capture of their state legislature, and in 1807 they elected their candidate, James Sullivan, to the governorship. It appeared that even in New England, Federalism was a dying cause.[2] It might well have disappeared from the political scene completely had not the young American republic become entangled again in the national and imperial rivalries of Europe.

The ordinary people of New Hampshire had observed the extraordinary rise of Napoleon Bonaparte with mixed emotions. To the Federalists in general he was the "heir of the French Revolution," and they hated him as fervently as they had despised the Jacobins. The more extreme Federalists, who regarded England as the bulwark of religion and civilization, saw Napoleon as the anti-Christ. This was especially true after his victories at Austerlitz and Jena, which left him virtually the master of continental Europe. "The Emperor of France is the wonder & astonishment of the world," exclaimed Senator Plumer. "Who can set limits to his conquests! . . . Tis fortunate for us that a vast ocean separates America from Europe. This, I hope, will prove a barrier against his great power."[3]

Republicans had no less reason to be grateful for the Atlantic Ocean rolling between them and their unpredictable friend in Saint-Cloud. That vulnerable avenue to his colonies had been at least one reason for his willingness to sell Louisiana, but his accommodating spirit had virtually stopped at that point. After Austerlitz and Trafalgar, which left Napoleon supreme on land and England in control of the seas, Americans were caught almost helplessly in the epic struggle between elephant and whale.

The demands of war brought immense profits and tremendous risks. Neither England nor France scrupled to fight with illegal blockades, interdictions, and confiscations when they could not effectively battle each other with arms. In the midst of this kind of economic warfare, Americans attempting to carry on a neutral trade with both belligerents were playing dangerous games.

Portsmouth merchants suffered heavily, as their ships were seized both by the British navy and by Napoleon's officers in continental ports. Profits far outweighed losses, however, as the trade grew by leaps and bounds, so the Federalist merchants were inclined to let well enough alone. British seizures under the Orders in Council, especially after the harsh *Essex* decision in 1805, were annoying and undoubtedly illegal, but the Anglophile Federalists were eager to overlook them in the interests of peace and prosperity. During the congressional debates on a proposed non-importation act in 1806, a Portsmouth merchant wrote:

> [Randolph] has hit off my idea exactly on the *fungus* trade, and the part Great Britain is now acting.—The most remote danger of war, for this extended carrying trade is absurd & ridiculous to the last degree. . . . In case the command of the ocean should go out of the hands of the English to the French, our state would be most probably very deplorable; Bonaparte would only have to take back the Mississippi New Orleans &c to be able to supply the principal part of his West Indies with every necessary without our trade or assistance & sure with his emmense resources in Europe he could depress the United States to any terms he might think proper to dictate.—If this reasoning be just we ought rather to allow G.B. every support to their naval power, that was consistent with our honor or security—But in my opinion the remaining malice for G.B.—& partiality for France will ruin these States.[4]

Federalist merchants were equally lenient toward Great Britain's practice of impressment, which, after all, did not affect them personally and had a certain grim rationale. James Sheafe, who had served in Congress and was one of Portsmouth's wealthiest importers, wrote in March 1806:

> The noise respecting Impressment of our Seamen is louder than the real evil requires . . . Beyond Measure half our Seamen are foreigners and none of them are without Protections which are daily procured by fraudulent Practises. . . . The British will always be justly jealous that we are cloaking their Subjects under false colours and deprive them of the services of Men from whom they depend almost altogether for their political Salvation at the present time from the almost omnipotent Power of France.[5]

Suddenly, in July 1807, word reached New Hampshire of an incredible British outrage—the attack of his majesty's warship the *Leopard* upon a virtually unarmed public vessel of the United States, the *Chesapeake*. The news of this disgraceful affair spread over the countryside as Americans were preparing to celebrate the thirty-first anniversary of their independence, and it united their sentiments as nothing had done since the XYZ excitement. Jefferson's proclamation ordering British warships out of American waters was universally approved, and "the federalists & republicans united in condemning the conduct of the British."[6]

The Atlantic coast burst into a flame of indignant memorials and resolutions. Portsmouth joined the other ports on July 13 with a set of resolutions adopted by a "large and respectable meeting." The townsmen called the *Leopard*'s attack "an act of hostility against the sovereignty and Independence of our country," declared they would "cheerfully submit to any sacrifices, which the necessity of the times may require," and warned those who might impede the measures that "our government may see fit to appoint" that the ominous Tory label—"enemies to our country"—would be revived against them.[7] Few there were who did not expect soon to be at war with Great Britain.

After the first hot flame of anger had cooled, however, and particularly after Jefferson's policy of commercial retaliation appeared to be as much pro-French as anti-British, Federalists began not only to criticize the administration but to excuse and justify Great Britain. This attitude of appeasement led some of the more nationalistic Federalists to break with their party. Senator John Quincy Adams attended a Republican indignation meeting in Boston and was subsequently recalled from his Washington post by the Federalist legislature of Massachusetts.[8] In New Hampshire his friend former senator William Plumer openly denounced the Exeter Junto and offered his support to President Jefferson.[9] New Hampshire's seven Republican members of Congress voted obediently for all of the president's embargo bills, although a former Granite State Federalist, Edward St. Loe Livermore, now representing the Newburyport district of Massachusetts, was a conspicuous opponent.[10] Even the people sympathetic with Jefferson, however, regarded the embargo as at best only a temporary nuisance and a necessary evil. Writing to an old friend in the Senate, William Plumer declared that

> I am an advocate for the freedom of commerce, but presume
> congress when they imposed the embargo, possessed information of
> danger to which our commerce was exposed, which it was then
> improper to disclose, but which if known, would have prevented
> prudent men from hazarding their ships on the ocean. When this
> danger shall, from any source whatever, be known to our merchants,

will the embargo be continued, or is it designed to operate against other nations? If the latter is the object, I fear while we are chastising them with *whips*, we shall be scourging ourselves with *scorpions*.[11]

It seems superfluous to say that New Hampshire suffered from the embargo. It was never supposed, even by the most sanguine Republican. that a sudden and violent enforcement of economic autarchy could be painless. New Hampshire's Jeffersonians regarded the measure with wry distaste, but defended it loyally. As their recently established organ, The *American Patriot* of Concord, admitted:

The embargo is a medicine prescribed by the government for the recovery of commerce, and although it is a little nauseous will produce eventual good. . . . There is one [other remedy]. It is *war*. But that . . . is a desperate medicine, and ought never to be used but in the last resort. A skilful physician never uses mercury when a milder preparation will suffice; And our administration have not thought it prudent to rack the republic with an agonizing specific whilst a more lenient application would answer.[12]

For New Hampshire, this somewhat specious argument held more validity than for other New England states. The immediate weight of the embargo fell upon the shipowners and shipbuilders of the Piscataqua region, yet the registered tonnage of New Hampshire vessels engaged in foreign trade decreased but slightly between 1807 and 1808.[13] The greatest sufferers were those whom many regarded as parasites anyway— the merchants engaged in the carrying trade. Reexports of foreign produce from Portsmouth plummeted from $314,072 to $2,765 during the embargo years.[14]

This staggering loss was proportionately greater than that of any other state except North Carolina and Georgia. Yet it affected but a small portion of the population—a few of the more speculative merchants in Portsmouth and their employees. The sailors, shipwrights, rope-walk workers, and artisans of the Piscataqua region must have been sore beset by unemployment and starvation, but they were few in number and they bore their trials with patriotic resignation. The fishermen of Rye and Newcastle, another class of humble men, also remained true to Republican principles in spite of the embargo, which reduced the general value of the fisheries by 70 percent.[15] It is a striking comment upon the doctrine of economic determinism that the area of New Hampshire most severely injured by the embargo—Portsmouth and the surrounding towns—remained loyal to the party and leader whose policy was the source of its pain.

Portsmouth, however, was far less representative of New Hampshire in

1808 than it had been during the days of prerevolutionary nonimportations. In 1775 the town had been one of the greater ports of New England, and the economy of New Hampshire had depended much upon its prosperity. In 1808 Portsmouth represented only a fragment of a population which was chiefly agricultural and which probably sent more than half of its surpluses to other ports. Measured by the exports shipped from Portsmouth, New Hampshire had fallen to thirteenth place among the nineteen states and territories in 1807, and its commerce was only a thirtieth of that of Massachusetts.[16]

The interests directly affected by the embargo therefore were small compared with the large agricultural concerns of the state. Farmers felt the pressure of trade restrictions belatedly and indirectly in the shape of falling prices or unmarketable surpluses. The degree to which they felt it at all depended on the extent to which they produced surpluses. The self-sufficient husbandmen on many a rocky New Hampshire hillside produced nothing to be embargoed. Only the landed proprietors of the rich valley farms, who raised beef or wool for export, and the lumbermen living along the large streams, whose boards, staves, shingles, spars, and hogsheads formed the major item in the West Indies trade, were immediately affected by the loss of foreign markets. The 74 percent decline in the value of lumber exports must have been peculiarly hard for some parts of the state to bear.[17]

Eventually, nearly all farmers were affected in some way by the decline in agricultural prices as surpluses accumulated in the markets. Potatoes lost 23 percent of their value, butter dropped 17 percent, cheese 5 percent, beef 9 percent, mutton 22 percent, and merchantable boards 12 percent.[18] The inhabitants of New Hampshire who purchased foreign luxuries could also justifiably complain of the exorbitant prices that they were soon forced to pay. But it should be emphasized again that, because of its rural population, its short seacoast, and the small proportion of its people directly interested in foreign trade, New Hampshire was probably less seriously hurt by the embargo than any other New England state, even Vermont.

These were the eventual effects, measured statistically, of a daring national experiment as it impinged upon a small and relatively unimportant part of the nation. That injuries were not immediately felt was indicated by the results of the spring elections in 1808. While the Federalists in Massachusetts and Rhode Island regained control of their state legislatures, Langdon carried his party to another easy victory in every elective branch of the government. In his speech to the assembly the governor did not mention the embargo, although he praised the administration for its "pacific disposition." He was inclined to ascribe "the gloomy prospect of our national affairs" to the righteous wrath of heaven rather than to either President Jefferson or King George, and he warned his fellow citizens that "we have not given God the glory, but have trusted too much to our own strength and wisdom."[19]

The house of representatives responded in an even more biblical strain, imputing righteousness to Jefferson but berating their fellow citizens in language that the skeptical president might have considered slightly extravagant: "We acknowledge, Sir, that this people have sinned: . . . we have neglected that means of heaven, the gospel of Jesus Christ; and have expected substantial good from the vanities of the world. Hence luxury, and avarice, and impiety, have opened a way to immorality and vice; and indeed we have too much reason to fear, that some among us even wish for a king to reign over us!"[20]

Several days later the legislature adopted an address of commendation that contrasted sharply with the anathemas hurled at Jefferson from other parts of New England. It was a noble composition, painting the first six years of Republican rule in glowing colors. Unfortunately the brightness had to fade when, almost reluctantly, the embargo was approached. After a recital of grievances against both England and France, the Republican legislators concluded that the Embargo Acts were the only means by which American commerce could be saved "from the rapacious grasp of a piratical power, and our seamen-citizens from insults, slavery, and death." Obedience to the law of the land did indeed "require the exercise of much virtue," but "we will suffer any privations, rather than submit to degradation, and we will cooperate with the General Government in all its measures." Then followed a panegyric to the retiring president and a slightly morbid sentiment: "On your exit from this world, that you may receive the plaudit of God, is, Sir, the wish and prayer of the people of New Hampshire."[21]

The address was adopted, 95–64, which may have indicated that it was not the prayer of two-fifths of the people of New Hampshire. Jefferson, however, ignored the minority and expressed particular gratitude for this testimonial from hostile New England. In his rather naive defense of the embargo, the president made an unfortunate reference to the growth of manufactures. "I see with satisfaction that this measure of self denial is approved and supported by the great body of our real citizens; that they meet with cheerfulness the temporary privations it occasions, and are preparing with spirit to provide for themselves those comforts and conveniences of life, for which it would be unwise ever more to recur to distant countries."[22] The Federalists pounced upon this innocent expression and twisted it into an admonition to abandon foreign commerce. Even after four years had passed, Jefferson had retired, and the embargo had been repealed, Daniel Webster recalled these words and thundered, "We do not hesitate to say, that we deem this language equally unconstitutional and arrogant."[23]

Jefferson accompanied his public acknowledgement with a private letter to Governor Langdon, couched in language of bitter disillusionment, which contrasted pointedly with the false optimism of his words to the legislature. He admitted that war was the only alternative to the embargo, unless "the whale of the ocean may be tired of the solitude it has made on that element, and return to honest principles; and his brother robber on the land may see that, as to us, the grapes are sour. I think one war enough for the life of one man; and you & I have gone through one which at least may lessen our impatience to embark in another. still, if it becomes necessary we must meet it like men, old men indeed, but yet good for something."[24]

Langdon's reply was a petulant denunciation of the Essex Junto for making political capital of the embargo. He insisted that they were sending emissaries into New Hampshire to secure the election of Federalist congressmen in August and were sparing neither pains nor money to achieve success.[25] It was evident that Langdon's patience had been sorely tried. He was indeed an old man, tired of politics and contention, and just when the state had become completely tranquil under his benign rule, his own party had awakened a virulent quarrel by a policy which was difficult even for its friends to swallow. The Federalists had taken advantage of Langdon's mercantile background to claim that he had privately expressed opposition to the embargo, and he had been forced to make a special announcement of denial and of support.[26] He had been subjected to the annoyance of issuing licenses to merchants for the importation of flour into Portsmouth, since the Piscataqua region did not raise its own wheat. Langdon had performed this unpleasant task much more circumspectly than had Governor Sullivan of Massachusetts, but it had inevitably exposed him to charges of favoritism and autocracy. He protested to Jefferson because the Additional Embargo Act had been construed unfavorably to New Hampshire, and he stoutly asserted: "This *revenue district* is as free from any evasion of the embargo laws, as any others in the United States; we are nearly all in favor of the embargo, and the Merchants of this place would not suffer a few enemies and speculators to make their fortune, while they themselves were suffering every inconsequence, and seeing (if permitted) it would defeat the intention of Government—I hope we shall have an equal chance with our sister States, and I will engage we shall be as honest."[27] In spite of Langdon's assurances, Gallatin listed Portsmouth, in November, as one of the places where violations of the laws had taken place.[28]

Friends of the administration surveyed the growing opposition to the embargo during the spring and summer of 1808 with anxiety. The breakdown of negotiations with George Rose, the British minister, in April convinced them of the necessity of maintaining the hated restrictions for a longer period. But the resolution of the Massachusetts legislature condemning the embargo and their proscription of John Quincy Adams boded ill for it in New England. Rather than lift the embargo in 1808, as New England Republicans had hoped it would do, Congress adopted still more stringent measures to enforce it. As the congressional elections drew near in August, Federalists made good use of the embargo's increasing unpopularity. The Essex Junto stepped up its propaganda campaign and probably circulated Timothy Pickering's *Letter to Governor Sullivan* throughout New Hampshire. "At no election since the establishment of our government, has their been so much time & money spent in New Hampshire, as at this," wrote William Plumer, who had openly switched to the Republican party. "The Federalists were bitter, malignant, & misrepresented the proceedings of the administration."[29]

The August elections seemed to indicate that a profound revolution had taken place in public opinion during the summer. The state that had given Langdon an overwhelming majority of 9,383 votes in March now elected the Federalist ticket of congressmen by an average majority of 1,300. This has been interpreted as a change in public opinion caused by the embargo. It was less a Republican defeat, however, than a Federalist recovery. The chief result of the antiembargo propaganda had been to arouse and consolidate the normally Federalist voters, who had been somnolent and scattered since 1805. The total vote drawn out by the first vigorous campaign in three years was nearly three times greater than the vote in the previous congressional election and, for the first time in New Hampshire history, far exceeded the vote in the previous gubernatorial contest. Both parties had made tremendous exertions to create this increase, but while the Republicans more than doubled their vote over that which had been sufficient for victory in 1806, they accounted for only 37 percent of the total gain. Nearly two-thirds of the newly aroused voters were Federalists, responding to the clarion call of their old party slogans.

The distribution of the vote for congressmen in 1808 bears out the conclusion that the economic stringency of the embargo was less responsible for the Federalist victory than was expert campaigning. The Federalists increased their vote sufficiently to produce majorities in thirty-six towns that had been Republican since 1805, although at the same time they lost five small towns. Fourteen of the recovered towns were in the Connecticut Valley and eight in the Merrimack Valley, while the net gain in the Old Colony and the Frontier was only five and four respectively.[30] Thus it is evident that the Federalists regained their ascendancy simply by recapturing the majorities in their old territory, leaving the party pattern of the map essentially undisturbed. The economic dislocations of the embargo seem to have had little effect in those areas where they might be supposed to have embittered the people. This is particularly evident in the Old Colony, where the unemployed sailors, fishermen, and artisans gave their usual majority for Republican candidates, who might be expected to keep them unemployed until Jefferson decreed otherwise. Such a phenomenon called forth an encomium from the *Independent Chronicle* in Boston:

> To prove that the federal success in New Hampshire was not the effect of any real pressure, of the Embargo, but was produced only by *Embargo clamor*, we need only mention that in almost every town near the sea-coast, and particularly concerned in trade, an increased democratic majority was given. In Portsmouth, the majority was vast and unexpected—and surely if the embargo were felt severely in any part of the State, it must have been there. The Portsmouth Republicans have gained immortal glory, and deserve the applause of every American.[31]

In spite of Portsmouth's loyalty, however, it was apparent that New Hampshire was being "federalized," as was all the rest of New England, by antiembargo propaganda, if not by embargo suffering. Governor Langdon informed candidate Madison that his election was endangered by the "enormous quantum of Treason dayly circulated" throughout the northern states by "venal papers."[32] Senator Nicholas Gilman began intriguing against Madison in favor of a northern antiembargo candidate, and Secretary Gallatin, closely in touch with embargo violations, reconciled himself to a Republican defeat in November.[33] As far as New England was concerned, his pessimism was justified. Every state but Vermont chose Federalist electors, and Madison's six votes from that state were secured only by the undemocratic expedient of choice by a rotten-borough legislature.[34] In New Hampshire the Federalist ticket won by the slender majority of about six hundred votes. The Republican legislature experienced the humiliating necessity in December of having to provide accommodations and expense money for seven political foes who gave the state's electoral vote to Charles Cotesworth Pinckney of South Carolina. Although Madison won the presidency without the help of New England, he faced a solid phalanx of Yankee opponents in Congress and an aroused Federalist minority throughout the country.

Federalist opposition to the embargo mounted to rebellious proportions during the winter of 1808–9, especially in Massachusetts. Nearly every issue of the New Hampshire newspapers during the early months of 1809 contained accounts of town meetings or county conventions in Massachusetts at which bold resolutions condemning the embargo and insulting memorials demanding its repeal were adopted. Even more ominous were the committees of correspondence that these meetings usually appointed and the appeals that they made to their state legislatures to protect them from the tyranny of the general government. "As far as they were able," noted Plumer, "they took measures similar to those which prevailed in the early stages of our revolution."[35] Newburyport even revived a company of minutemen.

Timothy Pickering's prominence in promoting these acts of defiance seemed to indicate that the extreme Federalists were plotting secession again, as they had in 1804. The activities of the Federalist state officials in New England gave further evidence of concert and collusion. Governor Trumbull of Connecticut refused to appoint militia officers to aid the collectors in enforcing the embargo, alleging that he had no authority to uphold an unconstitutional law. A few days later, the state legislature approved his conduct, threatened to nullify the embargo laws within the state's borders, and concurred with Massachusetts in demanding constitutional amendments that would secure the interests of commerce.[36] The Federalist majority in the Massachusetts legislature had already censured Republican Governor Lincoln for complying with the request that Trumbull had defied and had declared the latest embargo act to be "not legally binding on the citizens of this state."[37]

Republican control of the legislature in New Hampshire prevented that state from participating in the nullification gestures made by its neighbors. Addressing the second session in November 1808, Langdon had rather feebly attempted to explain and justify the embargo. Congress was then in session, he reminded his auditors, and "the Embargo which must be considered by all as a very great inconvenience, will without doubt be taken off at the moment it can be done, with safety to the public."[38] Jefferson himself, in his reply to the congratulatory address of June, had dealt largely in evasions. "Our first duty was to withdraw our seafaring citizens and property from abroad," he had written, "and to keep at home resources so valuable at all times, and so essential, if resort must ultimately be had to force."[39]

The Federalist minority seized upon these confessions of weakness with avidity. To replace the expressions of approbation that the majority's committee proposed as a reply to the governor, Thomas W. Thompson offered a series of strongly worded substitute amendments, pointedly questioning the necessity of interdicting trade with other neutral countries or with Canada if the embargo was merely designed to protect American shipping from belligerent decrees. The unlimited duration of the embargo, the severe restrictions on coastal traffic, the closing of American ports to foreign vessels, and the applause with which Jefferson's policy was greeted in France all pointed, said Thompson, to an interpretation of motives quite different from that offered by the administration. The minority summarized their argument in a cogent paragraph:

> Hence we believe that the conclusions are inevitable that the protection of our ships, property and seamen, was neither its [the embargo's] ultimate nor its principal object, and that its utility in that point of view has long since ceased; that as a measure of coercion it is perfectly futile; and that it is not to be considered an indignant refusal to submit to the decrees and orders of the belligerent nations. If we are correct in our views of this very important subject, no necessity now exists to continue the embargo in its present extent.[40]

These remarks served their purpose by appearing in the journals, but as amendments to the committee's report they were declared out of order by the Republican speaker and the orthodox, submissive reply was accepted by a party vote, 96–68. In order to appease public opinion, the Republicans permitted the creation of a committee to report on the expediency of petitioning Congress for a repeal of the embargo, but carefully packed it with partisan henchmen. Then they apparently decided to allow the question to expire quietly, but the Federalists again forced them into battle by introducing an independent resolution that the embargo was "unnecessary and ruinous to the country at large, unprecedented in the annals of other nations, and a prostration of the honor of the United States."[41] Thus confronted, the representatives of the people of New Hampshire voted 36–102 against petitioning for a removal of the embargo. The Republicans, of course, voted almost solidly against it, and they were joined by the representatives of fifteen Federalist towns, while a great many Federalists, particularly from the Old Colony and from Cheshire County, refrained from voting. This apparent reluctance of New Hampshire Federalists to follow their leaders was widely hailed as an embargo victory. Reporting on northern public opinion to Senator William B. Giles, John Quincy Adams interpreted the defeat of the resolution as "a strong indication that many of the federalists begin to perceive the danger of the ground to which they are thus drawn, and may possibly moderate the proceedings here."[42]

The August and November elections, however, had made the legislature elected in March something of a lame-duck institution and discredited the support that it gave the embargo. The real battle over the issue was being fought in the newspapers, the churches, and the taverns of New Hampshire. It was a battle in which the antiembargo forces enjoyed all the advantages of the offensive. Against such a measure it was easy to indulge in sweeping generalities, as did a pamphlet which was widely circulated before the August elections. "The embargo has destroyed our commerce, banished our seamen, reduced the value of the labors of our husbandmen to almost nothing, deprived many of our mechanics of the means of earning their bread, struck out of circulation the money of the country, multiplied lawsuits and executions, and will fill our jails with prisoners for debt."[43]

This address harped on all the old strings and ended on the familiar, ominous note of separation and civil war unless New England's influence in the Union was restored. The *Portsmouth Oracle* declared that "this powerful, flourishing, happy, enlightened country presents the *first spectacle* of voluntary debasement—of self-immolation."[44] Daniel Webster joined the war of words with a pamphlet that declared the embargo laws unconstitutional. "The individual states were originally complete sovereignties," wrote the man who was to deny this comforting doctrine to Calhoun and Hayne in 1830. "By the Constitution, they mutually agreed to form a General Government, and to surrender a part of their powers, not the whole, into the hands of this Government."[45] The power to impose an embargo, of course, was one of those which had *not* been surrendered.

The embargo may have destroyed New England commerce, but it was a great stimulant to Yankee wit. Sarcastic allusions to the American China and to the great American Turtle, usually labeled *O Grab Me*, filled the Federalist newspapers. One convivial satire, rather better than the average, was composed by a poet in Dover to be sung at a Fourth of July dinner in 1808. As usual on such occasions, it was interminable, but two stanzas are worthy of quotation:

> Our ships, all in motion,
> Once whitened the ocean,
>   They sail'd and return'd with a *cargo*;
> Now doom'd to decay
> They have fallen a prey
>   To Jefferson, worms, and *Embargo*.
>
>   . . .
>
> Thus Tommy destroys
> A great part of our joys;
>   Yet we'll not let the beautiful fair go;
> They all will contrive
> To keep Commerce alive,
>   There's nothing they hate like *Embargo*.[46]

The burden of journalistic defense was taken up largely by the new Republican organ established in Concord, the *American Patriot*. This paper, under the genius of its later editor, Isaac Hill, was destined to become the greatest rabble-rouser north of Boston. In its first issue,

October 25, 1808, it printed a savage attack against Federalist lawyers and clergymen, appealing to the poor and to the sectarians against these proud dictators. This was indicative of its persistent policy. It studiously avoided an open defense of the embargo, but directed a bitter counter-attack against the Federalists as warmongers and disunionists. In November the *Patriot* printed inflammatory appeals for class warfare at the polls. The embargo, it said, of course diminished the profits of bankers, shopkeepers, and lawyers, who therefore selfishly opposed it and would willingly drive honest farmers into the destructive alternative of war.[47]

As protests against the embargo swelled in volume, the *Patriot* turned its attention almost entirely to denunciations of the great Federalist secession plot, evidences of which it detected on every hand. Disunionist sentiments appearing in Federalist newspapers, the activities of British agents in the seaports, and disloyal town meetings were vigilantly brought to light and appropriately excoriated.[48] "Let me ask whether those who are in favor of a dissolution of the union, merit the appellation of federalists?" queried the editor.[49] In contrast to Federalist antipathy toward Virginia, the *Patriot* featured the articles of *Algernon Sydney*, who observed sensibly that New England ought to be grateful for membership in a Union that included economies complementary to her own. Even her loss of political control was fortunate, he told her people. "You ought not to forget that direct influence is solely charged with the duty of making the nation happy, while indirect influence enjoys every national benefit without responsibility."[50]

The frequent denunciations in the *Patriot* of Congregationalist ministers as fomenters of treason clearly indicated that the embargo was attacked from the pulpit. On every Sabbath day the meetinghouses throughout New Hampshire reverberated with anathemas hurled at Jefferson, and some of the northern preachers were not unwilling to repeat Timothy Dwight's famous sermon on the text "Come out therefore from among them and be ye separate, saith the Lord." This political intolerance caused many an orthodox New Hampshire Republican to find himself in the dilemma well described by Matthew Carey: "That portion of the congregation differing from the preacher, are reduced to the alternative of either absenting themselves from divine worship, or sitting patiently silent under the undeserved reproaches, and abuse, and maledictions of a man who flies in the face of all his duties, and to whom they cannot offer a reply."[51]

Few orthodox Republicans, perhaps, were driven into dissenting sects by their ministers' politics, but it is certain that the Republican politicians cultivated the Baptists, Quakers, and Methodists more assiduously than ever before. They also proved that even if they could not quote scriptures quite as pertinent as those which the ministers found to their purpose, they could at least write clever parodies. According to one satirist, the robed politicians should have preached from II Kings 18:29–32, rendered thus: "Let not Jefferson deceive you, neither let Madison make you trust in the Lord, saying the Lord will surely deliver us; hearken not unto them, but hearken to George the third: and make an agreement with him, to pay him tribute, and come out to him, and he will give you liberty. Yea, he will let you, every man, eat of his own vine, and every one of his own fig tree, and drink every one of the water of his own cistern, and hearken not to your Rulers."[52]

In spite, however, of the agitation of pulpit, press, caucus, and bar, and despite the near rebellion brewing in Massachusetts, it does not appear that the people of New Hampshire became greatly exercised over the embargo. The "disorganizing seditious spirit . . . breathes here in whispers and low murmers," declared one observer.[53] In other parts of New England the revenue officers were resisted with bloodshed, but the hanging of Jefferson in effigy at Exeter seems to have marked the height of mob violence in New Hampshire. No county conventions or self-appointed congresses of antiembargo delegates were held in the state, and the *Patriot*, which had a keen nose for sedition, reported town meetings of protest only in Keene, Packersfield, and Gilmanton.[54] The only New Hampshire petition presented to Congress, in contrast to the dozens that poured in from Massachusetts, came from the Cheshire County town of Packersfield (now Nelson), which was probably as little affected by the embargo as any place in the state.[55]

Toward the end of the winter, however, the gap in prices between imported goods and agricultural products, as well as the scarcity of currency resulting from the loss of exports, brought a perceptible degree of suffering to the poor farmers of New Hampshire. Some relief was gained by the rise of domestic manufactures, and Republican leaders tried to encourage this trend by wearing homemade garments.[56] But prosperity waned, and symptoms of the hardships of the 1780s began to reappear. Banks overstrained their resources in meeting the demand for notes, the poor murmured against the lawyers, and debtors asked for tender laws. Nevertheless, the common people bore their sufferings patiently, since the embargo was the chosen policy of their great leader. Jefferson's hold over their affections was made clear to him in a warmly human letter that he received from a semiliterate follower in Charlestown.

> Sir I have respected your laws and your government for the younited State of merricia and I wish to have you continue your laws and goverment and keep the embargo on til you see fit to take it off, though it is very trying to the people in this country about there debts and it is my wish that you would make some laws to pay our

debts without paing the money and if the is a law to pay with produce & cattle and horses I think that the orter be a tender act so we can pay our debts without money I sopose that you think strange of my writing to you but . . . I hope that you will take som notis of me, and write to me as soon as you get my letter so I may know if your oner will do a little for me,

Jonathan Hall Capt.[57]

The credit for New Hampshire's obedience to the law, however, rested not alone with its Republicans. The moderate Federalists were equally responsible for a record which contrasted as favorably with Federalist Massachusetts's nullification as with Republican Vermont's evasion. The New Hampshire attitude toward Timothy Pickering and his plots was expressed probably as well as anywhere in a Federalist newspaper.

We are glad to see an impartial opinion obtain in regard to the conduct of France and England. . . . They both merit the appellation of Barbarians. . . . Yet we still regret the growing prevalence of party animosity respecting our internal regulations. . . . We regret that ideas of a separation of the States and civil war should be introduced for no good purpose—for the gratification of a few malicious individuals. . . . If, after one year's experience the situation of our foreign relations renders a continuance in the present anti-commercial system necessary, in view of our constitutional authority, for the preservation of our independence and interest, we must submit.[58]

Although New Hampshire played but a small part in that Yankee defiance which frightened Jefferson into abandoning the embargo, its citizens were not sorry to see it go. Senator Nicholas Gilman, who was essentially a Hamiltonian Federalist, had deserted the administration as early as December 1808, when he voted against the so-called Force Bill.[59] To a correspondent who had begged him not to "go against Admn . . . in the present crisis," Gilman replied savagely: "How shall one support the Administration, and who is to be confided in? . . . To follow them through all their twistings and turnings I should require a portion of your faith my own stock I fear will be insufficient."[60]

New Hampshire voters were not too much surprised at this volte-face by Gilman, but they were a bit startled by the defection of Congressman Francis Gardner, who lived in the Republican town of Walpole but who voted not only against the Force Bill but against the Non-Intercourse Act.[61] The parting word from his neighbors, he said, was, "For God's sake take off the embargo before you return," and he followed their injunction by introducing a resolution for its repeal in December. Senator Parker, from the same area, joined Gardner and Gilman in voting against the Non-Intercourse Act, which superseded the act creating the embargo.[62] Thus, half the New Hampshire delegation in Congress had deserted the administration at a crucial moment, and the incoming quintet of Federalist representatives was sure to offer the most persistent opposition. The embargo had gone far to undermine the work that Langdon had done for Jefferson in the Granite State.

In Amherst the *Farmer's Cabinet* expressed a strong hope that the repeal of the embargo would reconcile all parties and bring peace once more to the political atmosphere.[63] The hope was illusory. It now became apparent that the Federalist revival had struck deep roots into the nourishing soil of foreign controversy and that the political war in America would rage until peace descended upon the battlefields of Europe. The Federalists simply shifted their attack from embargo to nonintercourse and played the dangerous game of shouting for war measures on the erroneous assumption that the Republicans "could not be kicked" into fighting.[64]

Langdon's followers had some hope that the skies would clear again in June 1809, when David Erskine, the new British minister, promised withdrawal of the Orders in Council and President Madison suspended nonintercourse with Great Britain. Disappointment was all the more bitter when Erskine's promises were repudiated and Madison was forced to resume the interdiction of British trade in August. A large amount of shipping sent out under the relaxed laws was captured, Republicans were humiliated, Federalists were confounded, and stagnation once more descended upon the ports. Erskine was recalled; Francis James Jackson, who succeeded him in Washington, soon revealed that he had nothing to offer, and was given his passports. Relations between Great Britain and the United States were no better in 1809 than they had been in 1807, before embargo and nonintercourse had been suffered for the sake of their improvement.

The repeal of the embargo came too late to help the New Hampshire Republicans in the March elections of 1809. The Federalist renaissance, begun in August of 1808 and continued in November, swept on to a third resounding victory. There is fascinating mystery in this resurrection of what had seemed to be a dead party. For three years the New Hampshire Federalists had stayed away from the polls or had scattered their votes among sectional favorites without any apparent direction from a party organization. Then in 1808 the caucus suddenly agreed upon candidates for all state and national offices and the central committee waged a series of expertly conducted campaigns.

This was more than a popular revolt against the embargo; it was discernment by a previously discouraged party machine that the embargo furnished a golden opportunity for vaulting back into power. Republicans cast about to find the secret of their foe's remarkable success. Noting the substitution of Jeremiah Smith and Oliver Peabody, both lawyers, for James Sheafe and John Taylor Gilman, both traders, on the Federalist electoral ticket in 1808, the Republican papers darkly hinted that the New Hampshire party had fallen under the vigorous control of the Essex Junto and that through the agency of Edward St. Loe Livermore it was being reorganized by the lawyers.[65]

However that may be, there is certainly no doubt about the party's increased efficiency. It was said to rest upon corruption by a writer who called himself Junius. Federalists bought votes, he charged, with money and liquor, threatened to foreclose mortgages, spread patronage abroad, prostituted the pulpit and the classroom, and sold out to the lawyers. "Have not many of the country traders been brought under the yoke of the British importing Merchant, and made to plough among the stubble, that the seeds of sedition may be scattered for a plentiful harvest?" he inquired.[66]

For some unaccountable reason, Jeremiah Smith was persuaded in 1809 to resign his seat on the superior court, where by patient and indefatigable labor he had for seven years been reforming the jurisprudence of the state, in order to become the Federalist candidate for governor. Republicans, not surprisingly, ascribed his decision to unworthy motives —vanity and the "love of . . . vulgar popularity."[67] It is difficult to understand, even on that score, why Smith left a secure, nonpolitical position which was congenial and peculiarly honorable to him to hazard his career for a political bombshell which offered three hundred dollars less salary and infinitely more trouble. At any rate, he had the immediate satisfaction of beating the popular Langdon by 369 votes out of a total twice as great as that cast in 1808. More significant than the gubernatorial victory were the changes in the legislature, where the Federalists obtained majorities of two in the senate and about fifteen in the house of representatives. In accomplishing this, they had recovered four senatorial districts and thirty in the lower house which their opponents had held in 1808.

The Federalist victories of August and November 1808 and March 1809 may fairly be accepted as a measure of the political consequences of the embargo in New Hampshire.[68] When the smoke of battle cleared away in March, it appeared that the Federalists had recovered or captured from their opponents some fifty-five towns, while twelve others had been shaken from their Republican allegiance in at least one of the three elections. The Federalists had improved their percentage of the total vote in every section of the state and had built up majorities in the Connecticut Valley and the Frontier. Table 14-1 tabulates the incomplete newspaper statistics.

The Federalist revival was accomplished by gains almost evenly distributed over the state. The increases in the Old Colony and the Merrimack Valley were insufficient to give the Federalists control of these regions, but Smith's party won the Frontier away from the Republicans and greatly increased its preponderance in the Connecticut Valley. This vote distribution cannot be interpreted as a reflection of actual economic hardship. In the Old Colony, the area which depended most directly on foreign trade, the Federalist gain of 7 percent appeared in the country towns, such as Epping, Barrington, and Southampton, while the ports— Dover, Rye, and Portsmouth—remained unswervingly Republican. The Federalists made their greatest gains in the Merrimack Valley, where they recovered such important towns as Chester, Concord, and Gilmanton, building up nearly solid control of the actual river valley. Boston's grip on the economic life of the river towns paid political dividends when a tangible grievance such as the embargo could be exploited by the Essex Junto. It is significant that the Republicans suffered absolute losses from their totals of 1805 in the two river valleys, where Massachusetts and Connecticut influence was strong, rather than on the seacoast, where the direct pinch of the embargo was actually felt.

Although the Federalists were unable to continue their ascendancy in 1810, the renewal of internal divisions on questions of foreign policy had created a new political balance in the state. From 1809 until 1816 the

TABLE 14-1

		1805	Percent of vote	1809	Percent of vote	Percentage gain
Old Colony	Federalist	1,943	33	2,708	40+	7
	Republican	3,968	67	4,018	60−	
	Totals	5,911		6,726		
Merrimack Valley	Federalist	3,707	37−	5,244	47	10
	Republican	6,417	63+	5,827	53	
	Totals	10,124		11,071		
Connecticut Valley	Federalist	4,746	55−	5,389	61+	6
	Republican	3,860	45+	3,390	39−	
	Totals	8,606		8,879		
Frontier	Federalist	1,296	45+	2,023	55+	10
	Republican	1,546	55−	1,655	45−	
	Totals	2,842		3,678		

two parties were almost evenly matched, neither winning by more than a 10 percent margin in any election. Each party won four of the eight annual contests. The votes were not only evenly divided but remained distributed according to a fairly uniform pattern. Exeter once more divided the Old Colony with Portsmouth, the trading towns of the two great river valleys pulled away from the hill towns of the interior, and the Frontier split again into western Federalist and eastern Republican halves. This was to remain the basic topography of politics in New Hampshire until the Era of Good Feelings brought the Federalist disintegration which might have come a decade earlier had Jefferson not tempted fate with his embargo.

CHAPTER 15

DRIFTING TOWARD WAR

O Governor, don't be afraid! It doesn't take much of a man to govern New Hampshire. —Anonymous

The repeal of the Embargo Act erased the problems of foreign relations from the consciousness of the average New Hampshire citizen and restored his faith in the republic.[1] Commerce revived under the Non-Intercourse Act, and prosperity returned in sufficient degree to keep the Yankee farmer devoted to his own affairs, unless he took too seriously the dreary pessimism of the Federalist press. The nation drifted toward war but in such a tortured fashion that the man on the farm could hardly follow its course. Distant matters disturbed the tenor of New Hampshire politics only fitfully until a presidential election and the outbreak of war concurred in 1812.

This situation was a misfortune for Governor Jeremiah Smith. He had been elected on the already dead issue of the embargo, and the resumption of commerce under the Non-Intercourse Act deprived his party of its war cry even before he took office in June. Smith's leadership was intellectual and symbolic rather than political; as a judicial officer, he had built up no great personal following. Most trying of his difficulties was to be the fact that three of his five councillors were Republicans; he could not make a single appointment without the concurrence of at least one of those opponents. Smith's year in the state's highest office proved to be the most frustrating in the life of the eminent jurist.

Faced with the necessity of giving up offices in which they had acquired an almost proprietary interest, Langdon and his followers did all they could to embarrass their dispossessors. The Republican governor and his council spent their last hours in Concord filling up vacant posts with deserving Republicans. The midnight appointments of John Adams were models of propriety compared with this hasty entrenchment against the incoming administration. In December the Republican legislature had passed a resolution authorizing the executive to fill vacancies occasioned by officers who had reached the constitutional age of retirement, whether or not they had resigned.[2] Acting under this resolution, Langdon removed two senescent sheriffs and Judge Wingate of the superior court without troubling to obtain legal proof that they were overage.[3] Then, even before he had notified the ousted sheriffs of their removal, he appointed two members of his council, Benjamin Pierce and William Tarleton, to replace them. One of the other councillors had died, and of the two remaining, one had already been made a judge. Thus, three of the four retiring councillors feathered their nests by approving jobs for one another. Even Republicans regarded this as a "course of conduct improper & impolitic," while Federalist newspapers, of course, cried shame and corruption.[4] General Amasa Allen, the Republican councillor from Cheshire County, had refused to participate in the bargaining, thereby earning the plaudits of the Federalist press and escaping "the disgrace and infamy which rightfully belongs to his colleagues."[5]

In filling the vacancy left on the superior court by Wingate's retirement, Langdon used still less discretion and propriety. For this place he proposed a political crony from Portsmouth, Richard Evans, who had risen to the chairmanship of the Republican central committee in 1808.[6] Evans was an enterprising, self-made merchant who had acquired a respectable position in society through sheer ability, but he was not a lawyer. According to his own statement, he accepted the judicial appointment "to gratify the wishes of many who thought it important to have one judge who possessed some practical knowledge of commercial affairs and the ordinary pursuits of life, and who, not having engaged in the active practise of the law, although possessing some knowledge of its general principles acquired by a course of private study, might be free from those prejudices which too often attach to those whose pursuits are confined to the practical part of professional life."[7]

Such a modest statement, so poorly composed that it even failed to say what the uneducated author had intended, must have scraped like a file upon the nerves of such men as Judge Livermore and the Federalist lawyers Webster, Mason, Sullivan, and Thompson. Actually, Evans had merely restated, however ineptly, a theoretical principle upon which Governor Gilman had frequently based his appointments, but after seven years of meticulous legal administration by Jeremiah Smith, the principle had become an anachronism. "As a partizan politician," wrote William Plumer in dismay, "he [Evans] has been industrious, persevering & decided. But as a judge he will be deficient in legal science, judgment, accuracy & decision of character."[8]

The new judge soon had reason to regret his acceptance of the appointment, for he had to deal with some of the most brilliant and ruthless attorneys in New England and they delighted in publicly exposing his ignorance of the law. For the succeeding half-decade, New Hampshire's political battles were fought not only at the polls, in the newspapers, and on the floor of the legislature but before the superior court bench as well.[9]

Perhaps in retaliation for Langdon's petty partisanship, the Federalists followed up their victory at the polls in March by a general proscription in June. Declaring that a suffrage law passed by the Republican legislature in 1808 was unconstitutional, they accepted election returns that did not conform to its requirements in order to give Smith a clear majority.[10] Officials dependent upon the legislature for their positions, from secretary of state to doorkeeper, were replaced with zealous Federalists.

After this distribution of the spoils, Governor Smith delivered an address curiously reminiscent of Jefferson's First Inaugural, disclaiming party feeling and pleading for political unity. It was longer by many pages and far more polished than the efforts of any of his predecessors, but its eloquence served rather to bewilder than to guide the governor's supporters. They heard generous declarations of respect for the national government which were contradicted by every issue of the Federalist newspapers. In one paragraph, Smith extended the olive branch to the Republicans; in another he assailed them for passing unconstitutional laws and arbitrarily removing unoffending officials. The governor proved himself an execrable politician but an excellent prophet by expressing regret that the people had voted for him and given him the prospect of nothing but toil and trouble during his administration.[11] The reality was to exceed his worst fears.

Governor Smith's biographer asserts that his primary purpose in moving from bench to executive office was to superintend a general reform in the judicial establishment and to "introduce into the executive and legislative, what he had already accomplished with such remarkable success in the judiciary department."[12] If this was indeed his purpose, he made but a poor exposition of it to the legislature. It is true that he painted a glowing picture of the importance of a good judiciary. "Next to the power of religion," he said, "a strict, able and impartial administration of justice is the best security of morals. It is indispensable to the peace, happiness, and good order of society."[13] But to attain this object, Governor Smith recommended no change in the judicial system, no reforms of procedure, no clarification of the laws. His sole suggestion, to which he devoted a major part of his speech, was the provision of larger salaries for the judges as a means of securing the best-qualified incumbents. Necessary as this may have been, Smith's exaggerated emphasis upon it, when combined with his own record of incessant importunity, gave false impressions to his friends and grounds for attack to his enemies. Toward the great project of establishing a reformed judiciary, the Federalist legislature subsequently did nothing more than appoint a committee on salaries and then slash by more than half the increases recommended by the committee.[14]

The contributions that Governor Smith was able, in his executive capacity, to make to the judiciary were equally disappointing. In an oblique criticism of Langdon's partisan appointments he had made a statement of policy which, while evidently sincere, became a mockery during the following decade: "To me it would be a source of great regret to find this office, or this department of government, subject to the revolutions of political parties, or at all affected by party feelings. All parties are bound to unite in a subject involving in it everything dear to all. . . . As far as depends on me, you may rest assured, that no considerations of that nature, will have the smallest influence on such appointments."[15] It could fairly be said that, until the appointment of Evans, the Republican revolution had not affected the judiciary, although this had been due chiefly to the longevity of Federalist judges. From 1809 until 1816, however, the judiciary was to become the most battered football in state politics. Smith had hoped to appoint Jeremiah Mason to the office of chief justice, but when that giant of the law refused to surrender his lucrative practice, Arthur Livermore was elevated to the place that Smith himself had vacated. Even in modesty the governor could not consider this an improvement, and Plumer said flatly that Livermore would "neither acquire fame or promote the public interest."[16] Since a vacancy yet remained on the superior court bench, Smith asked each of two councillors, a Federalist and a Republican, and then George Sullivan, who was a political hybrid, to accept the office, but all refused. He then nominated, in succession, three mediocre Federalists, each of whom was vetoed by the Republican majority in the council. The council proposed Clifton Claggett and then William Plumer, but Smith rejected them as deficient in legal knowledge.[17] Governor and council finally and reluctantly agreed upon the appointment of Jonathan Steele, the brother-in-law of George Sullivan. Since the day when Jefferson had offended him by appointing Sherburne rather than himself to the federal bench in Portsmouth, Steele had been gravitating toward Federalism, but he was still Republican enough to satisfy the councillors. Nevertheless, they were severely criticized for assenting to this appointment—perhaps justly so, since neither party gained much satisfaction from Steele's brief career on the bench.[18]

Thus, at the very beginning of his administration, Governor Smith made the painful discovery that the possession of jealously guarded power in a government of checks and balances did not by any means guarantee the realization of political dreams. The superior court that he had remodeled was much weaker than the one over which he had presided, and his opportunities for further judicial appointments proved to be scant. Nor did the legislature pay any further attention to the matter of judicial reform. Only one session of the assembly—a short one—was held during Smith's year in office, and it was not marked by any notable legislation, other than a generous grant, in which both Federalists and Republicans joined, to help Dr. Nathan Smith erect a medical school at Dartmouth.[19]

In the wake of the embargo, perhaps the most embarrassing event of Jeremiah Smith's administration was the failure of three of the state's ten banks. The directors of two of these faltering institutions, the Cheshire Bank at Keene and the Coös Bank at Haverhill, were nearly all Federalists, but the president of the Hillsborough Bank at Amherst was Samuel Bell, a prominent Republican politician and a member of the council. The two Federalist banks ultimately survived, but Bell's institution never reopened, and its stockholders and depositors alike took heavy losses. The political repercussions were severe but were almost equally felt by both sides; Bell's career suffered a temporary setback, but Smith and his associates were blamed as well.[20]

The tide of public opinion changed swiftly in 1810 and carried the Federalists out of office almost as quickly as it had brought them in. Smith's difficulties as governor had caused dissension in the Federalist ranks; the same clique which had urged him to run now proposed that he give way to John Taylor Gilman.[21] But when Smith indignantly refused, the ranks closed behind him and the Essex Junto sent emissaries from headquarters to support the field general in this beleaguered outpost.[22] Nothing prevailed. Although Smith's popular vote actually increased by about 2,500, Langdon's support grew even more and he returned to office with a majority of 1,100 (16,300 to 15,200).[23] By recovering doubtful districts four and six, the Republicans reversed the political balance in the senate and turned the Federalist majority of twelve in the house into a minority of eleven. In senate district two, the successful Republican candidate was William Plumer of Epping, who had confirmed his shift of party allegiance by taking an active part in the campaign and lampooning his former friend Governor Smith in the *Patriot*.[24] Plumer was promptly made president of the senate, and Nathaniel Gilman was reelected state treasurer. The Republicans perfected their control of the state by maintaining their three to two advantage in the council.

Thus, New Hampshire Federalists were thoroughly routed after only a single year in office, but defeat did not lead to quiescence, as it had in 1805. The continued harassment of neutral commerce and President Madison's inability to deal with it by diplomacy, boycott, or intrigue gave constant ground for discontent and a platform for the opposition. Jeremiah Smith, again engaged in the private practice of law, ran once more in 1811, but lost to Langdon by a margin of more than three thousand votes. The Republicans also increased their majorities in both houses of the legislature, thus continuing the trend toward the recovery of domination which had begun in 1810. The Federalists lost ground chiefly in the Merrimack Valley and on the Frontier, where Essex Junto propaganda had produced their adventitious gains in 1809.[25] In the

Connecticut Valley they maintained their position with relatively small losses. The Old Colony, however, showed the most interesting results, for there the Republicans failed to make any notable gains and they even lost the town of Durham. The long strain of the national restrictive policy toward commerce was beginning to shake the Republican loyalty of the seaboard area. The situation in the state as a whole, however, where forty-seven towns had returned to their Republican allegiance, was distinctly encouraging to the national party leaders.

Although the political horizon was fairly serene in 1810, the bank failures of the previous year had stirred up enough trouble to demand attention. Ignoring Samuel Bell's involvement, Governor Langdon denounced the bank failures as a "great injury to the public" which had "put it in the power of a swarm of speculators to plunder the citizens in a most bare-faced and shameful manner."[26] Legislative committees exonerated the bankers of intentional wrongdoing, but the necessity for state regulation had been painfully demonstrated, and the lesson was gradually applied.[27] So much prejudice, however, had been created among New Hampshire people against banks that the project of a state-owned bank, favored by many Republican leaders, was allowed to suffer a quiet demise. The failures of 1809 also resulted in a strong sentiment against the United States Branch Bank in Portsmouth. Its unfriendly attitude was one of the difficulties to which the directors of the Hillsborough Bank attributed their disaster.[28] It is not surprising, therefore, to find the New Hampshire delegation in Congress voting solidly against renewal of the United States Bank charter in 1811.

Governor Langdon, a former merchant-prince who had long since disposed of his ships, had become converted to the possibility of American economic independence from Great Britain. He particularly urged the legislature to encourage the introduction of merino sheep, with an eye to the development of woolen mills in New Hampshire.[29] But neither his own party nor the Federalists were disposed to do more for manufactures than was already being done. New England capital, at the moment, was moving toward improvements in transportation, particularly in the effort to make the Merrimack River navigable from Lake Winnepesaukee to the Middlesex Canal. Many plans for internal improvements were approved by the legislature without even a record vote.

The condition of the judiciary became a subject of considerable agitation in New Hampshire during the last two years of Langdon's administration. There had been complaints against Jeremiah Smith because of his lofty ideas of judicial prerogative, but he had at the same time kept the superior court efficient and respectable. Under Livermore, Evans, and Steele it lost all claim to these attributes, particularly after Judge Evans, afflicted with a fatal disease and a persecution complex, began to absent himself from many of the sessions. The inferior courts were, if possible, even less satisfactory. It was said of the Rockingham court of common pleas in 1810 that "the justices of that court are incompetent to perform their duties. They have no dignity & preserve no order—they are fickle and irresolute; & their decisions were often illegal."[30]

Although Langdon's appointments were responsible for much of the fumbling and delay, the "sinking" reputation of the courts was due much more to the inherent weaknesses that the reformers had been trying to eradicate since 1790. The old governor was sensitive to the public criticism, and he annually recommended reforms in the judiciary. In 1810 he called particular attention to the procrastination and expense that characterized the lower courts and the frequent setting aside of jury verdicts by judges, which was a thrust at former chief justice Smith. A bill to prevent this latter practice had been introduced by the administration in 1808, while Smith was still on the bench, but had failed to pass because nearly thirty Republicans voted against it.[31] There was more agreement on a proposition to pay judges a salary, rather than expect them to live on their fees, thereby removing one incentive for procrastination in the lower courts. A bill for this purpose failed in 1810, but passed the next year in the house by the triumphant margin of 111–28. Three of the seven Republicans and four of the five Federalists gave the bill a 7–5 majority in the senate.[32]

The evidence points to the fact that until the Federalists regained control of the state in 1813 and resorted to judicial head-hunting, reform of the courts was recognized as a necessity by progressive leaders on both sides and was supported by a bipartisan bloc in the legislature. Weare, a consistently Republican town in the Merrimack Valley, and Londonderry, a Federalist stronghold in the same area, voted for reform, while Exeter and Portsmouth, in the Old Colony, having little else in common, opposed it. Projects of reform were considered on their merits, and if the work proceeded with less than deliberate speed, it had at least kept within the limits of conservative restraint and constitutionality. If the Federalists had remained content with this slow and compromising progress, it might have proceeded on a bipartisan basis throughout the bitter quarrels of the war period. Unfortunately, they made it a party issue in 1813 and thereby killed the possibility of even a gradual reform.

When they returned to power in 1810, one minor embarrassment for the Republicans was the former secretary of state Philip Carrigain. Leaders in his own party thought him "destitute of that stability & weight of character which were requisite."[33] In spite of this, they felt obliged to nominate him for his old position, then suffered the anxiety of seeing him fail to win a majority on the first ballot. They were able to defeat the Federalist incumbent only by abandoning Carrigain and nominating Samuel Sparhawk, a much more suitable candidate, who was elected. The legislators had an example of Carrigain's rash enthusiasm constantly before them in the form of petitions regarding a state map. Carrigain and a partner had agreed in 1806 to furnish the state with five hundred copies of a projected map within one year, free of charge, in return for the copyright.[34] That he had reckoned without the cost was evident at the next session of the legislature, when it became necessary to extend his time for furnishing the map to 1810 and to make him a loan of $5,000.[35] It was known to everyone, now that his time had expired, that he was still far from ready to furnish the maps, and that he would petition again for relief. "Instead of being a support to the party he hangs a dead weight upon their wings," wrote one of the younger Republicans.[36]

The same tendency to rely upon weak candidates brought the Republicans to grief in the congressional elections of 1810. The five candidates nominated by the caucus were, in Plumer's opinion, "noisy, boisterous young men [who] prevailed in their claims against modest merit."[37] The people of New Hampshire must have been of the same mind, for in August they divided their votes so evenly that only the two leading Republicans received clear majorities and four of the six next highest were Federalists. In the runoff election, the two eligible Republicans and George Sullivan received majorities, so that for the first time since the parties began presenting regular tickets, the New Hampshire delegation to the House of Representatives was divided.[38] So was it also in the Senate, where Nicholas Gilman was openly opposing Madison and Gallatin. Nevertheless, by a narrow margin, Gilman was reelected to the Senate in 1810 because the party could not agree on another candidate.[39] It was a bad omen that the Republicans could not send a full complement of Madisonians to a Congress that badly needed unity in the face of imminent war.

John Langdon, the heart and soul of the Republican cause in New Hampshire, now presented a problem to the party. With memory, sight, and hearing impaired, he refused a proffered nomination for the vice-presidency of the United States in 1811 and made it clear to his followers that he also wanted to retire from the governorship. The Republican caucus offered the nomination to John Goddard, who refused it, and then to Nathaniel Gilman, who temporized.[40] Eventually, convinced that they otherwise faced defeat, the party leaders prevailed upon Langdon to serve for one more year. The venerable Republican was in the miserable and remarkable position of being unable to refuse what some men would have seized unasked. He offered to contribute two thousand dollars to a campaign fund if William Plumer would consent to run. He threatened, if elected, to resign so that Plumer, as president of the senate, might succeed him. But no stratagem could release Langdon from the responsibility he had incurred as the founder of the Republican party in New Hampshire, and eventually he had to submit "to the will of the republicans."[41]

Langdon distrusted Nathaniel Gilman and determined to make Plumer his successor. During the legislative session in June 1811 the two men took rooms at the same house in Concord and worked together in planning party strategy. When the Republican caucus met, it renominated Langdon as a matter of course, but he unequivocally refused to run again. The caucus then unanimously nominated Plumer, the president of the senate, who had only nine years previously been elected to the United States Senate by a Federalist legislature. Plumer pointed out to the committee that called upon him with this offer that he would face not only the inveterate hostility of his former Federalist friends but a national crisis that could break upon them with overwhelming force. Nevertheless, he accepted the nomination and then confided to his diary, "If a Langdon & a Gilman had sufficient abilities to perform the duties of a governor, I may perform the task, in case I am elected."[42]

Unfortunately, at this point Americans were more divided in their loyalties, perhaps, than at any time since 1795. The long effort to remain neutral in Europe's unending war had cost too much in prejudice, humiliation, and inconsistency on both sides to allow, after twenty years of indecision, a vigorous policy of any kind to receive national support. It is doubtful that a single prominent American had maintained a steady and temperate adherence to any particular line of foreign policy during those shameful years—even to a policy of enlightened opportunism. The two great parties had so completely exchanged positions that, while John Quincy Adams, William Plumer, Timothy Dexter, and many another Federalist had become Republicans, DeWitt Clinton, Nicholas Gilman, Robert Smith, and dozens of lesser Republicans had moved in the opposite direction. For two decades, under both Federalist and Republican administrations, the United States had submitted to insults and violations of neutrality which might at any time have justified war. But the insults had been swallowed, and resort to nearly every other conceivable expedient had convinced nearly everyone, both in Europe and America, that the republic would not fight. It is not therefore surprising that when a train of comic-opera circumstances forced the party that had eschewed war since 1800 to declare it in 1812, the party that had been willing to fight France in 1798 and England, perhaps, in 1807 looked upon the conflict as sectional and artificial.

When the New Hampshire Republicans came back into office in 1810, they had felt more cheerful about the nation's foreign policy than when they had been compelled to defend the embargo. Governor Langdon had addressed the legislature in words of exultation: "Gentlemen, you will permit me most sincerely to congratulate you and my country in general on the successes of our National Government, whose wisdom and firmness, amidst the convulsions of contending nations and party spirit, have, under the direction of Divine Providence, hitherto preserved the peace and Independence of the United States. Surely it is our highest duty as a people so greatly favored, to praise the Lord for his goodness and for his wonderful works to the children of men."[43] But even as John Taylor Gilman had praised the Lord and denounced Jacobinism with the same breath in 1798, so Langdon could not forbear to pounce upon the Anglomaniac fifth columnists in 1810: "It is much to be lamented, that the difference in political sentiments among our citizens should be carried so far as to produce a most violent opposition to our General Government, distract the public mind, and greatly disturb the peace and tranquility of the State. It is painful to hear some men among us eulogizing foreign nations, who are greatly inimical to us, and at the same time calumniating our own most excellent Government."[44]

The Federalists remained quiet under this thinly veiled attack, contenting themselves with voting against the parrotlike response composed by the house Republicans. With the revival of commerce, the abandonment of nonintercourse, and even the prospect of relaxations in the belligerent decrees against neutral shipping, the Federalists had hardly been in a position to feel sensitive. But this promising situation had not long endured. Instead of repealing their old restrictions, both England and France had issued new and more stringent orders for their enforcement. Reexport of foreign goods from Portsmouth, which had risen from the embargo low of $2,765 to $85,532 after repeal, had dropped again to $9,027 in 1810.[45]

Napoleon's diplomacy had led Madison, on a flimsy pretext, to remove all bans against commerce with France in November 1810 and to reinstitute nonintercourse with England on March 2, 1811. Federalists criticized the partiality and naiveté of this procedure and clamored instead for naval protection, which would have led inevitably to the war they did not want. Republicans stubbornly adhered to an outworn formula of passive resistance, which would lead with equal certainty to a war for principles in which they had no interest. With foreign relations in such a sorry state, Langdon had to admit to the legislature in 1811 his disappointment at not being able to announce a settlement of European difficulties. He took occasion again, however, to castigate those who opposed a government which he considered "to be the freest and the best that the world now produces."[46] The house of representatives replied to this part of the address with fulsome praise of the national administration for preserving peace, but devoted most of its attention to an outrageous attack upon the Federalist minority. Some paragraphs were deliberately insulting and inflammatory, for example:

> We sincerely regret, that any portion of our beloved fellow-citizens should be so infatuated with a political phrenzy, as to pursue measures which are derogatory to our national character and independence, and which may either invite, encourage or *countenance* the aggressions of foreign nations. The obvious tendency of this must be, to divide our national councils, distract the people, diminish public confidence, mislead the uninformed, enervate law, encourage insurrection and civil war, and produce destruction.[47]

The Republicans here borrowed from the Federalist speeches of 1798 the device of identifying political opposition with national treason. It proved to be no more acceptable to their opponents in 1811 than it had been to them when they were the minority. John Taylor Gilman, representing Exeter in the legislature, demanded evidence to support the allegations made by the majority committee, and David Morrill, a rising young politician from Goffstown, undertook to answer him by quoting from Federalist sermons, newspapers, and town resolutions. There followed an angry debate in which Gilman condemned ideas he had himself propounded in 1798, and the Federalists were finally driven to defend, rather than deny, their opposition.[48] They moved to amend the address by adding to the paragraph quoted above the following sentence:

> The House of Representatives, however, would not be understood by the foregoing remarks in any degree to infringe the constitutional liberty of free and temperate discussion of political subjects, holding it to be the undoubted right of the people, at all times, to inquire into, consider, approve or disapprove, as they may see cause, the conduct of their representatives and agents, and holding it also to be no indication of a spirit hostile to the principles of the government, to oppose, in a peaceable and constitutional manner, any measures of any administration which are thought to merit disapprobation.[49]

This shrewd and totally inconsistent maneuver gave the Federalists the appearance of championing the principle of free speech which they had prohibited by law in 1799. It also jockeyed the Republicans into the position of voting against the liberal doctrine for which they had then suffered martyrdom. They could think of nothing better to do than defeat the amendment and adopt the original address, 99–73. Elated by the embarrassment of their opponents, a group of leading Federalists, which included John Taylor Gilman, Thomas W. Thompson, and Ezekiel Webster (Daniel's older brother), drew up a protest against the address, had it signed by sixty-nine representatives, and, on the last day of the session, entered it upon the journals. Ostensibly, the document was a noble defense of the right of free speech, but in their enthusiasm the authors became incautious and, as a more moderate Federalist complained, "exposed too broad a front to a vigilant enemy." Their claim that the legislature's answer was calculated "either by accident or design, to discourage free inquiry, and to intimidate our fellow citizens from expressing any disapprobation of the measures of the administration," was a much more relevant condemnation of their own Sedition Act than of the Republican majority's perfectly legal expression of opinion.[50] They termed the majority's exercise of its freedom to condemn the criticisms of the minority unconstitutional. Finally, the protest included a one-sided review of foreign policy, the spirit of which moved Plumer to write: "These protesters deny the existence of opposition to the government, yet in their protest, with the spirit and temper of enemies, they arraign, censure & condemn the measure of our government."[51]

It was indeed the divisions between Americans themselves, rather than the enmity of either France or England, which constituted the greatest danger to the Republic. Differences of opinion over trade, impressment, the navy, war or peace, and politics were not only unavoidable but desirable. These matters were so involved in circumstance that both parties had thoroughly inconsistent records in their twenty years of dealing with them. But two principles rose far above these incidental questions—national unity and national allegiance. William Plumer, the apostate candidate, had come to recognize that all other loyalties, even the loyalties to party and friends, were subordinate to this primary allegiance. "In the event of war, I hope we will unite as Americans," he had written as early as 1807.[52] But the hope was to prove tragically illusory. New England Federalist extremists not only continued to bluster about secession at a time of impending catastrophe but heightened the peril by giving aid and comfort to the potential enemy. It was from Amherst, New Hampshire, that Joseph Henry, the self-appointed British spy, wrote to the governor-general of Canada that Federalist opposition had paralyzed the administration's will to resist. "They will risk anything but the loss of power," he informed a government already unwilling to make the slightest concessions.[53] It was this "degeneracy from the just and honorable *principles* which alone could ever have attached us to them," wrote John Quincy Adams to Plumer, that had alienated these New Englanders from the Federalist party.[54] "Both of us are reviled in the high-toned federal papers," Plumer told his friend, "but I trust posterity will say we deserved well of our country & the world."[55]

Events proved that Plumer had not deceived himself as to the passions aroused by his candidacy. The Federalist newspapers denounced him as an apostate, an atheist, and a usurer. Some of the older Republicans, led by Nathaniel Peabody and the Bartlett brothers, conducted a devious intrigue to supplant him with Nicholas Gilman as the party's candidate.[56] He was vigorously supported by the Republican newspapers, however, and especially by Isaac Hill, the new editor of the *New Hampshire Patriot*. Hill answered the charges of apostasy against his candidate with a blistering counterattack which excoriated the Federalist leaders who "openly avowed the intention" of "resisting the laws" and of "dismembering the Union."[57]

The Republicans, in fact, evinced a great deal more visible unanimity in supporting their new candidate than did the Federalists in choosing between their old ones. Smith had failed in two successive elections, and the older Federalists demanded the return of their popular favorite, John Taylor Gilman. In the middle of February the *Portsmouth Oracle* announced Gilman as the candidate, while the Boston *Centinel* and the remaining Federalist papers in New Hampshire declared for Smith. A week later, after some apparently hasty but unsynchronized consultations, the *Oracle* came out for Smith, while the *Centinel* announced that it had learned Gilman was to be the candidate. Isaac Hill sardonically offered the Federalists a solution for their dilemma by suggesting that since Smith had no support and Gilman was in his dotage, they discard both men.[58] These public embarrassments culminated in the publication at Exeter of a handbill which denounced Smith and the lawyers who had imposed him upon the party against the wishes of the vast majority of Federalists. Gilman, it said, was the choice of the people.[59] Soon afterward, a rumor that Smith had indignantly refused the nomination when he learned that Plumer was to be his opponent gained currency.[60] The palace revolution, it appeared, had been successful, for the Federalists ultimately gave their united support to Gilman and New Hampshire voters were faced with a choice between candidates from neighboring villages who had once been political associates.

National issues played a larger part than usual in this campaign. The Republicans harped upon Federalist opposition to the general government and tenderness toward Britain, interpreting both as treason. For this purpose they regretted deeply the fact that the Henry letters were not published in time to influence the elections, supposing that they "would have made thousands of votes difference in this State."[61] The Federalists, for their part, accused their opponents of rushing headlong toward a senseless war with England that would result in misery, defeat, and bankruptcy. Secretary of the Treasury Gallatin gave unintentional force to these claims by publishing his opinion that the Congress should levy direct taxes in preparation for war. The *Patriot* hastened to assure its readers that a war could be won without taxes and that Gallatin was evidently turning Federalist.[62] Nevertheless, the Treasury had touched a sensitive nerve in New Hampshire agrarianism, and local Republicans estimated the cost of Gallatin's statement at another thousand votes lost to the Federalists.[63]

In the face of these numerous handicaps it is surprising that Plumer was not badly defeated. Newspaper reports showed the voting to be so close that the final result could not be predicted before the legislature's official count in June. Contrary to Republican hopes, the Federalists had not divided between their candidates but had supported Gilman with disciplined vigor. Plumer, too, had run well, but against a strong ebb tide. In Portsmouth, the Republican stronghold, Plumer received only 525 votes to Gilman's 514 in a town meeting which had chosen Daniel Webster as moderator. In voting for the town's five representatives many Republicans tore the name of a notorious deist off their ballots and left the meeting before it was announced that, as a result of their action, only four representatives had won the necessary majority.[64] This suggests one reason why Plumer, known himself to be a deist, received 2,000 fewer votes from Republicans throughout the state than had Langdon in 1811.[65] Webster himself was the Federalist candidate for the fifth representative from Portsmouth and might have been elected if a zealous Republican had not recalled his departed comrades by ringing the meetinghouse bell, thus securing a triumphant majority of 100 for Colonel Upham.

When the ballots were counted by the legislature in June, it was learned that Gilman had received 15,612 votes, just three more than the number that had elected Smith in 1809, while Plumer's total of 15,492 was considerably less than the Langdon vote in 1810 or 1811. Neither candidate had a majority, however, for 877 scattering votes had been cast by Republicans who disliked Plumer and Federalists who were still loyal to Jeremiah Smith. The new Republican candidate had done well in the Old Colony and the Frontier, both of which he carried by comfortable margins. But Plumer ran much less strongly in the Merrimack Valley, where Chester and a great block of towns north of Concord turned against him. In the Connecticut Valley he was a thousand votes behind Gilman, and it was this region, in consequence, which made him a minority candidate.

The Federalists were less successful in the legislature than in the gubernatorial election. They definitely recovered the tenth senatorial district and in the second and eighth they managed to gain pluralities, owing to divisions among the Republicans. They had lost seats in the lower house, however, where the Republicans had a clear majority of twenty. This victory determined all the rest. The two houses, meeting in convention, elected Plumer to the governorship by a vote of 104–82.[66] A Republican was chosen in each of the two undetermined senatorial districts, giving the party a 7–5 majority in the senate. The Republicans also retained control of the council, 3–2. Plumer was thus elected as a minority governor, but popular opinion still backed his party and gave him legislative majorities that seemed sufficient for concerted action.

CHAPTER 16

IN THE WAR WITH ENGLAND

*And I trust that the good citizens of N.Hampshire will cordially unite,
and at all hazards steadily support those measures which the government
of their own choice may adopt, and that we shall have no interest or
feeling discordant to that of the Nation.* —William Plumer

Although the March elections had left his political future unsettled, William Plumer had prudently begun the composition of an inaugural address in April.[1] In this task he was embarrassed by uncertainty as to the probable state of affairs in the world when and if he should take office. John Harper, a New Hampshire war hawk in the Twelfth Congress, had assured Plumer, as early as December 2, that "the present Session will not be closed, without an *arrangement*, or an actual *war* with Great Britain."[2] Tremendous paper preparations had been made, but when Plumer wrote his speech, most of the congressmen were home on leave and nothing really decisive had been done. His own conviction was, however, that within a few weeks "if Great Britain does not make concessions we must declare war, or . . . submit to British exaction."[3]

As far as Plumer was concerned, the time for submission was past. The message that he wrote in May was a war message, more vigorous because less academic than the document that Madison sent to Congress on June 1. When he stood before the legislature and a throng of visitors in the north-end meetinghouse in Concord on June 6, Governor Plumer knew that Congress even then was debating in secret a resolution to declare war. His task, he felt, was to justify and support that resolution. "Though war is a great calamity," acknowledged the governor, "the sacrifice of our essential rights is greater."[4] Plumer declared that the war would be fought neither for the carrying trade nor against impressments, but because the nation "cannot long survive the loss of its spirit."[5] Such a struggle would be hopeless, however, unless the United States were indeed united upon a ground of common interest. Plumer therefore avoided the partisan attacks that New Hampshire governors had so often made in their speeches, and instead appealed eloquently for unity. "Union is the vital strength of a nation, particularly so of a Republic, whose authority rests on public opinion. Our union is our safety—*a house divided against itself cannot stand.* An indissoluble union of the States is essential, not only to our own prosperity, but even to our existence as a nation."

Plumer's appeal for unity, however, did not bring his Federalist opponents to the mourner's bench. Although the newspapers grudgingly admitted some virtue in his address, Federalist legislators consumed the better part of a day in attacking the official response, written by David Morrill.[6] They obtained some amendments, but the report was finally adopted, 88–62. At the end of the session the Federalists presented a resolution that whereas a war with Great Britain "under existing circumstances would be highly inconvenient, destructive of the prosperity and happiness of our country, burdensome to the people, and eminently hazardous to the existence of our republican form of government," their congressmen be directed to vote against it.[7] Consideration of the resolution was postponed to the next session by a vote of 98 to 70. Even though the Federalists had not been won over, Republican members maintained unbroken ranks and promised strong support for the war policy of the administration.

In spite of the imminence of war, however, the state Republicans, like their national brethren, preferred not to think about the unpleasant aspects of the subject. They refused to answer Plumer's requests for effective regulation of the militia or for adequate armament.[8] In another particular, the governor betrayed his old Federalist leanings and was rebuked by the old Republican majorities. He believed that in this critical year of 1812, as in 1800, the presidential electors should be chosen by the legislature rather than by popular vote. He was consequently irritated to find several veteran party leaders who were "afraid to choose themselves & insist upon the subject being submitted to the people."[9] It was so ordered, the only change being a decision to elect both congressmen and electors at the same town meetings in November. "Before that period arrives I presume the aspect of our affairs will be changed, & I hope public opinion will be more fully united in support of the measures of the general government," wrote Plumer hopefully.[10] How sadly was he destined to be disillusioned!

Notice that the nation was actually at war first reached Governor Plumer at nine o'clock on the evening of June 23, three days after the legislature had adjourned. It came in the form of dispatches from Major General Henry Dearborn, commander of the Northern Division of the United States Army, stating that war had been declared against Great Britain and requesting the governor to order out two companies of the detached militia for the defense of Portsmouth harbor.[11] Although no militia had been detached for federal service in New Hampshire, Plumer immediately issued the necessary orders and placed two companies from the First Brigade under the command of Major Upham of the United States Army, stationed at Portsmouth.[12] Two days later, the governor received official notice from James Monroe, secretary of state, that war had been declared. "You may with confidence assure the president of the

United States, that I will promptly afford my aid and assistance to the full extent of my power, to mitigate the evils of war to our citizens, & render it effectual against the enemies of our beloved country," he answered.[13]

As captain-general of his state's armed forces, the governor was responsible for its defense against any persons who should "in a hostile manner, attempt or enterprise the destruction, invasion, detriment, or annoyance of this state."[14] This responsibility should have been relatively easy to discharge, but it was complicated by unnecessary and sometimes malevolent interference. Defense of the state revolved around two possibilities: that of an assault upon Portsmouth harbor by the British fleet and that of raids from Canada against the northern frontier. These were also, and primarily, concerns of the national government; only in the absence of adequate national defenses would the governor be expected to call upon the state militia. Unfortunately, neither the nation nor the state was prepared for war in 1812. The frontier was completely bare of either national or state forces, and the two dilapidated forts on either side of the entrance to Portsmouth harbor, Fort Constitution on Great Island and Fort McClary in Kittery, were garrisoned only by a single company of United States regulars. No one believed that these forces could save Portsmouth from a spirited attack.

Federal and state responsibilities were complicated by the Jeffersonian tradition of dependence upon the militia for the peacetime military establishment. A federal law of April 10, 1812, had ordered the state executives to detach their respective proportions of a body of one hundred thousand men from the regular militia, to be ready to march "at a moment's warning" under the command of the War Department.[15] This, of course, was a continuation of a glorious tradition—the minutemen of the Revolutionary War.

New Hampshire's proportion of the total detachment amounted to thirty-five hundred soldiers and officers. Langdon, who was still in office when the orders came for this detachment, had promptly issued his own orders for compliance. Not a single militia officer, however, had made his returns by June 23; consequently there was no detached militia in New Hampshire when war was declared. In this dilemma it was fortunate that General Clement Storer, commander of the First Militia Brigade, to whom Governor Plumer issued his special orders for an immediate detachment, was an ardent Republican and eager to support the government. He chose his companies prudently and the first little crisis of the war was easily surmounted. The governor, in the meantime, addressed himself to the task of finishing the organization of the detached militia. After a month of prodding his officers, the adjutant general and the War Department, he finally finished the job that should have been done in

April and had the New Hampshire detached militia properly organized into a division, officered, and ready to function as a whole or by companies, if necessary. Whether it would actually fight remained to be seen, but Plumer professed "entire confidence in the zeal & patriotism of the officers & privates composing this detachment."[16]

Although General Dearborn's first concern had been for the defense of Portsmouth, it was the New Hampshire frontier that felt the earliest apprehensions of attack. Two weeks before the declaration of war, a petition had come to Plumer from many of the towns in Coös County, begging in the most urgent tones for armed forces to protect them from Indians and old Tory neighbors in Canada. Having no constitutional authority to act except in case of actual invasion, Plumer had sent the petition to the legislature, where it was ignored. Alarming letters continued to pour in, describing potential dangers in such terms as the following:

> There is of the St Francois Tribe of Indians now at their Village 50 Warriors who have for their Chief Officer, a person of the name of Caswell a celebrated hunter who went from Coos some years ago, these Indians are provided with Arms & Ammunition, receive regularly Blankets and Rations, are organized and held ready to form scouting parties.—Several of the towns in Canada adjoining our lines are settled by runaways from different parts of this & other of the States Cheifly from Coos, they consist of Counterfeders of bank notes, theives, swindlers, violators of all laws, prison breakers & other escapes from Justice; some of them have threatened in case of a rupture, that they will avenge themselves on their former prosecutors, the inhabitants of Coos are in great terror and I think in real danger.[17]

Governor Plumer now lost no time in suggesting to General Dearborn that a company of detached militia be sent to guard the United States frontier in the region of the Upper Connecticut. Dearborn generously gave the necessary orders, which Plumer hastened to carry out by detaching a company from the northernmost brigade under Captain Ephraim Mahurin and stationing the major part of it at Stewartstown, while a small scouting party was posted on the shores of Lake Umbagog to the eastward. By the latter part of August the little band of fifty soldiers had reached Stewartstown and built a blockhouse, which they called Fort Plumer.

Whether the danger had been real or imaginary, there was no invasion of New Hampshire during the war and Captain Mahurin's little company completely quieted the fears of the inhabitants, allowing them to remain on their farms and even to bring new lands into cultivation. The plan of committing defense to the detached militia shifted the burden of expense from the townspeople and the state to the national treasury. It also provided escape for the government from the odium of abandoning the frontier. Since the legislature had neither appropriated money for munitions nor authorized the furnishing of any to the towns, the governor would have been helpless if General Dearborn had not come to his aid.

Local historians with a Federalist bias have charged that the militia were placed on the frontier to prevent trading with the enemy.[18] There is nothing in the correspondence to justify this assertion, although Captain Mahurin did report that "the check which has been put to smuggling by the men stationed at this place has excited much warmth & irritation among the friends of Great Britain in this part of the State."[19] Whether Dearborn's original alacrity was influenced by this consideration, or whether Plumer shrewdly avoided sending arms to a band of potential smugglers, the fact is that the actual presence of United States militiamen did discourage illegal activities.

A paradoxical situation developed on the northern frontier. The inhabitants who had begged for protection in June now did all they could to frustrate the soldiers who had responded to their call. Finding that the Canadians were much more disposed to buy their cattle than to invade their borders, and being chiefly Federalists, they quickly came to oppose the war and those who were trying to win it. False rumors, which caused serious trouble between militia officers, were spread, and the soldiers were made mutinous by carefully sown propaganda. Some time before the six-months' term of Captain Mahurin's company expired in January, Governor Plumer issued orders for the dispatch of another company to replace him. It was not until three months later that these commands were carried out. For trivial reasons, the officers ordered to relieve Captain Mahurin refused to go, and the privates were, of course, infected by the disobedience of their officers. The malingering of these New Hampshire militiamen would have left their own homes unprotected during a favorite raiding season of the Indians, had not a company from Maine marched to Stewartstown. The difficulty had unquestionably been political. In apologizing for his own delay, Brigadier General Montgomery wrote, "I sincerely regret that so much division and party spirit prevails in our country as to render it almost impossible for an Officer in my situation to do his duty to acceptance."[20]

It was fortunate for New Hampshire that it was not invaded, for the state was woefully unprepared. The law required each militiaman to own a serviceable musket and each town to have a supply of powder, but the law was not enforceable.[21] Militiamen passed a few guns from hand to hand so that each might have a weapon on muster day, but the towns made no pretense of keeping stores of military supplies. Since the end of the Revolutionary War, the armament belonging to the state had been allowed to disappear or to deteriorate. Governor Plumer labored diligently to replenish this miserable supply, but his efforts were often balked by the accumulated carelessness of years or by partisan noncooperation. He was able to wheedle from the United States authorities a supply of bullets for the frontier guard and a stand of one thousand arms for the state militia. In November he advised the legislature to reorganize the militia, to authorize the distribution of the arms he had received from the War Department, to provide enough additional compensation for the militia in detached service to make their pay equal to that of regular troops, and, finally, to create a supply of armaments for the state.[22]

The first of these the legislature refused to do; the second it bungled, so that Plumer had to return the resolution for the inclusion of proper safeguards; the third it did reluctantly after instructing the state's congressmen to see that the United States would eventually assume payment.[23] But on the last and most important matter, the legislature procrastinated until Plumer feared that nothing would be done. Thereupon he called in the leading men of both parties and expostulated with them, pointing out that, no matter how opinion might differ on the justice of the war, it actually existed, that the state might be invaded before the legislature sat again, and that the law of self-preservation ought to deter even the Federalists from sending their sons out to fight barehanded.[24] Plumer's personal appeal was effective in securing an appropriation to purchase two thousand pounds of powder, five thousand pounds of lead, and twelve thousand flints.[25] This was virtually the total extent of New Hampshire's military preparation during the War of 1812.

Governor Plumer shared with President Madison the persistent illusion that an actual war would force unity upon the political factions that divided the country. "When once the declaration is made the state of parties in New England will be changed," he had confidently written to Congressman John Harper in April. "Many of the federal leaders who are in fact more attached to Great Britain than to our own govt. will be compelled to be silent—& many of their present followers will abandon them & rally round the standard of our Country."[26] No expectation could have been more cruelly deceptive. Federalist opposition increased with each step toward war and progressed steadily toward treason as the conflict lengthened. The defense loan from which Congress expected to realize $11 million in 1811 was thoroughly sabotaged by the New England Federalists, who were largely in control of the financial interests of their section. Not only did they themselves refrain from purchasing federal securities but they used every means of threat and persuasion to prevent others from doing so.[27] The loan failed to produce even $1 million in New England, or more than $6 million in the entire country.

The war had not been many weeks in progress before the Federalists found stronger methods of sabotage than keeping their pocketbooks closed. "Too many of the leaders of federalism in New Hampshire, in imitation of those in Massachusetts, are doing everything they can to embarrass & perplex the measures of the general government," wrote Governor Plumer to General Dearborn. "They not only discourage in-listments into the army, but do all they dare to prevent the detached officers & privates performing their duty agreeably to your former req-uisitions. They justify the government of the enemy, & condemn that of our own."[28]

The evidence on which this indictment rested lay on the governor's desk in the form of a letter from Major Timothy Dix, Jr., of the New Hampshire Volunteers. Just before the time when he was to leave the troop rendezvous at Concord and proceed with his regiment to join General Dearborn on Lake Champlain, he had been arrested on civil process and his march effectively delayed.[29] It probably could not have been proven in a court of law that Dix's arrest was due to Federalist plotting, any more than it was possible to attribute to their machinations the necessity of a court-martial among the militia at Portsmouth or the mutiny in Coös County or the constant stream of smuggled goods which Levi Bartlett witnessed passing through Kingston from Portland to Boston. But the war party had no doubts on the subject and was all the more angry because the opposition was covert and nonindictable.

Federalism generated much of the energy for its revival from the or-ganization of so-called Washington Benevolent Societies. Although such a society sprang up in Portsmouth and probably in every town where the Federalists had much strength, the idea caught on most favorably, as might have been expected, in the Connecticut Valley. On February 11, 1812, the *New Hampshire Patriot* declared that societies had been founded in Concord, Boscawen, Plymouth, Thornton, Newport, Haver-hill, Piermont, Orford, Lyme, Hanover, Plainfield, Walpole, and Keene (the latter nine in the Connecticut Valley) during the preceding week.[30] These town clubs were quickly gathered into county societies, of which the two in Grafton and Cheshire counties were particularly active, and remained as formidable political combinations for the duration of the war.[31] They were denounced in direct proportion to their effectiveness. Young Isaac Hill shrewdly proposed to fight fire with fire by organizing Tammany Societies among the Republicans, but it does not appear that his suggestion produced results.[32] Ezra Bartlett, writing from Haverhill, asserted that the Washington Benevolent Society members were pledged to vote together in every election and that with this disciplined cohort they expected to "make a schism among the Repubs" at the ensuing presidential election by bringing forward De Witt Clinton.[33] He proved to be well informed!

Throughout the summer of 1812 war party and peace party faced each other with increasing antagonism. Governor Plumer accepted an invitation to attend the Fourth of July celebration at Portsmouth, for the purpose not only of "countenancing" the Republicans but of sounding public opinion on state and national issues. At half past ten that morning, a company of uniformed militia escorted Plumer and Langdon to the North Meeting House, where they listened to a "spontaneous effusion . . . of patriotic ardor" from the lips of William Claggett, grandson of the quick-witted rebel, Wyseman Claggett, and a rising young lawyer-politician since his graduation from Dartmouth in 1808.[34] At noon they returned to Frost's Hotel, where more than one hundred gentlemen sat down with the governor to an excellent dinner and a formidable series of patriotic toasts. Plumer gave, "The United States—The *spirit* which produced will *support* the independence of our country, & vindicate its injured rights. *God nerves the patriot's arm.*" It was downed with nine cheers.[35]

But Portsmouth had *two* Independence Day celebrations in 1812. At the same moment that Claggett was holding forth in the Congregational meetinghouse, Daniel Webster, another Dartmouth graduate, was proclaiming to the Washington Benevolent Society, assembled, by ironic contrast, in the Universalist Church, that the war was "premature and inexpedient."[36] The occasion was a symbol of the nation's sadly distracted condition, and the orator, by reason of his forceful eloquence, became immediately the local spokesman of the distractors. Webster was elected by the Portsmouth Federalists to represent them at a Rockingham County convention held at Brentwood in August. Dr. Samuel Tenney, ex-congressman from Exeter, presided; the Reverend Peter Holt from Epping prayed for Heaven not to bless the armed forces, and George Sullivan denounced the war against which he had voted in Congress. Then Daniel Webster read the famous Rockingham Memorial, which was to prove a source of considerable embarrassment to him in later life. Assuming to speak for the trading interests of New Hampshire, he remonstrated against the administration's hostility to commerce, denied any grievance to exist in impressment, warned that the subordination of one great interest to another would lead to a separation of the states, and threatened civil war in case of an alliance with France.[37]

A month later the Republicans of Rockingham County held their convention at Kingston. Although they did not pretend to speak for commerce, they could, with more propriety, have presented a memorial to President Madison from the majority of Rockingham's citizens. But they had no Webster to compose such a document. William Plumer, Jr., the governor's son, made a speech on the subject of sailors' rights which was greatly admired by his friends but did not create much stir outside the boundaries of the county.[38] Instead of counteracting the far-reaching effect of Webster's memorial, the Republicans wasted their energies in factional bickering. Only one of their congressmen was renominated, and the younger party workers became thoroughly disgusted.

The political effect of the war had been, not to reunite the people in its support, but to drive some of the Republicans into opposition. New Hampshire's congressional delegation had supported the declaration of war by a bare majority of four votes to three.[39] One of the dissidents had been Senator Nicholas Gilman, an apostate Republican since the days of the embargo. The other two were Republican Josiah Bartlett and Federalist George Sullivan, whose conduct involved an interesting story. They had returned to New Hampshire on leave in May, Sullivan to attend to legal business and Bartlett to be married. While the latter was still at his bride's house, he had been visited by John Goddard and Captain McClintock, prominent Portsmouth Republicans, who begged him to return at once to Washington in order to help prevent an immediate declaration of war, which they deemed "an extraordinary hasty step considering the immense property in Britain & on the ocean."[40] Goddard estimated the possible loss, if war cut off the return of this property, at $100 million, of which his own share was much too large, and he "appeared very anxious and warm" to have hostilities postponed until he could get his goods safely home. Bartlett and Sullivan were impressed; leaving bride and legal briefs, they took the stage for Washington immediately and voted, in vain as it proved, against the inconvenient declaration of war.[41] Yet the war hawks had more reason to be alarmed than amused, for although the New Hampshire congressmen failed to postpone the war, the three who voted against it all came from the Old Colony, which was supposed to be a Republican stronghold.

During the summer other dangerous defections from the Republican ranks took place. One of the backsliders was the state treasurer, Nathaniel Gilman, who attended the convention of the "Friends of Peace" at Brentwood in August and was placed on Webster's committee to draw up the memorial to President Madison. With the younger Gilmans, John Goddard, Josiah Bartlett, and many a lesser Republican opposed to war, it had not been difficult to organize a "Peace Ticket," ostensibly bipartisan but heavily Federalist in composition. Under cover of a coalition effort to elect De Witt Clinton to the presidency, the Federalists of New Hampshire cleverly used the Peace ticket to regain complete partisan control of the state.

Their timing was excellent. The combined congressional and presidential election was scheduled for the second of November. On October 14, Dr. Goddard, who headed the Republican electoral slate, published a letter to his constituents explaining that they must not consider him pledged to vote for any particular candidate; if elected, he would use his independent judgment.[42] A Federalist elector immediately withdrew his name, and Goddard replaced him at the head of the Peace ticket. The *Patriot* as promptly erased the Portsmouth merchant's name from the Republican slate, but it was too late to repair the damage. Hundreds of rural voters went to their town meetings without knowledge of these extraordinary events and voted for Goddard, never suspecting that he was no longer a Madisonian.

Governor Plumer, who was an old hand at writing popular political satires, tried to offset this disaster by sarcastic attacks upon Goddard and Gilman in the *New Hampshire Patriot*.[43] Even this unusual effort, however, could not provide the impetus necessary for a Republican victory in November. The political timetable in New Hampshire turned anti-Republican after 1804; both of the succeeding presidential elections came at times when the national administration had arrayed the strongest forces in New England against itself. The Clinton ticket prevailed in New Hampshire by an average of 1,700 votes. At the same town meetings, but by a smaller margin, the people elected the entire Federalist congressional ticket, headed by Daniel Webster.[44] These five Federalist representatives proceeded to embarrass the administration in Washington to the limit of their greater-than-average abilities throughout the war. The Federalist victory in 1812 was not overwhelming, but it was the first of an unbroken series that prevailed for four years.

Governor Plumer had inherited a poor set of officeholders from his predecessor, particularly in the judiciary. In addition to appointing completely unqualified judges to the bench, Langdon had placed an alcoholic, Daniel French, in the office of attorney general. Plumer had few opportunities to improve this branch of the state government, but one did occur in the middle of the summer, when Judge Steele, who had alienated both parties, resigned from the superior court under a cloud of ugly rumor. Governor Plumer tried valiantly to put Samuel Bell into this office, but found two of his own Republican councillors adamantly opposed to the unlucky financier because of his connection with the Hillsborough Bank failure.[45] Bell was actually a man of strict integrity and great ability who did eventually become an excellent judge, governor, and senator, but in those days when banks were personally identified with the men who organized them, farmers who lost their deposits were inclined to hold the banker rather than the bank responsible. Eventually,

Plumer found it necessary to accede to the appointment of Clifton Clag-gett, an undistinguished but persistent and faithful party worker whom the three Republican councillors insisted upon rewarding.[46]

The superior court now consisted of Arthur Livermore, a judicial des-pot, Richard Evans, a chronic invalid, and Clifton Claggett, a mediocrity, while the attorney who argued the state's causes before this bench was usually inebriated. Of these four men, the only one with superior ability was Livermore, who was also the only Federalist. Through no particular fault of his own, Governor Plumer transmitted to his successor a judiciary which even he admitted could be reformed only by heroic measures.[47]

In spite of their nominal majorities in the legislature, the Republicans of New Hampshire in 1812 were fatally weakened by the defection of their Peace party members. This not only led to their defeat in the presi-dential and congressional elections but made itself dramatically evident in their failure, during two full sessions, to elect a United States senator. Responsibility for this debacle lay with Josiah Sanborn of Epsom, who had been elected to the senate as a Republican but who belonged in spirit to the Peace party.[48] He voted against all Republicans nominated by his colleagues and insisted upon the election of John Goddard, who, since his electoral vote against Madison, had of course become anathema to the party stalwarts. The legislature finally adjourned without electing a senator, thus permitting the Federalists to send Jeremiah Mason to the Senate in 1813.

Plumer and Gilman were both renominated in December by their party caucuses, and the gubernatorial campaign began immediately in the newspapers. The act of Plumer's administration which the Federalists most forcefully condemned was the one in which he most gloried—his prompt compliance with national requests for the service of the detached militia. During his twelve months in office, Plumer received four such requisitions, each of which he unhesitatingly fulfilled. His obedience gave him a certain claim to distinction, for he and Governor Galusha of Ver-mont were the only New England executives who recognized the author-ity of the United States in this matter. The governors of Massachusetts, Connecticut, and Rhode Island, all Federalists, took it upon themselves to declare unconstitutional the law of April 10, 1812 (and by implication, the Federalist statute of 1794, which it superseded).[49]

Some historians have accepted the Federalist argument on this point that the withdrawal of the regular army for the invasion of Canada left the New England coast defenseless and justified the governors in keeping their militia at home.[50] The fact is, however, that General Dearborn's first requisitions were precisely for the purpose of defending New En-gland's ports and it was the governors' defiance of federal law and the War Department which left their own coasts bare of troops.[51] Although

Plumer would undoubtedly have done so if required, he was not asked to send New Hampshire militia outside the state.[52] All the requisitions were for internal defense, paid for by the national government. This made no difference to the Federalists; Plumer was guilty of obeying a law passed by a Republican Congress. Yet, by a curious inversion of logic, the Federalists of Portsmouth pronounced curses upon Madison's administration for leaving them exposed to enemy attack.

The most reasoned version of the Federalist position on this question occurred in a minority protest against the Republican majority's reply to the governor's address at the November session of the legislature. "We have no disposition to weaken the arm of the General Government," insisted the seventy protestants, "but we cannot forget, that New Hampshire is a *free, sovereign* and *independent* State, and that we have sworn to support her Constitution." A sovereign state could not surrender control of its armed forces to an outside authority except voluntarily, they believed, and then only if the exigencies mentioned in the federal Constitution as warrant for such a surrender actually existed. They considered it the *duty* of the governor to determine whether they did. Governor Plumer, however, had made no inquiry, but had blindly surrendered discretion to the president. "We can find no clause in the Constitution, conferring on the President the sole power of determining, whether a Constitutional occasion of calling forth the militia does exist," declared these members of the party of loose construction and high prerogative.[53]

Such reasoning reduced the national government to the impotence of the Confederation period, from which the Federalists had been so eager to rescue it. Plumer's address to the legislature had contained a defense of his action so clear that the Federalist argument had been refuted before it was made.[54] If each of eighteen local sovereigns was to decide when the militia ought to be turned out, the British might very well conquer all the rest of North America while New Hampshire was waiting to be invaded. But Plumer based his case on precedent as well as reason. The earliest law placing state militia under the control of the president had been passed during Washington's administration by a Federalist Congress. Governor Gilman had not only failed to find this act of 1794 unconstitutional but had persuaded his legislature, in the same year, to sanction marching the militia out of the state if President Washington found it convenient so to ordain.[55] The bare suggestion that this might be done in 1812 made the Federalists hysterical. Yet the resolution of 1794 had never been repealed, and by its provisions Plumer could legally have sent New Hampshire militiamen to Louisiana.

Governor Plumer was eventually vindicated by compelling circumstances, as well as by logic and law. British control of the sea and the existence of a navy yard on Great Island subjected Portsmouth to constant danger of attack and its citizens to frequent alarms. Besides detaching four companies of militia on General Dearborn's orders for harbor defense, Plumer established on his own authority a guard of thirty men to watch the channel entrance.[56] The incoming Federalist administration raised a tremendous outcry because these few men had to be paid. They were immediately dismissed. Then the Portsmouth people, Federalists as well as Republicans, began to clamor for adequate protection. Prodded by Daniel Webster, Governor Gilman had to repeat Plumer's defensive measures on a much larger scale in 1814.[57] The British threat grew so serious that more than three thousand militiamen were called to Portsmouth, and when Gilman ran out of funds with which to pay them, he was forced to do exactly what Plumer had done in 1812—comply with a federal requisition.[58] Governor Strong of Massachusetts was likewise compelled to call out his militia. The Federalists feared that a British army of invasion would be no respecter of persons.

So far as the national conduct of the war was concerned, the Federalists found ample ground for condemnation. It was a record of monotonous disaster, beginning with Hull's surrender of Detroit, continuing with futile attempts to invade Canada, and culminating in the capture of the national capital by a British army. These fateful results of executive inefficiency could only embarrass the Republicans of New England, who suffered the constant derision of their opponents. "We are far from being in a pleasant situation here," wrote John Harper from Washington. "Many of the friends of the Administration believe, that the Executive are not disposed to prosecute the war with vigor, provided they can find any *hole* through which they can creep out and avoid the contest."[59]

Republicans, furthermore, had to resign themselves to the inevitability of direct federal taxes, and were thereby forced not only to swallow their own promises but to give up the New England farmers to Federalism. "The *hobgoblin* that the republican party raised against the necessary system of taxes in 1798 & 1799, & the violent prejudices they then unjustly excited, will now give them, & our country, much trouble," wrote Plumer to the patriarch, John Adams.[60]

These were the influences that swayed the town meetings in March 1813. The election depended less upon state issues than any since 1798— it was the attitude toward the war which determined the outcome. The campaign attracted a larger number of voters than any previous New Hampshire election, and both gubernatorial candidates shared in the increase. Gilman's gain was the larger, however, and he was elected over Plumer by a plurality of 797 votes, but with a majority of only 242 more than the number requisite to make a choice.[61] Since little more than two additional votes from each town would have returned Plumer to the chair, he attributed his defeat to the absence of Republican voters in the army and on privateers.[62] However, the Federalists also elected nine of the twelve senators and gained a dependable majority of more than twenty in the lower house of the legislature. They even won a precarious advantage of 3–2 in the council. The Federalist victory in New Hampshire was solid but no such landslide as occurred in the other New England states.[63]

The Republican decline in 1812 may best be measured not in gubernatorial, congressional, or presidential elections but in the change in the state legislature. Thirty-three constituencies that had sent Republicans to the lower house in 1812 elected Federalist representatives in 1813. One might expect to find these thirty-three concentrated in the area most immediately injured by the war, but as a matter of fact they were well distributed over the state. The Federalists made net gains of six seats in the Old Colony, five in the Merrimack Valley, nine in the Connecticut Valley, and nine on the Frontier.

The Old Colony, as the shipping and mercantile area of the state, should have responded most favorably to Federalist propaganda against the war. The political complexion of the area did indeed change, for Federalist control increased from only one-third of the towns to half of them. The Federalists also recovered senatorial districts two and five, which were chiefly in this area. They reestablished their ascendancy in the commercial centers of Dover and Barrington and snatched the agricultural towns of Milton, Northwood, Candia, Nottingham, Poplin, Kingston, and Hampstead from the Republicans. But they failed to capture Portsmouth. The war served as had no previous experience to emphasize the phenomenal character of Portsmouth politics. Just after the March elections in 1812, William Plumer had predicted pessimistically that "Portsmouth will eventually be federal—& that at no distant period. So will all the other commercial towns in the union—the reason is obvious."[64]

Goddard's defection, which came so shortly afterward, added weight to Plumer's prophecy. Webster and Mason in Congress gave national prominence to the impression that Portsmouth had at last committed its fortunes to the party that would cherish its commercial interests. Yet the fact remains that throughout the three years of war, when its shipping was idle, its commerce destroyed, and its sailors unemployed, Portsmouth continued perversely Republican. Webster's constant championship of the commercial interests was endorsed only by a minority of his constituency. He lived in a city which, had New Hampshire been divided into congressional districts, would never have sent him to Washington.

Throughout the years of Federalist ascendancy, 1813–15, Portsmouth gave Plumer a majority for governor and elected five Republicans to the legislature at every annual meeting. William Ham, the Republican senator from district one, and Elijah Hall, the Republican councillor from Rockingham County, held their seats throughout this period. The Federalists believed that this infallible Republican resource was maintained by fraud. In 1814 the legislature rejected all the votes from Portsmouth and expelled the five Republican city representatives on the ground that their election had been illegal.[65] By this rash and ill-considered action, the Federalists destroyed whatever chance they might ever have had of building up a strong following in the state's metropolis.

The Merrimack Valley was less affected by the war than any other section, to judge by political results. A Federalist gain of eight towns in 1813 was partially offset by the loss of three others, while each party added a new representative. The Federalists recovered the important towns of Gilmanton (although Gilford, set off in 1812, remained Republican), Mason, and Amherst, but the situation remained otherwise little changed. The area as a whole remained slightly Republican by thirty-one votes to thirty in the legislature, with the Federalist towns concentrated east of the Merrimack and the Republican towns west of it.

By recovering nine towns and adding a representative from Hanover the Federalists achieved an overwhelming preponderance of thirty-seven to sixteen in the Connecticut Valley. The Republicans lost their hold in Westmoreland, Walpole, Plainfield, Croyden, Orford, Piermont, and Haverhill, giving Federalism unbroken possession of the east bank of the river. Grateful Federalist leaders rejoiced that the Connecticut "like the Nile in Egypt fertilizes its banks from its source to the ocean and causes them to produce abundant harvests of Federalism and unwavering attachment to right principles."[66]

The loss of eight representatives in the Frontier region turned a slight Republican advantage into a one to three handicap, seven to twenty-one. Direct taxes and the profits of smuggling may have been the chief factors in this development. It is one of the ironies of a paradoxical war that the region that cried so loudly for protection promptly turned against the protector. Even Meredith, the home town of John Harper, the war hawk, turned Federalist.

Some historians of the War of 1812 have postulated its principal cause as the land hunger of the frontiersman. In this connection, Julius Pratt called attention to the views of Congressman Harper as significant because he represented a frontier section.[67] On the floor of the House of Representatives, on January 4, 1812, this young New Hampshire lawyer gave utterance to one of the earliest trumpetings of Manifest Destiny: "To me, sir, it appears that the Author of Nature has marked our limits in the south, by the Gulf of Mexico; and on the north, by the regions of perpetual frost."[68] Harper fought persistently in Congress for a pledge that Canada would be conquered and retained after the war. Other New

Hampshire Republicans, such as Daniel French, hoped for the conquest of the Canadas, and Governor Plumer did not wish to make peace until they had been secured. "We want those provinces, & sooner or later they will & must be annexed to the U.S.," he wrote to John Quincy Adams.[69]

It is easy, however, to misinterpret such statements. They resulted, not so much from land hunger among the New Hampshire backwoodsmen, nor even from the more voracious appetites of the speculators, as from the strategic advantage of holding Canada which had inspired Benjamin Franklin in 1782 and from the northern desire to insure a quid pro quo to match the southern appetite for Florida. Compared with the constant statements of irritation elicited in New Hampshire by British maritime aggression, these expressions of expansionist sentiment appear as after-thoughts.[70] At any rate, they did not represent the views of a majority in New Hampshire, nor even of its frontier area. Harper, it is true, happened to live in a frontier town, but he voiced the opinions of his party rather than of his constituents. If he had run for Congress on a district rather than a general ticket, he might not have been elected in 1810, and he actually was defeated in 1812. The New Hampshire frontier supported strong Federalist resolutions of opposition to the imperialism of "Mr. Madison's War" and, together with the state as a whole, gave its votes to the party that tried to sabotage the nation's war effort.[71] The supporters of Manifest Destiny lived in Portsmouth and Henniker far from the frontier.[72] As for the frontiersmen themselves, they were more interested in smuggling goods than marching armies into Canada.

CHAPTER 17

THE INDIAN SUMMER
OF FEDERALISM

*We believe that this war, so fertile in calamities and so threatening in
its consequences, has been waged with the worst possible views, and carried on in the worst possible manner; forming a union of wickedness
and weakness which defies, for a parallel, the annals of the world.*
—Resolution in the Massachusetts legislature, February 1814

The Federalists who returned to the seats of power in June 1813 were
convinced that their losses of 1812 had only been temporary aberrations.[1] Their defeat of a strong governor and recovery of control in the
legislature convinced them that they were the true exponents of public
opinion in their opposition to "Mr. Madison's War." The Federalists in
the lower house elected Thomas W. Thompson their speaker and, with
their majority in the convention of the two houses, chose a Federalist
councillor from Grafton County and thus gained a 3–2 majority in that
body. "At this moment the bells are ringing & cannon firing, in demonstration of the people's joy," wrote Ezekiel Webster triumphantly to his
brother in Congress.[2]

Bell ringing was quickly succeeded in the legislature by more decided
means of celebration. Governor and legislators first denounced "the war
in which our beloved country is unhappily involved with Great Britain;
the consequences of which cannot be foreseen; the necessity of which we
have never been able to discover."[3] They then implemented their policy
of noncooperation in the national war effort by deciding not to raise a
state tax for the year.[4] Having thus disposed of national issues, they
turned with relish to the business of remodeling the state judiciary.

Here the New Hampshire Federalists faced very much the same situation that had confronted Jefferson and his national administration in
1801—triumphs at the polls which gave them executive and legislative
control of the government, but had no effect on the opposition's entrenchment in the judicial establishment. Like Jefferson, they regarded
this state of things as unfair, but they had even more reason to complain
about the quality of the courts in possession of the enemy. Justice had
been delayed interminably not only by the ineffectiveness of the common
pleas courts but also by the absences of Evans and the ignorance of
Claggett in the superior court. Former governor Plumer's apprehensions

regarding his appointment were fully justified by Claggett's conduct during his short tenure; it proved him "deficient in quickness of apprehension, soundness of judgment and decision of character."[5] New Hampshire lawyers were convinced that questions of law were never given proper consideration by the overburdened superior court, with the result that judgments were "inconstant, fluctuating, perpetually changing."[6] Feeling against the judges had mounted to the point that Evans had been warned by friends that unless he resigned, he would be removed by address as soon as the Federalist legislature convened.[7]

Evans did not resign; nor was he removed by either of the constitutional means available to the legislature—address or impeachment. These procedures were too slow and too uncertain. The triumphant Federalist majority turned, instead, to the device that had served Jefferson so well in 1802—removal of the office from the judge. This was accomplished under the guise of a complete overhauling of the state court system by the Judiciary Act of June 24, 1813.[8] A supreme court with three judges replaced the old superior court, but the state was divided into three circuits, in each of which a single supreme court judge was to hold three sessions of the court annually. The judges were to come together only once a year to hold a "law session" at which questions of law postponed from the circuit courts were to be decided. The old courts of common pleas, with their eighteen judges, were replaced by two circuit courts, each with three judges. This was supposed to expedite original jurisdiction and prevent a large number of the appeals to the supreme court.

The Federalists, as had Jefferson in 1801, made a strong case for these radical changes as necessary reforms in an antiquated legal system.[9] But the really essential part of the bill, in the eyes of the average Federalist legislator, was its incidental effect of removing twenty-one Republican judges from office and permitting the governor to appoint nine Federalists in their places.[10] Gilman did not fail to do his duty. For the new chief justice of the new supreme court he named Jeremiah Smith, and for a circuit judgeship another Exeter neighbor, Oliver Peabody. Staunch Federalists were rewarded with all but two of the remaining offices, and the only nominal Republican reappointed to the bench was Nahum Parker, who, like Goddard, had departed from Jeffersonian orthodoxy when the war began and now reaped his reward. Arthur Livermore, former chief justice and a nominal Federalist, was also reappointed, but demoted at the same time to an associate justice's place under Judge Smith. No one could deny, however, that the new judiciary was infinitely superior in ability to the old—even the raging *Patriot* printed the argument that good judges could not compensate for unconstitutional appointments.[11]

The judicial coup d'etat came as a surprise, if not indeed as a shock, to most New Hampshire citizens, Federalists as well as Republicans. Everyone had expected the legislature to remove Evans from office and perhaps even to impeach Livermore, but the wholesale purge effected under the guise of law was a remedy wholly devised and executed by a well-organized and relatively narrow caucus of Federalist lawyers. It is not difficult to discern the ideas of Jeremiah Smith in those parts of the bill which attempted drastic reform of court procedure. It was in fact because Smith was the spiritual father of the new judicial system and felt a sincere obligation to accomplish reforms for which he had striven since the day when he was a neophyte in the profession that he accepted an appointment which could only bring financial loss, merciless criticism, and an indelible blot upon his reputation for consistency.[12] Smith had been one of the sixteen federal circuit judges deprived of office by Congress in 1801 and had signed the protest that this group had addressed to President Jefferson. Republican orators now quoted from this document with telling effect: "That Judges shall not be deprived of their offices, or compensations, without misbehaviour, appears to us to be among the first and best established principles in the American Constitutions."[13] Even more devastating was a reference to Smith's inaugural speech in 1809, when he had said, "It would be a source of great regret to find this . . . department [the judicial] of government subjected to the revolutions of political parties or at all affected by party feelings."[14] Smith at the head of the bench was a constant reminder of judicial subservience to partisan politics.

Although neither party could promote this view with consistency, the strongest argument against the Judiciary Act of 1813 was its alleged unconstitutionality.[15] If removal of the federal judges by the act of 1801 was contrary to the federal Constitution, then removal of the state judges by the act of 1813 was contrary to the state constitution. Both documents provided for judicial tenure on the basis of good behavior. Federalists, however, now stood foursquare for the doctrines of legislative supremacy, democratic responsibility to the voter, and opposition to vested judicial power, which had hitherto been Republican property, while Republicans railed against such heresies. "Why change the system?" inquired Isaac Hill, an editor not hitherto noted for contentment with the status quo. "Curse on the Innovating hand attempts it."[16] The now conservative Mr. Hill also opened his columns to "Vox Populi," who was horrified that the administration of justice had become a party question. He hurled this anathema at the Federalists:

> If your construction of the Constitution be legitimate, the Judges, from the high standing in which we have been accustomed to view them, that of being independent of any body on earth, so long as they behaved well, and placed altogether beyond the orbit of party

influence, are sunk down to become altogether dependent upon, and the miserable subservient minions of a ferocious and vindictive party spirit, in the shape of a legislative majority.[17]

The defrocked state judges refused to acknowledge their demise as gracefully as had Judge Smith in 1802. At the appointed times for holding the superior court in Strafford, Rockingham, and Hillsborough counties, Evans and Claggett took the bench and went through the form of holding sessions. The sheriffs in the latter two counties attended them, but clerks, lawyers, and suitors, with the single unimpressive exception of William Claggett, refused to obey their instructions or to do business in their court. The two repudiated judges took the line that the legislature had authority to establish as many new courts as it wished, so long as these did not interfere with the jurisdictions fixed by the state constitution or with the tenure of existing judges.[18]

Under this reasoning, new courts and old courts might have functioned side by side, had both parties been willing. It so happened that the terms of old and new courts coincided at Dover, where Arthur Livermore, appearing in his new capacity as an associate justice of the supreme court, dismayed the Federalists by joining with his former associates in denouncing the act under which he held his new appointment.[19] This erratic behavior was typical of the Livermores, but Arthur had at least the courage of consistency. "Let any man read the debates in Congress on the repeal of a Judicial act in the year 1802," he wrote later, "and compare the Constitution of this State with that of the United States, and hold a different opinion if he can."[20] Jeremiah Smith lacked this kind of consistency, but he won public respect for the new courts by the dignity and patience with which he submitted to the burlesque performance of the two disgruntled judges at the Exeter term, where they even insisted on occupying the same bench with the new chief justice.[21] Staged by two contentious politicians whose ignorance and disability had been chiefly responsible for their own misfortunes, these ridiculous spectacles unquestionably turned public opinion toward a favorable view of the Federalist judiciary.[22]

The collusion of the two Republican sheriffs with the Republican judges made it virtually impossible for the new supreme court to function in Rockingham and Hillsborough counties and thus imposed upon Governor Gilman the disagreeable necessity of calling a special session of the legislature to deal with the situation. Josiah Butler and Benjamin Pierce, the two offending sheriffs, were removed by address, and a committee report which condemned the behavior of Evans and Claggett in language little less scurrilous than that employed by the newspapers was adopted.[23]

Republican legislators lodged a protest against these arbitrary measures, which deprived the accused individuals of the right to be heard in their own defense and "placed them in such a situation, that there is no tribunal on earth, before whom they can appear in defence of themselves."[24] The minority further developed the interesting doctrine that since the sheriffs were accused of criminal acts, they should have been impeached rather than removed by address. The constitutional provision for address and removal, they asserted, was intended for use only in cases of sickness, insanity, and other contingencies in which no misbehavior was involved.[25]

Ignoring these ineffective words, the majority denounced opponents of the Judiciary Act as traitors and defended the legislature's right to dominate executive and judicial officers in terms which the most dogmatic Republican of 1798 would have found extravagant.[26] It then proceeded to amend its own Judiciary Act by abolishing Jeremiah Smith's brainchild, the law term. This left the judicial organization essentially what it had been before June, except for the change in the politics of the judges. The Federalists of New Hampshire had succeeded in their assault on the state judiciary beyond anything which Jefferson had dreamed of accomplishing in the national courts. There was nothing left for Republicans to do but fume in their newspapers and promise a reformation when they returned to power. Evans and Claggett abandoned their ridiculous crusade, and the remaining good citizens of New Hampshire accepted the Federalist judicial purge as a fait accompli.

The role of New England's Congregational clergy in helping to foment and sustain rebellion against England in the 1770s has been fully documented by American historians. Less attention has been paid to the contradictory fact that this same body of men defended Britain and bitterly opposed the struggle for maritime freedom which has sometimes been called the "Second War of Independence." Congregationalist churchgoers in 1813 listened every Sabbath to statements that would have placed their authors behind the bars of a federal penitentiary in 1918. The Reverend Dr. Osgood of Medford, Massachusetts, told those members of his congregation who volunteered for army service or lent their money to the government or even encouraged the prosecution of the war by conversation that they were murderers in the sight of God, "*and no murderer hath eternal life*."[27] "Do not, I beseech you, do not move a finger to promote this wicked war," thundered Dr. Elijah Parish from the pulpit in Byefield, Massachusetts. But he went even further and urged New England to separate from the southern states and proclaim itself neutral. "Let *southern* heroes fight their own battles," he urged. "Rise in the majesty of your unconquerable strength, burst these chains under which you have sullenly *murmered*, during the long, long reign of *democracy*."[28]

In order to discredit the Congregational preachers and thus weaken their alliance with the Federalist party, Isaac Hill attacked their legal establishment and accused them of using the exigencies of war as a means of imposing an even tighter stranglehold upon religion in New England. He found a spokesman for this position in former governor William Plumer, a deist who had never been fond of the Congregationalists, even in his own Federalist days, and was now convinced by their extremism that they sought to profit by their country's destruction. In December 1813, Plumer wrote and Hill published in the *Patriot* a series of articles entitled "An Address to the Clergy of New England by a Layman." Plumer actually gave additional publicity to the preachers' denunciation of the war by quoting sermons in which it was called an "outrage against heaven," "this profligate measure," a "contest between Christ and Antichrist," in which the officials of the Republican administration were labeled "murderers," "Virginia vassals of a French emperor," "malignant and infernal beings," comparable to Pharaoh and Judas, and "Devils" to whom "Satan, blushing, owns himself outdone in the work of deception." Dr. Parish had even declared that "though our government ... rush forward with the torch of war blazing in their hands, the English are determined to give the contest every feature of mildness and humanity which the nature of the case will admit."[29]

Plumer denounced this subversive attack upon the federal government in much the same terms that he had used against Republicans for objecting to the Adams administration in 1799. He was answered in the *Concord Gazette* by the Reverend Asa McFarland, Congregational minister in Concord, who pointed out the fallacy in Plumer's identifying criticism of rulers with opposition to laws, but attempted no defense of the open encouragement to resistance and secession which Plumer had quoted.[30] He made it clear that the war was a religious issue in the eyes of the clergy—a war in which the Republicans were the allies of degenerate, atheistic France against a "people, who, with all their faults, do more than all the rest of the world beside to extend the knowledge of revealed religion."[31]

In the meantime, the war dragged on, and except for a few victorious naval duels, the Republicans had nothing cheerful to offer the voters at town meeting. New Hampshire troops died in vain beyond the Niagara River and retreated ignominiously from Canada with Wilkinson. Necessity had finally driven Congress to the passage of the first direct tax bill since the hated Federalist measure of 1799. The unpopularity of the idea had not diminished during the intervening fourteen years, even though the parties had changed sides on the issue. New Hampshire's share of the levy was nearly ninety-seven thousand dollars, which seemed intolerable to people accustomed to a state tax of less than thirty thousand dollars a year.[32] The assessors of the direct tax, said the *Concord Gazette*, were the Federalists' best allies in New Hampshire.[33]

The *Gazette*'s analysis may well have been correct, for in the spring of 1814, Gilman won another year in the governorship by an official plurality over Plumer of 881 votes. His majority, however, would have dropped to a mere 118 out of 38,542 votes cast if the returns from three Republican towns had not been rejected by the legislature.[34] The Federalists held an advantage of about twelve votes in the lower house of the legislature and a safer 8–4 margin in the senate. The three eastern counties, however, elected Republican councillors, thus depriving Gilman of his party's majority in the body with which he had to work most closely and most continuously. This proved to be an embarrassing impediment to the full Federalist program.

The summer of 1814 was a time of hovering terror for the inhabitants of Portsmouth and of vexation for Governor Gilman. Freed from its more onerous duties in European waters, the British fleet drove America's valiant little frigates from the high seas and ranged the Atlantic coast at will, threatening every port of any consequence with dire calamity. Portsmouth, with its federal navy yard and a 74-gun warship in the ways, presented a tempting prize. In Portsmouth's virtually defenseless state, a sudden raid up the Piscataqua might pay rich dividends. As early as March, and again in April, Commodore Isaac Hull, in command of the navy yard, begged the governor for some attention to the deplorable military situation of this exposed seaport. Major General Storer of the New Hampshire militia added his own plea for authority at least to resume the military watch at Little Harbor, which Governor Plumer had first established and the Federalists had promptly disbanded in 1813.[35] On April 22 a Portsmouth committee visited Governor Gilman and demanded a militia force of at least eight hundred to garrison the harbor fortifications.[36]

These cries of alarm placed Gilman in a distressing situation. They could hardly be ignored; yet his political fortunes rested securely upon an antiwar platform, the strongest plank of which was that New Hampshire soldiers should not be expected to fight Mr. Madison's battles. All during the spring, while Portsmouth was thrown into periodic panics by the appearance of British cruisers off the coast, Gilman attempted without notable success to shift the burden of defense to the federal government, which his party was trying so desperately to paralyze.[37] He was finally forced to call out eight companies of the detached militia for sixty days—more men than Plumer had been reviled for ordering out in 1812—and the end was not yet in sight.[38] In September, Gilman suffered his greatest humiliation when rumors of a British attack multiplied more alarmingly than ever before. The frightened citizens of Portsmouth dispensed with politics for the duration of the crisis. Both parties joined at town meeting in calling upon the inhabitants to repair the fortifications, which the state and federal governments had seemed unable to mend. Tradition has it that Daniel Webster was the hero of this occasion, proposing the joint action and wielding a shovel at the head of his fellow townsmen as they marched upon the ramparts the next day.[39] Be that as it may, after a bipartisan committee from Portsmouth had been put off by Gilman's evasions, Webster called upon his nominal party chief and told him plainly that the peril to Portsmouth admitted of no further temporizing or political gambits. Gilman thereupon called the two eastern regiments of militia to the Portsmouth defenses, the soldiers, Plumer noted, being "more prompt in obeying the orders than the governor was in issuing them."[40]

Governor Gilman's cup of bitterness was filled to the brim shortly thereafter when President Madison made a requisition upon him for another portion of the detached militia to defend the seacoast. Since the troops were demanded by the people, Gilman had either to comply with the president's orders or call out the militia again upon his own authority. Unfortunately, the latter alternative required financial resources that Gilman could not obtain without approval from the legislature, and people were murmuring too much about the excessive cost of the special session in 1813 to make the prospect of another one very inviting. Gilman bowed to the inevitable and complied with the president's letter, thus doing exactly what Governor Plumer had done at the beginning of the war. Thereafter, the Federalist newspapers showed a strong reluctance to comment upon Plumer's subservience to the national military.

According to the Portsmouth Federalists, the militiamen who swarmed in their neighborhood served a purpose beyond that of preventing a possible attack upon the navy yard. Charging that the Republican town officials had used militiamen to cast more than five hundred fraudulent votes in the March election, the Federalist legislature in June rejected Portsmouth's election returns and expelled its representatives.[41] Not quite satisfied with this exhibition of arbitrary power, some extremists wished to deprive the councillor from Rockingham County of his office, since the rejection of Portsmouth's votes reduced his majority to a mere plurality. Although this same legislature elected Ezekiel Webster, who had only *four* popular votes, to a vacancy in the senate, the moderates decided that they had gone far enough, and allowed Councillor Hall to take his seat.[42] This compromise bargain, for so it seemed, disgusted Daniel Webster, since it left a Republican majority on the council.[43] It subsequently developed that New Hampshire was probably saved from participation in the Hartford Convention by this political deal.

While the vexations of the spring and summer may have betrayed the Federalists into excesses, their political fortunes did not seem to wane. The opportune death of Nicholas Gilman, who had been more a dissident Republican than a genuine Federalist, permitted them to place one of their stalwarts, Thomas W. Thompson, in the United States Senate, where he teamed with Jeremiah Mason to oppose the administration. As the congressional elections approached in August, strenuous attempts were made to retire the five Federalists who then spoke for New Hampshire in the House of Representatives.[44] It would be more proper to say the four who sat and the one who spoke, for Daniel Webster was the only son of the Granite State who favored the newly finished House chamber with his oratory. His notable maiden speech against the war in the previous session occasioned a slashing attack in the Republican press against "a man reared in the woods of Salisbury, [and] educated in the *wilds* of Hanover,"[45] who pretended to speak for the interests of commerce. This was a specious argument, but Webster's championship of New England particularism in a time of national peril was less defensible. The future defender of the Union attacked the proposed conscription bill of 1814 as an unconstitutional, despotic, "horrible lottery" and declared that the states should interpose to protect their citizens against its enforcement.[46] South Carolina did no more in 1833. But for the time, Webster seemed to have his state's support; his ticket was reelected, though by a diminished majority. Only in the governor's council could New Hampshire Republicanism in 1814 speak with authority in either state or national government.

Even without speaking, this slender thread of potential Republican power proved to be a major influence in New Hampshire's history. From Massachusetts came tidings that a state convention had been elected to choose delegates for a more pretentious meeting at Hartford, and Republican papers immediately assumed that this meeting would commit acts of treason.[47] Shortly after the Massachusetts convention had issued an official call to neighboring states, an emissary of Governor Strong dropped in upon John Taylor Gilman with the circular letter and left the old man in much confusion. The governor of New Hampshire professed deep respect for the governor of Massachusetts, but his legislature was not in session and he hesitated to call it together in an inclement season. His advisers in Exeter and Portsmouth thought it would be bad politics, even if the council agreed to it. There indeed was the chief stumbling block; who would suppose that the Republican majority on the council would consent to give him such advice? He wished the convention well, however, and if the situation became noticeably worse within the next twelve days, there would still be time to call the legislature.[48]

It is not improbable that Gilman secretly welcomed the political impasse that excused him from the necessity of acting in this matter.[49] Isaac Hill, in the columns of the *Patriot*, was giving him a vivid forecast of the lashing he would receive if he committed himself to the project. "While the hot-heads in Massachusetts think this is the most favorable time for such a project to be carried into complete effect in co-operation with His Brittanic Majesty's fleets and armies now hovering on our coasts for the avowed purpose of relieving us from the trouble of *governing ourselves*— more moderate men of the federal party view the plan with the abhorrence and indignation it so justly merits."[50]

When the Boston *Centinel* hailed the election of Rhode Island and Connecticut delegates to "the Henryite Convention" as the second and third pillars of a new federal edifice, Hill scornfully commented that it seemed doomed to remain a tripod.[51] Vermont declared the convention to be inexpedient, and the further growth of the structure had to come from New Hampshire or nowhere. The ardent Federalists in the Connecticut Valley decided to wrest the initiative from Gilman's palsied hand. A county convention at Walpole elected the venerable Benjamin West a delegate to represent Cheshire County at Hartford, and a week later came the news that Mills Olcott, son of the former chief justice and senator, had been similarly elected by a Grafton County convention at Hanover. "This fourth pillar, from its extreme shortness, will make but a poor prop to Major Russell's tripod," jeered the *Patriot*.[52]

What these two irregulars were expected to accomplish or did accomplish at Hartford is not certain. No one at the time knew what went on behind the closed doors of the Connecticut State House, and this in itself was suspicious. If nothing was rotten in Hartford, reasoned the Republicans, why was it being matured in the dark?[53] Some of the delegates were known secessionists, and it was predicted that their debates would lead to conspiracy and violence. William Plumer, however, believed that the controlling delegates had too "much *cunning* mixt with *fear* to proceed further than addresses, remonstrances, & resolves."[54] What he apprehended was a rapid growth of the rebellious spirit that had been materialized at Hartford and its seizure by more unprincipled leaders than Harrison Gray Otis. When the published resolutions of the convention appeared in the papers, they went far to confirm both Plumer's analysis and his fears. There were remonstrances and resolves enough, but there was also the threat of a second meeting in case events did not develop according to the Federalist way of thinking.

The historical significance of the Hartford Convention, however, was not that it posed a serious threat to the Union but that it demonstrated how weak that threat had been. New England had not united under convention leadership; the convention had been more strongly opposed by Republicans in New England than by outsiders; it had been led, in the end, not by the secessionists but by Federalists cautious in their approach to disunion. The three commissioners who carried the demands of the Hartford Convention toward Washington in January 1815 represented only a slender majority in three out of the eighteen United States.

Fortunately perhaps for everyone except the Hartford Convention commissioners, a treaty of peace had been unexpectedly signed on Christmas Eve in Ghent and the character of its terms became known in New Hampshire by February. "It leaves all our territory entire," wrote William Plumer, thankfully, "& has secured us the respect of the civilized world."[55] New Englanders hastened to resume business as usual and political passions were muted. Both Gilman and Plumer had been renominated by their respective caucuses in 1814, but the former was supported with considerable reluctance by the Federalists and the latter had lost most of his enthusiasm for campaigning.[56] In the desultory March elections of 1815, the Federalists won their last political victory in New Hampshire, but with diminished majorities in both houses of the legislature. John Taylor Gilman, at the age of sixty-one, capped his long public career by earning a fifteenth term as governor, defeating William Plumer for the third time by only 259 votes.

In the meantime, however, General Jackson had won his remarkable victory at New Orleans, the Treaty of Ghent had arrived in Washington, and the Hartford Convention commissioners had discreetly abandoned their mission. As a national institution, the Federalist party had committed suicide. Without energy or enthusiasm it barely managed to garner thirty-four electoral votes from Massachusetts, Connecticut, and Delaware for its last presidential candidate, Rufus King of New York, in 1816, and then expired forever.

CHAPTER 18

PEACE ABROAD:
WAR AT HOME

The college was formed for the public good, not for the benefit or emolument of its trustees; and the right to amend and improve acts of incorporation of this nature, has been exercised by all governments, both monarchical and republican. —William Plumer

While belated dispatches from Vienna, where the assembled diplomats were remaking the map of Europe, and from Paris, where Napoleon had reestablished his empire and was preparing to march toward Waterloo, continued to titillate the readers of New Hampshire's journals after the Peace of Ghent, their real interests began to focus once more upon events nearer at hand.[1] Preeminent among these was a cloud arising in the west, from the campus of Dartmouth College. Trouble had been brewing in that sylvan retreat for many years, but not until the spring of 1815 did it become public property.

Just before the meeting of the legislature, prominent men all over New England received copies of a pamphlet entitled *Sketches of the History of Dartmouth College*, which proved to be an anonymous and bitter attack upon the college trustees.[2] Readers readily deduced that the pamphlet had been written by no less a person than John Wheelock, the president of Dartmouth College, with the sole purpose of arousing public feeling against his own trustees.[3] Those who were disposed to believe what they read were assured that the trustees had perverted the college into an agency for the accomplishment of long-maturing plans to establish a politico-religious hierarchy in New England based upon the close alliance of Federalism and Congregationalism.[4]

Hardly had the shocked people of New Hampshire begun to recover from their amazement at this revelation of alleged rottenness in Hanover before Wheelock struck another well-timed blow by appealing to the New Hampshire legislature for an investigation of conditions at Dartmouth College. Calling on the lawmakers to perform their sacred duty of overseeing literary establishments and rectifying abuses, Wheelock begged them to "make such organic improvements, and model reforms in its system and movements as, under Divine Providence, will guard against the disorders and their apprehended consequences . . . that instead of a theatre for the purpose of a few terminating in public calamity, it may become an increasing source of blessings to the State, and to mankind of the present and succeeding ages."[5]

By thus plunging into the political arena, President Wheelock precipitated a struggle which was to go far beyond the college campus, and even beyond the confines of New Hampshire. The trustees professed to see no need for a legislative investigation, but did not attempt to block it. They welcomed it, in fact, since the legislature was controlled by Federalists and the investigating committee subsequently appointed had a Federalist majority. Hoping that "the Committee's Report should effectually put down a CERTAIN MAN,"[6] they persuaded the members to set an early date for the hearing without first consulting Wheelock. In August the president received official notice of the visitation, by which time it was too late for him to secure counsel, although the trustees had been gathering affidavits against him from his own faculty since July.[7] The three investigators appointed by Governor Gilman visited the campus, listened impassively to the testimony of both parties, and prepared to submit a report of the facts in the case to the next session of the legislature.[8] At this point, when patience might have brought them a resounding victory, the trustees committed a serious blunder by summarily dismissing John Wheelock from the presidency and immediately replacing him with the Reverend Francis Brown, a young Dartmouth alumnus then preaching in Maine. This precipitate action seemed peculiarly imprudent at a time when the controversy had been, in effect, placed "under the eyes of the sovereign body."[9] At one stroke the trustees created a martyr, insulted the state government, and delivered themselves into the hands of their enemies.

It was the perverse genius of Isaac Hill that recognized the priceless political opportunity so providentially offered the Republican party by the Dartmouth College trustees. Immediately after the circulation of Wheelock's pamphlet, Hill had written an editorial of righteous indignation, professing astonishment that the management of the college had become "so much a *party* concern as to persecute in a spirit of the most inveterate malignity the venerable man, who, by his own indefatigable labors and perseverance, had given that seminary its whole character for eminence and respectability."[10] Throughout the summer the *Patriot* kept up a steady drumfire of innuendo, while the Federalist press maintained a neutral attitude and insisted that the only politics involved were those that Hill was manufacturing so feverishly.[11] With Wheelock's dismissal, Hill's campaign attained a furious crescendo. The "venerable" president "had become the victim of a religious intolerance as despotic as it is wicked. . . . If before we thought these men to exhibit an unbecoming zeal in favor of their own religious party, we must now be convinced that that zeal will, when they shall have attained to the summit of their wishes, lead them to bind the object of its vengeance to the stake, and set fire to the faggots that surround him!"[12]

At the beginning, Hill was fighting a straw man, for Federalist opinion was much divided on the Dartmouth question and might never have united had Hill not forced the issue. President Wheelock himself, all but one of the trustees, the town of Hanover, and most of the alumni of Dartmouth College were Federalist and Calvinist. Governor Gilman, who was an elected rather than an ex officio trustee, and Judge Stephen Jacob of Vermont, both Federalists, dissented sharply from the vote to remove Wheelock.[13] The Reverend John Smith, the only college instructor who was also a trustee, likewise adhered to Wheelock. It was the remaining eight members of the board who had accomplished his ouster, and the most bitterly anti-Wheelock member of this group, Judge Nathaniel Niles of Vermont, was also the only Republican. The board included two more Vermonters, Elijah Paine and Charles Marsh, both strongly opposed to Wheelock. The rest were unrelenting New Hampshire Federalists. Two of them—Seth Payson of Rindge and Asa McFarland of Concord—were Congregationalist ministers. The remaining two were familiar political figures—Judge Timothy Farrar and the newly elected United States senator, Thomas W. Thompson. The sharpest legal mind in the Federalist party, Jeremiah Mason, had warned these men against dismissing Wheelock while their quarrel was being examined by the legislature. Such precipitance, he told them frankly, would arouse against them all the religious liberals, "nothingarians," and Democrats in New Hampshire—an accurate prediction.[14]

Having sought to end their dispute by the destruction of the other party, the trustees now somewhat belatedly published their official apologia entitled A *Vindication of the Official Conduct of the Trustees of Dartmouth College.* "It was written with much acrimony & displays a littleness & meanness of spirit dishonorable to the authors,"[15] declared William Plumer, in a description that would have applied to most of the extensive literature eventually appearing on both sides of the Dartmouth issue. Many Federalist papers were now beginning to match Hill's vituperation with poisoned shafts of their own, aimed at Wheelock and his loyal friends. Assailed by this barrage of propaganda, it was difficult for contemporaries to sort out truth from fiction; it is even more difficult now to follow the tortured controversy. The essential facts in the situation, however, can be briefly summarized.

Begun as an Indian mission school in Lebanon, Connecticut, in 1754, and moved to Hanover in 1770, Dartmouth College was the creation and lifework of one man, Eleazer Wheelock, a Presbyterian minister. Its corporate existence was based on a charter granted in 1769 by John Wentworth, last royal governor of the colony of New Hampshire, acting in his capacity as viceroy of George III. Surprisingly liberal for its time, the charter prohibited the exclusion of students on the ground of religious opinion, stipulated that seven of the twelve trustees be laymen, and divided the membership of the original board among Congregationalists, Episcopalians, and Presbyterians. However, the board was made self-perpetuating. Wheelock was named president, and was given the extraordinary right to choose his own successor, subject to the approval of the trustees. There was from the beginning some uncertainty as to whether Dartmouth was an Indian school (as the earl of Dartmouth believed) or an English boys' college (which Wheelock intended), and this was reflected in an overly complicated organization. Moor's Charity School was an entirely separate corporation from Dartmouth College, and the confusion had been compounded by the further creation of the Union Academy. Each of these had its own treasury, and there were special sources of income, such as the Phillips Fund, apart from all of them. Much of the confusion surrounding the Dartmouth College case, even in the mind of John Marshall, arose from these complications.[16]

For ten years after Dartmouth College was established in Hanover, Eleazer Wheelock had continued to guide its infant steps with success and benevolent despotism. At his death in 1779, he had bequeathed the presidency to his son, John, who continued to perpetuate the dynasty for thirty-six years. Thus from its very beginning, Dartmouth College had been inseparably identified with the Wheelock name, and New Hampshire people were accustomed to thinking of them as synonymous.

John Wheelock apparently had a capacity for making loyal friends, but casual acquaintances saw in him a pompous, dull, and rigidly orthodox figure with more pretensions to scholarship than performance merited. His chief ability lay in administration, and he had made Dartmouth College a going concern. In religion he was a far more uncompromising Presbyterian than his father had been; in politics he had been an equally firm but less active Federalist. He was well known in the state capital as a lobbyist, interceding year after year with the legislature for donations to his beloved institution.[17]

It was inevitable that such a man as Wheelock, obstinate, tactless, and dictatorial, should quarrel with such a board as governed the college in the second decade of the 1800s. Strong differences of opinion had appeared as early as 1793 between Wheelock and the newly elected trustee Judge Niles. Gradually the board, which had originally been subservient to the president, acquired more members of Judge Niles's opinion. In 1809, during the one-year regime of Governor Jeremiah Smith, who took his ex officio membership on the board seriously, Asa McFarland and Charles Marsh were elected to membership by the governor's casting vote. They were already aligned with the anti-Wheelock faction, and their recruitment gave that group a decided majority. From that moment until Wheelock threw the controversy before the public in 1815, there was constantly increasing friction between the trustees and the president.

Seven of the eight trustees who voted for Wheelock's ouster were "high-toned" Federalists, and all eight of them were strong Calvinists. This almost exclusive representation of orthodoxy in politics and religion was contrary to the spirit of the college charter and gave strong color to Wheelock's charge that "the Octagon," as Isaac Hill dubbed them, advocated the establishment of a "law-religion." Indeed, trustee Marsh declared flatly that the animus against Wheelock came from the fear that he would convert the college "into a seminary of Socinianism"—an event which would cause the "hearts of the faithful to faint."[18]

The breach between Wheelock and the trustees was, in fact, considerably widened by one of the church schisms so characteristic of New England Congregationalism. Wheelock's Presbyterianism clashed with the theological views of a group in the Hanover church who were supported by the trustees and the college professor of theology. By virtue of duplicity and stubbornness on both sides, this petty quarrel, which should never have gone beyond the confines of Hanover, became state property, being debated in the newspapers in such brotherly terms as "dastardly meanness," "jesuitical conduct," "scurrilous aspersions," and "manifest fraud." The innumerable and almost impenetrable pamphlets in which it was presented to the reading public buried the truth beyond hope of resurrection, but made it clear enough that a theoretically nonsectarian college government which involved itself in such a feud stood much in need of reform.[19]

In spite of all the heat generated by these disputes, however, the Dartmouth College case might have died in infancy had not Wheelock's determination and Isaac Hill's ingenuity lifted it to a level of national importance. Bold piling up of circumstantial evidence and skillful connection of unrelated events produced in the columns of the *Patriot* a diabolical alliance between the college trustees and the classes they represented—Congregational clergy, Federalist lawyers, orthodox squires—for the permanent suppression of democracy in New England. If the Federalists could not win at the polls, they could perpetuate their privileges in the churches and schools of the country. They would be supported by a "law-religion" and an established hierarchy culminating in a "Pope of New Hampshire"—to which eminence Asa McFarland already aspired.[20] Clerical sedition during the recent war, according to Hill, had been a major element in the plot. Others were now being revealed.

First, there was the Sabbath observance law, passed by the last Federalist legislature at the behest of the clergy. Forbidding even the most necessitous travel or patronage of taverns on Sunday, it had created a host of local tyrants and had given the clergy complete control of people's lives for at least one day of the week. It was obviously a part of the scheme to create law-religion by the "rigidly righteous."[21] So were the "moral societies" being incorporated everywhere by those who pretended that the church alone was not able to drive sin out of New England. Actually, said Hill, these were political machines for the election of religious bigots, who, once in power, would establish a hierarchy of Congregational jesuits to terrorize the people. Added to this mounting pile of evidence were the decisions of the Federalist courts against dissenters who sought to escape religious taxes, and the refusals of the Federalist legislature to incorporate dissenter societies while permitting Congregationalists to organize freely for any purpose. To cap the climax, Judge Smith, in supreme court session, December 1815, had decided that the settled clergy were exempt from direct taxation by the federal government, thus setting up, according to Hill, a privileged class and moving toward a union of church and state.[22]

Keystone of the plot to establish a law-religion, maintained a "Baptist" in the columns of the *Patriot*, was the seizure of the colleges by the Hopkinsian Calvinists.[23] Andover Academy, founded by the disgruntled fundamentalist seceders from Harvard and backed by a million-dollar endowment, was the fountainhead of aggressive orthodoxy. Williams, Yale, and, to an alarming extent, even Harvard had already succumbed to the attack. Dartmouth was only the latest victory in a campaign that was bound to continue until the hierarchs were triumphant in every college north of the Delaware.

The grain of truth in this lurid fantasy was not much bigger than a mustard seed, but the Republican politicians planted and watered it with loving care. "Every Man in every Town & State," wrote Levi Bartlett of Kingston, "should pointedly set his face against the insidious plans of the diabolical Clergy, who are endeavoring to subvert all Religious & Civil liberty."[24] The democratic papers did not fail to point out to "Every Man" that a remedy lay in his upraised hand for the right candidates at the March meetings. Dartmouth College was the point at which the counterattack could be launched, and there was nothing improper about making its affairs a matter of political concern. The state had been a liberal patron of the college, and every citizen had something of a vested interest in its welfare.[25] Therefore, unless a majority of the legislature were dupes of the trustees, "something will be done, as well to relieve the venerable Wheelock from his disagreeable dilemma, as to arrest the government of the College in a course no less destructive to the interests of the institution than to the intentions of its liberal founders and its generous patron, the State of New-Hampshire."[26]

Although he had been renominated by the Republican caucus before the Dartmouth imbroglio became a major political issue, William Plumer was well qualified to lead the forces demanding reform. As a champion of religious freedom and a well-publicized opponent of the Congregational clergy, he was ready to lead a crusade against intolerance at Dartmouth.[27] Whose name, Hill inquired rhetorically, could better grace the leading place on a ticket of "Religious Freedom, the Rights of the Baptist, Quaker, Methodist, and of all denominations—in room of a Law Religion, imposed by an intolerant sect, who boast that they 'will manage the Civil Government as they please' "?[28]

Once it entered the political arena, the Dartmouth College donnybrook created some strange bedfellows. Plumer, himself a deserter from the ranks of Federalism, looked upon Wheelock's apostasy with some skepticism. His previous acquaintance with the dismissed president had been confined to the legislature, where Wheelock had been "an importunate beggar" for state funds, and to the rumor that he had been an active critic of the late war.[29] Plumer's doubts were undoubtedly enhanced on Christmas Day 1815, when Colonel Brewster of Hanover and Dr. Cyrus Perkins, professor of the Dartmouth medical school, both Wheelock partisans, appeared unannounced at Plumer's country home and proposed that he allow Wheelock to replace him for a single year as head of the Republican party in New Hampshire and as candidate for governor. After the ex-president's vindication at the polls, they said, and the opportunity to frustrate the designs of the Octagon through the legislature, he would gladly relinquish the governorship to Plumer.[30]

It is a tribute to the Epping statesman that he shot down this weird proposal so adroitly that the two Hanoverians became his friends and supporters. Perkins established a pro-Wheelock newspaper in Hanover, to which Plumer subscribed and offered editorial advice. The Republicans, he assured Perkins, were "united in opinion that President Wheelock's removal from office was arbitrary and unjust & that means ought to be taken for his restoration."[31] Plumer found other curious allies in this cause. A visit to Exeter resulted in a long conversation with Governor Gilman, who condemned Thompson and McFarland for the part they played against Wheelock.[32] Letters came from the military hero and nephew of Wheelock, Major General Eleazer Wheelock Ripley, who sought an interview with the prospective governor.[33] Plumer would have been peculiarly blind had he not sensed the political value to the Republican party of Wheelock's martyrdom, and peculiarly naive had he not exploited it.

William Plumer, however, was interested in more than the mere restoration to office of John Wheelock. Almost alone among the New Hampshire citizens of his day, he saw the Dartmouth crisis as an opportunity to bring genuine educational reform into the government of the institution.

"If I should have any part to act in the government," he promised Amos Brewster, "I will make at least one effort to redress the wrongs he [Wheelock] has suffered, & repair the injuries that have been arbitrarily inflicted on the literary institution which he has nurtured, and over which he has so long & ably presided." So much for politics. But in his next paragraph, Plumer displayed the statesman's consideration of the problem. "Will it not be requisite that his friends in your vicinity should before June devise a system not only to restore him to his rights, but to prevent the college being again exposed to similar evils?"[34]

As a political issue, Dartmouth College was an acute embarrassment to the Federalist party. For several years its younger leaders had wanted to drop the venerable pilot, John Taylor Gilman, but his popularity had become almost an indispensable asset. The governor's personal friendship for Wheelock, however, increased the lawyers' discontent with him. Taking advantage of some tentative remarks about the blessings of retirement, they persuaded the Federalist caucus in June 1815 to abandon Gilman and to nominate Timothy Farrar for the governorship. Since Judge Farrar was one of the trustees opposed to John Wheelock, this was taking up Isaac Hill's gauntlet with a vengeance, and the moderate Federalists objected. Josiah Dunham warned Daniel Webster that he had "better undertake to drag old President Wheelock from his tomb, than Judge Farrar into the Governors Chair. There is no other man, (unless it be Mason,) who can run successfully against Plumer, but Gov. Gilman."[35] Under such pressures, Farrar withdrew his candidacy, thus compelling the Federalists to hold another nominating caucus, which Daniel Webster, absenting himself from Congress, attended.[36] After Jeremiah Mason refused to permit the use of his name, their choice fell upon the apostate Republican and Peace party man, John Goddard, who had helped gain a senatorship for them in 1812. This time, however, the singular hardware merchant declined to play the role of Judas goat.[37] According to Isaac Hill, the desperate Federalists then turned back to John Taylor Gilman, who scornfully spurned their advances, and to several other unwilling possibilities before they finally persuaded James Sheafe to accept their offer.[38]

Sheafe was a levelheaded Portsmouth merchant and a lifelong Federalist, who was free of any particular connection with the Dartmouth controversy, but who was otherwise a choice of desperation. His earlier political career had consisted of a term in the notorious Sixth Congress, where he had voted thirty-six times to put Aaron Burr into the presidency, and a subsequent election to the Senate, from which he had resigned after attending only one session. His most serious liability was his reputation as an aristocrat and a Tory who had been arrested by the patriots during the Revolution and who had refused to subscribe to government loans during the recent war with Great Britain.[39] In the afterglow of chauvinism kindled by the victory at New Orleans and the heat of the controversy at Dartmouth College, the campaign of 1816 became one of the most abusive in New Hampshire's history. William Plumer's eldest son composed a vigorous personal attack upon Sheafe and urged Federalists to desert their sinking ship and "Come Over To The Republicans In A Body."[40] The Federalist papers predictably rang all the changes on Plumer's apostasy from his early attachment to their party; this *"wheeling about,"* sneered the *Concord Gazette*, had presumably been sufficient in the eyes of his new party friends to "change the *spots* of the Leopard and the skin of the Ethiopian."[41] The *Portsmouth Oracle* turned Plumer's own propaganda guns against him by asserting that he had been arrested by Grafton County patriots during the Revolution for preaching submission to George III under the guise of Baptist exhortation.[42]

The troubles of Dartmouth College and the personalities of the gubernatorial candidates loomed so large as campaign issues in 1816 that little room could be found for other matters in the newspapers. The only national issue involved was one already settled—the war; and here the Republicans pressed their advantage hard. "THE UNION***98," announced the *Patriot*, under a very bad woodcut of a frigate in full sail, "will meet the enemy on Tuesday next, with their Blue-Light Hartford Convention Crew and Tory Commander, and give them, as we gave the British, TWO BROADSIDES FOR ONE."[43] On the question of the judiciary, which had been debated so bitterly in 1813, the Republicans simply made it clear that their victory would mean a restoration of the old courts.[44] Federalists warned that this would also mean a restoration of the old judges and payment of their claims for back salary, but they were conscious that having set the precedent for making the courts dependent upon the elections, they were in an indefensible position.[45] Stung by Hill's superb invective, they accused him first of being Plumer's servile and pliable tool, later shortened the designation to "Plumer's puny Patriot man," and finally descended to the phrase "Plumer's Pimp."[46]

The Dartmouth issue made what would probably have been a moderate Republican victory into a decisive turnabout. Plumer received a majority of 2,688 votes—nearly 53 percent of the second largest vote thus far cast in a gubernatorial election. The Federalists lost fifteen seats in the lower house of the legislature and four in the senate, surrendering control of both legislative houses to their rivals. By also maintaining their three-to-two advantage in the governor's council, the Republicans had won control of every branch of the government except the judiciary, and there was little doubt that they would move immediately to capture that bastion.[47]

The Federalists were sure that the Dartmouth issue alone had unhorsed them, and they gave full credit to Hill for inventing and to Plumer for elaborating that fortuitous weapon.[48] Election statistics, however, do not bear out this claim of Federalist defection. It is true that Plumer received more than a 2,000-vote majority over Sheafe, but the Federalist papers neglected to notice that the total vote in the state increased by nearly the same amount. While the Republicans won 2,500 more votes than in 1815, few of these were at the expense of the Federalist party, which lost only 363 from its total of the previous year. If their losses were due to Dartmouth, they were not defections but the excitement of a live issue, which brought out more than 2,000 additional voters, most of whom were Republicans. The number of Federalists who voted for Plumer and Wheelock was probably not greater than 350.[49]

The election maps tell the story clearly (see Maps 18 and 19).[50] The Republicans won from their opponents only about fifteen towns, and these were mostly the same ones they had lost in 1813. Plumer's hometown, Epping, returned to the fold, but his only major converts were Dover and Amherst. The distribution pattern also returned to normal, Plumer deriving his principal strength from the eastern counties and Sheafe inheriting the Federalist majorities of the Connecticut Valley. Only the Frontier changed, returning to its democratic allegiance now that the hardships of the war were over. In the Connecticut Valley it is true that Sheafe, although maintaining a majority, lost about 500 votes from Gilman's customary totals, while Plumer gained almost the same number over his 1815 record. This is the only indication of a major disturbance in the normal pattern wrought by the Dartmouth question, and it was obviously compensated for to some extent in other parts of the state.

It was in the leadership of the Federalist party, rather than in the rank and file, where the Dartmouth controversy created schism. Such prominent Hanoverians as Amos Brewster, Cyrus Perkins, and William Woodward became outright Republicans, while Aaron Hutchinson, the Freeman brothers, and Josiah Dunham kept their party name, but rebelled against their party leadership. The entry of pro-Wheelock candidates against the regular nominees in senatorial districts eleven and twelve prevented solid Federalist majorities there for the first time since the days of the embargo.[51] There were other defections, probably inspired by the scent of ripening political plums. George Sullivan and Arthur Livermore changed sides again, and Jotham Lawrence, who had been a fanatical member of the Exeter Junto, even betrayed the strategy of the Federalist campaign to Republican leaders. "How changeable is man!" philosophized Plumer, with his own transfer of allegiance only eight years past.[52]

Unquestionably the most urgent, but at the same time the most difficult, issue facing the triumphant Republicans in 1816 was the future of

Dartmouth College. The college trustees had convinced themselves that Plumer's party had callously used Wheelock to hoist itself into office and would now abandon the old man.[53] Sternly refuting this canard, Isaac Hill called upon the legislature to "make this Seminary what every institution of the kind should be—a nursery of Science conducted on such liberal principles that every American, be his political or religious principles what they may, would feel an interest in its welfare."[54] This was for public consumption. Privately, Hill pointed out that "the future governance of D. College . . . judiciously managed, will be a means of perpetuating the republican majority in the State."[55]

Thus, even before the meeting of the legislature in June, the dual nature of the Dartmouth problem had become apparent. Was the solution to be simply political—an overthrow of the Octagon, a restoration of Wheelock, and a return to the status quo with Dartmouth a Republican rather than a Federalist rampart—or was there to be a genuine educational reform in the institution? Incoming governor Plumer definitely aligned himself with those who advocated the latter change. There was a mild "state university" fever in the air, stimulated by the writings of Jeremy Bentham, Noah Webster, Benjamin Rush, and others, as well as the minor reforms imposed by state legislatures upon several of the old colonial colleges and the actual establishment of state-supported institutions of higher learning in Vermont, Virginia, and Georgia.[56] These examples were thoroughly discussed in the newspaper warfare over the fate of Dartmouth, and they unquestionably influenced Plumer's thinking.[57] It became his avowed intention to transform Dartmouth College into a state university.

Perhaps it might be more accurate to say that Governor Plumer already regarded Dartmouth as a state institution. In his inaugural address to the legislature on June 6 he declared that "the college was formed for the public good, not for the benefit or emolument of its trustees; and the right to amend and improve acts of incorporation of this nature, has been exercised by all governments, both monarchical and republican."[58] He reminded his auditors that the college charter had been granted by a "monarchical government" and that its provisions were more suitable to a royal colony than to an independent republic. The condition of the college, he said, was a legitimate concern of the legislature, particularly since an appeal had been made to that body for an investigation and since the state had been a liberal contributor to its support. He therefore called upon the legislature to "make such further provisions as will render this important institution more useful to mankind." Among these provisions, he specifically recommended that the number of trustees be increased, that the board cease to be self-perpetuating, and that the college president be required to make an annual report to the legislature.

While there was a degree of political exaggeration in Plumer's address, there was also a good deal of historical truth. The line between private and public corporations in colonial times was often undetectable, particularly in the patronage and control exerted by colonial assemblies over the colleges within their borders. The colleges were themselves so nearly always on the verge of bankruptcy that they not only accepted government aid but begged for it. This is a historical fact, neatly sidestepped by John Marshall and largely overlooked in subsequent discussion of the Dartmouth College case. The private donations in England, Scotland, and New England, which Marshall cited so convincingly in 1819, had been made to Moor's Indian school, not to the college created by the charter of 1769.[59] The colony and state of New Hampshire, on the other hand, had given three townships of land to Dartmouth College, had made a donation of $900 in 1805 to clear up a deficit, and had granted $3,450 in 1809 for the erection of a medical school building.[60] These may not have been "generous" manifestations of support, but they were tangible. In their frequent petitions to the legislature for further donations, the trustees invariably stressed the constitutional mandate "to cherish the interest of . . . seminaries" and declared that it was "only under the patronage and by the aids of the public" that the college could succeed.[61] On several occasions the colonial or state government had cherished the interest of Dartmouth College by legislative alterations in its government, such as in 1807 when it placed Moor's Charity School under the direction of the college trustees.[62] With these precedents in mind, Plumer was not entirely unjustified in supposing that he was asking the legislature merely to alter the charter of a state university.

General Eleazer Wheelock Ripley had promised his uncle in December that he would have a bill ready for the legislature in June, and he presented a skeleton measure to Governor Plumer as soon as he arrived in Concord.[63] After the governor had eliminated some of its eccentricities, this bill was presented to the grand Committee of Eighteen, which had been named by the legislature to consider the Dartmouth problem.[64] The Ripley-Plumer bill would have made sweeping changes in Dartmouth. The existing board of trustees would have been removed and the name of the institution changed to Dartmouth University. Two new boards, one of fifteen trustees and another of thirty to fifty overseers, were to be created, the original members of each to be named in the act itself. Vacancies on the board of overseers were to be filled by the governor and council; those on the board of trustees alternately by the state executive and by the board of overseers. The new board of trustees was to elect a new president at its first meeting, and the governor and council of the state were to make a formal and supervisory visit to the university at least once every five years.[65]

Governor Plumer admitted to his son that the future of this bill was uncertain. As he surmised, the strategy employed by the trustees against it was diversion, delay, and postponement.[66] A strong weapon in their hands was the report of the committee that the Federalist legislature of 1815 had authorized to investigate the situation at Dartmouth College. Dispassionate and purely factual, it tended to throw cold water upon Wheelock's extravagant charges. The Republicans, who might have been frightened into an effort to suppress this document, managed, however, to turn it cleverly to their own advantage. Plumer transmitted it immediately to the legislature, and it was given wide publicity.[67] The college party was permitted to move for a special committee to consider the report—a committee which was, of course, appointed by their opponents. This special committee (on the report of a committee) pointed out that the discovery of constant friction between the governing bodies at Dartmouth demonstrated convincingly the need of reform and that it was not the legislature's business to arbitrate between factions that ought not to exist but to remove the source of factionalism by excising the defects in Dartmouth's charter.[68] In spite of desperate efforts by the Federalists now to block this report, it was, of course, accepted. The Republicans had turned the tables on their enemy.

On June 18 the Committee of Eighteen reported a version of the bill to amend the charter of Dartmouth College which differed markedly in several respects from the Ripley-Plumer bill.[69] It did not propose to remove any of the incumbent college trustees, but instead moved simply to enlarge the board by the appointment of two to nine additional members at the discretion of the governor and council. A further provision, however, that none but citizens of New Hampshire would be eligible for board membership would automatically have removed the four Vermont trustees and thus given the executive an opportunity to appoint thirteen new men in a possible board of twenty-one. The board of overseers remained, and vacancies in both boards were to be filled by the governor and council. An important clause guaranteed "perfect freedom of religious opinions" to all officers and students of the university, but added the Ripleyesque provision that "any man or body of men shall have the right to endow Colleges or Professorships of any sect of the Christian Religion; And the Trustees shall be held and obliged to appoint Professors of Learning and Piety of such sect." No stipulation was made that the new board of trustees elect a new president, but they were given the significant power "to revise, correct, confirm or annul any act of the Trustees of the College."[70]

This version of the Dartmouth University bill corresponded in most respects to Governor Plumer's views on the subject, and probably resulted from the influence he had been able to exert upon the Committee of Eighteen. "My object," he wrote later, "was to establish not a nominal, but real authority in the civil government over the college; in such a manner that the rights of the legislature to superintend it so as to promote the public good should not hereafter be drawn in question."[71] Unfortunately for Plumer's object, he began to encounter subtle opposition on his own side. Although the partisans of Wheelock had been among the foremost in their original demands for material changes in the college charter, they now began to have serious second thoughts about the consequences of state control. Ripley and Allen decided that once the board of trustees had been properly reconstituted, it should remain a self-perpetuating body. At the same time, party lines were drawing closer and the Dartmouth question became definitely a partisan issue. The former Federalists whose loyalty to Wheelock was greater than their Federalism changed parties and were accepted into the Republican caucus.[72] Other pro-Wheelock Federalists, such as John Taylor Gilman, now abandoned the president and either rallied to the support of the trustees or withdrew from the struggle. As an organization, the Federalist party adopted the cause of the Octagon and submitted to its leadership.

With a strong minority in the legislature firmly behind them, the trustees began a long and adroit campaign against the Dartmouth bill by trying the seductive effects of a compromise. On June 19 they addressed to the general court a lengthy remonstrance against the proposed legislation, but averred that they had no objection to "a law connecting the Government of the State with that of the College, and creating every salutary check and restraint . . . that can be reasonably required."[73] Their conception of a reasonable check was a board of eighteen overseers consisting of New Hampshire's twelve senators, its five councillors, and the speaker of the house, with full veto power over the acts of the trustees. A willingness to concede so much in order to save the rest vitiated the later protests by the trustees against political control over educational institutions. Fortunately for them, the Republican majority rejected their compromise bait.[74] Thomas W. Thompson, acting as minority leader in the house, then submitted a petition that the trustees be given an open hearing before the Dartmouth bill passed to second reading. This was a reasonable request and was referred in the usual way to a special committee composed of one minority and two majority members. In order to force this hostile committee into action, the Federalists moved to delay further consideration of the Dartmouth bill until its report was submitted, but their maneuver was defeated, 84–97.[75]

This parliamentary battle had been proceeding simultaneously with an equally severe struggle over the judiciary and with debates upon other issues only a little less bitterly contested than these. By persistent filibustering the college party had already forced five roll calls in the house of representatives and thoroughly exhausted both themselves and the patience of their opponents. "We are all well but almost worn out by College business," wrote Thompson to his friends in Hanover.[76] Governor Plumer was finding Thompson's labors only too effective. The "leaders of both parties . . . have conducted in a very improper manner," he complained to his son; "each have offended & disquieted their friends & enflamed their opponents."[77] By a stern exercise of discipline, he and David L. Morrill, the speaker, finally closed the Republican ranks and brought the two principal measures to second reading. "Such is now the state of the battle—the Trustees failed & oscillating—their next movement doubtful," exulted Levi Woodbury, the young senate clerk, and added that the Republicans would stay in session until October, if necessary, in order to pass the Dartmouth and the judiciary bills.[78]

The trustees had by no means failed, however, for at this point Governor Plumer lost control of his party and had to surrender his own plans for the college, probably in order to save the rest of his legislative program. On second reading, seven of the ten sections of the college bill were recommitted, while the repeal of the judiciary act moved on without modification.[79] Since these motions were passed without roll call, it is impossible to analyze them accurately, but it would appear highly probable that the Wheelock faction voted with the Federalist minority in order to carry the recommitment against Plumer's followers. The committee was instructed to allow the new trustees to fill up their own vacancies on the board. This had been the chief point of contention between the faction interested only in restoring John Wheelock and the Republicans who really wanted a state university.[80]

In the hands of the Committee of Eighteen again, the Dartmouth bill underwent important changes. The board of overseers remained, but with membership limited to twenty-five, all to be appointed by the governor and council, "now and evermore."[81] The number of trustees was definitely fixed at twenty-one, but the existing members of the board were not to be removed and the limitation of membership to citizens of the state was dropped. This, of course, left the Octagon intact but supposedly rendered harmless by the nine new members to be appointed by the state executive. The most significant change, however, was a return to the old charter in the matter of filling vacancies in the board of trustees. After the governor and council had once filled the board to the required number, it was to become self-perpetuating, as it had always been. Here was evidence enough that the Wheelock party was less interested in reform than in restoration. Once the college was safely returned to their hands, they were apparently no more desirous of state control than were the old trustees.

In this respect, the Dartmouth bill was a severe defeat for Governor

Plumer at the hands of his own party, exposing him to newspaper jibes at the inconsistency between the statements in his inaugural address and his signature on the statute.[82] Sorely disappointed, he threatened to veto the bill unless it was amended in this particular, yet in the end he allowed the objectionable provision to stand.[83] His excuse was the one employed throughout American history by frustrated executives—"as it may hereafter be amended, I did not feel myself at liberty to place my veto upon it."[84]

The governor's willingness to accept an unsatisfactory bill was undoubtedly produced by the realization that he was fortunate to obtain any kind of bill at all. The amended measure finally passed the house on June 26 by the narrow margin of ten votes and the senate two days later, 8–4.[85] Inspired perhaps by the arrival in Concord of Daniel Webster, the Federalists fought shrewdly and desperately to the end, using every conceivable parliamentary device to divide and confuse their enemies, but none of these maneuvers shook the small Republican majorities. Ignoring all protests, leaving the trustees' request for a hearing buried in committee, responding with disciplined solidarity to every demand for a roll call, the Republicans carried the bill through, making it a test of party loyalty. For their part, the Federalists were equally unanimous in their defense of the Octagon. If Dartmouth College had not been a party issue before the legislature met, it certainly emerged from this session as simon-pure politics.[86]

While the Dartmouth College bill had been struggling for survival, the legislature had also been deeply involved in dealing with Governor Plumer's recommendations on the state judiciary. The Republicans had made it clear from the beginning that they would repeal the Federalist Judiciary Act of 1813 as soon as they obtained the power to do so. This made the legislative program much simpler than the uncertain business of how to modify the Dartmouth charter. Governor Plumer had recommended repeal and reforms in the protection of jury verdicts. The Republican caucus cut itself an easier pattern by ignoring the reforms and confining itself to the single issue of repeal.[87]

It required a fortnight for a joint committee to report a repeal bill, but the time had been spent not in deciding upon a course of action but in composing a lengthy apology for it. This was an able document, but it could hardly say anything new on the subject. It repeated the standard arguments: that the law of 1813 had destroyed the independence of the judiciary; that there was no reason why the judges in that year could not have been removed by either or both of the constitutional processes of impeachment and address if they deserved removal; and that the courts had been unfortunately brought into the arena of politics. The weakest part of the report was the justification of what it proposed to do after the unconstitutional system of 1813 had been destroyed—bring back the archaic structure of 1812. "And it is not doubted that the public good most imperiously demands a restoration of things as nearly as may be to the state in which they stood previously to the late unhappy changes—not only for the purpose of discouraging forever in future any similar attempts, but of restoring to the good people of this State their former confidence in their courts and constitution."[88]

Three days after a bill incorporating the recommendations of the committee had been placed on the calendar, Plumer remarked that there had been little discussion, but that Webster was in town to lobby against it.[89] Webster's sounding of public opinion in Portsmouth had led him to hope that there was Republican sentiment in favor of keeping the new courts, but Plumer thought differently.[90] "If the bill does not pass," he commented positively, "it will disgrace the Republicans."[91] Senator Mason had also appeared in Concord, not with Webster's false optimism, but with some idea of persuading Plumer to reappoint the existing judges after the old courts had been reorganized.[92] Even the Republican lobbyists were more concerned about prospective appointments than with the bill in the legislative hopper. After all, there could not be much room for maneuver in a repeal bill; it was an either-or proposition.

Since there was little to debate, the Federalists were reduced almost entirely to delaying tactics, but they pursued these relentlessly. Six roll calls on motions for amendment or postponement were demanded before the repeal bill, unharmed by the sniping, passed to third reading.[93] On the next day the weary Republicans added a house rule that the names of members who demanded roll calls should be recorded. Aided by this antifilibustering device, the judiciary bill passed the house on the following day by a strict party vote, 97–83,[94] and reached the desk of Governor Plumer on June 27, shortly before the Dartmouth College measure. Although he felt that "the bill was susceptible of amendments," Plumer believed it to be "substantially correct" and approved it, thus bringing the two great objectives of his party to a successful consummation on the same day.[95]

What remained was a somewhat messy but necessary mopping-up operation. Both houses passed resolutions addressing the executive for the removal of the seven judges who occupied the supreme and appellate court benches under the law just repealed.[96] This maintained the orthodoxy of the Republican doctrine that a judge could not be dismissed by the abolition of his court, but it raised the question of whether the party was not employing the provision for removal by address in an unconstitutional and purely partisan manner. Many discussions of this subject have maintained that there was no essential difference between the Federalist purge of 1813 and this Republican grand sweep of 1816.[97] The

Republicans, however, were at least consistent, and Governor Plumer made an ingenious argument in defense of these removals. The purpose of the impeachment and address clauses in the state constitution, he declared, was to provide for the removal of judges who had lost their ability to judge properly, either through criminal behavior or physical incapacity. Willingness to hold a judicial office under a law that he knew violated the constitution he had sworn to uphold and defend indicated indifference to the sanctity of an oath, which rendered a man unfit to be a judge.[98] If this reasoning was somewhat strained, it was at least logical, and contrasted forcefully with the weak rationalizations by which Jeremiah Smith persuaded himself to accept his appointment to the chief justiceship in 1813.

But the legislature, unfortunately, was not yet finished with the state judiciary. The preposterous claims of Claggett and Evans to a resumption of their old places on the bench and to their full salaries with interest for the three years since they had been ousted by the Federalists forced the legislature to address the governor again, this time for the removal of all surviving judges "whose offices have not been otherwise legally vacated."[99] This ultimate action could not be supported by arguments either logical or constitutional, but it had at least the merit of clearing away all the debris of claims and counterclaims. It made a clean sweep of the judiciary in the only possible manner, leaving the executive free to rebuild the courts from foundation to superstructure.

With such major problems as Dartmouth College and the judiciary engaging its attention, it would seem impossible for the legislature to have dealt with many more, yet this was far from being the case. When the unusually long session of twenty-five days had ended, the general court had added ninety-six laws to the statute books, elected David Morrill to the United States Senate, decided to build a new statehouse, and transferred the state's printing contract to Isaac Hill. It had followed the recommendations of Governor Plumer not only in the big matters but in the incorporation of sixteen religious societies, half of them sectarian, in the passage of a new militia act, and in a law for the relief of imprisoned debtors. It had reposed unusual confidence in the governor by allowing him and the council to let the contract and choose the site for the new statehouse and to take whatever measures he thought necessary to adjust the state's claims for military compensation against the federal treasury. It had refused, however, to adopt the more liberal of Plumer's recommendations, such as the one by which the Republican majority would surrender its chance to elect a solid slate of congressmen and electors. Most remarkable of all in the relations between executive and legislature, perhaps, was the calm acceptance of Plumer's vetoes, which ranged from his objections to a loosely drawn "act for the suppression of vice and immorality" to the return of a Walpole bank charter and the rejection of an act to relieve Daniel Webster from one of his financial indiscretions.[100]

When the state lawmakers finally packed their bags and rode out of Concord on the afternoon of June 29, they had every reason to feel pleased with themselves and their accomplishments. Behind them, Governor Plumer and his council were still at work, for the executive duties of this extraordinary year had only begun.

CHAPTER 19

TRIBULATIONS

It is an important question . . . whether a minority *of the trustees of a literary institution, formed for the education of your children, shall be encouraged to inculcate the doctrine of resistance to the law, and their example tolerated, in disseminating principles of insubordination and rebellion against government.* —William Plumer

When they assembled in executive session on Saturday morning, June 29, 1816, Governor Plumer and his council faced a monumental task.[1] The reestablishment of the old courts and the creation of a new university left them with the awesome responsibility of appointing seventeen judges,[2] nine university trustees,[3] and twenty-one overseers.[4] Furthermore, there were militia and other civil officers to appoint, a site for the new statehouse to be chosen, construction plans to be made, and a miscellany of minor matters to be settled. It is remarkable that all this was accomplished in less than a week.

The appointments might have taken even less time had not Governor Plumer insisted upon a nonpartisan or bipartisan bench. He proposed that the reconstituted superior court consist of chief justice Jeremiah Mason and puisne justices William Richardson and Samuel Bell. For a Republican governor to place Senator Mason, a veritable titan of Federalism, at the head of the state judiciary, required a degree of nonpartisan courage which his colleagues could neither appreciate nor support. The three Republican councillors adamantly refused even to consider the possibility of Mason's appointment.[5]

Richardson and Bell, however, were approved by the council, the former unanimously. This was unexpected good fortune, for while even the Federalists seemed to recognize Richardson's competence, he had only two years previously returned to New Hampshire from a long residence in Massachusetts, and his rapid rise to the forefront of the bar was regarded with jealousy by some of his fellow Republicans.[6] The two Federalist councillors from Cheshire and Grafton counties voted against Samuel Bell on the ground that his disastrous career in banking rendered him odious to citizens who might appear in his court. The Republican councillors supported him, however, and Plumer declared that his elevation to the bench would cause his character to "rise superior to that odium which the zeal & industry of party had excited against him."[7]

For the third place on the superior court bench, the governor now proposed the name of George B. Upham, "a federalist, a good lawyer, & a man of a fair irreproachable character," and finally obtained a majority for him in the council.[8] William H. Woodward was unanimously reappointed chief justice of the western circuit court, and, on the second try, a majority voted for Daniel M. Durell to head the eastern circuit. The remaining judicial appointments gave little trouble. Six of the seventeen were Federalists, and Plumer confidently expected his olive branch to be accepted by his former associates.

In contrast to the trouble with judicial appointments, the council displayed rare harmony in unanimously approving the thirty names that Governor Plumer submitted for membership on the Dartmouth governing boards.[9] Only two of the nominees, both to the board of overseers, were clergymen. The remarkable concurrence of the two Federalist councillors, both from the Connecticut Valley, in all these appointments is an unexplained circumstance which suggests interesting conjectures.

Among the new trustees were two men who had long been closely associated with Dartmouth—Dr. Cyrus Perkins, the distinguished head of the medical school, and William H. Woodward, nephew of John Wheelock and treasurer of the institution. The remaining appointments went to prominent politicians, such as Josiah Bartlett and Aaron Hutchinson, who, with the notable exception of the youthful Levi Woodbury, were no more and no less endowed with learning and ability than members of the Octagon. In the appointment of overseers, Plumer sought to enlist the services of nationally known figures, such as General Dearborn, Justice Story, cabinet members Benjamin Crowninshield and Levi Lincoln, the wealthy Boston merchant William Gray, Elisha Ticknor, and Jonathan Hubbard. To them were added such eminent New Hampshire men as John Langdon, George Sullivan, and Clement Storer.[10] There was natural criticism of the apparent inconsistency in loading the government of an aspiring "state" university with out-of-state personnel, but even the Federalist press admitted that the boards were "highly respectable."[11]

The men nominated to Dartmouth University's boards accepted their appointments, some with genuine enthusiasm for the new experiment.[12] During the early summer it also appeared that Plumer's bold stroke in favor of a bipartisan bench might succeed.[13] At least one opposition newspaper believed that, although some of the appointments were "exceptionable," others were gratifying and "ought to give general satisfaction."[14] Isaac Hill came loyally to the support of his chief in the unfamiliar role of a peacemaker. "Let party spirit be hereafter banished from our Courts of Justice," he pled, but could not help adding the more characteristic observation that the executive "in placing our Judiciary on *Con-*

stitutional Ground . . . were not actuated by that spirit of meanness and malignancy which induced federalism in 1813 to wrest from that Judiciary its constitutional barriers."[15]

Unfortunately for the prospect of political peace, the Federalist newspapers soon changed their tone from moderate approval to vicious attack. The governor was accused of courting cheap notoriety by offering offices to Federalists he knew would refuse them and by claiming credit for rewarding such turncoats as Woodward.[16] Richardson was berated as a foreigner who had hardly resided in the state long enough to know its laws,[17] and Bell's failure as a banker was denounced as criminal negligence. Inspired by some political pieces that Bell had published under the classical pseudonym of "Marcellus," the *Concord Gazette* broke into rhyme: "*And more true joy* Marcellus exiled *feels* / *Than Bell did, with* a Sheriff at his heels."[18] Noting that suits against Bell's defaulting bank were likely to be tried in his own court, the *Gazette* resorted again to literary analogy by quoting from *King Lear*: "Change places; handy-dandy; which is the justice, which is the thief?"[19]

It soon became evident that political passions had not yet subsided sufficiently to make Governor Plumer's dream of a bipartisan judiciary possible. Such Federalist leaders as Webster, Thompson, and Farrar insisted that his overtures be rejected.[20] Unable to resist such pressure, all six of the Federalist appointees refused their commissions, and even Jeremiah Mason, pressed by Plumer a second time to become chief justice, refused to consider the appointment, although he declared that "political considerations, which in these times are often supposed to determine almost everything, have with me on this subject no influence."[21]

To such party stalwarts as Benjamin Pierce, the councillor from Hillsborough County, it was axiomatic that the judicial vacancies should go to deserving Republicans, and no one, in his opinion, was more deserving than Clifton Claggett, who had been deprived of office by the Federalists in 1813. Claggett himself was emphatically of the same opinion and had repeatedly informed Governor Plumer that he expected to be reappointed to the superior court.[22] Samuel Quarles, the Republican councillor from Strafford County, however, voted with the two Federalist councillors against every nomination of Claggett made by Benjamin Pierce.[23] This did not prevent Clifton Claggett and his son William from holding the governor personally responsible for the father's failure to receive an appointment.[24]

Governor Plumer probably turned with relief from these cabinet dissensions to his plans for Dartmouth University, which he described in a letter to John Quincy Adams, now in London. The affairs of the college, he told his old friend, had fallen into the hands of "certain priests and their political partizans" who had long contemplated to raise the sect, the calvinist, to power, & form a legal religious establishment." Taking advantage of the public excitement in favor of the college, "the interest of which the State has too long neglected," Plumer declared that his party had amended "the charter of that institution so as to render it more useful." Again, the governor expressed his somewhat debatable conviction that a self-perpetuating governing board was more likely to become the property of a political faction than was one that was to some degree responsible to and under control of the state government.[25]

For the moment, however, Plumer could look forward to working with colleagues of his own choosing in the task of organizing Dartmouth University. On July 17 he exercised the authority conferred upon him by the statute to call the first meeting of the newly constituted boards.[26] On the same day, Charles Marsh had written to President Brown, advising him to withhold all active cooperation with the new boards until the old trustees had met to consider their future course.[27] They had found a loophole in the statute—the fact that the new trustees would require the presence of at least two of the old ones to form a quorum—and they hoped to take advantage of it. The politely noncommittal acknowledgments of their notices which the members of the Octagon returned to Plumer would alone have aroused his suspicions but rumors of their plans leaked out from other sources and caused a flurry of exhortative letter writing among members of the university party.[28] The governor could have felt no great degree of confidence when he alighted from the Concord stage in Hanover on the evening of August 20 and walked into the Dartmouth Hotel.[29] He carried in his pocket an invitation from President Brown to attend a meeting of the *college trustees* which had been called for the twenty-third.

For the next ten days, the little village of Hanover was the stage setting for a comedy which the genius of Beaumarchais could not have equaled. In response to Plumer's invitation, eminent men from Massachusetts and Vermont had come to meet with the board of overseers, while college party members and university party adherents of every description crowded the streets. It was college commencement time, and all the visitors had theoretically come to honor a few boys who had successfully completed four years of lectures, including those on moral principles and Christian ethics. The men behaved in ways which would have brought condign punishment upon the heads of the boys. Nevertheless, the social amenities were observed with elaborate care. Governor Plumer lodged with the Woodwards and banqueted with John Wheelock, just then recovering from a slight paralytic stroke. Visits were exchanged with the lieutenant governor of Vermont, "a plain unassuming man," and with General Dearborn, who had come to help democratize Dartmouth.[30]

From the enemy camp came President Brown himself, who "talked with apparent candor" and told Plumer (with something less than candor) that the old trustees had not yet decided whether to resist. Brown was soon followed by "the old metaphysical hair-splitting Judge Niles," who spent four hours in the governor's private chamber.[31] As the only Republican in the Octagon, Niles's strategy was to stress the advantages that would accrue to the party from leaving Dartmouth alone and establishing a purely Republican university in the state capital.[32] When Plumer replied that such a plan would require large funds, Niles shrewdly asked him whether the state would make a liberal donation to *any* college. The governor was forced to admit a negative opinion; his plans for Dartmouth University apparently covered only the spending of private donors' money. The Vermont Republican intimated that the June law was a political error which would restore Federalist supremacy to New Hampshire. This remark gave Plumer a chance to end the interview on a lofty note; he doubted the prediction, but, in any case, he thought it unfortunate "that any friends of literature and science should attempt to connect the subject with a political party."[33]

The next morning, after futile requests to Francis Brown to provide a meeting place and to Professor Shurtleff for the key to the library, Governor Plumer notified the university trustees that they would be convened in Treasurer Woodward's office.[34] Only eight men responded to his call. Although most of them were in Hanover, none of the old college board attended except Judge Jacob of Vermont. John Taylor Gilman had remained at home, unwilling to work either with the Octagon or with the Republicans. The absence of two of the governor's own appointees, who pled illness as their excuse, made it impossible to achieve the attendance of the eleven necessary for a quorum.[35]

On the next day, a tenth trustee appeared in response to urgent summons, but the Octagon remained aloof and the university board still lacked one of making a quorum. Someone suggested that the governor send for the Grafton County sheriff, take possession of the stage, and hold commencement, if necessary, without faculty, graduates, or spectators. Plumer refused; he was not a man of violence. Instead, he wrote another letter to President Brown, requesting his "attendance as required by statute to preside over their meeting."[36] Brown replied that he did not suppose himself bound by the new law to act as a trustee of the university against his will and that he would not decide upon his course of action until the trustees under the old law had determined theirs.[37] A complete stalemate had been reached.

Commencement Day, which was always a climactic, if not riotous, occasion in early American colleges, lived up fully to tradition on Wednesday, August 28, 1816. The "Decagon," as the Federalist papers derisively labeled the impotent university trustees, met early again in Woodward's office and asked him formally to continue acting as treasurer until an official appointment could be made. Their chairman then took up his pen again, this time addressing requests to the two Dartmouth professors, Adams and Shurtleff, to attend, recommend the candidates for degrees, and otherwise indicate their inclination to obey the law. The professors, however, like the president, had decided to cast their lot with the college party.[38] There seemed to be no further means by which the university trustees could insinuate themselves into control. President Brown added insult to injury by addressing a polite invitation to the governor to attend the *college* commencement exercises in his ex officio capacity, as New Hampshire governors had done since 1769. Plumer loftily refused to come in any capacity other than that of a trustee of Dartmouth University, accompanied by his fellow trustees.[39] With the door thus effectually closed, the governor and his friends spent the morning perforce in Woodward's office, missing the excitement of senior oratory in the chapel.

The old trustees, grim and united in the face of peril, had been in constant session since August 23, chiefly engaged in drafting a very lengthy declaration of their causes for taking up arms. On the morning of August 28 they resolved to reject the act of June 27 and expressly refused to act under its provisions. President Brown immediately transmitted a copy of this resolution to Governor Plumer and later in the afternoon sent the lengthy preamble. Plumer and his colleagues answered this act of defiance by warning the old trustees that everything they had done since June 27 was null and void.[40] The issue was thus clearly joined between the college and the university parties.

Without a quorum, Plumer and his colleagues could take no official action, but they decided, upon sound precedent, that they could recommend measures which a future, legal meeting might ratify. The final hours of their session on August 28 were devoted to this kind of wishful thinking.[41] It was resolved that the officers of Dartmouth University should be a president, secretary, treasurer, librarian, steward, and inspector of buildings. Professorships for the "general course of instruction" were to be instituted as follows:

1. Mathematics and natural philosophy
2. Logic, metaphysics, and ethics
3. Rhetoric, oratory, and the belles lettres
4. Latin and Greek literature
5. English and modern literature
6. Civil history

The first four of these professorships were to be instituted immediately and the last two as soon as funds could be obtained for the purpose. Also planned for the more prosperous future were three advanced colleges for "particular instruction of those who have made requisite progress in a general course of education." Each of these was to have a "principal officer" under the general superintendence of the university president and was to consist of the following departments:

The College of Theology: divinity and sacred eloquence; Hebrew and Oriental languages; sacred history.

The College of Medicine: anatomy and surgery; theory and practice of physic; chemistry and materia medica; natural history and botany.

The College of Law: civil law; natural and national law; science of government and political economy.

This scheme, of course, was visionary if not altogether fantastic, as the Federalist press was quick to point out.[42] Nevertheless, judged by its paper merits alone, it represented one of the most modern concepts of a university's proper function to be found in all America, and a vivid contrast to the eccentric ideas of General Ripley. If this paper university could have come into immediate corporeal existence, New Hampshire would have possessed an institution of higher learning far superior to the jumbled structure of Dartmouth College with its Moor's Charity School, its Phillips Fund, its Scotch Fund, its lotteries, and its state grants. The college supporters answered, of course, that while the Decagon built universities in the ethereal realms of the imagination, the Octagon was faced with the hard problems of physical reality, and that their task was not made easier by the interference of the state. "It was a dispensation of Providence which prevented the Trustees of Dartmouth University from making a quorum," they concluded.[43]

Providence had been equally unkind to the university board of overseers in the matter of a quorum, and General Dearborn had also had his journey for nothing. A public dinner provided by the citizens of Hanover on the evening of August 28 may have restored bruised egos to some degree, but it added nothing to inadequate numbers.[44] The trustees convened once more, the next morning, and voted to adjourn until September 17. Plumer sent a polite notice of this action to President Brown and then went home to ponder the predicament in which he had been placed.[45] He was checkmated not through the obduracy of the Octagon, which he had expected, but by the delinquency of a fellow Republican, whose reported illness Plumer suspected "was strongly tinctured with hypocondriac affections."[46] Before many days, his problems were greatly increased by the resignation of this same trustee and the death of Stephen Jacob.

After mature reflection, Governor Plumer decided that the actions taken by the rump university boards at Hanover had been illegal and he canceled their proposed meeting in September.[47] In making this decision, he was advised by the new chief justice, Judge Richardson, who also doubted the legality of a postponed meeting.[48] At this point, Governor Plumer made a serious political blunder by proposing to his council, which met on September 18, that the executive request the superior court for an opinion on the constitutionality of the Dartmouth University Act.[49] The two Federalist councillors withheld their assent, one arguing that the legislature ought to make the request, the other saying that he would never have consented to appointments under the act of June 27 if he had doubted its constitutionality.[50] Federalist newspapers seized upon these incidents as evidence that the governor doubted the validity of his own law, and Richardson and Bell excused themselves from "forming an opinion upon a question supposed to affect private rights alone, till those who may think themselves interested in the question, have an opportunity to be heard."[51] This left the future of Dartmouth University squarely in the hands of the legislators.

The September meeting of the executive council also faced the problem of the six judicial vacancies left by the noncooperative Federalists. Governor Plumer made one more effort toward bipartisanship by proposing John Harris, a respected Concord attorney of mildly Federalist persuasion, for the vacancy on the superior court. Harris had been recommended by Republicans in Hillsborough County and by both Richardson and Bell.[52] The council finally agreed upon the appointment of Harris by a vote of 3–2, and upon four moderate Republicans to fill the remaining vacancies. After some hesitation, Harris returned his commission, and Governor Plumer finally decided that he would have no more dealings with Federalists.[53] Turning from his unwilling or incompetent contemporaries, he decided to gamble on the next generation; he prevailed upon his council to offer the appointment to Levi Woodbury.[54]

This youth of twenty-six, nearly a year younger than Plumer's own son, was already marked as a rising luminary on the Republican horizon. He had been admitted to the bar only four years previously, after graduation from Dartmouth College and study of the law under the recondite guidance of Jeremiah Smith. If his preceptor had managed to impart any of his own judicial experience to his brilliant pupil, Woodbury could not have been entirely unprepared to understand the business of the superior court. He had already become an aggressive leader of the younger Republican group and a strong supporter of Plumer's administration. In June 1816, young Woodbury had become clerk of the senate; the governor had made him his military aide and had appointed him a trustee of Dartmouth University. They were both roomers in Isaac Hill's boardinghouse during sessions of the legislature in Concord, and Plumer had ample opportunity to be impressed by Woodbury's talents.

In spite of the difficulties encountered in putting it together, the new superior court proved to be an excellent judicial body. Judge Richardson served as head of the state judicial system for twenty-two years and, in the opinion of legal historians, did more than any other man save Jeremiah Smith to shape the jurisprudence of the state.[55] Neither Bell nor Woodbury remained long on the bench, but both advanced to the governorship of New Hampshire and to the United States Senate. Woodbury had frankly told Plumer that his object in life was political advancement and that he could stay only a few years in the court. True to his ambition, he went on, as is well known, to the president's cabinet, the Supreme Court, and what seemed to be an assured election to the presidency before death robbed him of the final goal.[56]

In his address to the November session of the legislature, Governor Plumer dealt with the Dartmouth fiasco bluntly. The humiliating events at Hanover in August he attributed to defects in the law of June 27, which he now called upon the legislature to remedy.[57] Describing the actions of the college trustees and quoting directly from the memorial they had sent him, he posed a rhetorical challenge: "It is an important question, and merits your serious consideration, whether a law, passed and approved by all the constituted authorities of the state, shall be carried into effect; or whether *a few individuals*, not vested with *any judicial authority*, shall be permitted to declare your statutes *dangerous and arbitrary, unconstitutional* and *void*."[58]

A bill embodying the governor's specific proposals was introduced on the second day of the session and ultimately carried by the Republican majority in both houses.[59] This measure authorized the state executive, for an extended time, to fill vacancies in the boards and fixed their respective quorums at nine rather than eleven for the trustees, and twelve rather than fifteen for the overseers.[60] In the latter part of the session a statute in amendment of the first was passed, prescribing stiff penalties to which anyone who assumed to perform official duties for the purported institution, Dartmouth College, might be subjected by suit.[61]

During this second session of the legislature the tensions that inevitably appear within a dominant majority party began to crack the Republican facade. Many Republican politicians did not willingly accept the leadership of a converted Federalist, and they seized several opportunities during the November session to embarrass William Plumer. In spite of having been elected to Congress, Clifton Claggett still believed that the governor should appoint him a judge and his son William established a newspaper in Portsmouth, the *People's Advocate*, which became more vicious than any Federalist journal in its slander of the administration.[62] Benjamin Pierce and Samuel Quarles, councillors, David Morrill, speaker of the house and senator-elect, Josiah Butler, congressman-elect from

Nottingham, and, to a lesser extent, the Bartlett brothers, John Langdon, Jr., a nephew of the former governor, and Estwicke Evans, brother of the deceased judge, were among the malcontents.[63] The stresses within the Republican party were, aside from personality conflicts, the natural results of conflicting forces—Plumer's lifelong conception of a vigorous executive authority and a growing maturity in the legislative branch of the government as the society for which it made law became more complex.[64]

In his address to the legislature, Governor Plumer reported briefly on the council's choice of location for the new statehouse, the appointment of a three-man building commission to superintend the construction, and the progress that had been made since June.[65] Two days later he transmitted to the legislature a report from the construction committee which showed that title to the land had been conveyed to the state, bonds had been executed, contracts had been let, stone cut, and the work started with the laying of heavy foundations which, from the viewpoint of the committee members, exhibited "a specimen of workmanship, not deficient in beauty, and in strength not exceeded by any work of the kind . . . in the United States."[66] Sixteen hundred and fifty tons of stone had been quarried from Rattlesnake Hill north of Concord and carried to the state prison, where convict labor hammered and dressed it for final use in the building; a thousand tons had already gone into the foundations.

Although this progress report, which legislators could verify with their own eyes, would seem to have precluded any rational possibility of changing sites, it had already engendered a local quarrel which was quickly taken up by the malcontents. Since 1788 the legislature had met in the town house, which was in the north end of Concord, and the individual lawmakers had roomed and boarded in the homes of north-end residents.[67] The site chosen for the new statehouse, however, was in the south end, and citizens in the older section of town immediately began to clamor against their prospective loss of revenue.[68] William Claggett, quick to perceive any opportunity for mischief, published an article in the *Advocate*, declaring that the chosen spot was "a low, sunken, boggy hole" where a cellar fourteen feet high would have to be built to keep out water and that the three-man construction committee that the executive had appointed included two members who were signers of the bond given by the town of Concord for compliance with the legislature's resolution.[69] Although Claggett retracted several of his charges in the next issue, he had aroused suspicions that the Federalist papers were not loath to repeat.

A legislative committee appointed by Speaker Morrill to inquire whether the resolution on the building of the statehouse had been followed "agreeably to [its] true meaning and provision"[70] questioned the governor and councillors by letter, after obtaining the aid of Pierce, Quarles, Claggett, and a disgruntled Concordian in framing the questions. Governor Plumer consulted his notes of the council meeting and replied that Quarles had obtained leave on July 2 for the following day and agreed to the council's proceeding in his absence with regular business. On July 3, the remaining five members of the executive committee had selected "the Green lot" by a vote of 3–2, Benjamin Pierce and Levi Jackson, a Federalist, constituting the minority.[71] Quarles had returned on July 4 and confirmed the previous day's action. In spite of the clear legality of this procedure, the committee decided that "the location of the lot . . . never was made agreeably to the true meaning and provisions of the resolve."[72]

In the debate on the committee's report, Claggett and Butler enlarged upon the unfortunate precipitancy and indiscretion of the executive, but other speakers pointed to the legislature's inconsistency in first delegating the choice of the site to an executive committee and then presuming to interfere in the committee's selection.[73] The rising edifice was actually in the center of Concord's main street, and the town would soon grow up around it. These sensible arguments finally prevailed with the legislature, which rejected its committee's report by a vote of 73–84.[74] A resolution to replace the construction committee appointed by the executive with a single agent responsible only to the legislature was also rejected. Instead, a report exonerating and commending the building committee was adopted and another four thousand dollars was appropriated to speed the work.[75]

Before the lawmakers assembled again in the spring of 1817, so much progress had been made with the new building that all opposition was silenced. As the building grew and the town moved southward to surround it, the people of New Hampshire became fully satisfied with its location and with the edifice itself.[76] It was finished in 1819, just at the end of Plumer's administration, at a cost which was more than modest for a structure which still houses the legislative chambers.[77] Plumer was vindicated by events, and as a dedication speaker said, "In the obloquy that was heaped upon him, he bore himself like the man he was in conscious rectitude."[78]

An even more personal attack upon Governor Plumer grew out of his efforts to relieve the state of its financial embarrassment. Governor Gilman had left his successor less than one hundred dollars in the treasury, a number of unpaid bills, and a heavy indebtedness to the banks.[79] Pending the assessment of taxes in November, the legislature authorized bank loans to meet current expenditures, but Plumer applied for such funds to every bank in Portsmouth without success. Fortunately, the adjustment of New Hampshire's claims against the federal government for the services of its detached militia during the recent war promised some relief.[80] An urgent letter to the secretary of the Treasury explaining the financial predicament of the state and asking for an advance on the unadjusted accounts produced a miracle.[81] Within a month, Governor Plumer had received forty thousand dollars on account from the United States Treasury.[82]

The advance, however, came in the form of treasury notes rather than cash, and since the banks would not accept the notes at par, the governor decided to convert them at face value into United States stock, earning 6 percent interest. On Governor Gilman's advice, the state treasurer had so funded more than seventeen thousand dollars in treasury notes which had been received during the year 1815, and the transaction had been commended by the Republican legislature in June.[83] However, Governor Plumer was guilty of serious indiscretions in the way he handled the transaction. Completely ignoring the state treasurer, Nathaniel Gilman, through whom such matters should normally have been routed, but whom Plumer mistrusted, he sent the notes by his own son, Samuel, to the Portsmouth federal loan office.[84] The federal loan commissioner, newly appointed to that office at the solicitation of the governor himself, was his oldest son, William, Jr. The whole transaction was a family affair, conducted with suspicious haste and secrecy. A brief reference to it in his November speech to the legislature gave Plumer's Republican enemies a springboard for malicious attack.

Acting under a resolution presented by Butler and Claggett, Speaker Morrill appointed a committee of four Federalists and one Republican to report upon the treasury note transaction.[85] The senate took the extraordinary step of adding to the committee another Federalist, John Vose, whom Isaac Hill promptly denounced as a speculator in state bank notes.[86] Without even questioning Plumer, the committee asked the state treasurer a few perfunctory questions and then turned over the writing of its report to Vose. While seeming to be factual and objective, the report managed to convey the idea that by proper manipulation, through the state treasurer, the notes could have been made to produce four thousand dollars more of United States stock than the amount that Plumer had placed in the treasury.[87] The legislature accepted this report on December 13 and ordered it printed, so that it received wide publicity, especially in the Federalist press.[88] "We refrain at present from saying much on the . . . development of Gov. Plumer's financial talents," remarked a contributor to the *Exeter Watchman*. "It remains to be discovered whether his Excellency has enriched himself, or the national treasury by the four thousand dollars which is thus lost to the State by his officiousness."[89] The *Concord Gazette* charged that Plumer and his son had colluded at the loan office for their personal gain. "Gov. Plumer is not an ignorant man in money matters," the *Gazette* reminded its readers. "He knows as well as any man in the State what will be the result of nine percent in 40,180 dollars."[90] If the governor had not gained by his speculation, it was asserted cynically, he was guilty of "gross negligence"; if he had, he had "*defrauded* the public." The one was a weakness, the other a wickedness, and either was sufficient to disqualify him for the governorship.[91]

Although the legislature ultimately voted to recommit the Vose report and it was subsequently forgotten, it had aroused suspicions on one side and intense indignation on the other.[92] Both Governor Plumer and his son published newspaper articles in their own defense, and Isaac Hill counterattacked with his usual vigor.[93] "Had Governor Plumer been as great an adept in speculation as the gentleman who . . . framed the report," sneered the *Patriot*, "he might possibly have been less reluctant in the unprofitable and dishonorable employment of petty brokerage."[94] The governor justified his actions by saying that he had disposed of the state's notes as he did his own[95] and as he thought best for the public interest, that the funded stock was a sound investment, paying interest quarterly, and that it would soon sell above par.[96] This prediction was verified before the end of May, when the state treasurer found it possible to sell the 6 percent stock at one and a quarter above par and to apply the proceeds upon the state debt.

In all of Governor Plumer's troubles, Isaac Hill and the *New Hampshire Patriot* had given unswerving support, even to policies that Hill did not personally approve, such as the appointment of Federalists to the bench. Hill's newspaper had long since become the most powerful in New Hampshire, and its effectiveness was increased considerably in 1816 by the employment of a new journalistic device—the direct reporting of debates in the legislature. An example of Hill's artistic talents in this medium was his satiric report of a speech made by one of the country legislators during the debate on the location of the new statehouse: "Mr. Speaker, . . . *that there* place was *nothin* but a Frog Pond! . . . When I got off *aginst* there, I was surprised—I had no *idee*—I couldn't conceive how any set of men whatever should be so tarnal blind. . . . So important a buildin should be placed on an *emanance*, on a hill, where you can see it; not in a low, sunken, *frog-pond!* . . . Now railly, Mr. Speaker, should we want to have the house split in the middle and the frogs peeping up through the crack? They might make as much noise as I do now."[97]

Stung by this rendition of his sentiments, the speaker introduced a resolution to censure Hill,[98] who, of course, claimed that freedom of the press was endangered and raised echoes of the old Federalist Sedition Act that carried as far away as Washington.[99] In a public hearing on the floor of the house, Hill's counsel had no difficulty showing that every newspaper in the state had printed more scurrilous statements than the article cited by the committee. As for the report of Prescott's speech, added the lawyer dryly, it was more favorable to him than the one he delivered. A resolution was then passed acknowledging that Hill's alleged offense was not cognizable by the legislature and that the "House deem it improper to express their disapprobation."[100] Claggett and two other disgruntled Republicans joined the Federalists in a petulant vote against this motion.

As the stormy autumn session of the legislature drew to its close, a few of Governor Plumer's friends felt a premonitory chill of defeat. The year had not been a good one for weather, crops, or business, and the Federalists, of course, could blame it all on the government. While Plumer, they said, labored to win the votes of the ignorant by bleating about economy and by niggardly administration, the affairs of the state were going from bad to worse. New Hampshire's only college had been wrecked, the judiciary entrusted to boys, the statehouse located in a bog, the state's money frittered away, the people heavily taxed—and for all this, the only return was a few dollars saved from official salaries.[101] The *People's Advocate* summarized the situation in much the same way; the legislature had ignored the governor's recommendations, declined noticing his speech, and openly censured his malfeasance. Did the people place their greatest confidence in a single man, or in their representatives elected from every part of the state?[102] The Federalists could hardly contain their elation at what seemed to be a major split in the Republican party. "It appears that the Woodenheads and those who belong to the Brickbat family in Portsmouth, all true blue Democrats, have just found out that each other were knaves," exulted the *Concord Gazette*, "and pell-mell they are at it."[103] On December 22, William Plumer, Jr., wrote to his father in great agitation that Claggett was home from Concord reporting that the Republican caucus had voted to support Levi Bartlett for governor and that his father had received only eighteen votes.[104]

Actually, the Republican caucus renominated Plumer by a vote of 85–8, with one vote for Morrill and only seven for Levi Bartlett.[105] After this overwhelming vote of confidence in Plumer's leadership opposition melted rapidly away. Morrill, Butler, and Claggett were soon removed from domestic politics by terms in Congress, and the last's small stature within the party was demonstrated by the legislature's impatient rejection of his claim for services rendered as a nonofficiating judge.[106] His son, however, persisted in a vindictive opposition to Plumer by making a prodigious effort to put Josiah Bartlett in his place. Dr. Bartlett, son of New Hampshire's first elected governor, enjoyed the advantage of a distinguished family name with an undeviating record of republicanism extending back to the signing of the Declaration of Independence. He was president of the state medical society, treasurer of Rockingham County, and a former state senator, congressman, and presidential elector.[107] In casting about for a suitable instrument of his vengeance, Clag-gett had discovered some pro-Bartlett sentiment, which he carefully nurtured through the columns of the *Advocate* until, in January 1817, he publicly announced the doctor's candidacy.[108] This step was to have been followed by endorsements in the county conventions, but the Bartlett bandwagon failed to roll. After the Strafford and Rockingham conventions enthusiastically endorsed Plumer's administration, Bartlett wrote a letter of formal withdrawal from the gubernatorial race and insisted that it be printed in the *Advocate*.[109] This blow killed the *Advocate* party.

In March 1817 the voters of New Hampshire put a decisive end to all dissent. Federalist voters, 2,358 fewer than in 1816, divided their ballots between Mason, the caucus candidate, and Sheafe, neither of whom had campaigned actively. Although Plumer's vote was 1,250 less than the previous year, the majority of 2,801 which he won over all his opponents, Republican and Federalist combined, was greater than he had obtained in 1816.[110] His share of the total vote increased to nearly 54 percent, while his majority, even over the combined Federalist vote, was far greater than anything that had appeared in election statistics since the days of John Langdon. Most interesting of all the election results, per-haps, was the evident fact that, in spite of all the furor in the newspapers, the New Hampshire voters were not very much exercised over Plumer's reported derelictions; nearly three thousand of them who had voted in 1816 stayed away from the polls in the following spring, and at least two-thirds of these absentees were obviously Federalists. The sovereign people of New Hampshire had made it very clear that Federalism was finally dead, that there was no genuine disunity in Republican ranks, and that William Plumer was the unquestioned leader of his party.[111]

Plumer's triumphant vindication at the hands of the electorate knocked the last prop from under the *Advocate*'s crazy structure, and the Ports-mouth paper suspended publication in May.[112] Perhaps the greatest trib-ute to Plumer's administration came from an ally whom he had once condemned with unlimited severity. In admiration of the way Plumer had held the legislature to its duty in regard to Dartmouth University, the Reverend Elijah Parish wrote to congratulate him upon his reelection—and added that he considered it indicative that Plumer would be governor for life.[113]

CHAPTER 20

THE DEMISE OF
FEDERALISM

*When the Federalists shall become completely disgusted and tired of the
disease with which the body politic of the State is infected, and shall
unitedly come forward with a determined and purifying spirit, we shall
take pride in recording their success.* —Concord Gazette

After Governor Plumer's vindication at the polls in 1817, the Federalist
party in New Hampshire disintegrated with even more dramatic speed
than did the national organization of which it was a part.[1] Plumer was
reelected in 1818 by more than 59 percent of the votes against a divided
Federalist ticket (Jeremiah Mason, William Hale) and a token opposition
of young Republicans in Portsmouth.[2] He bequeathed to his chosen successor, Samuel Bell, the habit of victory. In 1819 the Federalists cast only
35 percent of the total vote; in 1820 less than 3 percent; after that, there
was no semblance of an organized party effort at the polls.[3] Federalist
representation in the legislature decreased in the same way: in 1818 there
was not a single Federalist in the senate.[4]

In the November elections of 1816, Daniel Webster and his Federalist
colleagues in Congress had been defeated by a somewhat less than solid
Republican team, including Josiah Butler, Salma Hale, and Arthur Livermore. The Republican legislature of 1816–17 replaced Senator Thomas
W. Thompson with David Morrill and elected Clement Storer to complete Jeremiah Mason's term after he resigned. It could hardly be argued
that these changes increased the distinction of New Hampshire's representation at Washington, but they brought it more in harmony with the
rest of the nation. So too did the choice of presidential electors. New
Hampshire apparently preferred James Monroe to William H. Crawford
or Rufus King as President Madison's successor, and its eight Republican
electors voted for Jefferson's protégé in December with no apparent
objection to a continuation of the Virginia dynasty.[5] After 1817 no Federalist from New Hampshire ever again held a federal office.

The demise of Federalism occurred not so much because the nation
had opted for the agrarian, decentralized, laissez-faire principles of
Thomas Jefferson but because Jefferson himself and his successors had
stolen the Federalist party's platform, while the heirs of Alexander Ham-

ilton had become antinational, states' rights provincials. As the old ex-president John Adams observed to William Plumer, "Our two great parties have crossed over the valley and occupied each other's mountain."[6]

Adams's aphorism was well illustrated by the actions of the Fourteenth Congress, which had assembled in December 1815. When, in his last message to Congress, President Madison advocated a Hamiltonian program of a national bank, a protective tariff, and heavy expenditures for national defense, he was ardently supported by young Jeffersonians from the south and west, such as John C. Calhoun and Henry Clay, but opposed by Federalists from New England. New Hampshire's congressional delegation voted 6–1 against establishing the Second Bank of the United States.[7] Strangely enough, Jeremiah Mason, who registered one of the negative votes, resigned his seat in the Senate to become manager of the Portsmouth branch of the bank. Daniel Webster, who later served as the great champion of protection for New England's textile industry, declared in 1816 that he "was not prepared to say that the Government was bound to adopt a permanent protection."[8] New Hampshire's congressmen voted 3–1 against the tariff of 1816, which was carried by votes from every state in the Union except North Carolina and Louisiana.[9] The only representative from New Hampshire who had supported the national bank and the tariff was the son of Joshua Atherton of Amherst, Charles Atherton, who presented to the House a petition from six cotton mills in New Ipswich and Mason for a prohibition on the import of foreign cotton goods.[10] He seemed to see a national significance in these measures which escaped the vision of his Federalist colleagues.

The relative tranquility that marked the political scene in New Hampshire after 1816 did not extend to national affairs, in spite of the so-called Era of Good Feelings. There were strong disagreements among the Republicans in Congress over federal subsidies for internal improvements, over the encouragement of emigration to the western states and territories, over national fiscal policies, over recognition of the Latin American revolutionary governments, but, most of all, over the growth and extension of slavery. A few of these issues evoked an ideological response and some set class against class, but congressmen reacted to most of them on a regional basis. In the early months of 1817, New Hampshire's Federalist contingent in Congress voted 6–2 against Calhoun's Bonus Bill to devote revenues derived from chartering the national bank to internal improvements.[11] New Hampshire's Republican congressmen, however, were not essentially different in their suspicions of western development. They voted twice against appropriations for the Cumberland Road, 3–2 in 1818 and 3–1 in 1820.[12] In 1818 they voted

3–1 against the admission of Illinois to the Union.[13] Their Republican colleagues in Kentucky and Ohio, meanwhile, were voting solidly for these measures.

The most divisive national issue during these years, however, was one which pitted North against South—the terrible "alarm bell in the night," clanging over the institution of slavery. A bill introduced in the Fifteenth Congress to strengthen the Fugitive Slave Act met with vigorous opposition from New Hampshire's contingent in Washington. Senator Morrill flaunted his sectional feeling in the matter by boasting that in "New England we believe all men are born equally free and independent—thus commences our 'Bill of Rights'. Whatever their color, powers of mind, property, or rank in society, they are freemen—citizens, not slaves."[14] New Hampshire's congressmen voted against this bill, which passed with both Federalist and Republican votes from the slave states and Republican votes from the free states outside New England.[15] The running battle over the admission of Missouri as a slave state aroused even stronger passions on both sides. Senator Morrill and representatives Livermore, Claggett, and William Plumer, Jr., made eloquent speeches against the extension of slavery, ranging in character from closely reasoned constitutional and legal arguments to ringing denunciations of "the peculiar institution." Arthur Livermore's oratory in support of the Tallmadge Amendment bordered on provocation. "In the present slaveholding States let slavery continue, for our boasted Constitution connives at it," he flung out, "but do not, for the sake of cotton and tobacco, let it be told to future ages that, while pretending to love liberty, we have purchased an extensive country to disgrace it with the foulest reproach of nations."[16] Almost without exception, New Hampshire's senators and congressmen voted consistently against every proposal to tolerate or compromise with slavery in the trans-Mississippi area until in March 1820 they reluctantly accepted the final Missouri Compromise bill. Senator Morrill held out even against this concession.[17] No Federalist could have resisted the Virginia Republican aristocracy any more fiercely.

While Congress was demonstrating clearly enough that the term "Era of Good Feelings" was a highly inaccurate description for the administration of President Monroe, New Hampshire's eccentric governor, William Plumer, was giving further proof of it at home. Plumer would have preferred to see his old friend John Quincy Adams in the White House and was not much impressed by Monroe's performance.[18] When the president made his celebrated tour of the northern states in the summer of 1817, New Hampshire provided a rather conspicuous exception to the enthusiasm with which he was generally received.

President Monroe left Washington on the last day of May and slowly made his way northward in time to celebrate the Fourth of July in Boston.[19] In Massachusetts he was officially escorted everywhere by the local militia (which had refused to serve under federal officers during the war), squired about by Governor Brooks (whose predecessor had defied the president's orders in 1812), and greeted officially by the state legislature. The governor of New Hampshire, however, who had mobilized the detached militia in 1812 with alacrity at Madison's request, now discovered that he had no constitutional authority to order the militia into service merely for the escort of "dignified characters who might visit the state."[20] Although Portsmouth's leading citizens of both parties, including Richardson and Mason, united in declaring the governor's scruples groundless and in urging him to change his mind, they could not shake his convictions.[21] Not only did Governor Plumer refuse to order a militia escort but he himself fell seriously ill just before Monroe entered the state and was therefore unable to welcome the president officially to Portsmouth. He sent a handsome letter of apology and explanation of his constitutional limitations, which the old strict-constructionist president professed to understand and appreciate.[22] Nevertheless, it is probable that had John Quincy Adams been the state's guest, Governor Plumer would have greeted him in a very different way.

The governor's political opponents could not have been expected to overlook this opportunity for indignant criticism, and New Hampshire readers were soon treated to the strange spectacle of Federalists shedding crocodile tears over the disrespect shown a Republican president. The *Portsmouth Oracle* found Plumer's reasoning on the constitutional question "frivolous and trifling" and asked what militia officer in the state, "(the Captain General excepted) would have declined so reasonable a service."[23] The president, fumed one journalist, had been forced to depend upon "stage drivers and guide posts" to find his way to Portsmouth.[24] The Exeter Federalists poured scorn upon Plumer's intensive study of the constitution "to determine how far a compliment would be *lawful.* Other executives have . . . overwhelmed the President with *unconstitutional escorts.* Not so Mr. Plumer."[25] Even the distant *Albany Gazette* punned that the cold reception afforded by the Republicans of Greenland (where Monroe was met by a Portsmouth escort) "must have come like a *cutting northwester* across the President who had entered the state *smoking hot* from the *warm fires* and *roast beef* and *plumb pudding feasts* of the *Boston Rebels.*"[26]

In spite of such partisan sarcasm, the record shows that President Monroe did not suffer much neglect in New Hampshire. The militia turned out voluntarily in ample numbers, as Plumer had expected, and the citizens of Portsmouth could not have been far behind their Boston brethren in the warmth of their welcome.[27] The president heard and answered an address by the towering Federalist Jeremiah Mason and submitted later in other New Hampshire towns to repetitive welcoming remarks by Daniel Durell, William K. Atkinson, Amos Brewster, and Mills Olcott.[28] From Portsmouth, Monroe crossed the Piscataqua into the District of Maine, reentered New Hampshire at Dover two days later, and traveled westward through Concord to Hanover. Here public harmony reigned, and the president impartially received honorary degrees from both Dartmouth University and Dartmouth College.[29] Nowhere did he lack for military escort; nor does it appear that he could have enjoyed more than an occasional minute of privacy, except in bed. Perhaps Governor Plumer had actually done the president a favor by permitting him some travel without a thundering escort and its accompanying cloud of dust. "I wish he had stayed at home," remarked a Republican congressman who shared Plumer's point of view, "and not given his people a chance to play the fool. But Boston has outdone the rest, & that is some comfort."[30] It is certain that Plumer, and not even unlikely that Monroe, did take comfort from this spectacle of Federalists swarming back to the fleshpots.

William Plumer's apparently quixotic prejudices were recalled three years later when the former governor cast the only electoral vote in the nation against President Monroe's reelection. Unfortunately, the true significance of Plumer's uniquely independent gesture in 1820 has been obscured by the uncritical acceptance of the myth that his vote was cast in order to preserve for George Washington alone the distinction of unanimous election to the presidency.[31] Plumer's motives were far more rational and practical; he simply thought that Monroe had done a poor job as president and that John Quincy Adams could do a better one. The story of how he came to act on that conviction is an interesting one.

The moribund Federalist party in New Hampshire did not even nominate electors in 1820, and the Republican leaders anticipated no opposition to Monroe. Their decision to put former governor Plumer at the head of their electoral ticket was a purely perfunctory gesture of respect, which the retired statesman accepted with reluctance.[32] His lukewarm feeling for Monroe was no secret in New Hampshire, but Isaac Hill chose to ignore it. On October 31 the *New Hampshire Patriot* announced an electoral ticket with "the venerable William Plumer" at its head. "The universal sentiment of the people of this state," it continued complacently, "is in favor of the re-election of MONROE and TOMPKINS, and the Electors of course will represent that sentiment. . . . New Hampshire has not within her bosom a son so degenerate as to forget our national benefactors."[33]

Plumer's defiance of this "universal sentiment" apparently grew out of a Federalist plot in Massachusetts to prevent the reelection of Vice-

President Tompkins. Daniel Webster, who had moved from Portsmouth to Boston in 1816 and become a Massachusetts elector in 1820, was willing to vote for Monroe but not for Tompkins.[34] He and his fellow electors thought of voting instead for John Quincy Adams, the only New Englander in the cabinet. In order to discover whether Adams would accept such support, he asked his close friend, Jeremiah Mason, to see if he could get this information from Adams's friend William Plumer.[35] Through his son in Washington, William Plumer, Jr., the New Hampshire elector learned that Adams was completely opposed to the idea, but not until after he had been inspired to cast his own vote for Adams, and not as vice-president but as president.[36] In Concord on December 6 he repudiated Monroe and Tompkins before his fellow electors and voted for Adams and Richard Rush.[37]

The only newspapers that criticized Plumer's independence in his own state were Federalist. The *Portsmouth Oracle* declared that he would not have received a hundred votes had his opposition to Monroe been anticipated.[38] "But this vote is to be regretted," declared the *New Hampshire Sentinel*, "because it will probably be the only one throughout the United States in opposition to the re-election of the present incumbent, and thus to prevent a unanimous election will be pronounced sheer folly."[39] What the Federalist editors really regretted was the negative vote's coming from New Hampshire and thus focusing unfavorable attention from Washington upon the little state. So intense was now the Federalists' eagerness to bury the hatchet that they even protested the attachment of party labels to any of the electors.[40]

Embarrassed by this unexpected rebellion within their ranks, the great majority of Republican editors followed the example of Isaac Hill in refraining from public comment on Plumer's vote.[41] William Plumer, Jr., in Washington, however, reported that several of his congressional colleagues applauded his father's act and expressed the wish that "there had been more such votes in every part of the Union."[42] The fact is that the New Hampshire elector had unwittingly given expression to a considerable, though inarticulate, element of opposition to Monroe which was completely obscured by the cumbersome electoral system, even more undemocratic in 1820 than it is now. The situation gave rise to a demand echoing down to our own day for a constitutional amendment that would make the electoral machinery "more analagous to the general usage of our country."[43]

While the New Hampshire Republicans were winning their decisive victories at the polls from 1817 to 1820, they were fighting another battle in the courts, which terminated in a complete rout. At the beginning of 1817 it seemed that the struggle to bring Dartmouth University to life might succeed. Armed with the new powers given him by the amended charter act, Governor Plumer called a meeting of the university trustees for February 4 in Concord.[44] When he arrived, only seven other trustees were in town, and it seemed for the moment that the fiasco of the previous August might be repeated. The eight could now legally adjourn from day to day, however, and they did so until the essential ninth trustee rode into Concord on the evening of February 6 and made a quorum.[45]

The next day was crowded with delayed activity. A strong sentiment existed among the less cautious members of the board for the summary dismissal of all the Dartmouth College officers, but Plumer insisted that charges be specified and an opportunity for defense granted. The board accordingly drew up letters requiring President Brown, professors Adams and Shurtleff, and six of the college trustees to appear at a meeting on the twenty-second of the month to show cause why they should not be removed from office for flagrant neglect of their duties under the laws passed by the general assembly in June and December. Encouraged by this decisive move against his enemies, John Wheelock, through his nephew Judge Woodward, presented the university with deeds to about twelve thousand dollars worth of property and a release of his claims against the college. It seemed that finally Dartmouth University was about to become something more than a disembodied legislative apparition.[46]

It is improbable that Plumer expected to meet a penitent Octagon when he returned to Concord two weeks later. Nothing at all, in fact, was heard from the six trustees, although the professors had written a polite letter declining their invitations to appear. Brown again stated his doubts as to the validity of the laws under which the governor and his fellows were acting and declared that he placed his confidence in the judiciary, before whom a suit to try the constitutionality of the law was pending.[47] The trustees, ten strong this time, waited until the afternoon and then voted unanimously to remove Brown from his presidency and trusteeship, Adams and Shurtleff from their professorships, and McFarland, Payson, and Farrar from the board.[48] Action against the remaining members of the Octagon was postponed on various technicalities, but they were all removed for the same reasons at subsequent meetings. This action marked the final break between the university and the college parties; it was a declaration of war.[49]

The restoration of John Wheelock to the titular headship of the institution he had so long served was the next order of business.[50] His triumph proved to be short-lived; within six weeks he was dead. In the meantime, the actual duties of the presidency had been conferred by the trustees upon his son-in-law, William Allen.[51] A professor of mathematics was also appointed, and committees were named to prepare a public address upon the state of the university and to devise ways and means of raising funds for its support. The latter, at least, was to become an arduous assignment.[52]

The threat of the penalties contained in the December law produced discouragement among some college partisans and defiance from others. McFarland wrote that he was through hoping anything from man and believed that only God could save Dartmouth from "the immoderate measures" of "Gov Pl & Judge Woodward."[53] Consociations of Congregationalist ministers were devoting an hour each day to addressing God for that purpose, however, and friends of Dartmouth College from every quarter were offering advice and encouragement.[54] The temptation to abandon the struggle at this point must have been especially strong with President Brown, who had received from Hamilton College a flattering offer of their presidency. The trustees held firm, however, and promised complete support for the college officers in spite of the Penalties Act.[55] Encouraged by this spirit, Brown decided to stay, and assumed the initiative in the fight for Dartmouth College.[56]

The key man on the other side was William H. Woodward, who, as the former treasurer of Dartmouth College, held the charter, great seal, official records, and deeds to all its properties in his safekeeping. Had he sided with the trustees against Wheelock, the university party could never have obtained a foothold in Hanover. Woodward, however, one of his uncle's most faithful adherents, continued to serve as treasurer of the university and had been appointed to its board of trustees by Governor Plumer. The college trustees, of course, severed his connections with the institution, which they still assumed to control, and appointed Mills Olcott, the Hartford Convention delegate, to the vacated offices of treasurer and secretary. Shortly afterward, Olcott called upon Woodward with a formal demand for the surrender of the records and property of Dartmouth College, an institution which Woodward declared to be nonexistent and therefore could have no legal claim to the possessions of Dartmouth University under his stewardship.[57] On February 11, only four days after the university trustees had finished their first legal meeting, Woodward wrote in considerable agitation to Plumer that a writ of trover had been served upon him for the return of Dartmouth College properties to the value of fifty thousand dollars which were in his possession. Although Judge Woodward suffered the peculiar embarrassment of having the suit begun in his own court, Olcott had informed him that the trustees intended to carry it to the superior court immediately. Woodward therefore requested that the governor inform the judges of that court of the impending suit.[58]

From its beginning the celebrated case of *Trustees of Dartmouth College* versus *Woodward* was a political as much as a judicial contest. The defendant, peculiarly obnoxious to his opponents as an apostate Federalist, represented not himself, or the university of which he was treasurer, so much as he did the Republican party. The college trustees received the solid backing of the Federalists, who had voted to a man against the Dartmouth Act and had refused to participate in the government of Dartmouth University. Beaten by the combined forces of the executive and the legislature, they now looked to the judiciary as their only remaining hope. And since the state courts had also come under the control of the Republicans, they intended from the beginning to carry their case to Washington and the sympathetic ear of John Marshall. The university men hoped, on the other hand, to prevent an appeal to the national courts. They would get a favorable decision, they felt sure, in the state superior court, and there would then be an end, once and for all, to the troublesome opposition in Hanover.[59]

The suit against Woodward was entered in the February term of common pleas and transferred immediately, by agreement of counsel, to the May term of the superior court, meeting at faraway Haverhill. Here there assembled a colorful set of personalities. The judges, of course, were all Republicans, appointed by the administration allied with the defendant and occupying a bench which had been cleared of Federalist judges by the same legislature that had caused the injury to the plaintiffs. If this made the court the mere instrument of Plumer's will, the Federalists had no one but themselves to blame.[60] Had Plumer not been balked by their intransigence, the chief counsel for the plaintiffs, Jeremiah Mason, might have been instead the chief justice of the court. He served the cause more effectively, perhaps, with his forceful arguments as counsel than he could have with a minority vote as judge.[61] His conduct of the college case in the state courts was notable for its compactness, logic, and legal acumen.

The strategist of the trustees' cause was Jeremiah Smith, who had so recently occupied Richardson's place at the head of the bench. He could not have served the college better even in his old place than he did as an attorney. He virtually won the case at the very beginning by drawing the special verdict that was agreed upon in common pleas as its factual basis. This special verdict cited the college charter as the principal evidence in the case and omitted many of the facts, both as to its origin and its later historical development, which would have been favorable to the university side.[62] Both Mason and Webster leaned heavily upon Smith for the legal citations and constitutional niceties that distinguished their arguments.[63] As the third member of the plaintiff's solicitors, Daniel Webster held an equivocal position, which he never satisfactorily explained. During the earlier stages of the disputes at Hanover, he had only regretted the feud at his alma mater without taking sides. He was somewhat fond of President Wheelock, had discussed his problems with him during the 1815 session of the legislature, and had even accepted money from the old man, which may not technically have been a retainer but for which he certainly rendered no services. As soon as the college quarrel became a political issue, however, Webster took his stand with Thompson, McFarland, and Farrar; he may even have participated in the scheming to remove Wheelock from office. His opposition to Plumer's plans for Dartmouth University was implacable.[64]

Against the mighty triumvirate of Smith, Mason, and Webster, Judge Woodward, doubly handicapped by illness and a scarcity of Republican talent, employed the second-rate team of George Sullivan and Ichabod Bartlett. These men bore famous New Hampshire names, but they represented a weaker second generation. Sullivan, the attorney general and son of the revolutionary hero, had inherited his father's Irish wit and some of his ability, but little of his fire. He had lived his political career in a shadow zone between the two parties, managing nearly always to obtain office from the one currently in power. As senior counsel for Woodward's defense, he was responsible for serious errors, including the careless acceptance of Smith's special verdict. Ichabod Bartlett added much more strength to the university cause. Although this young attorney was relatively new to the state bar, Governor Plumer had recommended him to Woodward in extravagant terms.[65] Bartlett's argument of the university cause at Haverhill and Exeter was the best that it received anywhere, not excluding Washington.[66] Plumer had bound both men as closely to the interests of the university as possible by making Sullivan an overseer and Bartlett a trustee.[67]

These formidable warriors descended upon the frontier village of Haverhill in May for the first argument of the case, Mason and Smith appearing against Sullivan and Bartlett. At the request of the plaintiff's counsel, who declared themselves insufficiently prepared, the case was continued to the September term of the court at Exeter. Webster entered the case at this point and favored the court with a rehearsal of the impassioned peroration that he later used to such good effect at Washington, which admirers of his eloquence assumed to have been extemporaneous.[68] It reduced the Exeter spectators to tears, even as it later did the more exalted auditors at Washington, but it had less influence with the judges. "The College or University question has been this week elaborately and eloquently discussed," wrote young Judge Woodbury to Governor Plumer. "We have had, however, more language than *light*."[69]

At the next term, only a month later in Plymouth, the court pronounced its decision, which was, to no one's surprise, unanimously for the defendant. "It would be a queer thing if Gov. P's Court should refuse to execute his Laws," Webster had written as early as June.[70] The university men were elated by Richardson's "conclusive" opinion, which was admitted even by his opponents to be "able, ingenious and plausible."[71]

While the *Portsmouth Oracle* declared sourly that "every dominant faction" in the state government could thereafter repeal the charter of any literary or charitable institution and take over its funds, the friends of Wheelock felt that Dartmouth had finally been rescued from the grip of faction.[72] Elijah Parish wrote to Plumer in a transport of delight to congratulate him on the "late Decision. This," he declared, "seems to be the propitious moment for the friends of the University to come forward in the dignity of their power. It is only for you, my dear Sir, to say 'the University shall rise', & it will rise with new splendor. The historian will date its brilliant era from the *administration of Gov. Pr.*"[73]

The rising was not so splendid, however, and the historian must record a different story. While the university cause was winning in the courts, among friends, it was making but little headway in Hanover, where sympathy was scarce. Woodward sent Governor Plumer a constant stream of letters reciting in detail the humiliations that university adherents were forced to suffer in his neighborhood. This was all due to the remarkable, even fanatical spirit of resistance displayed by President Brown and professors Shurtleff and Adams, who declared their intention of holding Dartmouth College together until their cause had been heard by the highest court in the land. In this struggle, they claimed a great sense of peculiar responsibility, as if assigned by "Divine Providence to perform a part, which, in its consequences, may deeply affect the interests not only of this institution, but of all similar Institutions in this country."[74]

It seemed, indeed, that Providence supported them, for the majority of the Dartmouth student body followed its old faculty into exile, while Allen and his cohorts occupied the empty college buildings with less than a handful of shamefaced boys whose fathers adhered to the Wheelock faction.[75] At the end of his first year with the university, President Allen complied with a provision of the 1816 law by sending his first annual report to Governor Plumer. It was a discouraging document. The student body numbered sixteen, the board of overseers had not yet made a quorum, and the treasurer was too ill to give a particular account of the funds. Allen estimated that the university's debts amounted to three thousand dollars and its annual income to one thousand dollars. The only remedy for this situation, he believed, was a generous grant-in-aid from the state legislature. Plumer's optimistic conception of a university controlled by the state but supported by private donations had obviously failed to materialize.[76]

The problem of filling the two university boards with well-qualified men consumed much of Governor Plumer's time and patience. He was required to make forty-six appointments in all during the brief life span of the institution, seventeen to the board of trustees and twenty-nine to the board of overseers. Fortunately for his peace of mind, the Federalist councillors interposed no serious obstacle, although in May 1817 they combined with Quarles to block action upon appointments until after the state courts had declared an opinion upon the law.[77] Plumer's chief difficulties came from the appointees themselves. His high hopes for a board of overseers with national prestige and democratic zeal were never to be realized, for Story, Gray, Crowninshield, and Lincoln were either too cautious or too indifferent ever to attend a meeting of the board.

After February 1817 the trustees were usually able to make a quorum, but there was little stability in their membership. In the end, Plumer found himself forced to fill the board with young men, able enough in their own right, but hardly known beyond the borders of New Hampshire. One of his best appointments was that of Salma Hale, future historian but then a young Republican congressman from Keene, who after some hesitation, because he himself was not a college graduate, accepted his appointment and served the university cause faithfully in Washington as well as in New Hampshire.[78]

After their victory in the New Hampshire courts, the members of the university party became fatally overconfident. At first they deluded themselves with the opinion that there was no legal ground on which the trustees could carry their case to the federal courts.[79] When that expectation proved to be false, they were equally sure that "the decision will be in affirmance of the judgment of our own court, & settle the question for other States as well as this."[80] At their commencement meeting in August 1817 the university trustees assumed responsibility for Woodward's defense and assigned to Congressman Salma Hale the task of making on-the-spot arrangements in Washington.[81] Unfortunately, they tied his hands with previous arrangements and long-distance interference, but at the same time gave him little support.

There was a vivid contrast in the two groups supposedly fighting this battle. The college trustees felt a deep sense of responsibility for the institution they had nearly ruined, and they were constantly alert to raise money, supply information, invigorate their counsel, and stand solidly behind young President Brown; meanwhile, the university men, many of whom continued to be free enough with their advice, were not really willing to make sacrifices for their cause. Whether from overconfidence or from indifference, their preparations for the Washington hearings were woefully inadequate. Plumer protested their original decision to rest their cause in the hands of one attorney, John Holmes, a stump orator from Maine with a highly inflated reputation, after which Hale decided to employ the attorney general, William Wirt, to strengthen the university argument.[82]

The famous so-called Dartmouth College case was argued in March

1818 before the Supreme Court of the United States, with Daniel Webster and Francis Hopkinson appearing for the plaintiffs, John Holmes and William Wirt for the defendant. The scene enacted in the crowded judicial chambers in Washington was made vividly if somewhat spuriously familiar to generations of American schoolboys by the sentimental, second-hand reminiscences of Rufus Choate.[83] Salma Hale, a contemporary and more realistic witness, admitted that "Mr. Webster was as usuall able— very able—but also very disingenuous."[84] "He appeared himself to be much affected," Hale wrote a bit later, "and the audience was silent as death. He observed that in defending the college he was doing his duty— that it should never accuse him of ingratitude—nor address him in the words of the Roman dictator." Hale confided, furthermore, that Holmes was "below our moderate expectations." He believed, however, whether the enthralled Supreme Court justices did or not, that Webster's argument was "unfair." It appeared to him that "Mr. Wirt grasped the cause with the mind of a giant, and made Webster lower his crest and sit uneasy." According to Hale's account, Wirt even turned Webster's oratorical guns against him by dwelling upon John Wheelock's long and sacrificial years of service to Dartmouth, "his cruel persecution, dismissal & death of a broken heart." Wheelock's talents, Wirt had said, were evident in the eloquence just displayed by his pupil—the pupil to whom his ghost must now turn and exclaim, "Et tu, Brute?"[85] In the light of Webster's questionable professional relations with Wheelock in the summer of 1815, this must have been rather a telling blow.

Contrary to the hopes of both parties, the Supreme Court adjourned without announcing a decision in the college case. It was generally known that, in spite of Webster's tears, the judges were divided in their opinions, and Plumer had no doubts of their ultimate position—"they will decide in favour of the University," he predicted.[86] President Allen was not in a position to accept a year's delay quite so philosophically. "It is to us a great disappointment," he wrote to Plumer. "I believe you are aware of the difficulties under which we labor, and which will render it important that we receive pecuniary aid from the next legislature in order that we may continue the institution."[87]

William Plumer, Jr., now the representative from Epping in the state legislature, worked diligently in committee and on the floor for the university cause and succeeded in obtaining, not an appropriation, but a loan of four thousand dollars.[88] This money kept the university alive for a few more months, but hardly "routed" the Octagon party, as one enthusiastic Republican asserted. Criticism of the lackadaisical way in which the university cause had been argued in Washington became intense. General Ripley, who did not allow a transfer to distant New Orleans to curb his propensity for offering belated advice, declared, "I

never knew anything so lamely managed as this thing has been."[89] The
university party now did what it should have done a year earlier: William Pinkney of Baltimore, then perhaps the most eminent attorney in
America, was employed to open the case for reargument; Allen dug up a
mass of data from the Wheelock papers which seemed to place the relations of the college and the state in a light which had not been presented
to the court in March; and Cyrus Perkins went to Washington to help
Pinkney prepare himself as neither Holmes nor Wirt had done.[90]

It was too late. The "very imperfect" special verdict, as Pinkney properly complained, could not be repudiated, and none of Allen's "new
evidence" had any bearing on the case as long as the college charter was
accepted at face value.[91] Furthermore, Marshall had been confidently
preparing an opinion based entirely upon the concept of the college
charter as a contract, which he had no trouble persuading all but two of
his colleagues to accept. On February 2, 1819, at the beginning of the
new court term, Marshall entered his courtroom and, ignoring Pinkney,
who rose to move a reargument, announced that the court had come to
an agreement in the case of *Trustees* versus *Woodward*.[92] He then proceeded to read his famous decision, which ended the brief career of
Dartmouth University and blighted all the designs of its founders.[93]

Governor Plumer was especially disappointed at the support given to
Marshall by his friend Judge Story, who had expressed strong approval
of Plumer's policies in general. "It was known to judge Story," Plumer
reported to Hale, "that Pinkney was engaged to argue it again, & he said
'[that] was the only wise thing the University had done.'" The judges,
Plumer complained, "have evinced a strong disposition to extend their
jurisdiction beyond what I think either the constitution or law contemplated."[94] Hale assured Plumer that the Dartmouth decision excited great
astonishment in Washington and was considered as the greatest stride yet
taken over the states.[95] "This power must be restrained," Plumer agreed,
"or the States will in process of time be reduced to corporations and be
restricted to making by-laws and the legality of them subject to the
decisions of that tribunal."[96]

In spite of John Marshall's shattering blow, the university struggled on
for a few months, sustained by a faint ray of hope which, curiously
enough, had been kindled by its enemies. In addition to their trover
against Woodward, the college trustees had engineered three suits by
residents of Vermont against New Hampshire tenants of college property.[97] After the decision in *Trustees* versus *Woodward* was announced,
these cases were remanded, with consent of counsel, to the circuit court
at Portsmouth for consideration of the alleged "new facts" that might be
introduced into a new special verdict.[98] This gave the university men
some encouragement, for the arguments would be made before Justice

Story, who had been a Jeffersonian Republican and who was thought by some of them to favor their side of the case. Sustained by this naive faith, they determined to fight the cases in the circuit court as vigorously as they should have conducted their defense at Washington. Governor Plumer was still confident that "the fact of the State's being the principal donor [could] be proved so as to remove the doubts of even an unwilling judge."[99] Judge Story, however, as Webster had known beforehand, proved to be even more than unwilling.[100] At a special hearing in Boston on May 27, 1819, he dismissed the "new evidence" and gave the university its final coup de grace. Meanwhile, Governor Plumer had received an agitated letter from President Allen announcing that he had been deprived by force of most of the university buildings and had found it necessary to suspend instruction, although he still retained the key to a library which he could no longer use.[101] A month later, Amos Brewster wrote to announce "the funeral of the University."[102]

Whether John Marshall was right about the constitutionality of the acts of 1816 is a question that generations of brilliant legal historians have debated without arriving at a conclusive answer. It is certainly doubtful whether he or any of his contemporaries foresaw the momentous consequences that the decision was to have in shaping American legal practice and the development of the social fabric. As far as the limited question of educational institutions was concerned, the winners of the Dartmouth College case believed that they had saved American private education from "legislative despotism and party violence," while the losers felt that Marshall had wrongly deprived them of a chance to "render the institution useful, respectable, & honorable to the State & to our country."[103] Both were partly right. It was many years after Marshall's decision before Dartmouth College recovered the prestige that it had lost in New Hampshire or gave any indication of becoming the flourishing institution that it is today.[104] On the other hand, such a blow had fallen upon the principle of public support for higher education in New Hampshire that it was decades before it achieved any popularity again.[105]

CHAPTER 21

REFORM AND FREEDOM

The welfare of society requires that the prosperity of the many *should be preferred to the conflicting interest of the* few.—William Plumer

The last half of the second decade of the nineteenth century was a period of remarkable social advance in New Hampshire.[1] It saw the culmination of some reform movements initiated by the Revolution, a steady but more deliberate development of others, and the first stirrings of still more which were to blossom at a later era. William Plumer, governor of the state from June 6, 1816, to June 5, 1819, had a hand in most of these changes. This remarkable man, strong willed and self-educated, sometimes inscrutable to his contemporaries, often inconsistent but always supremely confident, was the epitome of his age.

With political opposition fading rapidly during the later years of his administration, Plumer might have rivaled John Taylor Gilman for length of gubernatorial tenure had not illness induced him to decline renomination in 1818.[2] In spite of Samuel Bell's connection with the Hillsborough Bank failure, Plumer believed that he was the best Republican available for the governorship and persuaded him to accept the caucus nomination that William Plumer, Jr., had worked hard to obtain for him.[3] Bell was easily elected in March 1819 and was reelected for four successive terms, serving without much criticism during a period of political calm. In 1823 he went to the United States Senate and ultimately became a Whig.[4] Both Plumer and Bell were advocates of moderate reform.

Nature had not been kind to New Hampshire in 1816, which became fixed in folklore as "The Year without a Summer." The spring had been cold and rainy; heavy frosts persisted into June and began again in September; crops failed and livestock perished.[5] Federalists regarded these disasters, together with their loss of political power, the attack on Dartmouth College, and the removal of the judges, as signals that Providence itself had turned against them and that further struggle was useless. Conservatism became unpopular. Revolutions in Latin America, westward migration, financial panic, and the deadly quarrel over slavery across the Mississippi all contributed to a restlessness and a questioning of old institutions which created a climate of reform, even in staid New England.

Governor Plumer, always something of an enigma to his friends as well as to his enemies, launched a small program of austerity in 1816 by persuading the legislature to reduce his own salary as well as those of the judges and the state treasurer.[6] Trifling as its practical effect on the public purse might be, this revival of a virtually extinct tenet of pure republicanism aroused intense excitement.[7] Thomas Jefferson, who had been one of the earliest American politicians to exploit the popularity of public economy, gave Plumer a warm word of approval. "I remark the phaenomenon of a chief magistrate recommending the reduction of his own compensation," he wrote. "This is a solecism of which the wisdom of our late Congress cannot be accused."[8] Nor could the New Hampshire legislators be so accused, for they took care not to slash their own stipends. Federalist newspapers regarded this whole business as sheer demagoguery. They scoffed at the "half-price Governor" and ridiculed the idea that the paltry savings in salary payments would make a noticeable difference in the tax schedules.[9] "A more Jesuitical, time-serving, popularity-hunting Speech never was delivered from the Executive Chair," declared the usually mild *New Hampshire Sentinel*.[10] Plumer's own record on this issue was inconsistent; as a Federalist member of the legislature in the 1790s, he had strongly advocated higher salaries for the governor and judges. In order to maintain an adequate superior court he was forced, in 1817 and 1818, to ask for a restoration of the judges' salaries.[11]

Although Plumer was not unaware of the political appeal of a program of governmental economy, his belief in its soundness was genuine. The failure of the state prison, which had been finished at a cost of thirty-seven thousand dollars in 1813, during his first term as governor, to become a self-supporting institution greatly disturbed him.[12] By the end of 1816 the debt on the prison had nearly doubled and a legislative committee admitted ruefully that no way to reduce it could be found.[13]

The New Hampshire prison was administered by a warden and a board of three directors, all appointed by the governor. The directors were supposed to supervise the warden and his accounts, and the prison was subject to annual inspections by the governor, council, and judges of the superior court.[14] In performing this duty, Governor Plumer always found the prison clean and apparently in good order, but he was disturbed by the fact that the directors kept no record of their proceedings and were seldom all present for the annual inspections. After his spring visit in 1817 he wrote in his journal, "I am convinced that the accounts are not perfectly correct, & think it probable the State is defrauded of some of its property."[15]

Noting that the prison had cost more than sixty-one thousand dollars since its founding, he called upon the state legislature to find a solution for the problem. A joint committee was appointed to investigate thoroughly the affairs of the institution, with an eye to possible economies. It was even empowered to receive offers from private individuals to operate the prison on a contract basis.[16] The committee presented an elaborate report on June 19, 1818, basing all of its conclusions on the assumption that New Hampshire could not farm out its responsibilities. Plumer's suspicions were corroborated by the committee's declaration that it had been forced to abandon any effort to disentangle the hopelessly muddled accounts of the institution. There was no accusation of fraud, but much criticism of carelessness and a strong implication that the effort to make the prison pay for itself interfered with its original purpose as a penitentiary institution for the reform of the criminal. Suggestions were made for improving prison discipline, bookkeeping techniques, and institutional administration, but although it declared "a material change in the present system to be expedient," the committee confessed its inability to prescribe anything more than temporary remedies.[17] Equally baffled, the legislature listened to this elaborate report and accepted it for the record, then did nothing.

Meanwhile, Governor Plumer and his council found a simpler solution for the problem by the appointment of a new warden. Trueworthy Dearborn, the incompetent warden originally appointed by Governor Gilman in 1813, was allowed to resign, and Moses C. Pillsbury was appointed to the vacant position.[18] With the governor's backing and the aid of subsequent legislation, Pillsbury not only turned the prison deficit into a surplus but made the prison itself a model of its kind in "management and progress" in the United States.[19] When former governor Plumer was asked in 1820 by a New York committee appointed to report on the general results of the penitentiary system in the United States to supply information from his own state, he could well respond, "From my own knowledge of the effects of the penitentiary system in New Hampshire, & from information received from other states, I am fully convinced, that it has more effectually suppressed crimes than any other mode of punishment previously established."[20]

Governor Plumer devoted his entire message to the legislature in June 1818 to a proposed remodeling of judicial practices.[21] His approach was remarkably liberal, if not actually socialist; he believed that the existing laws permitted and indeed encouraged the exploitation of what young Karl Marx was soon to call "the masses" by pettifogging lawyers, conniving judges, relentless creditors, corrupt officials, and an indifferent society. "If your republican governments, the glory and security of man, are to be preserved in its purity," he wrote in ungrammatical earnestness, "legislators must enact and cause to be rigidly enforced laws to reform abuses and protect the laboring class of people against the encroachments of the privileged orders of unproductive laborers."[22]

Plumer's recent perusal of Jeremy Bentham's works and the writings of Robert Owen undoubtedly influenced his thinking.[23] "The welfare of society," declared the governor, "requires that the prosperity of the *many* should be preferred to the conflicting interest of the *few*. And we are under high obligations to our constituents, not only to take care that the laws be duly executed but to improve and perfect our civil institutions, so as to render them conformable to natural justice and to the actual state of society."[24] Natural justice, Plumer believed, was being thwarted by the vast amount of trivial litigation in the state, which fell with peculiar weight upon the poorest people, bringing ruin to the individual and economic burdens to society. The laws encouraged litigation, numerous appeals, vexatious delay, and excessive fees, leading to outrageous costs, even where justice was finally obtained. Petty criminal prosecutions were encouraged by the laws that granted a moiety of the fines recovered upon conviction to informers or individuals who instituted suits, and thus gave legal sanction to collusion, fraud, envy, malice, and greed. A tax equal to the amount annually taken from the pockets of hapless litigants by these archaic practices would, declared Plumer, if levied by the legislature, produce a political revolution.

The governor, accordingly, recommended a number of specific changes in the laws governing the jurisdiction of the courts, the recovery of damages, the assessment of costs, the collection of fees, and the assignment of forfeitures—all designed to discourage unnecessary suits, capricious appeals, and mounting bills of costs. Much to the sardonic amusement of Jeremiah Smith, no doubt, he also advocated an annual law term for the superior court, a feature of the despised judiciary act of 1813 which Levi Woodbury had advised him to revive.[25] In proposing these reforms, Plumer anticipated the opposition of "the host of third & fourth rate lawyers" who, in his opinion, constituted too large a proportion of the membership of the legislature.[26] They did not disappoint him. According to the testimony of his son, who led the fight for enactment of the reform measures in the lower house, it was a bitter battle, and it should not be surprising that many of the governor's proposals were ignored.[27] The legislature did agree to measures designed to diminish the number of appeals and raised the salaries of the superior court judges.[28]

Plumer devoted a large part of his message in 1818 to an eloquent plea for the abolition of imprisonment for debt in New Hampshire. Reviewing the history of debt legislation, he pointed out that in colonial times New Hampshire's laws for delinquent debtors were as harsh as those of England, permitting imprisonment until the debt was fully paid or death came to the relief of the debtor. The creditor was compensated from the public treasury if the prisoner escaped. On the eve of the Revolution the first great step in softening this grim picture was taken when "a prison yard was established, in which the debtor, by giving bond, was permitted to breathe the common air without the limits of the prison house" and "indigent debtors were authorized, in any case, to make oath that they were unable to pay their debts. Even then, an unfeeling creditor had authority to retain his debtor during life, by paying a small sum for his weekly support."[29]

In the following years New Hampshire had done much to ameliorate the lot of the poor debtor.[30] These changes represented progress, but as Plumer insisted, "the cause of humanity and of natural justice [required] further legislative aid." It was still possible for a man to be arrested for a trifling debt and to rot in jail until judgment was obtained against him in court and for thirty days thereafter before he could even apply for permission to take the poor debtor's oath. An interval of many weeks' imprisonment was thus possible when the courts were behind in their dockets, as they usually were. It was also possible for a man of some property to be stripped of most of it and then to be imprisoned for life by a vindictive creditor, who arranged matters so that his victim could neither qualify for the poor debtor's oath, obtain sureties on his bond in order to gain the freedom of the prison yard, nor pay the remainder of his debt. Perhaps the most vicious part of the system was that the great majority of debts for which persons were imprisoned, usually on writs issued from a justice of the peace, were for sums less than ten dollars.

Plumer moved with the rising tide of public opinion, which regarded this entire system of enforcing financial contracts as archaic. "The time appears to be approaching," he informed the legislature, "when imprisonment for debt will no longer exist in any case, but creditors will consider the industry, fidelity and property of their debtors, and not the power of depriving them of liberty, as their only real and sufficient security." The governor admitted, however, that society was not yet prepared for so clean a sweep. He asked therefore only for minor changes in the laws to require creditors who insisted upon the incarceration of their debtors to bear the entire burden of their support in prison, to simplify and speed up the process of taking the poor debtor's oath, and to exempt the body of the debtor entirely from arrest on any process issued by a justice of the peace. "Let frauds in concealing property subject the offender to punishment," Plumer said in summarizing his case, "but preserve, as far as may be, the personal freedom of the citizen; for every unnecessary restraint on his natural liberty is a degree of tyranny, which no wise Legislature will inflict."[31]

As was the case everywhere, Plumer's reform proposals were bitterly resisted by "the lawyers and rum dealers," who profited most from the follies and vices of the poor.[32] The only act passed "for the Relief of Poor Debtors" by a reluctant legislature exempted those whose debt was less than $13.33 from imprisonment "on any judgment on contract."[33] Plumer was not at all pleased with the act, particularly since it did not specifically prohibit arrest and detention prior to court judgment in these petty cases, but "because it was a point gained in favor of the liberty of the person" and because defects might "be remedied by a future legislature," he signed the bill.[34] As a matter of fact, the succeeding legislature amended the act in a way that met Plumer's objections.[35]

This legislation placed New Hampshire well near the forefront of the movement for the abolition of debt imprisonment. The law of 1818 probably eliminated half of these cases and left the institution of the debtor's gaol in New Hampshire little more than a shadow of its former self.[36] So salutary was this reform in depopulating the county jails and thus inhibiting the education of professional criminals that the inmates in the state prison numbered only half as many as in Vermont and a third as many as in Connecticut during the decade of the 1830s.[37] The legislature did not formally abolish imprisonment for debt until 1840, after at least five other states had already done so, but New Hampshire had long been recognized as one of the most enlightened jurisdictions in the world in this respect.[38]

The reformers of this period derived much of their inspiration from the English rationalists and utilitarians William Cobbett, Henry Hunt, Robert Owen, and Jeremy Bentham, especially the last. As the language of his messages to the legislature clearly reveals, Governor Plumer was strongly influenced by Bentham's writings on judicial, penal, and social reform. He was the only chief executive in the world who took seriously Bentham's offer to draw up "a code of statutory laws . . . to supercede the *unwritten law*" for any state wishing to avail itself of such a gratuitous service.[39] Writing immediately to the Englishman, he joined in deploring the "numerous errors and gross absurdities" of the common law and predicted that the project would encounter "a host of prejudices" from "a body of lawyers, many of whom here, as in all other countries, dread reform, fearing it would diminish their individual profits."[40]

That is exactly what happened when Governor Plumer laid Bentham's proposal before the legislature in 1818, earnestly recommending it as "worthy of . . . mature consideration."[41] New Hampshire's lawmakers had read excerpts from Plumer's letter, which Bentham had published in England and which had been subsequently copied by American newspapers. Professional patriots and "practical" scoffers had a field day with this trans-Atlantic brand of utopianism. "New Hampshire Millenium" headlined the *Salem* [Massachusetts] *Gazette*, which ridiculed Plumer for wishing to make his state "a Pattern Form for experiments in Legislation."[42] Even so broadminded a man as Jeremiah Mason wrote that Bentham's utopian plans might "suit metaphysicians, but would make sad work with everybody else."[43] In spite of heroic efforts by William Plumer, Jr., to get a fair hearing for it in the house of representatives, consideration of the Bentham proposal was postponed until 1819 and never taken up again.[44] The younger Plumer and the "extraordinary" Englishman, however, continued a correspondence for some time, and Bentham's influence eventually made a permanent impress upon New Hampshire through the lifelong concern of William, Jr., with prison reform and the care of the insane.[45]

The long struggle for complete religious toleration in New Hampshire drew near its close during these years of reform. The final steps were marked not so much by any convulsive death grapple as by a series of almost comic paradoxes. Governor Plumer, a deist presiding over a population of Calvinists and "enthusiasts," experienced these contradictions firsthand. He had trouble composing Thanksgiving proclamations in language that expressed both his own rationalism and his constituents' piety.[46] The Republican legislature encountered an equally baffling problem. In 1817 they rewarded their political allies by inviting a Baptist minister, for probably the first time in New Hampshire, to preach the election sermon. The unfortunate result was a tactless denunciation of "the whole posse of Christians from the Pope of Rome to the Shaking Quakers" (Baptists, of course, excepted), with the choicest insults reserved for the Congregational clergy, many of whom were present.[47] Feelings in the legislature were so lacerated by this performance that the two houses quarreled disgracefully both in 1817 and 1818 over selection of a chaplain, resorting at one time to alternating prayers by the three preacher-members.[48] "Our chaplains cost more than they are worth," wrote Plumer disgustedly, but in view of the fact that the three member-chaplains graciously declined payment for their services, that statement seems to have been unduly cynical.[49]

Most paradoxical of all the sects that challenged Calvinist fundamentalism were perhaps the Shakers, living in their communal villages at Canterbury and Enfield. Governor Plumer, who visited Enfield in 1816, remarked upon the neatness, cleanliness, and hospitality of the Shaker community, but noted also that "this sect has more despotism than there is in the army & navy. Its foundation is superstition; & the civil authority has not the means of correcting the evil."[50]

The Shakers paid their taxes cheerfully, supported their own poor, and stayed out of politics, but their conscientious objection to military service brought them into conflict with the civil authority. The militia laws of both state and nation had generally recognized the right of religious pacifists to exemption from military duty, but an attempt was made to amend the bill for reorganizing the militia in 1816 by requiring that every able-bodied Shaker and Quaker pay an annual two-dollar tax in lieu of his service. This provision passed by a substantial majority, but by a much closer vote the entire bill was postponed until the 1817 session.[51]

With this threat hanging over them, the Shakers appealed to the known liberalism of their governor for assistance. "Men in thy station," wrote one of them to Plumer, "have it in their power . . . to be of eminent use in the world; and to gain to themselves a name and a praise, that will not only be as lasting as time but as eternity."[52] A deputation of Shaker elders visited Plumer to remonstrate against the tax, claiming that they could no more conscientiously support war with their money than with their bodies. The governor assured them that he opposed the principle of the equivalent tax and advised that they memorialize the legislature against the measure. The proposal was dropped during the 1817 session, but the next year, when feeling against the Shakers was especially inflamed, a committee was appointed to "inquire into the expediency" of taxing them in lieu of military service.[53] The Shaker communities petitioned against the proposed measure, and it was finally abandoned.

An element of that despotism to which Plumer referred in the Shakers' community life was their method of recruiting. Since their religion prohibited normal sexual relations, no one was ever born a Shaker. The sect would have died out long before it actually did had not a vigorous campaign of proselyting brought fresh blood, usually in the form of family groups, into the Shaker villages. If either partner of a Shaker marriage tired of the abnormal situation, as was bound frequently to be the case, the dissatisfied mate was inevitably expelled from the community while spouse and children remained behind. This problem was brought forcibly to the attention of the New Hampshire legislature in 1817 by one Mary Dyer, a woman "not wanting in talents, whatever might have been the sincerity of her motives," whose case became a cause célèbre in New England's annals.[54] With her husband, Joseph, and children, she had joined the Shaker community at Enfield; then, falling out with the elders, she had left community, husband, and children behind. Applying to the legislature for custody of her children, she appeared in person to support her cause with such ready wit and sharp rejoinder that she soon excited great public sympathy.[55] After hearing Mrs. Dyer and her "sensible" but less-spirited husband testify the legislature passed an ambiguous bill, giving the superior court power to grant a divorce, settle alimony, and determine custody of children in cases in which one partner of a marriage joined a Shaker community and remained with it for six months.[56] On the evening before the last day of the session this measure was presented to Governor Plumer for his signature.

Plumer was thus presented with an embarrassing dilemma. He detested Shaker "despotism" as much as any man, and he could hardly help feeling a natural sympathy for Mrs. Dyer and others in her position. On the other hand, he believed that the legislature had acted too hastily in allowing dissolution of the marriage bonds for a religious reason when it was permitted for very few others.[57] Harried by the rush of last-minute business, Plumer allowed the bill to die by a pocket veto.[58] This did not stop Mary Dyer. She was back again in 1818, more determined and more persuasive than ever, as William Plumer, Jr., now a legislator exposed to her eloquence, could testify. "Her statements about Shaker practises were sufficiently piquant; and some of her repartees and retorts were such as could hardly have been surpassed in keenness and efficiency," he later wrote. As a member of the committee to whom her petition was assigned, he visited the Shakers at Canterbury, but returned "without making any very alarming disclosures."[59] His father, meanwhile, had prepared himself for a possible divorce bill by studying similar legislation in other states and had concluded to use his veto if necessary.[60] This time the legislature agreed with him that this singling out of the Shakers for invidious attention would do more harm than good. "The sect," wrote Plumer, "would consider all laws having a particular reference to them as a species of persecution [which] seldom fails to build up the sect agt. which it is directed. . . . Nothing is more fatal to enthusiasm than toleration and neglect; it damps its ardor and cools its frantic spirit."[61]

It was not, however, because of any possible dampening effect but from a genuine instinct for liberty of conscience that the Republican officials from 1816 on pursued a steady campaign toward disestablishment in New Hampshire.[62] In his first message to the legislature in June of that year, Governor Plumer insisted that it was the duty of the legislature to grant acts of incorporation to any religious association which requested them. "The correctness of their tenets, is a subject that lies between God and their own consciences, and is one that no human tribunal has any right to decide. While therefore it becomes every man scrupulously to examine the foundations of his own belief, he cannot guard with too much jealousy against the encroachments of the civil power on his religious liberties."[63] The legislature not only accepted Plumer's reasoning on religious incorporations but took a significant step toward the ultimate secularization of New Hampshire with the passage of a bill to tax the property of ministers of "every denomination" in the same manner as other people were taxed. The loss of tax exemption by the settled clergy was attributed to "democratic malignity and abuse," but one of the Republicans in the legislature, a Baptist minister from Durham, argued that the clergy were much better able to pay taxes than war veterans and widows, many of whom had seen their only cows "sold at the post to pay ministerial taxes."[64] Passed in the house by a majority of 82–73 and signed without comment by Governor Plumer, this measure was condemned in Boston and applauded as far away as Rochester, New York.[65]

With their solid majority in both houses of the legislature in 1816, the

Republicans were also able to elect, for the first time in the state's history, a Republican senator from district twelve in Grafton County, where no candidate had a majority. The man they chose was the minority candidate, Dan Young, a Methodist preacher from Gunthwaite who, according to his own story, had entered politics solely for the purpose of ending the religious establishment in New Hampshire.[66] At his first session he brought in a bill to repeal the establishment law of 1791 and to replace it by the provision that "all persons voluntarily associating to build a house of worship, or hire a minister of the Gospel, should be held to the fulfilment of their contract, but no person should be compelled to go into such a contract."[67] This bill received only four votes in the senate. Young reintroduced it annually thereafter; in 1817 it received half the votes in the senate; in 1818 it passed the senate but was defeated by a tie vote in the house. By 1819 the combination of ecclesiastical solons, liberal lawyers, and Republican Congregationalists in the legislature was strong enough to prevail.

Also by this time, New Hampshire and Massachusetts were the only remaining states in the Union with religious establishments. Vermont had separated church and state as early as 1807. Even Maine, contemplating separation from Massachusetts, had formed a provisional constitution in which no guarantee of state support for any church was mentioned.[68] Most encouraging of all, a seeming miracle had occurred in Connecticut, the land of "steady habits" and unwavering Federalism. In 1818 a split had occurred in the dominant Federalist party, and a "reform" group composed of dissident Federalists and Republicans had carried the state, written a new constitution, and ended the legal support of religion.[69] New Hampshire liberals determined not to be the last state to opt for religious freedom.

In 1819 the New Hampshire senate passed Dan Young's so-called toleration bill for the second time and sent it down to the house, where Dr. Thomas Whipple, a Republican representative from the frontier town of Wentworth, became its champion. This famous measure did *not* propose to separate church and state in New Hampshire, as has so often been stated. The conviction that "morality and piety . . . will give the best and greatest security to government . . . by the institution of the public worship of the Deity" was so firmly rooted in the New England mind and in Article 6 of New Hampshire's Bill of Rights that a complete withdrawal of civil support from religion was unthinkable. What the toleration bill actually proposed to do was to amend the establishment act of 1791 by giving any sect or denomination of Christians the right to tax the polls and property of their members and to have the same powers of collecting such assessments as town officers had, provided that no person could be forced to join any society or to remain a member if he gave legal notice of withdrawal.[70] It also provided that all contracts already in effect would be honored until the dates of their expirations, which in some cases were twenty years in the future.[71] The idea of extending tax support to all Christian churches would obviously dilute the system to a point of virtual unenforceability, but the fact that the legislature seriously contemplated such a future was evidenced by their incorporation, in this same session, of seventeen Baptist, Methodist, Universalist, Free Will Baptist, and Congregational societies, all with legal authority to assess and collect religious taxes from their members.[72]

Although the toleration bill did not actually deprive ministers of civil support and did carefully guard their existing privileges, the Congregational clergy and their allies fought the measure with astonishing determination. They aroused a storm of popular hysteria, based largely on the fear that the toleration act, like the decrees of the French National Assembly in 1793, would abolish religion. "Pass the bill now on the table," shouted Representative Hubbard of Claremont, "and the temples consecrated to the worship of the Saviour of the world will soon be deserted and forsaken."[73] Such arguments were answered with a somewhat lesser degree of exaggeration by Dr. Whipple, Ichabod Bartlett of Portsmouth, and several other young lawyers in the legislature. The Inquisition, the Saint Bartholomew Massacre, and the Revocation of the Edict of Nantes were introduced as witnesses to the evil effects of religion enforced by law. New England's own beginnings for conscience's sake were held up before the opposition to embarrass them. "Such is the effect of fanaticism," noted Bartlett, "that those yet bleeding with the stripes and wounds of persecution, themselves become persecutors."[74] The advocates of toleration insisted that the act of 1791, unmodified, was a violation of article 5 and of the saving clause in article 6 of the state constitution. Dr. Whipple pointed to the folly of civil courts engaging in theological casuistry, as Judge Jeremiah Smith had done at such length in his decision in *Muzzy* versus *Wilkins* in 1803.[75]

Opponents of the measure fought with parliamentary tactics as well as invective. Roll-call votes were demanded in efforts to prevent the senate's bill from being suitably amended, to prevent passage to third reading, and to postpone consideration rather than proceed to the final vote.[76] Proponents won on the earlier roll calls by narrow margins of seven or eight votes. Those opposed even attempted a diversionary tactic by introducing an amendment of their own, which seemed to grant even greater freedom to dissenters, but left the town fathers still in charge of meetinghouse and settled clergy.[77] This smoke screen did not seem to fool many representatives, and those who were deceived came about equally from either side, so the tactic was a failure. The two sides held to their original strength with remarkable tenacity until the final roll call (on the motion to postpone), when ten representatives who had been voting consistently with the opponents of the measure switched over and voted against a postponement, helping to raise the triumphant majority to 103 votes against 79.[78]

The troops on both sides in this campaign were well disciplined, but who gave the orders and marshaled the forces? Although Governor Bell, President of the Senate Jonathan Harvey, and Speaker of the House Matthew Harvey all favored the toleration act, it could hardly be called a party or administration measure. The representatives from such Republican strongholds as Rye, Greenland, New Boston, Francestown, Washington, Richmond, and Canterbury voted against the act, while those from such solidly Federalist towns as Gilmanton, Holderness, Orford, and Sandwich voted steadily in its favor.[79] On the other hand, a glance at the map shows that formerly Federalist towns, such as Exeter, Londonderry, Amherst, Keene, Claremont, Hanover, and Plymouth, furnished most of the opposition votes while the traditional areas of Republican strength formed the core of the toleration forces. Evidence of party breakdown is furnished by Portsmouth, Rochester, Deerfield, and Concord, which elected representatives who appeared on both sides of the contest. Federalism had virtually disappeared, and Republicanism attempted to include everyone, but the old party loyalties still had a part to play, hidden though it might be.

The votes on the toleration bill, however, illustrated the waning of party loyalties as well as their fundamental perseverance. Both trends developed even further in 1820 when several minor issues that might have been expected to arouse partisan passions were introduced. Isaac Hill, newly elected senator from district four, submitted a resolution criticizing the Supreme Court of the United States for its decision in the Dartmouth College case.[80] It was defeated by a body which was supposed to contain not a single Federalist member. Senator George Long of Portsmouth then went to the other extreme and introduced a resolution which expressed unbounded confidence in the Supreme Court and the general government. This was postponed indefinitely by a majority of eleven to one. The New Hampshire senate in 1820 apparently knew not where it stood in relation to Monroe's administration.

Other grim echoes of the Dartmouth controversy reached this legislature in the form of resolutions to provide three professors of the defunct university the unpaid portions of their contracted salaries out of state funds and also to compensate the widow of William H. Woodward for services he had rendered as treasurer of the short-lived institution. After some bickering between the two houses as to exact amounts, these resolutions were finally passed without roll call in the senate and by majorities of seven to eleven votes in the house.[81] The voting pattern generally

followed that for the toleration act, with Portsmouth, Chester, Claremont, and Sandwich dividing their votes and such political stalwarts as
Exeter, Londonderry, and Hanover stoutly resisting any concessions to
the university party, while Dover, Hopkinton, Swanzey, Piermont, and
Meredith gave it their continued support.

The question of the Republican state government's accepting responsibility for financial obligations that it unquestionably had created was
complicated, however, by other factors. One of them was the currently
depressed condition of the economy, which may have induced representatives from the Republican towns of Weare, Henniker, and Haverhill to
vote against the resolutions. Respect for the obligation of contracts, on
the other hand, probably motivated Jeremiah Mason, now a representative from Portsmouth, to support the resolutions. The most astonishing reaction came from Governor Bell, who, as a superior court justice,
had participated in the decision supporting Dartmouth University, which
Marshall's court had overturned. He vetoed the resolutions to compensate the professors on the ground that the state had no obligation to
assume the defunct university's debts and in a time of financial hardship
it had no right to squander the taxpayers' money. An attempt to override
the veto enlisted the support of a dozen or so previous opponents, but
failed (98–78) to reach the necessary majority.[82]

Although the battle over the toleration act in the legislature, the newspapers, the churches, and the streets had been bitter and intense, it was
soon over. The salutary effects of the new arrangement developed so
quickly that the opposition was disarmed. Vexatious quarrels with dissenters were ended, irritating conflicts between town and congregation
had no further basis for existence, and the greatest barrier to peace
between Christian denominations was removed. Instead of being destroyed, religion flourished more than ever, and in the very year after the
passage of the act a tremendous revival affecting even the Congregationalist churches swept over New Hampshire. The churches, sectarian and
established alike, found it unnecessary or undesirable to enforce the taxing and collecting powers granted to all of them by the new law and soon
developed techniques for obtaining the voluntary support of their adherents without requiring legal intervention. Thus, the separation of church
and state came about naturally, unintentionally, almost imperceptibly,
within a few years. The results of the toleration act were so beneficial,
even to the Congregationalist clergy, that it soon won universal approval.

The Panic of 1819, which in any case did not affect New Hampshire
severely, gave way quickly to a burgeoning prosperity in the 1820s. Political harmony reigned, at least outwardly, with the demise of Federalism.
Religious animosities softened, as special privilege was taken away from
a favored sect. The bitter quarrel over Dartmouth College had been

settled by the Supreme Court; the state courts, reformed and streamlined, were functioning smoothly. Former partisan enemies joined hands to do honor to a president whose record in office, in earlier days, would have been the subject of heated controversy. Citizens of New Hampshire who had lived through all the forty years since 1780 might well have thought that they had at last reached a golden age.

Perhaps one citizen, the almost legendary hero of the Revolution John Stark, might have taken a more realistic view. In 1818 the United States Congress voted to grant the ninety-year-old veteran a life pension of sixty dollars a month, which some southern senators thought to be excessive.[83] Stark lived to enjoy this bounty for four more years. He had been born in Londonderry shortly after it was settled by his Scotch-Irish family. As a boy, he had been captured by Indians. During the French and Indian war he had enlisted in Rogers's Rangers. He had settled with his equally legendary wife on a farm in Dunbarton, which was then virtually on the frontier and from which he had marched off to fight the British in Boston.[84] In 1777 he had mortgaged the farm to pay his troops and rout the Hessians at Bennington.

After peace came in 1783, he had found himself, like many another veteran, in debt, in trouble over his land title, and bewildered by the sudden changes taking place in the new nation that he had helped bring to birth. He had seen his state go through three constitutions and his nation through two. He had seen former friends and companions-in-arms divide themselves into hostile political parties and fight savagely at town meetings for the votes that would open the way to privilege and pelf. He had seen his country come to blows with its former ally France and fight another war with the old enemy, the lobster-backs. He had seen newspapers multiply, roads cut through the wilderness, the nearby Merrimack turned into an avenue of commerce, farmlands extended to the base of the White Mountains, lawyers, physicians, and schools established in nearly every village, and the great Jehovah, who in his youth had been intimate almost exclusively with Congregationalists, now addressed familiarly by Baptists, Methodists, Quakers, Shakers, Unitarians, Universalists, Episcopalians, Presbyterians, and even Roman Catholics. John Stark had certainly lived through an era of momentous change. Had it all been worth sixty dollars a month? As far as we know, he never asked himself that question.

APPENDIX

MAPS AND EXPLANATIONS

MAP 1. NEW HAMPSHIRE REGIONS IN 1775

By the end of the colonial period, most of New Hampshire except the White Mountain region and the headwaters of the Connecticut River had been carved up into townships and granted to proprietary corporations or favored individuals by the royal governors or the Masonian Proprietors. Many of these grants, however, in the upper reaches of the Connecticut River, the Lake Winnepesaukee region, and the area beyond the White Mountains were still unpeopled. There were even extensive tracts, such as the Society Land, the Peterborough Slip, the Wilmot Gore, and so forth, within the older regions which were still only thinly settled and unincorporated. This map names the 158 towns that were incorporated and to some degree settled in 1775.

The regional boundary lines are of course arbitrary and only suggestive, but they are less illogical than the county boundaries. They are used only to suggest the very real tripartite division of the colony along geographical lines and the extension of two of the three regions into the northern frontier.

Ten of the twelve towns that protested against adoption of the state constitution in 1776 were in the Old Colony. Also shown are the seventeen Merrimack Valley towns that participated in the Hillsborough County congresses during the war and the thirty-four towns in the Connecticut Valley that seceded from New Hampshire and joined Vermont in 1781. These all help to illustrate the regional divisions of the state.

NOTE: *Named* towns were those entitled to representatives in Fifth Provincial Congress; *un-named* towns were not so entitled.

Every effort has been made to ensure accuracy, but since my husband's original maps were never located, I had to work from his copies and other materials in preparing these maps for publication. I regret any errors that may have resulted from the misinterpretation of his markings.

V. A. T.

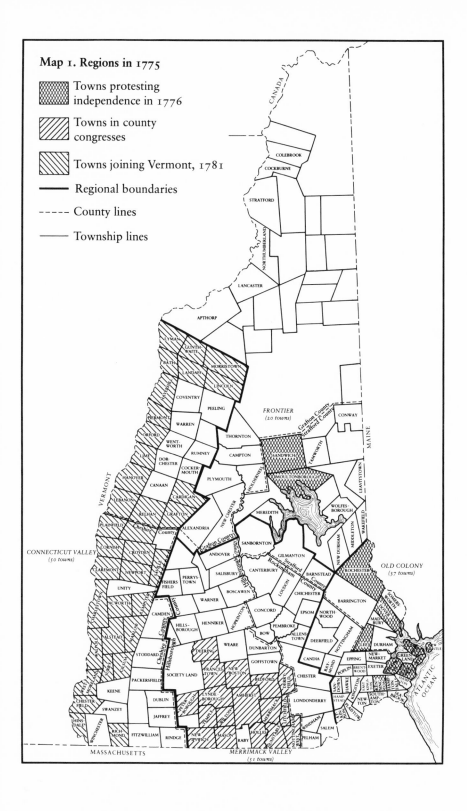

Map 1. Regions in 1775

Towns protesting
independence in 1776

Towns in county
congresses

Towns joining Vermont, 1781

Regional boundaries

County lines

Township lines

CANADA

COLEBROOK

COCKBURNE

STRATFORD

NORTHUMBERLAND

LANCASTER

APTHORP

LYMAN

GUNTH-
WAITE

BATH

MORRISTOWN

LANDAFF

LINCOLN

COVENTRY

PEELING

FRONTIER
(20 towns)

Grafton County
Stratford County

CONWAY

PIERMONT

WARREN

ORFORD

THORNTON

WENT-
WORTH

RUMNEY

CAMPTON

TAMWORTH

MAINE

LIME

DOR-
CHESTER

COCKER-
MOUTH

PLYMOUTH

HOLDERNESS

SANDWICH

LEAVITTSTOWN

HANOVER

CANAAN

MOULTONBOROUGH

WAKEFIELD

LEBANON

CARDIGAN

WOLFES-
BOROUGH

MIDDLETON

BELHAM

GRAFTON

NEW CHESTER

MEREDITH

PLAINFIELD

Cheshire County

ALEXANDRIA

NEW DURHAM

CORNISH

CROYDEN

Grafton County

SANBORNTON

GILMANTON

VERMONT

CONNECTICUT VALLEY
(50 towns)

CLAREMONT

NEWPORT

ANDOVER

CANTERBURY

Rockingham

Stratford

BARNSTEAD

ROCHESTER

OLD COLONY
(37 towns)

UNITY

FISHERS
FIELD

PERRYS
TOWN

SALISBURY

LOUDON

CHICHESTER

County

BARRINGTON

WARNER

BOSCAWEN

SOMERS-
WORTH

ACWORTH

CAMDEN

HOPKINTON

CONCORD

EPSOM

NORTH-
WOOD

MADBURY

ALSTEAD

HILLS-
BOROUGH

HENNIKER

PEMBROKE

DEERFIELD

NOTTINGHAM

DURHAM

STODDARD

DEERING

WEARE

BOW

ALLENS-
TOWN

CANDIA

RAY-
MOND

EPPING

NEW-
MARKET

GREEN-
LAND

PACKERSFIELD

SOCIETY LAND

FRANCES-
TOWN

NEW
BOSTON

GOFFSTOWN

DUNBARTON

CHESTER

POPLIN

BRENT-
WOOD

EXETER

SOUTH-
AMP-
TON

KEENE

DUBLIN

Cheshire County

Hillsborough

BEDFORD

SAN-
DOWN

HAWKE

KINGS-
TON

CHESTER-
FIELD

JAFFREY

LYNDE-
BOROUGH

AMHERST

LONDONDERRY

HAMP-
STEAD

KINGSTON

NEW-
TON

SWANZEY

FITZWILLIAM

RINDGE

NEW
IPSWICH

MASON

RABY

HOLLES

WINDHAM

SALEM

PELHAM

ATLANTIC
OCEAN

HINS-
DALE

WINCHESTER

RICH-
MOND

MASSACHUSETTS

MERRIMACK VALLEY
(51 towns)

MAP 2. POPULATION IN 1775

This map is based on the results of a census ordered by the fourth provincial congress and actually taken by town authorities. Although the town reports were incomplete and in many cases inaccurate, they provided the only information available on New Hampshire's population at the beginning of the Revolutionary War—a total of a little more than 84,000. Most of these people were concentrated in the Old Colony and the actual valley of the Merrimack River. The towns in the Connecticut Valley and on the Frontier were only just beginning to attract settlers.

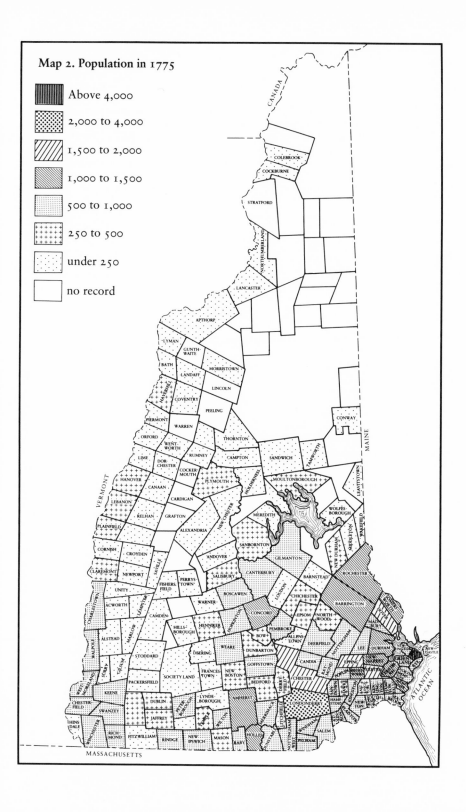

Map 2. Population in 1775

Above 4,000

2,000 to 4,000

1,500 to 2,000

1,000 to 1,500

500 to 1,000

250 to 500

under 250

no record

MAP 3. TOWNS REPRESENTED IN THE LAST PROVINCIAL ASSEMBLY, MAY 1775

This map shows clearly how inadequate was the representation of the newly settled parts of the colony in the royal assembly. Only 49 of the 158 incorporated towns were entitled to elect delegates. Of these, 32 were in the Old Colony. Only 11 towns in the Merrimack Valley, 5 in the Connecticut Valley, and 1 on the Frontier elected representatives to this last legal assembly. In the fourth provincial congress (see Map 4) meeting at the same time, 112 towns represented themselves with 151 delegates.

NOTE: 36 towns represented by 37 delegates. Towns with more than one representative: Portsmouth, 3; Hampton, 2; Exeter, 2; Dover, 2. Multiple constituencies (enclosed in heavy black line): Newcastle and Rye; Plaistow and Hampstead; Salem and Pelham; Nottingham West and Litchfield; Bedford and Amherst; Hawke and Sandown; Lee and Madbury.

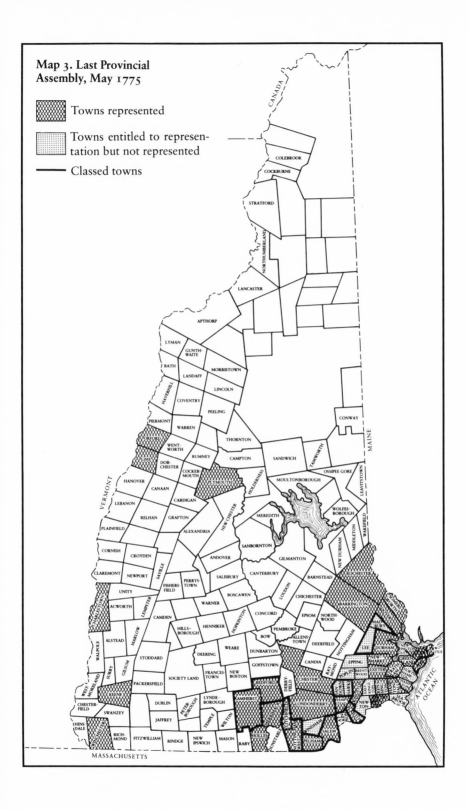

**Map 3. Last Provincial
Assembly, May 1775**

Towns represented

Towns entitled to representation but not represented

Classed towns

MAP 4. TOWNS REPRESENTED IN THE FOURTH PROVINCIAL
CONGRESS, 1775

The contrast between this map and Map 3 is striking. Sixty-three of the towns outside the Old Colony which were unrepresented in the provincial assembly elected one or in some cases two (Hanover, Canterbury) delegates to this revolutionary congress. Some towns which were combined by law to elect a single representative to the assembly separated to elect their own delegates to the congress (Sandown and Hawke, Madbury and Lee). A few towns combined voluntarily to elect a single delegate (Keene and Surry; Unity, Newport, and Croyden). It is certainly clear that the fourth provincial congress was a more democratic body than the contemporary provincial assembly, or than the fifth congress which succeeded it.

NOTE: 112 towns represented by 151 delegates. Towns with more than one delegate: Portsmouth, 5; Newington, 2; Greenland, 3; Northampton, 2; Hampton, 2; Hampton Falls, 2; Stratham, 2; Exeter, 5; Newmarket, 2; Epping, 2; Brentwood, 2; Poplin, 2; East Kingston, 2; Kingston, 2; Atkinson, 2; Durham, 2; Lee, 2; Dover, 2; Somersworth, 2; Rochester, 2; Windham, 2; Londonderry, 2; Chester, 2; Canterbury, 2; Litchfield, 2; Dunstable, 3; Amherst, 2; Holles, 3; Wilton, 2; Temple, 2; New Ipswich, 2; Packersfield, 2; Hanover, 2; Orford, 2. Multiple constituencies: Keene and Surry; Unity, Newport and Croyden; Plymouth and Rumney; New Chester and Campton.

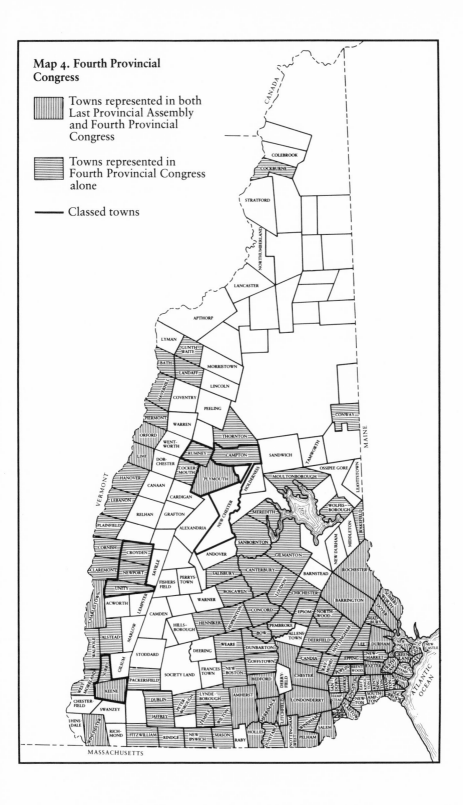

Map 4. Fourth Provincial Congress

Towns represented in both Last Provincial Assembly and Fourth Provincial Congress

Towns represented in Fourth Provincial Congress alone

—— Classed towns

CANADA

COLEBROOK
COCKBURNE

STRATFORD

NORTHUMBERLAND

LANCASTER

APTHORP

LYMAN
GUNTH-WAITE
BATH
LANDAFF
MORRISTOWN
HAVERILL
LINCOLN
COVENTRY
PEELING
PIERMONT
WARREN
ORFORD
WENT-WORTH
THORNTON
LYME
DOR-CHESTER
RUMNEY
CAMPTON
SANDWICH
TAMWORTH
CONWAY
HANOVER
COCKER-MOUTH
PLYMOUTH
HOLDERNESS
MOULTONBOROUGH
OSSIPEE GORE
CANAAN
CARDIGAN
NEW CHESTER
MEREDITH
WOLFES-BOROUGH
LEAVITTSTOWN
LEBANON
RELHAN
GRAFTON
SANBORNTON
NEW DURHAM
MIDDLETON
WAKEFIELD
PLAINFIELD
ALEXANDRIA
ANDOVER
GILMANTON
ROCHESTER
CORNISH
CROYDEN
SAVILLE
SALISBURY
CANTERBURY
BARNSTEAD
CLAREMONT
NEWPORT
PERRYS-TOWN
FISHERS-FIELD
BARRINGTON
UNITY
LEMPSTER
BOSCAWEN
GORHAM
CHICHESTER
ACWORTH
WARNER
CONCORD
EPSOM
NORTH WOOD
BARRINGTON
MADBURY
CHARLESTOWN
CAMDEN
HENNIKER
HAMPTON
PEMBROKE
ALLENS-TOWN
DEERFIELD
LEE
DURHAM
NEW CASTLE
WALPOLE
ALSTEAD
MARLOW
HILLS-BOROUGH
BOW
DUNBARTON
CANDIA
EPPING
NEW MARKET
WEST MOOR
GILSUM
STODDARD
DEERING
WEARE
GOFFSTOWN
DERRY-FIELD
CHESTER
RAY
BRENT WOOD
KINGSTON
PACKERSFIELD
SOCIETY LAND
FRANCES-TOWN
NEW BOSTON
BEDFORD
LONDONDERRY
KEENE
DUBLIN
PETER-BOROUGH
LYNDE-BOROUGH
AMHERST
CHESTER-FIELD
TEMPLE
WILTON
HOLLES
PELHAM
SALEM
SWANZEY
JAFFREY
HINS-DALE
RICHMOND
FITZWILLIAM
RINGE
NEW IPSWICH
MASON
RABY
NOTTINGHAM WEST

VERMONT

MAINE

ATLANTIC OCEAN

MASSACHUSETTS

MAP 5. TOWNS REPRESENTED IN THE FIFTH PROVINCIAL CONGRESS, 1776

This map shows the result of the system of representation which was adopted by the fourth provincial congress for the election of its successor body, the fifth congress, and by that body written into the constitution of 1776. It remained the basic system of representation in the New Hampshire legislature until after 1820, considerably modified in piecemeal fashion.

The number of represented towns was actually increased to 150 but the number of representatives reduced to ninety. This was accomplished by combining or "classing" towns with fewer than a hundred eligible voters, so that anywhere from two to eight towns were "classed" to elect a single representative. The map shows that no less than 112 towns were thus classed for the election of thirty-eight representatives. Obviously the dominant town in such a grouping elected one of its citizens and the rest were left voiceless. The device was reduced to absurdity in the far north, where Conway and Shelburne were expected to cross the White Mountains to join Apthorp, Lancaster, Northumberland, Stratford, Cockburne, and Colebrook in electing a single delegate. The plan was unworkable, and Conway ignored it by electing its own representative and petitioning for the right to do so. The petition was soon granted, as were many others (Hanover, Newport, Bath, Northampton, and so forth), and the classes were constantly shifting as populations grew and towns complained.

The system originally permitted only 33 towns to elect a single representative, and only 6 towns to elect more than one. These towns, especially Portsmouth, were seriously underrepresented after 1784 when the "mean increasing number" of taxpayers for an additional representative became three hundred. Thus Portsmouth, with more than nine times the population of Hinsdale, had only three representatives in the legislature to Hinsdale's one.

NOTE: 77 delegates present representing 123 towns; 13 delegates absent representing 27 towns. Towns with more than one representative: Portsmouth, 3; Exeter, 2; Dover, 2; Londonderry, 2; Chester, 2; Amherst, 2. Classed towns: Seabrook and Hampton Falls; Raymond and Poplin; Kingston and East Kingston; Hawke and Sandown; Newton and Southampton; Atkinson and Plaistow; Deerfield and Northwood; Allenstown, Epsom and Chichester; Raby and Mason; Canterbury and Loudon; Bow and Dunbarton; Derryfield and Goffstown; Nottingham West and Litchfield; Merrimack and Bedford; Wilton and Lyndeborough; New Boston and Francestown; Henniker, Hillsborough, Deering, and Society Land; Peterborough and Temple; Andover, Perrystown, Fishersfield, and Warner; Salisbury and Boscawen; Hinsdale and Chesterfield; Fitzwilliam and Swanzey; Dublin and Marlborough; Jaffrey and Rindge; Packersfield, Gilsum, Stoddard, and Camden; Surry, Alstead, and Marlow; Acworth, Lempster, Unity, Newport, and Croyden; Cornish, Plainfield, Grantham, and Protectworth; Lebanon, Relhan, Grafton, Hanover, Canaan, and Cardigan; Lime, Orford, Dorchester, Wentworth, Warren, and Piermont; Haverhill, Bath, Lyman, Gunthwaite, Landaff, and Morristown; Apthorp, Lancaster, Conway, Northumberland, Stratford, Colebrook, Cockburne, and Shelburne; Plymouth, Alexandria, New Chester, Cockermouth, and Rumney; Thornton, Campton, and Holderness; Wakefield, Middleton, and Leavitstown; Wolfborough, New Durham and Ossipee Gore; Moultonborough, Sandwich, and Tamworth; Sanbornton and Meredith; Gilmanton and Barnstead.

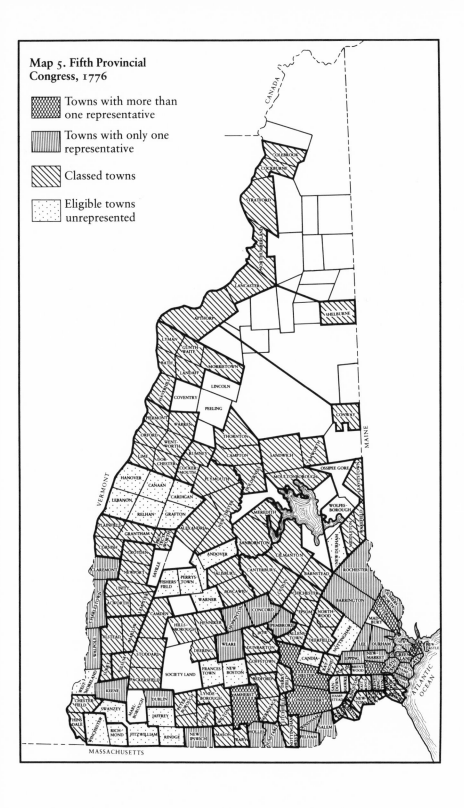

Map 5. Fifth Provincial Congress, 1776

Towns with more than one representative

Towns with only one representative

Classed towns

Eligible towns unrepresented

MAP 6. TOWNS REPRESENTED IN THE CONSTITUTIONAL CONVENTION OF 1778–1779

This map simply indicates the ninety-four towns which were represented by seventy-five delegates in the convention. Many towns obviously classed themselves to send a composite delegate, although several sent more delegates than they were entitled to representatives in the legislature. The map shows clearly the fifty-five towns, mostly in the Connecticut Valley and on the Frontier, that were not represented.

NOTE: 75 delegates representing 94 towns.

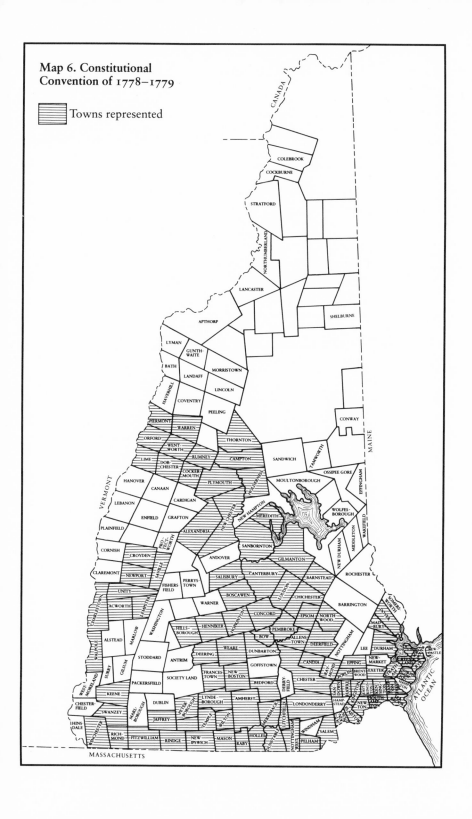

Map 6. Constitutional
Convention of 1778–1779

Towns represented

MAP 7. CONSTITUTIONAL CONVENTION OF 1781–1783

This rather complicated map attempts to show two different things: (1) how the towns' representatives voted in the legislature on the resolution to call the convention (*New Hampshire State Papers*, 8:897), and (2) the towns that elected delegates to the convention. There are thus six possibilities which are shown by different devices on the map. The representatives of twenty-seven towns that elected delegates to the convention had voted for the convention resolution. Thirty-three additional towns whose representatives had not voted for the resolution were represented in the convention, and, finally, eleven towns whose representatives voted against the resolution sent delegates to the convention. This made a total of seventy-one towns represented by fifty-eight delegates. On the other hand, there were twenty-five towns whose representatives voted in favor of the resolution but which did not elect delegates. Seventeen additional towns whose representatives voted against the resolution failed to elect delegates. But there were also forty-two towns neither voting for the resolution nor represented in the convention; most of these were in the Connecticut Valley. Altogether, there were eighty-four normally politically active towns unrepresented in the convention–thirteen more than *were* represented.

It is instructive to compare this map with Map 6 of the convention of 1778, and with Map 11 of the convention of 1791. The constitution, much modified, under which New Hampshire still operates today was made by the least representative of its many conventions.

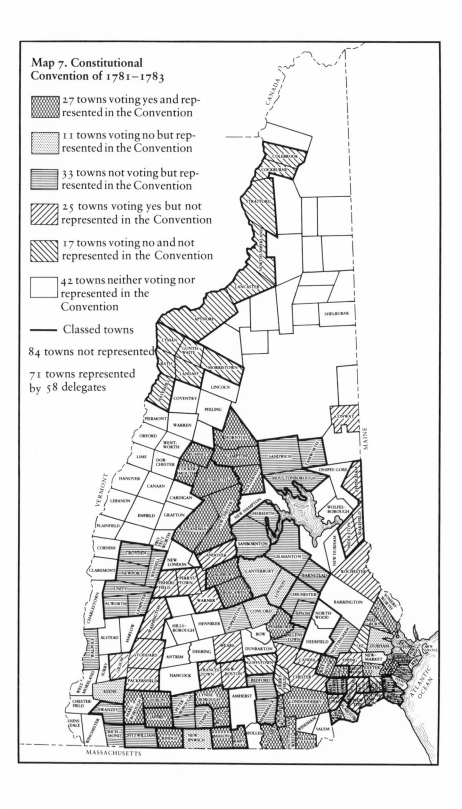

Map 7. Constitutional Convention of 1781–1783

27 towns voting yes and represented in the Convention

11 towns voting no but represented in the Convention

33 towns not voting but represented in the Convention

25 towns voting yes but not represented in the Convention

17 towns voting no and not represented in the Convention

42 towns neither voting nor represented in the Convention

—— Classed towns

84 towns not represented

71 towns represented by 58 delegates

MAP 8. VOTE ON THE LEGAL TENDER ACT OF 1781

This map well illustrates the fact that the passage of this deflationary measure was a legal coup d'etat, succeeding in a very "thin house" by the majority of a single vote, 22–21. Forty-two percent of the members of this legislature (thirty-one representatives) had gone home and did not participate in the vote. In addition to this, fifty-six towns entitled to eighteen representatives had not even elected them to this legislature. In other words, the Legal Tender Act was passed by men representing only 24 percent of the voting population of the state—none of them from the Connecticut Valley, only one from the Frontier, nine from the Merrimack Valley, and the remaining twelve from the Old Colony.

This vote is recorded in *New Hampshire State Papers*, 8:913. The roll of the assembly is printed on page 90.

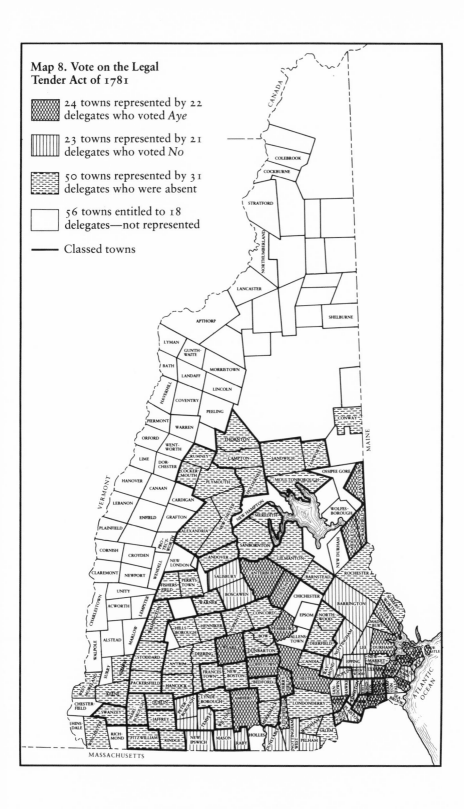

Map 8. Vote on the Legal Tender Act of 1781

24 towns represented by 22 delegates who voted *Aye*

23 towns represented by 21 delegates who voted *No*

50 towns represented by 31 delegates who were absent

56 towns entitled to 18 delegates—not represented

—— Classed towns

MAP 9. PAPER MONEY

This map represents in some degree the consequences of the action portrayed in Map 8. Amherst and Canterbury were the only towns voting for the Legal Tender Act which later showed any sympathy for paper money. However, it is a composite map showing not only the town representatives' votes in the legislature but direct town votes and petitions on the subject as well. It is based on the following four records: (1) Votes in the legislature on the reestablishment of metallic legal tender, September 1, 1781. See Map 8. (2) Vote in the legislature to accept the report of the committee on the Paper Money Plan of September 14, 1786. Recorded in *New Hampshire State Papers*, 20:696. Roll of the assembly on page 609. (3) Town votes on the paper money plan of 1786. Collected from town histories and the Town Paper series in New Hampshire State Papers, vols. 9–13. (4) Petitions from towns for paper money. Same sources.

It is assumed that a negative vote on (1), favorable votes on (2) and (3), and a petition in group (4) indicate positive paper money towns, strongly so in such cases as Londonderry, which registered in all four categories. The opposite positions would indicate a town strongly opposed to paper money, such as Portsmouth. As the map shows, there were few of these. The paper money fever infected at least 111 towns in the state to a greater or lesser degree.

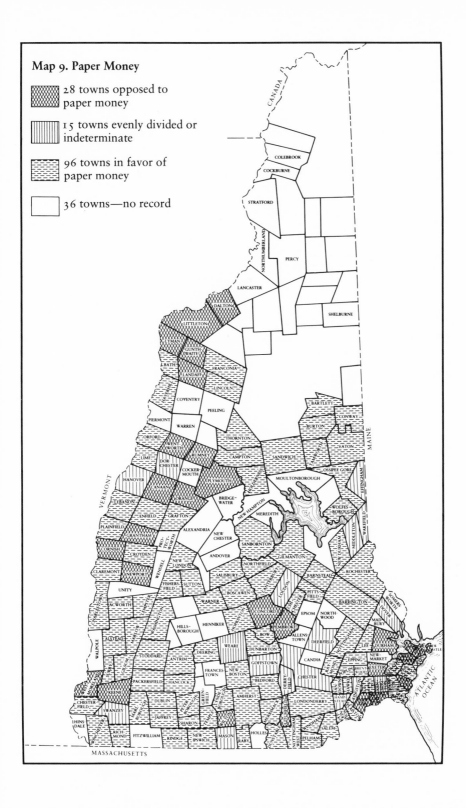

Map 9. Paper Money

28 towns opposed to
paper money

15 towns evenly divided or
indeterminate

96 towns in favor of
paper money

36 towns—no record

CANADA

COLEBROOK

COCKBURNE

STRATFORD

NORTHUMBERLAND

PERCY

LANCASTER

SHELBURNE

DALTON

LITTLETON

LYMAN

GUNTH-
WAITE

BATH

LANDAFF

FRANCONIA

LINCOLN

COVENTRY

PEELING

PIERMONT

WARREN

BARTLETT

CONWAY

ORFORD

THORNTON

BURTON

WENT-
WORTH

EATON

LIME

RUMNEY

CAMPTON

SANDWICH

OSSIPEE GORE

DOR-
CHESTER

COCKER-
MOUTH

EFFINGHAM

HANOVER

PLYMOUTH

MOULTONBOROUGH

ANAN

ORANGE

LEBANON

BRIDGE-
WATER

NEW HAMPTON

MEREDITH

WOLFES-
BOROUGH

ENFIELD

GRAFTON

VERMONT

PLAINFIELD

ALEXANDRIA

NEW DURHAM

MIDDLETON

WAKEFIELD

GRANTHAM

PROT-
ECT-
WORTH

NEW
CHESTER

SANBORNTON

CORNISH

CROYDEN

ANDOVER

GILMANTON

CLAREMONT

NEWPORT

WENDELL

NEW LONDON

NORTHFIELD

MAINE

UNITY

FISHERS-
FIELD

SUTTON

SALISBURY

BARNSTEAD

ROCHESTER

SOMERS-
WORTH

ACWORTH

LEMPSTER

WARNER

BOSCAWEN

PITTS-
FIELD

BARRINGTON

HILLS-
BOROUGH

HENNIKER

CONCORD

EPSOM

NORTH-
WOOD

MAD-
BURY

WALPOLE

ALSTEAD

STODDARD

BOW

PEMBROKE

ALLENS-
TOWN

DEERFIELD

LEE

DURHAM

ANTRIM

WEARE

DUNBARTON

CANDIA

EPPING

NEW-
MARKET

CASTLE

PACKERSFIELD

DEERING

FRANCES-
TOWN

NEW
BOSTON

GOFFSTOWN

BEDFORD

CHESTER

BRENT-
WOOD

EXETER

HANCOCK

GREEN-
FIELD

AMHERST

LONDONDERRY

HAMP-

CHESTER-
FIELD

DUBLIN

PETER

SWANZEY

JAFFREY

SHARON

MASON

HOLLES

PELHAM

SALEM

HINS-
DALE

RICH-
MOND

FITZWILLIAM

RINDGE

NEW
IPSWICH

RABY

WEST

WINDHAM

ATLANTIC
OCEAN

MASSACHUSETTS

MAP 10. VOTE ON THE RATIFICATION OF THE FEDERAL CONSTITUTION

The map indicates that participation in the ratifying convention was very nearly complete, only seven well-populated towns and a handful of remote wilderness settlements being unrepresented. The map also shows clearly that opposition to the Constitution came largely from the center of the state, in the Merrimack Valley and the hill region between the two great rivers. Comparison with Map 9 shows a certain degree of correlation, but by no means complete, between enthusiasm for paper money and opposition to the Constitution. Atkinson, Londonderry, Rochester, Amherst, and Haverhill, for instance, show this identity of interest, but Northampton, Windham, Hopkinton, and Lebanon do not. Portsmouth, Exeter, Hampton, Wilton, Keene, and Cornish opposed paper money and voted for the Constitution, but again, Stratham, Concord, Barrington, Newport, and Bath failed to show this correlation. The map shows very clearly that votes from the Connecticut Valley and the Frontier secured the ratification of the Constitution in New Hampshire.

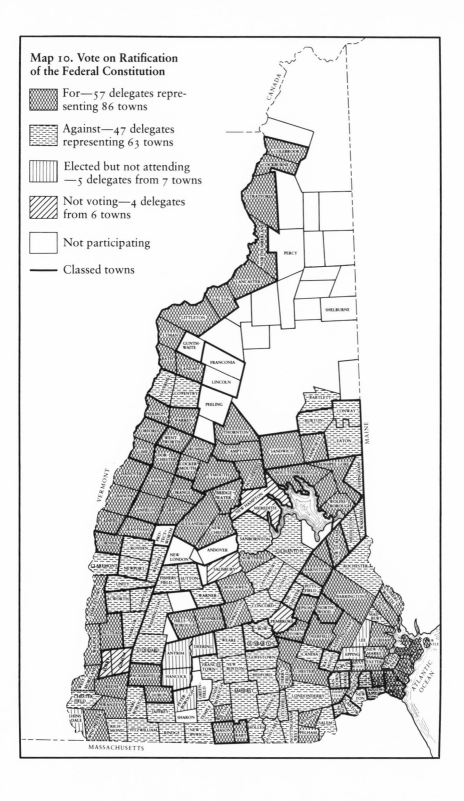

Map 10. Vote on Ratification
of the Federal Constitution

For—57 delegates repre-
senting 86 towns

Against—47 delegates
representing 63 towns

Elected but not attending
—5 delegates from 7 towns

Not voting—4 delegates
from 6 towns

Not participating

Classed towns

CANADA

COLEBROOK

COCKBURNE

PERCY

SHELBURNE

LANCASTER

DALTON

LITTLETON

GUNTH-
WAITE

FRANCONIA

LINCOLN

PEELING

BARTLETT

CONWAY

BURTON

EATON

LANDAFF

COVENTRY

ORFORD

THORNTON

WENT-
WORTH

CAMPTON

SANDWICH

LIME

DORCHESTER

COCKER-
MOUTH

PLYMOUTH

MOULTONBOROUGH

OSSIPEE GORE

HANOVER

ORANGE

BRIDGE-
WATER

NEW HAMPTON

MEREDITH

WOLFES
BOROUGH

WAKEFIELD

ENFIELD

ALEXANDRIA

GRANTHAM

PRO-
TECT-
WORTH

NEW
HOLT

SANBORNTON

NORTHFIELD

GILMANTON

CORNISH

CROYDEN

NEW
LONDON

ANDOVER

CLAREMONT

NEWPORT

SALISBURY

BARNSTEAD

ROCHESTER

UNITY

FISHERS
FIELD

SUTTON

WARNER

PITTS-
FIELD

HARRINGTON

ACWORTH

CONCORD

NORTH-
WOOD

MAD-
BURY

HILLS-
BOROUGH

HENNIKER

PEMBROKE

DEERFIELD

LEE

DURHAM

ALSTEAD

BOW

ALLEN-
STOWN

CANDIA

EPPING

NEW-
MARKET

EXETER

STODDARD

ANTRIM

DEERING

WEARE

DUNBARTON

GOFFSTOWN

PACKERSFIELD

HANCOCK

FRANCES-
TOWN

NEW
BOSTON

BEDFORD

LONDONDERRY

HAMP-
STEAD

NEW-
TON

CHESTER-
FIELD

DUBLIN

PETER-
BOROUGH

GREEN-
FIELD

AMHEST

JAFFREY

SHARON

RICH-
MOND

FITZWILLIAM

NEW
IPSWICH

MASON

HOLLES

PELHAM

SALEM

VERMONT

MAINE

ATLANTIC
OCEAN

MASSACHUSETTS

MAP 11. CONSTITUTIONAL CONVENTION OF 1791–1792

Like Map 7, this map attempts to show two things: (1) the towns that sent delegates to the constitutional convention in 1791, and (2) the way the towns voted on the final set of amendments presented to them. Both sets of data are recorded in *New Hampshire State Papers*, 10:23, 164. The two factors produce six kinds of combinations, which are shown by different shadings on the map.

In the convention 106 towns were represented by 108 delegates. Of these towns 66 subsequently gave majorities in favor of the amendments proposed by the convention, and 22 gave adverse majorities. Among represented towns 18 failed to vote on the amendments, and 26 towns not represented in the convention voted on the amendments, 16 of them with favorable majorities and 10 unfavorable. Opposition to a stronger state government tended to center in the same areas that opposed a strong federal government, but there are some interesting variations. Exeter, Hampton, and Dover, for example—all federal towns—opposed a strong state executive, while Londonderry, Amherst, and Claremont, which voted against the federal Constitution, now favored strengthening the state constitution.

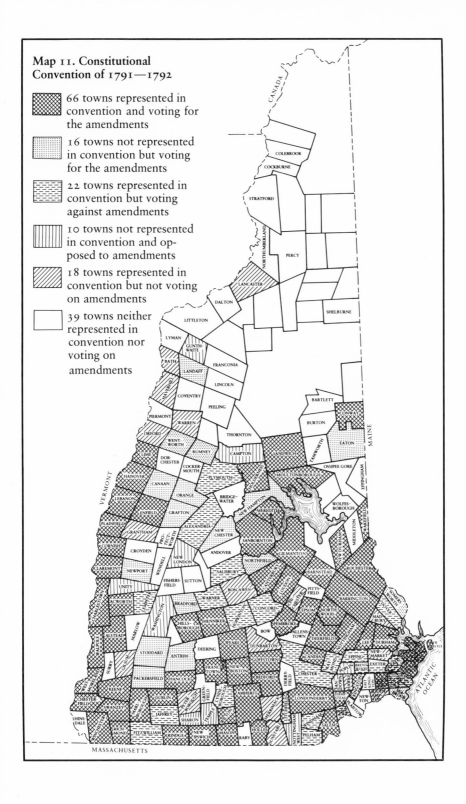

Map 11. Constitutional
Convention of 1791—1792

66 towns represented in
convention and voting for
the amendments

16 towns not represented
in convention but voting
for the amendments

22 towns represented in
convention but voting
against amendments

10 towns not represented
in convention and op-
posed to amendments

18 towns represented in
convention but not voting
on amendments

39 towns neither
represented in
convention nor
voting on
amendments

MAP 12. RELIGIOUS FREEDOM

This map is based on the votes taken in the constitutional convention of 1791 on three proposals to modify the church establishment in New Hampshire. These were: (1) A motion on September 8, 1791, to expunge article 6 from the state constitution in order to introduce a more liberal article, defeated 15–89. See *New Hampshire State Papers*, 10:41–42. (2) A motion on September 10, 1791, to remove the Protestant qualification for officeholding, also defeated 33–51. See ibid., p. 46, vote recorded on p. 24. (3) A motion on February 21, 1792, to accept report of a special committee on article 6, which would have required all persons regardless of religious persuasion to pay the ecclesiastical tax. Passed, 57–35. See ibid., p. 108, vote recorded on p. 58.

Town whose delegates consistently took the conservative position, that is, voted nay on 1 and 2 but aye on 3 are shown as "strongly opposed to religious freedom" (Dover). Those whose delegates voted 2–1, 2–0, or 1–0 for the conservative position are shown as "opposed to religious freedom" (Chester).

Towns whose delegates voted the conservative position on one issue and the liberal one on another are shown as "undecided" (Portsmouth).

Towns whose delegates voted 2–1, 2–0, or 1–0 in favor of the liberal position are shown as "favored religious freedom" (Hanover). Those whose delegates voted consistently for the liberal position are shown as "strongly favored religious freedom" (Epping).

Three things are clearly evident on the map. The first is that sympathy for greater religious freedom existed largely in the more recently settled towns of the north and west, especially where the sectarians were strong (as in Richmond), and that the religious establishment prevailed in the older towns of the Old Colony and the Merrimack Valley. The second and less easily explained phenomenon is that religious liberalism and economic radicalism certainly did not go hand in hand. Londonderry, Atkinson, and Amherst, which fought for paper money and voted against the federal Constitution, are consistently orthodox on these establishment issues. The third and most evident fact shown is that New Hampshire was still religiously very conservative in 1792. Only six delegates voted consistently for the liberal position, and it is certain that at least one of these, William Plumer, spoke only for himself and not for his constituency, Epping.

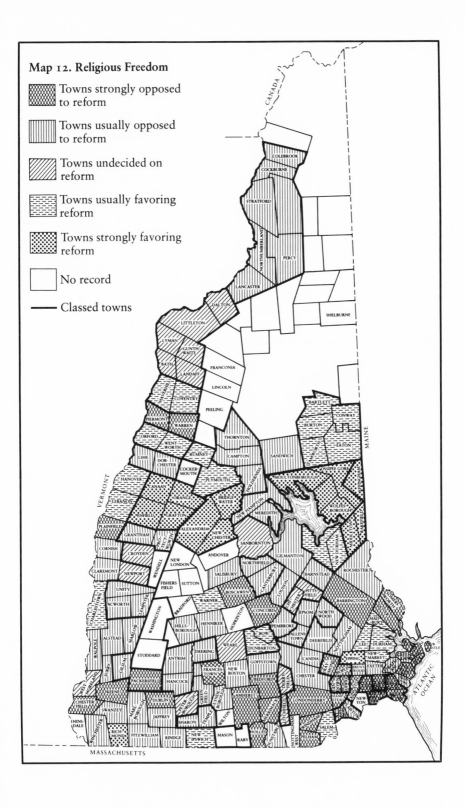

Map 12. Religious Freedom

Towns strongly opposed to reform

Towns usually opposed to reform

Towns undecided on reform

Towns usually favoring reform

Towns strongly favoring reform

No record

Classed towns

MAP 13. GUBERNATORIAL ELECTION OF 1800

This map is based on newspaper reports of the town votes in 1800, the first year for which anything like complete statistics are available. Although newspaper reporting was still inaccurate and far from complete, there are enough data in 1800 to reflect the political situation with some fidelity. Since this was the first year in which the Republicans made a determined drive against Gilman, it can be assumed that the map shows the Republican party at its maximum strength during the decade of the nineties. It is immediately apparent that the Republicans had developed three areas of control: (1) Portsmouth and its neighboring towns in the Old Colony (Newcastle, Newington, Greenland, Northampton, and Stratham, unreported, probably also had majorities for Walker); (2) the central portion of the Merrimack Valley, particularly in the upper part of Hillsborough County; and (3) around Lake Winnepesaukee in the Frontier area.

The remainder of the state, including a majority of the towns in each of the areas already mentioned and all but two of the towns in the Connecticut Valley, was Federalist. Only 40 of the 127 towns where the vote was recorded showed any Republican tendencies prior to 1801.

The basic political pattern in this period of New Hampshire history already appears in 1800. Exeter, Dover, Durham, Chester, Keene, Cornish, and Plymouth, which opposed paper money and favored the federal Constitution, had become and would generally remain Federalist. Hawke (now Danville), Goffstown, Canterbury, Wakefield, and New Boston, which favored paper money and voted against the federal Constitution had become Republican. But there are some surprises. Most unexpected of all, perhaps, is Portsmouth, which was staunchly federalist in 1788 and was Republican in 1800. Londonderry, Claremont, and Haverhill, on the other hand, favored paper money and opposed the Constitution but had become strongly Federalist. The overwhelming Federalist complexion of the map in 1800 shows how strongly New Hampshire voters reacted against Jacobinism.

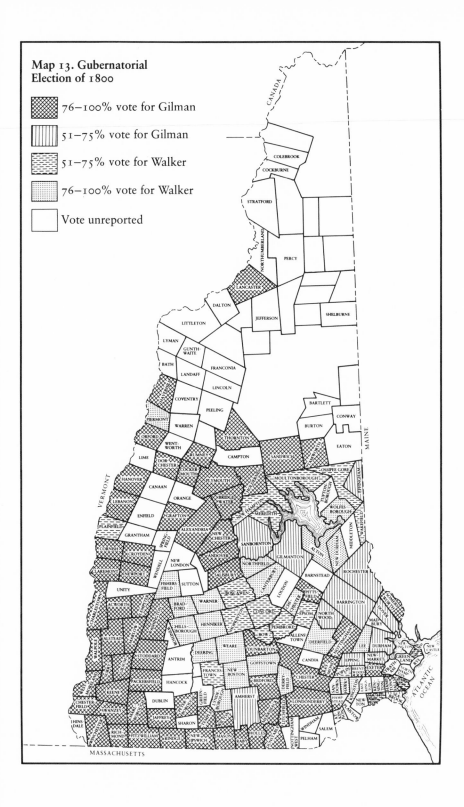

Map 13. Gubernatorial
Election of 1800

76–100% vote for Gilman

51–75% vote for Gilman

51–75% vote for Walker

76–100% vote for Walker

Vote unreported

MAP 14. REPUBLICAN TRIUMPH, 1800–1806

John Langdon and his Republican colleagues came to power in 1805 by persuading more than twice as many New Hampshire voters to exercise their franchise as had done so in 1799. Both parties benefited by this increased activity at the polls, that is, more Federalists voted in Portsmouth and more Republicans in Exeter, but the Republican increase was so much greater as to change the political complexion of more than sixty towns in the state. This change of allegiance is shown on the map.

The map is based on the vote in the seven gubernatorial elections from 1800 to 1806 so far as it was reported in the newspapers, which are the only sources for this data. Their reporting was not very complete until about 1803; for that year and the ensuing two we have very satisfactory data, but interest fell off again after 1805 and ceased completely by 1807.

Sixty towns in New Hampshire remained faithfully Federalist from 1800 to 1806; that is, they gave a majority for Gilman in 1800 or in the first election reported after that and continued to do so as long as the votes were recorded. Most of these were in the lower Merrimack Valley and the upper Connecticut.

Twelve towns changed from Republican to Federalist; they are not significant.

Fifty-five towns remained consistently Republican from 1800 to 1806. Note that they predominate in clusters around Portsmouth and Kingston in the Old Colony, in the upper part of the Merrimack Valley, and around Lake Winnepesaukee.

Sixty-six towns made the difference—by switching from Federalist to Republican majorities after 1800 (including two towns, Milton and Mount Vernon, created after 1800). They are pretty well distributed throughout the state and include many towns of importance—Epping, Dover, Durham, Rochester, Amherst, Walpole, Barrington, and Hollis.

These changes made the Old Colony and the Merrimack Valley definitely Republican, the Connecticut Valley still predominantly Federalist, and the Frontier equally divided.

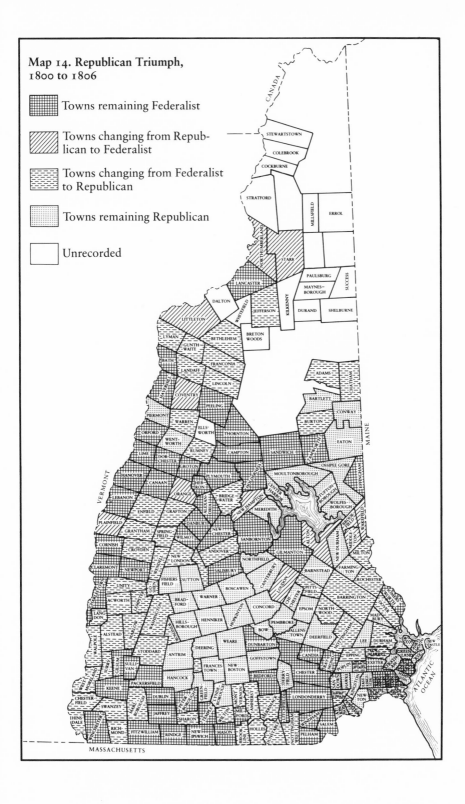

Map 14. Republican Triumph, 1800 to 1806

Towns remaining Federalist

Towns changing from Republican to Federalist

Towns changing from Federalist to Republican

Towns remaining Republican

Unrecorded

MAP 15. VOTE ON THE UNION BANK

The most warmly contested state issue which helped to produce the political revolution portrayed in Map 14 was the Union Bank of Portsmouth, which was not simply a financial institution but a Republican political machine as well. This map shows very well how the issue of incorporating the Union Bank helped to achieve Republican victory. The map is based on two roll-call votes in the state legislature: (1) June 12, 1800, on a motion to accept an adverse report from a committee appointed to consider a petition for the incorporation of the bank. Passed, 86–59, and the petition was dismissed. (2) June 10, 1801, on a motion to grant the Union Bank petitioners leave to bring in a bill for incorporation. Passed, 84–60, and the bank was subsequently chartered.

Note that the legislature reversed itself by almost exactly the same majority on these two votes.

Towns denoted "voted against" are those whose representatives voted both times against the bank, or who voted once against and were absent the other time. Thirty-five of these towns also remained Federalist during the period 1800–1806.

Towns whose representatives voted both times in favor of incorporation or who voted once in favor and were absent the other time are shown as "voted in favor." Thirty-seven of these towns also remained Republican during the period 1800–1806.

The representatives of fifty-six towns voted once against and once in favor of incorporation, most of them in that order. Their change in voting brought victory for the bank. Twenty-four of these towns also changed from Federalist to Republican during the years 1800–1806.

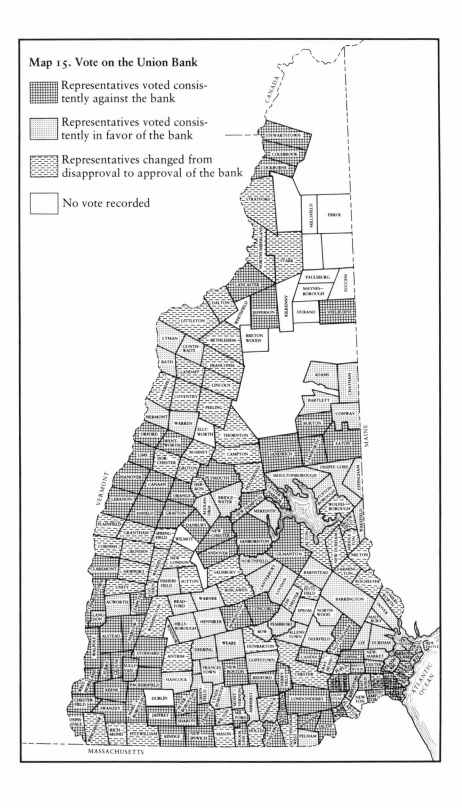

Map 15. Vote on the Union Bank

Representatives voted consistently against the bank

Representatives voted consistently in favor of the bank

Representatives changed from disapproval to approval of the bank

No vote recorded

CANADA

VERMONT

MAINE

MASSACHUSETTS

ATLANTIC OCEAN

STEWARTSTOWN
COLEBROOK
COCKBURNE
STRATFORD
MILLSFIELD
ERROL
NORTHUMBERLAND
STARK
LANCASTER
PAULSBURG
SUCCESS
MAYNES-BOROUGH
DALTON
KILKENNY
DURAND
SHELBURNE
WHITEFIELD
JEFFERSON
LITTLETON
BRETON WOODS
LYMAN
BETHLEHEM
GUNTH-WAITE
BATH
FRANCONIA
ADAMS
LANDAFF
CHATHAM
LINCOLN
COVENTRY
BARTLETT
CONWAY
PEELING
PIERMONT
WARREN
BURTON
EATON
ORFORD
ELLS-WORTH
WENT-WORTH
THORNTON
LIME
DOR-CHESTER
RUMNEY
CAMPTON
SANDWICH
OSSIPEE GORE
HANOVER
GROTON
PLYMOUTH
MOULTONBOROUGH
CANAAN
HEB-RON
LEBANON
ORANGE
BRIDG-WATER
MEREDITH
WOLFES-BOROUGH
ENFIELD
GRAFTON
PLAINFIELD
DANBURY
GRANTHAM
SPRING-FIELD
WILMOT
NEW CHESTER
SANBORNTON
CORNISH
MILTON
CROYDEN
NEW LONDON
ANDOVER
GILMANTON
CLAREMONT
NEWPORT
NORTHFIELD
SALISBURY
BARNSTEAD
FARMING-TON
FISHERS-FIELD
SUTTON
ROCHESTER
UNITY
BOSCAWEN
PITTS-FIELD
BARRINGTON
ACWORTH
WARNER
CONCORD
EPSOM
NORTH-WOOD
BRAD-FORD
LANG-DON
HILLS-BOROUGH
HENNIKER
PEMBROKE
MAD-BUR
ALLENS-TOWN
DEERFIELD
BOW
LEE
DURHAM
NEW-CASTLE
WALPOLE
STODDARD
DEERING
WEARE
DUNBARTON
NEW-MARKET
NEW-HAMP-TON
ANTRIM
GOFFSTOWN
CANDIA
EXETER
STODDARD
HANCOCK
FRANCES-TOWN
NEW BOSTON
BEDFORD
CHESTER
LONDONDERRY
PACKERSFIELD
KEENE
DUBLIN
AMHERST
HAMP
SWANZEY
JAFFREY
SHARON
MIL-FORD
HOLLES
PELHAM
CHESTER-FIELD
RICH-MOND
FITZWILLIAM
RINDGE
NEW IPSWICH
MASON
HINS-DALE
SALEM

MAP 16. FEDERALIST RECOVERY, 1805–1809

This map shows the effect of antiembargo propaganda and, to a certain degree, of the embargo itself in stimulating Federalist voters to return to the polls and even in converting some Republicans. It is based on (1) votes in the gubernatorial elections of 1805 and 1809, the congressional election of 1808, and the presidential election of 1808, as reported in the New Hampshire newspapers; (2) votes in the legislatures of 1808 and 1809 on party issues as recorded in the journals; (3) the senatorial election of 1809 in the state house of representatives.

These data show that sixty-five towns voted consistently Federalist throughout this period. Fifty-four of these had voted Federalist ever since 1800; they were the bedrock of the Federalist party—Exeter, Somersworth, Londonderry, Peterborough, Keene, Hanover, Plymouth, and so forth.

Seventy towns voted Republican throughout this period, in spite of the embargo. Of these, thirty-nine had been Republican since 1800—Portsmouth, Deerfield, Canterbury, Weare, Goffstown, Piermont, Meredith, and so forth; these were the basis of Republican strength.

There were fifty-six towns, however, which changed their voting pattern from Republican to Federalist during this period and helped elect Federalist congressmen in 1808 and a Federalist governor in 1809. Thirty-four of these had been Federalist before 1805; they now returned to their allegiance. Even such Republican strongholds as Atkinson and Madbury wavered.

Amazingly, six towns reversed the trend and changed from Federalist to Republican during these embargo years—for no discernible reason. They were Northampton, Effingham, New Chester, Hebron, Sandown, and Raymond.

Essentially, there were about sixty towns in New Hampshire where the parties were so evenly matched that major shifts in public opinion sent them over to one side and back again to the other. Their fence-jumping was largely responsible for the shifting majorities in the state legislature.

This map also shows the boundaries of the state senatorial districts in 1809 when districts III, IV, VI, IX, X, XI, and XII elected Federalist senators. The latter four districts, in the Connecticut Valley and the Frontier, together with district III in the lower Merrimack Valley, nearly always elected Federalists, while districts I and V in the Old Colony and VII and VIII in the Merrimack Valley consistently voted Republican. Districts II, IV, and VI were the "swingers," whose change of opinion determined the political majorities in the state senate. Federalists controlled the senate until 1803, Republicans from 1804 to 1808, Federalists in 1809, Republicans again from 1810 to 1812, Federalists from 1813 to 1815, and Republicans from 1816 to 1820 and beyond.

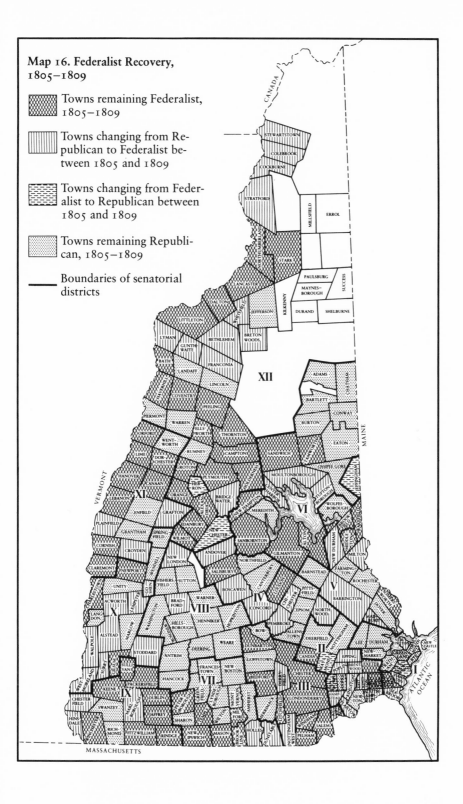

Map 16. Federalist Recovery,
1805–1809

Towns remaining Federalist,
1805–1809

Towns changing from Re-
publican to Federalist between 1805 and 1809

Towns changing from Federalist to Republican between
1805 and 1809

Towns remaining Republi-
can, 1805–1809

Boundaries of senatorial
districts

MAP 17. REPUBLICAN RECOVERY, 1810–1812

This map shows the means by which the Republicans regained control of the state government in 1810 and retained it until 1813. The data used are the statistics for the gubernatorial elections of the three years as reported in the newspapers, the roll-call votes on party issues in the house of representatives, taken from the journals and the party affiliations in the senate. Senatorial districts III, IX, XI and XII remained Federalist for all these years, while districts I, II, IV, V, VI, VII and VIII were consistently Republican. District X was Federalist in 1810 and 1812, Republican in 1811.

Seventy-two towns remained consistently Federalist during those three years. Nineteen of these seventy-two had been converted to Federalism after 1805; the remainder had been Federalist since before 1800.

Two towns, populous Durham in the Old Colony and newly settled Jefferson on the far northern frontier, reversed the trend and converted to Federalism in 1810. Durham had been a Republican town since 1805. Six other towns—Kensington, Poplin, Madbury, Wakefield, Peterborough, and Piermont—switched back and forth throughout this period.

Seventy-four towns remained consistently Republican throughout this period. Sixty-eight of them had been Republican since 1800. Note again that they were concentrated around Portsmouth in the Old Colony, in the upper Merrimack Valley, and around Lake Winnepesaukee.

Forty-four towns switched from Federalist to Republican after 1809. Twenty-five of these had shifted the other way after 1805. Most of these "swing towns" which made the difference in closely contested elections were in the southwest corner of the Old Colony, around the shores of Lake Winnepesaukee and in the hill country between the Merrimack and Connecticut valleys. They made the state Republican from 1810 to 1813.

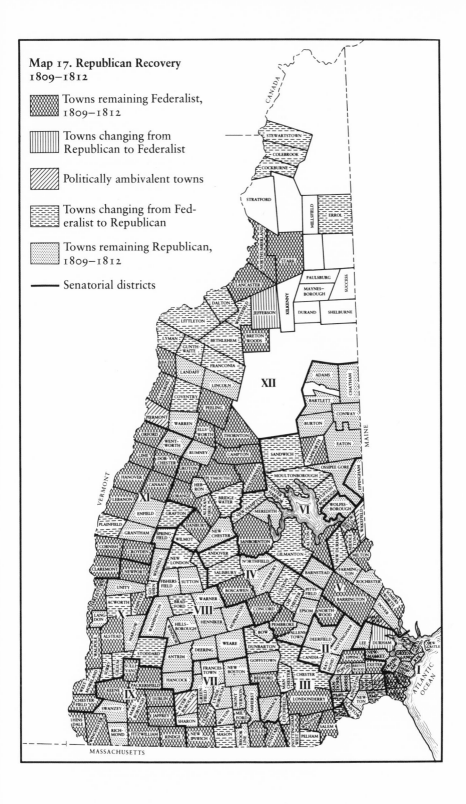

Map 17. Republican Recovery
1809–1812

Towns remaining Federalist,
1809–1812

Towns changing from
Republican to Federalist

Politically ambivalent towns

Towns changing from Fed-
eralist to Republican

Towns remaining Republican,
1809–1812

Senatorial districts

MAP 18. FEDERALIST WAR GAINS, 1812–1813

This map shows the political changes in the memberships of the legislatures in 1812 and 1813. Political affiliations of the members were determined by five test votes in 1812 and eleven in 1813. The voting was remarkably uniform on these issues and readily disclosed the party connections of the members. Data taken from the house journals.

Eighty-two towns elected Federalist representatives in both 1812 and 1813. Eighteen of these towns had voted Federalist in 1810 but had already switched allegiance by 1812. The remaining sixty-four—Exeter, Londonderry, Somersworth, Rindge, Keene, Hanover, Plymouth, and so forth—were hard-core Federalist.

Seventy-six towns elected Republican representatives both in 1812 and 1813. Some sixty of these—Portsmouth, Rochester, Weare, Richmond, Enfield, and so forth—had been consistently Republican since 1805.

Four towns elected Federalists in 1812 and Republicans in 1813—a strange reversal of the trend.

Thirty-eight towns, gathered into thirty-three constituencies, changed from Republican representatives in 1812 to Federalist in 1813. These were the towns that turned against the war policy of the national and state governments.

The Federalists not only had a majority of fifteen to twenty votes in the house of representatives during these years but enjoyed control of the senate, where the balance changed from 7–5 in favor of the Republicans in 1812 to 9–3 for the Federalists in 1813. Districts II, IV, V, and VI reversed their majorities to accomplish this result.

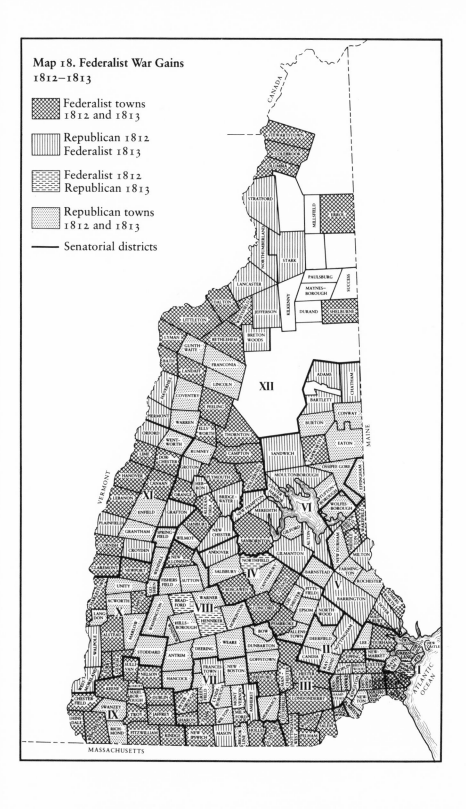

Map 18. Federalist War Gains
1812–1813

Federalist towns
1812 and 1813

Republican 1812
Federalist 1813

Federalist 1812
Republican 1813

Republican towns
1812 and 1813

— Senatorial districts

MAP 19. REPUBLICAN TRIUMPH, 1816

This map illustrates the process by which the Republican party returned to power in New Hampshire in 1816 and remained in control until the Federalist party had disappeared as an organized opposition.

It is based on the town votes in the gubernatorial election of 1816 as reported in the newspapers and two votes on distinct party issues in the house of representatives—the bill to amend the charter of Dartmouth College and the bill to repeal the Federalist Judiciary Act of 1813.

Ninety-five towns gave a majority of their votes for William Plumer in the March town meetings and also elected representatives who voted for the Dartmouth Act and the Judiciary Repeal bill. (Nine representatives of ten Plumer towns voted for one of the bills and were absent for the other.) Seventy of these towns were traditionally Republican towns from 1800 on.

Eighty-seven towns are shown here as Federalist. Most of them voted for Sheafe and elected representatives who voted against one or both of the bills, although there are some variations—Hanover and Gilmanton representatives divided on the college bill: one for, one against. Most of these were hard-core Federalist towns, although some, such as Barrington and Walpole, had defected during the earlier period of Republican ascendancy, 1805–8.

It was the twenty-nine towns changing from Federalist to Republican which provided the Republican majorities in the house of representatives from 1816 on. They also provided the votes for Republican recovery of senatorial districts IV and V. Together with the four districts which they normally controlled and districts XI and XII, where their minority candidates were elected by convention of the two houses, the Republicans gained an 8–4 advantage in the senate.

Federalists never again increased their strength in state elections; in fact, each year their votes decreased until by 1820 they had virtually disappeared.

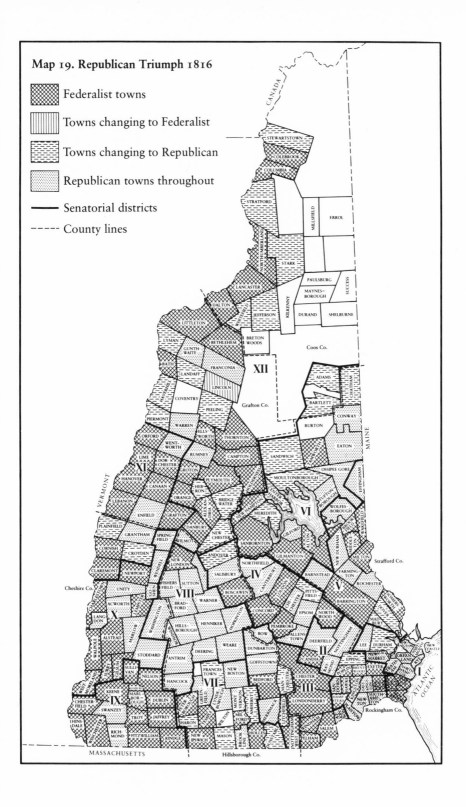

Map 19. Republican Triumph 1816

Federalist towns

Towns changing to Federalist

Towns changing to Republican

Republican towns throughout

Senatorial districts

County lines

MAP 20. TOLERATION ACT, 1819

The so-called Toleration Act of 1819, which was actually an act to amend the law of 1791 authorizing towns to collect taxes for the support of ministers and churches, elicited four roll-call votes in the house of representatives before it finally passed. Each of the 192 representatives, elected from 201 towns, responded to roll call on at least one of these occasions. (Of the towns entitled to elect representatives to the legislature, 6 failed to do so in 1819). Assuming that each representative voiced the majority opinion of his constituents, which in most cases is a valid assumption, we have in this map a pretty complete survey of popular opinion on the question of religious toleration.

The first roll-call vote was taken on an amendment offered in the house to the bill brought down from the senate. It passed, 96–88, with nearly all those in favor voting consistently for the passage of the bill.

The second roll call came on the amendment that was introduced by opponents of the bill as a diversionary tactic. It was defeated by almost exactly the same margin, 87–96, but actually by a different line-up of towns. Nine opponents of toleration and five proponents voted against the majorities of their colleagues on this amendment. Most of the towns indicated on the map as not consistently opposed to or in favor of toleration were those which were apparently misled by this amendment.

The third roll call came on the motion to pass the bill to third reading, which passed 95–88. This was probably the most accurate measure of the strength of the two sides: note that there were only *seven* votes difference.

The final roll call was requested on a motion at third reading to postpone the bill until the next session, which was defeated, 79–103. Ten members failed to answer this roll call. Their previous votes indicate that five of them were opponents and four were proponents; the tenth was the speaker, Matthew Harvey of Hopkinton—a proponent. Comparison with previous votes would indicate that proponents of the bill gained 7 or 8 votes from the other side and opponents lost about the same number. Actually, 11 representatives who had voted almost consistently against the bill on the three previous roll calls opposed the postponement on this final vote. Either they experienced a genuine conversion or recognized the futility of further opposition. One representative (from Whitefields), however, shifted from consistent support to opposition on this last roll call. After the postponement was defeated, the bill was enacted without further opposition.

Comparing this map with the previous political maps in this series is instructive in showing both the degree to which religious freedom was still a political issue and the degree to which it had ceased to be. Traditionally, the Federalist party had been associated with religious conservatism and the established connection between church and state, while the Republicans had proclaimed themselves to be the friends of religious liberty. In this showdown vote in 1819, a goodly number of towns followed the "party line"—Exeter, Londonderry, Peterborough, Rindge, Keene, Claremont, Hanover, Bath, Plymouth, Wakefield, and others which had been unshakeably Federalist voted against the Toleration Act, while Newington, Atkinson, Hawke, Madbury, Henniker, Weare, Swanzey, Piermont, Conway, and Meredith, which had been unswervingly Republican, followed the script by voting for toleration. However, there are many exceptions to this traditional pattern, some of them startling. Barrington, Gilmanton, Sandwich, Holderness, and Charlestown—old Federalist towns—voted for the Toleration Act, while such Republican strongholds as Rye, Canterbury, Francestown, Richmond, and Lyndeborough voted to maintain the establishment. Especially interesting is the way the issue split the larger towns. Portsmouth voted 3–2 for the Toleration Act, while Chester, Rochester, Deerfield, and Concord gave a vote to each side. The Rockingham Republican enclave was broken up by Portsmouth's division and the defection of Rye, Greenland, and Stratham, while the orthodoxy of

(continued on page 400)

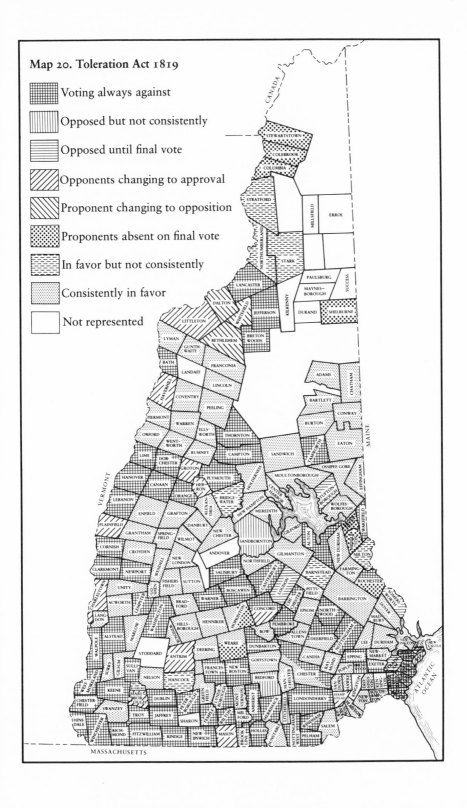

Map 20. Toleration Act 1819

- Voting always against
- Opposed but not consistently
- Opposed until final vote
- Opponents changing to approval
- Proponent changing to opposition
- Proponents absent on final vote
- In favor but not consistently
- Consistently in favor
- Not represented

Boscawen, Warner, Francestown, and Lyndeborough demonstrated a loosening of the Republican grip on the Merrimack Valley. In the Winnepesaukee region, the Connecticut Valley, and the Frontier, however, the friends of toleration gained more than they lost elsewhere. Six of the 10 representatives whose switch on the last vote brought the majority up to 103 came from these areas. If the vote on the Toleration Act was political, it proclaims a disintegration of older patterns and a groping toward new alignments.

MAP 21. POPULATION IN 1820

This map, when compared with Map 2, illustrates in detail the 190 percent increase in population which took place in New Hampshire during this forty-five-year period. It is instructive to notice the changes that occurred in the different categories. In 1775, only one town, Portsmouth, had more than 4,000 inhabitants, and only one other, Londonderry, had more than 2,000. Forty-five years later, Portsmouth was still the only town with more than 4,000, but the number with more than 2,000 had risen to twenty-four, and three of these, Londonderry, Gilmanton and Sanbornton had more than 3,000. The category of 1,500–2,000 had only four towns in 1775, but thirty in 1820. Eleven towns came in the 1,000–1,500 class in 1775; fifty-three had reached that status by 1820. The number of towns in the 500–1,000 group almost exactly matched at the beginning and end of this period, forty-eight in 1775, forty-nine in 1820, although of course most of them were different towns. There were actually fewer of the 250–500 class in 1820 (twenty-four) than there had been in 1775 (thirty), while the number of towns with fewer than 250 people had shrunk from fifty-eight in 1775 to sixteen in 1820. Of these sixteen, only three had had any settlers at all in 1775.

Most of New Hampshire's towns grew during this period—some of them phenomenally. In spite of being divided and sometimes divided again, Rochester, Amherst, Gilmanton, New Chester, and Charlestown had more people within their narrow borders in 1820 than they had had in their larger territories in 1775. In all of the area west of the Merrimack River and north of Lake Winnepesaukee there had been only three towns with as many as a thousand occupants in 1775. By 1820, the great majority of these towns had at least doubled their population, while many which had only been charter names on a map before the Revolution were now thriving settlements. Only in the agricultural towns of the Old Colony had growth begun to slow down; here were at least a dozen little towns which had fewer people in 1820 than in 1775.

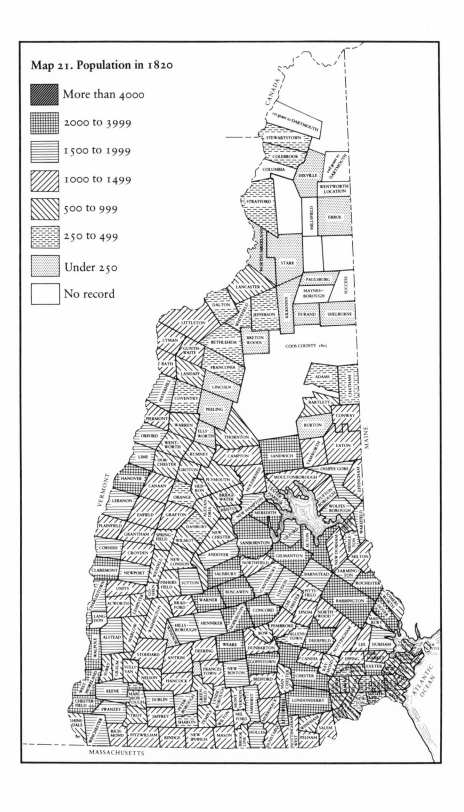

Map 21. Population in 1820

More than 4000

2000 to 3999

1500 to 1999

1000 to 1499

500 to 999

250 to 499

Under 250

No record

NOTES

CHAPTER I

1. The epigraph is drawn from Belknap's *The History of New Hampshire*, 3 vols., 2d ed. (Boston, 1813), 3:191. William Plumer, "Autobiography," William Plumer Papers, Library of Congress, Washington, D.C., pp. 15–16.

2. Richard Francis Upton, *Revolutionary New Hampshire* (Hanover, N.H., 1936), p. 211.

3. Nathaniel Adams, *Annals of Portsmouth* (Portsmouth, N.H., 1825), pp. 276–78.

4. Matthew Patten, *The Diary of Matthew Patten of Bedford, N.H., 1754–1788* (Concord, N.H., 1903), p. 467.

5. Upton, *Revolutionary New Hampshire*, p. 105.

6. Belknap, *New Hampshire*, 3:177. The figure for 1767 is that of an actual census taken by the towns upon order of the royal governor. The figure for 1780 is Belknap's estimate.

7. Ibid., p. 191.

8. Timothy Dwight, *Travels in New England and New York*, 4 vols., 2d ed. (London, 1823), 4:162. This statement was written in 1813. It is a curious fact that New Hampshire's sectional divisions in early times, so obvious to contemporary observers, were not apparent to such later historians as George Barstow, J. N. McClintock, E. D. Sanborn, and Nathan Batchellor. Other lines of division, such as those between political parties and between proslavery and antislavery sentiment, were more obvious in their day.

9. *Documents and Records Relating to the Province [Towns and State] of New Hampshire* (1623–1800), 39 vols., hereafter cited as *New Hampshire State Papers*. Volumes 1–10 were edited by Nathaniel Bouton, volumes 11–18 by I. W. Hammond, and volumes 19–31 by A. S. Batchellor. Most were published at Concord, although volume 7 was published at Nashua and volumes 20–22 at Manchester. Volumes used in this study are: 1,7,8,9,10,11,12,13,18,20,21,22,27,29. The population statistics in this regional survey are computed from the census of 1790, volume 13 (Concord, N.H., 1884), pp. 767–74.

10. The statement of relative wealth is based on tax assessments in 1768. This may not have been an accurate criterion twelve years later, but it is assumed that relative positions would not have diminished between the Old Colony and other regions. Although a great deal of ratable estate was created outside the Old Colony during these years, it is also true that the intangible wealth of the investors in Portsmouth, which was not subject to taxation, would have increased in proportion. See the seventh volume of the *New Hampshire State Papers* (Nashua, N.H., 1873), 7:166–67, for the tax lists of 1768.

11. John Adams, *Diary and Autobiography of John Adams*, ed. Lyman H. Butterfield, 4 vols. (Cambridge, Mass., 1961), 1:355. Jere B. Daniell, *Experiment in Republicanism: New Hampshire Politics and the American Revolution, 1741–1794* (Cambridge, Mass., 1970), though somewhat burdened with a debatable thesis, is an interesting analysis of the transformation from royal colony to republican state government.

12. Nathaniel Bouton, *History of Concord* (Concord, N.H., 1856), chap. 7.

13. Edward Parker, *History of Londonderry* (Boston, 1851), pp. 97–99.

14. *New Hampshire State Papers* (1873), 7:370–71.

15. Ibid., pp. 665–69. See also Daniell, *Experiment in Republicanism*, p. 107. In the

lawful provincial assembly of 1775, there were 37 members representing 35 towns, fewer than 26 percent of the incorporated places in the colony. At the contemporary fourth provincial congress there were 153 delegates representing 113 towns, nearly 80 percent of the total number.

16. Ibid., p. 701.

17. Edward Boylston, *Hillsborough County Congresses* (Amherst, N.H., 1884).

18. *New Hampshire State Papers* (Concord, N.H., 1877), 10:398–401.

19. Donald B. Cole, *Jacksonian Democracy in New Hampshire* (Cambridge, Mass., 1970), also stresses regionalism within the state as a factor influencing political and social developments, but he divides New Hampshire into eight sections rather than the four that I have suggested. This helps to eliminate some of the internal conflict within each section that I have mentioned, but the basic interpretation remains the same. All boundary lines are, of course, arbitrary. The ones that Cole has chosen help to explain voting patterns and social changes in the Jacksonian era. Mine serve equally well to identify the developments of an earlier and simpler period. See appendix, Map 1, "Regions in 1775."

CHAPTER 2

1. The epigraph is from a letter to George Wythe, "Thoughts on Government," in Charles Francis Adams, ed., *Works of John Adams*, 10 vols. (Boston, 1851), 4:200.

2. Richard Francis Upton, *Revolutionary New Hampshire* (Hanover, N.H.), 1936, pp. 73–74.

3. Worthington Chauncey Ford et al., eds., *Journals of the Continental Congress*, 34 vols. (Washington, D.C., 1904–37), 3:319.

4. J. F. Colby, *Manual of the Constitution of New Hampshire*, rev. ed. (Concord, N.H., 1912), pp. 69–72. The record of the adoption of this constitution may be found in the journal of the so-called fifth provincial congress, printed in *New Hampshire State Papers* (Concord, N.H., 1884), 13:1–4. A facsimile of the original printed copy of the constitution is included in the appendix of *New Hampshire State Papers* (Concord, N.H., 1882), 11:738.

5. *New Hampshire State Papers* (Concord, N.H., 1874), 8:341.

6. Ibid. (Concord, N.H., 1877), 10:234. The Grafton Address was probably written by Bezaleel Woodward, a professor at Dartmouth College and son-in-law of Eleazer Wheelock, the founder of the college.

7. Colby, *Manual*, p. 7.

8. *New Hampshire State Papers* (1874), 8:11, 18–19, 23–24, 28, 50, 57, 139. As a single example, John Hurd of Haverhill was elected a delegate to the fifth provincial congress, then appointed by the legislature to be councillor from Grafton County, county treasurer, recorder of deeds and conveyances, and justice of the inferior court of common pleas. See *Historical New Hampshire* 22 (Summer 1968): 31–32.

9. *New Hampshire State Papers* (1882), 11:328.

10. Ibid. (Nashua, N.H., 1873), 7:657–60.

11. The population figures for 1775 are taken from New Hampshire Historical Society, *Collections* 1 (1824): 231–35. The membership roll of the assembly in 1775 is printed in *New Hampshire State Papers* (1873), 7:370–71. See appendix, Map 3, "Last Provincial Assembly."

12. The membership roll of the fourth provincial congress is found in *New Hampshire State Papers* (1873), 7:665–69. See appendix, Map 4, "Fourth Provincial Congress."

13. Jeremy Belknap, *The History of New Hampshire*, 3 vols, 2d ed. (Boston, 1813), 2:308.

14. Frank Sanborn, *New Hampshire: An Epitome of Popular Government* (Cambridge, Mass., 1904), p. 221.

15. "Grafton County Address," *New Hampshire State Papers* (1877), 10:229–35. See also appendix, Map 5, "Fifth Provincial Congress."

16. Colby, *Manual*, pp. 21–22, 282. In 1943 the house reached a membership of 443, making it larger than the House of Representatives. A constitutional amendment subsequently reduced its membership to not more than 400 nor less than 375. Forty-fifth in population among the fifty states, New Hampshire has by far the largest state legislature.

17. *New Hampshire State Papers* (1874), 8:775. The possibility exists that this plan for a constitutional convention, by complying with demands made by a group of delegates from western towns who had met at Hanover in June 1777, may have been an honest attempt to woo the Connecticut Valley back into allegiance toward Exeter. At any rate, this Hanover convention had laid down the classical formula for constitution making by delegates elected for that purpose only. See New Hampshire State Library, Legislative Reference Service, *New Hampshire Constitutional Conventions* (Concord, N.H., 1956), p. 6.

18. *New Hampshire State Papers* (1874), 8:778.

19. Allan Nevins, *The American States during and after the Revolution* (New York, 1927), pp. 175, 183.

20. *New Hampshire State Papers* (1874), 8:778. See appendix, Map 6, "Constitutional Convention of 1778–79."

21. Colby, *Manual*, p. 79. This analysis is made from the membership rolls of the various bodies as follows: the constitutional convention of 1778 in Parker Lyon, ed., *New Hampshire Register* (Concord, N.H., 1852), pp. 18–21. This list was compiled by Lyon from town records and is consequently incomplete. The state legislature of 1778 in *New Hampshire State Papers* (1874), 8:766–67; note the absence of representatives from the Grafton County towns. The fifth provincial congress, 1775, in *New Hampshire State Papers* (1873), 7:690–93.

22. Colby, *Manual*, pp. 78–79.

23. The proposed constitution of 1779 is printed in Colby, *Manual*, pp. 80–84; *New Hampshire State Papers* (Concord, N.H., 1875), 9:837–42; New Hampshire Historical Society, *Collections* 4 (1834). A facsimile copy appears in *New Hampshire State Papers* (1882), vol. 11, appendix. In the absence of firm evidence, this statement about the authorship of the 1779 constitution is admittedly a leap in the dark—but it is a leap of faith. The few known facts about the 1778 convention are confusing. John Pickering, who strove valiantly to put more executive strength into the later constitution of 1784, may have led the party that made a similar effort in 1778, but at this time he was a delegate from Exeter, the center of the ruling oligarchy. There is also some evidence that Meshech Weare advocated a governor for New Hampshire, which would not be consistent with his leadership of the squirearchy. It is relatively clear, however, that the mercantile interests of Portsmouth, led by the Langdon brothers and George King, were beginning to reclaim authority from the Exeter politicians. On these points, see Jere B. Daniell, *Experiment in Republicanism* (Cambridge, Mass., 1970), pp. 136–45.

24. *New Hampshire State Papers* (1877), 10:333 ff.

25. Lawrence Shaw Mayo, "Jeremy Belknap's Apologue of the Hen at Pennycook," Colonial Society of Massachusetts, *Publications* 27 (1932): 31–34.

26. (Portsmouth) *New Hampshire Gazette*, August 17, 1779.

27. Massachusetts Historical Society, *Collections*, 5th series 2 (1877): 10.

28. Ibid., p. 168.

29. William Plumer, Jr., "Constitutions of New Hampshire," ms. in New Hampshire State Library, Concord, N.H.

30. Albert S. Batchellor, in George Willey, ed., *State Builders* (Manchester, N.H., 1903), p. 22.

31. *New Hampshire State Papers* (1874), 8:908.

32. Ibid., p. 897.

33. Ibid. (1875), 9:895n. See also New Hampshire State Library, *N.H. Constitutional Conventions*, p. 9. Seven more months were added to this total before the constitution went into effect, the whole period stretching from June 1781 to June 1784.

34. *New Hampshire State Papers* (1877), 10:398–401. See appendix, Map 7, "Constitutional Convention of 1781–83."

35. Edward Stackpole, *History of New Hampshire*, 4 vols. (New York, 1916) 2:235.

36. *New Hampshire State Papers* (1875), 9:845–52.

37. Colby, *Manual*, p. 96.

38. Ibid., p. 95.

39. Ibid., pp. 93–101. One of the seven hundred copies of this address and the proposed constitution of 1781, which were printed at Portsmouth and Exeter, is preserved in the Widener Library at Harvard University.

40. The proposed constitution of 1781 may be found in *New Hampshire State Papers* (1875), 9:852–77.

41. Colby, *Manual*, p. 99.

42. Upton, *Revolutionary New Hampshire*, p. 177.

43. Colby, *Manual*, pp. 97–98.

44. Stackpole, *New Hampshire*, 2:235.

45. Plumer's "Biographical Sketches," printed in *New Hampshire State Papers* (Concord, N.H., 1893), 22:840–41.

46. Reasoning from the record of how consistently Concord voted against a strong executive, it is not implausible to conjecture that Timothy Walker, the Concord delegate, led the fight against Pickering and Sewall. However, Walker was later an advocate of the federal constitution.

47. Jeremy Belknap to Ebenezer Hazard, November 16, 1781, Massachusetts Historical Society, *Collections*, 5th series 2 (1877): 111. Belknap carried on a voluminous correspondence with the postmaster general in Philadelphia.

48. Joseph Dow, *History of Hampton, N.H.*, 2 vols. (Salem, Mass., 1893), 1:267.

49. *New Hampshire Gazette*, January 5, 1782.

50. Ibid., December 15, 1781.

51. *Concord Town Records, 1732–1820* (Concord, N.H., 1894), pp. 198–99.

52. Salma Hale, *Annals of the Town of Keene* (Keene, N.H., 1851), pp. 60–63. Daniel Newcomb's influence and Keene's opposition to the Vermont intrigues, which were rife in nearly all of the neighboring towns, probably accounted for this vote.

53. This endorsement is written on the back of the copy preserved in the Widener Library at Harvard University.

54. Colby, *Manual*, p. 86n.

55. Massachusetts Historical Society, *Collections*, 5th series 2 (1877): 161.

56. Belknap, *New Hampshire*, 2:336.

57. The draft of 1782 may be found in *New Hampshire State Papers* (1875), 9:882–95.

58. The constitution of 1783–84 may be found in *New Hampshire State Papers* (1859), 9:896–919, and in Colby, *Manual*, pp. 101–23. Copies of the original printed edition (Portsmouth, N.H., 1783) are preserved in the state libraries of New Hampshire and Massachusetts, the Widener Library at Harvard University, and elsewhere.

59. Fortunately, the convention felt strong enough to resist the demand made by some towns that the entire executive power be left in the hands of the legislature and the interim committees of safety.

60. Massachusetts Historical Society, *Collections*, 5th series 2 (1877): 161.

61. Ibid., p. 113, Hazard to Belknap, December 18, 1781. Hazard thought that he "could live very comfortably" under the 1781 constitution.

62. Gaspar Bacon, "The State Constitution, 1777–1780," in Albert Bushnell Hart, ed., *The Commonwealth History of Massachusetts*, 5 vols. (New York, 1929), 3:189. The identical guarantee of civil liberties in the two constitutions had the simultaneous effect of emancipating the few remaining slaves in both states.

63. Samuel Eliot Morison, "The Struggle over the Adoption of the Constitution of Massachusetts," Massachusetts Historical Society, *Proceedings* 50 (1917): 400–401.

CHAPTER 3

1. The epigraph is from *New Hampshire State Papers* (Concord, N.H., 1883), 12:765.

2. Otis Hammond, ed., *Letters and Papers of Major-General John Sullivan*, New Hampshire Historical Society, *Collections* 15 (1939): 357.

3. *New Hampshire State Papers* (Manchester, N.H., 1891), 20:152.

4. Ibid., pp. 697–99.

5. Allan Nevins, *The American States during and after the Revolution* (New York, 1927), p. 651n.

6. New Hampshire Historical Society, *Collections* 15 (1939): 355 ff.

7. Nathaniel Adams, *Annals of Portsmouth* (Portsmouth, N.H., 1825), pp. 268, 275.

8. Samuel Bemis, *Jay's Treaty: A Study in Commerce and Diplomacy* (New York, 1923), p. 103n.

9. (Portsmouth) *New Hampshire Gazette*, January 6, 1786.

10. New Hampshire Historical Society, *Collections* 15 (1939): 354–55.

11. Massachusetts Historical Society, *Collections*, 5th series 2 (1877): 282. New Hampshire was the only state that defined personal belief in British sovereignty as treasonable. See Robert McCluer Calhoon, *The Loyalists in Revolutionary America* (New York, 1965), pp. 306 ff.

12. *New Hampshire State Papers* (Concord, N.H., 1882), 11:564, 20:217.

13. Salma Hale, *Annals of the Town of Keene* (Keene, N.H., 1851), pp. 66–67.

14. Wilbur Henry Siebert, *The Loyalist Refugees of New Hampshire* (Columbus, Ohio, 1916), pp. 22–23.

15. *New Hampshire State Papers* (1882), 11:317.

16. Jeremy Belknap, *The History of New Hampshire*, 3 vols., 2d ed. (Boston, 1813), p. 326.

17. Richard Francis Upton, *Revolutionary New Hampshire* (Hanover, N.H., 1936), p. 136.

18. Ibid., p. 137. The equivalent of $1,331,590 in uninflated dollars.

19. A motion to compel payment of overdue taxes passed the legislature on December 26, 1786, by a vote of 39–27, with nearly all the negative votes coming from towns in the interior parts of the Merrimack and Connecticut valleys and the Frontier (*New Hampshire State Papers*, 20:761–62).

20. *New Hampshire State Papers* (1883), 12:406–9.

21. Ibid. (Concord, N.H., 1884), 13:122.

22. Ibid. (1882), 11:502–3.

23. Ibid. (1891), 20:506, 531. This arrangement gave the western towns the equivalent of a 66$^2/_3$ percent discount. See *New Hampshire Gazette*, June 3, 1785. Reconciliation was also encouraged by offices conferred upon former rebels (Bezaleel Woodward was commissioned a justice of the peace) and by the fact that the Vermont assembly had renounced

jurisdiction over the east bank of the Connecticut River (Jere B. Daniell, *Experiment in Republicanism* [Cambridge, Mass., 1970], pp. 158–62).

24. *New Hampshire State Papers* (1884), 13:118, 578.

25. Upton, *Revolutionary New Hampshire*, p. 143.

26. W. C. Ford, ed., *Journals of the Continental Congress*, 34 vols. (Washington, D.C., 1933), 29:767.

27. Nevins, *American States*, p. 477.

28. Upton, *Revolutionary New Hampshire*, p. 137.

29. *New Hampshire State Papers* (1891), 20:666.

30. *American State Papers, Finance*, 38 vols. (Washington, D.C., 1832), 1:29.

31. *New Hampshire Gazette*, June 3, 1785.

32. Upton, *Revolutionary New Hampshire*, p. 141.

33. Ibid., p. 142. New Hampshire's proportion of the "old issue," which was entirely collected and paid into the treasury after 1780, was $5,200,000. This measured approximately the amount which circulated in the state.

34. *New Hampshire State Papers* (Concord, N.H., 1874), 8:907. For an excellent survey of revolutionary finance see E. James Ferguson, *The Power of the Purse: A History of American Public Finance, 1776–1790* (Chapel Hill, University of North Carolina Press, 1961). See also Merrill Jensen, *The New Nation* (New York, 1950), chaps. 15, 16.

35. Matthew Patten, *The Diary of Matthew Patten of Bedford, N.H., 1754–1788* (Concord, N.H., 1903), p. 433.

36. Jane Marcou, *Life of Jeremy Belknap, D.D.* (New York, 1847), pp. 33 ff.

37. Massachusetts Historical Society, *Collections*, 5th series 2 (1877): 267.

38. Jensen, *New Nation*, pp. 52–56. Sullivan was himself a candidate for the newly created post of secretary of war, but was defeated by the bitter opposition of Sam Adams.

39. Ibid., pp. 48–49.

40. Upton, *Revolutionary New Hampshire*, pp. 136–37.

41. *New Hampshire State Papers* (1874), 8:913. See appendix, Map 8, "Vote on the Legal Tender Act of 1781."

42. *New Hampshire State Papers* (1874), 8:907; Upton, *Revolutionary New Hampshire*, p. 143.

43. Ralph Harlow, *Economic Conditions in Massachusetts during the American Revolution*, Colonial Society of Massachusetts, *Publications* 20 (1920): 183. See also William Plumer, "Autobiography," William Plumer Papers, Library of Congress, p. 21.

44. *New Hampshire State Papers* (1883), 12:765.

45. Ibid.

46. Bemis, *Jay's Treaty*, pp. 21 ff.

47. Copied in *New Hampshire Gazette*, August 5, 1785.

48. Upton, *Revolutionary New Hampshire*, p. 157.

49. *New Hampshire State Papers* (1874), 8:898.

50. Upton, *Revolutionary New Hampshire*, p. 158.

51. Nevins, *American States*, p. 642.

52. *New Hampshire State Papers* (1891), 20:108, 197, 201, 215, 356.

53. Ibid., pp. 385, 416.

54. Maurice Robinson, *A History of Taxation in New Hampshire* (New York, 1903), p. 135.

55. Lawrence S. Kaplan, *Colonies into Nation: American Diplomacy, 1763–1801* (New York, 1972), p. 156. See also Jensen, *New Nation*, p. 297.

56. Bemis, *Jay's Treaty*, p. 24.

57. *New Hampshire State Papers* (1891), 20:504.

58. Ibid., p. 419.

59. Ibid., pp. 502, 514, 518.

60. Ibid., pp. 502–4.

61. When Dr. Jeremy Belknap announced that his *History of New Hampshire* could be had "in boards," his Dover parishioners asked him how many boards he wanted for a copy.

62. *New Hampshire State Papers* (1884), 13:341.

63. Ibid. (1891), 20:625.

64. Article signed "Independence" in *New Hampshire Gazette*, March 27, 1784.

65. Protest of a Portsmouth merchant, ibid., February 3, 1786.

66. *New Hampshire State Papers* (1891), 20:760.

67. Otis Hammond, *The Mason Title and Its Relations to New Hampshire and Massachusetts* (Worcester, Mass., 1916).

68. See petitions and protests from the inhabitants of Marlow to the Masonian Proprietors in *New Hampshire State Papers* (Concord, N.H., 1896), 27:465–68.

69. Ibid. (1883), 12:575.

70. Ibid. (Concord, N.H., 1896), 29:334.

71. Plumer, "Autobiography" (LC), p. 22. For interesting comments about Nathaniel Peabody as a land speculator, see Harriet S. Lacy, "Nathaniel Peabody Papers," *Historical New Hampshire* 22 (Summer 1968): 39 ff.

72. See petitions printed in *New Hampshire State Papers* (1882), 11:319 (from Chester), 484 (from Hawke, now Danville) (1883), 12:93 (Hampstead), 479 (Londonderry) (1884), 13:408 (from Sandown).

73. *New Hampshire Gazette*, May 27, 1785.

74. *New Hampshire State Papers* (Manchester, N.H., 1890), 18:767–69.

75. Ibid., 20:525; Plumer, "Autobiography" (LC), p. 23.

76. Hammond, *Mason Title; New Hampshire State Papers* (1891), 20:525, 660, 739, 779, 788; ibid. (Concord, N.H., 1896), 29:335–42.

77. Marcou, *Belknap*, p. 120.

78. Plumer, "Autobiography" (LC), pp. 22–23.

79. *New Hampshire State Papers* (1890), 18:721, 723.

80. For the law prescribing imprisonment for debt in New Hampshire in this period, see Peter J. Coleman, *Debtors and Creditors in America: Insolvency, Imprisonment for Debt, and Bankruptcy, 1607–1900* (Madison, 1974), chap. 5.

81. *New Hampshire State Papers* (1883), 12:54.

82. *New Hampshire Gazette*, May 20, 1785.

83. Ibid., October 7, 1785.

84. Ibid., October 14, 1785. "CRISIS," writing in the *New Hampshire Gazette* for July 20, 1786, remarked that "even leather buttons, when stamped with authority and funded with realities, will answer for internal commerce as well as silver and gold." Jensen, *New Nation*, p. 315.

85. *New Hampshire Gazette*, June 3, 1785.

86. (Portsmouth) *New Hampshire Mercury and General Advertiser*, June 21, 1785.

87. Plumer, "Autobiography" (LC), p. 23.

88. *New Hampshire Gazette*, June 10, 1785. In February 1785, Major General Sullivan urged the citizen-soldiers in New Hampshire's militia to manufacture their own uniforms and to avoid the purchase of foreign goods, which lowered the value of all property and left debtors at the mercy of their creditors. Jensen, *New Nation*, p. 283.

89. *New Hampshire Gazette*, October 5, 1786.

90. *New Hampshire State Papers* (1891), 20:434, 445, 502, 518.

91. Plumer, "Autobiography" (LC), pp. 22–23.

92. Belknap, *New Hampshire*, 2:356.

93. *New Hampshire Gazette*, May 25, 1786.

94. *New Hampshire State Papers* (1891), 20:450; Plumer, "Autobiography" (LC), p. 382; Massachusetts Historical Society, *Collections*, 5th series 2 (1877): 423.

95. Ibid., p. 433.

96. *New Hampshire Gazette*, May 25, 1786.

97. Plumer, "Autobiography" (LC), p. 24.

98. Ibid., p. 25.

99. *New Hampshire State Papers* (1891), 20:661. As a member of the council in 1784–85, Peabody had taken advantage of Meshech Weare's illness to get himself and his cronies appointed to lucrative offices (Daniell, *Experiment in Republicanism*, p. 189).

100. William Plumer, "Biographies," 5 vols., William Plumer Papers, New Hampshire Historical Society Library (Concord, N.H.), 5:307. Plumer to John Hale, October 14, 1786, Letters 1, William Plumer Papers, Library of Congress.

101. Joseph Dow, *History of Hampton, N.H.*, 2 vols. (Salem, Mass., 1893), 1:278.

102. Colonial Society of Massachusetts, *Publications* 11 (1893): 388.

103. This petition, dated September 28, 1784 is printed in *New Hampshire State Papers* (1883), 12:173–74. See editor's note. Hanover voted against the paper money proposal of 1786.

104. *New Hampshire State Papers* (1882), 11:122–27. A careful study of the numerous petitions for paper money printed in these volumes indicates that while the soft-money party was strong and strident, it was hopelessly divided. It included ruined gentlemen whose debts might be drowned in a flood of paper, baffled farmers who honestly wished to discharge their debts but had not the specie, and simpletons who demanded paper currency so "that this State may never More be looked upon as Inferior to the other States in the Union." The amount of paper requested ranged from just enough to liquidate state securities to multiplied millions. Some wanted it to be a comprehensive legal tender; others a tender only for taxes or for executions on judgments. Some wanted it to carry 5 percent interest; others emphatically opposed interest bearing. Atkinson wanted to prohibit its depreciation by law and to punish counterfeiters with death; Bath wanted to establish an automatic rate of depreciation, reaching zero in twenty-five years. Stratham reasoned that if the bills were loaned out at 6 percent interest but carried only 3 percent, the difference of £3000 annually would pay all the current expenses of government and eliminate the necessity for taxes. Atkinson thought that the bills could be given to individuals who would promise, within two years, to pay the same sums in specie to the nation's foreign creditors and thus liquidate New Hampshire's proportion of the national debt. But the citizens of Goffstown were becomingly modest. They were positive about every feature of their petition except a method of redemption. This they were willing to "refer to your Honours wisdom or some future Assembly to determine, knowing that Time will Solve what we cant foresee."

105. Ibid., pp. 127–30. A curious feature of the plan provided for the collection of future taxes in six different kinds of tender, ranging from lumber to specie.

106. *New Hampshire State Papers* (1891), 20:699. This vote is incorrectly cited in Orin G. Libby, *Distribution of the Vote on the Federal Constitution* (Madison, 1894), p. 54.

107. Plumer, "Autobiography" (LC), pp. 27–28.

108. Charles H. Bell, *The Bench and Bar of New Hampshire* (Boston, 1894), pp. 96–97.

109. New Hampshire Historical Society, *Collections* 3 (1832): 119; Plumer to John Hale, September 20, 1786, Letters 1, Plumer Papers (LC).

110. *New Hampshire State Papers* (1891), 20:707.

111. Marcou, *Belknap*, p. 125.

112. New Hampshire Historical Society, *Collections* 3 (1832): 122.

113. Plumer, "Autobiography" (LC), p. 30.

114. Ibid.

115. Colonial Society of Massachusetts, *Publications* 11 (1893): 395.

116. *New Hampshire State Papers* (1890), 18:744.

117. New Hampshire Historical Society, *Collections* 15 (1939): 482.

118. Belknap, *New Hampshire*, 2:360.

119. New Hampshire Historical Society, *Collections* 15 (1939): 483.

120. Edward Parker, *History of Londonderry* (Boston, 1851), p. 118. Several contemporary accounts of the Exeter riot, including eyewitness stories by Jeremy Belknap, William Plumer, and Jeremiah Smith, have been preserved. They agree with each other remarkably well. See Colonial Society of Massachusetts, *Publications* 11 (1893): 390–96; Marcou, *Belknap*, pp. 124–25; Charles Brewster, *Rambles about Portsmouth*, 2 vols. (Portsmouth, N.H., 1869), 2:139–42; New Hampshire Historical Society, *Collections* 3 (1832): 122; *Historical Magazine* 15 (January 1869): 37–38. The legislative journals are printed in *New Hampshire State Papers* (1891), 20:671–713, and a few documents connected with the affair may be found there in volume 18 (1890).

121. *New Hampshire State Papers* (1891), 20:772.

122. See appendix, Map 9, "Paper Money."

123. New Hampshire Historical Society, *Collections* 15 (1939): 484–85.

124. Ibid.

CHAPTER 4

1. The epigraph comes from a letter, Belknap to Hazard, Massachusetts Historical Society, *Collections*, 5th series 2 (1877): 434.

2. Matthew Patten, *The Diary of Matthew Patten of Bedford, New Hampshire, 1754–1788* (Concord, N.H., 1903), p. 432. At an advanced age, Colonel Abiel Rolfe of Concord read a paper of reminiscences before the New Hampshire Historical Society in which he recalled the town meetings of his youth in the days of Isaac Hill. Although this was four decades later than the period with which I am dealing here, the institution had not changed much (Abiel Rolfe, *Recollections of Seventy Years in Concord, N.H.* [Penacook, N.H., 1901], pp. 37–41).

3. Massachusetts Historical Society, *Collections*, 5th series 2 (1877): 314.

4. Plumer to Hale, October 14 and 22, 1786, Letters 1, William Plumer Papers, Library of Congress; Jere B. Daniell, *Experiment in Republicanism* (Cambridge, Mass., 1970), p. 189.

5. Plumer to Hale, October 14, 1786, Letters 1, Plumer Papers (LC).

6. William Plumer, Jr., *Life of William Plumer* (Boston, 1856), pp. 67–71.

7. New Hampshire Historical Society, *Collections* 15 (1939): 348, 355.

8. Plumer to Hale, October 22, 1786, Letters 1, Plumer Papers (LC).

9. See Belknap's correspondence with Hazard in Massachusetts Historical Society, *Collections*, 5th series 2 (1877): 23.

10. When Sullivan was president of the state he complained constantly that although Langdon's salary had been paid, his was not. The fact is that Langdon had accepted payment of his salary in treasury orders on the impost fund with which he then paid the duties on his imported merchandise. Sullivan, not being a merchant, could extract no such comfort from an empty treasury. See John Taylor Gilman to John Sullivan, April 9, 1787, New Hampshire Manuscripts, Library of Congress.

11. *New Hampshire State Papers* (Concord, N.H., 1893), 22:824. Atkinson had been born George King. His name had been changed by the state legislature to permit him to inherit the Atkinson fortune.

12. Ibid. (Manchester, N.H., 1891), 20:307.

13. Massachusetts Historical Society, *Collections*, 5th series 2 (1877): 433.

14. New Hampshire Historical Society, *Collections* 15 (1939): 439. The available data from town records permit no certain conclusions, but do suggest the possibility that Sullivan was the favorite candidate of the conservatives, while the depressed towns pinned their hopes on Langdon.

15. William Plumer to Samuel Plumer, Jr., June 6, 1786, Letters 1, Plumer Papers (LC).

16. *New Hampshire State Papers* (Manchester, N.H., 1891), 20:617.

17. New Hampshire Historical Society, *Collections* 15 (1939): 454.

18. Massachusetts Historical Society, *Collections*, 5th series 2 (1877): 443, 446.

19. "Milices du Newhampshire, 1787," *New England Quarterly* 1 (1928): 82–83.

20. Edward Parker, *History of Londonderry*, p. 232.

21. *New Hampshire State Papers* (Concord, 1892), 21:41.

22. William Plumer to John Sullivan, March 14, 1787, Letters 1, Plumer Papers (LC).

23. Massachusetts Historical Society, *Collections*, 5th series 2 (1877): 434.

24. *New Hampshire State Papers* (1892), 21:305.

25. Ibid., p. 299.

26. Massachusetts Historical Society, *Collections*, 5th series 2 (1877): 308–15, 439.

27. *New Hampshire State Papers* (Manchester, N.H., 1890), 18:783–85.

28. Ibid. (1891), 20:783.

29. Ibid., p. 839.

30. Ibid. (1890), 18:773.

31. Ibid. (1891), 20:840–43.

32. Lawrence Shaw Mayo, *John Langdon of New Hampshire* (Concord, N.H., 1937), p. 196.

33. Ibid., p. 199. Forrest McDonald, *We, the People* (Chicago, 1958), p. 38, labels Langdon "the archtype of the personal property interest." In addition to real estate in Portsmouth, ships, warehouses, and wharves, Langdon owned shares in the Bank of North America and the Bank of Massachusetts, New Hampshire and Connecticut state securities, and $26,572.78 in continental securities.

34. *New Hampshire State Papers* (1892), 21:871–74.

35. Charles Beard, *An Economic Interpretation of the Constitution of the United States* (New York, 1914), p. 122. See also McDonald, *We, the People*, pp. 38–39.

36. Beard, *Economic Interpretation*, pp. 93–95; McDonald, *We, the People*, pp. 39–41. In analyzing Gilman's economic interests, McDonald overlooks the impact of his family connections.

37. *New Hampshire State Papers* (1892), 21:835.

38. Beard, *Economic Interpretation*, p. 93. The French chargé d'affaires at Philadelphia, who kept his government much better informed on American affairs than were Americans themselves by their newspapers, believed that Gilman's election indicated a paucity either of talent or of talented men wealthy enough to hold office in New Hampshire.

39. Mayo, *Langdon*, pp. 203–5.

40. Ibid., p. 204.

41. William Plumer to Daniel Tilton, December 16, 1787, Letters 1, Plumer Papers (LC).

42. New Hampshire Historical Society, *Collections* 15 (1939): 557.

43. *New Hampshire State Papers* (1892), 21:875.

44. Ibid., pp. 157–58. McDonald, *We, the People*, pp. 236–37, states that "less than forty of the hundred-odd members appeared for the special session. Lacking a quorum, the legislature hesitated a few days, then proceeded to do business without a quorum." Reasoning from this premise, he further states that the ratifying convention was illegally called and that New Hampshire therefore never actually ratified the Constitution. There is

clear evidence that these statements are incorrect. Forty-eight representatives responded to the single roll-call vote taken during the session on a day when other members may have been temporarily absent. The attendance roll for this special session was not preserved, but the journal explicitly states that on Tuesday, December 11, the house "made a quorum and proceeded to business."

45. Fifteen representatives from the Old Colony, eighteen from the Merrimack Valley, eleven from the Connecticut Valley, and two from the Frontier, plus two who cannot be placed geographically, responded to the roll-call vote on December 12.

46. *New Hampshire State Papers* (1892), 21:160. In *We, the People*, p. 237, McDonald interprets this motion as a "clever maneuver" by a "handful of Federalist legislators" to assure a "disproportionate number of delegates from towns around Portsmouth." He attributes the failure of the motion to the alleged facts that "only eight representatives from Rockingham County and none from Portsmouth itself were in attendance." His facts are wrong, and I cannot agree with his conclusions. Seventeen representatives from Rockingham County responded to the roll call vote, and twelve of them, including *three* representatives from Portsmouth, voted *against* the motion to double representation in the ratifying convention. Of the fourteen towns whose representatives voted in favor of the motion, ten sent delegates to the convention who voted against ratification. I interpret this "clever maneuver" as one instigated by that master intriguer Nathaniel Peabody and his associate Runnels of Londonderry to assure the defeat of the Constitution.

47. *New Hampshire State Papers* (1892), 21:160–61, 165.

48. McDonald's statement in *We, the People*, p. 237, that the convention "was the most nearly complete representation of the towns the state had ever witnessed" is technically correct by virtue of the word "state," since the larger fourth provincial congress assembled while New Hampshire was still a colony. The ratifying convention consisted of 112 delegates; there had been 150 in the fourth provincial congress. Attendance in the regular house of representatives usually peaked at around 80.

49. Mayo, *Langdon*, p. 211.

50. Newspaper accounts support Langdon's statement. See Orin G. Libby, *Distribution of the Vote on the Federal Constitution* (Madison, 1894), pp. 72–74.

51. Mayo, *Langdon*, p. 210. In *We, the People*, pp. 237–38, McDonald says that "most of the fourteen delegates from the towns on the northern frontier" were originally committed to opposing the Constitution. He gives Samuel Livermore credit for "privately" persuading "several" of them to change their minds. I have found no evidence to support either McDonald's count or Langdon's.

52. Libby, *Vote on the Constitution*, pp. 73–74; Joseph Walker, *A History of the New Hampshire Federal Convention* (Boston, 1888), pp. 27–30.

53. *New Hampshire State Papers* (1892), 21:845. Lawrence Guy Stevens, "Reactions of Supporters of the Constitution to the Adjournment of the New Hampshire Ratification Convention, 1788," *Historical New Hampshire* 23, no. 3 (Autumn 1968): pp. 37–50.

54. The brief journal of the convention is printed in *New Hampshire State Papers* (Concord, N.H., 1877), 10:1–22.

55. Joseph Walker included brief biographical sketches of the prominent delegates in his little book. See also the valuable notes on nearly all of the delegates, compiled from microfilmed town records as well as printed sources and concentrating on economic and professional status, in McDonald, *We, the People*, pp. 246–51.

56. *New Hampshire State Papers* (1892), 21:851.

57. Ibid., pp. 844–53.

58. Ibid. (1890), 18:791; Beard, *Economic Interpretation*, p. 94.

59. George Barstow, *History of New Hampshire* (Concord, N.H., 1842), p. 280.

60. Atherton to Lamb, June 11, 1788, John Lamb Papers, box 5, no. 16, New York His-

torical Society; quoted in Charles P. Whittemore, *A General of the Revolution: John Sullivan of New Hampshire* (New York, 1961), p. 217. It is ironic that Atherton, a Tory aristocrat, and Jack Lamb, leader of New York's revolutionary mob, worked together in the attempt to prevent the establishment of what they thought would be a new tyranny. It is easier to understand Lamb than Atherton.

61. Walker, *Federal Convention*, p. 116.

62. Ibid., p. 27n.

63. Whittemore, *John Sullivan*, p. 214.

64. Libby, *Vote on the Federal Constitution*, pp. 71–72.

65. *New Hampshire State Papers* (1877), 10:5.

66. Walker, *Federal Convention*, p. 43n; John Dearborn, ed., *History of Salisbury* (Manchester, N.H., 1890), pp. 114–15; *New Hampshire State Papers* (1892), 21:833n.

67. *New Hampshire State Papers* (1892), 21:851.

68. Libby, *Vote on the Federal Constitution*, pp. 97–98.

69. *New Hampshire State Papers* (1892), 21:228, 293. Patterson is listed in the journal of the convention as representing Lincoln and Franconia, but these towns were virtually unpopulated at the time, and Patterson was a resident of Piermont. The town records state that he was elected in March "as agent to attend the convention at Concord to act for or against the Federal Constitution." He voted *for* and thus canceled out Haverhill's adverse vote in the final reckoning. See *Granite Monthly* (Concord, N.H., 1889), 12:39, 59.

70. Libby, *Vote on the Federal Constitution*, pp. 97–98.

71. *New Hampshire State Papers* (1891), 20:846. A. S. Batchellor, who edited this volume, stated that the population represented by the affirmative vote was 68,766; by the negative 59,640; by those not voting 10,661. What he meant by "not voting" was not explained, but there is good reason to believe that the not-voting constituency was antifederal. If it was added to the actual negative group, the population in opposition to the Constitution would outnumber the federal constituencies by almost 2 percent.

72. Massachusetts Historical Society, *Proceedings* 16 (1902): 385–86.

73. Walker, *Federal Convention*, pp. 115–16.

74. Ibid., pp. 112–14.

75. Dearborn, *Salisbury*, p. 115; Edwin D. Sanborn, *History of New Hampshire* (Manchester, N.H., 1875), p. 239; James Patterson, "Anniversary Address," New Hampshire Historical Society, *Proceedings* 2 (1895): 33–34.

76. Whittemore, *John Sullivan*, p. 212.

77. Ibid., p. 213.

78. Newington, Walpole, and Boscawen.

79. *New Hampshire State Papers* (1877), 10:17–18; Samuel Harding, *Contest over Ratification in Massachusetts* (New York, 1896), pp. 88–89.

80. *New Hampshire State Papers* (1877), 10:18.

81. Ibid.

82. Whittemore, *John Sullivan*, p. 216.

83. Mayo, *Langdon*, p. 216; Walker, *Federal Convention*, pp. 54–55.

84. *New Hampshire State Papers* (1892), 21:854–55.

85. It is curious that the significance of this distribution has been appreciated chiefly by outsiders and even denied by state historians. John Bach McMaster, *History of the People of the United States*, 8 vols. (New York, 1883), 1:484, recognized that it was the hostility of the "country members" that made the adjournment in February necessary. Ten years later, Orin Libby demonstrated the areal groupings of the final vote in detail. Yet A. S. Batchellor, in 1891, declared that "if a township map of the state were to be colored, according to the vote in this convention, it would have very little significance" (*New Hampshire State Papers*

[1891], 20:846). Had he colored such a map he would surely have changed his mind. See appendix, Map 10, "Vote on Ratification of the Federal Constitution."

86. Maps which summarize the votes in the legislature on these issues during the 1780s have been prepared. They do show such a general correspondence, but there were many towns which were exceptions, some being very inconsistent on these matters.

87. Data on town petitions are taken from several volumes of *New Hampshire State Papers*, principally 9–13 (1875–84). The vote in the legislature on the paper-money plan of 1786 is recorded in volume 20 (1891), p. 696. Data on town votes in the paper-money referendum come from McDonald, *We, the People*, pp. 242–43. None of these data is very precise. Town petitions for paper money varied widely in what was requested. The vote in the legislature for and against the peculiar paper-money proposal of 1786 did not necessarily reflect simple approval of or opposition to paper money. For instance, the two anti-federal towns whose representatives voted against the proposal were Atkinson and Plaistow, notorious leaders of the paper-money agitation. Their representative in 1786, Major Joseph Welch, voted against the plan because it did not make the paper a legal tender. It must also be noted that in constituencies consisting of more than one town, the representative usually came from the largest or oldest town and may or may not have expressed the views of the other townspeople. A clear case in point was the classed constituency of Haverhill (a paper-money, anti-federal town), Coventry, Piermont (a federal town), and Warren, which would have increased the anti-federal vote in the ratifying convention had it not been divided in 1788.

88. Compare Map 9, "Paper Money," with Map 10, "Vote on Ratification," in appendix. While I agree with McDonald that Beard and Libby exaggerated the degree of concurrence between paper-money and anti-federal sentiment, I certainly cannot agree that "there was almost no correlation" (McDonald, *We, the People*, p. 242). A positive correlation is clearly evident in such towns as Londonderry, Atkinson, Rochester, Amherst, Bedford, Stoddard, Claremont, and Haverhill. An equal concurrence between antipaper and pro-federal sentiment can be seen in Portsmouth, Hampton, Exeter, Durham, Wilton, Keene, Westmoreland, Cornish, Plymouth, and Littleton.

89. Libby, *Vote on the Federal Constitution*, p. 46.

90. Albert S. Batchellor, *Brief View of the Influences for Adoption of the Constitution by New Hampshire* (Concord, N.H., 1900), pp. 22–23.

91. Quoted in Libby, *Vote on the Federal Constitution*, p. 11.

92. This point can best be illustrated by the table below:

Area	Towns	Population	Federal	Anti-federal
Old Colony	41	40,471	24	8
Merrimack Valley	55	53,518	11	25
Connecticut Valley	53	37,159	16	12
(Cheshire County)			(10)	(11)
(Grafton County)			(6)	(1)
Frontier	33	10,870	6	2
Totals	182	142,018	57	47

CHAPTER 5

1. The epigraph may be found in Alvah Hovey, *A Memoir of Isaac Backus* (Boston, 1858), pp. 195–97.

2. "An Act for the Maintenance and Supply of the Ministry," 13th Anne, *Laws of the Province of New Hampshire*, reprint (Portsmouth, N.H., 1761), pp. 57–58.

3. Paul Lauer, *Church and State in New England* (Baltimore, 1892), Johns Hopkins University Studies in Historical and Political Science, 10:57.

4. Edgar Pennington, *The Reverend Arthur Browne* (Hartford, Conn., 1938), p. 7.

5. Isaac Backus, *History of New England Baptists*, 3 vols., 2d ed. (Newton, Mass., 1871), 2:533.

6. Joseph Fullonton, "Early History of the Baptists in New Hampshire," *Granite Monthly* 1 (1878): 156–58.

7. Hovey, *Memoir of Isaac Backus*, p. 196.

8. Backus, *New England Baptists*, 2:308–9.

9. Franklin Jameson, *The American Revolution as a Social Movement* (Princeton, 1926), pp. 133 ff.

10. J. F. Colby, *Manual of the Constitution of New Hampshire*, rev. ed. (Concord, N.H., 1912), pp. 101–2.

11. Ibid.

12. Charles B. Kinney, Jr., *Church and State: The Struggle for Separation in New Hampshire, 1620–1900* (New York, 1955), p. 93. It is notable that, whereas New Hampshire merely authorized the use of this contractual power, the laws of Massachusetts and Connecticut enjoined it upon towns in the same way that they compelled towns to maintain schools. Timothy Dwight criticized New Hampshire's laxity in this regard. See Timothy Dwight, *Travels in New England and New York*, 4 vols., 2d ed. (London, 1823), 4:161.

13. Occasionally these quarrels originated in theological disputes and ended with the establishment of a new denominational affiliation as well as a new town. Thus, before the Revolution, a Presbyterian minority had seceded from Hampton Falls and its Congregational church to form the town of Seabrook and a Presbyterian church (Charles Wingate, *The Life of Paine Wingate*, 2 vols. [Medford, Mass., 1930], 1:118).

14. Jeremy Belknap, *The History of New Hampshire*, 3 vols., 2d ed. (Boston, 1813), 3:245.

15. Quoted in Backus, *New England Baptists*, 2:533–34.

16. According to the Baptist historians, this phenomenon occurred in Deerfield, where the Congregational minister himself and a majority of his parishioners were proselytized and the town meetinghouse became a Baptist sanctuary. See Ebenezer Cummings, *Annals of Baptist Churches in New Hampshire* (Concord, N.H., 1836), p. 29; Backus, *New England Baptists*, 2:535. Methodists gained control of South Newmarket, installed a Methodist minister in the glebe, took over the meetinghouse, and taxed all property owners for their support (Kinney, *Church and State*, pp. 92–93).

17. Kinney, *Church and State*, pp. 86–89, cites several examples of towns that exempted Baptists and others from church taxes or abolished the church tax altogether.

18. In 1796, Christopher Erskine sued the selectmen of Claremont for return of a tax of $4.49 which he had been compelled to pay for support of the Congregational minister. A jury in common pleas court awarded him damages, but, on appeal, Chief Justice Simeon Olcott of the superior court reversed the decision, stating that Universalists were not a sect differing from Congregationalists, according to law (Kinney, *Church and State*, pp. 94–95). William Plumer, defending another Universalist before Judge Wingate, suggested to the court that "it did not require either argument or testimony to shew there was an essential difference between . . . the doctrine of eternal salvation for *all* men, & the everlasting misery

of nearly the whole human family." In spite of, or perhaps because of this succinct exegesis, he lost his case (William Plumer, "Autobiography," William Plumer Papers, Library of Congress, p. 79).

19. Backus, *New England Baptists*, 2:539.

20. Cummings, *Annals of Baptist Churches*, pp. 32, 35.

21. Isaac Stewart, *History of the Freewill Baptists*, 2 vols. (Dover, N.H., 1862), 1:144.

22. There are general descriptions of persecutions in John McClintock, *History of New Hampshire* (Boston, 1889), p. 527, and George Barstow, *History of New Hampshire* (Concord, N.H., 1842), pp. 422–28.

23. Maria L. Greene, *Development of Religious Liberty in Connecticut* (Boston, 1905), p. 377.

24. Belknap to Hazard, Massachusetts Historical Society, *Collections*, 5th series 2 (1877): 49.

25. Dwight, *Travels in New England*, 4:161–62.

26. Quoted in Nathaniel Bouton, "History of Education in New Hampshire," New Hampshire Historical Society, *Collections* 4 (1834): 10.

27. Belknap, *New Hampshire*, 3:217.

28. George Bush, *History of Education in New Hampshire* (Washington, D.C., 1898), p. 55.

29. Massachusetts Historical Society, *Collections*, 5th series 2 (1877): 287–88.

30. Belknap, *New Hampshire*, 3:218.

31. Colby, *Manual*, p. 120. This paragraph, with additions, forms article 82 of the present state constitution.

32. *New Hampshire State Papers* (Concord, N.H., 1893), 22:136, 239.

33. George Martin, *Evolution of the Massachusetts Public School System* (New York, 1908), p. 78.

34. Plumer, "Autobiography" (LC), p. 9.

35. Thomas Amory, *Life of John Sullivan* (Boston, 1868), p. 263.

36. Nathaniel Adams, *Annals of Portsmouth* (Portsmouth, N.H., 1825), pp. 344–45.

37. *Laws of the State of New Hampshire* (Portsmouth, N.H., 1792), pp. 276–77.

38. New Hampshire Historical Society, *Collections* 4 (1834): 20.

39. Charles Bell, *Phillips Exeter Academy* (Exeter, N.H., 1883), p. 17; Belknap, *New Hampshire*, 3:218.

40. Bush, *Education in New Hampshire*, p. 40.

41. Belknap, *New Hampshire*, 3:222.

42. *New Hampshire State Papers* (Concord, N.H., 1892), 21:405, 499. This land grant bill was said to have been carried in the house of representatives only by the dramatic appearance of General Sullivan, who rose from a sick bed to plead for its passage. The house journal, however, shows that a comfortable majority of thirty-two votes was obtained.

43. William Plumer to Jeremiah Smith, January 4, 1793, Letters 1, Plumer Papers (LC); Leon Richardson, *History of Dartmouth College*, 2 vols. (Hanover, N.H., 1932), 1:216.

44. This information is extracted from the section on New Hampshire periodicals in Clarence Brigham, "Bibliography of American Newspapers, 1690–1820," pt. 5, American Antiquarian Society, *Proceedings*, new series 26 (April 1916): 96–184, and Caroline Whittemore, "A Checklist of New Hampshire Imprints, 1756–1790," microfilmed M.S. thesis, Columbia University, 1929.

45. *New Hampshire State Papers* (1893), 22:412.

46. New Hampshire Library Association, *Centenary of Establishment of Public Libraries* (Peterborough, N.H., 1933). It was not until 1833 that the town of Peterborough established the first free public library in America.

47. Nathaniel Bouton compiled an interesting table of the comparative numbers in the

various professions as an appendix to his discourse on the history of education before the New Hampshire Historical Society in 1833. See their *Collections* 4 (1834): 38.

48. Information in this paragraph is taken from Irving Watson, "Notes on the Medical Profession in New Hampshire," in George Willey, ed., *State Builders* (Manchester, N.H., 1903), p. 166. I very much regret that J. Worth Estes's *Hall Jackson and the Purple Foxglove: Medical Practice and Research in Revolutionary America, 1760–1820* (Hanover, N.H., 1979) came to my attention too late to permit me to profit from its excellent portrayal of the work of a notable New Hampshire physician of this period. I recommend it as a most illuminating enlargement of my brief sketch of medicine and medical practitioners. Dr. Hall Jackson, whom I had previously known only as an army surgeon during the Revolutionary War and therefore overlooked in my catalog of politico-physicians, was actually a well-known practitioner in Portsmouth from 1763 to 1797, well trained and well read, open to scientific observation and at the same time an active revolutionary. William Plumer gave him credit for having introduced the use of digitalis (derived from the purple foxglove) into America for the treatment of cardiovascular diseases, and Estes substantiates this claim with carefully researched evidence.

49. Francis Packard, *History of Medicine in the United States* (New York, 1931), pp. 341, 433 ff.

50. Dr. William Douglas of Boston wrote that frequently there was "*more Danger* from the Physician, than from the Distemper." The mode of practice, he said, was "bleeding, vomiting, blistering, purging, Anodyne, etc. If the illness continued, there was *repetendi* and finally *murderendi*" (Whitfield J. Bell, *The Colonial Physician and Other Essays* [New York, 1975], p. 8).

51. The earlier organizations were in New Jersey, 1766; Massachusetts, 1781; South Carolina, 1789; New York, 1791. (William G. Rothstein, *American Physicians in the Nineteenth Century* [Baltimore, 1972], p. 70).

52. New Hampshire Medical Society, *Records, 1791–1854* (Concord, N.H., 1911), pp. 28–29.

53. Ibid., pp. 20–21, 24–25, 58, 69, 83, 116.

54. Rothstein, *American Physicians*, pp. 88, 93.

55. Willey, *State Builders*, p. 168.

56. An example of this prejudice is given in the humorous story of an encounter between the Methodist circuit rider, Jesse Lee, and two young lawyers, in Abel Stevens, *Memorials of the Introduction of Methodism into New England*, 2 vols. (Boston, 1852), 2:411.

57. *New Hampshire Gazette*, August 26, 1785.

58. William Plumer, Jr., *Life of Plumer* (Boston, 1856), pp. 153–54.

59. Edwin Dexter, *History of Education in the United States* (New York, 1904), pp. 316–18.

60. Albert S. Batchellor, "Outline of New Hampshire History," in Willey, *State Builders*, pp. 22–23.

61. *New Hampshire State Papers* (Concord, N.H., 1874), 8:810–12.

62. These biographical facts are derived from Batchellor's article in *State Builders*, Charles H. Bell's *Bench and Bar of New Hampshire* (Boston, 1894), and Plumer's "Biographical Sketches." Thirty-four of Plumer's unusual characterizations were published as appendixes to volumes 21 and 22 (1892–93) of the *New Hampshire State Papers*, but the great majority of them remain in manuscript in the New Hampshire Historical Society library at Concord.

63. New Hampshire Historical Society, *Collections* 4 (1834): 38.

64. William Plumer kept a record of the minutes of the state organization and of the Rockingham County meeting in 1788 in his "Repository," vol. 4, Plumer Papers, New Hampshire State Library, pp. 271–76.

65. Lawrence Mayo, *John Wentworth* (Cambridge, Mass., 1921), p. 36.

66. Belknap, *New Hampshire*, 2:311–12.

67. Albert S. Batchellor and Henry Metcalf, eds., *Laws of New-Hampshire*, 10 vols. (Bristol, N.H., 1904–22), 3:524.

68. *Journal of the Senate, December session, 1793* (Portsmouth, N.H., 1794), p. 87.

69. *Laws of New-Hampshire, 1792*, p. 67.

70. *New Hampshire Gazette*, June 1, 1786.

71. William Plumer to Jeremiah Smith, February 5, 1793, Letters 1, Plumer Papers (LC).

72. *Laws of New-Hampshire, 1792*, pp. 67–70.

73. Lawrence Shaw Mayo, *John Langdon of New Hampshire* (Concord, N.H., 1937), p. 253.

74. *New Hampshire State Papers* (1893), 22:842.

75. Ibid., p. 837.

76. William Fry, *New Hampshire as a Royal Province* (New York, 1908), p. 647.

77. *New Hampshire State Papers* (1893), 22:837.

78. Bell, *Bench and Bar*, p. 45.

79. Smith to Plumer, April 27, 1796, Plumer Papers (NHSL).

80. William Plumer, Jr., *Life of Plumer*, p. 155.

81. *New Hampshire State Papers* (1892), 21:817.

82. William Plumer, Jr., *Life of Plumer*, p. 151.

83. Ibid., p. 154.

84. John Farmer and Jacob Moore, eds., *Collections Relating Principally to New Hampshire*, 3 vols. (Concord, N.H., 1824), 3:205.

85. John Shirley, "Early Jurisprudence of New Hampshire," New Hampshire Historical Society, *Proceedings* 1 (1885): 312, 326.

86. Fry, *Royal Province*, p. 438.

87. From the royal commission issued to John Cutt, first president of the province of New Hampshire in 1680, printed in *New Hampshire State Papers* (Concord, N.H., 1867), 1:376.

88. William Plumer, Jr., *Life of Plumer*, p. 206.

89. *Laws of New-Hampshire, 1792*, p. 218.

90. Fry, *Royal Province*, p. 431.

91. Peter J. Coleman, *Debtors and Creditors in America* (Madison, 1974), p. 59.

92. Tracy Carleton, "Abolition of Imprisonment for Debt," *Yale Review* 17 (1908): 339–44.

93. New Hampshire Historical Society, *Proceedings* 1 (1885): 235–36.

94. John H. Morison, *The Life of Jeremiah Smith* (Boston, 1845), p. 38; *Laws of New Hampshire, 1792*.

95. Plumer, "Repository," 4:303–6, Plumer Papers (NHSL). See also Walter Dodd, "The Constitutional History of New Hampshire, 1775–1792," New Hampshire Bar Association, *Proceedings* 2, no. 3 (1906): 399–400; *New Hampshire State Papers* (1893), 22:22, 59, 67, 104, 113, 156, 168.

96. G. J. Clark, ed., *Memoirs of Jeremiah Mason* (Boston, 1917), reprint of G. S. Hilliard, *Memoirs* (1837), pp. 25–26. The quote is from Mason's autobiography, which forms the first section of the *Memoirs*.

CHAPTER 6

1. The epigraph is from John H. Morison, *The Life of Jeremiah Smith* (Boston, 1845), p. 47.

2. *New Hampshire State Papers* (Concord, N.H., 1892), 21:357, 359, 415.

3. Ibid., p. 876.

4. Parker Lyon, ed., *New Hampshire Register, 1860* (Concord, N.H., 1859), p. 29.

5. *New Hampshire State Papers* (1892), 21:441–45.

6. Langdon resigned from the state presidency in order to enter the Senate, and John Pickering was elected to fill out his unexpired term.

7. *New Hampshire State Papers* (1892), 21:597.

8. *New Hampshire Register, 1860*, p. 40.

9. William Plumer, "Autobiography," William Plumer Papers, Library of Congress, p. 49.

10. Orin Libby, "Political Factions in Washington's Administrations," *Quarterly Journal of the University of North Dakota* 3 (July 1913): 298, 304.

11. One reason for New Hampshire's wavering support of Washington's administration was the frequent change of personnel in its congressional delegation. Its rate for returning incumbents during the first five congresses was only 67 percent, although seven other states had lower percentages. See Rudolph M. Bell, *Party and Faction in American Politics: The House of Representatives, 1789–1801* (Westport, Conn., 1973), p. 8, Table 1.

12. Charles Wingate, *The Life of Paine Wingate*, 2 vols. (Medford, Mass., 1930), 2:406.

13. Morison, *Smith*, p. 56.

14. *Annals of Congress* (Washington, D.C., 1834–56), Second Congress, pp. 106, 482; Bell, *Party and Faction*, pp. 40–42. Bell is mistaken in his interpretation of New Hampshire's attitude toward this issue. It *gained* a representative under the legislation for which it voted. However, his general thesis that "issue-oriented" factions prevailed in the first two congresses is well reasoned, although I would not call these impermanent factions "cohesive" or "polarized." See p. 16.

15. Smith to Plumer, November 16, 1791, Plumer Papers, New Hampshire State Library.

16. Lawrence Shaw Mayo, *John Langdon of New Hampshire* (Concord, N.H., 1937), p. 230.

17. Wingate, *Life of Paine Wingate*, 2:310–11.

18. Mayo, *Langdon*, p. 238.

19. Foster to Plumer, May 10, 1790, Plumer Papers (NHSL).

20. Morison, *Smith*, pp. 53–54.

21. Gilman to Sullivan, July 25, 1790, New Hampshire Manuscripts, Library of Congress.

22. John C. Miller, *The Federalist Era, 1789–1801* (New York, 1960), p. 46, is incorrect in saying that "every New England representative except one wished to see assumption carried." Two New Hampshire representatives and one senator voted against the assumption bill.

23. Morison, *Smith*, p. 58.

24. Charles Beard, *Economic Origins of Jeffersonian Democracy* (New York, 1915), p. 181.

25. George Barstow, *History of New Hampshire* (Concord, N.H., 1842), p. 292.

26. William Plumer to Abiel Foster, June 28, 1790, Letters 1, Plumer Papers, Library of Congress.

27. *New Hampshire State Papers* (Concord, N.H., 1893), 22:146, 227.

28. Ibid., pp. 339–41; Wingate, *Life of Wingate*, 2:543–44. Wingate was the author of this memorial to himself and his fellow congressmen.

29. Smith to William Plumer, March 15, 1792, Plumer Papers (NHSL).

30. *Annals of Congress*, First Congress, 2:1748, 1960.

31. Wingate, *Life of Wingate*, 2:323.

32. *Annals of Congress*, First Congress, 1:783, 796, 820.

33. Barstow, *New Hampshire*, pp. 305–6.

34. Herman Ames, *State Documents on Federal Relations*, 6 vols. (Philadelphia, 1900–

1906), 1:11–13.

35. Ibid., pp. 13–15; *Journal of the House of Representatives*, December session, 1794 (Portsmouth, N.H., 1795), p. 37.

36. *Penhallow et al v. Doane's Administrators*, in Benjamin Curtis, *Reports of Decisions of the Supreme Court of the United States*, 5th ed. (Boston, 1870), p. 84.

37. Morison, *Smith*, p. 47.

38. Plumer, "Autobiography" (LC), pp. 47–48; *New Hampshire State Papers* (1893), 22:177, 231–32, 237.

39. Plumer to Jeremiah Smith, January 2, 1792, Letters 1, Plumer Papers (LC); *New Hampshire State Papers* (1893), 22:444, 451; *Laws of New Hampshire* (Portsmouth, 1792), p. 191. The clerk's copy of this tax bill was actually stolen from his file by a senator who hoped by this act of political piracy to prevent passage of the law, which would diminish his own property.

40. Plumer, "Autobiography" (LC), pp. 47–48; *New Hampshire State Papers* (1893), 22:177, 231–32, 237.

41. Plumer, "Autobiography" (LC), pp. 51–52.

42. *New Hampshire State Papers* (1893), 22:385, 394, 446, 475.

43. See p. 111.

44. *New Hampshire State Papers* (Manchester, N.H., 1891), 20:652–53.

45. Ibid. (1892), 21:78–79.

46. Ibid., p. 813.

47. William Plumer, "Repository," 4:241, Plumer Papers (NHSL). Plumer's "Repositories" were scrapbooks of miscellaneous information, some of it quite valuable. His copy of this letter is the only one extant.

48. *New Hampshire State Papers* (1893), 22:76, 82.

49. Ibid., p. 754 and (1892), 21:814; William Plumer to Woodbury Langdon, March 26, 1791, Letters 1, Plumer Papers (LC).

50. Mayo, *Langdon*, p. 257.

51. Plumer, "Repository," 4:245–49, Plumer Papers (NHSL). Records of the senate sitting as a court of impeachment are printed in *New Hampshire State Papers* (1893), 22:751–56.

52. Plumer, "Autobiography" (LC), pp. 43–45; *New Hampshire State Papers* (1893), 22:171–73.

53. *New Hampshire State Papers* (1892), 21:815, (1893), 22:117, 177; Plumer, "Autobiography" (LC), p. 45.

54. President Bartlett and the five councillors did not, in fact, vote on the removal resolutions, although they were not prohibited from doing so by the constitution.

55. Morison, *Smith*, pp. 38–40.

56. Plumer, "Autobiography" (LC), p. 43.

57. William Page to Plumer, June 26, 1792, Letters 1, Plumer Papers (LC).

58. Plumer to Abiel Foster, June 28, 1790, Letters 1, Plumer Papers (LC).

CHAPTER 7

1. The epigraph is from a letter, Jeremy Belknap to Ebenezer Hazard, Massachusetts Historical Society, *Collections*, 5th series 2 (1877):314–315.

2. New Hampshire's extensive revision of its constitution in 1791–92 was part of a general movement toward a stronger executive authority which affected several states of the Union. Pennsylvania abolished its unicameral legislature, Georgia and South Carolina gave their western sections more equal representation, and South Carolina did away with its ap-

pointive council. See John C. Miller, *The Federalist Era, 1789–1801* (New York, 1960), p. 4.

3. William Plumer to Jeremiah Smith, February 8, 1792, Letters 1, William Plumer Papers, Library of Congress.

4. Henry Saunderson, *History of Charlestown, N.H.* (Claremont, N.H., 1876), p. 498.

5. Plumer, "Autobiography," William Plumer Papers, Library of Congress, pp. 49–50.

6. Plumer to Smith, February 8, 1792, Letters 1, Plumer Papers (LC).

7. Plumer preserved a copy of this resolution in his "Repository," 4:33, Plumer Papers, New Hampshire State Library. Its basic provisions were that "the free exercise & enjoyment of religious profession & worship, without discrimination or preference, shall forever hereafter be allowed within this State to all mankind. . . . Nor shall any person within this State ever be obliged to pay tithes taxes or any other rates for the purpose of building or repairing any other church or churches . . . or for the maintenance of any minister or ministry, contrary to what he beleives to be right, or has deliberately or voluntarily engaged himself to perform."

8. *New Hampshire State Papers* (Concord, N.H., 1877), 10:41, 46. The journal of this convention is printed in this volume, pp. 23–168.

9. Plumer, "Repository," 4:331 ff., Plumer Papers (NHSL).

10. *New Hampshire State Papers* (1877), 10:106, 108, 113–14. See appendix, Map 12 "Religious Freedom."

11. Ibid., p. 141.

12. Ibid., p. 48.

13. Ibid., pp. 67–68, 93, 104; Plumer, "Repository," 4:331 ff., Plumer Papers (NHSL).

14. *New Hampshire State Papers* (Concord, N.H., 1884), 13:772. The disparity is illustrated in the table below:

Counties	Population	Proportion of Total Population (percentage)	Senators	Proportion of Total Number (percentage)
Rockingham	43,169	30+	5	41.67
Strafford	23,734	17−	2	16.67
Hillsborough	32,871	23+	2	16.67
Cheshire	28,772	20+	2	16.67
Grafton	13,472	9+	1	8.33

15. Ibid. (1877), 10:43–44, 51–52.

16. Ibid. (Concord, N.H., 1892), 21:588. The following few examples show the inconsistencies:

Towns	Population, 1790	Number of Representatives
Portsmouth	4,720	3
Londonderry	2,622	2
Rochester	2,857	1 (2 after 1792)
Gilmanton	2,613	1
Concord	1,747	1
Exeter	1,722	1

Table (continued)

Dover	1,998	1
Hinsdale	522	1
Lancaster, Percy, Northumberland, Stratford, Dartmouth, Cockburne, Colebrook[a]	638	1

a. These seven towns stretched for some forty miles along the upper Connecticut and included some four hundred square miles of mostly uninhabited forest.

17. Plumer, "Repository," 4:331 ff., Plumer Papers (NHSL).

18. *New Hampshire State Papers* (1877), 10:48–50.

19. *New Hampshire State Papers* (1877), 10:24–29.

20. Ibid., p. 96.

21. Ibid., p. 178.

22. Thorsten Kalijarvi and William Chamberlin, *The Government of New Hampshire* (Durham, N.H., 1939), pp. 59–60.

23. The New Hampshire senate now numbers 24, the house of representatives 400.

24. Winston Churchill made this situation the theme of his novel *Mr. Crewe's Career* (New York, 1908).

25. Plumer to Smith, December 10, 1791, Letters 1, Plumer Papers (LC).

26. Ibid.; Plumer, "Autobiography" (LC), p. 50.

27. Plumer, "Repository," 4:331 ff., Plumer Papers (NHSL). Plumer's copy of this judicial plan and of the explanatory report of the Committee of Ten seem to have been the only ones preserved.

28. Ibid.

29. *Some Remarks on the Proceedings of the Late Convention* (n.p., 1791), pp. 3–13.

30. William Plumer, "Biographical Sketches," 4:541, Plumer Papers, New Hampshire Historical Society.

31. *New Hampshire State Papers* (1877), 10:97.

32. Ibid., pp. 98–100.

33. Ibid., p. 57.

34. *Remarks on the Late Convention*, p. 10.

35. *New Hampshire State Papers* (1877), 10:53.

36. Ibid., pp. 111–12.

37. Page to Plumer, April 5, 1792, Letters 1, Plumer Papers (LC). Page had already been defeated for another year in the legislature and Plumer had decided not to be a candidate.

38. *Concord Town Records, 1732–1820* (Concord, N.H., 1894), pp. 271–72.

39. Massachusetts Historical Society, *Collections*, 5th series 2 (1877): 314–15.

40. Plumer, "Autobiography" (LC), p. 54.

41. *New Hampshire State Papers* (1877), 10:141.

42. Ibid., pp. 141–42.

43. Ibid., p. 142.

44. Ibid., p. 144.

45. Ibid., p. 164.

46. Samuel Eliot Morison, "The Struggle over the Adoption of the Constitution of Massachusetts," Massachusetts Historical Society, *Proceedings* 50 (1917): 400.

47. *New Hampshire State Papers* (1877), 10:167–68.

48. J. F. Colby, *Manual of the Constitution of New Hampshire*, rev. ed. (Concord, N.H., 1912), p. 93.

49. William Plumer, Jr., *Life of Plumer* (Boston, 1856), p. 124.

50. The full text of the 1792 revision is printed in *New Hampshire State Papers* (1877), 10:169 ff.

51. See appendix, Map 11, "Constitutional Convention of 1791–92."

52. Plumer to Smith, February 5, 1793, Letters 1, Plumer Papers (LC).

CHAPTER 8

1. The epigraph is from a letter, William Plumer to Jeremiah Smith, April 25, 1796, Letters 1, William Plumer Papers, Library of Congress.

2. The more recent students of party origins in American history—John Miller, Joseph Charles, J. T. Main, Noble Cunningham, Manning J. Dauer, Rudolph Bell, William Chambers—have generally moved away from the older emphasis on economics or political theory and toward recognition of the role of foreign relations in polarizing political opinion in the middle 1790s. None of them, however, in my opinion, gives quite enough weight to this decisive factor. The man perhaps most responsible for creating our two-party system, Thomas Jefferson, stated the matter succinctly in 1793 when he said that the French Revolution "kindled and brought forward the two parties with an ardour which our own interests merely, could never excite" (quoted by Arthur M. Schlesinger, Jr., in his introduction to *History of American Presidential Elections*, 4 vols. [New York, 1971], 1:xl).

3. Charles Wingate, *The Life of Paine Wingate*, 2 vols. (Medford, Mass., 1930), 2:429.

4. John H. Morison, *The Life of Jeremiah Smith* (Boston, 1845), p. 63.

5. Plumer to Smith, March 22, 1794, Letters 1, Plumer Papers (LC); Lawrence Shaw Mayo, *John Langdon of New Hampshire* (Concord, N.H., 1937), p. 265.

6. *Annals of Congress*, Third Congress, pp. 602–3. John Samuel Sherburne, a Portsmouth attorney and a brother-in-law of John Langdon, had a reputation for intrigue and was disliked by most of the Federalists.

7. Ibid., pp. 89, 114.

8. Plumer to Smith, March 22, April 28, 1794, Letters 1, Plumer Papers (LC).

9. Morison, *Smith*, p. 62.

10. Plumer, "Autobiography," William Plumer Papers, Library of Congress, pp. 47–48; *New Hampshire State Papers* (Concord, N.H., 1893), 22:177, 231–32, 237.

11. *Journal of the House of Representatives*, June session, 1794 (Portsmouth, N.H., 1794), p. 63.

12. *Journal of the Senate*, December session, 1794 (Portsmouth, N.H., 1795), p. 17.

13. Smith to Plumer, January 10, 1795, William Plumer Papers, New Hampshire State Library.

14. *Annals of Congress*, Fourth Congress, pp. 3, 862.

15. Nathaniel Adams, *Annals of Portsmouth* (Portsmouth, N.H., 1825), pp. 309–10.

16. Ibid., p. 311.

17. Plumer to Smith, September 15, 23, 1795, Letters 1, Plumer Papers (LC).

18. Ibid.

19. George Barstow, *History of New Hampshire* (Concord, N.H., 1842), p. 309.

20. Plumer to Smith, January 1, 1796, Letters 1, Plumer Papers (LC).

21. *Laws of New Hampshire* (Dover, N.H., 1805), pp. 210–12.

22. *Journal of the Senate*, June session, 1794 (Portsmouth, N.H., 1794), p. 51.

23. Plumer to Smith, January 27, 1795, Letters 1, Plumer Papers (LC).

24. *Journal of the House of Representatives*, December session, 1794 (Portsmouth, N.H.,

1795), p. 52; *Senate Journal*, December 1794, pp. 31, 36.

25. "Veritas," no. 3, in William Plumer, "Repository," 2:33–39, William Plumer Papers, Library of Congress.

26. Smith to Plumer, December 6, 1794, February 24, 1795, Plumer Papers (NHSL).

27. Plumer to Smith, June 30, 1795, Letters 1, Plumer Papers (LC).

28. Smith to Plumer, January 10, 1795, Plumer Papers (NHSL).

29. *House Journal*, December 1794, p. 60.

30. Plumer to Smith, December 23, 1794, Letters 1, Plumer Papers (LC).

31. *Journal of the House of Representatives*, December session, 1795 (Portsmouth, N.H., 1796), pp. 142–45.

32. Plumer to Smith, January 6, 1796, Letters 1, Plumer Papers (LC).

33. Parker Lyon, ed., *New Hampshire Register, 1860* (Concord, N.H., 1859), p. 40.

34. Smith to Plumer, March 30, 1796, Plumer Papers (NHSL).

35. Plumer to Smith, March 15, 1796, Letters 1, Plumer Papers (LC).

36. Plumer to Smith, April 19, 1796, Letters 1, Plumer Papers (LC).

37. John Langdon to James Madison, April 28, 1796, folio 19, Madison Papers, Library of Congress.

38. Plumer to Smith, April 25, 1796, Letters 1, Plumer Papers (LC).

39. *Annals of Congress*, Fourth Congress, first session, p. 1291; Plumer to Smith, March 31, 1796, Letters 1, Plumer Papers (LC). Sherburne voted on thirteen of the eighteen bills in the Fourth Congress which were classified as important party measures by Manning J. Dauer, *The Adams Federalists* (Baltimore, 1953), pp. 289, 293. Besides the Jay Treaty appropriations, these included bills on western lands, army and navy appropriations, and salaries. Sherburne voted twelve times against administration measures and only once with the Federalists—on a land issue. Dauer classifies him as a "Republican regular." Dauer's system breaks down in dealing with Nicholas Gilman and Jeremiah Smith, both of whom he classifies as "Federalist moderates." Gilman's voting record was 9 Federalist, 4 Republican, and 5 absences, but he was a political chameleon, changing sides with unpredictable frequency. Smith's record was 9–7 on administration measures with two absences. He voted against the heavy expenditure bills but he was actually a much stronger Federalist than Gilman. He was simply not a Hamiltonian Federalist. Foster voted 16–2 on administration measures. Dauer classifies him correctly as a "Federalist regular."

40. Morison, *Smith*, p. 105.

41. Plumer to Smith, July 14, 1796, Letters 1, Plumer Papers (LC).

42. Plumer to Smith, August 12, 1796, Letters 1, Plumer Papers (LC).

43. *New Hampshire State Papers* (Concord, N.H., 1892), 21:815.

CHAPTER 9

1. The epigraph from the *Village Messenger* is quoted in Daniel Secomb, *History of the Town of Amherst* (Concord, N.H., 1883), pp. 103–4.

2. William Plumer to Jeremiah Smith, March 23, 1797, Letters 1, William Plumer Papers, Library of Congress.

3. Plumer to William Gordon, February 5, 1798, Letters 1, Plumer Papers (LC).

4. Parker Lyon, ed., *New Hampshire Register, 1860* (Concord, N.H., 1859), p. 40.

5. Plumer to Smith, June 11, 1797, Letters 1, Plumer Papers (LC).

6. Plumer to Gordon, June 18, 1797, Letters 1, Plumer Papers (LC); *Journal of the House of Representatives*, June session, 1797 (Portsmouth, N.H., 1797), pp. 19–21, 35–37. Sprague continued his record of belligerent Federalism on the national level after his elec-

tion to Congress. He twice introduced a resolution to legalize the capture of unarmed French merchant vessels—a practice that would almost certainly have brought on a war with France. See Ralph Adams Brown, *The Presidency of John Adams* (Lawrence, Kan., 1975), p. 58.

7. Arthur Livermore to Plumer, May 16, 1798, Letters 3, Plumer Papers (LC).

8. (Concord) *Courier of New Hampshire*, June 5, 1798.

9. Plumer to Gordon, February 5, 1798, Letters 1, Plumer Papers (LC).

10. Plumer to Sarah Plumer, June 14, 1798, Letters 1, Plumer Papers (LC); William Plumer, "Autobiography," William Plumer Papers, Library of Congress, p. 72.

11. *Journal of the House of Representatives*, June session, 1798 (Portsmouth, N.H., 1798), p. 43.

12. Ibid., pp. 50–52.

13. Ibid., p. 36.

14. (Portsmouth) *Oracle of the Day*, June 1, 1799.

15. *Annals of Congress*, Fifth Congress, 2:1553, 1772, 1865. J. Manning Dauer, *The Adams Federalists* (Baltimore, 1953), pp. 298, 304, 311, classifies all New Hampshire representatives in the Fifth Congress as Federalist regulars. On the eighteen roll calls in the first session, voting on defense measures, direct taxation and naturalization, Foster, Freeman, Gordon, and Smith registered 63 votes for the administration, 4 votes opposed (to higher expenditures), and 5 absences. In the second session, which passed the Alien and Sedition Acts, abrogated the French treaty, and exposed the XYZ papers, New Hampshire congressmen, including Sprague (*vice* Smith), recorded 30 absences at the twenty-eight partisan roll calls, but gave 79 votes for administrative measures to only 3 opposed. In all three sessions, the four New Hampshire congressmen supported the administration with 172 votes and opposed it with only 13, 3 of these against a bankruptcy bill.

16. (Portsmouth) *Oracle*, March 23, 1799.

17. *Annals of Congress*, Fifth Congress, 2:1983–86, 2028, 2095, 2171, 3016. All four representatives from New Hampshire voted for the Sedition Act, and all except Sprague, who was absent, for the Alien Act. Professor Libby was incorrect in stating that New Hampshire furnished one vote against these measures. See Orin Libby, "Early Political Parties in the United States," *Quarterly Journal of the University of North Dakota* 2 (April 1912): 223.

18. (Concord) *Courier*, August 21, 1798.

19. (Portsmouth) *Oracle*, January 12, 1799.

20. Frank Anderson, "Contemporary Opinion of the Virginia and Kentucky Resolutions," *American Historical Review* 5 (1900): 231.

21. (Portsmouth) *Oracle*, March 23, 1799.

22. *Journal of the House of Representatives*, June session, 1799 (Portsmouth, N.H., 1799), pp. 60–61.

23. Anderson, "Contemporary Opinion," assumed that there were Republican members who refrained from voting on these resolutions, but only 3 members were absent at roll call, and they had voted in favor of the equally partisan reply to Governor Gilman's address. The 3 members who had not answered roll call on the reply vote were present and voted in favor of the response to the Virginia and Kentucky legislatures. Thus, every one of the 140 members of the House of Representatives and every one of the twelve senators had subscribed either to the reply to the governor, the reply to Virginia and Kentucky, or to both. This legislature included 9 of the 27 dissidents in 1797 and Moses Leavitt, the senator from the Portsmouth district, all of whom were undoubtedly Republicans. Nevertheless, these men rejected a doctrine enunciated by Thomas Jefferson himself and gave unqualified endorsement to the Adams administration. As far as national policy was concerned, New Hampshire could well be counted as unanimously Federalist in 1799.

24. Plumer, "Autobiography" (LC), p. 69.

25. Quoted in Secomb, *Amherst*, pp. 115–16.

26. John H. Morison, *The Life of Jeremiah Smith* (Boston, 1845), p. 139. "Peter Porcupine," the acidulous editor of the *Political Censor*, bestowed similar epithets upon Senator John Langdon in Philadelphia. Commenting upon a Republican dinner where Langdon was toasted as "an old whig," Porcupine defined the term for his readers. "It is a very ill looking, nasty, despised and neglected thing, fit for nothing but to be trodden under foot, or thrown in the dunghill" (Dauer, *Adams Federalists*, p. 34).

27. Plumer to Oliver Wolcott, June 8, 1798, Letters 1, Plumer Papers (LC). This incident is discussed in Carl R. Fish, *The Civil Service and the Patronage* (New York, 1905), pp. 19–20.

28. Plumer, "Autobiography" (LC), p. 70.

29. *Journal of the House of Representatives*, December session, 1797 (Portsmouth, N.H., 1798), p. 72; Plumer to Sprague, February 21, 1798, Letters 1, and "Autobiography" (LC), pp. 64, 76.

30. Plumer, "Autobiography" (LC), p. 65.

31. *House Journal*, June 1798, pp. 62, 71.

32. Plumer, "Autobiography" (LC), pp. 71–72.

33. For roll-call votes on measures to reform the judiciary, see *Journal of the House of Representatives*, December session, 1793 (Portsmouth, N.H., 1794), pp. 149, 194, 197.

34. *Journal of the House of Representatives*, June session, 1794 (Portsmouth, N.H., 1794), pp. 40, 48.

35. Plumer to Smith, January 25, 1797, Letters 1, Plumer Papers (LC).

36. Plumer to Smith, February 2, 1797, Letters 1, Plumer Papers (LC).

37. For roll-call votes on bills regarding judicial salaries during the decade of the 1790s, see *New Hampshire State Papers* (Concord, N.H., 1893), 22:228, 441; *Journal of the House of Representatives*, December session, 1795 (Portsmouth, N.H., 1796), p. 134, June, 1797, p. 48.

38. *House Journal*, June 1797, p. 48.

39. Edward Livermore to Plumer, June 3, 1797, Letters 3, Plumer Papers (LC).

40. Plumer, "Autobiography" (LC), p. 66.

41. Charles R. Bell, *The Bench and Bar of New Hampshire* (Boston, 1894), p. 55.

42. Plumer to Gordon, June 26, 1798, Letters 1, Plumer Papers (LC).

43. Plumer, "Autobiography" (LC), pp. 77–78.

44. Ibid., p. 77. When the federal judiciary was established during the first session of Congress, Livermore had opposed holding any terms of court at Exeter, "alledging that it had little or no commerce, & that its river was a *mud creek*."

45. (Concord) *Courier*, December 1, 1798.

46. Plumer, "Autobiography" (LC), p. 78.

47. For roll-call votes on these economic matters, see *New Hampshire State Papers* (1893), 22:239, 332, 475; *House Journal*, December 1793, pp. 73, 76, 115, June 1794, p. 67, December 1794 (Portsmouth, N.H., 1795), p. 107, December 1795 (Portsmouth, N.H., 1796), p. 144, June session, 1796 (Portsmouth, N.H., 1796), p. 53, December session, 1797 (Portsmouth, N.H., 1798), p. 57, December 1797 (Portsmouth, N.H., 1798), pp. 72, 98, June 1799, p. 55, December session, 1799, pp. 25, 80, November session, 1800 (Portsmouth, N.H., 1801), p. 65.

48. *House Journal*, December 1795, pp. 142–45.

49. Morison, *Smith*, pp. 124–25. See also George Leutscher, *Early Political Machinery in the United States* (Philadelphia, 1903), pp. 4, 122.

50. Charles Hazen, ed., *Contemporary American Opinion of the French Revolution* (Baltimore, 1897), pp. 182–83.

51. Charles Hanson, ed., *A Journal for the Years, 1739–1803 by Samuel Lane of Stratham, New Hampshire* (Concord, N.H., 1937), p. 58.

52. Daniel Webster to James Bingham, February 11, 1800, in Daniel Webster, *Writings and Speeches*, 18 vols. (Boston, 1903), 17:81.

53. *Journal of the House of Representatives*, November session, 1798 (Portsmouth, N.H., 1799), pp. 13 ff.

54. Ibid., June 1799, pp. 34–36.

55. (Concord) *Courier*, April 3, 1798.

56. George Aldrich, *Walpole as It Was and as It Is* (Claremont, N.H., 1880), pp. 79–80. See also Charles and Mary Beard, *The Rise of American Civilization*, 2 vols. (New York, 1930), 1:506.

57. (Walpole) *Newhampshire and Vermont Journal*, November 15, 1796.

58. Seth Ames, ed., *Works of Fisher Ames*, 2 vols. (Boston, 1854), 1:168.

59. (Boston) *Columbian Centinel*, February 13, 1796, quoted in Anson Morse, *The Federalist Party in Massachusetts to 1800* (Princeton, 1909), p. 165.

60. Seth Payson, *Election Sermon, 1799* (Portsmouth, N.H., 1799), p. 13.

61. Noah Worcester, *Election Sermon, 1800* (Concord, N.H., 1800), p. 26.

62. George Barstow, *History of New Hampshire* (Concord, N.H., 1842), p. 316.

63. *Journal of the House of Representatives*, June session, 1800 (Portsmouth, N.H., 1800), p. 70; Plumer, "Autobiography" (LC), pp. 85–86.

64. *House Journal*, November 1800, pp. 11–13.

65. Ibid., p. 16.

66. Charles Beard, *Economic Origins of Jeffersonian Democracy* (New York, 1915), p. 48; Lawrence Shaw Mayo, *John Langdon of New Hampshire* (Concord, N.H., 1937), pp. 240, 246, 266.

67. Charles Brewster, *Rambles about Portsmouth*, 2 vols. (Portsmouth, N.H., 1869), 2:120, 154.

CHAPTER 10

1. The epigraph is from William Plumer, "Autobiography," p. 91, William Plumer Papers, Library of Congress.

2. William Plumer, "Biographical Sketches," 4:486, Plumer Papers, New Hampshire Historical Society. Resentment against the direct taxes of Adams's administration was widespread in all the sixteen states.

3. (Portsmouth) *New Hampshire Gazette*, December 3, 1796; (Concord) *Courier of New Hampshire*, July 24, 1798.

4. Throughout this period New Hampshire congressmen continued to be elected on a general ticket. Until 1816 they were elected at special town meetings held every second year in August. Presidential electors were chosen, if not by the legislature, by another special town meeting held every fourth year in November. This, of course, was long before the day when New Hampshire earned political notoriety by holding the earliest presidential preferential primary in the election year. After 1816 both congressmen and electors were chosen at the same November town meeting. Donald B. Cole's statement in *Jacksonian Democracy in New Hampshire* (Cambridge, Mass., 1970), p. 13, that local, state, and congressional officers were all elected in the March town meetings is incorrect.

5. *Journal of the House of Representatives*, December 1799 (Portsmouth, N.H., 1800), p. 45.

6. (Concord) *Courier*, December 13, 1798.

7. Plumer to Jeremiah Smith, June 14, 1800, Letters 1, William Plumer Papers, Library of Congress.

8. *House Journal*, December 1799, pp. 49, 51. See appendix, Map 15, "Union Bank."

9. Samuel Curtis, ed., *New Hampshire Register, 1805* (Amherst, N.H., 1804), section on bank statements; (Boston) *Columbian Centinel*, March 22, 1800.

10. *Columbian Centinel*, March 22, 1800.

11. *New Hampshire Gazette*, February 26, 1805; *Laws of New Hampshire* (Dover, 1805), pp. 240–41.

12. *House Journal*, December 1799, p. 77. The law was not to go into effect, however, against existing institutions (i.e., the Union Bank) until August 1, 1800. Cole's statement in *Jacksonian Democracy*, p. 17, that the Federalist legislature forced John Langdon's new bank "to close down" is not accurate.

13. *New Hampshire Gazette*, February 26, 1805. These newspaper quotes come from attacks that were made five years later in editorials that reviewed the whole history of the bank wars in New Hampshire.

14. (Walpole) *Political Observatory*, February 2, 1805.

15. *House Journal*, December 1799, p. 100.

16. *Political Observatory*, February 2, 1805.

17. The Congregational pulpit was especially vigorous in denouncing "Jacobinism" and openly supporting Gilman in this campaign. Mark P. Kaplanoff, "Religion and Righteousness," *Historical New Hampshire* 23 (1968): 3–20, quotes from sermons preached in this vein by Joseph Buckminster, George Richards, and Timothy Alden of Portsmouth, Noah Worcester of Thornton, and Jacob Magaw at Merrimack, as well as from the correspondence of Federalist orthodox lawyers, such as Jeremiah Smith and George Sullivan.

18. Plumer to James Sheafe, March 19, 1800, Letters 1, Plumer Papers (LC). "Jog around the country then, ye disorganizers," complained a Federalist newspaper. "Foment malicious falsehoods. . . . make use of every species of intrigue—but before any person you propose is chosen Governor, you ALL will be suspended by a single rope." A Republican "runner" who interrupted a town meeting was strapped to a "Fandango" (a small ferris wheel) and given a spin. Kaplanoff, "Religion and Righteousness"; Cole, *Jacksonian Democracy*, p. 18.

19. Parker Lyon, ed., *New Hampshire Register, 1860* (Concord, N.H., 1859), p. 40.

20. *Columbian Centinel*, March 22, 1800.

21. Plumer to George Thatcher, March 11, 1800, Letters 1, Plumer Papers (LC).

22. *Concord Town Records, 1732–1820* (Concord, N.H., 1894), p. 337. See appendix, Map 13, "Election of 1800."

23. Plumer, "Autobiography" (LC), p. 84.

24. Plumer to Smith, June 14, 1800, Letters 1, and "Autobiography," p. 84, both in Plumer Papers (LC).

25. Charles Paullin, *Atlas of the Historical Geography of the United States* (Baltimore, 1932), pp. 89, 93.

26. Samuel Eliot Morison, *The Life and Letters of Harrison Gray Otis*, 2 vols. (Cambridge, Mass., 1913), 1:186–87.

27. Plumer to Smith, June 14, 1800, Letters 1, and "Autobiography," p. 85, both in Plumer Papers (LC).

28. *Journal of the House of Representatives*, November session, 1800 (Portsmouth, N.H., 1801), pp. 74, 105.

29. Plumer, "Autobiography" (LC), p. 86.

30. *Columbian Centinel*, January 7, 1801.

31. Edward Stanwood, *A History of the Presidency, 1789–1897*, 2 vols. (Boston, 1898),

1:72. New Hampshire's four congressmen, Abiel Foster of Canterbury, Jonathan Freeman of Hanover, Samuel Tenney of Exeter, and Jacob Sheafe of Portsmouth, also voted for the Judiciary Act of 1801 and for every other administrative bill introduced into the Sixth Congress. J. Manning Dauer, *The Adams Federalists* (Baltimore, 1953), pp. 317–18.

32. Plumer to Livermore, January 13, 1803, Letters 1, Plumer Papers (LC).

33. Lawrence Shaw Mayo, *John Langdon of New Hampshire* (Concord, N.H., 1937), pp. 267–77.

34. *Journal of the House of Representatives*, June session, 1806 (Portsmouth, N.H., 1801), pp. 6, 14; Plumer to Smith, June 13, 1801, Letters 3, Plumer Papers (LC).

35. Plumer, "Autobiography" (LC), p. 92; *House Journal*, June 1801, p. 64.

36. Charles H. Bell, *The Bench and Bar of New Hampshire* (Boston, 1894), p. 48.

37. John H. Morison, *The Life of Jeremiah Smith* (Boston, 1845), pp. 150–54.

38. *Journal of the Senate*, June session, 1801 (Portsmouth, N.H., 1801), p. 27; *House Journal*, 1801, pp. 36–38.

39. Plumer, "Autobiography" (LC), p. 93.

40. *House Journal*, June 1801, pp. 60–62; *Senate Journal*, June 1801, pp. 47–48.

41. Samuel Tenney to Josiah Bartlett, January 25, 1802, Bartlett Papers, Library of Congress.

42. Plumer to Henry Dearborn, June 1, 1801, Letters 3, Plumer Papers (LC); Dearborn to Plumer, June 13, 1801, William Plumer Papers, New Hampshire State Library.

43. Plumer, "Autobiography" (LC), p. 69. Joseph Whipple, one of the "notorious Jacobins," had written to President Jefferson asking for "re-establishment" as collector of customs "as a healing specific to a wound maliciously inflicted through the enemies of our country's peace and independence" (Leonard D. White, *The Jeffersonians: A Study in Administrative History, 1801–1829* [New York, 1951], pp. 365–66).

44. Plumer to George Upham, March 15, 1802, Letters 1, Plumer Papers (LC).

45. Plumer to David Hough, January 30, 1802, Letters 1, Plumer Papers (LC).

46. *New Hampshire Register, 1860*, pp. 40–41.

47. Thomas Jefferson to John Langdon, June 29, 1802, folio 124, Jefferson Papers, Library of Congress.

48. *Journal of the House of Representatives*, June session, 1802 (Concord, N.H., 1802).

49. Samuel Tenney to Josiah Bartlett, February 18, 1803, Bartlett Papers.

50. *New Hampshire Gazette*, August 10, 1802.

51. (Concord) *Republican Gazette*, June 22, 1802.

CHAPTER 11

1. The epigraph is from William Plumer, "Cincinnatus, No. 141, 'On Manufactures,' " published in the *Portsmouth Journal*, original manuscript in Plumer, "Essays," 3:191–96, William Plumer Papers, New Hampshire State Library.

2. George Tucker, *Progress of the United States* (New York, 1843), pp. 15, 32.

3. Statistics for this table come from John Farmer and Jacob Moore, *A Gazetteer of the State of New Hampshire* (Concord, N.H., 1823).

4. Harold Wilson, *The Hill Country of Northern New England* (New York, 1936), chap. 1.

5. Edward St. Loe Livermore to William Plumer, Jr., March 17, 1816, *Indiana Magazine of History* 35 (June 1939): 181–82.

6. Letter of T. Hands, reprinted from the (London) *Monthly Magazine*, September 1821, in *Magazine of History* 18 (1914): 111–13.

7. See appendix, Map 2, "Population in 1775," and Map 21, "Population in 1820."

8. Harold Wilson, "Population Trends in Northwestern New England, 1790–1930," *New England Quarterly* 7 (1934): 292.

9. Ibid., pp. 286, 291. See the very interesting maps on pages 276–77, showing the towns which lost population each decade, 1790–1930.

10. Farmer and Moore, *Gazetteer*, p. 7.

11. David McPherson, *Annals of Commerce*, 4 vols. (London, 1805), 3:570–71.

12. George Barstow, *History of New Hampshire* (Concord, N.H., 1842), p. 342.

13. Farmer and Moore, *Gazetteer*, pp. 30–31. In 1801, New Hampshire exported goods worth $555,055, a fourth of which were foreign reexports. Only three other states exported less (J. Manning Dauer, *The Adams Federalists* [Baltimore, 1953], p. 10).

14. In 1817, William Plumer, Jr., living in Portsmouth, reported to his father that goods from the Piscataqua were being sold to Boston and reshipped at a profit by Boston merchants to Concord, via the Middlesex Canal (Plumer, Jr., to Plumer, October 18, 1817, Plumer Papers [NHSL]).

15. Nathaniel Adams, *Annals of Portsmouth* (Portsmouth, N.H., 1825), pp. 306–7.

16. Tucker, *Progress of the United States*, p. 135.

17. Augustus Gould and Frederic Kidder, *History of New Ipswich* (Boston, 1852), p. 224.

18. Fred Lamb, "Amoskeag Manufacturing Company," *Granite State Monthly* 61 (1929): 192–95.

19. Frederick Irwin, "Glass-Making in New Hampshire," *Granite State Monthly* 60 (1928): 93.

20. Farmer and Moore, *Gazetteer*, p. 30.

21. *Granite State Monthly* 61 (1929): 192.

22. Plumer, "Autobiography," p. 270, William Plumer Papers, Library of Congress.

23. Report of a Committee on Manufactures, *Journal of the Senate*, June session, 1810 (Concord, N.H., 1810), p. 74.

24. *Journal of the Senate*, June session, 1819 (Concord, N.H., 1819), pp. 77–78.

25. *Annals of Congress*, Fourteenth Congress, First Session, pp. 331, 1344, 1352.

26. Farmer and Moore, *Gazetteer*, p. 29.

27. Mabel Hope Kingsbury, "Turnpikes, Toll-Gates and Stage Coach Days in New Hampshire," *Granite State Monthly* 52 (1920): 145–46.

28. Farmer and Moore, *Gazetteer*, pp. 15, 17. One of the best bridges was erected in 1796 by the White River Falls Bridge Company (chartered in 1792) across the Connecticut River between Hanover and Norwich, Vermont. Bridge companies were resisted by monopolists who operated licensed ferries. (W. R. Waterman, "The Story of a Bridge," *Historical New Hampshire* 20 [1965]: 3–26).

29. Edwin Bacon, *The Connecticut River* (New York, 1906), pp. 314–15.

30. Fred Lamb, "Canal Boat Days," *Granite State Monthly* 61 (1929): 277–80.

31. Thomas Amory, *Life of James Sullivan*, 2 vols. (Boston, 1859) 1:361–71.

32. *Granite State Monthly* 61 (1929): 426–28.

33. Ibid., p. 380; Farmer and Moore, *Gazetteer*, p. 14.

34. Plumer, "Autobiography" (LC), p. 262.

35. *Journal of the Senate*, June session, 1811 (Concord, N.H., 1811), p. 89.

36. Plumer, "Essays," 1:96, William Plumer Papers, New Hampshire State Library.

37. *Journal of the House of Representatives*, June session, 1812 (Concord, N.H., 1812), pp. 91, 112. The Concord Boating Company, as it was subsequently called, operated twenty boats, each sixty feet long and twenty feet wide. The business flourished until 1842, when it was absorbed by the Concord Railroad. Abiel Rolfe, *Recollections of Seventy Years in Concord, N.H.* (Penacook, N.H., 1901), pp. 50–51; Raymond P. Holden, *The Merrimack* (New York, 1958), pp. 150–61.

38. *Journal of the Senate*, November session, 1816 (Concord, N.H., 1817), pp. 107–17.

39. *Senate Journal*, June 1819, p. 36.

40. Bartlett's report is printed in the *Senate Journal*, June 1819, pp. 34–65.

41. See pp. 120–21, 178–81.

42. Farmer and Moore, *Gazetteer*, p. 40. Outside capital, of course, purchased much of New Hampshire's bank stock, but there are no reports on the exact amount.

43. Nathaniel Bouton, *History of Concord* (Concord, N.H., 1856), pp. 337–38; Joseph Walker, "Banking and Currency in New Hampshire," in William Davis, ed., *New England States*, 4 vols. (Boston, 1897), 2:1646.

44. Such notables as Charles H. Atherton, Colonel Robert Means, Judge Ebenezer Champney, and Robert Fletcher, the well-known land speculator, were among the petitioners and directors of the Hillsborough Bank. Its president was Samuel Bell, a future judge and governor. The charter permitted the bank to issue notes to double the amount of its stock, but within a year after its founding it had issued $490,000 in notes and made loans of $418,317 against a specie reserve of less than $20,000. More than six hundred suits were brought against the bank directors after its doors were closed. See Norman W. Smith, "The 'Amherst Bubble': Wildcat Banking in Early Nineteenth Century New Hampshire," *Historical New Hampshire* 20 (1965): 27–40.

45. Eliphalet Merrill, *Gazetteer of the State of New Hampshire* (Exeter, N.H., 1817), p. 44.

46. Adams, *Annals of Portsmouth*, p. 327. The company's office building, now headquarters of the Portsmouth Athenaeum, stands in Market Square and appears in most collections of Portsmouth photographs.

47. Henry Robinson, "The New Hampshire State Prison," *Granite State Monthly* 15 (1892): 216–18.

48. William Whitcher, *History of the Town of Haverhill* (Concord, N.H., 1919), pp. 362–63.

49. *Journal of the Senate*, June session, 1812 (Concord, N.H., 1812), p. 39.

50. As usual, New Hampshire followed the example of its neighbor state Massachusetts, where the state prison at Charlestown had been established in 1805. Orlando Lewis, *The Development of American Prisons and Prison Customs, 1776–1845* (Albany, N.Y., 1922), pp. 68–76.

51. *Journal of the Senate*, June session, 1814 (Concord, N.H., 1814), p. 103.

52. Farmer and Moore, *Gazetteer*, p. 44.

53. Lewis, *Development of American Prisons*, p. 149.

54. *Journal of the House of Representatives*, June session, 1806 (Portsmouth, N.H., 1806), p. 12.

55. *Senate Journal*, June 1814, p. 109.

56. Hosea Hildreth, *A Book for New-Hampshire Children*, 5th ed. (Exeter, N.H., 1839), p. 48.

57. Elias Smith, *The Life of Elias Smith* (Boston, 1840), pp. 206–7.

58. Isaac Stewart, *History of the Freewill Baptists*, 2 vols. (Dover, N.H., 1852), 336.

59. Abel Stevens, *Memorials of the Introduction of Methodism into New England*, 1:92, 356, and vol. 2 passim. The very first Methodist "missionary" to New Hampshire was Philip Embury, an Irish immigrant to New York, who had organized American Methodism's oldest church in New York City in 1766, and later took up land in Duane's tract, northeast of Albany. At James Robertson's invitation, he traveled across the "New Hampshire Grants" in the autumn of 1772 and preached the first Methodist sermon in Robertson's home in Chesterfield. (Arthur Bruce Moss, "Philip Embury's Preaching Mission at Chesterfield, New Hampshire," *Methodist History* 16 [January 1978]: 101–9).

60. Lucius Harrison Thayer, *Religious Condition of New Hampshire at the Beginning of the Nineteenth Century* (Rochester, N.H., 1901), pp. 16–17.

61. Massachusetts Historical Society, *Collections*, 5th series 2 (1877): 328.

62. Richard Eddy, *Universalism in America*, 2 vols. (Boston, 1886), 1:164.

63. Thayer, *Religious Condition*, p. 19.

64. This table is derived from information in John Farmer, *An Ecclesiastical Register of New Hampshire* (Concord, N.H., 1821).

65. *Laws of New Hampshire* (Dover, 1805), p. 393.

66. Everett Somerville Brown, ed., *William Plumer's Memorandum of Proceedings in the United States Senate, 1803–1807* (New York, 1923), p. 353. See also William G. McLoughlin, "The Bench, the Church, and the Republican Party in New Hampshire, 1790 to 1820," *Historical New Hampshire* 20 (Summer 1965): 3–31.

67. In Charles B. Kinney, Jr., *Church and State in New Hampshire* (New York, 1955), pp. 86–93, the author cites towns such as Loudon, Hopkinton, Hillsborough, and Gilmanton as abandoning ecclesiastical taxation prior to 1819.

68. John Peck, *A Short Poem on the Universal Plan*, 4th ed. (Boston, 1858).

69. Romans 16:17–18.

70. Ebenezer Cummings, *Annals of Baptist Churches in New Hampshire* (Concord, N.H., 1836), p. 32.

71. New Hampshire Historical Society, *Collections* 9 (1889): 55–58.

72. Jacob Cram, *Journal of a Missionary Tour* (Rochester, N.H., 1909).

73. William Patton, *The Last Century of Congregationalism* (Washington, D.C., 1878), p. 7.

74. Smith, *Elias Smith*, pp. 306–7.

75. Stevens, *Memorials of Methodism*, 1:461.

76. Thayer, *Religious Condition*, p. 12.

77. Elias Smith, *The Clergyman's Looking Glass* (Portsmouth, N.H., 1803), pp. 6, 8.

78. Stewart, *Freewill Baptists*, p. 154.

79. Isaac Backus, *History of New England Baptists*, 3 vols., 2d ed. (Newton, Mass., 1871), 2:542.

80. Thayer, *Religious Condition*, p. 15.

81. Stevens, *Memorials of Methodism*, 2:414.

82. Cummings, *Annals of the Baptists*, pp. 24, 51.

CHAPTER 12

1. The epigraph is from a letter, Jeremiah Smith to William Plumer, December 25, 1803, quoted in John H. Morison, *The Life of Jeremiah Smith* (Boston, 1845), p. 214.

2. John Langdon to Thomas Jefferson, January 26, 1803, folio 129, Thomas Jefferson Papers, Library of Congress.

3. Parker Lyon, ed., *New Hampshire Register, 1860* (Concord, N.H., 1859), p. 41.

4. Nathaniel Adams, *Annals of Portsmouth* (Portsmouth, N.H., 1825), pp. 324–25.

5. Smith to Plumer, December 28, 1802, William Plumer Papers, New Hampshire State Library.

6. Plumer to Smith, January 27, 1803, Plumer Papers (NHSL).

7. Everett Somerville Brown, ed., *William Plumer's Memorandum of Proceedings in the United States Senate, 1803–1807* (New York, 1923), p. 9.

8. *Journal of the House of Representatives*, November session, 1803 (Concord, N.H., 1804), p. 122.

9. Morison, *Smith*, pp. 148–49. The ousted judges met in Philadelphia in November 1802 and sent an ineffectual protest to Congress.

10. *New Hampshire State Papers* (Concord, N.H., 1877), 22:843. In the first edition of his *Thomas Jefferson* (Boston, 1883), p. 259, John T. Morse called Pickering "a worthless fellow, morally and mentally." Dr. Andrew Peabody published a communication in the Massachusetts Historical Society, *Proceedings* 20 (1883): 333–38, which took Morse to task for his hasty judgment. Morse subsequently admitted, in an appendix to the 1897 edition of his book (p. 345) that he had done "an unintentional injustice to the memory of a worthy man." See also Adams, *Annals of Portsmouth*, pp. 332–34.

11. *Annals of Congress*, Sixth Congress (Washington, D.C., 1851), p. 1545.

12. Affidavits of William Plumer, Jonathan Steele, et al. in *Annals of Congress*, Eighth Congress, First Session, pp. 336–37.

13. See "First Article of Impeachment" and Edward Livermore's deposition in *Annals of Congress*, Eighth Congress, First Session, pp. 446–47, 337–38.

14. *Documents relative to John Pickering* (Washington, D.C., 1803), pp. 2–14.

15. Deposition of Edward Livermore, note 13 above. For a more complete account of the Pickering case, see Lynn W. Turner, "Impeachment of John Pickering," *American Historical Review* 54 (1948–49): 489 ff.

16. Plumer to James Sheafe, December 13, 1802, Letters 1, William Plumer Papers, Library of Congress.

17. *Documents relative to John Pickering*, p. 3.

18. *Annals of Congress*, Seventh Congress, Second Session, pp. 460, 544, 642.

19. *Extracts from the Journal of the United States Senate in All Cases of Impeachment* (Washington, 1912), p. 17.

20. Dumas Malone questions whether either Gallatin or Jefferson realized that Pickering was actually insane. If they had, they might not have prosecuted the case so vigorously. William Plumer, however, had testified personally to both men that Pickering could not be responsible for his behavior. See Dumas Malone, *The First Term* (Boston, 1974), pp. 460–64.

21. James Bayard to Robert G. Harper, January 30, 1804, in Elizabeth Donnan, ed., *Papers of James A. Bayard*, American Historical Association, *Annual Report, 1913* (Washington, D.C., 1915), 2:150–61.

22. *Annals of Congress*, Eighth Congress, First Session, pp. 333–62; Plumer, *Memorandum*, pp. 156–68.

23. Charles Francis Adams, ed., *Memoirs of John Quincy Adams*, 12 vols. (Philadelphia, 1874–77), 1:299–303.

24. *Extracts in Cases of Impeachment*, p. 34.

25. Plumer, "Biographical Sketches," 5:327, William Plumer Papers, New Hampshire Historical Society.

26. Massachusetts Historical Society, *Proceedings* 20 (1883): 334.

27. Plumer to Thomas Thompson, March 19, 1804, Letters 4, Plumer Papers (LC).

28. For more on this plot see Hervey Prentiss, *Timothy Pickering as the Leader of New England Federalism* (Evanston, Ill., 1932), and Lynn W. Turner, *William Plumer of New Hampshire* (Chapel Hill, 1962), pp. 133–50, 345–46.

29. Smith to Plumer, January 28, 1804, Letters 4, Plumer Papers (LC).

30. Smith to Plumer, February 22, 1804, Letters 4, Plumer Papers (LC). Judge Smith was well informed, but his accusation that the Republicans had acted in secret was false. The Boston *Independent Chronicle*, a Republican paper, reported that a "General Convention" of Republican members of the legislature and other citizens met at Concord in December and created a "Grand Committee of Election and Correspondence" consisting of six per-

sons from each county with John Goddard as chairman (Noble Cunningham, *The Jeffersonian Republicans in Power: Party Operations, 1801–1809* [Chapel Hill, 1963], p. 142).

31. See Jefferson's letters to Elbridge Gerry and Gideon Granger in Andrew Lipscomb, ed., *The Writings of Thomas Jefferson*, 20 vols. (Library Edition, Washington, D.C., 1903), 11:15, 24. Granger kept the president minutely informed of the election returns throughout New England. See Jefferson Papers, folios 139, 140, 142.

32. Smith to Plumer, March 11 and 18, 1804, Letters 4, Plumer Papers (LC).

33. Parker Lyon, ed., *New Hampshire Register, 1860* (Concord, N.H., 1859), p. 41.

34. William Robinson, *Jeffersonian Democracy in New England* (New Haven, 1916), p. 77.

35. *New Hampshire State Papers* (Concord, N.H., 1892), 21:807.

36. John Lord, *A History of Hanover, N.H.* (Hanover, N.H., 1928), p. 163.

37. William Plumer, "Proceedings of the Federalists of New Hampshire in 1804," "Repository," 1:264–68, William Plumer Papers, New Hampshire State Library.

38. [Impartialis], *An Address to the Electors of New Hampshire* (Portsmouth, N.H., 1804), p. 3.

39. Gideon Granger to Thomas Jefferson, September 2, 1804, folio 143, Jefferson Papers.

40. Robinson, *Jeffersonian Democracy*, p. 64n.

41. *A Republican Address to the Electors of New Hampshire* (Walpole, N.H., 1804), p. 3.

42. *New Hampshire Register, 1860*, p. 22.

43. Samuel Eliot Morison, *The Life and Letters of Harrison Gray Otis*, 2 vols. (Cambridge, Mass., 1913), 1:262–63; James Truslow Adams, *New England in the Republic* (Boston, 1926), p. 170.

44. *Journal of the House of Representatives*, June session, 1804 (Portsmouth, N.H., 1804), p. 23. This quotation is actually taken from Gilman's opening address rather than from the veto message in which the same sentiment is expressed, but less forcefully.

45. *Journal of the House of Representatives*, November session, 1804 (Portsmouth, N.H., 1805), pp. 44–45.

46. John Bach McMaster, *History of the People of the United States*, 8 vols. (New York, 1883), 3:45–47.

CHAPTER 13

1. The epigraph is from a letter, William Plumer to Uriah Tracy, May 2, 1805, Letters 4, William Plumer Papers, Library of Congress.

2. William Robinson, *Jeffersonian Democracy in New England* (New Haven, 1916), pp. 68–69.

3. Richard Purcell, *Connecticut in Transition, 1775–1818* (Washington, D.C., 1918), pp. 310–11.

4. (Walpole) *Political Observatory*, March 9, 1805.

5. Ibid., February 2, 1805.

6. Claude Fuess, *Daniel Webster*, 2 vols. (Boston, 1930), 1:68.

7. [Webster] An Old Whig, *An Appeal to the Old Whigs of New Hampshire* (n.p., 1805).

8. Parker Lyon, ed., *New Hampshire Register, 1860* (Concord, N.H., 1859), p. 41. Between 1800 and 1805 the Republican vote for governor in New Hampshire increased 166 percent. This was part of a general trend in New England. The Republican vote in Massachusetts grew by 106 percent between 1800 and 1807; in Vermont 205 percent during the same years; and 792 percent in Connecticut from 1801 to 1806 (Robinson, *Jeffersonian*

Democracy, pp. 74–75). Edward Stackpole, *History of New Hampshire*, 4 vols. (New York, 1916), 3:6, makes the amazing declaration that William Plumer organized this Republican landslide.

9. Thomas Jefferson to John Langdon, January 9, 1805, folio 146, Thomas Jefferson Papers, Library of Congress.

10. *Journal of the House of Representatives*, June session, 1804 (Portsmouth, N.H., 1804), pp. 41–45.

11. *Journal of the Senate*, June session, 1804 (Portsmouth, N.H., 1804), p. 28.

12. Smith's long letter of application is printed in John H. Morison, *The Life of Jeremiah Smith* (Boston, 1845), pp. 156–65.

13. *House Journal*, June 1804, p. 45.

14. Smith to Plumer, January 1, 1805, Letters 4, Plumer Papers (LC).

15. Arthur Livermore to the Legislative Committee of Investigation, November 30, 1805, copy in Plumer, "Repository," 3:155, Plumer Papers (LC).

16. *Journal of the House of Representatives*, June session, 1805 (Portsmouth, N.H., 1805), pp. 73, 77.

17. *Journal of the House of Representatives*, December session, 1805 (Portsmouth, N.H., 1806), p. 93.

18. Samuel Eliot Morison, *The Life and Letters of Harrison Gray Otis*, 2 vols. (New York, 1913), 1:259–60.

19. Lawrence Shaw Mayo, *John Langdon of New Hampshire* (Concord, N.H., 1937), pp. 284–85.

20. *House Journal*, June 1805, pp. 9–11.

21. *Journal of the House of Representatives*, June session, 1806 (Portsmouth, N.H., 1806), pp. 56, 65, 77.

22. *House Journal*, December 1805, pp. 17–18.

23. *House Journal*, June 1805, p. 15; Everett Somerville Brown, ed., *William Plumer's Memorandum of Proceedings in the United States Senate, 1803–1807* (New York, 1923), p. 324.

24. *House Journal*, December 1805, p. 36. See Herman Ames, *Proposed Amendments to the Constitution of the United States*, in American Historical Association, *Annual Report, 1896* (Washington, D.C., 1897), 2:327.

25. Plumer to Langdon, February 3, 1806, Letters 4, Plumer Papers (LC).

26. *House Journal*, December 1805, pp. 74–75; Ames, *Proposed Amendments*, 2:157–58, 326–27.

27. *House Journal*, December 1805, p. 94.

28. *House Journal*, June 1806, p. 50.

29. *New Hampshire Register, 1860*, p. 31.

30. *House Journal*, June 1806, p. 27.

31. (Walpole) *Newhampshire and Vermont Journal*, March 14, 1806.

32. See appendix, Map 13, "Gubernatorial Election of 1800."

33. See appendix, Map 14, "Republican Triumph, 1800–1806."

34. The statistics in this paragraph are based on the votes in gubernatorial elections, 1799–1805, as officially counted by legislative committees and recorded in the journals. They may be regarded as reasonably accurate. They are conveniently collected in the *New Hampshire Register for 1860*, pp. 40–41.

35. The statistics in these tables are taken from newspaper reports of the votes in town meetings for governor. They are far from accurate, but sufficiently so to demonstrate the trend toward Republicanism.

36. Robinson, *Jeffersonian Democracy*, pp. 54–55.

37. Ibid., p. 55.

38. George Leutscher, *Early Political Machinery in the United States* (Philadelphia, 1903), pp. 122–24.

39. William Plumer, "Autobiography," William Plumer Papers, Library of Congress, pp. 55, 100, 158.

40. Jacob Meyer, *Church and State in Massachusetts, 1740–1833* (Cleveland, Ohio, 1930), p. 144.

41. Robinson, *Jeffersonian Democracy*, pp. 138–40.

42. Elias Smith, *Life of Elias Smith* (Boston, 1840), p. 272.

43. Lucius Harrison Thayer, *Religious Condition of New Hampshire at the Beginning of the Nineteenth Century* (Rochester, N.H., 1901), p. 11.

44. Quoted in Robinson, *Jeffersonian Democracy*, p. 141.

45. *Portsmouth Oracle*, March 11, 1809.

46. William G. McLoughlin, "The Bench, the Church and the Republican Party in New Hampshire, 1790 to 1820," *Historical New Hampshire* 20, no. 2 (Summer 1965): 3–31.

47. See appendix, Map 15, "Union Bank."

48. *House Journal*, June 1805, pp. 11, 69, 79.

49. On a resolution to accept a committee report in favor of creating congressional districts in 1790, the vote was 22 yeas, 39 nays (*New Hampshire State Papers* [Concord, N.H., 1893], 22:70). In 1799, the House of Representatives refused even to appoint a committee on the subject by a vote of 22 yeas, 104 nays. (*Journal of the House of Representatives*, December session, 1799 [Portsmouth, N.H., 1800], p. 45).

50. The vote on the districting bill in 1803 was 69–75 (*Journal of the House of Representatives*, November session, 1803 [Concord, 1804], p. 106). Roll-call vote on the bill, finally passed in 1804 but vetoed by Governor Gilman, was 83–69 (*House Journal*, June 1804, p. 53). Exeter, Barrington, Londonderry, Bedford, Dublin, Gilmanton, Sanbornton, Plymouth, Sandwich, Claremont, Hanover, Bath, and Lancaster held out against districting to the bitter end.

CHAPTER 14

1. The epigraph is from a poem written by an anonymous poet in Dover, New Hampshire, to be sung at an Independence Day celebration on July 4, 1808. Quoted in Walter Jennings, *The American Embargo, 1807–1809* (Iowa City, 1921), pp. 128–29.

2. Vermont and Rhode Island were also safely in the Republican column by 1806. Only Connecticut remained under Federalist control in all New England (William Robinson, *Jeffersonian Democracy in New England* [New Haven, 1916], chap. 5).

3. Everett Somerville Brown, ed., *William Plumer's Memorandum of Proceedings in the United States Senate, 1803–1807* (New York, 1923), p. 528.

4. John Peirce to William Plumer, April 7, 1806, Letters 4, William Plumer Papers, Library of Congress.

5. James Sheafe to Plumer, March 2, 1806, Letters 4, Plumer Papers (LC).

6. William Plumer, "Autobiography," William Plumer Papers, Library of Congress, p. 230.

7. Nathaniel Adams, *Annals of Portsmouth* (Portsmouth, N.H., 1825), pp. 343–44.

8. Charles Francis Adams, ed., *Memoirs of John Quincy Adams*, 12 vols. (Philadelphia, 1874–77), 1:468–69; W. C. Ford, "The Recall of John Quincy Adams in 1808," *Massachusetts Historical Society, Proceedings* 45 (1912): 357.

9. Plumer to J. Q. Adams, February 12, 1808, Plumer Papers, New Hampshire State Library; Plumer, "Autobiography" (LC), p. 230.

10. *Annals of Congress*, Tenth Congress, First Session, 1:51, 372, 1222, 1271.

11. Plumer to Samuel Mitchell, January 26, 1808, Letters 3, Plumer Papers (LC).

12. (Concord) *American Patriot*, December 6, 1808.

13. Jennings, *American Embargo*, pp. 219–20.

14. Ibid., pp. 216–17.

15. Ibid., p. 213.

16. See tables in Jennings, *American Embargo*, pp. 214, 216.

17. Ibid., p. 213.

18. Ibid., p. 186. These prices are for Massachusetts. New Hampshire losses may not have been quite so great, although their prices were usually fixed by the Boston and New York markets.

19. *Journal of the House of Representatives*, June session, 1808 (Concord, N.H., 1808), pp. 12–14.

20. Ibid., pp. 34–36.

21. Ibid., pp. 72–77.

22. *Journal of the House of Representatives*, November session, 1808 (Dover, N.H., 1809), pp. 25–27.

23. Daniel Webster, *Writings and Speeches*, 18 vols. (Boston, 1903), 15:600–601.

24. Jefferson to Langdon, August 2, 1808, folio 179, Jefferson Papers, Library of Congress.

25. Langdon to Jefferson, August 13, 1808, folio 180, Jefferson Papers.

26. *New Hampshire State Papers* (Concord, N.H., 1892), 21:808.

27. Langdon to Jefferson, May 14, 1808, folio 177, Jefferson Papers.

28. Jennings, *American Embargo*, p. 122. Joseph Whipple, whom Jefferson had restored to the collector's post in Portsmouth, was especially vigilant in preventing embargo infractions. The areas of the state bordering Canada were less responsive to Langdon's control. See Dumas Malone, *The Second Term* (Boston, 1974), p. 599.

29. Plumer, "Autobiography" (LC), p. 239.

30. See appendix, Map 16, "Federalist Recovery."

31. (Boston) *Independent Chronicle*, May 30, 1808, quoted in Louis Sears, *Jefferson and the Embargo* (Durham, N.C., 1927), p. 177.

32. John Langdon to James Madison, November 3, 1808, vol. 35, Madison Papers, Library of Congress.

33. Jennings, *American Embargo*, p. 130.

34. Robinson, *Jeffersonian Democracy*, p. 82.

35. Plumer, "Autobiography" (LC), p. 242.

36. Sears, *Jefferson and the Embargo*, pp. 186–87.

37. Samuel Eliot Morrison, *The Life and Letters of Harrison Gray Otis*, 2 vols. (Cambridge, Mass., 1913), 2:12.

38. *House Journal*, November 1808, pp. 7–10.

39. Ibid., pp. 25–27.

40. Ibid., p. 17.

41. Ibid., p. 127.

42. W. C. Ford, ed., *The Writings of John Quincy Adams*, 7 vols. (New York, 1913–17), 3:288.

43. *Address to the Citizens of New Hampshire*, by "A Citizen" (n.p., 1808).

44. *Portsmouth Oracle*, December 24, 1808.

45. Webster, *Writings*, 15:564.

46. Quoted in Jennings, *American Embargo*, pp. 128–29.

47. *American Patriot*, November 1, 1808.

48. Ibid., January 31, February 14, 1809.

49. Ibid., February 7, 1809.

50. Ibid., February 21, 1809.

51. Matthew Carey, *The Olive Branch*, 10th ed. (Philadelphia, 1818), p. 306.

52. *American Patriot*, February 14, 1809.

53. William Plumer to Daniel Durell, February 7, 1809, Plumer Papers (NHSL).

54. *American Patriot*, February 7, March 7, 1809.

55. *Annals of Congress*, Tenth Congress, First Session, 2:1375.

56. Plumer, "Autobiography" (LC), p. 245.

57. Quoted in Sears, *Jefferson and the Embargo*, p. 105.

58. (Amherst) *Farmer's Cabinet*, December 13, 1808.

59. *Annals of Congress*, Tenth Congress, Second Session, p. 298.

60. Nicholas Gilman to unnamed correspondent, December 8, 1808, Gilman Papers, Library of Congress. See also *New Hampshire State Papers* (1892), 21:803.

61. *Annals of Congress*, Tenth Congress, Third Session, pp. 1024, 1541.

62. Ibid., pp. 436, 903.

63. *Farmer's Cabinet*, April 18, 1809.

64. Morison, *Otis*, 2:33.

65. *American Patriot*, October 25, 1808.

66. Ibid., March 7, 1809.

67. Plumer, "Autobiography" (LC), p. 248.

68. See appendix, Map 16, "Federalist Recovery."

CHAPTER 15

1. The epigraph comes from an observation supposedly made by a member of the legislative committee that notified John Langdon in 1811 that he had been reelected governor of New Hampshire (Frank Sanborn, *New Hampshire: An Epitome of Popular Government* [Cambridge, Mass., 1904], p. 337).

2. *Journal of the House of Representatives*, November session, 1808 (Dover, N.H., 1809), pp. 67–69.

3. Wingate became seventy on May 14, 1809, during the Cheshire term of court. He did not attend the Grafton term, commencing May 23, although notice of his being superseded did not reach him until May 30. (Charles Wingate, *The Life of Paine Wingate*, 2 vols. [Medford, Mass., 1930], 2:476, and *New Hampshire State Papers* [Concord, N.H., 1892], 21:827).

4. William Plumer, "Autobiography," William Plumer Papers, Library of Congress, p. 247.

5. *Portsmouth Oracle*, June 17, 1809.

6. The Walker Papers in the New Hampshire Historical Society Library contain a printed letter of instructions sent by Evans as "Chairman of the Conventional Committee" to Timothy Walker, the Concord Republican leader in 1809 (Walker Papers, folio 1, p. 162, New Hampshire Historical Society).

7. Plumer's biography of Richard Evans in William Plumer, "Biographical Sketches," 5:103, William Plumer Papers, New Hampshire Historical Society.

8. Plumer, "Autobiography" (LC), p. 246.

9. Charles H. Bell, *The Bench and Bar of New Hampshire* (Boston, 1894), pp. 67–68.

10. Plumer to Nahum Parker, June 16, 1809, Letters 3, William Plumer Papers, Library of Congress.

11. *Journal of the House of Representatives*, June session, 1809 (Concord, N.H., 1809), p. 40.

12. John H. Morison, *The Life of Jeremiah Smith* (Boston, 1845), p. 246.

13. Ibid., pp. 246–47.

14. *House Journal*, June 1809, p. 89.

15. Morison, *Smith*, p. 249.

16. Plumer, "Autobiography" (LC), p. 250.

17. Morison, *Smith*, p. 252.

18. Plumer to Samuel Bell, April 16, 1810, Letters 3, Plumer Papers (LC).

19. (Concord) *New Hampshire Patriot*, March 6, 1810. This was the continuation of the *American Patriot*, renamed after Isaac Hill took it over.

20. William Davis, ed., *New England States*, 4 vols. (Boston, 1897), 2:1646.

21. Morison, *Smith*, p. 254.

22. *New Hampshire Patriot*, March 10, 1810.

23. Parker Lyons, ed., *New Hampshire Register, 1860* (Concord, 1859), p. 41.

24. After seventeen years of close friendship and political cooperation, Plumer and Smith fell out over a court case in 1805 and subsequently became bitter enemies. Plumer published five articles under the pen name "Aristides," February 6 to March 6, 1810, in the *New Hampshire Patriot*. They were abusive, personal attacks against Smith and the Federalist party's opposition to the general government. Plumer's authorship was easily detected, and he was subjected to savage reprisals as an "apostate" by the Federalist press. See *Portsmouth Oracle*, March 3, 1810. See also Isaac Hill to Plumer, February 20, 1810, Letters 6, Plumer Papers (LC); William Kent to Daniel Webster, February 28, 1810, Daniel Webster Papers, Library of Congress.

25. See appendix, Map 17, "Republican Recovery."

26. *Journal of the Senate*, June session, 1810 (Concord, N.H., 1810), p. 12. Captain Eli Brown, one of the directors of the Hillsborough Bank, was sued for the arrears in his accounts. He petitioned the legislature in 1810 for an investigation of the bank. An investigating committee visited Amherst and asked to examine the bank's books, but a majority of the directors refused. Both Bell and Brown published defenses of their positions; Brown was supported by the *Patriot*. He attacked Joshua Atherton on the streets of Amherst and was committed to gaol. Norman W. Smith, "The 'Amherst Bubble'; Wildcat Banking in Early Nineteenth Century New Hampshire," *Historical New Hampshire* 20 (1965): 27–40.

27. *Journal of the Senate*, June session, 1806 (Portsmouth, N.H., 1806), p. 76; Davis, ed., *New England States*, 3:1645–47.

28. Daniel Secomb, *History of the Town of Amherst* (Concord, N.H., 1883), p. 450.

29. *Senate Journal*, June 1810, p. 13.

30. Plumer, "Autobiography" (LC), p. 259.

31. *House Journal*, November 1808, p. 93.

32. *Senate Journal*, June 1811, p. 89.

33. Plumer, "Autobiography" (LC), p. 256.

34. *Journal of the House of Representatives*, June session, 1806 (Portsmouth, N.H., 1806), p. 76.

35. *Journal of the House of Representatives*, June session, 1807 (Portsmouth, N.H., 1807), p. 88.

36. William Plumer, Jr., to Plumer, June 12, 1810, Letters 6, Plumer Papers (LC).

37. Plumer, "Autobiography" (LC), p. 257.

38. *New Hampshire Register, 1860*, p. 32. The four Republican representatives were Josiah Bartlett, Jr., of Stratham, John A. Harper of Meredith, Samuel Dinsmoor of Keene, and Obed Hall of Bartlett.

39. *Senate Journal*, June 1810, p. 66.

40. John Parrott to Plumer, July 18, 1810, Letters 3, Plumer Papers (LC).

41. Plumer, "Autobiography" (LC), p. 260. It was after this nomination, and in response to Langdon's ritual remarks about distrusting his ability to fill so responsible a post, that the

naive country member of the notification committee was supposed to have made the remark quoted in the introduction to this chapter.

42. Ibid., p. 263.

43. *Senate Journal*, June 1810, p. 11.

44. *Senate Journal*, June 1810, p. 11.

45. Walter Jennings, *The American Embargo, 1807–1809* (Iowa City, 1921), p. 216.

46. *Senate Journal*, June 1811, pp. 12–13.

47. *Journal of the House of Representatives*, June session, 1811 (Concord, N.H., 1811), p. 57.

48. Plumer, "Autobiography" (LC), pp. 261–62.

49. *House Journal*, June 1811, p. 59.

50. Ibid., p. 98.

51. William Plumer, "Diary" (1807–36), entry for June 24, 1811, William Plumer Papers, Library of Congress.

52. Plumer to Joseph Varnum, December 25, 1807, William Plumer Papers, New Hampshire State Library.

53. *American State Papers, Foreign Relations*, 38 vols. (Washington, D.C., 1832–61), 3:548.

54. W. C. Ford, ed., *The Writings of John Quincy Adams*, 7 vols. (New York, 1913–17), 3:508.

55. Plumer to J. Q. Adams, May 18, 1810, Letters 3, Plumer Papers (LC).

56. Levi Bartlett to Josiah Bartlett, February 4, 1812, Bartlett Papers, Library of Congress.

57. *New Hampshire Patriot*, February 11, March 7, 1812. The major part of Isaac Hill's remarkable career came after 1820, but he was already making his presence felt by 1812. Born in Cambridge, Massachusetts, into a family marked by insanity, ignorance, and poverty, crippled by a childhood injury, slight, short, and unprepossessing in appearance, Hill surmounted every obstacle and by sheer determination and a sure instinct for the jugular became not only a dominant figure in New Hampshire politics but an eminent backstairs politician on the national scene. See Cyrus Parker Bradley, *Biography of Isaac Hill of New Hampshire* (Concord, N.H., 1835), a campaign eulogy, and Donald B. Cole, *Jacksonian Democracy in New Hampshire* (Cambridge, Mass., 1970), pp. 3–5.

58. *New Hampshire Patriot*, February 11, 1812.

59. Plumer, "Autobiography" (LC), pp. 266–67.

60. Levi to Josiah Bartlett, January 1812, Bartlett Papers.

61. Plumer to William Claggett, March 24, 1812, Plumer Papers (NHSL).

62. *New Hampshire Patriot*, February 11, 1812.

63. William Plumer, Jr., to Obed Hall, March 11, 1812, Plumer Papers (NHSL).

64. Samuel Plumer to William Plumer, Jr., March 14, 1812, Plumer Papers (NHSL).

65. *New Hampshire Register, 1860*, p. 41.

66. *Journal of the Senate*, June session, 1812 (Concord, N.H., 1812), p. 10.

CHAPTER 16

1. The epigraph is from William Plumer's inaugural address, *Speech of His Excellency, William Plumer, to the Legislature, June, 1812* (n.p., 1812).

2. John Harper to William Plumer, December 2, 1811, Letters 6, William Plumer Papers, Library of Congress. Harper's assurance was based on inside information, gained from his appointment by Speaker Clay to the Foreign Relations Committee. By the middle of May he was alerting Plumer to committee decisions recommending a declaration of war, the is-

suance of letters of marque and reprisal, and an address to Canadians promising their incorporation into the Union. See Roger H. Brown, *The Republic in Peril: 1812* (New York, 1964), pp. 54–56, 122.

3. William Plumer, "Autobiography," William Plumer Papers, Library of Congress, p. 266.

4. *Journal of the House of Representatives*, June session, 1812 (Concord, N.H., 1812), pp. 23–30.

5. It is interesting to see how historical scholarship, after wandering pretty far afield a few decades ago, has come around generally to agreement with Governor Plumer's analysis of the casus belli. Reginald Horsman, *Causes of the War of 1812* (New York, 1975), relegates land hunger to a minor role in stimulating belligerence. Bradford Perkins, *Prologue to War, England and the United States, 1805–1812* (Berkeley, 1961), reemphasizes British arrogance on the high seas as the exacerbating factor. Norman Risjord, "1812: Conservatives, War Hawks, and the Nation's Honor," *William and Mary Quarterly*, 3rd series 18 (April 1961), virtually echoes Plumer's contention that the nation had to choose between war and degradation.

6. *Portsmouth Oracle*, June 13, 1812.

7. *House Journal*, June 1812, p. 117.

8. Ibid., p. 76.

9. Plumer to William Plumer, Jr., June 8, 1812, William Plumer Papers, New Hampshire State Library. The Federalist legislature of New Jersey was less timorous. It repealed a law of 1807 that had provided for popular elections and then proceeded to choose eight Federalist electors in November (Edward Stanwood, *A History of the Presidency 1789–1897*, 2 vols. [Boston, 1898], 1:103).

10. Plumer to John Harper, June 12, 1812, Letters 6, Plumer Papers (LC).

11. General Dearborn to Governor Plumer, June 22, 1812, Letters 3, Plumer Papers (LC).

12. General orders to Brigadier-General Clement Storer, June 24, 1812, copy in Plumer, "Essays," 1:97–98, William Plumer Papers, Library of Congress.

13. Plumer to James Monroe, June 27, 1812, Letters 3, Plumer Papers (LC).

14. *Constitution of New Hampshire* (as of 1812), part 2, article 51.

15. *Annals of Congress*, Twelfth Congress, First Session, p. 2267.

16. General orders by the Captain-General, July 23, 1812, copy in Plumer, "Essays," 1:100–101, Plumer Papers (LC).

17. Joseph Whipple to Governor Plumer, June 1812, Letters 6, Plumer Papers (LC).

18. W. A. Fergusson, comp., *History of Coös County* (Syracuse, 1888), pp. 95 ff.

19. Ephraim Mahurin to Plumer, December 14, 1812, Letters 6, Plumer Papers (LC).

20. John Montgomery to Plumer, May 19, 1813, Letters 6, Plumer Papers (LC).

21. Chandler Potter, "Military History of New Hampshire," *Adjutant-General's Report for 1866*, 2 vols. (Concord, N.H., 1866), 2:387, 393.

22. William Plumer, *Speech of His Excellency, William Plumer, to the Legislature, November, 1812* (Concord, N.H., 1812), pp. 7–8.

23. *Journal of the House of Representatives*, November session, 1812 (Concord, N.H., 1813), pp. 46–47, 122, 136, 171.

24. Plumer, "Autobiography" (LC), p. 286.

25. *House Journal*, November 1812, p. 148.

26. Plumer to John Harper, April 13, 1812, Letters 4, Plumer Papers (LC). See also Henry Adams, *The Life of Albert Gallatin* (Philadelphia, 1879), p. 460.

27. Plumer to John Harper, May 11, 1812, Letters 6, Plumer Papers (LC). See also Marshall Smelser, *The Democratic Republic* (New York, 1968), pp. 230–32.

28. Plumer to Henry Dearborn, July 29, 1812, Letters 3, Plumer Papers (LC).

29. Timothy Dix, Jr. to Plumer, July 24, 1812, Letters 6, Plumer Papers (LC).

30. *New Hampshire Patriot*, February 4, 11, 1812.

31. John Lord, *A History of Hanover, N.H.* (Hanover, N.H., 1928), pp. 8–9.

32. Isaac Hill to William Plumer, Jr., July 10, 1811, Plumer Papers (NHSL).

33. Ezra Bartlett to Josiah Bartlett, February 14, 1812, Bartlett Papers, Library of Congress.

34. *New Hampshire Gazette*, July 7, 1812.

35. Plumer, "Autobiography" (LC), p. 274.

36. Daniel Webster, *Writings and Speeches*, 18 vols. (Boston, 1903), 15:595.

37. Ibid., pp. 599–610.

38. William Plumer, Jr., "Journal," entry for September 15, 1812, William Plumer, Jr., Papers, New Hampshire State Library.

39. *Annals of Congress*, Twelfth Congress, 1:297, 2:1637. Those who voted *for* the war were Senator Charles Cutts and Representatives Harper, Dinsmoor, and Hall.

40. Josiah Bartlett to Ezra Bartlett, May 30, 1812, Bartlett Papers.

41. Plumer to Harper, May 4, 1812, Letters 6, Plumer Papers (LC). See also Brown, *Republic in Peril*, p. 123.

42. Plumer, "Autobiography" (LC), p. 280.

43. "Demosthenes" in *New Hampshire Patriot*, October 27, 1812.

44. The other four congressmen elected were Bradbury Cilley of Nottingham, Samuel Smith of Peterborough, Roger Vose of Walpole, and Jeduthan Wilcox of Orford—a well-balanced ticket.

45. Plumer, "Autobiography" (LC), p. 277.

46. Ibid., p. 294.

47. Plumer, "Diary," May 19, 1813, Plumer Papers (LC).

48. Plumer to William Plumer, Jr., December 5, 1812, Letters 4, Plumer Papers (LC).

49. James Truslow Adams, *New England in the Republic* (Boston, 1926), p. 270.

50. Samuel Eliot Morison, *The Life and Letters of Harrison Gray Otis*, 2 vols. (Cambridge, Mass., 1913), 2:64.

51. See Governor Strong's speech to the Massachusetts legislature, October 14, 1812, *Resolves of the Commonwealth of Massachusetts*, May 1812, p. 74.

52. Donald B. Cole, *Jacksonian Democracy in New Hampshire* (Cambridge, Mass., 1970), p. 26, states that Governor Plumer sent New Hampshire militia units off to Lundy's Lane, Sackett's Harbor, and Ogdensburg. This statement is wrong on every count. Plumer did not send detached militia units *anywhere*; even under command of army officers rather than the governor, detached militia were not sent out of the state; the New Hampshire troops at Lundy's Lane, and so forth, were volunteers in the United States Army; and, finally, Plumer was no longer in office when these engagements occurred.

53. *House Journal*, November 1812, pp. 160 ff.

54. Plumer, *Speech to the Legislature*, November 1812, pp. 4–6.

55. *Journal of the House of Representatives*, June session, 1794 (Portsmouth, N.H., 1794), p. 49.

56. Plumer, "Autobiography" (LC), p. 293.

57. Emma Watts, "New Hampshire in the War of 1812," *Granite State Monthly* 30 (1898): 357–66.

58. Plumer, "Autobiography" (LC), p. 305.

59. Harper to Plumer, February 6, 1813, Letters 6, Plumer Papers (LC).

60. Plumer to John Adams, March 19, 1813, Letters 3, Plumer Papers (LC).

61. Parker Lyon, ed., *New Hampshire Register, 1860* (Concord, 1859), p. 41.

62. Plumer to James Madison, March 27, 1813, folio 51, James Madison Papers, Library of Congress.

63. William Robinson, *Jeffersonian Democracy in New England* (New Haven, 1916),

chap. 4. The Republican vote in Rhode Island decreased by 80 percent during the war. Caleb Strong, the Federalist governor of Massachusetts, defeated Samuel Dexter in 1814 by more than ten thousand votes.

64. Plumer to Clifton Claggett, March 24, 1812, Plumer Papers (NHSL).

65. *Journal of the House of Representatives*, June session, 1814 (Concord, N.H., 1814), p. 135.

66. Quoted in Robinson, *Jeffersonian Democracy*, p. 165.

67. Julius Pratt, *Expansionists of 1812* (New York, 1925), pp. 49, 126–27.

68. *Annals of Congress*, Twelfth Congress, First Session, 1:657.

69. Plumer to John Quincy Adams, January 24, 1814, Letters 3, Plumer Papers (LC).

70. New Hampshire attitudes strongly support the view expressed by Warren H. Goodman, "The Origins of the War of 1812: A Survey of Changing Interpretations," *Mississippi Valley Historical Review* 28 (1941): 171–86.

71. *Journal of the House of Representatives*, June session, 1813 (Concord, N.H., 1813), pp. 59–60.

72. Matthew Harvey of Henniker demanded war and the annexation of Canada in a Fourth of July oration in 1811. Cole, *Jacksonian Democracy*, p. 15.

CHAPTER 17

1. The epigraph is extracted from a resolution adopted by the Massachusetts legislature in February 1814.

2. Daniel Webster, *Writings and Speeches*, 18 vols. (Boston, 1903), 17:233. New Hampshire Federalists were not alone in their elation. Every state in New England, including Vermont, came under Federalist control in the spring elections of 1813.

3. *Journal of the Senate*, June session, 1813 (Concord, N.H., 1813), p. 58.

4. Ibid., p. 55. For the geographical distribution of Federalist legislators, see appendix, Map 18, "Federalist War Gains."

5. William Plumer, "Clifton Claggett," "Biographical Sketches," 5:459, William Plumer Papers, New Hampshire Historical Society.

6. *Portsmouth Oracle*, July 10, 1813.

7. Plumer, "Richard Evans," "Biographical Sketches" (NHHS), 5:104.

8. *Laws of New Hampshire*, 1813, vol. 8, chap. 36.

9. See, for example, the *Portsmouth Oracle*, July 10, 1813, quoting the *Exeter Constitutionalist*.

10. [William Plumer, Jr.], Phocian, "The Federalism of New Hampshire for 1813," manuscript in William Plumer, Jr., Papers, New Hampshire State Library, no. 7.

11. *New Hampshire Patriot*, August 10, 1813.

12. So Smith himself admitted. He was under heavy pressure from Mason, Webster, Thompson, and Gilman to accept the appointment as his patriotic duty (John H. Morison, *The Life of Jeremiah Smith* [Boston, 1845], pp. 268–71).

13. *Speech of William Claggett, Esq. on the Repeal of the Judiciary Act of 1813* (n.p., 1814).

14. Ibid.

15. Phocian, "Federalism of New Hampshire," no. 7.

16. *New Hampshire Patriot*, June 15, 1813.

17. Ibid., July 20, 1813.

18. *Opinions of Claggett and Evans on an Act of the Legislature of 1813* (Concord, N.H., 1813).

Notes to Pages 287–92 445

19. Ezra Stearns, "Arthur Livermore," Grafton and Coös Counties Bar Association, *Proceedings*, 1892, pp. 439–42.

20. *New Hampshire Patriot*, October 19, 1813.

21. The prospect of a violent clash between the old and new courts had attracted a crowd of spectators to Exeter. William Plumer, Jr., who came from Epping to join the spectators, left an interesting account of these proceedings in his "Journal," 1:449 ff., Plumer, Jr., Papers (NHSL). See also an entertaining but highly prejudiced account in the *Exeter Constitutionalist*, reprinted in the *Portsmouth Oracle*, October 9, 1813.

22. *Portsmouth Oracle*, October 23, 1813.

23. *Journal of the Senate*, special session, October 1813 (Concord, N.H., 1813), pp. 34–40.

24. *Journal of the House of Representatives*, special session, October 1813 (Concord, N.H., 1813), pp. 67–69.

25. For a lawyer's and historian's endorsement of this doctrine, see A. S. Batchellor, "The Tenure of Office of the Judges of the Supreme Court of the State under the Constitution," Bar Association of New Hampshire, *Proceedings, 1902* 6 (1902): 531.

26. *Senate Journal*, October 1813, pp. 57–70.

27. Quoted in [William Plumer], A Layman, *Address to the Clergy of New England on Their Opposition to the Government* (Concord, N.H., 1812), no. 2.

28. Ibid., no. 3.

29. Ibid., nos. 2 and 3.

30. [Asa McFarland] W, "A Defence of the Clergy of New England," nine articles in the *Concord Gazette*, December 28, 1813, to February 22, 1814.

31. [Asa McFarland] A Clergyman, letter in *Concord Gazette*, August 16, 1814.

32. *Nile's Register* (Baltimore, 1813), 5:17; Maurice Robinson, *History of Taxation in New Hampshire* (New York, 1903), p. 111.

33. *Concord Gazette*, March 29, 1814.

34. Parker Lyon, ed., *New Hampshire Register, 1860* (Concord, 1859), p. 41; *Journal of the Senate*, June session, 1814, (Concord, N.H., 1814), p. 9.

35. William Plumer, "Autobiography," William Plumer Papers, Library of Congress, pp. 293, 301–2.

36. *Journal of the House of Representatives*, June session, 1814 (Concord, N.H., 1814), p. 127.

37. Ibid., pp. 128–31.

38. Plumer, "Autobiography" (LC), p. 302.

39. Emma Watts, "New Hampshire in the War of 1812," *Granite State Monthly* 30 (1898): 360.

40. Plumer, "Autobiography" (LC), p. 305.

41. *House Journal*, June 1814, pp. 25, 80, 98, 135.

42. Ibid., p. 117; *Journal of the Senate*, June session, 1814 (Concord, N.H., 1814), pp. 88–89; Plumer, "Autobiography" (LC), p. 303.

43. Daniel Webster to Moses Payson, June 1813 [should be 1814], Daniel Webster Papers, vol. 1, New Hampshire Historical Society. Evidence for the compromise is purely circumstantial. The Portsmouth votes were thrown out for technical noncompliance with an election law passed by a previous legislature. The Republican minority introduced a resolution to reject the votes of all towns which had failed to comply with the law. Since few town clerks had followed the law's provisions faithfully, this resolution, if passed, would have emptied the legislature. In a Federalist-dominated legislature, the resolution was postponed and Hall was elected to the council, both by voice votes.

44. [William Plumer, Jr.], Gracchus, *An Address to the Electors of New Hampshire on*

the Choice of Representatives to Congress (Concord, N.H., 1814). This pamphlet was written at the request of Isaac Hill and other Republican leaders. Hill to Plumer, Jr., June 23, 1814, Letters 6, William Plumer Papers, Library of Congress.

45. [William Plumer], A Farmer, "To the People of New Hampshire," no. 2, Plumer, "Essays," 2:126–31, printed in *New Hampshire Patriot*, August 9, 1814. Claude Fuess, *Daniel Webster*, 2 vols. (Boston, 1930), 1:168, attributes this statement to Isaac Hill.

46. Webster, *Writings*, 14:65, 68. This was a period of tragedy in Webster's personal life. His house in Portsmouth was destroyed by a devastating fire on December 22, 1813, and this was followed by the death of a beloved daughter in 1817 (Ralph Nading Hill, *Yankee Kingdom: Vermont and New Hampshire* [New York, 1973], p. 190).

47. William Plumer to Joshua Darling, December 3, 1814, Letters 3, Plumer Papers (LC).

48. Samuel Eliot Morison, *The Life and Letters of Harrison Gray Otis*, 2 vols. (New York, 1913), 2:181–82.

49. It has been asserted that Governor Gilman's Republican council prevented his calling a special session of the legislature in November 1814. This is true only in the sense of its deterrent effect. See the (Hanover) *Dartmouth Gazette*, November 29, 1815.

50. *New Hampshire Patriot*, October 18, 1814.

51. Ibid., November 15, 1814.

52. Ibid., November 29, 1814.

53. Ibid., January 3, 1815.

54. William Plumer to Jeremiah Mason, December 29, 1814, Letters 3, Plumer Papers (LC). That Plumer gauged the attitude of the delegates, at least those from New Hampshire, shrewdly is confirmed by a long letter of advice from T. W. Thompson to Mills Olcott, December 20, 1814, Dartmouth Manuscripts, 814670, Baker Library, Hanover, N.H.

55. Plumer, "Autobiography" (LC), p. 307. Plumer had urged J. Q. Adams, as one of the peace commissioners, to hold out for the cession of Canada, but had abandoned that hope by 1815. Plumer to John Quincy Adams, January 24, 1814, Letters 3, Plumer Papers (LC).

56. Plumer, "Autobiography" (LC), p. 307. Many of the Federalist lawyers were opposed to Gilman's candidacy, and there were efforts to persuade Mason or Farrar or even the elderly Benjamin West to accept the nomination. When Daniel Webster learned that "Gov. G. is to run again," he wrote to his brother Ezekiel, "I do not at all like this. . . . I think it a very foolish affair" (Daniel to Ezekiel Webster, January 30 [1815], Dartmouth Mss., 815130). Other letters in this collection which reveal these intrigues are John Wheelock to T. W. Thompson, May 7, 1814, 814307; Daniel to Ezekiel Webster, November 29, 1814, 814629; H. Chase to P. M. Olcott, January 10, 1815, 815110.

CHAPTER 18

1. The epigraph is from William Plumer, *Speech of His Excellency, William Plumer, Governor of New Hampshire, Before the Legislature* (Concord, N.H., 1816).

2. [John Wheelock], *Sketches of the History of Dartmouth College* (Newburyport, Mass., 1815). Wheelock sent copies of the *Sketches* to his son-in-law, William Allen, to be distributed in Connecticut, Massachusetts, and New York (Wheelock to Allen, May 22, 1815, Dartmouth Manuscripts, 815322, Baker Library, Hanover, N.H.).

3. William Plumer, "Diary," entry for July 18, 1815, William Plumer Papers, Library of Congress.

4. An excellent analysis of this pamphlet may be found in Leon Richardson, *History of Dartmouth College*, 2 vols. (Hanover, N.H., 1932), 1:304–5. Strangely enough, this attack on clerical influence was prepared with the aid and enthusiastic support of the Reverend Elijah Parish, whom William Plumer had accused of seeking to create a priestly hierarchy.

See William North, "The Political Background of the Dartmouth College Case," *New England Quarterly* 18 (June 1945): 181–203.

5. *Documents Relative to Dartmouth College*, published by order of the general court (Concord, N.H., 1816).

6. T. W. Thompson to Ebenezer Adams, July 13, 1815, Dartmouth Mss., 815413; This letter fell into the hands of the Republicans, by felonious means according to the Federalists, and its intemperate references to Wheelock were given wide publicity. See (Hanover) *Dartmouth Gazette*, November 29, 1815.

7. John Shirley, *The Dartmouth College Causes and the Supreme Court of the United States* (Chicago, 1895), pp. 86–90.

8. Josiah Dunham, *An Answer to the Vindication of the Trustees* (Hanover, N.H., 1816), p. 17. As an elected trustee of Dartmouth College, but a friend of President Wheelock, Governor Gilman appointed a balanced investigating committee consisting of two religious liberals, Daniel A. White and Nathaniel A. Haven, and a conservative Presbyterian, Ephraim P. Bradford—all Federalists (North, "Political Background," pp. 192–93).

9. Dunham, *Answer to the Vindication*, p. 18.

10. *New Hampshire Patriot*, May 23, 1815.

11. *Portsmouth Oracle*, July 8, 1815; *Dartmouth Gazette*, July 19, 1815.

12. *New Hampshire Patriot*, September 5, 1815.

13. Shirley, *Dartmouth College Causes*, p. 100; William Plumer, "Autobiography," p. 313, William Plumer Papers, Library of Congress.

14. Shirley, *Dartmouth College Causes*, p. 96.

15. William Plumer, "Diary," entry for October 15, 1815, William Plumer Papers, Library of Congress.

16. Francis N. Stites, *Private Interest and Public Gain: The Dartmouth College Case, 1819* (Amherst, Mass., 1972), helps to untangle the complicated legal and financial web woven by Eleazer Wheelock in his successful efforts to extract gifts and grants from diverse sources for conflicting purposes. The earl of Dartmouth, for example, disapproved of the charter granted by Governor Wentworth for a "college," so Wheelock set up a double trust, with English trustees administering the Dartmouth fund for the benefit of "Moor's Charity School" and its projected enrollment of Indian lads, while American trustees controlled the other funds in maintaining the college. Wheelock himself disregarded the distinction and used income from the English funds to support his entire enterprise.

17. See, for example, *New Hampshire State Papers* (Concord, N.H., 1892), 21:73, 439, 476; Plumer, "Diary" (LC), entry for July 18, 1815.

18. Richardson, *Dartmouth College*, 1:348.

19. Anyone courageous enough to wish further details of this dreary ecclesiastical vendetta can find them in Wheelock's *Sketches*; [Elijah Parish], *A Candid, Analytical Review of the "Sketches"* (Newburyport, Mass., 1815), written before the "Sketches" were published by a man who had helped prepare them; *A Vindication of the Official Conduct of the Trustees of Dartmouth College* (Concord, N.H., 1815); Josiah Dunham's *Answer to the Vindication*; Peyton Freeman, *A Refutation of Sundry Aspersions in the "Vindication"* (Portsmouth, N.H., 1816); Benoni Dewey, James Wheelock, *A True and Concise Narrative of the Origin of the Church Difficulties in Dartmouth College* (Hanover, N.H., 1815), which runs to 68 pages, etc. The evidence, such as it is, shows that John Wheelock and the trustees were about equally responsible for mixing the affairs of the church and the college and dragging ecclesiastical questions into college concerns.

20. *New Hampshire Patriot*, February 13, 1816.

21. Ibid., January 16, 1816. William Plumer had been alarmed by the appearance of voluntary "Sabbath associations," which circulated petitions for strict Sabbath observance as early as the summer of 1814. He believed they were designed principally to interfere with

the work of recruiting officers and government officials during the war. "Perhaps we are approaching a state of religious intolerance & bigotry greater than existed in the last generation," he wrote (Plumer, "Autobiography" [LC], pp. 305–6).

22. [The Reverend Humphrey] *Moore* v. [Benjamin] *Pool*, reported in the *New Hampshire Patriot*, January 2, 1816. See also, William G. McLoughlin, "The Bench, the Church and the Republican Party in New Hampshire, 1790 to 1820," *Historical New Hampshire* 20, no. 2 (Summer 1965): 3–31. Smith ruled that clergymen under contract to a town corporation were civil officials and were therefore exempt from the federal tax. Few sectarian preachers were a part of the establishment and did not, therefore, come under the exemption.

23. *New Hampshire Patriot*, February 20, 27, 1816. The same idea is expressed in a letter from Samuel Allen to John Wheelock, July 1, 1815, Dartmouth Mss., 815401.1.

24. Levi Bartlett to Ezra Bartlett, January 30, 1816, Bartlett Papers, Library of Congress. "My opinion of the Dartmouth affair is that the Legislature will (as they ought) take up the hearing & remove the whole board of Trustees annull their illegal proceedings & let Mr F Brown go home again."

25. *New Hampshire Patriot*, June 13, 1815.

26. Ibid., May 23, 1815.

27. Ibid., February 23, 1816.

28. Ibid., March 5, 1816.

29. Wheelock voiced the common Federalist attitude of hostility to "an unjust war, conducted in weakness and folly" (Wheelock to Nicholas Gilman, February 15, 1814, Dartmouth Mss., 814155).

30. Plumer, "Autobiography" (LC), p. 314.

31. Plumer to Cyrus Perkins, February 15, 1816, William Plumer Papers, New Hampshire State Library. This is a draft copy of Plumer's reply, written on the back of Perkins's letter to him, February 11, 1816.

32. Plumer, "Autobiography" (LC), p. 313. The practice of nominating candidates for the March elections by legislative caucus during the preceding June left Gilman in the embarrassing position of being a lame-duck governor for practically all of his last year in office.

33. William Plumer, Jr., to E. W. Ripley, November 1, 1815, Plumer Papers (NHSL).

34. Plumer to Amos Brewster, March 22, 1816, draft copy on back of a letter from Brewster to Plumer, March 13, 1816, Plumer Papers (NHSL).

35. Josiah Dunham to Daniel Webster, August 10, 1815, Dartmouth Mss., 815466.

36. *New Hampshire Patriot*, January 2, 1816.

37. Jeremiah Mason to Mrs. Mason, January 24, 27, 1816, quoted in G. S. Hilliard, ed., *Memoirs of Jeremiah Mason*, pp. 130–31. Mason worried about these developments, but was not sorry that he himself had declined the nomination.

38. *New Hampshire Patriot*, January 23, February 6, 1816. That Hill's sources of information were very good is confirmed by a letter from Peyton to Jonathan Freeman, February 17, 1816, Dartmouth Mss., 816167, which contains an illuminating discussion of the political situation between two embarrassed Federalists who supported Wheelock.

39. *New Hampshire Patriot*, February 6, 13, March 5, 1816.

40. [William Plumer, Jr.] *General Address to the Freemen of New Hampshire* (Concord, N.H., 1816), pp. 32, 34–35.

41. *Concord Gazette*, March 9, 1816.

42. *Portsmouth Oracle*, February 10, 17, 24, 1816.

43. *New Hampshire Patriot*, March 5, 1816.

44. Ibid., February 6, April 21, 1816.

45. *Concord Gazette*, February 27, 1816.

46. Ibid., February 6, March 5, April 30, 1816.

47. Parker Lyon, ed., *New Hampshire Register, 1860* (Concord, N.H., 1859), pp. 41–42.

48. *Portsmouth Oracle*, March 16, 1816; (Keene) *New Hampshire Sentinel*, March 16, 1816.

49. The statistics of the election were:

	1815	1816
Total number of votes	36,194	38,407
Increase in total vote		2,213
Votes for Gilman and Sheafe	18,357	17,994
Loss in total Federalist vote		363
Votes for Plumer	17,779	20,338
Increase in Plumer's vote		2,559
Increase additional to total increase		346
Necessary to elect	18,098	19,204
Federalist surplus and deficit	+ 259	− 1,210
Plumer's deficit and surplus	− 319	+ 1,134

50. See appendix, Map 18, "Federalist War Gains," and Map 19, "Republican Triumph."

51. Timothy Farrar to Francis Brown, April 8, 1816, Dartmouth Mss., 816258; Isaac Hill to William Plumer, Jr., April 22, 1816, Plumer Papers (NHSL).

52. Plumer, "Autobiography" (LC), pp. 310, 316.

53. Elijah Paine to Francis Brown, April 12, 1816, Dartmouth Mss., 816262.

54. *New Hampshire Patriot*, April 21, 1816.

55. Isaac Hill to William Plumer, Jr., April 22, 1816, Plumer Papers (NHSL).

56. Charles Arrowood, *Thomas Jefferson and Education in a Republic* (New York, 1930), pp. 31–37; Donald Tewksbury, *The Founding of American Colleges and Universities before the Civil War* (New York, 1932), p. 167.

57. Plumer, "Autobiography" (LC), p. 317; Elmer Brown, *The Origin of State Universities* (Berkeley, 1903), pp. 1–45.

58. Plumer, *Speech Before the Legislature* (Concord, N.H., 1816); *Journal of the Senate*, June session, 1816 (Concord, N.H., 1816), p. 13.

59. Shirley, *Dartmouth College Causes*, pp. 44–52; Stites, *Private Interest and Public Gain*, pp. 4–5.

60. These and other donations are partially summarized in Shirley, *Dartmouth College Causes*, pp. 7–9. Shirley made rather too much of these infrequent legislative grants, some of which were of very doubtful value. Dartmouth completely lost the Landaff grant, for example, to speculators led by Nathaniel Peabody who bought out the proprietors of an earlier, presumably forfeited grant and pushed their claims with brutal aggression, unhindered by courts or legislature. See Frederick Chase, *A History of Dartmouth College and the Town of Hanover, New Hampshire*, 2d ed. (Brattleboro, Vt., 1928), pp. 121, 600 ff.

61. "Memorial of the Trustees of Dartmouth College to the Legislature of New-Hampshire, December, 1795," ms. in New York Public Library; "Memorial of the Trustees," December 14, 1803, Dartmouth Mss.

62. Draft of an "Act More Effectually to Define and Improve . . . Moor's Charity School," Dartmouth Mss., 807360.11. The act was passed in a different form on June 10, 1807.

63. Eleazer W. Ripley to John Wheelock, December 6, 1815, Dartmouth Mss., 815656.

Lawyer, army officer, alumnus of Dartmouth College, grandson of its founder, son of its first theology professor, and nephew of its deposed president, General Ripley was certainly the most colorful lobbyist to appear in Concord during the June session of the legislature. As one of New England's few military heroes in the War of 1812, he enjoyed a considerable popularity, even in Federalist Concord, which honored him with a public dinner. His interest in the Dartmouth business was a curious blend of family loyalty and political intrigue. See Thomas Spaulding, "Ripley, Eleazer Wheelock," *Dictionary of American Biography*, ed. Allen Johnson and Dumas Malone, 20 vols. (New York, 1928–36), 15:621–22.

64. *Journal of the House of Representatives*, June session, 1816 (Concord, N.H., 1816), pp. 30, 45, 46; *Senate Journal*, June 1816, pp. 45, 47. Ripley's bill proposed to establish within Dartmouth University colleges of Arts, Law, Medicine, Politics, and two colleges of Theology, one Baptist and one Methodist, each with a complete set of teachers and officers. Governor Plumer preserved this curious plan in his "Repository," 4:667, Plumer Papers (NHSL).

65. These details were reported in a letter from Governor Plumer to William Plumer, Jr., June 10, 1816, Plumer Papers (NHSL).

66. This is what Daniel Webster was advising from Portsmouth and T. W. Thompson was attempting in Concord. Webster to William Henderson, June, 1816, Dartmouth Mss., 816390.1; Thompson to Francis Brown, June 10, 1816, ibid., 816360.

67. The house of representatives passed a resolution to print three hundred copies of the report and of Wheelock's original memorial to the legislature (*House Journal*, June 1816, pp. 51, 60). Richardson's statement that "the party devoted to the president now endeavored to suppress this document" is obviously incorrect (Richardson, *Dartmouth College*, 1:318). For the printed report, see note 5 of this chapter.

68. *Senate Journal*, June 1816, p. 104; *House Journal*, June 1816, pp. 124–29.

69. *House Journal*, June 1816, p. 90.

70. Copies of this version of the bill were printed and publicly distributed. See *An Act to Amend, Enlarge and Improve the Corporation of Dartmouth College* (Concord, N.H., 1816). Copy among Moore's Pamphlets, Library of Congress.

In 1822, John Farmer and Jacob Bailey Moore began the publication of *The Literary Journal*, or *Collections, Topographical, Historical and Biographical relating principally to New Hampshire*. This enterprise began as a scholarly periodical but was superseded by the publications of the state historical society after 1824. Thereafter, they published pamphlets, among the earliest and most valuable of which was their *Gazetteer of the State of New Hampshire*, published in Concord in 1823. Their pamphlets covered a wide range of subject matter, and when John Farmer withdrew from the enterprise, Jacob Moore carried on alone. The Library of Congress has an extensive collection of these pamphlets.

71. Plumer, "Autobiography" (LC), p. 319.

72. *Portsmouth Oracle*, June 29, 1816.

73. Shirley, *Dartmouth College Causes*, pp. 9–10.

74. *House Journal*, June 1816, pp. 119, 121. Had a bill incorporating these changes been passed and enforced, the trustees could not have claimed violation of contract, since they themselves had proposed the changes.

75. Ibid., pp. 124, 132.

76. T. W. Thompson to Mills Olcott, June 21, 1816, Dartmouth Mss., 816371.

77. Plumer to Plumer, Jr., June 24, 1816, Plumer Papers (NHSL).

78. Levi Woodbury to Plumer, Jr., June 21, 1816, Plumer Papers (NHSL).

79. *House Journal*, June 1816, pp. 133, 165.

80. T. W. Thompson to Mills Olcott, June 21, 1816, Dartmouth Mss., 816371.

81. T. W. Thompson to Mills Olcott, June 21, 1816, Dartmouth Mss., 816371. It is significant that Thompson reported essentially all the amendments made by the committee

on the day after the bill was recommitted.

82. *Concord Gazette*, August 6, 1816.

83. Plumer to Plumer, Jr., June 24, 1816, Plumer Papers (NHSL).

84. Plumer, "Autobiography" (LC), p. 323.

85. *House Journal*, June 1816, pp. 194–99; *Senate Journal*, June 1816, pp. 142–43. It was a party vote, with all the Federalists and two Republicans making up the minority.

86. The Dartmouth Bill as finally passed may be found in *Laws of New Hampshire*, ed. A. S. Batchellor, 10 vols. (Bristol, N.H., 1920), 8:505–8.

87. William Plumer, Jr., "Journal," 2:318, William Plumer, Jr., Papers, New Hampshire State Library.

88. *Senate Journal*, June 1816, pp. 90–98.

89. *House Journal*, June 1816, p. 95; Plumer to Plumer, Jr., June 24, 1816, Plumer Papers (NHSL).

90. Daniel Webster to William Henderson, June 1816, Dartmouth Mss., 816390.1.

91. Plumer to Plumer, Jr., June 24, 1816, Plumer Papers (NHSL).

92. Plumer, "Autobiography" (LC), pp. 319–21.

93. *House Journal*, June 1816, pp. 151–70.

94. Ibid., p. 185.

95. Plumer, "Autobiography" (LC), p. 323. The repeal bill is printed in *Laws of New Hampshire*, 8:501–5.

96. *House Journal*, June 1816, p. 148. There were two vacancies at the time.

97. A. S. Batchellor, "The Tenure of Office of the Judges of the Supreme Court of the State under the Constitution," New Hampshire Bar Association, *Proceedings, 1902* 6(1902): 527. The next judicial purge after 1816 in New Hampshire did not occur until 1855. Then there were two more in 1874 and 1876. Batchellor noted that although Massachusetts had the same constitutional provisions for removal as New Hampshire, no judge had ever been removed by address in that state (up to 1902) and no court had ever been abolished.

98. Plumer vitiated his own reasoning, however, by reappointing William Woodward to the western circuit court after he had been removed by the first address. The Republican majority of the council insisted on thus rewarding a man who had defected to their party.

99. *Senate Journal*, June 1816, pp. 162–63. A comic result of this action was Arthur Livermore's double removal, once by each address.

100. *House Journal*, June 1816, pp. 179–82, 223–58.

CHAPTER 19

1. The epigraph is taken from Plumer's speech recorded in the *Journal of the Senate*, November session, 1816 (Concord, N.H., 1817), p. 14.

2. The seventeen judicial appointments were: three judges to the restored superior court, two justices in each of the six restored courts of common pleas, and one chief justice in each of the two common pleas circuit courts that were retained from the 1813 act.

3. In addition to the twelve incumbent trustees, one of whom was the governor of the state, ex officio.

4. In addition to the four ex officio members: the president of the senate and the speaker of the house of representatives in New Hampshire; the governor and lieutenant governor of Vermont.

5. William Plumer, "Autobiography," p. 319, William Plumer Papers, Library of Congress.

6. Charles Bell, *Life of William M. Richardson* (Concord, N.H., 1839), p. 31; C. S.

Lobingier, "Richardson, William Merchant," *Dictionary of American Biography*, ed. Allen Johnson and Dumas Malone, 20 vols. (New York, 1928–36), 15:579–80.

7. Plumer, "Autobiography" (LC), p. 325.

8. Ibid., p. 326.

9. Ibid.

10. Appointments to the Boards of Dartmouth University, certified by Samuel Sparhawk, July 27, 1816, Dartmouth Manuscripts, 816427, Baker Library, Hanover, N.H.

11. (Keene) *New Hampshire Sentinel*, July 13, 1816.

12. Aaron Hutchinson to William Plumer, Jr., July 9, 1816, William Plumer, Jr., Papers, New Hampshire State Library.

13. Levi Bartlett to Ezra Bartlett, July 18, 1816, Bartlett Papers, Library of Congress. Levi had been offered a commission in common pleas, and Ezra had received a similar appointment to the Grafton County court. Both brothers hesitated to accept, but finally did. The Bartletts and the Plumers were not the best of friends. See letters from Plumer to Ezra Bartlett, June 28, July 9, September 23, 1816, Bartlett Papers.

14. *New Hampshire Sentinel*, July 13, 1816.

15. *New Hampshire Patriot*, July 9, 1816.

16. *Concord Gazette*, July 23, 1816.

17. *Portsmouth Oracle*, July 13, 1816.

18. *Concord Gazette*, July 30, 1816.

19. Ibid., August 13, 1816.

20. Plumer, "Autobiography" (LC), p. 331. A friend reported to Plumer that Farrar had insulted the governor by posting his commission in a grog shop (H. W. Gordon to Plumer, July 24, Plumer to Gordon, July 27, 1816, William Plumer Papers, New Hampshire State Library).

21. Jeremiah Mason to Plumer, August 18, 1816, Plumer Papers (NHSL).

22. Plumer, "Autobiography" (LC), p. 320. Richard Evans had been removed by death from making similar demands upon the new administration.

23. Ibid., p. 326. Later, after being elected to Congress, Claggett insisted on being made clerk of both courts in Hillsborough County and judge of probate. William Richardson to Plumer, October 6, 1816, Plumer Papers (NHSL).

24. William Claggett to Plumer, Jr., July 30, 1816, Plumer Papers (NHSL).

25. Plumer to J. Q. Adams, July 30, 1816, Letters 3, William Plumer Papers, Library of Congress.

26. Copy of notice sent to Nathaniel Niles et al. of meeting to be held in Hanover, August 26, 1816, Dartmouth Mss., 816417.

27. Marsh to Brown, July 17, 27, 1816, Dartmouth Mss., 816417.1, 816417.2.

28. The governor received acknowledgments from Paine, Farrar, Thompson, Smith, McFarland, Brown, and Payson, all preserved among Dartmouth Mss., 816429.1–3, 196459, 816462, and 816470. Most of these managed to convey in subtle language their intention of resisting the new regime. For the panic in the university party, see Levi Woodbury to Plumer, Jr., August 7, 1816, Plumer Papers (NHSL); Josiah Bartlett to Clement Storer, August 13, 1816, and Joshua Darling to Josiah Bartlett, August 20, 1816, Bartlett Papers.

29. Plumer, "Autobiography" (LC), p. 331.

30. Ibid., pp. 331–32.

31. Plumer to Plumer, Jr., August 25, 1816, Plumer Papers (NHSL).

32. This was a favorite diversionary tactic with the college party. Prior to the meeting of the legislature in June, Daniel Webster had suggested to President Brown an elaborate resolution for investigating the possibilities of such an institution, to be introduced by "somebody who has been favorably inclined to Dr. W., but who would wish to prevent violent

measures" (Webster to Brown, June 4, 1816, Daniel Webster, *Writings and Speeches*, 18 vols. [Boston, 1903], 1:259–60).

33. Plumer, "Autobiography" (LC), p. 332.

34. These notes are all preserved among the Dartmouth Mss., 816476.1–10.

35. (Hanover) *American*, September 11, 1816. This was the short-lived newspaper set up by Perkins and Brewster as the voice of Wheelock's party.

36. Plumer to Brown, August 27, 1816, Dartmouth Mss., 816477.

37. Brown to Plumer, August 27, 1816, Dartmouth Mss., 816477.1.

38. Plumer to Shurtleff and reply, August 28, 1816, Dartmouth Mss., 816478.

39. Brown to Plumer and reply, August 28, 1816, Dartmouth Mss., 816478.1–2.

40. These documents were printed in the *American*, September 11, 1816.

41. The minutes of this meeting were printed in full in the *American*, September 11, 1816. Plumer kept two manuscript copies, one of which was purchased by Dartmouth College at the sale of his library in 1910 and is now preserved in Dartmouth Mss., 816900. The other is in Plumer, "Repository," 4:671–90, Plumer Papers (NHSL).

42. *Concord Gazette*, September 17, 1816.

43. Ibid., November 26, 1816.

44. Plumer, "Autobiography" (LC), p. 333.

45. Plumer to Brown, August 29, 1816, Dartmouth Mss., 816479.2.

46. Plumer to Plumer, Jr., September 2, 1816, Plumer Papers (NHSL). The delinquent trustee was Jonathan Harvey, a state senator.

47. Plumer to Josiah Bartlett, September 10, 1816, Bartlett Papers; Plumer to Levi Woodbury, September 9, 1816, folio 4, Woodbury Papers, Library of Congress.

48. In seeking and receiving this opinion, the governor used his son, William, Jr., as an intermediary. Plumer, Jr. to Plumer, September 3, 1816, Plumer Papers (NHSL).

49. Questions proposed by governor and council to superior court, September 1816, extract from the council minutes, Dartmouth Mss., 816540.1.

50. Plumer, "Autobiography" (LC), p. 335.

51. *Journal of the House of Representatives*, November session, 1816 (Concord, N.H., 1817), pp. 200 ff. In refusing later to comply with the summons to show cause why they should not be removed from office, Brown, Adams, and Shurtleff declared that their opinion of the unconstitutionality of the act of 1816 had "received no small degree of confirmation . . . from the doubts entertained on this subject by his Excellency . . . and the honorable Council, as implied in their application to the judges of the Superior Court for their opinion; and from the answer of said judges, in which they expressly state that they had not formed any opinion on the question" (John Shirley, *The Dartmouth College Causes and the Supreme Court of the United States* [Chicago, 1895], p. 135).

52. Plumer, "Autobiography" (LC), p. 334.

53. The governor's son was vehement in warning his father against any further Federalist appointments (Plumer, Jr., to Plumer, December 1, 1816, Plumer Papers [NHSL]).

54. Plumer, "Autobiography" (LC), p. 338. Judge Richardson had already mentioned Woodbury as probably the best man available except for his youth. Plumer, Jr., to Plumer, November 27, 1816, Plumer Papers (NHSL). A native of Francestown, Woodbury launched his political career with a rousing Independence Day oration at Lyndeborough in 1815. His exuberant partisanship is well illustrated in a letter to Plumer, Jr., August 7, 1816, Plumer, Jr., Papers (NHSL), in which he said, "I had considerable expectation that Federalism would bury the hatchet—and unite in the support of our common country—and leave you, and myself, & others, to study the science of government—meditate on the sublimities of philosophy—and bask in the Elysium of literature with those we love—But they appear inclined to throw away the scabbard; and if so, 'my voice is still for war.'"

55. Charles H. Bell, *The Bench and Bar of New Hampshire* (Boston, 1894), p. 72; A. S.

Batchellor, "The Tenure of Office of the Judges of the Supreme Court," New Hampshire Bar Association, *Proceedings* 6(1902): 528. The son of Jeremiah Smith compared Richardson favorably with John Marshall.

56. William Smith, "Woodbury, Levi," *Dictionary of American Biography*, 20:488–89.

57. *Senate Journal*, November 1816, pp. 13–14.

58. Ibid., p. 14.

59. The legislative history of the measure may be traced in the *House Journal*, November 1816, pp. 33, 116–23, 237; *Senate Journal*, November 1816, pp. 101, 104, 153.

60. *Laws of New Hampshire*, 8:555–56.

61. Ibid., p. 584.

62. Claggett announced that he expected to lose a thousand dollars on his newspaper, but would have the satisfaction of effecting the removal of Governor Plumer. William Plumer, Jr., "Journal," vol. 2, entry for September 22, 1816, Plumer, Jr., Papers (NHSL).

63. Ibid., entry for August 13, 1816.

64. For the first time in the state's history, the house of representatives failed to return an answer to the governor's opening address. This created extraordinary excitement in the newspapers. See *New Hampshire Sentinel*, January 11, 1817; *Portsmouth Oracle*, January 4, 1817; *New Hampshire Patriot*, January 7, 1817. Plumer's reaction was one of indifference (Plumer, "Autobiography" [LC], pp. 344, 359–60).

65. *Senate Journal*, November 1816, pp. 8–9. Some accounts state that Governor Plumer laid the cornerstone on September 24, but he returned to his home from Hanover on September 20 and makes no mention of another journey to Concord for this event in his autobiography.

66. Ibid., pp. 36–38.

67. The old Concord Town House stood on the site of the present Merrimack County Courthouse.

68. Plumer, "Autobiography" (LC), pp. 337–38; Fred Leighton, "Evolution of New Hampshire State House," *Granite State Monthly* 62 (1930): 323.

69. *People's Advocate*, November 18, 1816.

70. *House Journal*, November 1816, p. 119.

71. "Committee of the House to His Excellency William Plumer" [June session, 1816], in Plumer Letters 3, Plumer Papers (LC).

72. *House Journal*, November 1816, pp. 185–92.

73. This debate was reported in the *New Hampshire Patriot*, December 24, 1816.

74. *House Journal*, November 1816, p. 192.

75. *Senate Journal*, November 1816, pp. 143, 156.

76. John Farmer and Jacob Moore, *A Gazetteer of the State of New Hampshire* (Concord, N.H., 1823), p. 41. The *New Hampshire Patriot*, September 2, 1817, carried an elaborate and laudatory description of the building at the time the outer walls were completed.

77. The original statehouse forms today the central part of the building, which has been extensively remodeled and enlarged. The lower floor is devoted principally to a lobby and hall of flags. A copy of the Hoit portrait of Governor Plumer hangs in the council chamber, located in an addition built in 1909.

78. Albert Annett, "The Builders: Address at Dedication of Remodeled State House," *Granite State Monthly* 62 (1930): 388. The original building is pictured on page 325. Visitors to Concord today would be surprised to learn that the beautiful civic center which has grown up around the capitol and which seems to be ideally located just at the north end of the business section is in an area once considered too far south of the town's residences.

79. Plumer, "Autobiography" (LC), p. 330.

80. *House Journal*, June 1816, p. 331.

81. Plumer to William Crawford, July 11, 1816, Letters 3, Plumer Papers (LC).

82. Letters to Plumer from George Jackson, War Department, July 24, 1816; Peter Hagner, War Department, July 25, 1816; Thomas Tucker, treasurer, July 31, 1816; Joseph Nourse, register, August 2, 1816, all in Plumer Papers (NHSL).

83. *Senate Journal*, June 1816, pp. 64–70.

84. Plumer to Plumer, Jr., August 14, 1816, Plumer Papers (NHSL).

85. Plumer, "Autobiography" (LC), p. 351.

86. *New Hampshire Patriot*, December 17, 1816.

87. *House Journal*, November 1816, pp. 125–26.

88. The *People's Advocate* had already printed an attack upon the governor's funding operation which corresponded suspiciously with the report later published by the Vose committee. Plumer, Jr., "Journal," vol. 2 (NHSL), entry for January 12, 1817; *People's Advocate*, December 14, 1816.

89. Quoted in *Concord Gazette*, December 31, 1816.

90. Ibid., January 28, 1817. See also (Amherst) *Farmer's Cabinet*, February 15, 1817.

91. *Concord Gazette*, February 25, 1817.

92. *Senate Journal*, November 1816, p. 150.

93. Plumer, Jr., "Journal," vol. 2 (NHSL), entry for January 12, 1817.

94. *New Hampshire Patriot*, December 17, 1816.

95. This, of course, was a strong and legitimate ground of complaint against Plumer. His public and his private business were too closely associated. The same letter in which Plumer instructed his son to fund the treasury notes "not in my name but in that of the *State of New Hampshire*" carried an order to credit the governor with $325 of the new stock, purchased with the interest earned on his extant holdings (Plumer to Plumer, Jr., August 14, October 4, 1816, Plumer Papers [NHSL]).

96. [William Plumer], *Veritas*, "Funding Treasury Notes," in "Essays," 2:136–40, Plumer Papers, New Hampshire State Library, published in *New Hampshire Patriot*, January 28, 1817.

97. *New Hampshire Patriot*, December 24, 1816.

98. *House Journal*, November 1816, pp. 219 ff.

99. *New Hampshire Patriot*, December 31, 1816, January 21, 1817. The committee exposed itself to these charges by ignoring the other newspapers and shifting the attack from Hill's report of Prescott's speech to his criticism of the Vose report. Hill quoted an attack on this "persecution" by the *National Intelligencer* in his issue of January 21.

100. *House Journal*, November 1816, pp. 249–54.

101. *New Hampshire Sentinel*, February 1, 1817. See also the (Boston) *Daily Advertiser*, January 3, 1817, for a long article of the same character.

102. *People's Advocate*, December 28, 1816.

103. *Concord Gazette*, October 22, 1816.

104. Plumer, Jr., to Plumer, December 22, 1816, Plumer Papers (NHSL).

105. Plumer, "Autobiography" (LC), pp. 342–43.

106. *House Journal*, November 1816, p. 197. Governor Plumer's difficulties with the Claggetts were complicated by the marriage of his only daughter, Sarah, to William Claggett, and by the fact that his son William, Jr., made his home with his sister and brother-in-law in Portsmouth.

107. Plumer, "Josiah Bartlett," "Biographical Sketches," 5:608, Plumer Papers, New Hampshire Historical Society.

108. *People's Advocate*, January 18, 1817.

109. William Claggett to Josiah Bartlett, February 10, 17, 1817, Bartlett Papers; Josiah Bartlett to editors of the *New Hampshire Gazette*, February, 1816, printed in *New Hampshire Gazette*, clipping in Plumer, Jr., "Scrapbook" (NHSL).

110. Parker Lyon, ed., *New Hampshire Register, 1860* (Concord, 1859), p. 41. Election statistics were as follows:

Whole number of votes cast	35,375
Necessary for a choice	17,688
Scattering	112
Josiah Bartlett	539
Jeremiah Mason	3,607
James Sheafe	12,029
William Plumer	19,000

111. The geographical distribution of the vote, as nearly as can be determined by very incomplete newspaper reports, remained relatively unchanged. Although Plumer lost his own hometown and felt himself betrayed (Plumer to Plumer, Jr., March 11, 1817, Plumer Papers [NHSL]), he increased his majority considerably in the Old Colony and still more in the Merrimack Valley. The Federalists held their own, or probably even increased their margin in the Connecticut Valley.

112. Plumer, Jr., to Plumer, May 17, 1817, Plumer Papers (NHSL). An unsavory aftermath of the *Advocate*'s demise was a suit against William Claggett by his publisher to force payment of subscribers' monies which Claggett denied having received. William Weeks to Josiah Bartlett, July 24, 1817, Bartlett Papers.

113. Elijah Parish to Plumer, April 8, 1817, Plumer Papers (NHSL).

CHAPTER 20

1. The epigraph is drawn from the *Concord Gazette* of March 15, 1818.

2. William Plumer, "Autobiography," pp. 359–60, William Plumer Papers, Library of Congress. The authoritative study of the Federalist party in its declining years is Shaw Livermore's *The Twilight of Federalism, 1815–1830* (Princeton, 1962). By 1816 the Federalists had already lost Vermont and New Hampshire, as well as every state outside New England except Maryland and Delaware. They surrendered Connecticut in 1817.

3. Parker Lyon, ed., *New Hampshire Register, 1860* (Concord, N.H., 1859), p. 41.

4. (Amherst) *Farmer's Cabinet*, May 23, June 6, 1818.

5. Plumer to Samuel Connor, January 20, 1816, Plumer Papers, New Hampshire State Library; Plumer to James Monroe, March 7, 1816, Monroe Papers, New York City Public Library. "I congratulate you & the nation on the circumstance of the leading Republicans in the eastern States having generally united in favor of your being the candidate for the next presidential election, notwithstanding the senseless clamor of your being born in the same State that gave birth to a Washington, a Jefferson & a Madison." In light of the fact that on the previous day, Plumer had written to John Quincy Adams in London, regretting his absence from the country which prevented his being "brought forward" as a candidate, this letter to Monroe was obviously political window dressing.

6. John Adams to William Plumer, January 10, 1813, quoted in William Plumer, Jr., *Life of William Plumer* (Boston, 1856), p. 403.

7. *Annals of Congress*, Fourteenth Congress, First Session, p. 281, records the vote in the Senate, Mason nay, Thompson not voting. Page 1219 records the vote in the House, Charles Atherton aye, the other five New Hampshire representatives, including Daniel Webster, nay.

8. Ibid., p. 1270.

9. Ibid., p. 1352. Hale, Vose, and Wilcox voted against the bill, Atherton for it. Webster and Cilley are not recorded as voting.

10. Ibid., p. 719.

11. *Annals of Congress*, Fourteenth Congress, Second Session; Senate vote, 20–15, recorded on page 191, Mason aye, Thompson nay; House vote, 86–84, on page 934, Webster aye, the other five nay.

12. *Annals of Congress*, Fifteenth Congress, First Session. Appropriation of 1818, page 1664, passed 74–56, Livermore and Parrott aye, Claggett, Hale, and Upham nay. Ibid., Sixteenth Congress, First Session, p. 1649, appropriation of 1820 passed 90–66, William Plumer, Jr., aye, Buffum, Butler, and Claggett nay, Livermore and Upham not voting.

13. *Annals of Congress*, Fifteenth Congress, Second Session, p. 311. Upham voted for this bill; Claggett, Hale, and Livermore opposed; Butler and Parrott not voting. It will be noticed that New Hampshire's Republican congressmen were not very diligent about answering final roll calls. Josiah Butler, in particular, continued the habit he had developed in the New Hampshire legislature of avoiding final commitments.

14. *Annals of Congress*, Fifteenth Congress, First Session, p. 102.

15. Ibid., pp. 262, 840. This bill passed in the Senate, 17–13, and in the House, 84–69. Neither New Hampshire senator voted on the bill, and Butler failed to vote on it in the House.

16. *Annals of Congress*, Fifteenth Congress, Second Session, pp. 1191–93. New Hampshire congressmen were at first strongly supported by public opinion at home. A public meeting in Portsmouth in December 1819 voted to exclude slavery from Missouri, and Isaac Hill, in the *Patriot*, labeled slavery "the foulest stain on our national character." By February 1820, however, he was singing a different tune, suspecting Rufus King and DeWitt Clinton of "reviving sectional prejudices . . . for sinister party purposes" (Donald B. Cole, *Jacksonian Democracy in New Hampshire* [Cambridge, Mass., 1970], p. 41). See also George Dangerfield, *Era of Good Feelings* (New York, 1963), pp. 223–25.

17. *Annals of Congress*, Fifteenth Congress, Second Session, pp. 273, 1214–15; Sixteenth Congress, First Session, pp. 118, 359, 427, 455, 1572.

18. Plumer announced Adams as the preference of New Hampshire, but he was speaking primarily for himself. In March, Plumer had conveyed this wish directly to Adams in London, but conceded that his absence from the country had made it impossible for the eastern states to "bring [him] forward." He added as consolation a statement somewhat ironic in the light of subsequent history. "This may be a fortunate circumstance to you, for should you succeed at your present time of life, after eight years, the country would have been deprived of your official services; for custom has declared he that has held that high office cannot afterwards take any other" (Plumer to J. Q. Adams, March 6, 1816, Letters 3, William Plumer Papers, Library of Congress).

19. The story of the president's pilgrimage is related in detail in Samuel Waldo, *The Tour of James Monroe, President of the United States, in the Year 1817* (Hartford, Conn., 1818).

20. Plumer, "Autobiography" (LC), pp. 353–54.

21. Ibid., p. 355.

22. Plumer to Monroe, July 18, 1817, Letters 3, Plumer Papers (LC). This is a rough copy of the letter actually sent to Monroe, which is printed in Waldo, *Tour of Monroe*, pp. 193–94. President Monroe to Governor Plumer, July 21, 1817, Plumer Papers (NHSL).

23. *Portsmouth Oracle*, July 26, 1817. This Federalist attitude toward ordering out the militia contrasted so glaringly with their objections to such orders when they were really needed in 1812 that one Republican editor wrote in disgust, "Now look ye! gentlemen of the *martial spirit* . . . when you wish again to gratify your natural propensity for *grumbling*, in the name of consistency, choose some other subject than that of *calling out the militia*" (*New Hampshire Gazette*, July 29, 1817).

24. *Portsmouth Oracle*, August 2, 1817.

25. *Exeter Watchman*, quoted in *Portsmouth Oracle*, August 2, 1817.

26. Quoted in *Portsmouth Oracle*, August 2, 1817.

27. For a full description of the festivities, see Waldo, *Tour of Monroe*, pp. 166–70.

28. Copies of several of these speeches, including Mason's, are preserved in the James Monroe Papers, New York City Public Library.

29. Minutes of the Trustees of Dartmouth University, August, 1817, Dartmouth Mss., Baker Library, Hanover, N.H., 817490.4; Francis Brown to President Monroe, August 30, 1817, Dartmouth Mss., 817480.

30. Salma Hale to Plumer, July 18, 1817, Plumer Papers (NHSL). See also remarks by William Plumer, Jr., as "Gracchus" in *New Hampshire Patriot*, September 9, 1817.

31. For a full account of the myth-making process in this instance, see Lynn W. Turner, "The Electoral Vote against Monroe in 1820—An American Legend," *Mississippi Valley Historical Review* 42 (September 1955): 250–73.

32. Plumer, "Autobiography" (LC), p. 378.

33. *New Hampshire Patriot*, October 31, 1820.

34. Lynn W. Turner, "Elections of 1816 and 1820," *History of American Presidential Elections*, ed. Arthur M. Schlesinger, Jr., and Fred L. Israel, 4 vols. (New York, 1971), 1:316–17.

35. Daniel Webster to Jeremiah Mason, November 12, 1820, Webster Papers, 1:155, New Hampshire Historical Society.

36. Plumer to Plumer, Jr., November 15, 1820; Plumer, Jr., to Plumer, November 24, 1820, both in Plumer Papers (NHSL); Everett Brown, *The Missouri Compromises and Presidential Politics, 1820–1825* (St. Louis, 1926), pp. 53–54; Charles Francis Adams, ed., *Memoirs of John Quincy Adams*, 12 vols. (Philadelphia, 1874–77), 5:205–6.

37. Plumer, "Autobiography" (LC), pp. 378–79.

38. *Portsmouth Oracle*, December 30, 1820. Plumer's vote and the reasons for it were widely noticed over the country. See (New York) *National Advocate*, December 21; (New York) *Columbian*, December 21; (New York) *American*, December 22; *Boston Intelligencer & Evening Gazette*, December 23; (Albany) *New York Statesman*, December 26; *Richmond Enquirer*, December 28, 1820.

39. *New Hampshire Sentinel*, December 16, 1820.

40. *Boston Intelligencer*, December 9, 1820. "Now if voting for Mr. Monroe be the touchstone of Republicanism," complained this Federalist paper, "We suspect that [after the election, people] will be puzzled to find any but Republicans in the Union."

41. Although completely discomfited by Plumer's vote, Hill exercised remarkable self-restraint. "For my part at the time," he wrote to Plumer, Jr., "I regretted that the vote should have been given; and I regret still more that the subject should be handled to the disadvantage of any one. As it respects yourself, I pray it make no difference at Washington, as I think it will not in this State" (Hill to Plumer, Jr., January 3, 1821, Plumer, Jr., Papers [NHSL]).

42. Plumer, Jr., to Plumer, January 16, 1821, January 15, 1822, Plumer Papers (NHSL).

43. (Washington) *National Intelligencer*, December 12, 1820. An amendment to require all electors and congressmen to be elected from districts within the states was approved by the Senate in 1819 but tabled by the House. New Hampshire's senators voted for it, its representatives 3–1 against it (*Annals of Congress*, Fifteenth Congress, Second Session, pp. 207, 1421).

44. Plumer to Francis Brown, December 29, 1816, Dartmouth Mss., 816670.

45. Plumer, "Autobiography" (LC), pp. 345–46.

46. Plumer to Plumer, Jr., February 11, 1817, Plumer Papers (NHSL). This letter was written on the back of a printed report of the trustees' meeting.

47. Francis Brown et al. to Plumer, "Repository," 9:29–31, Plumer Papers, New Hampshire State Library.

48. The university board acted on legal advice from Judge Richardson. Plumer, Jr. to Plumer, January 18, 1817, Plumer Papers (NHSL).

49. Plumer, "Autobiography" (LC), p. 347.

50. Minutes of the Trustees of Dartmouth University, Dartmouth Mss., 817854.

51. Allen was a minister in Pittsfield, Massachusetts. In a letter to Plumer, January 13, 1817, Plumer Papers (NHSL), he had asked that his father-in-law be reinstated, but hinted at his own availability.

52. Plumer to William H. Woodward, March 21, 1817, Letters 3, Plumer Papers (LC).

53. Asa McFarland to Francis Brown, January 29, 1817, Dartmouth Mss., 817122.

54. Jonathan Freeman to Peyton Freeman, February 5, 1817, Dartmouth Mss., 817155; William Thurston to Francis Brown, December 28, 1816, Dartmouth Mss., 816678.

55. T. W. Thompson to Brown, January 9, 1817, Dartmouth Mss., 817119.

56. Plumer to William H. Woodward, April 5, 1817, Plumer Papers (NHSL). Though slight and scholarly, Brown was a man of iron will, great invention, and tremendous energy. He compelled the reluctant admiration of Governor Plumer, whose personal relations with him were invariably friendly in spite of their public hostility. See Plumer to Brown, March 5, 1817, Letters 3, Plumer Papers (LC).

57. John Shirley, *The Dartmouth College Causes and the Supreme Court of the United States* (Chicago, 1895), pp. 116–17.

58. Woodward to Plumer, February 11, 1817, Plumer Papers (NHSL).

59. Plumer to Woodward, March 21, 1817, Letters 3, Plumer Papers (LC).

60. Shirley, *Dartmouth College Causes*, p. 131.

61. Mason based his argument upon the eleemosynary character of the college as intended by its founders and protected by the inviolability of its charter (Francis N. Stites, *Private Interest and Public Gain: The Dartmouth College Case, 1819* [Amherst, Mass., 1972], pp. 46 ff).

62. See Shirley, *Dartmouth College Causes*, p. 144; Charles Marsh to William Allen, April 22, 1819, Dartmouth Mss., 819272.

63. Webster to Smith, December 8, 1817, Daniel Webster, *Writings and Speeches*, 18 vols. (Boston, 1903), 17:267–68.

64. This whole matter, which is sidestepped by most of Webster's biographers, is fairly well covered, with supporting documents, in Shirley, *Dartmouth College Causes*, pp. 88–92. Webster's sentiment for his alma mater was not altogether eleemosynary—his fee for arguing the case in Washington was $1,000. Webster to Francis Brown, November 15, 1817, Dartmouth Mss., 817615.3.

65. Plumer to Woodward, April 5, 1817, Plumer Papers (NHSL); G. J. Clark, ed., *Memoirs of Jeremiah Mason* (Boston, 1917), p. 427.

66. Timothy Farrar, *Report of the Dartmouth College Case* (Portsmouth, N.H., 1819), pp. 116–206. Bartlett's argument, accepted by the superior court, was that corporations were public or private according to their functions and that Dartmouth functioned as a public corporation and therefore was legally subject to legislative supervision (Stites, *Private Interest and Public Gain*, pp. 50 ff.).

67. An interesting, if not particularly significant, fact is that of the eight men associated with the Dartmouth College case as counsel or judges in the New Hampshire courts, four were Dartmouth alumni, but only one of these, Webster, took the college side. Bell, Woodbury, and Bartlett favored the proposed reform of their alma mater.

68. *Farmer's Cabinet*, September 27, 1817; *New Hampshire Patriot*, September 7, 1817. Hill reported that Webster made a "very pathetic appeal to the Court as *alumni* of the College."

69. Levi Woodbury to Plumer, September 19, 1817, Plumer Papers (NHSL).

70. Webster to Jeremiah Mason, June 28, 1817, vol. 1, Webster Papers, New Hampshire

Historical Society.

71. Nathaniel Adams, ed., *Reports of Cases Argued and Determined in the Superior Court* (Exeter, N.H., 1819), pp. 113–36. "All agreed that some corporations were controllable by the legislature, but there was, as the arguments in the Superior Court demonstrated, disagreement about the criterion for classifying corporations as public, for permitting regulation. Richardson . . . emphasized the objects; College counsel had stressed the origins, the sources of funds. The case would ultimately turn on that criterion" (Stites, *Private Interest and Public Gain*, p. 54).

72. *Portsmouth Oracle*, November 15, 1817. Delegates from Harvard, Yale, Bowdoin, Middlebury, Williams, Andover, Dartmouth, and the University of Vermont met in Boston in May 1818 to consider the implications of the Dartmouth situation for each of them (Stites, *Private Interest and Public Gain*, p. 70).

73. Elijah Parish to Plumer, November 14, 1817, Letters 9, Plumer Papers (LC).

74. Shirley, *Dartmouth College Causes*, pp. 137–40; Rufus Choate to David Choate, March 12, 1817, Dartmouth Mss., 817212.

75. Woodward to Plumer, March 8, 13, 1817, Plumer Papers (NHSL). There was even violence in Hanover. In the fall of 1817 the procollege students seized the library, carried off the books, and locked the doors. The university professors broke in with axes, were locked in a closet by the students, and indicted by a local magistrate for breaking and entering.

76. William Allen to Plumer, July 7, 1818, Letters 9, Plumer Papers (LC).

77. Plumer, "Autobiography" (LC), p. 349.

78. Salma Hale to Plumer, January 3, 1817; Plumer to Hale, January 8, 1817, both in Plumer Papers (NHSL).

79. Plumer to Plumer, Jr., March 4, 1817, Plumer Papers (NHSL); Plumer to Woodward, October 11, 1817, Letters 8, Plumer Papers (LC). See also Maurice G. Baxter, *Daniel Webster and the Supreme Court* (Amherst, Mass., 1966), chap. 4, for an excellent treatment of the legal aspects of the case.

80. Plumer to Salma Hale, January 15, 1818, Plumer Papers (NHSL).

81. Hale to Plumer, January 26, 1818, Letters 9, Plumer Papers (LC).

82. Plumer to Hale, February 5, 1818, Plumer Papers (NHSL).

83. Baxter, *Webster and the Supreme Court*, p. 84.

84. Hale to Plumer, March 12, 1818, Letters 9, Plumer Papers (LC). Stites gives a lucid review of Webster's argument in *Private Interest and Public Gain*, pp. 60–64.

85. Hale to Plumer, Jr., March 24, 1818, Plumer Papers (NHSL), misdated December 24 by writer. "From this," Hale commented, "you will perceive how much the speakers in our highest courts of law are indulged in their flights."

86. Plumer to Hale, March 26, 1818, Plumer Papers (NHSL).

87. Allen to Plumer, March 26, 1818, Letters 9, Plumer Papers (LC).

88. *Journal of the House of Representatives*, June session, 1818 (Concord, N.H., 1818), pp. 97, 152.

89. General Ripley to William Allen, August 14, 1818, Dartmouth Mss., 818464.1.

90. Allen to Plumer, October 15, 1818, Letters 9, Plumer Papers (LC). Allen's documents and arguments are preserved in a thick envelope in the Baker Library at Dartmouth College. Woodward had died on August 9, 1818, so Allen carried on as the defendant.

91. Cyrus Perkins to William Allen, January 28, 1819, Dartmouth Mss., 819128. Webster understood this situation very well and was not alarmed by Pinkney's entry into the case. Webster to Jeremiah Smith, February 28, 1819, 1:139, Webster Papers (NHHS).

92. Perkins to Allen, February 2, 1819, Dartmouth Mss., 819152. No one seemed to have expected Marshall's immediate decision. Perkins wandered into the courtroom when the chief justice was halfway through his reading, and Pinkney was the only university lawyer present at the opening of the session.

93. Albert J. Beveridge, *The Life of John Marshall*, 4 vols. (Boston, 1916–19), 4:261–74.

94. Plumer to Hale, February 13, 1819, Plumer Papers (NHSL).

95. Hale to Plumer, February 21, 1819, Letters 9, Plumer Papers (LC).

96. Plumer to Hale, April 8, 1819, Letters 9, Plumer Papers (LC).

97. Webster was originally eager to have these suits come to Washington, for he had little faith in the obligation of contract clause as the salvation of the college. The "cognate" cases threatened to backfire when Webster won his case on the original suit. Webster to Jeremiah Smith, December 8, 1817, Daniel Webster, *Writings and Speeches*, 18 vols. (Boston, 1903), 17:267–68.

98. For the university side of this development see Salma Hale to Levi Woodbury, February 12, 1819, folio 5, Woodbury Papers, Library of Congress. For the college side, see letters from Webster to Jeremiah Mason, quoted in Clark, *Memoirs of Mason*, pp. 213, 219, 221, 223.

99. Plumer to Hale, April 8, 1819, Plumer Papers (NHSL).

100. For Webster's foreknowledge of Story's decision see Shirley, *Dartmouth College Causes*, p. 304. The history of the "cognate" cases is even more tangled than that of *Dartmouth College Trustees v. Woodward*. Baxter, *Webster and the Supreme Court*, and Stites, *Private Interest and Public Gain*, trace it in detail.

101. Allen to Plumer, March 13, 1819, Letters 9, Plumer Papers (LC).

102. Brewster to Plumer, April 18, 1819, Letters 9, Plumer Papers (LC); Plumer to Brewster, April 21, 1819, Dartmouth Mss., 819271.

103. Shirley, *Dartmouth College Causes*, p. 304; Plumer to William H. Woodward, March 21, 1817, Letters 3, Plumer Papers (LC).

104. See Leon Richardson, *History of Dartmouth College*, 2 vols. (Hanover, N.H., 1932), 1:345–46, for an appreciative appraisal of Marshall's decision and Webster's services. Only two years after the decision, however, the college trustees wanted to apply to the state legislature again for patronage and were only prevented by Webster, who wrote that "if the College must die, it is better it should die a natural death" (Shirley, *Dartmouth College Causes*, pp. 11–13).

105. In 1821 the state legislature established a "literary fund," raised by a tax on bank stock, which was to be applied toward endowing a state college. The money was actually spent, however, on elementary schools (Samuel Bartlett, "History of Education in New Hampshire," in William Davis, ed., *The New England States*, 4 vols. [Boston, 1897], 3:1610, 1614).

CHAPTER 21

1. The epigraph is taken from *Speech of His Excellency, William Plumer, to the Legislature, June 4, 1818* (Concord, N.H., 1818).

2. William Plumer, Jr., *Life of William Plumer* (Boston, 1856), p. 479.

3. William Plumer, "Autobiography," pp. 352, 359, 362, William Plumer Papers, Library of Congress; William Plumer, Jr., "Memoirs," vol. 1., May and June 1818, William Plumer, Jr., Papers, New Hampshire State Library.

4. William Alexander Robinson, "Bell, Samuel," *Dictionary of American Biography*, 2:162–63.

5. Edwin D. Sanborn, *History of New Hampshire* (Manchester, N.H., 1875), p. 265. The mean annual temperature in southern New Hampshire in 1816 was 43 degrees.

6. *Journal of the Senate*, June session, 1816 (Concord, N.H., 1816), p. 161.

7. Ibid., pp. 23–24.

8. Jefferson to Plumer, July 21, 1816, folio 207, Jefferson Papers, Library of Congress.

John Quincy Adams, who was later to be accused of extravagance in the White House, also approved of Plumer's parsimony, remarking that "the appetite of ambition for place is sufficiently sharp-set, without needing the stimulant dram of avarice to make it keener" William Plumer, Jr., *Life of Plumer*, p. 436. Plumer's example of Spartan virtue aroused so much interest that his speech was printed in the London *Morning Chronicle* of September 20. See (Boston) *Daily Advertiser*, November 2, 1816.

9. *Portsmouth Oracle*, June 15, 1816.

10. (Keene) *New Hampshire Sentinel*, June 15, 1816. See also (Boston) *Daily Advertiser*, June 10, 1816.

11. *Laws of New Hampshire*, 10 vols. (Concord, N.H., 1920), 8:743.

12. During its first ten years of operation, the prison cost the state $5,676.67 more than it produced. John Farmer and Jacob Moore, eds., *A Gazetteer of the State of New Hampshire* (Concord, N.H., 1823), p. 44.

13. Henry Robinson, "The New Hampshire State Prison," *Granite State Monthly* 22 (1890): 216–18.

14. *Journal of the Senate*, November session, 1816 (Concord, N.H., 1817), pp. 136–40.

15. Plumer, "Autobiography" (LC), p. 349.

16. *Journal of the House of Representatives*, June session, 1817 (Concord, N.H., 1817), pp. 240–41.

17. *Journal of the House of Representatives*, June session, 1818 (Concord, N.H., 1818), pp. 166–94. Also published separately as *Report of the Committee to Investigate the State Prison* (Concord, N.H., 1818).

18. Plumer, "Autobiography" (LC), p. 366. Shortly after Pillsbury's appointment, Plumer wrote letters of inquiry about their penitentiaries and penal codes to the governors of Virginia, Pennsylvania, New York, Vermont, and Massachusetts. Copies in Letters 8, Plumer Papers (LC).

19. Orlando Lewis, *The Development of American Prisons and Prison Customs, 1776–1845* (Albany, N.Y., 1922), p. 149.

20. Plumer to Cadwallader Colden, September 21, 1820, Letters 9, Plumer Papers (LC). This is a remarkable letter, showing a grasp of the problem which goes far to explain why New Hampshire succeeded with its penitentiary system.

21. Plumer, *Speech to the Legislature, June 4, 1818*.

22. Plumer to Jesse Hawley, July 11, 1818, Letters 9, Plumer Papers (LC).

23. Plumer to Robert Owens [sic], September 17, 1817, Letters 8, Plumer Papers (LC).

24. *House Journal*, June 1818, pp. 14–15.

25. Woodbury to Plumer, August 18, 1817, Plumer Papers (NHSL).

26. Plumer, "Autobiography" (LC), p. 360.

27. William Plumer, Jr., *Life of Plumer*, p. 474.

28. *Laws of New Hampshire*, 8:704, 736, 743.

29. *House Journal*, June 1818, pp. 24–25; *Laws of New Hampshire*, 3:619.

30. The more important legislation on this subject may be found in *Laws of New Hampshire*, 5:704, 6:321, 7:583, 8:50, 343, 499. See also Peter J. Coleman, *Debtors and Creditors in America* (Madison, Wis., 1974), chap. 5.

31. *House Journal*, June 1818, pp. 19–25.

32. Tracy Carlton, "Abolition of Imprisonment for Debt in the United States," *Yale Review* 18 (1909): 344.

33. *Laws of New Hampshire*, 8:743. According to Cole, the legislature passed this law for the specific release of Captain Amos Brewer, a seventy-year-old Revolutionary War veteran who had been imprisoned for four years on an unpaid debt of eight dollars. If this was the case, the law failed of its purpose, for Brewer was soon back in jail for failure to pay the accumulated jailer's bill of three hundred dollars. Isaac Hill gave publicity to the case, and Benjamin Pierce rescued Brewer by paying his debt to the jailer from his own pocket (Don-

ald B. Cole, *Jacksonian Democracy in New Hampshire* [Cambridge, Mass., 1970], p. 44).

34. Plumer, "Autobiography" (LC), p. 367.

35. *Laws of New Hampshire*, 8:870.

36. In New Hampshire, as elsewhere in the nation, it had still been possible in earlier days for even distinguished men to end their lives in debtor's prison, yet it had also been true that the great majority of prisoners held in the filthy county gaols were hapless small debtors whose incarceration served no good purpose. The Prison Discipline Society of Boston estimated in 1829 that seven-tenths of all imprisoned debtors owed less than twenty dollars (Carlton, "Abolition of Imprisonment," p. 340). See Edwin T. Randall, "Imprisonment for Debt in America: Fact and Fiction," *Mississippi Valley Historical Review* 39 (June 1952): 89–102, for a criticism of the figures given in the society's report in the light of the many laws passed for the amelioration of debt imprisonment before 1830. Randall, however, overlooks the many loopholes that existed in these laws. There are too many tragic cases of debt imprisonment on record to call it a fiction.

37. Lewis, *American Prisons*, p. 151.

38. David M. Ludlum, *Social Ferment in Vermont* (New York, 1939), pp. 213–14; Carlton, "Abolition of Imprisonment," pp. 339, 342; *Laws of the State of New-Hampshire, Passed in November Session, 1840* (Concord, N.H., 1840), p. 469. As a matter of fact, the 1840 statute abolished arrest or imprisonment only for contract debt and left a large area of financial liability in which arrest and imprisonment were still possible. It required three pages in the latest revision of the New Hampshire code to print the law still covering imprisonment for debt.

39. Adams, the secretary of state, transmitted Bentham's offer to all the state governors. See John Quincy Adams to Plumer, October 27, 1817, Plumer Papers (NHSL). James Madison wrote, in response to Bentham's proposition, "Either I overrate or he underrates the task he wished to undertake" Madison to Adams, December 23, 1817, folio 65, James Madison Papers, Library of Congress.

40. Plumer to Jeremy Bentham, October 2, 1817, Letters 9, Plumer Papers (LC).

41. *House Journal*, June 1818, p. 30.

42. *Concord Gazette*, June 6, 1818, copying item from the *Salem Gazette*; *New Hampshire Patriot*, commenting on article in (Boston) *Daily Advertiser*, June 21, 1818. The tone in the Federalist press was uniformly sarcastic, but the best job of it was done by the *Salem Gazette*.

43. Jeremiah Mason to Rufus King, May 15, 1818, printed in G. J. Clark, ed., *Memoirs of Jeremiah Mason* (Boston, 1917), p. 206.

44. Plumer, Jr., to Jeremy Bentham, October 2, 1818, "Plumer, Jr., Letter-Book," vol. 3, William Plumer, Jr., Papers, New Hampshire State Library.

45. Bentham to Plumer, Jr., n.d., 1819, Plumer Papers (NHSL); William Plumer, Jr., *Life of Plumer*, pp. 475–76. William Plumer, Jr., served in later years as president of the New Hampshire Insane Asylum Board of Trustees.

46. Plumer, "Autobiography" (LC), p. 358.

47. *New Hampshire Sentinel*, June 28, 1817; Plumer, "Autobiography" (LC), p. 351.

48. *House Journal*, June 1817, pp. 44, 58, 60, 63–66, 73–74.

49. Plumer, "Autobiography" (LC), p. 351.

50. Ibid., p. 331.

51. *Journal of the House of Representatives*, November session, 1816 (Concord, N.H., 1817), p. 122.

52. Daniel Coolidge to Plumer, February 9, 1818, Letters 9, Plumer Papers (LC).

53. *House Journal*, June 1818, p. 82.

54. *New Hampshire Gazette*, July 8, 1817.

55. Plumer, "Autobiography" (LC), p. 352.

56. *House Journal*, June 1817, p. 186.

57. New Hampshire law did not, for example, allow divorce upon grounds of incompatibility, drunkenness, or conviction of crime.

58. Plumer, "Autobiography" (LC), pp. 352–53.

59. William Plumer, Jr., *Life of Plumer*, p. 465.

60. Plumer asked the governor of New York for a copy of the objections made by his council of revision to a bill of divorcement passed in favor of Mrs. Eunice Chapman, whose situation was virtually identical with that of Mrs. Dyer (Plumer to DeWitt Clinton, May 18, 1818, Letters 8, Plumer Papers [LC]).

61. Plumer to Jesse Hawley, July 11, 1818, Letters 9, Plumer Papers (LC).

62. I cannot agree with Professor McLoughlin's thesis that the Republican party had no genuine interest in religious reform and used the issue only for political purposes. See William G. McLoughlin, "The Bench, the Church and the Republican Party in New Hampshire," *Historical New Hampshire* 20, no. 2 (Summer 1965): 3–31.

63. *Senate Journal*, June 1816, pp. 25–26.

64. *New Hampshire Patriot*, December 24, 1816, and January 14, 1817, quoting from the *Boston Gazette*.

65. *House Journal*, November 1816, p. 209.

66. William Peter Strickland, ed., *The Autobiography of Dan Young* (New York, 1860), pp. 279–81.

67. John N. McClintock, *History of New Hampshire* (Boston, 1889), p. 528.

68. Paul G. Lauer, *Church and State in New England* (Baltimore, 1892), pp. 99, 102.

69. Maria Louise Greene, *The Development of Religious Liberty in Connecticut* (Boston, 1905), pp. 466–80.

70. *Laws of New Hampshire*, 8:820–21.

71. Disposition of property interests in meetinghouses and glebe lands also posed difficult problems for many years. As late as 1865 Presbyterian church trustees in Bedford were collecting tax money fraudulently in lieu of glebe rents (Charles B. Kinney, *Church and State: The Struggle for Separation in New Hampshire* [New York, 1955], pp. 110–11).

72. *Laws of New Hampshire*, 8:821.

73. George Barstow, *History of New Hampshire* (Concord, N.H., 1842), p. 434.

74. Ibid., p. 437. The battle was also fought in the newspapers, with the Republican press—*New Hampshire Patriot*, *New Hampshire Gazette*, (Dover) *Strafford Register*—supporting the bill, and some of the old Federalist papers—*New Hampshire Sentinel*, *Concord Observer*—strongly opposing it (Kinney, *Church and State*, p. 104).

75. For Smith's opinion, which concluded that Presbyterians and Congregationalists were different sects, see McLoughlin, "Bench, Church and Republican Party."

76. *Journal of the House of Representatives*, June session, 1819 (Concord, N.H., 1819), pp. 224–28, 239–42, 286–88, 293–96.

77. Ibid., pp. 239–42.

78. Ibid., pp. 293–96.

79. See Map 20, "Toleration Act, 1819."

80. *Journal of the Senate*, November session, 1820 (Concord, N.H., 1821), pp. 192–94.

81. *Journal of the House of Representatives*, November session, 1820 (Concord, N.H., 1821), pp. 111–18, 174–79, 235–40.

82. Ibid., pp. 292–98.

83. *Annals of Congress*, Fifteenth Congress, First Session, p. 1770; Second Session, pp. 337–39.

84. One of the legends connected with John Stark's career is that when he deployed his troops for their attack on the Hessians at Bennington, he shouted, "There they are boys. We beat them today, or Mollie Stark's a widow." Mrs. Stark's name was actually Elizabeth.

INDEX

10